CONSTITUTIONAL AND ADMINISTRATIVE LAW
Casebook

3rd edition

Edited by Michael T Molan
BA, LLM (Lond), Barrister
Senior Lecturer at South Bank Polytechnic

HLT Publications

HLT PUBLICATIONS
200 Greyhound Road, London W14 9RY

First published 1988
3rd edition 1991

© The HLT Group Ltd 1991

All HLT publications enjoy copyright protection and the copyright belongs to The HLT Group Ltd.

All rights reserved. No part of this publication may be reproduced or transmitted in any form or by any means, electronic, mechanical, photocopying, recording or otherwise, or stored in any retrieval system of any nature without either the written permission of the copyright holder, application for which should be made to The HLT Group Ltd, or a licence permitting restricted copying in the United Kingdom issued by the Copyright Licensing Agency.

Any person who infringes the above in relation to this publication may be liable to criminal prosecution and civil claims for damages.

ISBN 1 85352 908 7

ACKNOWLEDGEMENT
The publishers and author would like to thank The Incorporated Council of Law Reporting for England and Wales for kind permission to reproduce extracts from the Weekly Law Reports.

British Library Cataloguing-in-Publication.

A CIP Catalogue record for this book is available from the British Library.

Printed and bound in Great Britain

Ravi Dabydeen

CONTENTS

CONTENTS

iv

PREFACE

This HLT Casebook can be used as a companion volume to the *Constitutional and Administrative Law Textbook,* but also comprises an invaluable reference tool in itself. Its aim is to supplement and enhance students' understanding and interpretation of this particular area of the law, and to provide essential background reading. Where appropriate, the subject matter dealt with within a chapter is broken down into separate sections.

The structure and content of this latest edition of the *Constitutional and Administrative Law Casebook* reflect the increasing importance of community law, and the impact of community law on the British constitution.

The law is stated as of 1 January 1991.

TABLE OF CASES

1 THE NATURE AND SOURCES OF CONSTITUTIONAL LAW

Attorney-General v Jonathan Cape Ltd [1976] QB 752 Queen's Bench Division (Lord Widgery CJ)

Confidentiality and cabinet discussions

Judicial recognition of conventions

Facts

Richard Crossman kept a political diary 1964-70 while a Cabinet minister. After his death his diary was edited for publication and submitted to the Secretary to the Cabinet in accordance with custom. The diary contained detailed accounts of discussions at Cabinet meetings and the Secretary refused to consent to publication. Crossman's literary executors went ahead with publication, and the Attorney-General sought an injunction to stop it.

Held

The court had power to restrain the improper publication of information acquired by a Minister in confidence, and the doctrine of collective responsibility justified the restriction of confidential Cabinet discussions. However, the court should and would only act where need for continuing confidentiality had been clearly shown. On the facts, publication in 1975 of Cabinet discussions during 1964-6 should not be restrained.

Lord Widgery CJ :

'It has always been assumed by lawyers and, I suspect, by politicians, and the Civil Service, that Cabinet proceedings and Cabinet papers are secret, and cannot be publicly disclosed until they have passed into history. It is quite clear that no court will compel the production of Cabinet papers in the course of discovery in an action, and the Attorney-General contends that not only will the court refuse to compel the production of such matters, but it will go further and positively forbid the disclosure of such papers and proceedings if publication will be contrary to the public interest.

The basis of this contention is the confidential character of these papers and proceedings, derived from the convention of joint Cabinet responsibility whereby any policy decision reached by the Cabinet has to be supported thereafter by all members of the Cabinet whether they approve of it or not, unless they feel compelled to resign. It is contended that Cabinet decisions and papers are confidential for a period to the extent at least that they must not be referred to outside the Cabinet in such a way as to disclose the attitude of individual Ministers in the argument which preceded the decision. Thus, there may be no objection to a Minister disclosing (or leaking, as it was called) the fact that a Cabinet meeting has taken place, or, indeed, the decision taken, so long as the individual views of Ministers are not identified.

There is no doubt that Mr Crossman's manuscripts contain frequent references to individual opinions of Cabinet Ministers, and this is not surprising because it was his avowed object to obtain a relaxation of the convention regarding memoirs of ex-Ministers to which Sir John Hunt referred. There have, as far as I know, been no previous attempts in any court to define the extent to which Cabinet proceedings should be treated as secret or confidential, and it is not surprising that different views on this subject are contained in the evidence before me. The Attorney-General does not attempt a final definition but his contention is that such proceedings are confidential and their publication is capable of control by the courts at least as far as they include (a) disclosure of Cabinet documents or proceedings in such a way as to reveal the individual views or attitudes of Ministers;

(b) disclosure of confidential advice from civil servants, whether contained in Cabinet papers or not;
(c) disclosure of confidential discussions affecting the appointment or transfer of such senior civil servants.

The Attorney-General contends that all Cabinet papers and discussions are prima facie confidential, and that the court should restrain any disclosure thereof if the public interest in concealment outweighs the public interest in a right to free publication. The Attorney-General further contends that, if it is shown that the public interest is involved, he has the right and duty to bring the matter before the court. In this contention he is well supported by Lord Salmon in *R* v *Lewes Justices, ex parte Secretary of State for the Home Department* [1973] AC 388, 412, where Lord Salmon said:

> "when it is in the public interest that confidentiality shall be safe-guarded, then the party from whom the confidential document or the confidential information is being sought may lawfully refuse it. In such a case the Crown may also intervene to prevent production or disclosure of that which in the public interest ought to be protected."

I do not understand Lord Salmon to be saying, or the Attorney-General to be contending, that it is only necessary for him to evoke the public interest to obtain an order of the court. On the contrary, it must be for the court in every case to be satisfied that the public interest is involved, and that, after balancing all the factors which tell for or against publication, to decide whether suppression is necessary.

The defendants' main contention is that whatever the limits of the convention of joint Cabinet responsibility may be, there is no obligation enforceable at law to prevent the publication of Cabinet papers and proceedings, except in extreme cases where national security is involved. In other words, the defendants submit that the confidential character of Cabinet papers and discussions is based on a true convention as defined in the evidence of Professor Henry Wade, namely, an obligation founded in conscience only. Accordingly, the defendants contend that publication of these Diaries is not capable of control by any order of this court.

If the Attorney-General were restricted in his argument to the general proposition that Cabinet papers and discussion are all under the seal of secrecy at all times, he would be in difficulty. It is true that he has called evidence from eminent former holders of office to the effect that the public interest requires a continuing secrecy, and he cites a powerful passage from the late Viscount Hailsham to this effect. The extract comes from a copy of the Official Report (House of Lords) for 21 December 1932, in the course of a debate on Cabinet secrecy. Lord Hailsham said; col 527:

> "But, my Lords, I am very glad that the question has been raised because it has seemed to me that there is a tendency in some quarters at least to ignore or to forget the nature and extent of the obligations of secrecy and the limitations which rigidly hedge round the position of a Cabinet Minister. My noble friend has read to your Lordships what in fact I was proposing to read - that is, the oath which every Privy Councillor takes when he is sworn of His Majesty's Privy Council. Your Lordships will remember that one reason at least why a Cabinet Minister must of necessity be a member of the Privy Council is that it involves the taking of that oath. Having heard that oath read your Lordships will appreciate what a complete misconception it is to suppose, as some people seem inclined to suppose, that the only obligation that rests upon a Cabinet Minister is not to disclose what are described as the Cabinet's minutes. He is sworn to keep secret all matters committed and revealed unto him or that shall be treated secretly in Council."

Lord Hailsham then goes on to point out that there are three distinct classes to which obligation of secrecy applies. He describes them as so-called Cabinet minutes, secondly, a series of documents, memoranda, telegrams and despatches and documents circulated from one Cabinet Minister to his colleagues to bring before them a particular problem and to discuss the arguments for and against a particular course of conduct; and, thirdly, apart from those two classes of documents, he says there is the recollection of the individual Minister of what happens in the Cabinet. Then the extract from

Lord Hailsham's speech in the House of Lord's report continues in these words:

"I have stressed that because, as my noble and learned friend Lord Halsbury suggested and the noble Marquis, Lord Salisbury, confirmed, Cabinet conclusions did not exist until 16 years ago. The old practice is set out in a book which bears the name of the noble Earl's father, Halsbury's Laws of England, with which I have had the honour to be associated in the present edition."

Then the last extract from Lord Hailsham's speech is found in col 532, and is in these words:

"It is absolutely essential in the public interest that discussions which take place between Cabinet Ministers shall take place in the full certainty of all of them that they are speaking their minds with absolute freedom to colleagues on whom they can explicitly rely, upon matters on which it is their sworn duty to express their opinions with complete frankness and to give all information, without any haunting fear that what happens may hereafter by publications create difficulties for themselves or, what is far more grave, may create complications for the King and country that they are trying to serve. For those reasons I hope that the inflexible rule which has hitherto prevailed will be maintained in its integrity, and that if there has been any relaxation or misunderstanding, of which I say nothing, the debate in this House will have done something to clarity the position and restate the old rule in all its rigour and all its inflexibility."

The defendants, however, in the present action, have also called distinguished former Cabinet Ministers who do not support this view of Lord Hailsham, and it seems to me that the degree of protection afforded to Cabinet papers and discussion cannot be determined by a single rule of thumb. Some secrets require a high standard of protection for a short time. Others require protection until a new political generation has taken over. In the present action against the literary executors, the Attorney-General asks for a perpetual injunction to restrain further publication of the Diaries in whole or in part. I am far from convinced that he has made out a case that the public interest requires such a Draconian remedy when due regard is had to other public interests, such as the freedom of speech: see Lord Denning MR in *In re X (A Minor) (Wardship: Jurisdiction)* [1975] Fam 47.

Some attempt has been made to say that the publication of these Diaries by Mr Crossman would have been a breach of his oath as a Privy Councillor, and an echo of this argument is, of course, to be found in Lord Hailsham's words recently quoted. This is, however, not seriously relied upon in the two actions now before me, and the Attorney-General concedes that the present defendants are not in breach of the Official Secrets Acts. It seems to me, therefore, that the Attorney-General must first show that whatever obligation of secrecy or discretion attaches to former Cabinet Ministers, that obligation is binding in law and not merely in morals.

I have read affidavits from a large number of leading politicians, and the facts, so far as relevant, appear to be these. In 1964, 1966 and 1969 the Prime Minister (who was in each case Mr Harold Wilson) issued a confidential document to Cabinet Ministers containing guidance on certain questions of procedure. Paragraph 72 of the 1969 edition provides:

"The principle of collective responsibility and the obligation not to disclose information acquired whilst holding Ministerial office apply to former Ministers who are contemplating the publication of material based upon their recollections of the conduct of Cabinet and Cabinet committee business in which they took part."

The general understanding of Ministers while in office was that information obtained from Cabinet sources was secret and not to be disclosed to outsiders.'

[His Lordship then turned to consider submissions by counsel for the publishers to the effect that there was no evidence to support the doctrine of collective responsibility]

'I find overwhelming evidence that the doctrine of joint responsibility is generally understood and practised and equally strong evidence that it is on occasion ignored. The general effect of the evidence is that the doctrine is an established feature of the English form of government, and regarded as confidential. Furthermore, I am persuaded that the nature of the confidence is that spoken for by the Attorney-General, namely, that since the confidence is imposed to enable the efficient conduct of the Queen's business, the confidence is owed to the Queen and cannot be released by the members of the Cabinet themselves. I have been told that a resigning Minister who wishes to make a personal statement in the House, and to disclose matters which are confidential under the doctrine obtains the consent of the Queen for this purpose. Such consent is obtained through the Prime Minister. I have not been told what happened when the Cabinet disclosed divided opinions during the European Economic Community referendum. But even if there was here a breach of confidence (which I doubt) this is no ground for denying the existence of the general rule. I cannot accept the suggestion that a Minister owes no duty of confidence in respect of his own views expressed in Cabinet. It would only need one or two Ministers to describe their own views to enable experienced observers to identify the views of the others.

The other defence submissions are either variants of those dealt with, or submission with regard to relief.

The Cabinet is at the very centre of national affairs, and must be in possession at all times of information which is secret or confidential. Secrets relating to national security may require to be preserved indefinitely. Secrets relating to new taxation proposals may be of the highest importance until Budget day, but public knowledge thereafter. To leak a Cabinet decision a day or so before it is officially announced is an accepted exercise in public relations, but to identify the Ministers who voted one way or another is objectionable because it undermines the doctrine of joint responsibility.

It is evident that there cannot be a single rule governing the publication of such a variety of matters. In these actions we are concerned with the publication of diaries at a time when 11 years have expired since the first recorded events. The Attorney-General must show (a) that such publication would be a breach of confidence; (b) that the public interest requires that the publication be restrained, and (c) that there are no other facts of the public interest contradictory of and more compelling than that relied upon. Moreover, the court, when asked to restrain such a publication, must closely examine the extent to which relief is necessary to ensure that restrictions are not imposed beyond the strict requirement of public need.

Applying those principles to the present case, what do we find? In my judgment, the Attorney-General has made out his claim that the expression of individual opinions by Cabinet Ministers in the course of Cabinet discussion are matters of confidence, the publication of which can be restrained by the court when this is clearly necessary in the public interest.

The maintenance of the doctrine of joint responsibility within the Cabinet is in the public interest, and the application of that doctrine might be prejudiced by premature disclosure of the views of individual Ministers.

There must, however, be a limit in time after which the confidential character of the information, and the duty of the court to restrain the publication, will lapse. Since the conclusion of the hearing in this case I have had the opportunity to read the whole of volume one of the Diaries, and my considered view is that I cannot believe that the publication at this interval of anything in volume one would inhibit free discussion in the Cabinet of today, even though the individuals involved are the same, and the national problems have a distressing similarity with those of a decade ago. It is unnecessary to elaborate the evils which might flow if at the close of a Cabinet meeting a Minister proceeded to give the press an analysis of the voting, but we are dealing in this case with a disclosure of information nearly 10 years later.

It may, of course, be intensely difficult in a particular case, to say at what point the material loses its confidential character, on the ground that publication will no longer undermine the doctrine of joint Cabinet responsibility. It is this difficulty which prompts some to argue that Cabinet discussions should retain their confidential character for a longer and arbitrary period such as 30 years, or even for all the time, but this seems to me to be excessively restrictive. The court should intervene only in the clearest of cases where the continuing confidentiality of the material can be demonstrated. In less clear cases - and this, in my view, is certainly one - reliance must be placed on the good sense and good taste of the Minister or ex-Minister concerned.

In the present case there is nothing in Mr Crossman's work to suggest that he did not support the doctrine of joint Cabinet responsibility. The question for the court is whether it is shown that publication now might damage the doctrine notwithstanding that much of the action is up to 10 years old and three general elections have been held meanwhile. So far as the Attorney-General relies in his argument on the disclosure of individual ministerial opinions, he has not satisfied me that publication would in any way inhibit free and open discussion in Cabinet hereafter.

It remains to deal with the Attorney-General's two further arguments, namely, (a) that the Diaries disclose advice given by senior civil servants who cannot be expected to advise frankly if their advice is not treated as confidential; (b) the Diaries disclose observations made by Ministers on the capacity of individual senior civil servants and their suitability for specific appointments. I can see no ground in law which entitle the court to restrain publication of these matters. A Minister is, no doubt, responsible for his department and accountable for its errors even though the individual fault is to be found in his subordinates. In these circumstances, to disclose the fault of the subordinate may amount to cowardice or bad taste, but I can find no ground for saying that either the Crown or the individual civil servant has an enforceable right to have the advice which he gives treated as confidential for all time.

For these reasons I do not think that the court should interfere with the publication of volume one of the Diaries, and I propose, therefore, to refuse the injunction sought but to grant liberty to apply in regard to material other than volume one if it is alleged that different considerations may there have to be applied.'

Reference Re Amendment of the Constitution of Canada (1982) 125 DLR (3rd) 1 (Supreme Court of Canada)

Facts

The Canadian Supreme Court was asked to grant a declaration confirming the existence of a convention to the effect that there would be no changes to the Canadian constitution without the unanimous agreement of the Canadian provinces.

Held (by a majority, Martland, Ritchie, Dickson, Beetz, Chouinard, and Latimer JJ)

There was such a convention.

Extracts from the judgment of the majority

'The conventional rules of the Constitution present one striking peculiarity. In contradistinction to the laws of the Constitution, they are not enforced by the Courts. One reason for this situation is that, unlike common law rules, conventions are not judge-made rules. They are not based on judicial precedents but on precedents established by the institutions of government themselves. Nor are they in the nature of statutory commands which it is the function and duty of the Courts to obey and enforce. Furthermore, to enforce them would mean to administer some formal sanction when they are breached. But the legal system from which they are distinct does not contemplate formal sanctions for their breach.

Perhaps the main reason why conventional rules cannot be enforced by the Courts is that they are generally in conflict with the legal rules which they postulate and the Courts are bound to enforce the legal rules. The conflict is not of a type which would entail the commission of any illegality. It results from the fact that legal rules create wide powers, discretions and rights which conventions prescribe should be exercised only in a certain limited manner, if at all.'

[The majority endorsed the approach expounded by Sir Ivor Jennings (in *The Law and the Constitution*) 5th ed 1959 p136) to ascertaining the existence of a convention]

'We have to ask ourselves three questions: first, what are the precedents; secondly, did the actors in the precedents believe that they were bound by a rule; and thirdly, is there a reason for the rule? A single precedent with a good reason may be enough to establish the rule. A whole string of precedents without such a reason will be of no avail, unless it is perfectly certain that the persons concerned regarded them[selves] as bound by it.'

Madzimbamuto v Lardner-Burke [1969] 1 AC 645 House of Lords

Relationship between convention and statute

Facts

In 1961 the United Kingdom government had recognised the existence of a convention to the effect that the Parliament at Westminster would not legislate for colonies such as Southern Rhodesia without their consent. In 1965 the government in Rhodesia declared unilateral independence. This declaration was not recognised by the United Kingdom government, and Parliament at Westminster enacted the Southern Rhodesia Act 1965 seeking to invalidate the acts of the Southern Rhodesian government.

Held (by a majority)

Regardless of the existence of a convention, the courts would enforce legislation duly enacted by Parliament.

Lord Reid (referring to the convention in issue):

'That was a very important convention but it had no legal effect in limiting the legal power of Parliament.

It is often said that it would be unconstitutional for the United Kingdom Parliament to do certain things, meaning that the moral, political and other reasons against doing them are so strong that most people would regard it as highly improper if Parliament did these things. But that does mean that it is beyond the power of Parliament to do such things. If Parliament chose to do any of them the courts could not hold the Act of Parliament invalid. It may be that it would have been thought, before 1965, that it would be unconstitutional to disregard this convention. But it may also be that the unilateral Declaration of Independence released the United Kingdom from any obligation to observe the convention. Their Lordships in declaring the law are not concerned with these matters. They are only concerned with the legal powers of Parliament ...'

2 THE SEPARATION OF POWERS – THE RULE OF LAW – THE INDEPENDENCE OF THE JUDICIARY

Separation of Powers

Duport Steels Ltd v Sirs [1980] 1 WLR 142 House of Lords

Facts

The House of Lords was asked to consider an appeal from the Court of Appeal's restrictive interpretation of s13(1) of the Trade Union and Labour Relations Act 1974 (as amended). On the issue of the importance of the doctrine of the separation of powers, Lord Diplock commented :

'... My Lords, at a time when more and more cases involve the application of legislation which gives effect to policies that are the subject of bitter public and parliamentary controversy, it cannot be too strongly emphasised that the British constitution, though largely unwritten, is firmly based upon the separation of powers; Parliament makes the laws, the judiciary interpret them. When Parliament legislates to remedy what the majority of its members at the time perceive to be a defect or a lacuna in the existing law (whether it be the written law enacted by existing statutes or the unwritten common law as it has been expounded by the judges in decided cases), the role of the judiciary is confined to ascertaining from the words that Parliament has approved as expressing its intention what that intention was, and to giving effect to it. Where the meaning of the statutory words is plain and unambiguous it is not for the judges to invent fancied ambiguities as an excuse for failing to give effect to its plain meaning because they themselves consider that the consequences of doing so would be inexpedient, or even unjust or immoral. In controversial matters such as are involved in industrial relations there is room for differences of opinion as to what is expedient, what is just and what is morally justifiable. Under our constitution it is Parliament's opinion on these matters that is paramount.

A statute passed to remedy what is perceived by Parliament to be a defect in the existing law may in actual operation turn out to have injurious consequences that Parliament did not anticipate at the time the statute was passed; if it had, it would have made some provision in the Act in order to prevent them. It is at least possible that Parliament when the Acts of 1974 and 1976 were passed did not anticipate that so widespread and crippling use has in fact occurred would be made of sympathetic withdrawals of labour and of secondary blacking and picketing in support of sectional interests able to exercise "industrial muscle". But if this be the case it is for Parliament, not for the judiciary, to decide whether any changes should be made to the law as stated in the Acts, and, if so, what are the precise limits that ought to be imposed upon the immunity from liability for torts committed in the course of taking industrial action. These are matters on which there is a wide legislative choice the exercise of which is likely to be influenced by the political complexion of the government and the state of public opinion at the time amending legislation is under consideration.

It endangers continued public confidence in the political impartiality of the judiciary, which is essential to the continuance of the rule of law, if judges, under the guise of interpretation, provide their own preferred amendments to statutes which experience of their operation has shown to have had consequences that members of the court before whom the matter comes consider to be injurious to the public interest.'

Per Lord Scarman:

'When one is considering law in the hands of the judges, law means the body of rules and guidelines within which society requires its judges to administer justice. Legal systems differ in the width of the discretionary power granted to judges: but in developed societies limits are invariably set, beyond which the judges may not go. Justice in such societies is not left to the unguided, even if experienced, sage sitting under the spreading oak tree.

In our society the judges have in some aspects of their work a discretionary power to do justice so wide that they may be regarded as law-makers. The common law and equity, both of them in essence systems of private law, are fields where, subject to the increasing intrusion of statute law, society has been content to allow the judges to formulate and develop the law. The judges, even in this, their very own field of creative endeavour, have accepted, in the interests of certainty, the self-denying ordinance of 'stare decisis', the doctrine of binding precedent: and no doubt this judicially imposed limitation on judicial law-making has helped to maintain confidence in the certainty and evenhandedness of the law.

But in the field of statute law the judge must be obedient to the will of Parliament as expressed in its enactments. In this field Parliament makes, and un-makes, the law: the judge's duty is to interpret and to apply the law, not to change it to meet the judge's idea of what justice requires. Interpretation does, of course, imply in the interpreter a power of choice where differing constructions are possible. But our law requires the judge to choose the construction which in his judgment best meets the legislative purpose of the enactment. If the result be unjust but inevitable, the judge may say so and invite Parliament to reconsider its provision. But he must not deny the statute. Unpalatable statute law may not be disregarded or rejected, merely because it is unpalatable. Only if a just result can be achieved without violating the legislative purpose of the statute may the judge select the construction which best suits his idea of what justice requires. Further, in our system the rule 'stare decisis' applies as firmly to statute law as it does to the formulation of common law and equitable principles. And the keystone of 'stare decisis' is loyalty throughout the system to the decisions of the Court of Appeal and this House ...'

See further *R* v *HM Treasury, ex parte Smedley* [1985] QB 657.

Rule of law

Entick v Carrington (1765) 19 St Tr 1030 Court of Common Pleas

General search warrants - whether lawful

Facts

The plaintiff sued the King's messengers in trespass after they had entered and searched his house under authority of a 'general warrant'. The defendants were unable to show any statutory or common law authority for the issuing of such warrants.

Held

There was no legal basis for the issuing of such warrants

Per Lord Camden :

'When the officers of the Inland Revenue come armed with a warrant to search a man's home or his office, it seems to me that he is entitled to say: "Of what offence do you suspect me? You are claiming to enter my house and to seize my papers." And when they look at the papers and seize them, he should be able to say: "Why are you seizing these papers? Of what offence do you suspect me? What have these to do with your case?" Unless he knows the particular offence charged, he cannot take steps to secure himself or his property. So it seems to me, as a matter of construction of the statute and therefore of the warrant - in pursuance of our traditional role to protect the liberty of

2 THE SEPARATION OF POWERS – THE RULE OF LAW – THE INDEPENDENCE OF THE JUDICIARY

the individual - it is our duty to say that the warrant must particularise the specific offence which is charged as being fraud on the revenue. If no such excuse can be found or produced, the silence of the books is an authority against the defendant, and the plaintiff must have judgment ...

I come now to the practice since the Revolution, which has been strongly urged, with this emphatical addition, that an usage tolerated from the era of liberty, and continued downwards to this time through the best ages of the constitution, must necessarily have a legal commencement ...

With respect to the practice itself, if it goes no higher, every lawyer will tell you, it is much too modern to be evidence of the common law ...

This is the first instance I have met with, where the ancient immemorable law of the land, in a public matter, was attempted to be proved by the practice of a private office.

The names and rights of public magistrates, their power and forms of proceeding as they are settled by law, have been long since written, and are to be found in books and records ... [W]hoever conceived a notion, that any part of the public law could be buried in the obscure practice of a particular person?

To search, seize, and carry away all the papers of the subject upon the first warrant: that such a right should have existed from the time whereof the memory of man runneth not to the contrary, and never yet have found a place in any book of law; is incredible ...

But still it is insisted, that there has been a general submission, and no action brought to try the right.

I answer, there has been a submission of guilt and poverty to power and the terror of punishment. But it would be a strange doctrine to assert that all the people of this land are bound to acknowledge that to be universal law, which a few criminal booksellers have been afraid to dispute ...

It is then said, that it is necessary for the ends of government to lodge such a power with a state officer; and that it is better to prevent the publication before than to punish the offender afterwards ... [W]ith respect to the argument of state necessity, or a distinction that has been aimed at between state offences and others, the common law does not understand that kind of reasoning, nor do our books take notice of any such distinctions ...'

See *Liversidge* v *Anderson* [1942] AC 206, chapter 8. *Padfield* v *Minister of Agriculture* [1968] AC 997, chapter 11; *Commissioners of Customs and Excise* v *Cure and Deely* [1962] 1 QB 340, chapter 8.

Independence of the judiciary

Sirros v Moore [1975] QB 118; [1974] 3 All ER 776 Court of Appeal (Lord Denning MR, Buckley and Ormrod LJJ)

Immunity of the judiciary from liability for judicial acts

Facts

A circuit court judge by an erroneous procedure ordered the police to detain a Turkish citizen who had appeared before him. The plaintiff had obtained his liberty by a writ of habeas corpus, and sought to recover damages from the judge.

Held

The judge was entitled to immunity granted to every judge, including a justice of the peace, for acts committed in good faith in a judicial capacity. The plaintiff had recovered his liberty and was not entitled to further compensation from the judge.

3 PARLIAMENTARY SOVEREIGNTY

Attorney-General for New South Wales v Trethowan [1932] AC 526 Privy Council (Viscount Sankey LC, Lord Blanesburgh, Lord Hanworth, Lord Atkin and Lord Russell of Killowen) (Dixon J in the Australian High Court affirmed)

Limitations on the power of Parliament

Facts

The legislature of New South Wales, which however had only limited constitutional powers at that time, proposed and passed a measure which, under their constitution, should have then been put to the electorate. The Legislative Council (or those members of it other than the plaintiffs who were suing) proposed to put the measure to the Governor-General for approval without holding a referendum.

Held

An ex parte injunction would be granted to prevent this happening.

Dixon J:

> 'An act of the British Parliament which contained a provision that no Bill repealing any part of the Act including the part so restraining its own repeal should be presented for the Royal Assent unless the Bill was first approved by the electors, would have the forces of law until the sovereign actually did assent to a Bill for its repeal. In strictness it would be an unlawful proceeding to present such a Bill for the Royal Assent before it had been approved by the electors. If, therefore, before the Bill received the Assent of the Crown, it was found possible, as appears to have been done in this appeal, to raise for judicial decision the question whether it was lawful to present the Bill for that Assent, the Courts would be bound to pronounce it unlawful to do so. Moreover, if it happened that, notwithstanding the statutory inhibition, the Bill did receive the Royal Assent although it was not submitted to the electors, the Courts might be called upon to consider whether the supreme legislative power in respect of the matter had in truth been exercised in the manner required for its authentic expression and by the elements in which it had come to reside.'

Bonham's (Dr) Case (1610) Co Rep 118a King's Bench (Coke LJ)

The relations between the courts and statute

Coke LJ:

> 'And it appears in our books, that in many cases, the common law will control Acts of Parliament, and sometimes adjudge them to be utterly void: for when an Act of Parliament is against common rights or reason, or repugnant, or impossible to be performed, the common law will control it and adjudge such Act to be void.'

Edinburgh and Dalkeith Railway v Wauchope (1842) 8 Cl & F 710 House of Lords (Lords Cottenham, Brougham and Campbell)

No power in the courts to enquire behind the fact of the passing of an act

Facts

The company was incorporated by a private Act, under which the respondent claimed to be entitled to a payment for every passenger-carrying carriage which crossed his land. The company denied that he was so entitled, and in any case argued that the first Act had been repealed by a later Act under which he could not claim. The respondent claimed not to be bound by the later Act because it had been introduced into the House without his having been given proper notice, as required by the Standing Orders of the House. By the time the case came to the House of Lords the respondent had abandoned this claim, but it had been raised in the lower Courts and all their Lordships referred to it.

Held

The appeal would be dismissed.

Lord Campbell:

'... I think it right to say a word or two upon the point that ... an Act of Parliament [might be] ... held inoperative because the forms prescribed by the two Houses ... have not been exactly followed. There seems great reason to believe that an idea to that effect had prevailed ... in Scotland ... This defence was entered into in the court below ... and the Lord Ordinary ... gave great weight to [it] ... I cannot but express my surprise that such a notion should ever have prevailed. There is no foundation whatever for it. All that a Court of Justice can do is look to the parliamentary roll; if from that it should appear that a bill has passed both Houses and received the Royal Assent, no Court of Justice can enquire into the mode in which it was introduced into Parliament, nor into what was done previous to its introduction, or what passed in Parliament during its progress in its various stages through both Houses. I trust, therefore, that no such enquiry will again be entered upon in any court ... but that due effect will be given to every Act of Parliament private as well as public, upon what appears to be the proper construction of its existing provisions.'

Ellen Street Estates Ltd v Minister of Health [1934] 1 KB 590 Court of Appeal (Scrutton and Maugham LJJ, Talbot J)

Power of Parliament to alter its own provisions

Facts

The plaintiffs sought to have compensation for compulsorily acquired land paid on an earlier more favourable basis rather than that laid down in a later statute.

Held

The later statute must prevail.

Scrutton LJ:

'... The point advanced by [Counsel]... is this: the Acquisition of Land (Assessment of Compensation) Act 1919 lays down certain principles on which compensation for land taken is to be assessed. Section 7(1) says this:

"The provisions of the Act or order by which the land is authorised to be acquired ... shall, in relation to the matters dealt with in this Act, have effect subject to this Act, and so far as inconsistent with this Act, those provisions shall cease to have ... effect."

[The] ... contention is that if in a later Act provisions are found as to compensation ... which are inconsistent with those contained in the Act of 1919, the later provisions are to have no effect. Such a contention involves this proposition, that no subsequent Parliament by enacting a provision inconsistent with the Act of 1919, can give any effect to the words it uses. Section 46(1) of the Housing Act 1925 says this:

> "Where land included in any improvement or reconstruction scheme ... is acquired compulsorily", certain provisions as to compensation shall apply. These are inconsistent with those contained in the ... 1919 Act, and then s46(2) of the Act of 1925 provides: "Subject as aforesaid, the compensation to be paid for such land shall be assessed in accordance with the ... 1919 Act."

I asked [Counsel] ... what these last quoted words mean, and he replied they mean nothing. That is absolutely contrary to the constitutional position that Parliament can alter an Act previously passed, and it can do so by repealing in terms the previous Act ... and it can do it also in another way - namely, by enacting a provision which is clearly inconsistent with the previous Act. In Maxwell's Interpretation of Statutes I find three or four pages devoted to cases in which Parliament, without using the word "repeal", has effected the same result by enacting a section inconsistent with an earlier provision. It is impossible to say that these words that compensation shall be assessed in a particular way and, subject as aforesaid, shall be assessed in accordance with the provisions of the Act of 1919 have no effect. This point was not dealt with... because in *Vauxhall Estates Ltd* v *Liverpool Corporation* (1) a Divisional Court rejected [Counsel's] ... argument and held that the provisions of the Act of 1925, so far as they were inconsistent with, must prevail over, the Act of 1919. In the present case the matter is carried a step further, because s12 of the Housing Act 1930 says in effect that compensation shall be assessed in accordance with the provisions of the Act of 1919 except as altered in a series of matters which the Act of 1930 prescribed. In my opinion *Vauxhall Estates Ltd* v *Liverpool Corporation* was rightly decided and [the plaintiff's] ... point fails and the appeal must be dismissed.'

(1)   Infra, this chapter

Lee v Bude and Torrington Junction Railway Co (1871) LR 6 CP 576 Court of Common Pleas (Willes, Byles and Keating JJ)

No power in the court to examine procedure in passing of a statute

Facts

The plaintiffs were solicitors who had been instrumental in obtaining private acts which founded the defendant railways. The Act provided that their costs should be met by the companies, but as they had no assets the plaintiffs sued the shareholders. The defendants argued that the company was a sham which had never built a railway, but was merely a shell to allow the plaintiffs to run up bills of costs.

Held

The costs were recoverable.

Willes J:

'... I would observe, as to these Acts of Parliament, that they are the law of this land; and we do not sit here as a court of appeal from Parliament. It was once said - I think in Hobart - that, if an Act of Parliament were to create a man judge in his own case, the court might disregard it. That dictum, however, stands as a warning, rather than an authority to be followed. We sit here as servants of the Queen and the legislature. Are we to act as regents over what is done by Parliament with the consent of the Queen, Lords and Commons? I deny that any such authority exists. If an Act of Parliament has been obtained improperly, it is for the legislature to correct it by repealing it; but, so long as it exists as law the courts are bound to obey it. The proceedings here are judicial, not autocratic, which they would be if we were to make laws instead of administering them. The Act of Parliament makes these persons shareholders, or it does not. If it does, there is an end of the question. If it does not, that is a matter which may be raised by plea to the scire facias. Having neglected to take proper steps at the proper time to prevent the Act from passing into a law, it is too late now to raise any objections to it.'

Mortensen v Peters 1906 14 SLT 227 High Court of Justiciary Full Bench (The Lord Justice General, The Lord Justice Clerk, Lords Ardwall, Dundas, Johnston, Kyllachy, Low, Mackenzie, M'Laren, Pearson, Salvesen, and Stormont-Darling)

Rule of Law: Parliamentary Sovereignty and international law

Facts

The appellant was a Dane and had been convicted of trawling in the Moray Firth, contrary to a by-law issued by the Fishery Board for Scotland under the Herring Fishery (Scotland) Act 1889. He appealed, arguing that under international law a state could control fishing only within its territorial waters, which were limited to bays and estuaries of ten miles or less in breadth.

Held

Conviction upheld.

Lord Dunedin, Lord Justice General:

'In this Court we have nothing to do with the question whether the Legislature has or has not done what foreign powers may consider a usurpation in a question with them. Neither are we a tribunal sitting to decide whether an Act of the Legislature is ultra vires as a contravention of generally acknowledged principles of international law. For us, an Act of Parliament duly passed by Lords and Commons and assented to by the King is supreme, and we are bound to give effect to its terms.'

Pickin v British Railways Board [1974] AC 765 House of Lords (Lords Reid, Wilberforce, Morris of Borth-y-Gest, Simon and Cross)

No power in the courts to enquire into procedure behind the passing of an Act

Facts

The Bristol and Exeter Railway, to which the defendants were successors, was set up by private Act in 1836, and the statute provided that if the line ceased to be used the land should revert to the ownership of the landowners on either side of the track. The defendant Board in 1968 secured a private Act which (inter alia) took away those rights, and proposed to close the line. The plaintiff, an objector to the principle of closing branch lines, bought land alongside the track, and claimed a declaration that he was entitled to the land on which the abandoned line lay. He claimed that the 1968 Act had been secured fraudulently, because the preamble recited that lists of owners and plans had been deposited in Somerset County Record Office, which they had not.

Held

The House of Lords dismissed Mr Pickin's claim.

Lord Reid:

'... The idea that a court is entitled to disregard a provision in an Act of Parliament on any ground must seem strange and startling to anyone with any knowledge of the history and law of our constitution, but a detailed argument has been submitted to Your Lordships and I must deal with it.

I must make it plain that there has been no attempt to question the general supremacy of Parliament. In earlier times many learned lawyers seem to have believed that an Act of Parliament could be disregarded in so far as it was contrary to the law of God or the law of nature or natural justice, but since the supremacy of Parliament was finally demonstrated by the Revolution of 1688 any such idea has become obsolete.

The respondent's contention is that there is a difference between a public and a private Act. There are, of course, great differences between the methods and procedures followed in dealing with public and private Bills, and there may be some differences in the methods of construing their provisions. But the respondent argues for a much more fundamental difference. There is little in modern authority that he can rely on. The mainstay of his argument is a decision of this house, *Mackenzie* v *Stewart* in 1754 ...

At that period there were no contemporary reports of Scots appeals in this House. It would seem that quite often no other peer with legal experience sat with the Lord Chancellor and it seems to me to be probable that frequently no formal speech giving reasons was made at the conclusion of the argument. In comparatively few cases there have been preserved observations made in the courts of the argument. In the present case we have a note made by Lord Kames in his Select Decisions (1):

> "The Lord Chancellor, in delivering his opinion, expressed a good deal of indignation at the fraudulent means of obtaining the act; and said, that he never would have consented to such private acts, had he entered a notion that they could be used to cover fraud."

Lord Kames' Select Decisions cover the earlier period of his long tenure of office as a judge. We do not know how he came to add this passage at the end of his report of the case in the Court of Session. He must have got it, perhaps at second hand, from someone present during the arguments; so these observations may have been made during the argument or in a speech. Lord Hardwicke was Lord Chancellor both in 1754 and in 1739 when the Act was passed, so he may have had some part in passing the Act. In any case I do not read his observations as indicating the ground of the decision, but rather as a comment on what took place when the Act was passed ...

It appears to me that far the most probable explanation of the decision is that it was a decision as to the true construction of the Act ...

If the decision was only as to the construction of a statutory provision that would explain why the case has received little attention in later cases ... If *Mackenzie* v *Stewart* is found to afford no support to the respondent's argument the rest of the authorities are negligible.

In my judgment the law is correctly stated by Lord Campbell in *Edinburgh and Dalkeith Railway Co* v *Wauchope* (2) ... No doubt this was obiter but, so far as I am aware, no one since 1842 has doubted that it is a correct statement of the constitutional position.

The function of the court is to construe and apply the enactments of Parliament. The court has no concern with the manner in which Parliament or its officers carrying out its standing orders perform these functions. Any attempt to prove that they were misled by fraud or otherwise would necessarily involve an inquiry into the manner in which they had performed their functions in dealing with the Bill which became the British Railways Act 1868.

In whatever form the respondent's case is pleaded he must prove not only that the appellants acted fraudulently but also that their fraud caused damage to him by causing the enactment of Section 18. He could not prove that without an examination of the manner in which the officers of Parliament dealt with the matter. So the court would, or at least might, have to adjudicate upon that.

For a century or more both Parliament and the courts have been careful not to act so as to cause conflict between them. Any such investigations as the respondent seeks could easily lead to such a conflict, and I would only support it if compelled to do so by clear authority. But it appears to me that the whole trend of authority for over a century is clearly against permitting any such investigation ... I am therefore clearly of opinion that this appeal should be allowed ...'

(1)   Reported in Morison at p7445 (1 Pat App 578)

(2)   Supra, this chapter

Vauxhall Estates Ltd v Liverpool Corporation [1932] 1 KB 733 King's Bench Divisional Court (Avory J)

Power of Parliament to alter previous enactments

Facts

The plaintiffs wished to receive compensation for land which had been compulsorily acquired by the defendants on an earlier, more favourable basis than that provided in the statute under which the order was made.

Held

The provisions of the later Act must prevail.

Avory J:

> 'We are asked to say that by a provision of the Act of 1919 the hands of Parliament were tied in such a way that it could not by any subsequent Act enact anything which was inconsistent with the provisions of the Act of 1919. It must be admitted that such a suggestion as that is inconsistent with the principle of the constitution of this country. Speaking for myself, I should certainly hold until the contrary were decided, that no Act of Parliament can effectively provide that no future Act shall interfere with its provisions.'

4 THE EUROPEAN ECONOMIC COMMUNITY

Costa v ENEL [1964] ECR 585 European Court of Justice (Judgment anonymous)

Community law and national law

Facts

Italy had nationalised the production and distribution of electricity, and transferred the assets of the private undertakings to a new State body, ENEL. Costa, as a shareholder in one of the private undertakings which had been nationalised, and also as a consumer, claimed before an Italian court that the 1962 nationalisation legislation infringed provisions of the EEC Treaty. The matter went to the European Court, where the Italian government argued that it was obliged to apply its national legislation.

Held

Community law prevails over subsequent incompatible national law.

The Court:

'The EEC Treaty has created its own legal system which [has become] an integral part of the legal systems of the member states and which their courts are bound to apply. By creating a Community of unlimited duration, having its own institutions, its own personality, its own legal capacity ... and, more particularly, real powers stemming from a limitation of sovereignty or a transfer of powers from the states to the Community, the member states have limited their sovereign rights, albeit within limited fields, and have thus created a body of law which binds both their nationals and themselves. ... The executive force of Community law cannot vary from one state to another in deference to subsequent domestic laws, without jeopardising the attainment of the objectives of the Treaty.'

Export Tax On Art Treasures (No 2), Re [1972] CMLR 699 European Court of Justice

Self-executing provisions

Facts

The Italian Law No 1089 of 1 June 1939 on the protection of articles of artistic or historical interest contains several provisions relating to the exportation of such articles. In particular, it provides according to circumstances an absolute export prohibition (Article 35), the need for a licence (Article 36), a right of prior purchase inhering in the State (Article 39), and the imposition on exportation of a progressive tax on the value of the article, ranging by successive stages from 8 to 30 per cent. (Article 37).

In January 1960, the Commission asked the Italian Republic to remove the tax, as regards the other member-States, by the end of the first stage of the transitional period, ie before 1 January 1962 since it considered it to have the same effects as a customs duty on exportation and so contrary to Article 16 of the EEC Treaty. After a prolonged exchange of correspondence, the Commission by letter of 25 February 1964 commenced proceedings under Article 169 of the EEC Treaty, inviting the Italian Government to put forward its observations on the violation of the Treaty alleged of the Italian Republic. The observations which were thereupon made by the Italian Government did not satisfy the Commission which consequently issued the reasoned opinion provided for by Article 169(1) of the Treaty, by letter of 24 July 1964.

In that opinion the Commission gave the reasons for stating that the Italian Republic had failed to fulfil the obligations which bind it under Article 16, and gave a time limit of two months in which to remove the disputed tax from transactions with the other member-States. This time limit was extended to 31 December 1965 after the Commission was informed by the Italian Government that a parliamentary committee had been set up with the task of studying a protection system in the light of the Commission's observations.

On 16 May 1966, the Commission, in reply to a fresh request for an extension, informed the Italian Government that it had, in the light of the necessary parliamentary procedures, granted an extension sufficient for the removal of the tax in question and that it reserved the right to bring the matter before the Court of Justice at a suitable moment.

A government Bill to exempt exports to member-States of the communities from payment of the tax was approved by the Legislation Committee of the Italian Senate on 26 July 1967 and passed to the Chamber of Deputies. The Bill lapsed on dissolution of the Italian Parliament on 11 March 1968. Meanwhile, the Commission brought proceedings before the Court of Justice by application filed on 7 March 1968, where it was held admissible.

Following that decision, Italy failed to comply with the judgment of the Court. By letters in June and October 1970 the President of the Commission called on the Italian Government to take the measures necessary to comply with that judgment. The Italian Government introduced into its Parliament providing for (inter alia) the repeal of the tax. The Commission considered this to be insufficient and invited Italy to submit observations. In May 1971 the Commission called on Italy in a reasoned opinion to take the measures necessary to end the infringement within one month. As no measures were taken within that time the Commission brought the matter before the European Court of Justice. The Advocate-General presented his submissions in June 1972. Subsequently the Italian Government informed the Court that it had adopted a Decree-Law formally retrospectively abolishing the imposition of the tax and providing for repayment on request of taxes paid. The commission informed the Court that it intended to refrain from pursuing the action only after the Decree-law had been transformed into a formal statute.

Held

The laws of Community law should apply automatically, unconditionally throughout the Community. By imposing this tax Italy has failed to fulfil her Community obligations. The Court notes that an end has been put to the infringement as of 1 January 1962.

The judgment of the Court was in these terms:

'(1) By writ of 23 July 1971 the Commission brought before the Court under Article 169 of the Treaty an action for a declaration that Italy, by not complying with the judgment delivered on 10 December 1968 in *Re Export Tax on Art Treasures (No 1)*, case 7/68, infringed the obligations by which it was bound under Article 171 of the EEC Treaty.

In that judgment the Court had held that by continuing after 1 January 1962 to levy the progressive tax laid down in s3 of Law no 1089 of 1 June 1939 on the export to other member-States of the Community of objects of artistic, historical, archaeological or ethnological importance, Italy had failed to fulfil the obligations which rest upon it under Article 16 of the EEC Treaty.

(2) Italy, while recognising that it was bound to adopt the measures required for execution of that judgment, invokes the difficulties with which it was faced on the march through Parliament of the repeal of the tax and reform of the system of protection of the national artistic heritage. These measures necessarily had to be adopted in the forms and according to the processes laid down by its constitutional law. Since collection of the tax could only be terminated through repeal of the statute. and since the delays in making the repeal itself were due to circumstances independent of the will of the relevant authorities, there is no ground for holding that the obligations imposed by Article 171 of the treaty have been violated.

(3) The Commission submits that the repeal of the national provisions could have been made with greater diligence.

(4) Without it being necessary to examine the validity of these arguments, the court restricts itself to observing that, in its judgment of 10 December 1968, it resolved affirmatively the question in dispute between the Italian Government and the Commission of whether the tax in issue should be considered to be a tax with effect equivalent to a customs duty on exports within the meaning of Article 16 of the Treaty. Furthermore, in another judgment, delivered on 26 October 1971 in *SAS Eunomia di Porro EC* v *Italian Ministry of Education* (18/71), this Court expressly held that the prohibition laid down in Article 16 produces direct effects in the internal law of all the member-States.

(5) Since we are concerned with a directly applicable Community norm, the argument that its violation could be terminated only by the adoption of measures which are constitutionally proper for repealing the provisions incompatible with that norm would amount to affirming that the efficacy of the Community norm is subject to the law of each member-State and, more precisely, that its application is impossible so long as a national statute is opposed to it.

(6) In the present instance the efficacy of Community law, as held with binding effect against Italy, implied an absolute prohibition on the relevant national authorities applying a national provision which had been held incompatible with the Treaty and, where necessary, an obligation to adopt all measures necessary to facilitate the full efficacy of the Community law.

(7) The attainment of the aims of the Community requires that the norms of Community law, contained in the Treaty itself and enacted under it, should apply unconditionally, at the same instant and with identical efficacy in the whole territory of the Community, without the member-State being able to thwart them in any way.

(8) The grant to the Community by the member-States of the rights and powers envisaged by the provisions of the Treaty implies in fact a definitive limitation of their sovereign powers, over which no appeal to provisions of internal law of any kind whatever can prevail.

(9) It is therefore necessary to hold that by not complying with the judgment delivered by the Court on 10 December 1968 in *Re Export Tax on Art Treasures (No 1)*, case 7/68, Italy has failed to fulfil the obligations imposed upon her by Article 171, of the Treaty.

(10) By communication of 4 July 1972, the respondent informed the Court that the levy of the tax has ceased and that its effects have been abolished as from 1 January 1962, the date when the levy itself should have ceased.

Costs

(11) It follows from the foregoing that the Commission's action was well based. The infringement alleged ceased only after the conclusion of the written and oral stages. In those circumstances, the respondent is ordered to pay the costs.

The Court, for these reasons, hereby

1. Notes that with effect from 1 January 1962 an end has been put to the infringement of the obligations imposed on Italy by Article 171 of the EEC Treaty.

2. Orders that the respondent pay the costs.'

NV Algemene Transport-en Expeditie Onderneming van Gend en Loos v Nederlandse Administratie der Belastingen (Case 26/62) [1963] ECR 1

The European Court of Justice was asked (by the Nederlandse administratie der belastingen - Netherlands

Inland Revenue Administration) to rule upon the direct applicability of Article 12 of the Treaty of Rome.

The European Court of Justice:

'The first question of the Tariefcommissie is whether article 12 of the Treaty has direct application in national law in the sense that nationals of Member States may on the basis of this article lay claim to rights which the national court must protect.

To ascertain whether the provisions of an international treaty extend so far in their effects it is necessary to consider the spirit, the general scheme and the wording of those provisions.

The objective of the EEC Treaty, which is to establish a Common Market, the functioning of which is of direct concern to interested parties in the Community, implies that this Treaty is more than an agreement which merely creates mutual obligations between the contracting states. This view is confirmed by the preamble to the Treaty which refers not only to governments but to peoples. It is also confirmed more specifically by the establishment of institutions endowed with sovereign rights, the exercise of which affects member states and also their citizens. Furthermore, it must be noted that the nationals of the stages brought together in the Community are called upon to cooperate in the functioning of this Community through the intermediary of the European Parliament and the Economic and Social Committee.

In addition the task assigned to the Court of Justice under article 177, the object of which is to secure uniform interpretation of the Treaty by national courts and tribunals, confirms that the states have acknowledged that Community law has an authority which can be invoked by their nationals before those courts and tribunals.

The conclusion to be drawn from this is that the Community constitutes a new legal order of international law for the benefit of which the states have limited their sovereign rights, albeit within limited fields, and the subjects of which comprise not only member states but also their nationals. Independently of the legislation of member states, Community law therefore not only imposes obligations on individuals but is also intended to confer upon them rights which become part of their legal heritage. These rights arise not only where they are expressly granted by the Treaty, but also by reason of obligations which the Treaty imposes in a clearly defined way upon individuals as well as upon the member states and upon the institutions of the Community ...

The wording of article 12 contains a clear and unconditional prohibition which is not a positive but a negative obligation. This obligation, moreover, is not qualified by any reservation on the part of states which would make its implementation conditional upon a positive legislative measure enacted under national law. The very nature of this prohibition makes it ideally adapted to produce direct effects in the legal relationship between member states and their subjects.

The implementation of article 12 does not require any legislative intervention on the part of the states. The fact that under this article it is the member states who are made the subject of the negative obligation does not imply that their nationals cannot benefit from this obligation.

In addition the argument based on articles 169 and 170 of the Treaty put forward by the three Governments which have submitted observations to the Court in their statements of case is misconceived. The fact that these articles of the Treaty enable the Commission and the member states to bring before the Court a state which has not fulfilled its obligations does not mean that individuals cannot plead these obligations, should the occasion arise, before a national court, any more than the fact that the Treaty places at the disposal of the Commission ways of ensuring that obligations imposed upon those subject to the Treaty are observed, precludes the possibility, in actions between individuals before a national court, of pleading infringement of these obligations.

A restriction of the guarantees against an infringement of article 12 by member states to the procedures under article 169 and 170 would remove all direct legal protection of the individual rights of their nationals. There is the risk that recourse to the procedure under these articles would be ineffective if it were to occur after the implementation of a national decision taken contrary to the provisions of the Treaty.

The vigilance of individuals concerned to protect their rights amounts to an effective supervision in addition to the supervision entrusted by articles 169 and 170 to the diligence of the Commission and of the member states.

It follows from the foregoing considerations that, according to the spirit, the general scheme and the wording of the Treaty, article 12 must be interpreted as producing direct effects and creating individual rights which national courts must protect.'

Van Duyn v Home Office (Case 41/74) [1974] ECR 1337

Ms Van Duyn had been refused entry into the United Kingdom following the Home Secretary's announcement that foreign nationals would not be granted work permits where they intended to take up employment with the Church of Scientology. Ms Van Duyn sought a declaration that the minister's prohibition was in contravention of Article 48 of the Treaty of Rome, and was not permitted under Council Directive No 64/221. Pennycuick VC referred three questions under Article 177.

The European Court of Justice:

'*First question*

4 By the first question, the Court is asked to say whether article 48 of the EEC Treaty is directly applicable so as to confer on individuals rights enforceable by them in the courts of a member state.

5 It is provided, in article 48(1) and (2), that freedom of movement for workers shall be secured by the end of the transitional period and that such freedom shall entail "the abolition of any discrimination based on nationality between workers of member states as regards employment, remuneration and other conditions of work and employment".

6 These provisions impose on member states a precise obligation which does not require the adoption of any further measure on the part either of the Community institutions or of the member states and which leaves them, in relation to its implementation, no discretionary power.

7 Paragraph 3, which defines the rights implied by the principle of freedom of movement for workers, subjects them to limitations justified on the grounds of public policy, public security or public health. The application of these limitations is, however, subject to judicial control, so that a member state's right to invoke the limitations does not prevent the provisions of article 48, which enshrine the principle of freedom of movement for workers, from conferring on individuals rights which are enforceable by them and which the national courts must protect.

8 The reply to the first question must therefore be in the affirmative.

Second question

9 The second question asks the Court to say whether Council Directive No 64/221 of 25 February 1964 on the co-ordination of special measures concerning the movement and residence of foreign nationals which are justified on grounds of public policy, public security or public health is directly applicable so as to confer on individuals rights enforceable by them in the courts of a member state.

10 It emerges from the order making the reference that the only provision of the Directive which is relevant is that contained in article 3(1) which provides that "measures taken on grounds of public policy or public security shall be based exclusively on the personal conduct of the individual concerned".

11 The United Kingdom observes that, since article 189 of the Treaty distinguishes between the effects ascribed to regulations, directives and decisions, it must therefore be presumed that the

Council, in issuing a directive rather than making a regulation, must have intended that the directive should have an effect other than that of a regulation and accordingly that the former should not be directly applicable.

12 If, however, by virtue of the provisions of article 189 regulations are directly applicable and, consequently, may by their very nature have direct effects, it does not follow from this that other categories of acts mentioned in that article can never have similar effects. It would be incompatible with the binding effect attributed to a directive by article 189 to exclude, in principle, the possibility that the obligation which it imposes may be invoked by those concerned. In particular, where the Community authorities have, by directive, imposed on member states the obligation to pursue a particular course of conduct, the useful effect of such an act would be weakened if individuals were prevented from relying on it before their national courts and if the latter were prevented from taking it into consideration as an element of Community law. Article 177, which empowers national courts to refer to the Court questions concerning the validity and interpretation of all acts of the Community institutions, without distinction, implies furthermore that these acts may be invoked by individuals in the national courts. It is necessary to examine, in every case, whether the nature, general scheme and wording of the provision in question are capable of having direct effects on the relations between member states and individuals.

13 By providing that measures taken on grounds of public policy shall be based exclusively on the personal conduct of the individual concerned, article 3(1) of Directive No 64/221 is intended to limit the discretionary power which national laws generally confer on the authorities responsible for the entry and expulsion of foreign nationals. First, the provision lays down an obligation which is not subject to any exception or condition and which, by its very nature, does not require the intervention of any act on the part either of the institutions of the Community or of member states. Secondly, because member states are thereby obliged, in implementing a clause which derogates from one of the fundamental principles of the Treaty in favour of individuals, not to take account of factors extraneous to personal conduct, legal certainty for the persons concerned requires that they should be able to rely on this obligation even though it has been laid down in a legislative act which has no automatic direct effect in its entirety.

14 If the meaning and exact scope of the provision raise questions of interpretation, these questions can be resolved by the courts, taking into account also the procedure under article 177 of the Treaty.

15 Accordingly, in reply to the second question, article 3(1) of Council Directive No 64/221 of 25 February 1964 confers on individuals rights which are enforceable by them in the courts of a member state and which the national courts must protect.

Third question

16 By the third question the Court is asked to rule whether article 48 of the Treaty and article 3 of Directive No 64/221 must be interpreted as meaning that

"a member state, in the performance of its duty to base a measure taken on grounds of public policy exclusively on the personal conduct of the individual concerned is entitled to take into account as matters of personal conduct:

(a) the fact that the individual is or has been associated with some body or organisation the activities of which the member state considers contrary to the public good but which are not unlawful in that state:

(b) the fact that the individual intends to take employment in the member state with such a body or organisation it being the case that no restrictions are placed upon nationals of the member state who wish to take similar employment with such a body or organisation."

17 It is necessary, first, to consider whether association with a body or an organisation can in itself constitute personal conduct within the meaning of article 3 of Directive No 64/221. Although a person's past association cannot, in general, justify a decision refusing him the right to move freely

within the Community, it is nevertheless the case that present association, which reflects participation in the activities of the body or of the organisation as well as identification with its aims and its designs, may be considered a voluntary act of the person concerned and, consequently, as part of his personal conduct within the meaning of the provision cited.

18 This third question further raises the problem of what importance must be attributed to the fact that the activities of the organisation in question, which are considered by the member state as contrary to the public good are now however prohibited by natural law. It should be emphasised that the concept of public policy in the context of the Community and where, in particular, it is used as a justification for derogating from the fundamental principle of freedom of movement for workers, must be interpreted strictly, so that its scope cannot be determined unilaterally by each member state without being subject to control by the institutions of the Community. Nevertheless, the particular circumstances justifying recourse to the concept of public policy may vary from one country to another and from one period to another, and it is therefore necessary in this matter to allow the competent national authorities an area of discretion within the limits imposed by the Treaty.

19 It follows from the above that where the competent authorities of a member state have clearly defined their standpoint as regards the activities of a particular organisation and where, considering it to be socially harmful, they have taken administrative measures to counteract these activities, the member state cannot be required, before it can rely on the concept of public policy, to make such activities unlawful, if recourse to such a measure is not thought appropriate in the circumstances.

20 The question raises finally the problem of whether a member state is entitled, on grounds of public policy, to prevent a national of another member state from taking gainful employment within its territory with a body or organisation, it being the case that no similar restriction is placed upon its own nationals.

21 In this connexion, the Treaty, while enshrining the principle of freedom of movement for workers without any discrimination on grounds of nationality, admits, in article 48(3), limitations justified on grounds of public policy, public security or public health to the rights deriving from this principle. Under the terms of the provision cited above, the right to accept offers of employment actually made, the right to move freely within the territory of member states for this purpose, and the right to stay in a member state for the purpose of employment are, among others all subject to such limitations. Consequently, the effect of such limitations, when they apply, is that leave to enter the territory of a member state and the right to reside there may be refused to a national of another member state.

22 Furthermore, it is a principle of international law, which the EEC Treaty cannot be assumed to disregard in the relations between member states, that a state is precluded from refusing its own nationals the right of entry or residence.

23 It follows that a member state, for reasons of public policy, can, where it deems necessary, refuse a national of another member state the benefit of the principle of freedom of movement for workers in a case where such a national proposes to take up a particular offer of employment even though the member state does not place a similar restriction upon its own nationals.

24 Accordingly, the reply to the third question must be that article 48 of the EEC Treaty and article 3(1) of Directive No 64/221 are to be interpreted as meaning that a member state, in imposing restrictions justified on grounds of public policy, is entitled to take into account, as a matter of personal conduct of the individual concerned, the fact that the individual is associated with some body or organisation the activities of which the member state considers socially harmful but which are not unlawful in that state, despite the fact that no restriction is placed upon nationals of the said member state who wish to take similar employment with these same bodies or organisations ...'

5 EEC MEMBERSHIP AND PARLIAMENTARY SOVEREIGNTY

Blackburn v Attorney-General [1971] 1 WLR 1037 Court of Appeal (Lord Denning MR, Salmon and Stamp LJJ)

The Treaty of Rome and crown prerogative

Facts

The plaintiff sought declarations that by signing the Treaty of Rome, the Government would be acting in breach of the law by irreversibly surrendering part of Parliament's sovereignty.

Held

The power of the Crown to sign treaties was one based firmly within the prerogative, and its exercise would not be questioned by the courts.

Lord Denning MR:

'I do not think these courts can entertain these actions. Negotiations are still in progress for us to join the Common Market. No agreement has been reached. No treaty has been signed. Even if a treaty is signed, it is elementary that these courts take no notice of treaties as such. We take no notice of treaties until they are embodied in laws enacted by Parliament, and then only to the extent that Parliament tells us. That was settled in a case about a treaty between the Queen of England and the Emperor of China. It is *Rustomjee* v *The Queen* (1) Lord Coleridge CJ said, at p74:

"She" - that is the Queen - "acted throughout the making of the treaty and in relation to each and every of its stipulations in her sovereign character, and by her own inherent authority; and, as in making the treaty, so in performing the treaty, she is beyond the control of municipal law, and her acts are not to be examined in her own courts."

Mr Blackburn acknowledged the general principle, but he urged that this proposed treaty is in a category by itself, in that it diminishes the sovereignty of Parliament over the people of this country. I cannot accept the distinction. The general principle applies to this treaty as to any other. The treaty-making power of this country rests not in the courts, but in the Crown; that is, Her Majesty acting upon the advice of her Ministers. When her Ministers negotiate and sign a treaty, even a treaty of such paramount importance as this proposed one, they act on behalf of the country as a whole. They exercise the prerogative of the Crown. Their action in so doing cannot be challenged or questioned in these courts.'

(1)   (1876) 2 QBD 69

Factortame Ltd v Secretary of State for Transport (No 2) [1990] 3 WLR 818 House of Lords (Lord Bridge, Lord Brandon, Lord Oliver, Lord Goff, and Lord Jauncey)

Availability of injunctive relief against the ministers

Facts

Fishing quotas were introduced by the EEC to prevent over-fishing. The United Kingdom Parliament enacted the Merchant Shipping Act 1988 (Part II) to protect British fishing interests by restricting the number of vessels whose catch could be counted against the British quota. The Secretary of State issued regulations under the Act that required any vessel wishing to fish as part of the British fleet to be registered under the 1988 Act. Registration was contingent upon a vessel's owner being a British citizen or domiciled in Britain. In the case of companies, the shareholders would have to meet these requirements. The applicants were British registered companies operating fishing vessels in British waters. These companies now found it impossible to obtain registration because their shareholders and directors were Spanish. The applicants contended that the regulations effectively prevented them from exercising their rights under community law to fish as part of the British fleet. The Secretary of State contended that Community law did not prevent the United Kingdom from introducing domestic legislation determining which companies where 'British nationals' and which were not.

The applicants sought judicial review of:

a) the minister's decision that their registration should cease;

b) the minister's determination that they were no longer 'British' ships;

c) the relevant parts of the Act and Regulations which would have the effect of preventing them from fishing.

The applicants sought the following remedies:

a) a declaration that the minister's decision should not take effect because of its inconsistency with Community law;

b) an order of prohibition to prevent the minister from regarding the ships as de-registered;

c) damages under s35 of the Supreme Court Act 1981;

d) an interim injunction suspending the operation of the legislation pending the ruling of the European Court of Justice.

As regards the interpretation of Community law, the Divisional Court requested a preliminary ruling under Art. 177 of the Treaty of Rome so that the questions relating to the applicant's rights could be resolved. Pending that ruling, the court granted interim the applicants interim relief in the form of an injunction to suspend the operation of the legislation by restraining the minister from enforcing it, thus enabling the applicants to continue fishing. The Secretary of State sought to challenge the order for interim relief, which was set aside by the Court of Appeal. The applicants appealed to the House of Lords.

Held

The appeal would be dismissed. The court had no power to grant interim relief to prevent the operation of a statute passed by parliament. If the ultimate decision of the European Court went against the applicants they would have enjoyed approximately two years (the length of time it would take for the European Court to resolve the matter) unjust enrichment by being allowed to continue fishing.

Further, the court had no power to grant an interim injunction against the Crown. Sections 21(2) and 23(2)(b) of the Crown Proceedings Act 1947 preserved what had been the common law position ie that such relief was not available in judicial review proceedings on the Crown side. On this basis there was no way that the interim relief could be obtained, unless it was be shown that there is some overriding principle of Community law which provides that member states must provide some form of relief to litigants who claim that their rights are being interfered with, pending a decision of the European Court of Justice, a matter that would now have to be referred to the European Court of Justice under Art. 177.

The European Court of Justice held that Community law required the courts of member states to give effect to the directly enforceable provision of Community law. Such Community laws rendered any conflicting national law inapplicable. A court which would grant interim relief, but for a rule of domestic law, should set aside that rule of domestic law in favour of observing community obligations. On the reference back to the House of Lords :

Held: In determining whether interim relief by way of an injunction should be granted, the determining factor should not be the availability of damages as a remedy, but the balance of convenience, taking into account the importance of upholding duly enacted laws. Damages are not available against a public body exercising its powers in good faith. The court should not restrain a public authority from enforcing an apparently valid law unless it is satisfied, having regard to all the circumstances, that the challenge to the validity of the law is prima facie so firmly based as to justify so exceptional a course being taken.

Per Lord Bridge (at p857)

'Some public comments on the decision of the European Court of Justice, affirming the jurisdiction of the courts of member states to override national legislation if necessary to enable interim relief to be granted in protection of rights under Community law, have suggested that this was a novel and dangerous invasion by a Community institution of the sovereignty of the United Kingdom Parliament. But such comments are based on a misconception. If the supremacy within the European Community of Community law over the national law of member states was not always inherent in the EEC Treaty (Cmnd 5179-11) it was certainly well established in the jurisprudence of the European Court of Justice long before the United Kingdom joined the Community. Thus, whatever limitation of its sovereignty Parliament accepted when it enacted the European Communities Act 1972 was entirely voluntary. Under the terms of the Act of 1972 it has always been clear that it was the duty of a United Kingdom court, when delivering final judgment, to override any rule of national law found to be in conflict with any directly enforceable rule of Community law. Similarly, when decisions of the European Court of Justice have exposed areas of United Kingdom statute law which failed to implement Council directives, Parliament has always loyally accepted the obligation to make appropriate and prompt amendments. Thus there is nothing in any way novel in according supremacy to rules of Community law in those areas to which they apply and to insist that, in the protection of rights under Community law, national courts must not be inhibited by rules of national law from granting interim relief in appropriate cases is no more than a logical recognition of that supremacy.

Although affirming our jurisdiction, the judgment of the European Court of Justice does not fetter our discretion to determine whether an appropriate case for the grant of interim relief has been made out. While agreeing with Lord Goff's exposition of the general principles by which the discretion should be guided, I would wish to emphasise the salient features of the present case which, at the end of the argument left me in no doubt that interim relief should be granted. A decision to grant or withold interim relief in the protection of disputed rights at a time when the merits of the dispute cannot be finally resolved must always involve an element of risk. If, in the end, the claimant succeeds in a case where interim relief has been refused, he will have suffered an injustice. If, in the end, he fails in a case where interim relief has been granted, injustice will have been done to the other party. The objective which underlies the principles by which the discretion is to be guided must always be to ensure that the court shall choose the course which, in all the circumstances, appears to offer the best prospect that eventual injustice will be avoided or minimised. Questions as to the adequacy of an alternative remedy in damages to the party claiming injunctive relief and of a cross-undertaking in damages to the party against whom the relief is sought play a primary role in assisting the court to determine which course offers the best prospect that injustice may be avoided or minimised. But where, as here, no alternative remedy will be available to either party if the final decision does not accord with the interim decision, choosing the course which will minimise the risk presents exceptional difficulty.

If the applicants were to succeed after a refusal of interim relief, the irreparable damage they would have suffered would be very great. That is now beyond dispute. On the other hand, if they failed after a grant of interim relief, there would have been a substantial detriment to the public interest resulting from the diversion of a very significant part of the British quota of controlled stocks of fish from those who ought in law to enjoy it to others having no right to it. In either case, if the final decision did not accord with the interim decision, there would have been an undoubted injustice. But the injustices are so different in kind that I find it very difficult to weigh the one against the other. If the matter rested there. I should be inclined to say, for the reasons indicated by Lord Goff of Chieveley, that the public interest should prevail and interim relief be refused. But the matter does not rest there. Unlike the ordinary case in which the court must decide whether or not to grant interlocutory relief at a time when disputed issues of fact remain unresolved here the relevant facts are all ascertained and the only unresolved issues are issues of law, albeit of Community law. Now, although the final decision of such issues is the exclusive prerogative of the European Court of Justice, that does not mean that an English court may not reach an informed opinion as to how such issues are likely to be resolved. In this case we are now in a position to derive much assistance in that task from the decisions of the European Court of Justice in *R v Minister of Agriculture, Fisheries and Food, ex parte Agegate Ltd* (Case C3/87) [1990] 2 QB 151 and *R v Ministry of Agriculture, Fisheries and Food, ex parte Jaderow Ltd* (Case C216/87) [1990] 2 QB 193 and the interim decision of the President in the proceedings brought by the European Commission against the United Kingdom *(Commission of the European Communities v United Kingdom* (Case 246/89 R) The Times 28 October 1989) to which Lord Goff of Chieveley has referred. In the circumstances I believe that the most logical course in seeking a decision least likely to occasion injustice is to make the best prediction we can of the final outcome and to give to that prediction decisive weight in resolving the interlocutory issue. It is now, I think, common ground that the quota system operated under the common fisheries policy, in order to be effective and to ensure that the quota of a member state enures to the benefit of its local fishing industry, entitles the member state to derogate from rights otherwise exerciseable under Community law to the extent necessary to ensure that only fishing vessels having a genuine economic link with that industry may fish against its quota. The narrow ground on which the Secretary of State resists the applicants' claim is that the requirements of section 14 of the Merchant Shipping Act 1988 that at least 75 per cent of the beneficial ownership of a British fishing vessel must be vested in persons resident and domiciled in the United Kingdom is necessary to ensure that the vessel has a genuine economic link with the British fishing industry. Before the decision of the European Court of Justice in *Agegate* that would have seemed to me a contention of some cogency. But in *Agegate* it was held that a licensing condition requiring 75 per cent of the crew of a vessel fishing against the quota of a member state to be resident within the member state could not be justified on the ground that it was "irrelevant to the aim of the quota system:" p261. 1 confess that I find some difficulty in understanding the reasoning in the judgment which leads to this conclusion. But if a residence requirement relating to crew members cannot be justified as necessary to the maintenance of a genuine economic link with the local industry, it is difficult to see how residence or domicile requirements relating to beneficial owners could possibly fare any better. The broader contention on behalf of the Secretary of State that member states have an unfettered right to determine what ships may fly their flag raises more difficult issues. It would not be appropriate in the context of the present interlocutory decision to enter upon a detailed examination of the wide-ranging arguments bearing upon those issues. I believe the best indication that we have of the prospect of success of that contention is found in the interlocutory judgment of President Due in the case brought by the Commission against the United Kingdom. He concluded that the contention was of insufficient weight to preclude him from granting an interim order suspending the application of the nationality requirements of section 14 of the Act of 1988 to nationals of other member states. His reasoning persuaded me that we should reach the same conclusion in relation to the residence and domicile requirements.'

Per Lord Goff (at p870)

'I take the first stage. This may be affected in a number of ways. For example, where the Crown is seeking to enforce the law, it may not be thought right to impose upon the Crown the usual undertaking in damages as a condition of the grant of an injunction: see *F Hoffmann La Roche & Co A-G v Secretary of State for Trade and Industry* [1975] AC 295. Again, in this country there is no general right to indemnity by reason of damage suffered through invalid administrative action; in particular, on the law as it now stands, there would be no remedy in damages available to the applicants in the present case for loss suffered by them by reason of the enforcement of the Act of 1988 against them, if the relevant part of the Act should prove to be incompatible with European law: see *Bourgoin SA v Ministry of Agriculture, Fisheries and Food* [1986] QB 716. Conversely, an authority acting in the public interest cannot normally be protected by a remedy in damages because it will itself have suffered none. It follows that, as a general rule, in cases of this kind involving the public interest, the problem cannot be solved at the first stage, and it will be necessary for the court to proceed to the second stage, concerned with the balance of convenience. Turning then to the balance of convenience, it is necessary in cases in which a party is a public authority performing duties to the public that one must look at the balance of convenience more widely, and take into account the interests of the public in general to whom these duties are owed: see *Smith* v *Inner London Education Authority* [1978] 1 All ER 411, 422, *per* Browne LJ, and see also *Sierbein* v *Westminster City Council* (1987) 86 LGR 431. Like Browne LJ, I incline to the opinion that this can be treated as one of the special factors referred to by Lord Diplock in the passage from his speech which I have quoted. In this context, particular stress should be placed upon the importance of upholding the law of the land, in the public interest, bearing in mind the need for stability in our society, and the duty placed upon certain authorities to enforce the law in the public interest. This is of itself an important factor to be weighed in the balance when assessing the balance of convenience. So if a public authority seeks to enforce what is on its face the law of the land, and the person against whom such action is taken challenges the validity of that law, matters of considerable weight have to be put into the balance to outweigh the desirability of enforcing, in the public interest, what is on its face the law, and so to justify the refusal of an interim injunction in favour of the authority, or to render it just or convenient to restrain the authority for the time being from enforcing the law.'

Garland v British Rail Engineering [1983] 2 AC 751 House of Lords

Lord Diplock considered the way in which the English courts should deal with apparent conflicts between United Kingdom legislation and community law. He stated (at p771):

'My Lords, even if the obligation to observe the provisions of article 119 were an obligation assumed by the United Kingdom under an ordinary international treaty or convention and there were no question of the treaty obligation being directly applicable as part of the law to be applied by the courts in this country without need for any further enactment, it is a principle of construction of United Kingdom statutes, now too well established to call for citation of authority, that the words of a statute passed after the Treaty has been signed and dealing with the subject matter of the international obligation of the United Kingdom, are to be construed, if they are reasonably capable of bearing such a meaning, as intended to carry out the obligation, and not to be inconsistent with it. A fortiori is this the case where the Treaty obligation arises under one of the Community treaties to which section 2 of the European Communities Act 1972 applies.

The instant appeal does not present an appropriate occasion to consider whether, having regard to the express direction as to the construction of enactments "to be passed" which is contained in section 2(4), anything short of an express positive statement in an Act of Parliament passed after 1 January 1973, that a particular provision is intended to be made in breach of an obligation assumed by the United Kingdom under a Community treaty, would justify an English court in construing that provision in a manner inconsistent with a Community treaty obligation of the United Kingdom, however wide a departure from the prima facie meaning of the language of the provision might be needed in order to achieve consistency.'

Macarthys Ltd v Smith [1981] QB 180; [1979] 3 All ER 325 Court of Appeal (Lord Denning MR, Lawton and Cumming-Bruce LJJ)

Effect of EEC Treaty: direct effect: equal pay provisions

Facts

Macarthys Ltd employed a man to manage their stockroom at £60 per week. Four and a half months after he had left their employment, they took on a woman stockroom manager at £50 per week. She claimed that she was entitled to equal pay by virtue of s1(2)(a)(i) of the Equal Pay Act 1970. The employers contended that that section only applied where men and women were employed on like work at the same time. The Employment Appeal Tribunal dismissed the appeal on the grounds that s1(2)(a)(i) was to be construed so as to give effect to the principle contained in Article 119 of the EEC Treaty which clearly related to successive as well as contemporaneous employment. On appeal to the Court of Appeal.

Held

1) (Lord Denning MR dissenting) The 1970 Act was to be construed according to the ordinary canons of construction which did not include reference to the Treaty of Rome.

2) (Lord Denning MR dissenting) it was not clear whether Article 119 related to successive as well as concurrent employment.

3) (Lord Denning concurring) As there was doubt as to the ambit of Article 119 and as the court was bound by s2 of the European Communities act to give effect to the provisions of the EEC Treaty in priority to a United Kingdom statute, the question of the true interpretation would be referred to the European Court under Article 177.

Lord Denning MR:

'Macarthys Ltd are wholesale dealers in pharmaceutical products. They have warehouses in which they keep the goods and send them out to retailers. Each warehouse is divided into four departments. One of these is the stockroom. In 1974 the manager of the stockroom was a man named McCullough. He left on 20 October 1975. For four months the post was not filled. But on 1 March 1976 a woman was appointed to be manageress of the stockroom. Her duties were not quite the same as those of Mr McCullough. For instance she did not know anything about the maintenance of vehicles whereas he did: but he had assistants to help him whereas she did not. The tribunal found that her work was of equal value to his. They said:

"... whilst it cannot be said that (Mrs Smith's) work was the same as that of Mr McCullough, it was of a broadly similar nature and we do not think that the differences between the work of (Mrs Smith) and Mr McCullough were practical differences to warrant the terms and conditions of the contract being any different. We accordingly find that (Mrs Smith) was employed on like work with her immediate predecessor Mr McCullough."

Nevertheless, although they were employed on like work, the employers paid Mrs Smith only £50 a week whereas they had paid Mr McCullough £60 a week. The tribunal found that this difference was not due to any material difference other than the difference of sex. That is, it was due to the difference in sex. In short, because she was a woman and he was a man. In these circumstances the industrial tribunal held unanimously that she was entitled to be paid at the same rate as Mr McCullough. She remained in the employment as manageress from 1 March 1976 to 9 March 1977. The industrial tribunal awarded her extra remuneration accordingly. The Employment Appeal Tribunal affirmed that decision. The employers appeal to this court.

The employers say that this case is not within the Equal Pay Act 1970. In order to be covered by that Act, the employers say that the woman and the man must be employed by the same employer on like work at the same time: whereas here Mrs Smith was employed on like work in succession to Mr McCullough and not at the same time as he.

To solve this problem I propose to turn first to the principle of equal pay contained in the EEC Treaty, for that takes priority even over our own statute.

The EEC Treaty

Article 119 of the EEC Treaty says:

> "Each Member State shall during the first stage ensure and subsequently maintain the application of the principle that men and women should receive equal pay for equal work ..."

That principle is part of our English law. It is directly applicable in England. So much so that, even if we had not passed any legislation on the point, our courts would have been bound to give effect to Article 119. If a woman had complained to an industrial tribunal or to the High Court and proved that she was not receiving equal pay with a man for equal work, both the industrial tribunal and the court would have been bound to give her redress: See *Defrenne (Gabrielle)* v *Societe Anonyme Belge de Navigation Aerienne (Sabena)* (1) and *Shields* v *E Coomes (Holdings) Ltd* (2).

In point of fact, however, the United Kingdom has passed legislation with the intention of giving effect to the principle of equal pay. It has done it by the Sex Discrimination Act 1975 and in particular by s8 of that Act amending s1 of the Equal Pay act 1970. No doubt the Parliament of the United Kingdom thinks that it has fulfilled its obligations under the Treaty. But the European Commission take a different view. They think that our statutes do not go far enough.

What then is the position? Suppose that England passes legislation which contravenes the principle contained in the Treaty, or which is inconsistent with it, or fails properly to implement it. There is no doubt that the European Commission can report the United Kingdom to the European Court of Justice; and that the court can require the United Kingdom to take the necessary measures to implement Article 119. That is shown by Articles 169 and 171 of the Treaty.

That is indeed what is happening now. We have been shown a background report of the European Communities Commission dated 20 April 1979 which says:

> "The European Commission recently reported on how the nine member countries of the Community were implementing the Community equal pay policy for men and women. It found that in all countries practice fell short of principle ... where national legislation does not comply the Commission has written letters to the following governments outlining why it considers that their legislation does not conform ...

> United Kingdom: the concept of work of equivalent value seems to be given a restrictive interpretation on the basis of the Equal Pay Act ...

> The British position: The government has maintained that the Equal Pay Act 1970 and the Sex Discrimination Act 1975 fully comply with Community legislation against sex discrimination."

It is unnecessary, however, for these courts to wait until all that procedure has been gone through. Under s2(1) and (4) of the European Communities Act 1972 the principles laid down in the Treaty are "without further enactment" to be given legal effect in the United Kingdom; and have priority over "any enactment passed or to be passed" by our Parliament. So we are entitled and I think bound to look at Article 119 of the EEC Treaty because it is directly applicable here; and also any directive which is directly applicable here: see *Van Duyn* v *Home Office (No 2)* (3). We should, I think, look to see what those provisions require about equal pay for men and women. Then we should look at our own legislation on the point, giving it, of course, full faith and credit, assuming that it does fully comply with the obligations under the Treaty. In construing our statute, we are entitled to look to the Treaty as an aid to its construction; but not only as an aid but as an overriding force. If on close investigation it should appear that our legislation is deficient or is inconsistent with Community law by some oversight of our draftsmen then it is our bounden duty to give priority to Community law. Such is the result of s2(1) and (4) of the European Communities Act 1972.

I pause here, however, to make one observation on a constitutional point. Thus far I have assumed that our Parliament, whenever it passes legislation, intends to fulfil its obligations under the Treaty.

If the time should come when our Parliament deliberately passes an Act with the intention of repudiating the Treaty or any provision in it or intentionally of acting inconsistently with it and says so in express terms then I should have thought that it would be the duty of our courts to follow the statute of our Parliament. I do not however envisage any such situation. As I said in *Blackburn* v *Attorney-General* (4), "But if Parliament should do so, then I say we will consider that event when it happens". Unless there is such an intentional and express repudiation of the Treaty, it is our duty to give priority to the Treaty. In the present case I assume that the United Kingdom intended to fulfil its obligations under Article 119. Has it done so?

Article 119

Article 119 is framed in European fashion. It enunciates a broad general principle and leaves the judges to work out the details. In contrast the Equal Pay Act is framed in English fashion. It states no general principle but lays down detailed specific rules for the courts to apply (which, so some hold, the courts must interpret according to the actual language used) without resort to considerations of policy or principle.

Now consider Article 119 in the context of our present problem. Take the simple case envisaged by Phillips J. A man who is a skilled technician working single-handed for a firm receives £1.50 an hour for his work. He leaves the employment. On the very next day he is replaced by a woman who is equally capable and who does exactly the same work as the man but, because she is a woman, she is only paid £1.25 an hour. That would be a clear case of discrimination on the ground of sex. It would, I think, be an infringement of the principle in Article 119 which says "that men and women should receive equal pay for equal work". All the more so when you take into account the explanatory sentence in Article 119 itself which says:

"... Equal pay without discrimination based on sex means ... that pay for work at time rates shall be the same for the same job".

If you go further and consider the Council directive of 10 February 1975, it becomes plain beyond question:

"The principle of equal pay for men and women outlined in Article 119 of the Treaty, hereinafter called 'principle of equal pay', means, for the same work or for work to which equal value is attributed, the elimination of all discrimination on ground of sex with regard to all aspects and condition of remuneration."

That directive may be directly applicable in England; but, even if it be not, it is relevant as showing the scope of the principle contained in Article 119. It shows that it applies to the case of the skilled technician (which I have put) and that the difference between the woman and the man should be eliminated by paying her £1.50 an hour just like the man.

In my opinion therefore Article 119 is reasonably clear on the point; it applies not only to cases where the woman is employed on like work at the same time with a man in the same employment, but also when she is employed on like work in succession to a man, that is in such close succession that it is just and reasonable to make a comparison between them. So much for Article 119.

The Equal Pay Act 1970

Now I turn to our Act to see if that principle has been carried forward into our legislation. The relevant part of this act was passed not in 1970 but in 1975 by s8 of the Sex Discrimination Act 1975.

Section 1(2)(a)(i) of the Equal Pay Act 1970 introduces an "equality clause" so as to put a woman on an equality with a man "where the woman is employed on like work with a man in the same employment". The question is whether the words "at the same time" are to be read into that subsection so that it is confined to cases where the woman and the man are employed at the same time in the same employment.

Reading that subsection as it stands, it would appear that the draftsman had only in mind cases where the woman was employed at the same time as a man. The use of the present tense "is" and of the phrase "in the same employment" carry the connotation that the woman and the man are employed on like work at the same time.

Section 1(2)(a)(i) does not however carry the same connotation. It introduces an equality clause: "... where the woman is employed on work rated as equivalent with that of a man in the same employment ..." That subsection looks at the value of the work done in the job. If the job is rated as equivalent in value, the woman should get the rate for the job, no matter whether she is employed at the same time as the man or in succession to him.

Some light is thrown on the problem by reference to the Sex Discrimination Act 1975. It applies to all cases of discrimination against a woman in the employment field: see ss1 and 6(1) and (2) except where she is paid less money than the man: see s6(6). Now take a case where a man leaves his job and the employer discriminates against an incoming woman by offering her (not less money) but less benefits than he would offer a man for the same job: for instance, less holidays or less travelling facilities or the like. And she accepts them. That would be discrimination against her on the ground of her sex. It would be unlawful under ss1 and 6(1) and (2). In such a case you would think that there should be an "equality clause" introduced under s1(2) of the Equal Pay Act: so that, in regard to her holidays or her travel facilities, she would be put on equal terms with the man. But in order to achieve that just result, it is necessary to extend s1(2)(a), so that it extends not only to employment "at the same time" as the man but also to employment in succession to a man.

Now stand back and look at the statutes as a single code intended to eliminate discrimination against women. They should be a harmonious whole. To achieve this harmony s1(2)(a)(i) of the Equal Pay act should not be read as if it included the words "at the same time". It should be interpreted so as to apply the cases where a woman is employed at the same job doing the same work "in succession" to a man.

By so construing the Treaty and the statutes together we reach this very desirable result; it means that there is no conflict between Article 119 of the Treaty and s1(2) of the Equal Pay Act; and that this country will have fulfilled its obligations under the Treaty. This is a consideration which weighed very much with Phillips J in the very important "red circle" cases: *Snoxell* v *Vauxhall Motors Ltd*, *Charles Early and Marriott (Witney) Ltd* v *Smith* (5). In the reserved judgment of much value Phillips J said:

> "It is important to observe that Article 119 establishes a principle, with little or no detail of the way in which it is to be applied. It appears to us that the (Sex Discrimination Act 1975) and the (Equal Pay Act 1970) must be construed and applied subject to, and so as to give effect to, the principle."

In our present case Phillips J quoted that very passage and said:

> "What has to be given effect to is the principle of Article 119, and the principle is that men and women should receive equal pay for equal work. An Act which permitted discrimination (on succession of a woman to the same job) would not be a successful application of the principle."

So I would hold, in agreement with Phillips J, that both under the Treaty and under the statutes a woman should receive equal pay for equal work, not only when she is employed at the same time as the man, but also when she is employed at the same job in succession to him, that is, in such close succession that it is just and reasonable to make a comparison between them.

Now my colleagues take a different view. They are of opinion that s1(2)(a)(i) of the Equal Pay Act should be given its natural and ordinary meaning, and that is, they think, that it is confined to cases where the woman is employed at the same time as a man.

So on our statute, taken alone, they would allow the appeal and reject Mrs Smith's claim. My colleagues realise, however, that in this interpretation there may be a conflict between our statute and the EEC Treaty. As I understand their judgments, they would hold that if Article 119 was clearly in favour of Mrs Smith it should be given priority over our own statute and Mrs Smith should succeed. But they feel that Article 119 is not clear, and, being not clear, it is necessary to refer it to the European Court at Luxembourg for determination under Article 117 of the Treaty. If I had had any real doubt about the true interpretation of Article 119, I would have been disposed to agree with my colleagues, and refer it to the European Court at Luxembourg for the reasons which Lawton LJ will give. But I would not put it in the form which he has suggested; it is somewhat loaded. I would like it to be reviewed after counsel have had an opportunity to consider our judgments.

Conclusion

For myself I would be in favour of dismissing the appeal, because I agree with the decision of the Employment Appeal Tribunal. I have no doubt about the true interpretation of Article 119.

But, as my colleagues think that Article 119 is not clear on the point, I agree that reference should be made to the European Court at Luxembourg to resolve the uncertainty in that article.

Pending the decision of the European court, all further proceedings in the case will be stayed. It will be put in the list again as soon as the ruling of the European Court is received.'

Lawton J:

'This case started by raising what seemed to the parties to be an issue of fact, namely whether Mrs Smith had been employed on like work of a broadly similar nature to that done by her immediate predecessory, a Mr McCullough, in the job of taking charge of the employer's stockroom. It will end as a case of historical interest as being the first to be sent by this court to the Court of Justice of the European Communities (hereinafter referred to as the European Court of Justice) for an opinion on the construction and application of an article of the EEC Treaty. Further it may be of a constitutional importance if the opinion when given conflicts with the clear terms of a statute.

As Lord Denning MR has already recounted the history of this case and summarised the submissions made on both sides, I can start with the issues as I see them. They are these: first, is the meaning of the relevant parts of the Equal Pay Act 1970 as amended, (hereinafter referred to as "the Act") clear?

If it is, what is it? Secondly, if it is not clear, how is the Act to be construed? Thirdly, is the meaning of Article 119 of the EEC Treaty clear? If it is, what is it? Fourthly, if that clear meaning conflicts with the clear meaning of the relevant parts of the Act, what should this court do? Fifthly, if the meaning of Article 119 is not clear, what should this court do?

The Act envisages that women's contracts of employment shall contain an equality clause: see s1(1). Such a clause is to contain provisions having specified effects: see s1(2). In my judgment the grammatical construction of s1(2) is consistent only with a comparison between a woman and a man in the same employment at the same time. The words, by the tenses used, look to the present and the future but not to the past. They are inconsistent with a comparison between a woman and a man, no longer in the same employment, who was doing her job before she got it.

I find in the words used a clear indication of policy, namely that men and women in the same employment doing like work, or work of a broadly similar nature, should be paid the same. Before the act came into force, which was on 29 December 1979, women were often paid less than men, even though they were working side by side. This was the unfairness which was so obvious, which rankled and had to go. It was of a kind easy to identify. If a job is open, subject to a few statutory exceptions, women should be considered for it as well as men. The Sex Discrimination Act 1975 says so. If a woman is given the job she must be paid the same as any man in the same employment doing the like or broadly similar work. In such a situation there is no scope, nor should there be, for an economic argument: see 1(3) of the Act and Clay Cross (Quarry Service Ltd v Fletcher). But when a comparison is made between what a woman is being paid in a job with what her male predecessor was paid, the scope of the enquiry may widen. The lower pay of the woman may have been due, not to sex discrimination, but to economic pressures, such as diminishing profits, or to other factors such as a more accurate job evaluation. Some such factor as this may be present even when a woman takes over from a man without any time interval, the situation which troubled Phillips J and which counsel for Mrs Smith submitted was so anomalous. The employers may have gone on paying the man more than they could afford out of sympathy for his person position as a long service employee or his family commitments. Phillips J in his judgment accepted that such factors could exist. Parliament may have done so too and have decided to restrict the concept of equal pay to those cases in which men and women were doing side by side like or broadly similar work and not to burden industrial tribunals with the more complicated enquiries which would be required if economic factors had to be considered.

As the meaning of the words used in s1(2) and (4) is clear, and no ambiguity, whether patent or latent, lurks within them, under our rules for the construction of Acts of Parliament the statutory intention must be found within those words. It is not permissible to read into the statute words which are not there or to look outside the Act, as counsel for Mrs Smith invited us to do and Phillips J did, to read the words used in a sense other than that of their ordinary meaning. Counsel for Mrs Smith submitted that the Act should be read in harmony with the Sex Discrimination Act 1975; but that Act, as s6(6) expressly provides, "does not apply to benefits consisting of the payment of money when the provision of those benefits is regulated by the woman's contract of employment". It follows, so it seems to me, to be irrelevant that the Sex Discrimination Act 1975 does allow a comparison between the benefits, other than those consisting of money, which a man got when doing a job and which his successor, a woman, did not get when doing the same job, whereas under the Act relied on by Mrs Smith in this case comparison in relation to pay is outside it.

What led Phillips J to construe s1(2) and (4) of the Act so as to allow such a comparison where the provisions of Article 119 of the EEC Treaty to which Lord Denning MR has referred to its full terms. In this court counsel on both sides have submitted that the meaning of this article is clear; but they have differed as to what that meaning is. Counsel for Mrs Smith has submitted that under Article 119 a woman should receive the same pay as a man she follows in a job, unless there are factors, other than sex discrimination, which justify the difference. If this be right, Article 119 says something different from what I adjudge to be the plain, unambiguous meaning of s1(2) and (4) of the Act. When an Act and an article of the EEC Treaty are in conflict, which should this court follow? Counsel for Mrs Smith says the article, because s2 of the European Communities Act 1972 so provides, as does European Community law. Thus in *Amministrazione delle Finanze dello Stato* v *Simmenthal* the Court of Justice (6) adjudged:

> "A national court which is called upon, within the limits of its jurisdiction, to apply provisions of Community law is under a duty to give full effect to those provisions, if necessary refusing of its own motion to apply any conflicting provision of national legislation, even if adopted subsequently, and it is not necessary for the court to request or await the prior setting aside of such provisions by legislative or other constitutional means."

Counsel for the employers submitted that Article 119 envisages that men and women working side by side for the same employer and doing like or broadly similar work should be paid the same. He further submitted that the opening words of the article, "Each Member state shall ... ensure and subsequently maintain ..." envisages that the member states should enact their own legislation to ensure and maintain the application of the principle that men and women should receive equal pay for equal work. He argued that the United Kingdom had done so by amending the Equal Pay Act 1970 and that if the Commission of the European Communities ('the EEC Commission') thought that the United Kingdom had not done enough in this respect, it was not for this court to ignore what it had done by way of legislation but for the European Court of Justice to adjudge whether the United Kingdom had discharged its Treaty obligations.

As to meaning of Article 119, in my opinion, counsel for the employers is right in his submission that it envisages men and women working for the same employer. They are to receive "equal pay" for "equal work" and "pay" is defined as what the worker received from his employer. It follows that men and women doing "equal work" are to receive the same pay from their employer. For this to make sense they must each have the same employer. This construction is strengthened by the references to work at "time rates (which should) be the same for the same job". Counsel for the employers submission as in the meaning of statutes and deeds, its ambit was confined to men and women doing like or broadly similar work side by side at the same time. The part of the article which begins with the words "Equal pay without discrimination based on sex" takes in para (a) "the same work" and in para (b) "the same job" as the bases of comparison. A woman may do the "same work" or "the same job" after a man as well as alongside a man. In my opinion there is some doubt whether Article 119 applies to the facts of this case.

We cannot, as counsel for the employers submitted, ignore Article 119 and apply what I consider to be the plan meaning of the Act. The problem of the implementation of Article 119 is not for the EEC Commission to take up with the government of the United Kingdom and Northern Ireland, as counsel for the employers submitted it was. Article 119 gives rise to individual rights which our courts must protect. The European Court of Justice has already adjudged that this is so: see *Defrenne (Gabrielle)* v *Societe Anonyme Belge de Navigation Aerienne (Sabena)* (1). The doubts which I have about the meaning of Article 119 are not dissipated by Article 1 of the Council of the European Communities directive of 10 February 1975.

Being in doubt as to the ambit of Article 119 and being under an obligation arising both from the decisions of the European Court of Justice in the two cases to which I have referred and s2 of the European Communities Act 1972 to apply that article in our courts, it seems to me that this is a situation to which Article 177 of the EEC Treaty applies. I consider that a decision is necessary as to the construction of Article 119 and I would require the European Court of Justice to give a ruling on it. The question which I suggest tentatively should be answered is this: whether Article 119 applies to a case in which a woman has claimed that, because of discrimination based on sex, she was paid less than a man whose job she took over 4 1/2 months after he had left it, her work in that job being broadly similar in nature to what he had done.

Before saying au revoir, if not adieu, to this appeal, I would like to set out my reasons for deciding as I have that there should be a reference to the European Court of Justice. First, counsel on both sides persuaded me that it would be more convenient and less expensive to the parties for this court to request the European Court of Justice to give a ruling on the application of Article 119 than for the House of Lords to do so. The issue in the appeal is clear, even if by English concepts the construction of Article 119 is not. The ruling when given may decide the case; and when the ruling is given, there can be no appeal from it. There seems to be nothing else which would justify an appeal to the House of Lords. Further, I can see nothing in this case which infringes the sovereignty of Parliament. If I thought there were, I should not presume to take any judicial step which it would be more appropriate for the house of Lords, as part of Parliament, to take. Parliament by its own act in the exercise of its sovereign powers has enacted the European Community law shall "be enforced, allowed and followed" in the United Kingdom of Great Britain and Northern Ireland (see s2(1) of the European Community Act 1972) and that any enactment passed or to be passed ... shall be construed and have effect subject to (s2) (see s2(4) of that Act). Parliament's recognition of European Community law and of the jurisdiction of the European Court of Justice by one enactment can be withdrawn by another. There is nothing in the Equal Pay Act 1970 amended by the Sex Discrimination Act 1975, to indicate that Parliament intended to amend the European Communities Act 1972, or to limit its application. Secondly, as I am in doubt as to what is the right construction of Article 119 when our canons of construction are applied and in ignorance as to how the European Court of Justice would construe that article when it applies its own rules of construction, I consider myself under a judicial duty not to guess how that court would construe it but to find out how it does.'

Cumming-Bruce LJ (read by Lawton LJ):

'I agree with the reasoning and conclusion of Lawton LJ. The first question is: what does s1(2)(a)(i) of the Equal Pay Act 1970 as amended by the Sex Discrimination Act 1975 mean? This question has to be answered by applying the ordinary rules of construction which have been established in this country. One such rule is that words in an Act of Parliament have their natural and ordinary meaning unless such a meaning is manifestly inconsistent with the context or gives rise to such absurdity or injustice that Parliament cannot have intended such meaning.

At first sight s1(2)(a)(i) contemplates a man and a woman being employed by the same employer at the same time. The use of the present tense strongly points to that meaning, as both Lord Denning MR and Phillips J accepted. But three grounds are put forward for the contrary view.

(1) The fact that the draftsman in s1(2)(b)(i) evidently used the term "is employed on work rated as equivalent with that of a man in the same employment" - in a descriptive sense. In that clause attention is focussed on the rating of the work, and to that issue the time factor is irrelevant. The rating is the same whether the man and woman do the work at the same time or one after the other. As the phrase "is employed ... in the same employment" is used in a sense that describes the job and not the time when the job is done, in s1(2)(b)(i) it is evident that the same words in s1(2)(a)(i) are not as free from ambiguity as might appear on first impression; and there is sufficient doubt to justify a look at the consequences of the two alternative meanings to see if one produces absurdity or results apparently inconsistent with the general intention of the Act while the other does not.

(2) There are undoubtedly some results of the contemporaneous employment meaning which are odd and inconsistent with an attempt to achieve that any woman employed is paid the same as any man whom she has replaced on like work. Examples cited at the bar include: (a) where there is only one job, in which case the equal pay provision could never apply; (b) where the man and woman have worked together but the man is promoted the day before her claim to be paid as much as him; (c) where the man leave the job, and the woman succeeds him next day.

But these results are only anomalous or unfair if the intention of Parliament was to deal with situations extending beyond the cases of a man or woman working on like work at the same time. The argument of anomaly is circuitous. If the intention is clear, the anomaly is clear, but as the anomaly is relied on to discover the intention, the reasoning is chasing its own tail. I take the view that a scrutiny of the whole of the Act leads of the conclusion that it is perfectly possible that Parliament was regarding, and only regarding, the mischief of women working beside men for less money. If so, the anomaies relied on are not anomalies at all. And there is what may be described as a practical difficulty, rather than an anomaly, which is inherent in the other meaning. Whenever an employer reduced his wages and a man left because he would not work for lawsuit. This peril does not exist in the different case of job evaluation where the essence of the matter is the objective evaluation of the job.

(3) It is said that it is absurd that if the battle is about terms and conditions of employment other than pay the Sex Discrimination Act clearly gives the palm to the woman whether she is comparing herself with a previous employee or one with whom she works. The short answer is that s6(6) of the Sex Discrimination Act 1975 clearly provides that its rules are not to apply to equal pay.

I am left so far wholly unconvinced that there is any reason for giving s1(2)(a)(i) a meaning other than that which at first impression I thought was the ordinary and natural meaning of the words.

This is what Phillips J thought too. But he thought that the effect of Article 119 of the EEC Treaty was clear in the sense that Lord Denning MR has quoted from the judgment of Phillips J, and that it was permissible to use the article as an aid to construction of the English statute. Lord Denning MR agrees with Phillips J on both points. With respect to them both, I take a different view on each point. Like Lawton LJ I do not find it easy to discern the application of Article 119 to the circumstances contemplated by s1(2)(a)(i) of the English statute having regard to my construction thereof. I take the view that Article 119, which expresses a general principle, may be perfectly consistent with the English legislation as I construe it. But I am not sure about that, and therefore agree that the court at Luxembourg should give an authoritative answer to that question. Secondly, I do not think that it is permissible, as an aid to construction, to look at the terms of the Treaty. If the terms of the treaty are adjudged in Luxembourg to be inconsistent with the provisions of the Equal Pay Act 1970, European law will prevail over that municipal legislation. But such a judgment in Luxembourg cannot affect the meaning of the English statute.

For these reasons I agree with the order proposed by Lawton LJ, subject only to an appropriate revision of the question to be put to the European Court after counsel have had the opportunity to consider it.'

(1)   [1976] 2 CMLR 98   (4)   [1971] 1 WLR 1037

(2)   [1978] 1 WLR 1408   (5)   [1978] QB 11

(3)   [1974] ECR 1337   (6)   [1978] ECR 629

6 ELECTORAL SYSTEM – MEMBERSHIP OF PARLIAMENT

Fox v Stirk [1970] 2 QB 463 Court of Appeal (Lord Denning MR, Widgery and Karminski LJJ)

Interpretation of statute: meaning of residence in the Representation of the People Act.

Facts

University students were in residence at their Cambridge address on 10 October, the date for entry onto the electoral register. It was argued that as they were only in residence for part of the year, they were not eligible to register in Cambridge.

Held

They were sufficiently resident, using the dictionary definition, 'to dwell permanently, or for a considerable time, to have one's settled or usual abode ... in a particular place', to be registered at their university address. A person may be 'resident' at more than one address, so that they could also register at their home addresses, but not vote in both.

R v Boundary Commission for England, ex parte Foot [1983] QB 600 (Court of Appeal)

The reviewability of the Boundary Commissioners

Facts

The Leader of the Labour Party applied for judicial review and an order of prohibition or an injunction to prevent the Boundary Commission from laying before parliament its report on the redrawing of constituency boundaries. The grounds for the application were that in drawing up its report the Commission had failed to pay sufficient regard to its duty to produce substantially equal constituencies, and had not exercised its discretion to propose constituencies that crossed London borough boundaries. The application was rejected at first instance and renewed on appeal.

Held

The application would be dismissed.

Per Lord Donaldson MR:

[His Lordship commenced by considering the legal context within which the Commission operated, at p615]

'Under the terms of the House of Commons (Redistribution of Seats) Acts 1949-79, the Boundary Commissions are required to report to the Secretary of State from time to time on which changes, if any, they recommend. When the report is made, the Secretary of State is required to lay it before Parliament together, except in a case where the report states that no alteration is required to be made, with the draft of an Order in Council giving effect, with or without modifications, to the recommendations contained in the report. A Boundary Commission can make recommendations when particular local changes take place, but this appeal concerns a general review which has to be undertaken not less than 10 nor more than 15 years from their last review.

A Boundary Commission would face considerable problems if they received no guidance on the principles to be applied in their reviews. However, that is not the case. Such guidance is provided by Schedule 2 to the Act of 1949 read with section 2(2) of the Act of 1958.

The role of the court

Since a very large number of people are interested in this appeal and since it is most unlikely that our decision, whether for or against the applicants, will meet with universal approval, it is important that it should at least be understood. In particular it is important that everyone should understand what is the function and duty of the courts. Parliament entrusted the duty of recommending changes in English constituency boundaries to the commission. It could, if it had wished, have further provided that anyone who was dissatisfied with those recommendations could appeal to the courts. Had it done so, the duty of the court would, to a considerable extent, have been to repeat the operations of the commission and see whether it arrived at the same answer. If it did, the appeal would have been dismissed. If it did not, it would have substituted its own recommendations. Parliament, for reasons which we can well understand, did no such thing. It made no mention of the courts and gave no right of appeal to the courts.

There are some who will think that in that situation the courts have no part to play, but they would be wrong. There are many Acts of Parliament which give ministers and local authorities extensive powers to take action which affects the citizenry of this country, but give no right of appeal to the courts. In such cases, the courts are not concerned or involved so long as ministers and local authorities do not exceed the powers given to them by Parliament. Those powers may give them a wide range of choice on what action to take or to refrain from taking and so long as they confine themselves to making choices within that range, the courts will have no wish or power to intervene. But if ministers or local authorities exceed their powers – if they choose to do something or to refrain from doing something in circumstances in which this is not one of the options given to them by Parliament – the courts can and will intervene in defence of the ordinary citizen. It is of the essence of parliamentary democracy that those to whom powers are given by Parliament shall be free to exercise those powers, subject to constitutional protest and criticism and parliamentary or other democratic control. But any attempt by ministers or local authorities to usurp powers which they have not got or to exercise their powers in a way which is unauthorised by Parliament is quite a different matter. As Sir Winston Churchill was wont to say, "that is something up with which we will not put." If asked to do so, it is then the role of the courts to prevent this happening.

There are undoubtedly distinctions between the position of the commission and that of a minister or local authority taking executive action under statutory powers which affects the individual citizen. The commission have no executive power. Their function and duty is limited to making advisory recommendations. Furthermore the commission's task is ancillary to something which is exclusively the responsibility of Parliament itself, namely, the final decision on parliamentary representation and constituency boundaries. These are distinctions to which we will return when giving further consideration to what action should or should not be taken by the court in the circumstances of this case. At the moment all that need be said is that it is common ground that in some circumstances it would be wholly proper for the courts to consider whether the commission have, no doubt inadvertently, misconstrued the instructions which they have been given by Parliament and, if they have done so, to take such action as may be appropriate in order to ensure that the will of Parliament is done.

The commission's instructions from Parliament and their method of working

Parliament has laid down certain "Rules for Redistribution of Seats," which tell the commission the basis upon which they should formulate recommendations to the Secretary of State. We shall set out the relevant statutory provisions, and in particular these rules, later in this judgment. We shall also consider the proper construction to be placed on the rules, as to which there has been some argument. The rules indicate the number of constituencies in each part of the United Kingdom, and point to certain basic considerations, such as that constituencies shall, so far as practicable, not cross county or London borough boundaries (rule 4); that the electorate of each constituency shall be as near as practicable to what is called the electoral quota (rule 5); and the relevance of geographical considerations (rule 6). The manner of calculating the electoral quota for each constituency is also specified, and it is common ground that, for the purposes of the present review, the electoral quota is 65,753 electors for each constituency. Some provision is made for the procedures to be adopted by the commission. Thus they have to publish provisional recommendations and, in certain circumstances, to cause local inquiries to be held to investigate objections to those recommendations before making their report to the Secretary of State. However, subject to these somewhat limited requirements, the commission are entitled to regulate their own procedure.

The commission have to report not later than 15 years after their last general report, and they must begin their review in sufficient time to enable this to be done. In the present instance the report is due not later than May 1984 and the commission decided to begin their task in February 1976. Hence it is that figure for the electoral quota and the basic figures for the electorate are those for 1976. Having given formal notice of an intention to make a report, the procedure is as follows: the commission's first task is to formulate provisional recommendations and publish them in the localities which may be affected. Where they receive representations objecting to their proposals and the representation comes from a local authority in the area concerned or from a body of electors numbering 100 or more, the commission have to hold a local inquiry. These inquiries are conducted by non-political lawyers appointed by the Home Secretary and known as "assistant commissioners." After each inquiry is concluded, the assistant commissioner sends a written report to the commission and the commission then review their provisional recommendations in the light of that report and any other information or representations which have come to their attention. When this process has been gone through for the whole of the territory concerned – in this case England – the commission report to the Secretary of State.

These are the formal procedural steps, but in addition it is the practice of the commission to have informal meetings with the representatives of the political parties at which there are discussions on general matters. To give an example which is not directly material to the appeal, in November 1979 the commission and representatives of the political parties discussed whether in principle it was practicable to have "polo-mint" constituencies, ie a central urban constituency wholly surrounded by another and rural constituency, the alternative being to have two constituencies each with urban and rural parts. The commission are in no way bound by the advice or representations which they receive, but it is clearly sensible and useful that they should have the benefit of the experience of the political parties and their organisers.

[and at p619]

The relevant statutory provisions and their construction

Before we further consider these complaints and the application for judicial review, we must set out the relevant statutory provisions, and express our view of the construction to be placed on those provisions.

(i) The statutory provisions

The principal statutory provisions are contained in the House of Commons (Redistribution of Seats) Act 1949 and in certain rules set out in Schedule 2 to that Act as amended and qualified by the House of Commons (Redistribution of Seats) Act 1958. These provisions have, however, to be read in the light of the Local Government Act 1972, sections 251, 272(1), Schedule 29, Part II, paragraph 38, Schedule 30, which amended the rules to take account of substantial changes made by that legislation in the structure of local government.

Section 1 of the Act of 1949 (later amended by section 1 of the Act of 1958) provides for the establishment of four permanent boundary commissions, one each for England, Scotland, Wales and Northern Ireland.

Section 2(1) of the Act of 1949 provides:

"Each Boundary Commission shall keep under review the representation in the House of Commons of the part of the United Kingdom with which they are concerned and shall, in accordance with the next following subsection, submit to the Secretary of State reports with respect to the whole of that part of the United Kingdom, either – (*a*) showing the constituencies into which they recommend that it should be divided in order to give effect to the rules set out in Schedule 2 to this Act; or (*b*) stating that, in the opinion of the commission, no alteration is required to be made in respect of that part of the United Kingdom in order to give effect to the said rules."

Section 2(2) provided for the minimum and maximum periods which may elapse between the making of reports by the commission, periods which were later varied by section 2(1) of the Act of 1958. Section 2(5) of the Act of 1949 provides:

"As soon as may be after a Boundary Commission have submitted a report to the Secretary of State under this Act, he shall lay the report before Parliament together, except in a case where the report states that no alteration is required to be made in respect of the part of the United Kingdom with which the commission are concerned, with the draft of an Order in Council for giving effect, whether with or without modifications, to the recommendations contained in the report."

Section 3 of the Act of 1949 contains provision for the manner in which Parliament shall deal with any draft Order in Council so laid before it, giving Parliament the alternatives of either approving or declining to approve the draft Order. If approved, the draft Order is to be submitted by the Secretary of State to Her Majesty in Council; if a motion for approval of the draft Order is rejected, the Secretary of State may amend the draft and lay the amended draft before Parliament for approval.

It is therefore in Schedule 2 to the Act of 1949 that the rules are found to which the commission are required to give effect in making their recommendations under section 2(1) of that Act. These rules (as amended by the Act of 1958, two Local Government Acts and the House of Commons (Redistribution of Seats) Act 1979) are in the following terms:

"1. The number of constituencies in the several parts of the United Kingdom set out in the first column of the following table shall be as stated respectively in the second column of that table –

Part of the United Kingdom	Number of Constituencies
Great Britain	Not substantially greater or less than 613
Scotland	Not less than 71
Wales	Not less than 35
Northern Ireland	Not greater than 18 or less than 16

2. Every constituency shall return a single member.

3. There shall continue to be a constituency which shall include the whole of the City of London and the name of which shall refer to the City of London.

4. (1) So far as is practicable having regard to the foregoing rules – (*a*) in England and Wales, – (i) no county or any part thereof shall be included in a constituency which includes the whole or part of any other county or the whole or part of a London borough; [(ii) repealed by Local Government Act 1972]; (iii) no London borough or any part thereof shall be included in a constituency which includes the whole or part of any other London borough; [(iv) repealed by Local Government Act 1972]; (*b*) in Scotland, regard shall be had to the boundaries of local authority areas; (*c*) in Northern Ireland, no ward shall be included partly in one constituency and partly in another. (2) In paragraph (1) of this rule the following expressions have the following meanings, that is to say: – "area" and "local authority" have the same meanings as in the Local Government (Scotland) Act 1973; "county" means an administrative county.

5. The electorate of any constituency shall be as near the electoral quota as is practicable having regard to the foregoing rules; and a Boundary Commission may depart from the strict application of the last foregoing rule if it appears to them that a departure is desirable to avoid an excessive disparity between the electorate of any constituency and the electoral quota, or between the electorate thereof and that of neighbouring constituencies in the part of the United Kingdom with which they are concerned.

6. A Boundary Commission may depart from the strict application of the last two foregoing rules if special geographical considerations, including in particular the size, shape and accessibility of a constituency, appear to them to render a departure desirable.

7. In the application of these rules to each of the several parts of the United Kingdom for which there is a Boundary Commission – (*a*) the expression "electoral quota " means a number obtained by dividing the electorate for that part of the United Kingdom by the number of constituencies in it existing on the enumeration date; (*b*) the expression "electorate" means – (i) in relation to a constituency, the number of persons whose names appear on the register of parliamentary electors in force on the enumeration date under the Representation of People Acts for the constituency; (ii) in relation to the part of the United Kingdom, the aggregate electorate as hereinbefore defined of all the constituencies therein; (*c*) the expression "enumeration date" means, in relation to any report of a Boundary Commission under this Act, the date on which the notice with respect to that report is published in accordance with section 2 of this Act."

We shall refer to these rules as so amended as "the rules". Of the rules, we are concerned in particular with rules 4, 5 and 6, the construction of which we shall consider in a moment.

We should add that section 1(2) of the Act of 1949 provides that the procedure of the Boundary Commissions shall be regulated in accordance with Part III of Schedule 1 to that Act. Paragraphs 1 and 2 of Part III provide for meetings of the commissions. Paragraph 3 provides for the publication of provisional determinations to make recommendations affecting any constituency. Paragraph 4 empowers the commissions to cause local inquiries to be held in respect of any constituency or constituencies; though under section 4(2) of the Act of 1958, if a commission receive from an interested authority or from a body of electors numbering 100 or more any representation objecting to a proposed recommendation, a local inquiry must be held. Paragraph 5 makes certain provisions relating to procedure at local inquiries; and paragraph 6 provides that "subject to the foregoing provisions of this Schedule, each of the commissions shall have power to regulate their own procedure."

Finally, section 2(2) of the Act of 1958 provides as follows:

"It shall not be the duty of the Boundary Commission, in discharging their functions under the said section 2, to aim at giving full effect in all circumstances to the rules set out in Schedule 2 to the principal Act, but they shall take account, so far as they reasonably can, of the inconveniences attendant on alterations of constituencies other than alterations made for the purposes of rule 4 of those rules, and of any local ties which would be broken by such alterations; and references in that section to giving effect to those rules shall be construed accordingly."

(ii)   *Construction of the statutory provisions*

(a)   *Section 2(1)(a) of the Act of* 1949

Under section 2(1)(a) of the Act of 1949, the commissions are required to submit their reports to the Secretary of State showing that constituencies in which they recommend that their area should be divided "in order to give effect to the rules set out in Schedule 2 to this Act." The requirement in this subsection to give effect to the rules is plainly mandatory. We shall however have to consider in a moment the impact upon this requirement of section 2(2) of the Act of 1958.

(b) *The relationship between rule 4 and rule 5*

Turning to the rules themselves, rules 4, 5 and 6 are each concerned with separate matters. Rule 4 is concerned with county and London borough boundaries; rule 5 is concerned with the size of the electorate of each constituency, considered in relation to the electoral quota for that constituency; and rule 6 is concerned with geographical considerations. It is clear, in our judgment, that of these matters, although they may all be properly regarded as interlocking, the requirement in rule 4 that "so far as is practicable" constituencies shall not cross county or London borough boundaries must be regarded as taking precedence over the requirement in rule 5 concerning the size of the electorate for each constituency. This appears from the facts that (1) rule 4 is on its face not qualified by reference to rule 5, whereas rule 5 provides that the electorate of any constituency shall be as near the electoral quota as is practicable having regard to the foregoing rules, which of course include rule 4; and (2) the second limb of rule 5 authorises departure from rule 4 only in the circumstances there specified.

This point is not academic in the present case. Mr Williams, for the applicants, asserted in argument that the primary purpose of the rules is to achieve electoral equality between constituencies. On a true construction of the rules, this is not so. The requirements of electoral equality is, subject to the second limb of rule 5, subservient to the requirement that constituencies shall not cross county or London borough boundaries.

(c) *Construction of rules 4, 5, and 6*

The requirements of rule 4 and rule 5 are qualified by the words "so far as is practicable" or "as near … as is practicable."

Practicability is not the same as possibility. In part of his argument before us (and, it appears, also before the Divisional Court) Mr Williams came close to suggesting, particularly in relation to rule 5, that the two were the same. But this is plainly not so. Practicability not merely connotes a degree of flexibility: it contemplates that various matters should be taken into account when considering whether any particular purpose is practicable, ie capable in practical terms of achievement. We can see no limit to the matters which may be so taken into account, whether under rule 4 or rule 5, save that they must be relevant to the particular question, having regard to the terms of the relevant statutes and the rules themselves, of which rules 4 and 5 form part. It may be that the test of what is or is not practicable is objective; but in relation to the requirement in rule 5 (with which we are primarily concerned) this is for present purposes theoretical, because the power to depart from the requirement in rule 4 to respect local boundaries only arises if, in the subjective view of the commission, such departure is desirable to avoid any excessive disparity of the kinds specified (see the second limb of rule 5). Exactly the same comment can be made concerning the word "excessive" itself in this context. It may involve an objective, albeit flexible, standard, but whether it is to be treated as achieved is dependent upon the subjective judgment of the commission. Likewise the question whether there is to be a departure from the strict application of rules 4 or 5 by reason of special geographical considerations is made, by rule 6, dependent upon the subjective view of the commission whether such a departure is thereby rendered desirable. These considerations obviously have an inhibiting effect upon any judicial review of the kind sought by the applicants. We add in parenthesis that, since the Boundary Commissions are not subject to the provisions of the Tribunals and Inquiries Act 1971, they are not required to give reasons for their decision to make any particular recommendation. It follows that it cannot usually be known whether, or if so to what extent, any such decision has been affected by the matters referred to in rule 4; or those in rule 5; or those in rule 6; or, indeed, those referred to in the second limb of section 2(2) of the Act of 1958, to which we will shortly refer. This consideration alone must make it very difficult, indeed usually impossible, to seek judicial review of the kind now sought upon the basis that the commission have failed to construe or apply the rules properly.

(d) *Section 2(2) of the Act of 1958*

Overriding these various points however there is, in our judgment, the impact of section 2(2) of the

Act of 1958. There was considerable argument about the construction of this subsection, both before the Divisional Court and before us. For the applicants, Mr Williams made two submissions, both of which (if accepted) would limit the impact of the subsection. The first (which found favour with the Divisional Court) was that the first limb of the subsection (discharging Boundary Commissions from the duty to aim at giving full effect in all circumstances to the rules) was to be read subject to the second limb of the subsection. On this construction the dispensation in the first limb is effective only to take account of the two matters specified in the second limb, viz. inconveniences attendant on alterations of constituencies, and local ties which would be broken by such alterations. This argument found favour in particular with Oliver LJ in the Divisional Court, because he felt that otherwise no weight would be given to the conjunction "but" which provides the link between the two limbs of the subsection. We have formed a different view. We consider that the function of the first limb is to do just what it says, viz. to relieve Boundary Commissions from the duty to give effect in all circumstances to the rules, with the result that, although plainly Boundary Commissions must indeed have regard to the rules, they are not strictly bound to give full effect to them in all circumstances. The word "but" has a role to play because it points the contrast between the dispensation in the first limb of the subsection, and the mandatory requirement in the second limb, that Boundary Commissions shall nevertheless take account of the matters specified in the second limb. So read, we consider that effect is given to all parts of the subsection: whereas on Mr Williams's submission, which we feel unable to accept, no weight is given to the first limb which could, if he is right, for all practical purposes be deleted.

Mr Williams's second submission on the subsection related only to the second limb. It was that Boundary Commissions were required thereby only to take account of the specified inconveniences and local ties when considering *whether* to recommend the alteration of a constituency; but that, once they had decided to recommend an alteration, they were not required to take these matters into account when considering the *nature* of the alteration to be recommended. This submission, which underwent some refinement in the course of argument before us, we are quite unable to accept. We reject it as a matter of construction. Section 2(2) of the Act of 1958 is a statutory provision which modifies the duty placed upon Boundary Commissions under section 2(1) of the Act of 1949. The second limb of section 2(2) of the Act of 1958 requires Boundary Commissions to take account of the specified matters, and this must mean that they are required to take account of them when making recommendations which are the subject matter of a report to be submitted by them to the Secretary of State. If they are to take account of such matters for that purpose, they must plainly take account of them not only in deciding whether to alter a particular constituency, but for all purposes relative to their recommendations, which must include selection of the particular alteration which they decide to recommend. This view is, in our judgment, reinforced by the fact that we can see no practical sense in imposing any such restrictive meaning as that for which Mr Williams has contended. For these reasons we are unable to accept his argument on this point.

The broad construction of section 2(2) of the Act of 1958 which we prefer places yet another, very substantial, obstacle in the way of judicial review of a decision of a Boundary Commission to make any particular recommendation in a report to the Home Secretary. For the practical effect is that a strict application of the rules ceases to be mandatory so that the rules, while remaining very important indeed, are reduced to the status of guidelines. We also observe in parenthesis that the second limb of section 2(2) of the Act of 1958 underlines (if this is necessary) the importance placed by Parliament on respecting the county and London borough boundaries mentioned in rule 4, which will often also reflect local ties.

The course of the present review by the commission

We have already described the general methods of working adopted by the commission in the light of their statutory obligations. For the purposes of their present review, the commission for England gave notice on March 5, 1976, of their determination to make a report. That report has to be submitted before May 1984. Having given notice, the commission formulated proposals for the fixing of constituency boundaries. These were published at various times during the ensuing years;

but the proposals relating to all the London boroughs (except, for special reasons, Enfield) were published together on July 31, 1979. Before formulating and publishing their proposals, a meeting was held with the representatives of the main political parties in 1976; a further meeting was held in March 1978. At the second meeting, the representatives of all the political parties (including the representative of the Labour Party) expressed the opinion that none of the London borough boundaries should be crossed.

After the publication of their proposals, and the receipt of objections and counter-proposals, the commission caused a number of local inquiries to be held, presided over by assistant commissioners. The commission decided that where the proposed boundaries crossed district boundaries, one local inquiry should be held for both districts; where the proposed boundary did not cross district boundaries, it was decided that a separate local inquiry should be held for that district, unless counter-proposals had been received that constituencies should cross those district boundaries, in which event the same assistant commissioner was engaged to hold the local inquiries for both districts involved. The various local inquiries have all been held, and the reports of the assistant commissioners have all been received by the commission. In every case, the commission intimated whether, in the light of the report so received, they intended to make any, and if so what, change in their original proposals; and the commission fixed the last date for the submission of any further representations. In every case, that last date has now passed; the commission have carried out their final overall review of the various proposals, and are ready to submit their report to the Secretary of State as soon as there is no obstacle in their way. Against this background the applicants issued their application for judicial review, seeking prohibition against the submission by the commission to the Home Secretary of their report.'

[His Lordship then considered the dismissal of the application by the Divisional Court, and continued]

'The powers of the court to intervene

We have already pointed out that the relevant legislation has provided for no appeal against the commission's recommendations. Furthermore, the discretion in carrying out their functions conferred on the commission by the legislature is a very wide one. However, it is not absolute and unfettered, in view of the existence of the rules.

A long line of cases has established that if public authorities purport to make decisions which are not in accordance with the terms of the powers conferred on them, such decisions can be attacked in the courts by way of an application for judicial review; and furthermore, that even if such decisions on the face of them fall within the letter of their powers, they may be successfully attacked if shown to have been "unreasonable."

The situation of the commission differs from that of many other public authorities in that, even at the very end of their inquiries and deliberations, they make no final decision; they merely make a recommendation to the Secretary of State who, after making any modification to their report which he thinks appropriate, has to pass it on to Parliament for final approval or rejection. This distinctive nature of the function of the commission might well make the court in the exercise of its discretion more slow to intervene in regard to their activities than it would be in relation to those of many other public authorities. Nevertheless, it has not been suggested before this court, and in our opinion could not be correctly suggested, that the commission are above the law, in the sense that their activities are never susceptible to review by the courts.

In the present case, it has not been submitted that the commission have exceeded or are about to exceed the letter of their statutory powers. The complaint is more that they have unreasonably exercised or failed to exercise the various discretions conferred on them by statute. This submission necessitates a brief consideration of the meaning of "reasonableness" in this context.

As Professor H W R Wade says in *Wade, Administrative Law*, 5th ed. (1982), p362:

"The doctrine that powers must be exercised reasonably has to be reconciled with the no less important doctrine that the court must not usurp the discretion of the public authority which Parliament appointed to take the decision. Within the bounds of legal reasonableness is the area in which the deciding authority has genuinely free discretion. If it passes those bounds, it acts ultra vires. The court must therefore resist the temptation to draw the bounds too tightly, merely according to its own opinion. It must strive to apply an objective standard which leaves to the deciding authority the full range of choices which the legislature is presumed to have intended."

What then is this objective standard? The locus classicus on the subject is a passage from the judgment of Lord Greene MR in *Associated Provincial Picture Houses Ltd* v *Wednesbury Corporation* [1948] 1 KB 223, 230, in which he stated what has become known as "the *Wednesbury* principle." Mr Williams expressly accepted that this principle applies so as to govern and limit the powers of the court to intervene in regard to the activities of the commission. We need not cite the passage from Lord Greene's judgment verbatim. For present purposes it will suffice to say that the *Wednesbury* principle would or might in our opinion entitle the court to intervene if it was satisfied that the commission had misdirected themselves in law, or had failed to consider matters which they were bound to consider or had taken into consideration matters which they should have considered. It would not, however, entitle it to intervene merely because it considered that, left on its own, it might (or indeed would) have made different recommendations on the merits; if the provisional conclusions of the commission are to be attacked on the ground of unreasonableness, they must be shown to be conclusions to which no reasonable commission could have come. The onus falling on any person seeking to attack their recommendations in the courts must thus be a heavy one, which by its very nature may be difficult to discharge.'

Allighan (Garry) MP, Case of, HC 138 (1947)

Right of Parliament to regulate its own composition: power to expel a member

On 3 April 1947, Garry Allighan MP in a newspaper, World's Press News, alleged in an article that newspapers obtained their information about what happened at the private meetings of the various parliamentary parties held at Westminster in a variety of ways. These meetings (held regularly once or twice a week) were not open to the press but Allighan claimed in his article that newspapers paid MPs to reveal the information or gave them personal publicity in return and, in addition, some MPs gave the information under the influence of drink. On 16 April, the article was referred to the Committee of Privileges on the ground that the reflections in it were, prima facie, a breach of privilege. The Committee found, on investigation, that only Allighan and one other MP (Walkden) had disclosed information in the way claimed by Allighan, by giving information in return for payment.

The Committee reported:

'14. On any view this is a case of great seriousness. It is also one of much difficulty from the point of view of the law and custom of Parliament ... Your Committee are very mindful of the fact that Parliament has no right to extend its privileges beyond those to which recognition has already been accorded and they believe that it would be contrary to the interest both of Parliament and of the public so to do. On the other hand the absence of an exact precedent does not in itself show that a particular matter does not come within some recognised principle of Parliamentary privilege.

15. Moreover, it is to be remembered that the right to punish for contempt is by no means restricted to the case where some actual privilege has been infringed. The two matters are distinct.

16. Whether or not the matter has by analogy some relation to the privilege that Members are entitled to be free from molestation, it has long been recognised that the publication of imputations reflecting on the dignity of the House or of any Member in his capacity as such is punishable as a contempt of Parliament. It is true that the imputation upon a Member to come within this principle must relate to something which he has done as such, that is to say incidentally to and as part of his service to Parliament. Thus in an extreme case concerning the Times in 1887, an allegation that certain Members "draw their living ... from the steady perpetration of crimes for which civilisation demands the gallows" was held not to constitute a contempt in that it did not refer to the action of Members concerned in the discharge of their duties as such. Reflections upon Members, however, even where individuals are not named, may be so framed as to bring into disrepute the body to which they belong, and such reflections have therefore been treated as equivalent to reflections on the House itself. It is for the House to decide whether any particular publications constitutes such an affront to the dignity of the House or its Members in that capacity as amounts to a contempt of Parliament.

17. In modern times the practice of holding private meetings in the precincts of the Palace of Westminster of different parties has become well established and, in the view of Your Committee, it must now be taken to form a normal and everyday incident of parliamentary procedure, without which the business of Parliament could not conveniently be conducted. Thus, meetings held within the precincts of the Palace of Westminster during the parliamentary session are normally attended only by Members as such, and the information which is given at such meetings is, in Your Committee's view, given to those attending them in their capacity as Members. Your Committee therefore concludes on this matter that attendance of Members at a private party meeting held in the precincts of the Palace of Westminster during the parliamentary session, to discuss parliamentary matters connected with the current or future proceedings of Parliament is attendance in their capacity of

Members of Parliament. It does not, of course, follow that this conclusion attracts to such meetings all the privileges which are attached to the transactions of Parliament as a whole.

18. It follows that an unfounded imputation in regard to such meetings involves an affront to the House as such. Your Committee consider that an unjustified allegation that Members regularly betray the confidence of private party meetings either for payment or whilst their discretion has been undermined by drink is a serious contempt.

19. Where, as here, the contempt alleged is the making of such a charge against Members, proof that the charge was true would not, in Your Committee's view, of necessity provide a defence. If the publication were intended to bring to light matters which were true so that an end might be put to them, then, however discreditable the facts, Your Committee consider that such a publication for such a high purpose, would constitute a defence. It was not suggested the article in question here was published with any such object.

20. Whether the actual betrayal of information about a private meeting of Members held in a Committee Room of the House or its publication in the Press constitutes a distinct breach of privilege is a separate and more difficult matter ....

22. Your Committee consider that whilst the two cases which have come to light in the course of the inquiry involve a serious departure from that high standard of personal honour which is to be expected from all Members of Parliament, there is no evidence whatever to justify the general charges made by Mr Allighan; Your Committee regard these charges as wholly unfounded and constituting a grave contempt.

23. In the case of Mr Allighan, this contempt was aggravated by the facts that we were seeking to cast suspicion on others in respect of the very matter of which he knew himself to be guilty, and that he persistently misled the Committee ...

25. Your Committee consider that Mr Heighway, the Editor and Publisher of "World's Press News", should be reprimanded.'

The House debated the report on 30 October 1947. It resolved:

'(i) That the article written by Mr Allighan ... in its general tone, and particularly by its unfounded imputations against unnamed Members of insobriety in the precincts of this House, is an affront to this House; and that both Mr Allighan, as the writer of the article, and Arthur Heighway, the editor and publisher of the "World's Press News", are guilty of a gross contempt of this House.

(ii) That Mr Allighan, in persistently misleading the Committee of Privileges in his evidence, and in seeking to cast suspicion on others in respect of the very matter of which he knew himself to be guilty, has committed a grave contempt of this House in disregard of the Resolution of this House of 12 November 1946, "That if it shall appear that any person hath given false evidence in any case before this House, or any Committee thereof, this House will proceed with the utmost severity against such offender".

(iii) That Mr Allighan, a Member of this House, in corruptly accepting payment for the disclosure of information about matters to be proceeded with in Parliament obtained from other Members under the obligation of secrecy, is guilty of dishonourable conduct which deserves to be severely punished as tending to destroy mutual confidence among Members and to lower this House in the estimation of the people.'

On a division, the House voted by 187 votes to 75 to expel Mr Allighan rather than suspend him.

Mr Heighway was summoned to the bar of the House and reprimanded.

Mr Walkden, MP, who had admitted receiving payment for (inter alia) disclosing information about private party meetings, was also reprimanded.

Bradlaugh v Gossett (1884) 12 QBD 271 Court of Appeal (Lord Coleridge CJ, Matthew and Stephen LJJ)

Exclusive right of Parliament to regulate its own internal proceedings

Facts

Bradlaugh was an atheist who had been elected as MP for Northampton. Being an atheist he had, under the Parliamentary Oaths Act 1866, made a declaration in lieu of taking the Parliamentary Oath. In a previous case involving Bradlaugh - *Bradlaugh* v *Clarke* - the House of Lords had decided that Bradlaugh as an atheist should have taken the oath and was not in any of the categories of person entitled to make a declaration rather than take the oath. Bradlaugh wished, therefore, to take the oath. The House of Commons ordered that he should not be allowed to take the oath but was prepared to allow him to continue to sit and vote on the strength of his declaration. However, Bradlaugh, wished to take the oath (because in *Bradlaugh* v *Clarke* the House of Lords had held that the Crown was entitled to recover penalties from him for every day that he sat or voted in the House on the strength of his declaration along). Bradlaugh, therefore, disturbed the proceedings of the House. The House, therefore, resolved 'that the Serjeant-at-Arms do exclude Mr Bradlaugh from the House until he shall engage not further to disturb the proceedings of the House'.

Bradlaugh sought an injunction to restrain the Serjeant-at-Arms from excluding him by force. He also sought a declaration that the resolution of the House preventing him from taking the oath was void.

Held

The injunction and the declaration were refused. A resolution of the House of Commons cannot change the law of the land. However, even though the Commons were wrong in their interpretation of the Parliamentary Oaths Act 1866 so that on a correct interpretation Bradlaugh was entitled to take the oath, nevertheless a court of law has no right to inquire into the propriety of a resolution of the House (even though it was a resolution to restrain B from taking with oath, which by the general law of the land he was entitled to do). Nor will a court of law allow an action against the Serjeant-at-Arms for excluding a member from the House in obedience to a resolution of the House directing him to do so. This was a matter relating to the internal management of the procedure of the House of Commons and thus the court had no power to interfere.

Brown (WJ) MP, Case of, HC 118 (1947)

Actions calculated to influence an MP in the discharge of his duties

Mr Brown was elected MP for Rugby in 1942. He had been the General Secretary of the Civil Service Clerical Association. He now agreed to become its Parliamentary General Secretary. In his agreement with the Association it was provided (i) that he should be entitled to engage in his political activities with complete freedom; (ii) that he should deal with all questions arising in the work of the Association which required parliamentary or political action; (iii) that he did not have authority to represent the political views of the Association. Between 1945 and 1947 there was strong disagreement between Mr Brown and the Executive of the Association over matters such as the closed shop, affiliation to the trades Union Congress and the Association's attitude to the Labour Party. (Mr Brown was an Independent MP.) The Executive came to the conclusion that having Mr Brown as the Association's Parliamentary General Secretary was an embarrassment to the Association and weakened its position in the trade union movement. They therefore resolved to propose to the Association at the next Annual Conference that Mr Brown's appointment should be terminated on terms to be mutually agreed.

On 25 March 1947 Mr Brown raised the matter as a question of privilege suggesting that the action of the Executive was calculated improperly to influence him in the exercise of his parliamentary duties and therefore amounted to a breach of privilege. The House referred the matter to the Committee of Privileges.

The Committee reported:

'10. The nature and extent of any particular privilege claimed by Parliament has to be considered in relation to the circumstances of the time, the underlying test in all cases being, whether the right claimed as a privilege is one which is absolutely necessary for the due execution of the powers of Parliament. Not only has Parliament no legal right to extend its privileges beyond those which satisfy this test, but Your Committee feel that any attempt so to do would be contrary to the interest both of Parliament and the public.

11. Your Committee think that the true nature of the privilege involved in the present case can be stated as follows:

It is a breach of privilege to take or threaten action which is not merely calculated to effect the Member's course of action in Parliament, but is of a kind against which it is absolutely necessary that Members should be protected if they are to discharge their duties as such independently and without fear of punishment or hope of reward.

12. Not every action by an outside body which may influence the conduct of a Member of Parliament as such could now be regarded as a breach of privilege, even if it were calculated and intended to bring pressure on the Member to take or to refrain from taking a particular course. Thus a Resolution passed by some national organisation, or a town's meeting in a Member's constituency urging him to speak or vote in one way or another would not normally involve any breach of privilege, even though it expressly or by implication indicated that political support would be given or withheld according to the Member's response. Had the Civil Service Clerical Association or its Executive Committee not been in contractual relationship with Mr Brown, Your Committee think it clear that they would have been entitled, if so minded, to criticise Mr Brown's political and public activities and to urge him to take a difference course. In Your Committee's view the fact that a contractual relationship does exist is not in itself one which must completely tie the hands of the outside body if it desires to criticise or comment on a Member's activities.

3. The relationship between a Member and an outside body with which he is in contractual relationship and from which he receives financial payments is, however, one of great difficulty and delicacy in which there must often be a danger that the rules of privilege may be infringed. Thus it would certainly be improper for a Member to enter into any arrangement fettering his complete independence as a Member of Parliament by undertaking to press some particular point of view on behalf of an outside interest, whether for reward or not. Equally it might be a breach of privilege for an outside body to use the fact that a Member had entered into an agreement with it or was receiving payments from it as a means of exerting pressure upon that Member to follow a particular course of conduct in his capacity as Member.

It would also be clearly improper to attempt to punish a Member pecuniarily because of his actions as a Member. An example of such action is to be found in the resolution of the Newcastle branch of the Association condemning Mr Brown's activities and recommending that he be immediately placed on pension because of them. Your Committee have not referred to this incident in greater detail since the resolution was rejected by the Executive Committee and Mr Brown very properly sought to make no point about it and considered that the Resolution was passed in ignorance. We mention it now as an instance of the dangers resulting from financial relationships between Members and outside bodies.

14. It has long been recognised, however, that there are Members who receive financial assistance from Associations of constituents or other outside bodies, and whilst those who enter into such arrangements must of course exercise great discretion to ensure that the arrangements do not involve the assertion or the exercise of any kind of control over the freedom of the Member concerned. Your Committee do not think that the making of such payments in itself involves any breach of privilege. On the other hand, Your Committee regard it as an inevitable corollary that if an outside body may

properly enter into contractual relationships with and make payments to a Member as such, it must in general be entitled to terminate that relationship if it lawfully can where it considers it necessary for the protection of its own interests so to do. What, on the other hand, an outside body is certainly not entitled to do is to use the agreement or the payment as an instrument by which it controls, or seeks to control the conduct of a Member or to punish him for what he has done as a Member.

15. Your Committee appreciate that it may often be difficult to reconcile these principles and that the line between them may be a fine one. That is one of the evils which flows from the fact that these contractual relationships and payments are themselves permissible. Thus a decision by an outside body to terminate its relationship with a Member might in practice be a powerful factor in inducing that Member to change his course of conduct although the body concerned did not desire to put any pressure on him so to do. But Your Committee consider that where a Member voluntarily places himself in a contractual relationship of this kind with an outside body be must in general be taken to have accepted its possible termination as a matter which would not influence him in his Parliamentary duties and, therefore, must further be taken to require no protection against a bona fide attempt by the outside body to bring the relationship to an end. It must be assumed in the Member's favour that having voluntarily entered the relationship he has put himself beyond the reach of any improper influence to which either its continuance or its threatened termination might give rise. None the less, Your Committee consider that Parliament must be jealous to see that relationships of this kind are not allowed by Members or used by outside bodies to influence Members in their course of conduct.

20. It appears to your Committee that the Executive Committee were entitled to bring the question of the termination of the agreement before the Annual Conference of the Association, that they had in effect been invited by Mr Brown so to do, and that their action in proposing so to do was not calculated to, and did not in fact, affect Mr Brown in the discharge of his Parliamentary duties. Your Committee do not think it necessary for the due execution of the power of Parliament that the Association should be precluded from pursuing the proposed course. Your Committee therefore recommend that no further action should be taken in regard to the matter.'

His report was debated by the House of Commons on 15 July 1947. The House passed the following resolution (which is quoted in Erskine May's Parliamentary Practice as a resolution having permanent effect):

'That this House agrees with the report of the Committee of Privileges, and in particular declares that it is inconsistent with the dignity of the House, with the duty of a Member to his constituents, and with the maintenance of the privilege of freedom of speech, for any Member of this House, to enter into any contractual agreement with an outside body, controlling or limiting the Member's complete independence and freedom of action in Parliament or stipulating that he shall act in any as the representative of such outside body in regard to any matters to be transacted in Parliament; the duty of a Member being to his constituents and to the country as a whole, rather than to any particular section thereof.'

Church of Scientology v Johnson-Smith [1972] 1 QB 522 Queen's Bench Division (Browne J)

Absolute nature of privilege

Facts

The plaintiff was suing the defendant, an MP, for libel because of remarks made on television. To show malice, they wished to introduce evidence of other remarks made in Parliament.

Held

What was said in Parliament was absolutely privileged and could not be used in evidence even to support an action which arose from remarks made outside Parliament.

Browne J:

'A member must have a complete right of free speech in the House without any fear that his motives or intentions or reasoning will be questioned or held against him thereafter.'

Cook v Alexander [1974] QB 279 Court of Appeal (Lord Denning MR, Buckley and Lawton LJJ)

Parliamentary privilege and reports of proceedings: fair comment

Facts

The plaintiff, a teacher at an approved school, had criticised the way in which the school was run in letters to a newspaper. The Home Secretary ordered an inquiry. The school was ordered to be closed. There was a debate in the House of Lords on the closure of the school. In the debate a bishop strongly criticised the plaintiff. 'The Daily Telegraph', the next day, gave on its back page a short 'Parliamentary sketch' which consisted of a commentary describing the reporter's impression of the salient aspects of the debate. This sketch emphasised the bishop's attack and referred to a rebuttal of the attack and to a full report of the debate on an inside page.

The plaintiff claimed damages for libel in respect of the sketch against the defendants (the writer, editor and publishers concerned).

Held

The reporter of a sketch of parliamentary proceedings is entitled to select that part of a debate which appeared to him to be of special public interest and such a sketch was protected by qualified privilege if made fairly and honestly and without malice. Since this sketch had been made without malice and was a fair report of the proceedings, it was protected by qualified privilege.

Lord Denning MR:

'Ever since *Wason* v *Walter* (1) it has been settled that, in a report of proceedings in Parliament, there is a privilege - a qualified privilege - in the reporter. If his report is fair and honest, then he is not liable to an action.

... I would add that, not only is the report of the proceedings privileged, but also the reporter or the newspaper can make any fair comment on it. That follows inexorably from the fact that the proceedings are presumed conclusively to be of public interest; and accordingly that fair comment can be made upon it: see *Wason* v *Walter* (1), and *Mangena* v *Wright* (2).

Such being the position of a report of proceedings in Parliament, what is the position of a parliamentary sketch? When making a sketch, a reporter does not summarise all the speeches. He selects a part of the debate which appears to him to be of special public interest and then describes it and the impact which it made on the House. I think that a parliamentary sketch is privileged if it is made fairly and honestly with the intention of giving an impression of the impact made on the hearers. In these days the debates in Parliament take so long that no newspaper could possibly report the debates in full, nor give the names of all the speakers, nor even summarise the main speeches. When a debate covers a particular subject matter, there are often some aspects which are of greater public interest than others. If the reporter is to give the public any impression at all of the proceedings, he must be allowed to be selective and to cover those matters only which appear to be of particular public interest. Even then, he need not report it verbatim word for word or letter by letter. It is sufficient if it is a fair presentation of what took place so as to convey to the reader the impression which the debate itself would have made on a hearer of it. Test it this way: if a member of the House were asked: "What happened in the debate? Tell me about it.", his answer would be a sketch giving in words the impression it left on him, with more emphasis on one thing and less emphasis on another, just as it stuck in his memory. Such a sketch is privileged, whether spoken at the dinner table afterwards, or reported to the public at large in a newspaper. Even if it is defamatory of someone it is privileged because the public interest in the debate counter-balances the private interest of the individual.

Applying that in the present case, when the reporter said that the Bishop of Southwark "launched a scathing attack on Mr Ivan Cook" he was recording the impact made on him by the bishop's remarks. When he said "House amused", he was giving the reaction of the members of the House of Lords as he saw it. When he spoke of Lord Longford "in what was rather a bumbling reply", he was giving his impression of Lord Longford's manner. Such a sketch, which gives the impression on the hearer, so as it is fairly done, seems to me to be the subject of privilege - qualified privilege - for which the reporter is protected unless he is actuated by malice.

I would emphasise that it has to be fair. Here I come to the point particularly made by Mr Cook. He said it was unfair to give such large prominence to what the bishop had said and such little prominence to the rebuttal by Lord Longford, and it was unfair to describe Lord Longford as "bumbling" and so forth. But fairness in this regard means a fair presentation of what took place as it impressed the hearers. It does not mean fairness in the abstract as between Mr Cook and those who were attacking him. Applying that test, it seem to me that this parliamentary sketch is protected by the qualified privilege. It gives a fair presentation of the impression on the hearers. The bishop's speech made the most impact: so it was given particular prominence. If it had been unfairly distorted, it would not have been a fair presentation. If Lord Longford's rebuttal had been omitted, it would not have been a fair presentation. But, looking at it as a whole, there is only one reasonable conclusion to which a reasonable jury could come, and that is that it was a fair presentation of what took place.

There is one further point. The column on the back page - which contained the parliamentary sketch - gave specific references to the inner pages of the paper where there was a full report of the whole debate. I should have thought that any reader who was sufficiently interested in the case to take particular notice of what was said about Mr Cook, would have turned to the inner page where he could have read the full report. The two together, beyond all doubt, are protected by privilege ..."

(1)   Infra, this chapter

(2)   [1909] 2 KB 958

R v Graham-Campbell, ex parte Herbert [1935] 1 KB 594 King's Bench Division (Lord Hewart CJ, Avory and Swift JJ)

Power of the House to regulate its own affairs

Facts

Drinks were served in various bars of the Houses of Parliament while Parliament was sitting without reference to the ordinary licensing laws, and this action was an attempt to prosecute members of the House Kitchen Committee for breaches of the ordinary law.

Held

The action failed because the House had exclusive jurisdiction to regulate its own affairs as it wished and the courts could not interfere.

R v Rule [1937] 2 KB 375 Court of Criminal Appeal (Lord Hewart CJ, Humphreys and Du Parcq JJ)

Parliamentary privilege: qualified privilege: special interest

Facts

A constituent wrote two letters to his MP, complaining once about the conduct of a policeman, and once about a JP.

Held

The letters were not absolutely privileged, but a plea of qualified privilege was upheld.

Hewart CJ:

'A Member of Parliament to whom a written communication is addressed by one of his constituents asking for his assistance in bringing to the notice of the appropriate Minister a complaint of improper conduct on the part of some public official acting in that constituency in relation to his offices, has sufficient interest in the subject matter of the complaint to render the occasion of such a publication a privileged occasion.'

Ramsay (Captain) MP, Case of, HC 164 (1940)

Freedom of MPs from arrest

Section 1(2)(a) of the Emergency Powers (Defence) Act 1939_ authorised Defence Regulations to be made 'for the detention of persons who detention appears to the Secretary of State to be expedient in the interests of the public safety or the defence of the realm'. Regulation 18B of these Defence Regulations provided:

'If the Secretary of State has reasonable cause to believe any person to be of hostile origin or associations or to have been recently concerned in acts prejudicial to the public safety or the defence of the realm or in the preparation or instigation of such acts and that by reason thereof it is necessary to exercise control over him, he may make an order against that person directing that he be detained.'

The Home Secretary ordered the detention of Captain Ramsay, an MP, under that Regulation. The question was referred to the Committee of Privileges for consideration whether this order involved a breach of privilege.

The Committee reported:

'14. The Home Secretary ... gave evidence which Your Committee accept that the grounds on which he acted did not arise from anything said by Captain Ramsay from his place in Parliament. If the Home Secretary had taken action for that reason a breach of privilege would have been committed. Your Committee attached great importance to being satisfied on this point ...

15. Your Committee have examined the history of the privilege of freedom from arrest ... It is plain that arrest in civil proceedings is a breach of privilege and that arrest on a criminal charge for an indictable offence is not ...

17. The privilege originated at a time when our law made a free use of imprisonment in civil proceedings as a method of coercing debtors to pay their debts. Members of Parliament in attendance on the House were considered as engaged upon the King's business, and therefore not to be hindered in doing so by arrest at the suit of another subject of the King. Criminal acts were regarded as offences against the King, and the privilege, therefore, did not apply. Consideration of the general history of the privilege shows that the tendency has been to narrow its scope ...

19. ... privilege ... must have regard to the general principle laid down by the Commons in 1641 that "Privilege of Parliament is granted in regard to the Service of the Commonwealth and is not to be

used to the danger of the Commonwealth". It is granted to Members in order that they may be able to perform their duties in Parliament without let or hindrance; for example, the privilege of free speech protects a Member speaking in his place in Parliament because such freedom is necessary to the performance of his functions and duties as Member, but does not protect him from civil and criminal consequences of speeches made outside the House, although such speeches may be dealing with political matters. The House should be careful not to relinquish any established privilege, but it should be equally careful not to extend privilege beyond what is essential for its purpose and beyond what he has, in principle if not by precise precedent, been recognised in the past.

20. ... The relevant provisions of the Act ... and of the Regulation itself have already been set out. It is clear that Parliament gave and intended to give to the Secretary of State extensive powers of arresting and imprisoning citizens without trial in a court of law. There is, of course, a substantial difference between arrest and subsequent imprisonment on a criminal charge and detention without trial by executive order under this Regulation or under analogous provisions in the past. They have, however, this in common; the purpose of both is the protection of the community as a whole. In the present case the purpose ... defined in the Act ... is the public safety or the defence of the realm.

21. Arrest in the course of civil proceedings is, in principle, wholly different. It is a method of coercion to enforce a private right. Although different views were expressed in early days it is only in cases of arrest in civil proceedings that the privilege of freedom from arrest can be held to be clearly established. As Sir Gilbert Campion states "it is certain that during this period (the last two hundred years) privilege from arrest has not been successfully claimed except in civil cases". Applying the principles set out above, Your Committee came to the conclusion that the arrest of Captain Ramsay was not a breach of privilege.

25. ... It has already been pointed out that a power of arrest such as that in question here can be exercised by the Executive only in Parliament has itself conferred the power ... In the use, therefore, of these as of other powers, whether exercised against Members of the House or of the public, the Executive is subject to Parliamentary control.'

Stockdale v Hansard (1839) 9 Ad & E 1; 112 ER 1112 Queen's Bench Division (Lord Denman CJ, Litterdale, Patterson and Coleridge JJ)

Conflict between the Commons and the courts concerning privilege

Facts

Stockdale brought his first action against Hansard in November 1836. In that action he complained of defamation in a passage of a Report of the Inspector of Prisons, published by Hansard on the order of the House of Commons. Hansard raised two defences; (i) that the statements complained of were true and (ii) that they were published on the order of the House of Commons and so were protected by parliamentary privilege. The first defence succeeded but Lord Denman CJ, hearing the case, stated as regards the second defence: 'I am not aware of the existence in this country of any body whatever, which can privilege any servant of theirs to publish libels on any individual'.

In August 1836 Messrs Hansard published a reply by the Inspectors to criticisms made of their report by a committee. In this reply, the allegations about Stockdale were repeated. In May 1937 Stockdale therefore brought a second action against Hansard. Before the action came to trial, the House of Commons passed the following resolutions:

'Resolved, That the power of publishing such of its Reports, Votes and Proceedings as it shall deem necessary or conducive to the public interest, is an essential incident to the constitutional functions of Parliament, more especially of this House, as the representative portion of it ...

Resolved, That by the law and privilege of Parliament, this House has the sole and exclusive jurisdiction to determine upon the existence and extent of its privileges, and that the institution or prosecution of any action, suit or other proceeding, for the purpose of bringing them into discussion or decision before any court or tribunal elsewhere than in Parliament, is a high breach of such privilege, and renders all parties concerned therein amenable to its just displeasure, and to the punishment consequent thereon ...

Resolved, That for any court or tribunal to assume to decide upon matters of Privilege inconsistent with the determination of either House of Parliament thereon, is contrary to the law of Parliament, and is a breach and contempt of the Privileges of Parliament.'

The House of Commons instructed Hansard to defend the action relying solely on the defence that the statements were published on the authority of the House of Commons.

Held

The courts are not debarred from questioning an act simply because the act was done on the order of the House of Commons; that the House is not the sole judge of the existence and extent of its own privileges; and that the privilege here claimed by the House of Commons to be entitled to authorise the publication of defamatory material does not exist.

Lord Denman CJ:

'The grievance complained of appears to be an act done by order of the House of Commons, a Court superior to any Court of Law, and none of whose proceedings are to be questioned in any way ... The supremacy of Parliament, the foundation on which the claim is made to rest, appears to me completely to overturn it, because the House of Commons is not the Parliament, but only a co-ordinate and component part of the Parliament. That sovereign power can make and unmake the laws; but the concurrence of the three legislative estates is necessary; the resolution of any one of them cannot alter the law, or place any one beyond its control. The Proposition is therefore wholly tenable, and abhorrent to the first principles of the Constitution of England.

The next defence involved in this plea, is that the defendant committed the grievance by order of the House of Commons in a case of privilege, and that each House of Parliament is the sole judge of its own privileges ... In truth no practical difference can be drawn between the right to sanction all things under the name of privilege and the right to sanction all things whatever be merely ordering them to be done. The second proposition differs from the first in words only. In both cases the law would be superseded by one assembly; and, however dignified and respectable that body, in whatever egree superior to all temptations of abusing their power, the power claimed is arbitrary and irresponsible, in itself the most monstrous and intolerable of all abuses.

The proof of this privilege was grounded on three principles - necessity - practice - universal acquiescence. If the necessity can be made out, no more need be said: it is the foundation of every privilege of Parliament, and justifies all that it required. But the promise to produce that proof ended in complete disappointment. It consisted altogether in first adopting the doctrine of *Lake* v *King* (1), that printing for the use of the members is lawful, and then rejecting the limitation which restricts it to their use ... Another ground for the necessity of publishing for sale all the papers printed by order of the House was, that members might be able to justify themselves to their constituents, when their conduct in Parliament is arraigned, appealing to documents printed by authority of the House. This is precisely the principle denied and condemned by Lord Ellenborough and the Court in *R* v *Creevey* (2) ...

The practice of a ruling power in the state is but a feeble proof of its legality. I know not how long the practice of raising ship-money had prevailed before the right was denied by Hampden; general warrants had been issued and enforced for centuries before they were questioned in actions by Wilkes and his associates, who, by bringing them to the test of law, procured their condemnation and abandonment. I apprehend that acquiescence on this subject proves, in the first place, too much; for the admitted and grossest abuses of privilege have never been questioned by suits in Westminster Hall. The most obvious reason is, that none could have commenced a suit of any kind for the purpose, without incurring the displeasure of the offended House, instantly enforced, if it happened to be sitting, and visiting all who had been concerned. During the session, it must be remembered that privilege is more formidable than prerogative, which must avenge itself by indictment or information, involving the tedious process of law, while privilege, with one voice, accuses, condemns, and executes. And the other to "take him", addressed to the serjeant-at-arms, may condemn the offenders to persecution and ruin. Who can wonder that early acquiescence was deemed the lesser evil, or gravely argue that it evinced a general persuasion that the privilege existed in point of law? ...

I am of opinion, upon the whole case, that the defence pleaded is no defence in law, and that our judgment must be for the plaintiff on this demurrer.'

(1)   (1667) 1 Saunders 131

(2)   (1813) 1 M & S 273

Stourton v Stourton [1963] P 302 Divorce Division (Scarman J)

Parliamentary privilege: immunity from arrest: scope

Facts

Lord Mowbray had been ordered under the Married Women's Property Act to send property to his wife, and he had failed to do so. She applied for a summons for an order of attachment, but he defended, pleading immunity because Parliament was sitting.

Held

The Baron was protected from arrest under any attachment order where, as here, it was for a civil matter, to compel performance of a civil law obligation, not a criminal one, and therefore the immunity from arrest applied.

Strauss (GR) MP, Case of, HC 305 (1956-7); HC 227 (1957-8)

Parliamentary proceedings not to be questioned in the courts

GR Strauss MP had written to the minister responsible in the Commons for the nationalised electricity industry (the Paymaster-General) complaining of the methods of disposal of scrap metal followed by the London Electricity Board. As the Board saw a copy of this letter they complained vigorously about the contents of the letter to Mr Strauss and finally the Board's solicitors informed Mr Strauss that they had instructions to sue him for libel unless he withdrew his remarks and apologised.

Mr Strauss drew the attention of the Commons to this correspondence, raising the question of privilege. The House referred the matter to the Committee of Privileges. The central question for the Committee was whether the original letter from Strauss to the Paymaster-General was 'a proceeding in Parliament' within the meaning of the Bill of Rights.

The Committee concluded that it was 'a proceeding in Parliament', so that the threat made by the Board to sue for libel amounted to a threat to impeach or question a proceeding in Parliament 'in a Court or place outside Parliament'. Thus, the Committee concluded, the Board and their solicitors had acted in breach of privilege, but the Committee recommended the House to take no further action in the matter.

On 8 July 1958, however, the House decided on a free vote (218 to 213) to disagree with the Committee, resolving that the original letter from Strauss to the Paymaster-General was not 'a proceeding in Parliament' and that nothing in the subsequent correspondence constituted a breach of privilege.

Teach v Freeson [1972] QB 14 Queen's Bench Division (Geoffrey Lane J)

MP's communications: qualified privilege

Facts

The defendant, an MP, wrote a letter to the Law Society and an identical one to the Lord Chancellor, saying that he had been specifically requested by a constituent to refer the plaintiff's solicitor's firm to the Law Society for investigation. He set out the constituent's complaints and stated that he had complied with the request because this was not the first complaint he had received from constituents about the plaintiff's firm. The plaintiff sued the defendant for libel. The defendant did not deny that the letter was defamatory but set up the defence of qualified privilege.

Held

In general an MP had both an interest and a duty to communicate to the appropriate body any substantial complaint from a constituent concerning a professional man or firm in practice at the service of the public. The Law Society had a corresponding duty and interest in receiving such a complaint. Thus the letter to the Law Society and the subject of qualified privilege, being privileged in the absence of malice.

The Lord Chancellor, being the minister charged with the responsibility of ensuring that the machinery of justice ran smoothly, was sufficiently concerned with the proper behaviour of solicitors, who are officers of the court and eligible for certain judicial appointments, to give him an interest in receiving this letter. Thus the letter to the Lord Chancellor was also protected by qualified privilege.

Wason v Walter (1879) LR 4 QB 73 Queen's Bench (Cockburn CJ)

Parliamentary privilege and reports of debates

Facts

A debate had occurred in the House of Lords in which words were spoken which were disparaging to the character of the plaintiff. The subject of the debate was a petition which the plaintiff had presented to the House of Lords charging a high judicial officer with having, thirty years before, made a deliberately false statement in order to deceive a committee of the House of Commons, and praying inquiry and possible removal of the officer in question. The charge against the judicial officer was utterly refuted in the debate. The defendant published in a public newspaper both a report of the debate and an article commenting on it in terms disparaging of the plaintiff. The plaintiff brought actions for libel against the defendant for the publication of the report and the article.

Held

A faithful report in a public newspaper of a debate in either Houses of Parliament containing matter disparaging to the character of an individual which had been spoken in the course of the debate, is not actionable at the suit of the person whose character has been called in question. The publication is privileged on the same principle as an accurate report of proceedings in a court of justice is privileged, that is because the advantage of publicity to the community at large outweighs any private from publication.

As a subject of great public concern was involved, a writer in a public newspaper had full right to comment and therefore the comments in the article were privileged and not actionable so long as a jury should think them honest and made in a fair spirit and justified by the circumstances disclosed in the accurate report of the debate.

Cockburn CJ:

'... Our law of libel has, in many respects, only gradually developed itself into anything like a satisfactory and settled form. The full liberty of public writers to comment on the conduct and motives of public men has only in very recent times been recognised. Comments on government, on ministers and officers of state, on members of both Houses of Parliament, on judges and other public functionaries, are now made every day, which half a century ago would have been the subject of actions or ex officio informations, and would have brought down fine and imprisonment on publishers and authors. Yet who can doubt that the public are gainers by the change, and that, though injustice may often be done, and though public men may often have to smart under the keen sense of wrong inflicted by hostile criticism, the nation profits by public opinion being thus freely brought to bear on the discharge of public duties? Again, the recognition of the right to publish the proceeding of courts of justice has been of modern growth. Till a comparatively recent time the sanction of the judges was thought necessary even for the publication of the decisions of the courts upon points of law. Even in quite recent days judges, in holding publication of the proceedings of courts of justice lawful, have thought it necessary to distinguish what are called ex parte proceedings as a probable exception from the operation of the rule. Yet ex parte proceedings before magistrates, and even before this court, as, for instance, on application for criminal informations, are published every day, but such a thing as an action or indictment founded on a report of such an ex parte proceeding is unheard of, and, if any such action or indictment should be brought it would probably be held that the true criterion of the privilege is, not whether the report was or was not ex parte, but whether it was a fair and honest report of what had taken place, published simply with a view to the information of the public, and innocent of all intention to do injury to the reputations of the party affected.

It is to be observed that the analogy between the case of reports of proceedings of courts of justice and those of proceedings in Parliament being complete, all the limitations placed on the one to prevent injustice to individuals will necessarily attach on the other: a garbled or partial report, or of detached parts of proceedings, published with intent to injure individuals, will equally be disentitled to protection. Our judgment will in no way interfere with the decisions that the publication of a single speech for the purpose or with the effect of injuring an individual will be unlawful, as was held in the cases of *R* v *Lord Abingdon* (1) and *R* v *Creevey* (2). At the same time it may be as well to observe that we are disposed to agree with what was said in *Davison* v *Duncan* (3) as to such a speech being privileged if bona fide published by a member for the information of his constituents. But whatever would deprive a report of the proceedings in a court of justice of immunity will equally apply to a report of proceedings in Parliament.

It only remains to advert to an argument urged against the legality of the publication of parliamentary proceedings, namely, that such publication is illegal as being in contravention of the standing orders of both Houses of Parliament. The fact, no doubt, is, that each house of Parliament does, by its standing orders, prohibit the publication of its debates. But practically, each house not only permits, but also sanctions and encourages, the publication of its proceedings, and actually gives every facility to those who report them. Individual members correct their speeches for publication in Hansard or the public journals, and in every debate reports of former speeches contained therein are constantly referred to. Collectively, as well as individually, the members of both houses would deplore as a national misfortune the withholding their debates from the country at large. Practically speaking, therefore, it is idle to say that the publication of parliamentary proceedings is prohibited by Parliament. The standing orders which prohibit it are obviously maintained only to give to each house the control over the publication of its proceedings, and the power of preventing or correcting any abuse of the facility afforded. Independently of the orders of the houses, there is nothing unlawful in publishing reports of parliamentary proceedings. Practically, such publication is sanctioned by Parliament; it is essential to the working of our parliamentary system, and to the welfare of the nation. Any argument founded on its alleged illegality appears to us, therefore, entirely to fail. Should either house of Parliament ever be so ill-advised as to prevent its proceedings from being made known to the country - which certainly never will be the case - any publication of its debates made in contravention of its orders would be a matter between the house and the publisher. For the present purpose, we must treat such publication as in every respect lawful, and hold that, while honestly and faithfully carried on, those who publish them will be free from legal responsibility, though the character of individuals may incidentally be injuriously affected.

So much for the great question involved in this case. We pass on to ... the article in The Times commenting on the debate in the House of Lords, and the conduct of the plaintiff in preferring the petition which gave rise to it. We are of opinion that the direction given to the jury was perfectly correct. The publication of the debate having been justifiable, the jury were properly told the subject was, for the reasons we have already adverted to, pre-eminently one of public interest, and therefore one on which public commend and observation might properly be made, and that consequently the occasion was privileged in the absence of malice. As to the latter, the jury were told that they must be satisfied that the article was an honest and fair comment on the facts - in other words, that, in the first place, they must be satisfied that the comments had been made with an honest belief in their justice, but that this was not enough, inasmuch as such belief might originate in the blindness of party zeal, or in personal or political aversion; that a person taking upon himself publicly to criticise and to condemn the conduct or motives of another, must bring to the task, not only an honest sense of justice, but also a reasonable degree of judgment and moderation, so that the result may be what a jury shall deem, under the circumstances of the case, a fair and legitimate criticism on the conduct and motives of the party who is the object of censure.

Considering the direction thus given to have been perfectly correct ...'

(1)   (1795) 1 Esp 226

(2)   (1813) 1 M & S 273

(3)   (1857) 7 E & B 219

8 MINISTERIAL POWER – DELEGATED LEGISLATION

Ministerial power

Attorney-General v Jonathan Cape Ltd

See chapter 1

Carltona v Commissioners of Works [1943] 2 All ER 560 Court of Appeal (Lord Greene MR, Goddard and du Parcq LJJ)

The constitutional position of delegation of powers to officials by a minister

Facts

The appellants were manufacturers of food products. On 4 November 1942 their factory was requisitioned by the Commissioners of Works under the provisions of the Defence (General) Regulations 1939, reg 51(1) which read

> 'A competent authority, if it appears to that authority to be necessary or expedient so to do in the interests of the public safety, the defence of the realm or the efficient prosecution of the war, or for maintaining supplies and services essential to the life of the community, may take possession of any land, and may give such directions as appear to the competent authority to be necessary or expedient in connection with the taking of possession of that land.'

'A competent authority' included the Commissioners of Works. The appellants claimed a declaration that the Commissioners were not entitled to take possession on the ground that the order for requisition was invalid. Before the Court of Appeal the appellant contended, inter alia, that the order was invalid because the 'competent authority' had never brought their minds to bear on the question in that the decision had been taken by an Assistant Secretary (a civil servant) in the Ministry of Works.

Held

By statute the functions and powers of the Commissioners of Works were vested in the First Commissioner of Works viz. the Minister heading the Ministry of Works. It could not be supposed that reg 51 meant that the minister in person should direct his mind to the matter since this would be impossible in the case of every requisition. In the administration of government of this country so many functions are given to ministers that the minister could never attend to them all personally. Normally such functions are exercised under the authority of the minister by the officials in the department. Constitutionally, the decision of such an official is a decision of the minister, and constitutionally the minister is responsible to Parliament for the decision. The order was valid.

Lord Greene MR:

> '... The regulation under which their action was taken is regulation 51(1) of the Defence (General) Regulations ...
>
> ... The notice of 4 November is signed by a Mr Morse for and on behalf of the Commissioners of Works. It is on the headed letter-paper of the Ministry of Works and Planning, whose connection with the Commissioners of Works arises in a way which I will indicate in a moment. The letter says:

"I have to inform you that the department have come to the conclusion that it is essential, in the national interest, to take possession of the above premises occupied by you."

Then the appellants are asked to take the letter as formal notice, and they are directed to arrange for the removal of such chattels as are not requisitioned ...

In the administration of government in this country the functions which are given to ministers (and constitutionally properly given to ministers because they are constitutionally responsible) are functions so multifarious that no minister could ever personally attend to them. To take the example of the present case no doubt there have been thousands of requisitions in this country by individual ministries. It cannot be supposed that this regulation meant that, in each case, the minister in person should direct his mind to the matter. The duties imposed upon ministers and the powers given to ministers are normally exercised under the authority of the ministers by responsible officials of the department. Public business could not be carried on if that were not the case. Constitutionally, the decision of such an official is, of course, the decision of the minister. The minister is responsible. It is he who must answer before Parliament for anything that his officials have done under his authority, and, if for an important matter he selected an official of such junior standing that he could not be expected competently to perform the work, the minister would have to answer for that in Parliament. The whole system of departmental organisation and administration is based on the view that ministers, being responsible to Parliament, will see that important duties are committed to experienced officials. If they do not do that, Parliament is the place where complaint must be made against them ...'

Liversidge v Anderson [1942] AC 206 House of Lords (Viscount Maugham, Lords Macmillan, Wright, Atkin and Romer)

Conclusive nature of Minister's certificate under emergency conditions

Facts

The Defence (General) Regulations 1939, reg 18B, para 1 provided:

'if the Secretary of State has reasonable cause to believe any person to be of hostile origin or associations or to have been recently concerned in acts prejudicial to the public safety, or the defence of the realm ... and that by reason thereof it is necessary to exercise control over him, he may make an order against that person directing that he be detained'.

The Home Secretary, A, made such an order, detaining L, on 26 May 1940. The detention order recited was as follows:

'Whereas I have reasonable cause to believe Jack Perlzweig alias Robert Liversidge to be a person of hostile associations and that by reason thereof it is necessary to exercise control over him: Now, therefore, I, in pursuance of the power conferred on me by regulation 18B of the Defence (General) Regulations, 1939, hereby make the following order: I direct that the above-mentioned Jack Perlzweig alias Robert Liversidge be detained.

(Signed)   John Anderson

One of His Majesty's Principal Secretaries of State.'

The appellant, L, brought an action for damages for false imprisonment against A. L applied for particulars (a) of the grounds on which the respondent, A, had reasonable cause to believe the appellant to be a person of hostile associations and (b) of the grounds on which the respondent had reasonable cause to believe that by reason of such hostile associations it was necessary to exercise control over the appellant. Master Moseley refused to make any order for particulars and that was upheld by the judge in chambers.

Finally, an appeal to the House of Lords was allowed. The question which, in effect, arose, was whether the production of the detention order made by the Home Secretary and ex facie regular and duly authenticated was a sufficient defence to the action, or whether the Home Secretary was required to prove the reasonable grounds of his belief under reg 18B in order to establish his defence to the action for false imprisonment.

Held (Lord Atkin dissenting)

The production of the detention order was a sufficient defence. Although, in the absence of a context, the prima facie meaning of a phrase such as 'if AB has reasonable cause to believe' might be 'if there is in fact reasonable cause for believing', the context may make it clear that the meaning is rather 'if AB thinks (honestly) that he has reasonable cause to believe'. The present was just such a case. The legislators, when making the Defence Regulations, would have been well-aware that in many cases the Home Secretary would be acting on information of the most confidential character which could not be disclosed in court for reasons of public security. All that was required, therefore, was that the Home Secretary should honestly believe that he had reasonable grounds to believe the matters specified in reg 18B and thus the production of the detention order was a sufficient defence.

Viscount Maugham:

'... I propose, first, to deal with the important question of the construction of the words in the regulation, "If the Secretary of State has reasonable cause to believe, etc" that is, the question whether, as the appellant contends, the words require that there must be an external fact as to reasonable cause for the belief, and one, therefore, capable of being challenged in a court of law, or whether, as the respondents contend, the words, in the context in which they are found, point simply to the belief of the Secretary of State founded on his view of there being reasonable cause for the belief which he entertains.

Before dealing with the construction of the regulation, it is desirable to consider now the matter should be approached. The appellant's counsel truly say that the liberty of the subject is involved. They refer in emphatic terms to Magna Carta and the Bill of Rights, and they contend that legislation dealing with the liberty of the subject must be construed, if possible, in favour of the subject and against the Crown. Adopting the language of Lord Finay LC in this House in the case of *R* v *Halliday* (1) I hold that the suggested rule has "no relevance in dealing with an executive measure by way of preventing a public danger" when the safety of the state is involved ...

My Lords, I think we should approach the construction of regulation 18B of the Defence (General) Regulations without any general presumption as to its meaning except the universal presumption, applicable to Orders in Council and other like instruments, that, if there is a reasonable doubt as to the meaning of the words used, we should prefer a construction which will carry into effect the plain intention of those responsible for the Order in Council rather than one which will defeat that intention. My Lords, I am not disposed to deny that, in the absence of a context, the prima facie meaning of such a phrase as "if AB has reasonable cause to believe" a certain circumstance or thing, it should be construed as meaning "if there is in fact reasonable cause for believing" that thing and if AB believes it. But I am quite unable to take the view that the words can only have that meaning. It seems to me reasonably clear that, if the thing to be believed is something which is essentially one within the knowledge of AB or one for the exercise of his exclusive discretion, the words might well mean if AB acting on what he thinks is reasonable cause (and, of course, acting in good faith) believes the thing in question.

In the present case there are a number of circumstances which tend to support the latter conclusion.

First, regulation 18B, paragraphs (1) and (1A), alike require the Secretary of State to have reasonable cause to believe two different things. Taking the first paragraph, he must, in the first place, believe the person (a) to be of hostile origin or associations, or (b) to have been recently concerned in acts prejudicial to the public safety or the defence of the realm, or (c) in the preparation or instigation of such acts, or (d) to have been or to be a member of, or (e) to be active in the furtherance of the objects of organisations which are carefully defined by reference to the personal decision of the Home Secretary. Any one of these various circumstances is sufficient to satisfy the first fact which the Secretary of State must believe, and I do not doubt that a court could investigate the question whether there were grounds for a reasonable man to believe some at least of those facts if they could be put before the court. But then he must at the same time also believe something very different in its nature, namely, that by reason of the first fact, "it is necessary to exercise control over" the person in question. To my mind this is so clearly a matter for executive discretion and nothing else that I cannot myself believe that those responsible for the Order in Council could have contemplated for a moment the possibility of the action of the Secretary of State being subject to the discussion, criticism and control of a judge in a court of law. If, then, in the present case the second requisite, as to the grounds on which the Secretary of State can make his order for detention, is left to his sole discretion without appeal to a court, it necessarily follows that the same is true as to all the facts which he must have reasonable cause to believe.

Secondly, it is admitted that the Home Secretary can act on hearsay and is not required to obtain any legal evidence in such a case, and clearly is not required to summon the person whom he proposed to detain and to hear his objections to the proposed order. Since the Home Secretary is not acting judicially in such a case, it would be strange if his decision could be questioned in a court of law.

Thirdly, and this is of even greater importance, it is obvious that in many cases he will be acting on information of the most confidential character, which could not be communicated to the person detained or disclosed in court without the greatest risk of prejudicing the future efforts of the Secretary of State in this and like matters for the defence of the realm. A very little consideration will show that the power of the court (under section 6 of the Act) to give directions for the hearing of proceedings in camera would not prevent confidential matters from leaking out, since such matters would become known to the person detained and to a number of other persons. It seems to me impossible for the court to come to a conclusion adverse to the opinion of the Secretary of State in such a matter. It is beyond dispute that he can decline to disclose the information on which he has acted on the ground that to do so would be contrary to the public interest, and that this privilege of the Crown cannot be disputed. It is not ad rem on the question of construction to say in reply to this argument that there are cases in which the Secretary of State could answer the attack on the validity of the order for detention without raising the point of privilege. It is sufficient to say that there must be a large number of cases in which the information on which the Secretary of State is likely to act will be of a very confidential nature. That must have been plain to those responsible in advising His Majesty in regard to the Order in Council, and it constitutes, in my opinion, a very cogent reason for thinking that the words under discussion cannot be read as meaning that the existence of 'reasonable cause' is one which may be discussed in a court which has not the power of eliciting the facts which in the opinion of the Secretary of State amount to "reasonable cause".

Fourthly, it is to be noted that the person who is primarily entrusted with these most important duties is one of the principal Secretaries of State, and a member of the government answerable to Parliament for a proper discharge of his duties. I do not think he is at all in the same position as, for example, a police constable. It is not wholly immaterial to note that the Secretary of State is provided with one or more advisory committees (paragraph (3)), and that he has to report to Parliament at least once in every month as to the action taken by him and the orders he has made, and as to the number of cases in which he has declined to follow the advice of the advisory committee (paragraph (6)). These provisions seem to point to the fact that the Secretary of State will be answerable to Parliament in carrying out duties of a very important and confidential nature. I have heard no explanation of the circumstance that no express provisions are made in the regulation as to an appeal from the Secretary of State's decision unless it is the fact that no such appeal was intended. It seems to me that, if any such appeal has been thought proper, it would have been to a special tribunal with power to inquire privately into all the reasons for the Secretary's action, but without any obligation to communicate them to the person detained. The objections to an appeal in a case of mere suspicion and in time of war are not far to seek, but, however that may be, an application to the

High Court, with power to the judge to review the action of the Secretary of State, seems to be completely inadmissible, and I am unable to see that the words of the regulation in any way justify the conclusion that such a procedure was contemplated ...

I am of opinion that the arguments above enumerated in favour of the construction for which the Attorney-General contends must greatly outweigh any arguments which your Lordships have heard on the other side and that his construction must prevail. The result is that there is no preliminary question of fact which can be submitted to the courts and that in effect that is no appeal from the decision of the Secretary of State in these matters provided only that he acts in good faith ...'

(1)   [1917] AC 260

See also *Padfield* v *Minister of Agriculture* [1969] AC 997, Chapter 11.

Delegated legislation

Agricultural, Horticultural and Forestry Industry Training Board v Aylesbury Mushrooms Ltd [1972] 1 WLR 190; [1972] 1 All ER 280 Queen's Bench Division (Donaldson J)

Effect of failure to consult

Facts

In 1965 preliminary consultations took place between the Minister of Labour and the National Farmers Union ('the NFU') concerning the Minister's plans to set up a training board for the agricultural, horticultural and forestry industry under the provisions of the Industrial Training Act 1964. By April 1966 a draft had been prepared and a copy of the schedule defining the industry to which it related was circulated to a large number of addresses inviting comments. In addition a press notice was published summarising the activities which it was proposed should be covered by the new board and advising any organisation which considered that it had an interest in the draft schedule and had not received a copy to apply to the Minister. Among the addresses to whom the draft schedule was sent was the Mushroom Growers Association ('the association'). This was a specialist branch of the NFU, although largely autonomous. It was not represented on the NFU council but a representative was invited to attend when matters relating to mushroom growing were discussed. No comments on the draft schedule were received from the association. The order constituting the board was made and come into operation on 15 August 1966. In was discovered later that the association had never received a copy of the draft schedule and had no knowledge of the press notice or of the consultations between the NFU and the Minister.

In an action for a declaration, the association contended that it was not bound by the order (by virtue of which employers in the industry became subject to a levy to finance the operations of the training board) on the ground that, before making the order, the Minister had a duty to consult the association since it was an organisation 'appearing to him' to be within one of the categories of organisation which, under s1(4) of the 1964 Act (see above), he was bound to consult.

Held

In view of the importance which was attached to consultation in the scheme of the Act, and the fact that the Minister had not in terms stated in argument that the association did not appear to him to fall within s1(4) it followed that the association was a body which had to be consulted. Although, prima facie, consultation with a parent body would constitute consultation with the constitutent parts, this general rule did not apply in the present case since the Minister had attempted and intended direct consultation with the association as well as with the NFU. The mere sending of a letter which was not received was only an attempt to consult and did not constitute consultation; the essence of consultation was the actual communication of a genuine invitation, extended with a receptive mind, to give advice; *Rollo* v *Minister of Town and Country Planning* (1) applied. Statutory powers which involve taxation should be strictly construed, and so construed, the association should have been consulted and had not been consulted. Therefore the 1966 order had no application to persons engaged in the growing of mushrooms solely by reason of their being so engaged.

Donaldson J:

'... This leaves only the related questions whether the Mushroom Growers Association did in fact appear to the Minister to be an organisation falling within the categories set out in s1(4) with the consequence that he was under an obligation to consult them and whether in any event this consultations with the National farmers Union constituted consultation with the Mushroom Growers Association as a branch of the NFU. This is the heart of the problem.

Mr Devey has deposed in para 5 of his affidavit that:

"In accordance with practice the circulation of the draft schedule was not restricted to organisations that appeared to me to be representative of substantial numbers of employers engaging in activities specified in the draft schedule. This will appear sufficiently from a perusal of the document. In particular the Mushroom Growers Association was listed, although it was, and remains, a specialist branch of the National Farmers Union. The listed address of the Association is the same as that of the Union which is Agriculture House, Knightsbridge, London SW1 ..."

This only leaves the question of whether it was consulted vicariously, and it may be accidentally, by means of the consultations with the National Farmers Union. This is a nice point. Prima facie consultation with the parent body undoubtedly constitutes consultation with its constituent parts, but I think that this general rule is subject to an exception where, as here, the Minister has also attempted and intended direct consultation with a branch. The association's complaint has very little merit, because it seems to have been completely blind to all that was going on around it. Nevertheless it is important that statutory powers which involve taxation shall be strictly construed and, so construed, I consider that the association should have been consulted and was not consulted ...'

(1) [1948] 1 All ER 13

Bailey v Williamson (1873) LR 8 QB 118 Queen's Bench (Cockburn CJ, Blackburn and Quain JJ)

Laying before Parliament: directory

Facts

The appellant was convicted of contravening regulations concerning Hyde Park, which had been made pursuant to the Parks Regulations Act 1872. The Act provided that any regulation made thereunder should be laid before Parliament. The regulations in question were made and published on 30 September 1872 and appellant convicted in November, at which time Parliament was still in recess, and the regulations had not been laid.

Held

The regulations were still valid despite the fact that they had still not been laid as required by the parent Act at the time of the conviction.

Bates v Lord Hailsham [1972] 1 WLR 1373 Chancery Division (Megarry J)

The rules of natural justice do not apply to delegated legislation

Facts

A committee of which the Lord Chancellor was a member, was empowered by s56 of the Solicitors Act 1957 to make orders prescribing solicitors' remuneration in respect of non-contentious business. Section 56 (3) of the Act stated:

'Before any such order is made, the Lord Chancellor shall cause a draft to be sent to the council (of the Law Society), and the Committee shall, before making the order, consider any observations in writing submitted to them by the council within one month of the sending to them of the draft, and may then make the order ...'

A draft copy of proposals was sent to the Law Society, but not the British Legal Association of which the plaintiff was one of 2,900 members. He now sought a declaration that it would be ultra vires for the committee to confirm the making of the Order without first giving the British Legal Association an opportunity to give its views.

Held

The application for a declaration would be refused. The rules of natural justice could not be applied to what was clearly a legislative function.

Megarry J:

'... In the present case, the committee in question has an entirely different function: it is legislative rather than administrative or executive. The function of the committee is to make or refuse to make a legislative instrument under delegated powers. The order, when made, will lay down the remuneration for solicitors generally; and the terms of the order will have to be considered and construed and applied in numberless cases in the future. Let me accept that in the sphere of the so-called quasi-judicial the rules of natural justice run, and that in the administrative or executive field there is a general duty of fairness. Nevertheless, these considerations do not seem to me to affect the process of legislation, whether primary or delegated. Many of those affected by delegated legislation, and affected very substantially, are never consulted in the process of enacting that legislation: and yet they have no remedy. Of course, the informal consultation of representative bodies by the legislative authority is a commonplace; but although a few statutes have specifically provided for a general process of publishing draft delegated legislation and considering objections (see, for example, the Factories Act 1961, Schedule 4). I do not know of any implied right to be consulted or make objections, or any principle upon which the courts may enjoin the legislative process at the suit of those who contend that insufficient time for consultation and consideration has been given. I accept that the fact that the order will take the form of a statutory instrument does not per se make it immune from attack, whether by injunction or otherwise; but what is important is not its form but its nature, which is plainly legislative ...'

Commissioners of Customs and Excise v Cure and Deeley Ltd [1962] 1 QB 340; [1961] 3 WLR 798; [1961] 3 All ER 641 Queen's Bench Division (Sachs J)

Courts to be judges of extent of powers even when they may be used when 'necessary'

Facts

The Finance (No 2) Act 1940 provided: '33(1) The Commissioners may make regulations providing for any matter for which provision appears to them to be necessary for the purpose of giving effect to the provisions of this Part of this Act and of enabling them to discharge their functions thereunder ...' The Commissioners made Regulation 12 of the Purchase Tax Regulations 1945: 'If any person fails to furnish a return as required to these regulations or furnishes an incomplete return the Commissioners may, without prejudice to any penalties which may be incurred by such person, determine the amount of the tax appearing to them to be due from such person, and demand payment thereof, which amount shall be deemed to be the proper tax due from such person and shall be paid within seven days of such demand unless within that time it is shown to the satisfaction of the Commissioners that some other amount is the proper tax due which other amount shall immediately be paid to the Commissioners.'

The Commissioners made a determination and demand for payment under Regulation 12. The defendants argued that Regulation 12 was ultra vires and not authorised by s33(1) of the Finance Act.

Held

The words 'appear to them to be necessary' when used in a statute conferring powers on a competent authority do not necessarily make that authority the sole judge of what its powers are, and it is still open to the court to determine this.

Regulation 12 was ultra vires because:

(i) It is no part of the functions assigned to the Commissioners by the Finance Act 1940 to take upon themselves the powers of a High Court judge and decide issues of fact and law as between the Crown and the subject;

(ii) Regulation 12 renders the subject liable to pay such tax as the commissioners believe to be due, whereas the charging sections of the Finance Act only render the subject liable to pay such tax as in law is due;

(iii) Regulation 12 is capable of excluding the subject from access to the courts and of defeating pending proceedings. It thus purports to deny him the right to have his legal liability to taxation determined by the court.

Sachs J:

'... In the first place I reject the view that the words "appear to them to be necessary" when used in a statute conferring powers on a competent authority necessarily make that authority the sole judge of what are its powers as well as the sole judge of the way in which it can exercise such powers as it may have. It is axiomatic that to follow the words used by Lord Radcliffe in the *Canadian* case(1), "the paramount rule remains that every statute is to be expounded according to its manifest or expressed intention". It is no less axiomatic that the application of that rule may result in phrases identical in wording or in substance receiving quite different interpretations according to the tenor of the legislation under consideration. As an apt illustration of such a result it is not necessary to go further than *Liversidge* v *Anderson* (2) and *Nakkuda Ali* v *Jayaratne* (3), in which cases the words "reasonable cause to believe" and "reasonable grounds to believe" receive quite different interpretations.

To my mind a court is bound before reaching a decision on the question whether a regulation is ultra vires to examine the nature, objects and scheme of the piece of legislation as a whole, and in the light of that examination to consider exactly what is the area over which powers are given by the section under which the competent authority is purporting to act ...

It is against the background of the above examination of the relevant legislation that the court has to interpret the words "for the purpose of giving effect to the provisions of this Part of the Act and of enabling them to discharge their functions thereunder" to see what is the area over which the power of the commissioners to make regulations extends ...

On the above footing it is, to my mind, clear that regulation 12 is ultra vires on at any rate three grounds, which, to my mind, are distinct in law though they overlap in so far as they may be different ways of expressing the result of certain facts. First, it is no part of the functions assigned to the commissioners to take upon themselves the powers of a High Court judge and decide issues of fact and law as between the Crown and the subject. Secondly, it renders the subject liable to pay such tax as the commissioners believe to be due, whereas the charging sections impose a liability to pay such tax as in law is due. Thirdly, it is capable of excluding the subject from access to the courts and of defeating pending proceedings ...

In the result this attempt to substitute in one segment of the taxpayer's affairs the rule of tax collectors for the rule of law fails ...'

(1)   *A-G for Canada* v *Hallett and Carey Ltd* [1952] AC 427

(2)   Supra, this chapter

(3)   Infra, chapter 14

Kruse v Johnson [1898] 2 QB 91 Specially constituted Divisional court of seven judges of whom one dissented

By-laws: reasonableness and validity

Facts

A county council, claiming to act under their statutory powers, made a by-law prohibiting any person from playing music or singing in any public place or highway within 50 yards of any dwellinghouse after being requested by any constable, or an inmate of such house, or his or her servant, to desist. K had been conducting an open air religious service and had continued to sing a hymn after a constable had required him to stop. He was convicted under the by-law. On appeal to the Divisional Court, Lord Russell CJ and Matthew J had disagreed, and the case was referred to the full court of seven judges. Counsel for K argued that the by-law was invalid because it was unreasonable.

Held

The by-law was valid. In determining the validity of by-laws made by public representative bodies, such as county councils, the Court ought to be slow to hold that a by-law is void for unreasonableness. A by-law made by such a body ought not be declared invalid on grounds of unreasonableness unless it is manifestly partial and unequal in its operation between different classes, or manifestly unjust, or made in bad faith or involving such oppressive or gratuitous interference with the rights of those subject to it as could not be justifiable in the eyes of reasonable men.

Lord Russell CJ:

'... I have thought it well to deal with these points in some detail, and for this reason that the great majority of the cases in which the question of by-laws has been discussed are not cases of by-laws of bodies of a public representative character entrusted by Parliament with delegated authority, but are for the most part cases of railway companies, dock companies, or other like companies, which carry on their business for their own profit, although incidentally for the advantage of the public. In this class of case it is right that the Courts should jealously watch the exercise of these powers, and guard against their unnecessary or unreasonable exercise to the public disadvantage. But, when the Court is called upon to consider the by-laws of public representative bodies clothed with the ample authority which I have described, and exercising that authority accompanied by the checks and safeguards which have been mentioned, I think the consideration of such by-laws ought to be approached from a different standpoint. They ought to be supported if possible. They ought to be, as has been said, 'benevolently' interpreted, and credit ought to be given to those who have to administer them that they will be reasonably administered. This involved the introduction of no new canon of construction. But, further, looking to the character of the body legislating under the delegated authority of Parliament, to the subject-matter of such legislation, and to the nature and extent of the authority given to deal with matters which concern them, and in the manner which to them shall seem meet, I think courts of justice ought to be slow to condemn as invalid any by-law, so made under such conditions, on the ground of supposed unreasonableness. Notwithstanding what Cockburn CJ said in *Bailey* v *Williamson* (1), an analogous case, I do not mean to say that there may not be cases in which it would be the duty of the Court to condemn by-laws, made under such authority as these were made, as invalid because unreasonable. But unreasonable in what sense? If, for instance, they were found to be partial and unequal in their operation as between different classes; if they were manifestly unjust; if they disclosed bad faith; if they involved such oppressive or gratuitous interference with the rights of those subject to them as could find no justification in the minds of reasonable men, the Court might well say, "Parliament never intended to give authority to make such rules; they are unreasonable and ultra vires". But it is in this sense, and in this sense only, as I conceive, that the question of unreasonableness can properly be regarded. A by-law is not unreasonable merely because particular judges may think that it goes further than is prudent or necessary to convenient, or because it is not accompanied by a qualification or an exception which some judges may think ought to be there. Surely it is not too much to say that in matters which directly and mainly concern the people of the county, who have the right to choose those whom they think best fitted to represent them in their local government bodies, such representatives may be trusted to understand their own requirements better than judges ...'

Matthew J (dissenting):

'... I do not propose to refer at length to the cases cited in the argument where by-laws made under local authority have in recent times been condemned as unreasonable. In none of those cases is there any indication of the principle which I understand to be now contended for, namely, that such ordinances should receive a special kind of interpretation. The powers conferred on county councils have been spoken of in the discussion as something previously unknown to the law. But from the earliest times when charters were granted to towns municipal affairs have been managed by elected representatives of the inhabitants. The by-laws made by such bodies have been frequently declared to be invalid. Take, for instance, the by-laws which have been held to be unreasonable restraints of trade, and which are referred to in the judgment in *Mitchell* v *Reynolds* (2). No case has been cited in which there is any trace of the principle now contended for, that such by-laws are to be interpreted with any particular indulgence because of their popular origin. If this view be adopted, it seems to be the judges will be placed in an anomalous position. Where they differ from bodies not popularly elected their jurisdiction to pronounce upon the validity of a by-law would remain unimpaired; but where they differed from bodies like a county council, their position would be altogether different. They would be bound to uphold what in other cases they would be right in condemning ...

I regret to be unable to concur in the view of the majority of my colleagues. Their judgment appears to me to conflict with the recent decisions referred to in the course of the discussion and with the views expressed by Sir Henry Hawkins, the late Mr Justice Cave, the present Master of the Rolls, and the late Lord Justice Kay. In the case of *Alty* v *Farrell* (3), a by-law which gave a policeman an unqualified right to require a vendor of coals in small quantities to weigh the coal in the policeman's presence was held to be unreasonable and invalid, because the power might be exercised oppressively. This principle seems to me applicable to the present case. The decision of *Alty* v *Farrell* has the high authority of the Lord Chief Justice and Wright J ...'

(1)   Supra, this chapter

(2)   (1711) 1 P Wms 181

(3)   [1896] 1 QB 636

9   PREROGATIVE POWER

Attorney-General v De Keyser's Royal Hotel [1920] AC 508 House of Lords (Lords Dunedin, Atkinson, Moulton, Sumner and Parmoor)

The effect of statute on the prerogative

Facts

In May 1916, the Crown took possession of an hotel for the purposes of housing the headquarters personnel of the Royal Flying Corps, and denied the legal right of the owner to compensation. By a Petition of Right the owners asked for a declaration that they were entitled to compensation under the Defence Act 1842.

Held

Reg 2 of the Defence of the Realm Regulations issued under the Defence of the Realm Consolidation Act 1914, when read with s1(2) of the Act, conferred no new powers of acquiring land, but simply authorised the taking possession of land under the Defence Act 1842 which provided for the payment of compensation. Since statute required the payment of compensation, the crown could not claim any prerogative power to take possession of land without compensation; any prerogative power to this effect was in abeyance during the lifetime of the statute.

Lord Dunedin:

'... The prerogative is defined by a learned constitutional writers as "The residue of discretionary or arbitrary authority which at any given time is legally left in the hands of the Crown". Inasmuch as the Crown is a party to every Act of Parliament it is logical enough to consider that when the Act deals with something which before the Act could be effected by the prerogative, and specially empowers the Crown to do the same thing, but subject to conditions, the Crown assents to that, and by that Act, to the prerogative being curtailed.

... Those powers which the executive exercises without parliamentary authority are comprised under the comprehensive term of the prerogative. Where, however, Parliament has intervened and has provided by statute for powers, previously within the prerogative, being exercised in a particular manner and subject to the limitations and provisions contained in the statute, they can only be so exercised. Otherwise, what use would there be in imposing limitations, if the Crown could at its pleasure disregard them and fall back on prerogative?...

It is quite obvious that it would be useless and meaningless for the Legislature to impose restrictions and limitations upon, and to attach conditions to, the exercise by the Crown of the powers conferred by a statute, if the crown were free at its pleasure to disregard these provisions, and by virtue of its prerogative do the very thing the statutes empowered it to do. One cannot in the construction of a statute attribute to the Legislature (in the absence of compelling words) an intention so absurd. It was suggested that when a statute is passed empowering the crown to do a certain thing which it might therefore have done by virtue of its prerogative, the prerogative is merged in the statute. I confess I do not think the word "merged" is happily chosen. I should prefer to say that when such a statute, expressing the will and intention of the King and of the three estates of the realm, is passed, it abridges the Royal Prerogative while it is in force to this extent; that the Crown can only do the particular thing under and in accordance with the statutory provisions, and that its prerogative power to do that thing is in abeyance. Whichever mode of expression be used, the result intended to be indicated is, I think, the same, namely that after the statute has been passed, and while it is in force, the thing it empowers the Crown to do can thenceforth only be done by and under the statute and subject to all the limitations, restrictions and conditions by it imposed, however unrestricted the Royal Prerogative may theretofore have been ...'

Bate's Case: the Case of Impositions (1606) 2 State Trials 371 Court of Exchequer

Prerogative power to regulate trade

Facts

Bate refused to pay duty on imported currants imposed by the Crown, claiming that it was contrary to the Statute 45 Edw 3 c 4 which prohibited indirect taxation without the consent of Parliament.

Held

The King could impose what duties he pleased for the purpose of regulating trade, and the court could not go behind the King's statement that the duty was in fact imposed for the regulation of trade.

Burmah Oil Co (Burma Trading) Ltd v Lord Advocate [1965] AC 75 House of Lords (Lords Reid, Hodson, Pearce and Upjohn and Viscount Radcliffe)

Exercise of royal prerogative: right to compensation

Facts

The General Officer Commanding in Burma (in 1939-45) ordered the destruction of the installations of the appellant companies near Rangoon. This was because the Japanese army was advancing and UK Government policy was to deny resources to the enemy. The appellant companies (which had their registered offices in Scotland) commenced an action for compensation for the damage sustained.

Held (Viscount Radcliffe and Lord Hodson dissenting)

Although the demolitions were carried out lawfully in exercise of the royal prerogative, there is no general rule that the prerogative can be exercised, even in time of war or imminent danger, by taking or destroying property without making payment for it. The taking or the destruction of property in the course of actually fighting the enemy - 'battle damage' - does not give rise to any claim for compensation, but these demolitions did not fall under the head of battle damage, because, although the enemy was approaching, they did not arise out of the military operations. Thus the circumstances of the destruction gave the appellants a right to claim compensation.

Lord Reid:

'... We must now take it that these demolitions were carried out by an exercise of the royal prerogative, and the question for decision is whether such an exercise of the royal prerogative gives any legal right to compensation to the persons who have suffered loss thereby.

It is not easy to discover and decide the law regarding the royal prerogative and the consequences of its exercise. Apart from *In Re A Petition of Right* (1) and *Attorney-General* v *De Keyser's Royal Hotel Ltd* (2), there have been no cases directly raising the matter for some centuries, and obiter dicta and the views of institutional writers and text writers are not always very helpful.

What we have to determine in this case is whether or when, in a case not covered by any statute, property can be taken by virtue of the prerogative without compensation. That could only be an exceptional case, because it would be impracticable to conduct a modern war by use of the prerogative alone, whether or not compensation was paid. The mobilisation of the industrial and financial resources of the country could not be done without statutory emergency powers. The prerogative is really a relic of a past age, not lost by disuse, but only available for a case not covered by statute, so I think the proper approach is a historical one: how was it used in former times and how has it been used in modern times?

As regards modern times, extensive investigation in connection with the *De Keyser* case failed to disclose a single instance of asking or interfering with land without payment. And if movables had been taken without compensation at any time after 1660 I feel sure that historians would have found evidence of that. People in influential positions may have been very willing to give their services but they were very sensitive about property. It would certainly have been a grievance if property had been taken without payment, yet there is no mention of such a grievance either in 1688-9 - or at any other time. Negative evidence may not amount to proof, but it is so strong that I would hold it established that prerogative was never used or attempted to be used in that way in modern times before 1914 ...

Before turning to the cases which arose out of the 1914 war, I would make these observations. First, there is nothing novel in the idea that a prerogative right to take property carries with it an obligation to pay compensation: that has apparently always been recognised with regard to the prerogative rights of purveyance and angary. And, secondly, it was well established that taking or destroying property in the course of fighting the enemy did not give rise to any claim for compensation, whether that was done by the armed forces of the Crown or by individuals taking arms to defend their country or by the enemy. What had never been clarified was the question whether compensation was payable when property was taken deliberately for defence purposes, and in modern times such purposes would at least include training of troops, manufacture of munitions, obtaining the wide variety of supplies necessary to maintain the forces on active service, and economic warfare and various purposes essential to the conduct of the war but not immediately concerned with the maintenance of the fighting services. I may say at this point that it was rightly not argued that the fact that property is taken for destruction and not for use can make any difference ...

Such damage must include both accidental and deliberate damage done in the course of fighting operations. It cannot matter whether the damage was unintentional or done by our artillery or aircraft to dislodge the enemy or by the enemy to dislodge our troops. And the same must apply to destruction of a building or a bridge before the enemy actually capture it. Moreover, it would be absurd if the right to compensation for such a building or bridge depended on how near the enemy were when it was destroyed. But I would think that Vattel is right in contrasting acts done deliberately (librement et par precaution) with damage caused by inevitable necessity (par une necessite inevitable). His examples show that he means something dictated by the dispositions of the opposing forces. It may become necessary during the war to have new airfields or training grounds and the necessity may be inevitable, but that kind of thing would not come within the exception as stated by any of the commentators, and there are many other preparatory acts which are in a sense inevitably necessary because there is really no choice: for example, there may be only one factory in the country or one site suitable for a particular purpose.

The peculiarity of this case is that, although the destructions took place while the enemy was approaching, they were not done to hamper his advance. If HM Government had decided not to try to defend Burma and there had been no fighting there, the need to destroy these installations would have been just the same. On the pursuers' averments the purpose was "to deny to the enemy industrial resources and facilities" - really a form of economic warfare. Suppose that the appellants had held in Rangoon a stock of wolfram or some other material which it was important to keep out of enemy hands, and had been themselves unable to remove it. The Government would certainly have taken it: suppose they could have brought it home and used it, could it then have been said that no compensation was due because the enemy advance had made the taking inevitably necessary?'

Lord Pearce:

'... The general question, therefore, is whether at common law the Crown, by virtue of its war prerogative, can take the subject's property without any compensation. If there is a general duty to compensate, the particular question arises whether, in the circumstances averred, that general duty to compensate was excluded by the fact that the destruction was battle damage or was done in the course of military operations ...

It is plainly just and equitable that when the state takes or destroys a subject's property for the general good of the state it shall pay him compensation. Are there good grounds of authority or theory or practice for saying that in England the prerogative had no such general duty to compensate?

In my view, the matters on which the Crown relies are too slender to support such an infringement of the subject's rights. There are the imprecise dicta in the Year Books about coming on land in time of crisis to make bulwarks in defence of the King and his realm and the power of pulling down suburbs, and so forth. These are repeated in the *Saltpetre* (3) case, but the finding in the case is that the King must pay for his saltpetre and the King's servants must leave the inheritance of the subject in so good a plight as they find it, and have a duty to make the places in which they dig so well and commodious to the owner as before.

In Stuart times there are some admissions in 70 pages of learned argument by Hampden's counsel in the *Ship Money* (4) case, but it is unwise to regard the admissions of counsel as establishing the law. There is the decision in *In Re a Petition of Right* (1) but I agree with the observation of Atkin LJ and, in my view, it cannot stand in the light of the subsequent case of *De Keyser's Royal Hotel* (2). Nor can the incidental references of Lord Parker in *The Zamora* (5) to the law as it then stood.

These matters are greatly outweighed by the indications to the contrary. There are the thoughtful institutional writings which, on a balanced view, concluded that justice as it was in fact, or ought to be in theory, required compensation for losses inflicted on subjects for the benefit of the community. There is the absence of any decision that the Crown may seize without compensation. On the contrary, there is the *Saltpetre* (3) case which held that the crown must pay and make reparation for damage caused in a taking of saltpetre which was justified on the ground of war prerogative. There are the opinions of your Lordships' House in the *De Keyser's Royal Hotel* (2) case. Above all, there is the fact that from early days, by bargain or by statutory compensation, the Crown has always paid so far as records show. And the 1939 legislation shows, if any doubt on the matter could exist, that our modern view of what is equitable on this point accords with that of the institutional writers ...

It has not been contended before us that the deliberate destruction of property to deny it to the enemy is any less a taking than is the acquisition of it for use. Nor do I think that such a distinction is valid at common law. Both alike are taken for military purposes. There may, however, well be a distinction in terms of compensation. Petrol which is taken and used may be worth its full value. Petrol which is blown up when it is about to pass into the hands of an enemy, who will undoubtedly consume it without paying the owner, may be valueless. But that matter has not been argued and is not yet relevant. On the general question whether a right to compensation, be it substantial or minimal, exists I find myself unable to accept a dividing line between acquisition and destruction.

Whether one accepts in general terms the line indicated by de Vattel or by the dictum of Field J in the *Pacific Railroad* case, which was to some extent founded on it, or the lines indicated either by the Lord Ordinary or by the Inner House, it is clear that some line must be drawn. In cases that lie far from the line it is easy to see what justice requires. In respect of a house that has the misfortune to be in the centre of a battlefield and is inevitably demolished by the Crown's artillery, it is clear, on the principles which have been almost unanimously set out, that the subject can have no claim. In respect of a house that is demolished by the crown with wise forethought, long before any battle, to provide a fort or a clear field of fire in case of threatened invasion, I think it equally clear that the subject should obtain compensation. Cases which lie close to that line, wherever it be drawn, must depend on fact and degree. The Lord Ordinary wisely observed: "The real answer I think is that the line has to be drawn somewhere, and on one side of it, however artificial it may seem, legal consequences are different from what they may be on the other. The practical consequences may differ very little, and this may be the kind of case in which that is especially true. Although the principles of the common law direct me to decide that this case falls on that side of the line which means that compensation is payable, my decision says nothing as to the value of such right to compensation."

I think that the line drawn by de Vattel marks substantially the area in which damage ceases to be payable. I would define the line as excluding damage done in the battle or for the necessities of the battle. If an evacuating army destroys as it goes, I would exclude from compensation any damage which it does for the purposes of its survival, for example, by destruction of ammunition which will be turned against it by the enemy, or petrol which will be used by the enemy to pursue it, or food which will sustain the enemy during their attacks upon it. But more general damage done with a view to weakening or depriving the enemy in the not immediate future, especially when the scene of battle will have moved elsewhere, comes in the category of deliberate destruction done outside the battle. The destruction of oil wells, like various forms of economic warfare, is quite outside the battle damage, and the fact that the battle may have dictated the date of the destruction is irrelevant.

When the motive of destruction is a deliberate long-term strategy then, unless it be shown by the Crown that the damage has also an impact and importance for the purpose of the battle and would have been done for that purpose in any event, the subject is entitled to compensation.

It must not be thought that by compensation I mean the full cost of reinstatement. It was argued that the claim was irrelevant because it set out a demand for compensation on that basis. In my opinion, the pursuers are entitled to put forward their claim on that basis, since that is the starting point for a consideration of the amount payable as compensation for the value lost. The argument did not, however, go into the further questions which must, I think, be considered. For it would seem that the value of property that is about to pass, probably for ever, into the hands of the enemy must depend on the nature of the property and the chances of its survival and restoration, intact or damaged, to the pursuers...'

Commentary

Shortly after the pronouncement of this decision, the Government secured the passage of the War Damage Act 1965 which obviated the necessity for the Crown to pay compensation in cases such as the *Burmah Oil* case.

(1) [1915] 3 KB 649

(2) Supra, this chapter

(3) (1606) 12 Co Rep 12

(4) (1637) 3 Stake Trials 825

(5) [1916] AC 77

Chandler v DPP [1964] AC 763 House of Lords (Lords Reid, Devlin, Radcliffe, Hodson and Pearce)

Interests of the state: who is to decide

Facts

The appellants were members of the Committee of 100 who in the course of a political demonstration attempted to enter an air base to immobilise certain planes. They were tried and convicted of approaching a prohibited place for a purpose prejudicial to the interests of the state under s1(1) of the Official Secrets Act 1911. They appealed on the ground (inter alia) that their purposes were not prejudicial to the interests of the state.

Held

The appellants were properly convicted.

Lord Reid:

'Counsel for the accused said that they sought to adduce evidence that their purpose was not prejudicial to the interests of the State, and that the basis of their defence was that these aircraft used nuclear bombs and that it was not in the interests of the State to have aircraft so armed ... It would be beneficial to the State to immobilise these aircraft ... In reply the Attorney-General submitted that an objective test must determine whether the purpose of grounding aircraft was a prejudicial purpose, that the accused's belief was irrelevant, and so was the reasonableness of their beliefs. Havers J ... ruled that the defence were not entitled to call evidence to establish that it would be beneficial for this country to give up nuclear armament ...

... Who then is to determine what is and is not prejudicial to the interests of the State? ... I do not subscribe to the view that the Government or a Minister must always or even as a general rule have the last word about that ... It is in my opinion clear that the disposition and armament of the armed forces are, and for centuries have been, within the exclusive discretion of the Crown, and that no one can seek a legal remedy on the ground that such discretion has been wrongly exercised ...'

Lord Devlin:

'... there is no rule of the common law that whenever questions of national security are being considered by any court for any purpose, it is what the Crown thinks to be necessary or expedient that counts, and not what is necessary or expedient in fact ... In a case like the present, it may be presumed that it is contrary to the interests of the Crown to have one of its airfields immobilised ... but the presumption is not irrebuttable ... Men can exaggerate the extent of their interests, and so can the Crown. The servants of the Crown, like other men animated by the highest motives, are capable of formulating a policy ad hoc so as to prevent the citizen from doing something that the Crown does not want him to do. It is the duty of the courts to be as alert now as they have always been to prevent any abuse of the prerogative. But in the present case there is nothing at all to suggest that the Crown's interests in the proper operation of its airfields is not what it may naturally be presumed to be, or that it was exaggerating the perils of interference with their effectiveness ...'

China Navigation Co Ltd v Attorney-General [1932] 2 KB 197 Court of Appeal (Scrutton, Lawrence and Slessor LJJ)

Royal prerogative to demand payment for special protection

Facts

The plaintiffs, an English shipping company trading in the China seas, requested the Crown to provide armed guards to be placed on board their ships as a protection against internal piracy, which was a serious menace at that time. Armed guards were provided, it being agreed that they should be paid for by the plaintiffs.

The plaintiffs, however, sought a declaration that as British subjects they were entitled to this protection without payment.

Held

When Parliament has by the Army (Annual) Act sanctioned the raising and keeping of the army, the right of the Crown as to the disposition and use of the forces so raised is a prerogative right the exercise of which cannot be controlled by the courts. Thus there is no legal duty on the Crown to afford by its military forces protection to British subjects in foreign parts and if, in the exercise of its discretion, the Crown decides to afford such protection it may lawfully stipulate that it will only do so in return for payment.

Commentary

See also House of Lords in *Chandler v DPP* [1964] AC 763, supra.

Council of Civil Service Unions v Minister for the Civil Service [1984] 3 WLR 1174
House of Lords (Lords Fraser, Scarman, Roskill, Diplock and Brightman)

Judicial review of the royal prerogative

Facts

Since 1947 staff employed at GCHQ had been permitted to be members of trade unions. In December 1983 the Minister, with no prior consultation, peremptorily altered the conditions of service, forbidding membership of a union. The applicants sought judicial review on the ground of unfairness due to failure to consult. Gladwell J granted the application and declared the instrument to be invalid. The Court of Appeal allowed the Minister's appeal.

Held

The court will not intervene to review the decision of a minister where the requirements of national security outweigh other matters. The appeal was dismissed because although executive action based on common law or the use of a prerogative power was not therefore immune from review, the requirements of national security outweighed those of fairness, which was a matter for the executive to weigh and decide.

Lord Fraser said that the most important and difficult question raised by the appeal concerned the royal prerogative. The Order of Council of 1982 had been issued by the Sovereign by virtue of her prerogative, but of course on the advice of the Government of the day. The respondent submitted that it was not open to review by the courts because it was an emanation of the prerogative.

That submission involved two propositions. The first was that prerogative powers were discretionary, that is, they might be exercised at the discretion of the Sovereign (acting on advice in accordance with modern constitutional practice) and the way in which they were exercised was not open to review by the courts.

That proposition was vouched by an impressive array of authority. *Attorney-General* v *De Keyser's Royal Hotel Ltd* (1) showed that the courts would inquire into whether a particular prerogative power existed or not, and if it did exist, into its extent. But once the existence of the extent of a power were established to the satisfaction of the court, the court could not inquire into the proprietary of its exercise.

That was undoubtedly the position as laid down in the authorities and it was plainly reasonable in relation to many of the most important prerogative powers that were concerned with control of the armed forces and with foreign policy and other matters that were unsuitable for discussion or review in the law courts.

In the present case, the prerogative power involved was power to regulate the Home Civil Service, and his Lordship recognised that there was no obvious reason why the mode of exercise of that power should be immune from review by the courts. Nevertheless, to permit such review would run counter to the great weight of authority.

Having regard to the opinion that he had reached on the respondent's second proposition, it was unnecessary to decide whether her first proposition was sound or not and his Lordship preferred to leave that question open until it arose in a case where a decision on it was necessary. He therefore assumed, without deciding, that all powers exercised directly under the prerogative were immune from challenge in the courts.

The respondent's second proposition was that an instruction given in the exercise of a delegated power conferred by the Sovereign under the prerogative enjoyed the same immunity from review as if it were itself a direct exercise of prerogative power. That depended on whether the power conferred by article 4 of the 1982 Order in Council on the respondent of 'providing for ... the conditions of service' of the Civil Service was subject to an implied obligation to act fairly.

There was no doubt that, if the Order in Council had been made under the authority of a statute, it would have been so construed. His Lordship was unable to see why the words conferring the same powers should be construed differently merely because their source was an order in council made under the prerogative.

Whatever their source, powers that were are defined, either by reference to their object or by reference to procedure for their exercise, or in some other way, and whether the definition was expressed or implied, were in his Lordship's opinion normally subject to judicial control to ensure that they were not exceeded. By 'normally' he meant provided that considerations of national security did not require otherwise.

The courts had already shown themselves ready to control by way of judicial review the actions of a tribunal set up under the prerogative: see, for example, *R* v *Criminal Injuries Compensation Board, ex parte Lain* (2).

Lord Scarman said that he would dismiss the appeal for one reason only. He was satisfied that the respondent had made out a case on the ground of national security. He had no doubt that she had refused to consult the unions before issuing her instruction because she had feared that, if she did, union-organised disruption of the monitoring services of GCHQ could well result.

He was satisfied that that fear had been one that a reasonable minister in the circumstances in which she had found herself could reasonably have entertained and that she could reasonably have considered such disruption to constitute a threat to national security.

Like Lord Diplock, his Lordship believed that the law relating to judicial review had now reached the stage where it could be said with confidence that, if the subject matter in respect of which prerogative power was justifiable, the exercise of the power was subject to review in accordance with the principles developed in respect of the review of the exercise of statutory power.

The royal prerogative had always been regarded as part of the common law, and Sir Edward Coke had had no doubt that it was subject to the common law: 'the King hath no prerogative, but that which the law of the land allows him'.

It was, of course, beyond doubt that in Coke's time and thereafter judicial review of the exercise of prerogative power had been limited to inquiring into whether a particular power existed and, if it did, into its extent: *Attorney-General* v *De Keyser's Royal Hotel Ltd* (1). But that limitation had now gone, overwhelmed by the developing modern law of judicial review.

Just as ancient restrictions in the law relating to the prerogative writs and orders had not prevented the courts from extending the requirement of natural justice, namely the duty to act fairly, so that it was required of a purely administrative act, so also had the modern law extended the range of judicial review in respect of the exercise of prerogative power. Today, therefore, the controlling factor in determining whether the exercise of prerogative power was subject to judicial review was not its source but its subject matter.

His Lordship agreed, subject to his comments, with Lord Diplock and Lord Roskill.

Lord Diplock said that the English law relating to judicial control of administrative action had been developed on a case to case basis that had virtually transformed it over the last three decades.

His Lordship had derived little practical assistance from learned and esoteric analyses of the precise legal nature, boundaries and historical origin of the prerogative, which was a part of the common law, or of what powers exercisable by executive officers acting on behalf of central Government that were not shared by private citizens qualified for inclusion under the label.

Nevertheless, whatever label might be attached to them there had unquestionably survived into the present day a residue of miscellaneous fields of law in which the executive Government retained decision-making powers that were not dependent on any statutory authority but nevertheless had consequences on he private rights or legitimate expectations of other persons that would render them subject to judicial review if the power of the decision-maker to make them were statutory in origin.

From matters so relatively minor as the grant of pardons to condemned criminals, of honours to the good and great, of corporate personality to deserving bodies of persons, and of bounty from moneys made available to the executive Government by Parliament, they extended to matters so vital to the survival and welfare of the nation as the conduct of relations with foreign states and what lay at the heart of the present case - the defence of the realm against potential enemies, or 'national security'.

His Lordship said no reason why simply because a decision-making power was derived from a common law and not a statutory source it should, for that reason only, be immune from judicial review. Judicial review had developed to a stage when one could classify under three heads the grounds on which administrative action was subject to control by judicial review: 'illegality', 'irrationality' and 'procedural impropriety'.

As respected 'procedural impropriety', his Lordship saw no reason why it should not be a ground for judicial review of a decision made under powers of which the ultimate source was the prerogative.

The crucial point of law in the present case, which had never been identified or even adumbrated in the respondent's argument before Mr Justice Glidewell and so, excusably, found no place in an otherwise impeccable judgment, was whether procedural propriety must give way to national security when there was conflict between, on the one hand, the prima facie rule of 'procedural propriety' in public law, applicable to a case of legitimate expectations that a benefit ought not to be withdrawn until the reason for its proposed withdrawal had been communicated to the person who had theretofore enjoyed that benefit and that person had been given an opportunity to comment on the reason, and, on the other hand, action that was needed to be taken in the interests of national security, for which the executive Government bore the responsibility and alone had access to sources of information that qualified it to judge what the necessary action was.

To that, there could only be one sensible answer: 'Yes'.

Lord Roskill, also dismissing the appeal on the ground of national security, said that to speak today, as Blackstone had done, of the actions of the Sovereign as 'irresistible and absolute' when modern constitutional convention required that all such acts were done by the Sovereign on the advice of, and would be carried out by, the Sovereign's ministers currently in power was surely to hamper the continued development of administrative law by harking back to what Lord Atkin had once called, in a different context, the clanking of medieval chains of ghosts of the past.

His Lordship was unable to see, subject to what he should say later, that there was any logical reason why the fact that the source of a power under which the executive acted was the prerogative and no statute should today deprive the citizen of that right to challenge to the manner of its exercise that he would possess were the source of the power statutory.

That right of challenge could not, however, be unqualified. It must depend on the subject matter of the prerogative power that was exercised. Many examples were given during the argument of prerogative powers which as at present advised his Lordship did not think could properly be made the subject of judicial review.

Prerogative powers such as those relating to the making of treaties, the defence of the realm, the prerogative of mercy, the grant of honours, the dissolution of Parliament and the appointment of ministers as well as others were not, he thought, susceptible to judicial review because their nature and subject matter was such as not to be amenable to the judicial process. The courts were not the places wherein to determine whether a treaty should be concluded or the armed forces disposed in a particular manner or Parliament dissolved on one date rather than another.

Lord Brightman agreed that the appeal should be dismissed on the ground of national security. Like Lord Fraser, he would prefer to leave resolution of the quetion whether judicial reviewability might extend, in an appropriate case, to a direct exercise of a prerogative power to a case where it must necessarily be determined.

(1)   Supra, this chapter

(2)   [1967] 2 QB 864

Gouriet v Union of Post Office Workers [1978] AC 435 House of Lords (Viscount Dilhorne, Lords Diplock, Wilberforce, Edmund-Davies and Fraser of Tullybelton)

The courts and executive decisions

Facts

The union had resolved to refuse to handle mail destined for South Africa as part of a protest against apartheid. This was, arguably, an offence under the Post Office Act 1953. The plaintiff had requested the Attorney-General for his consent to act as plaintiff in relator proceedings against the union for an injunction.

The Attorney-General refused the consent sought, and the plaintiff proceeded to apply for injunctions against the union in his own name, and for a declaration that the Attorney-General had acted improperly in refusing to exercise his discretion in the plaintiff's favour.

The Attorney-General applied for the declaration against him to be struck out on the grounds that his discretion to consent or refuse to act as plaintiff in relator proceedings was absolute and could not be reviewed by the courts; that he did not have to give his reasons, and that the court was not entitled to inquire into them; and that if his decision was wrong he was answerable to Parliament alone.

The Court of Appeal held, by a majority (inter alia) that the discretion of the Attorney-General in such matters was unreviewable, and the matter was no longer a live issue by the time the main action reached the House of Lords. In the House of Lords, however, their Lordships did take the opportunity to comment upon Lord Denning's view that the Attorney-General's discretion was reviewable.

Viscount Dilhorne:

'On the Saturday the statement of claim was also amended to include a claim for a declaration that the Attorney-General had acted improperly in refusing his consent to relator proceedings and had wrongly exercised his discretion. At the hearing the following Tuesday the Attorney-General's refusal to give his reasons for withholding his consent was regarded by Lord Denning MR as a direct challenge to the rule of law, a statement with which I feel I must express my complete dissent.

In the course of his judgment on 27 January Lord Denning MR said that he accepted that the court could not inquire into the giving of consent by the Attorney-General to the institution of a relator action but in his opinion his refusal of consent could be reviewed by the courts. Lawton LJ and Ormrod LJ did not agree. On the last day of the hearing Mr Gouriet abandoned his contention that the courts had power to review the Attorney-General's exercise of his powers, but in view of Lord Denning's observations and those of Lawton LJ on the Saturday to which I have referred and the importance of the question, I feel I should say something with regard thereto.

The Attorney-General has many powers and duties. He may stop any prosecution on indictment by entering a nolle prosequi. He merely has to sign a piece of paper saying that he does not wish the prosecution to continue. He need not give any reasons. He can direct the institution of a prosecution and direct the Director of Public Prosecutions to take over the conduct of any criminal proceedings and he may tell him to offer no evidence.

In the exercise of these powers he is not subject to direction by his ministerial colleagues or to control and supervision by the courts. If the court can review his refusal of consent to a relator action, it is an exception to the general rule. No authority was cited which supports the conclusion that the courts can do so. Indeed such authority as there is points strongly in the opposite direction.

... in my opinion the view that refusal of consent to a relator action is an exception to the general rule and is subject to review by the courts must be rejected. It is because I think it undesirable that any judicial observations suggesting that the exercise by the Attorney-General of these functions and duties is subject to control, supervision and review by the courts should be left unanswered that I have ventured to make these observations.'

Lord Diplock:

'Although the majority of the Court of Appeal in the instant case accepted that they had no right to review the Attorney-General's refusal of consent to a relator action, they inconsistently held that where the proposed civil action aims at upholding the criminal law they can review such refusal and are free to express the view, for example, that "there is no discernible reason why threatened breaches of the criminal law should not be declared illegal and possibly restrained" (per Lawton LJ), and, having done so, to allow the private citizen to proceed. Such a conclusion strikes at the roots of the Attorney-General's unique role, and it is backed by no more authority than that available to support the view expressed obiter in *McWhirter's* case (1) that a private citizen may act if the Attorney-General unreasonably delays in giving his consent or refuses it in what was there described as "a proper case".

... And yet lip-service was paid to the proposition that the Attorney-General's exercise of his discretion cannot be reviewed by the courts. For my part, I venture to reiterate by way of a contrast the striking fact that my noble and learned friend, Viscount Dilhorne, has expressed the affirmative view that the Attorney-General may well have acted in the public interest in withholding his consent. This highlights the undesirability of making the matter one of disputation in the courts, instead of in Parliament.

Accepting as I do that the Attorney-General's discretion is absolute and non-reviewable, there was accordingly, in my judgment, no basis upon which the plaintiff should have been granted the final injunction he sought. It remains to be considered whether he should have been granted any relief or whether, as the three defendants submit, the proceedings should have been dismissed as showing no reasonable cause of action.'

(1)   [1973] QB 629

Laker Airways Ltd v Dept of Trade [1977] QB 643 Court of Appeal (Lord Denning MR, Roskill and Lawton LJJ)

Justiciability of extent of Crown prerogative powers. Acts inconsistent with general objectives of an administrative power are ultra vires

Facts

The Civil Aviation Authority, established by the Civil Aviation Act 1971, was required by s3(1) to perform its functions in the manner best calculated to secure the general objectives set out in paragraphs (a) to (d), subject to any current 'guidance' given by the Secretary of State for trade under s3(2) which read:

'... the Secretary of State may from time to time ... give guidance to the Authority in writing with respect to the performance of the functions conferred on it ...'

Section 3(3) provided that such guidance should be approved by a resolution of each House of Parliament.

Objective (b) was 'to secure that at least one major British Airline not controlled by' the state-owned airways board 'has opportunities to participate in providing ... air transport services ...'

The Authority considered an application by the plaintiffs, privately owned air service operators, for a licence to operate a cheap passenger service known as Skytrain between London (Stansted) and New York. After a full inquiry the Authority, in October 1972, granted the plaintiff a ten year licence to begin on 1 January 1973.

Before Skytrain could operate over United States territory, a permit, signed by the President, had to be obtained by the United States under an international treaty between the UK and the USA, the Bermuda Agreement 1946. In February 1973 the British Ambassador formally notified the USA of the designation of the plaintiff for operations on the specified route.

The plaintiffs, with the active help and encouragement of the executive, incurred capital expenditure in buying aircraft and preparing for Skytrain to start; they were further encouraged when in February 1975 the Authority refused an application by the state-owned airways board to revoke their licence.

However there had been a change of Government in February 1974 and in July 1975 the new Secretary of State reversed the policy of the previous Government and implemented this change in 1976 in a Command Paper which contained 'guidance' to the Authority and received parliamentary approval under s3(3) of the 1971 Act. Paragraph 7 of the guidance constituted in effect an instruction to the Authority to eliminate competition with the state-owned airline and to revoke the plaintiffs' licence. The Command Paper also stated that the plaintiffs' designation as a scheduled service operator under the Bermuda Agreement should be cancelled.

The plaintiffs brought an action against the Dept of Trade for declarations that paras 7 and 8 of the guidance were ultra vires and that the Department was not entitled to cancel the designation. The Department denied that the guidance was ultra vires but also claimed that the Crown had the prerogative right or discretion to withdraw the designation under the treaty and that the exercise of this prerogative right could not be questioned in legal proceedings.

Held

The Secretary of State had acted beyond his powers in formulating the new policy by the procedure of 'guidance' under s3(2), albeit with parliamentary approval under s3(3), for any 'guidance' under s3(2) should as a matter of construction be consistent with the general objectives laid down in s3(1)(a) to (d) and as paragraph 7 of the guidance was inconsistent with objective (b), the plaintiffs were entitled to a declaration that the guidance was ultra vires the powers of the Secretary of State.

Per Roskill and Lawton LJJ, although the exercise of the Crown's prerogative in relation to its treaty-making powers was not justiciable in the municipal courts, this was a question as to the extent of those prerogative powers. The Crown's prerogative power to cancel a designation under the Bermuda Agreement was impliedly fettered by the 1971 Act to the extent that it could not be used to achieve by an indirect method a result which could not lawfully be achieved by guidance under the 1971 Act. Dicta in *A-G* v *De Keyser's Royal Hotel Ltd* (1) considered.

(1)   Supra, this chapter

Proclamations, The Case of (1611) 12 Co Rep 74 Informal conference between Judges and Privy Council

Crown prerogative and proclamations

Facts

The King asked Coke what his powers were to issue proclamations, and in particular, whether he could prohibit new building in and around London, and prohibit the making of starch from wheat, by that means. Coke asked for time to consult his fellow judges, and a conference was held between the Chief Justice, the Chief Baron, Baron Altham, and the Privy Council.

Held

It was resolved that the King by his proclamation cannot create any new offence which was not an offence before; for then he may alter the law of the land by his proclamation in a high point: for if he may create an offence where none is, upon that ensues fine and imprisonment; also that the law of England is divided into three parts, common law, statute law and custom; but the King's proclamation is none of them; also malum aut est malum in se, aut prohibitum, that which is against common law is malum in se, malum prohibitum is such an offence as is prohibited by Act of Parliament, and not by proclamation.

Also it was resolved that the King hath no prerogative but that which the law of the land allows him. But the King for the prevention of offences may by proclamation admonish his subjects that they keep the laws, and do not offend them; upon punishment to be inflicted by the law. Lastly, if an offence be not punishable in the Star Chamber, the prohibition of it by proclamation cannot make it punishable there; and after this resolution, no proclamation imposing fine and imprisonment was afterwards made.

Prohibitions del Roy (1607) 12 Co Rep 63 Conference of all the Judges

Limits of Royal prerogative and the courts

'Note, upon Sunday the 10th of November in this term, the King upon complaint made to him by Bancroft, Archbishop of Canterbury, concerning Prohibitions, the King was informed, that when the question was made of what matters the Ecclesiastical Judges have cognizance, either upon the exposition of the statutes concerning tithes or any other thing ecclesiastical or upon the statute 1 E1 concerning the high commission or in any other case in which there is not express authority in law, the King himself may decide it in his royal person; and that the Judges are but delegates of the King, and that the King may take what causes he shall please to determine, from the determination of the Judges, and may determine them himself. And the Archbishop said, that this was clear in divinity, that such authority belongs to the King by the word of God in the Scripture. To which was answered by me, in the presence, and with the clear consent of all the Judges of England and Barons of the Exchequer, that the King in his own person cannot adjudge any case, either criminal, as treason, felony etc, or betwixt party and party, concerning his inheritance, chattels or goods, etc, but that this ought to be determined and adjudged in some court of justice, according to the law and custom of England ... And the judges informed the King, that no king after the Conquest assumed to himself to give any judgment in any cause whatsoever, which concerned the administration of justice within this Realm, but these were solely determined in the Courts of Justice ... The King said, he thought the law was founded upon reason, and that he and others had reason, as well as the Judges; to which it was answered by me, that true it was, that God had endowed His Majesty with excellent science and great endowments of nature; but His Majesty was not learned in the laws of his realm of England, and causes which concern the life, or inheritance, or goods, or fortunes of his subjects, are not to be decided by natural reason but by the artificial reason and judgement of law, which law is an act which requires long study and experience, before that a man can attain to cognizance of it; that the law was the golden met-wand and measure, to try the causes of the subjects; and which protected His Majesty in safety and peace: with which the King was greatly offended, and said, that then he should be under the law, which was treason to affirm, as he said; to which I said, that Bracton saith, quod Rex non debet esse sub homine, sed sub Deo et lege (that the King should not be subject to any man, but to God and the law).'

R v Secretary of State for Foreign and Commonwealth Affairs, ex parte Everett
[1989] 2 WLR 224 Court of Appeal (O'Connor, Nicholls and Taylor LJJ)

Royal prerogative and judicial review

Facts

The applicant lived in Spain and his British passport was endorsed by the Spanish for residence there. He applied for a new passport on the expiry of the old one, but the Consul in Malaga refused it. There was a warrant out for the applicant's arrest in the UK and it was policy not to renew passports for anyone in that situation. The applicant sought judicial review of the decision. Mann J granted the relief sought and the Secretary of State appealed.

Held

The appeal would be allowed.

O'Connor LJ:

'... a passport ... is a familiar document to all citizens who travel in the world and it would seem obvious to me that the exercise of the prerogative, because there is no doubt that passports are issued under the royal prerogative in the discretion of the Secretary of State, is an area where common sense tells one that, if for some reason a passport is wrongly refused for a bad reason, the court should be able to inquire into it. I would reject the submission made on behalf of the Secretary of State that the judge was wrong to review the case ...

It will be seen that the judge [stated] that the policy of not issuing passports to persons against whom there was a warrant of arrest outstanding was an intelligible and valid policy, and no appeal is made against that because it is obvious good sense. But the judge came to the conclusion that the fair application of the policy required that if a passport was refused because a warrant was outstanding against the applicant, inquiry had to be made of the applicant before refusing a passport, as to whether he had anything to say.

In my judgment the judge fell into error in concluding that that was required for the fair exercise of his discretion. It seems to me that the Secretary of State, in the fair exercise of his discretion, was entitled to refuse the passport but to give his reason for so doing, and the fair giving of the reason, if the reason be that there is a warrant for the applicant's arrest outstanding, was to tell him when the warrant was issued and what offence was charged. Once he has done that he has all but discharged his duty, but he should, when notifying the applicant that that was the reason for refusing the passport, tell him that if there were any exceptional grounds which might call for the issue of a passport he would consider them. We have been told very properly by counsel for the Secretary of State that it is possible that exceptions may arise on compassionate grounds, eg if such a person were desperately ill in hospital in a foreign country it might be that a passport would be issued or an exception made. Had that been done, no one could challenge the proper exercise of the discretion ...

That is not an end of the matter, because judicial review is a discretionary remedy and one must look at the position at the time when the application came before the judge. At that stage the applicant knew everything. He was fully armed with lawyers in this country, solicitors and counsel, and there is not a word from him of any sort. There is no suggestion that there are any exceptional circumstances in this case. There is no suggestion from him that there is anything wrong with the warrant, or that he was not wanted on a warrant for an offence of obtaining a false passport or obtaining a passport ... by deception; he knew everything which he ought to have been told. He certainly knew when he made representations in the launching of the proceedings.

In those circumstances I cannot see that there are any grounds for thinking that, had the decision letter contained the information which he got later and contained the offer to consider any representations as to exceptional circumstances, any different result would have come about. Where the court finds itself in that position, namely that the applicant has suffered no injustice and that to grant the remedy would produce a barren result there are no grounds for granting relief ...

In those circumstances I would allow this appeal and refuse the order for judicial review.'

Commentary

Applied: *Council of Civil Service Unions* v *Minister for the Civil Services* [1984] 3 WLR 1174.

See also, *R* v *Secretary of State for the Home Department, ex parte Northumbria Police* [1988] 1 WLR 356, extracted in Chapter 17.

10 CROWN LIABILITY – PUBLIC INTEREST IMMUNITY

10.1   Statutes and the Crown

British Broadcasting Corporation v Johns [1965] Ch 32 Court of Appeal (Diplock, Willmer and Danckwerts LJJ)

Public corporations and Crown immunity

Facts

The principal question arising was whether the BBC was entitled to Crown immunity from taxation.

Held

The BBC was created as an independent legal entity, quite separate from the Crown. It was not an instrument of the Government and enjoyed none of the Crown's immunities.

Diplock LJ:

'The Crown immunity question. The BBC is liable to pay income tax under schedule D upon any annual profits or gains accruing to it from its activities if it is included in the expression "any person" in s122(1)(a)(i) and (ii) of the Income Tax Act, 1952. The question is thus one of construction of a statute. Since laws are made by rules for subjects, a general expression in a statute such as "any person," descriptive of those upon whom the statute imposes obligations or restraints is not to be read as including the rule himself. Under our more sophisticated constitution the concept of sovereignty has in the course of history come to be treated as comprising three distinct functions of a rule: executive, legislative and judicial, though the distinction between these functions in the case, for instance, of prerogative powers and administrative tribunals is sometimes blurred. The modern rule of construction of statutes is that the Crown, which today personifies the executive government of the country and is also a party to all legislation, is not bound by a statute which imposes obligations or restraints on persons or in respect of property unless the statute says so expressly or by necessary implication. But to use the expression "the Crown" as personifying the executive government of the country tends to conceal the fact that the executive functions of sovereignty are of necessity performed through the agency of persons other than the Queen herself. Such persons may be natural persons or, as has been increasingly the tendency over the last hundred years, fictitious persons ' corporations. The question here is whether the BBC carries on all or any of its activities as agent for the executive government. Are they carried out in the performance of a duty or in the exercise of a power which is imposed upon or vested in the executive government of the United Kingdom by statute or by the prerogative? (cf *Pfizer Corporation* v *Minister of Health* (1).

Mr Bucher has submitted that because wireless telegraphy and telephony were new inventions the Crown had a prerogative right to a monopoly of their use and has chosen to exercise this monopoly as respects broadcasting, wholly before 1954 and partially thereafter, through the instrumentality of the BBC. This contention involves adopting what he described as a modern and I as a seventeenth' century, view of the scope of the prerogative. But it is 350 years and a civil war too late for the Queen's courts to broaden the prerogative. The limits within which the executive government may impose obligations or restraints upon citizens of the United Kingdom without any statutory authority are now well settled and incapable of extension. In particular, as respects monopolies the Crown's claim to a general prerogative right to the monopoly of any activity was denied and circumscribed by the Statute of Monopolies 1623. Today, save in so far as the power is preserved by the Statute of Monopolies, or created by other statutes, the executive government has no constitutional right either itself to exercise through its agents or to confer upon other persons a monopoly of any form of activity.'

(1)   [1964] Ch 614

Lord Advocate v Dumbarton District Council; Same v Strathclyde Regional Council
[1989] 3 WLR 1346 House of Lords (Lords Keith of Kinkel, Griffiths, Ackner, Lowry and Jauncey)

Statutes binding the Crown

Facts

The Ministry of Defence in order to carry out work on the perimeter fence of a submarine base in Scotland, proposed to cut off one mile of highway in order to store plant and equipment while the work was in progress. It was admitted that the closure would be contrary to the Roads (Scotland) Act 1984, but the Ministry contended that the Act did not bind the Crown or its contractors.

Held

In considering the issue the House restated the principle that it was a rule of construction applicable both to England and Scotland, that the Crown was not bound by a statute save where expressly named or by necessary implication.

Lord Keith of Kinkel:

'I come finally to *BBC* v *Johns (Inspector of Taxes)* (1965) Ch 32. That case was concerned with the liability of the BBC to pay income tax. A number of issues were raised, of which the first was whether the corporation was exempt from taxation as an instrument of government, and the second was whether or not surplus funds remaining out of its grant from Parliament constituted profits of a trade. The Court of Appeal held that it was not exempt from taxation but that the surplus funds did not represent a "profit" taxable under Sch D. In connection with the first point, Diplock LJ said ([1964] Ch 32 at 78–79):

"The Crown immunity question. The BBC is liable to pay income tax under Sch D on any annual profits or gains accruing to it from its activities if it is included in the expression 'any person' in s122 1(a)(i) and (ii) of the Income Tax 1952. The question is thus one of construction of a statute. Since laws are made by rulers for subjects, a general expression in a law such as 'any person' descriptive of those on whom the law imposes obligations or restraints is not to be read as including the ruler himself. Under our more sophisticated constitution the concept of sovereignty has in the course of history come to be treated as comprising three distinct functions of a ruler: executive, legislative and judicial, though the distinction between these functions in the case, for instance, of prerogative powers and administrative tribunals is sometimes blurred. The modern rule of construction of statutes is that the Crown, which today personifies the executive government of the country and is also a party to all the legislation, is not bound by a statute which imposes obligations or restraints on persons or in respect of property, unless the statute says so expressly or by necessary implication."

In my opinion this statement by Diplock LJ accurately and correctly expresses the effect of the authorities. I consider it to be no longer a tenable view that the Crown is in terms bound by general words in a statute but that the prerogative enables it to override the statute. As to the considerations which may be applicable for the purpose of finding a necessary implication that the Crown is bound, it is clear that the mere fact that the statute in question has been passed for the public benefit is not in itself sufficient for that purpose.'

Lord Jauncey of Tullichettle:

'I would only add a few further words in support of the proposition that a statute must, in the absence of some particular provision to the contrary, bind the Crown either generally or not at all. Any other approach would mean that the applicability of a particular statute to the Crown in any given circumstances could depend not on the terms of the statute but on matters extraneous thereto, namely the relevant common law rights of the Crown at the time. Such a result would, in my view, be wholly illogical.'

Town Investments Ltd v Department of the Environment [1978] AC 359

Facts

A lease on an office block was granted to the Secretary of State for the Environment 'for and on behalf of Her Majesty'. The block was occupied by civil servants. One of the questions before the House of Lords was to determine who the tenant was, the Secretary of State, or Her Majesty.

Held

The use of premises by government servants for government purposes constituted occupation of the premises by the Crown as tenant. The civil servants were servants of the Crown.

Lord Diplock (after expressing his view that when speaking of executive acts of government it might be less confusing to refer to 'the government' rather than 'the Crown'):

'Where ... we are concerned with the legal nature of the exercise of executive powers of government, I believe that some of the more Athanasian-like features of the debate in your Lordships' House could have been eliminated if instead of speaking of "the Crown" we were to speak of "the government" ' a term appropriate to embrace both collectively and individually all of the ministers of the Crown and parliamentary secretaries under whose direction the administrative work of government is carried on by the civil servants employed in the various government departments. It is through them that the executive powers of Her Majesty's government in the United Kingdom are exercised, sometimes in the more important administrative matters in Her Majesty's name, but most often under their own official designation. Executive acts of government that are done by any of them are acts done by "the Crown" in the fictional sense in which that expression is now used in English public law.'

10.2   Act of state

Buron v Denman (1848) 2 Ex 167 Court of Exchequer (Parke B, Alderson B, Rolfe B, and Platt B)

Act of state and acts against an alien abroad

Facts

The defendant was a British naval commander stationed on the coast of Africa with instructions to suppress the slave trade. Having made a treaty with the King of the Gallinas for the abolition of the slave trade in that country and in execution of that treaty, the defendant set fire to the barracoon of the plaintiff, a Spaniard carrying on the slave trade at the Gallinas, and carried away his slaves to Sierra Leone, where they were liberated. These proceedings were communicated to the UK Government which ratified the acts of the defendant. The plaintiff brought an action in trespass against the defendant.

Held

The ratification of the defendant's act by the ministers of state was equivalent to a prior command, and rendered it an act of state, for which the Crown alone was responsible. Thus no action would be maintained against the defendant.

Johnstone v Pedlar [1921] 2 AC 262 House of Lords (Viscount Finlay, Viscount Cave, Lords Atkinson, Sumner and Phillimore)

Act of state no defence to illegal act against a friendly alien

Facts

The plaintiff was a naturalised American citizen (born in Ireland). He returned to Ireland and took part in the rebellion of 1916 in Dublin. On 1 May 1918 he was arrested on a charge of illegal drilling. He was convicted and served a 6 month prison sentence in a Belfast goal. When he was arrested he had with him some money and a cheque which were seized and detained by the police. The seizure and detention were subsequently ratified by the Chief Secretary of Ireland. The plaintiff brought an action against the Chief Commissioner of the police for the recovery of the money and cheque. The Chief Commissioner pleaded that the plaintiff was an alien and that the money was detained by direction of the Crown as an act of state.

Held

The defence of act of state could not be used against the plaintiff as a friendly alien on British territory. Whilst on British territory the friendly alien owes temporary allegiance to the British Crown and is entitled to the protection of British law.

Viscount Finlay:

'... It is the settled law of this country, applicable as much to Ireland as to England, that if a wrongful act has been committed aganst the person or the property of any person the wrongdoer cannot set up as a defence that the act was done by the command of the Crown. The Crown can do no wrong, and the Sovereign cannot be sued in tort, but the person who did the act is liable in damages, as any private person would be.

This rule of law has, however, been held subject to qualification in the case of acts committed abroad against a foreigner. If an action be brought in the British courts in such a case it is open to the defendant to plead that the act was done by the orders of the British Government, or that after it had been committed it was adopted by the British Government. In any such case the act is regarded as an act of State of which a municipal Court cannot take cognizance. The foreigner who has sustained injury must seek redress against the British Government through his own Government by diplomatic or other means. This was established in 1848 in the well-known case of *Buron* v *Denman* (1) ...

This doctrine has no application to any case in which the plaintiff is a British subject. If authority be wanted for the proposition that a British subject's right of action for any wrong to his person or property is not subject to this qualification with regard to acts of State it is enough to refer to the case of *Walker* v *Baird* (2).

In that case the officers of the Crown had, with the authority of the Government, seized a lobster factory in Newfoundland belonging to British subjects. An action was brought in the Courts of Newfoundland against the officers engaged. The Superior Court of Newfoundland held that, in an action of this description, in which the plaintiffs are British subjects, for a trespass within British territory in time of peace, it was no answer to say in exclusion of the jurisdiction of the municipal Courts that the trespass was an act of State. An appeal to His Majesty in Council was dismissed. Lord Herschell said that the suggestion that these acts could be justified as acts of State was wholly untenable.

The cases in which the defence of "Act of State" has hitherto been recognised, have been cases in which the acts complained of were committed out of British territory. The plaintiffs have been foreigners, and no question arose as to their being in any sense subjects of the British Crown, as it might have arisen if the wrongs complained of had been done in British territory. An alien in British territory is normally regarded as a British subject for the time being in virtue of local allegiance, and it is for this reason that in dealing with the defence of "Act of State" it is often said that the act must have been abroad as well as against a foreigner in order that the defence should succeed.

The plaintiff is not a subject of the British Crown, but he was, at the time of his arrest, within British territory. It was contended for him that he must be treated for the purposes of the present case as a British subject, inasmuch as he was at the time resident in Ireland. Hale, in his *Pleas of the Crown* (vol i, p542) after discussing a statute of Henry VIII giving to any of the King's subjects whose goods have been taken away the right to a writ of restitution on conviction of the thief, says: "Though the Statute speak of the King's subjects, it extends to aliens robbed; for though they are not the King's natural born subjects, they are the King's subjects, when in England, by a local allegiance". The subject of a State at peace with His Majesty, while permitted to reside in this country, is under the King's protection and allegiance, and may be convicted of high treason in respect of acts committed here.

The proposition put forward on behalf of the appellant was that residence in this country does not put an alien in the same position as a British subject in respect of acts of State of the Government, and does not entitled him to bring an action against a tortfeasor, whose act has been ordered or adopted by the Government.

I am quite unable to accept this proposition as a correct statement of our law. On such a view of the law aliens in this country instead of having the protection of British law would be at the mercy of any department entitled to use the name of the Crown for an "Act of State". It would have effects upon aliens in this country of a far-reaching nature as to person and property. If an alien be wrongfully arrested, even by order of the Crown, it cannot be doubted that a writ of habeas corpus is open to him, and it would be surprising if he has not the right to recover damages from the person who has wrongfully imprisoned him. He has corresponding rights as regards his property ... the defence of act of State cannot be made good as to acts in the King's Dominions on a bare averment that the plaintiff is an alien ...'

Lord Atkinson:

'... By the common law of this country an alien enemy has no rights. He could be seized or imprisoned and could have no advantage from the laws of this country. He could not obtain redress for any wrong done to him in this country: *Sylvester*'s (3) case. The Crown may no doubt grant a licence to an alien enemy to reside in this country, which imports a licence to trade here, but in the absence of such a licence the property of an alien enemy may be seized for the use of the Crown: *The Johanna Emilie*. But while in this country with a licence any alien enemy may bring an action: *Wells* v *Williams* (4), *Janson* v *Driefontein Mines* (5). A mere non-interference with an alien enemy does not imply a licence to reside and trade. It is necessary for him to show that he resides in this country with the full knowledge and sanction of the Government: *Boulton* v *Dobree*. Aliens, whether friendly or enemy, can be lawfully prevented from entering this country and can be expelled from it: 1 Blackstone, 259; *Attorney-General for Canada* v *Cain* (6). And at any time the Crown may revoke its licence expressed or implied to an alien to reside: *The Hoop* (7). In Vattel, Book 2, s108, it is stated that a friendly alien can at any time leave the country, the Government have no right to detain him, except for a time and for very particular reasons, as, for instance, the apprehension in war, lest such foreigners acquainted with the state of the country and of the fortified placed should communicate knowledge to the enemy.

A friendly alien resident in this country can undoubtedly be prosecuted for high treason: *De Jager* v *Attorney-General of Natal* (8), because it can then be averred that he acted contra ligentiae suae debitum: *Calvin*'s case (9).

For the same reason an alien enemy can be prosecuted for high treason if he has accepted the protection of the Sovereign, but not otherwise: Foster 185.

I cannot find any authority for the proposition that if the property of a friendly alien resident in this country under the protection of the crown and not violating in any way the allegiance he owes to the Crown which protects him be seized and detained by an act of State of the sovereign authority the alien cannot sue the office of the Crown by whose act he is aggrieved in one of the municipal courts of the country. The major proposition for which the Crown contends, that is such a case that the alien could not sue here, is not, I think, sustainable. No authority was cited in support of it and it is not in harmony with the principles laid down in many cases as to the rights of a friendly alien such as I have described. The respondent in the present case is in a position wholly different from the friendly alien whom I have mentioned. The question is does his conduct deprive him of the remedy which would be open to a well conducted friendly alien resident peaceably with the realm?

He states in his evidence, which is uncontradicted, that he took part in the rebellion in 1916 in Dublin. It does not appear that any proceedings were ever taken against him for that crime. It does appear that he was interned in Frongoch (why, is not stated) and was released at Christmas 1916, that he returned to Ireland in March 1917, and was again deported, this time to Oxford; that he was released in May 1917, returned to Ireland, and after an entire year's residence there, was arrested in May 1918, for illegal drilling, and was presecuted, convicted and sentenced to four months' imprisonment, so that from April 1916, when the Irish rebellion took place, till 18 May 1918, about two years, he was only absent from Ireland for about nine months. During the rest of the time he was resident in Ireland, his presence being apparently as little objected to by any of the Government authorities as that of any ordinary citizen, though they must, I think, be taken to have been aware of his presence.'

(1)   Supra, this chapter

(2)   Infra, this chapter

(3)   (1703) 7 Mod Rep 150

(4)   (1697) 1 Ld Raymond 282

(5)   [1902] AC 484

(6)   [1906] AC 542

(7)   (1799) 1 C Rob 196

(8)   [1907] AC 326

(9)   (1608) 7 Co Rep 1A

Nissan v Attorney-General [1970] AC 179 House of Lords (Lords Reid, Morris of Borth-y-Gest, Pearce, Wilberforce and Pearson)

Nature of an act of state

Facts

During civil strife in Cyprus in December 1963, the British, Greek and Turkish governments jointly appealed to the Cyprus government and to the Greek and Turkish communities on the island to end the strife and to the Cyprus government to fix a suitable hour to arrange a cease-fire, and offered their good offices to help to resolve the difficulties on the island. The Cyprus government announced that it had accepted an offer that forces from the UK, Greece and Turkey (the truce force) be stationed in Cyprus and placed under British command to assist in the preservation of the cease-fire and the restoration of peace.

From 26 December 1963 to 27 March 1964, pursuant to the agreement between the UK and Cyprus government, the truce force operated in the island under British command. On 28 March the UN Peace-keeping force was established in Cyprus after recommendations to that effect by the Security Council of the UN with the consent of the Cyprus government.

The legal status of the UN force was the subject of an agreement set out in a letter from the Secretary-General of the UN to the Foreign Minister of Cyprus and ratified by law, and from 27 March the British elements of the truce-force became contingents in the UN force.

These facts were pleaded by the crown in its defence to a claim by the respondent, a British subject, in relation to the occupation of his hotel on Cyprus by the British forces from 29 December 1963 until 5 May 1964, when the British forces were replaced by Finnish forces.

Held

In respect of the events occurring in the first period (26 December – 27 March) the British forces were not acting as agents of the Cyprus Government so as to make their actions the acts of the Cyprus Government; they were acting as agents of the British Government. The same applied for the second period (27 March – 5 May). Thus, throughout, the acts of the British forces were the acts of the British Government.

However, (Lord Reid dissenting on this point) the act of the British troops in requisitioning the hotel was not in the nature of an act of state and thus the plaintiff could maintain his action against the UK Government in the English courts.

Per Lord Reid:

'A British subject – or at least a citizen of the U.K. and Colonies – can never be deprived of his legal right to redress by an assertion that the acts complained of were acts of state and for that reason the plaintiff could maintain his action.'

Lord Pearce:

'My Lords, all the judgments in this case are agreed that, on the facts pleaded, the British forces were not acting as agents for the Cyprus Government during the period before the arrival of the United Nations force. In this they were clearly right. There is nothing to prevent the Crown acting as agent or trustee if it chooses to do so, as Lord Atkin said in *Civilian War Claimants Association Ltd* v *The King* [1932] AC 14, 27. But none of the matters pleaded raises any such inference. They all point to the British forces coming on the scene as allies and helpers, not as agents, and making their own arrangements for their accommodation. There is nothing to suggest that they called in aid the Cyprus

Government or acted on their instructions or left it to them to arrange the occupation of the hotel.

All the judgments, however, took the view that during the second period the British troops no longer occupied the hotel in the Queen's name but in the name of the United Nations. I do not think so. The United Nations is not a super-state nor even a sovereign state. It is a unique legal person or corporation. It is based on the sovereignty of its respective members. But it is not a principal carrying out its policy through states acting as its agents. It is an instrument of collective policy which it enforces by using the sovereignty of its members. In carrying out the policies each member still retains its own sovereignty, just as any sovereign state, acting under its treaty obligations to another state, would normally still retain its sovereignty.

This view of the matter is strongly reinforced by the relevant letters and regulations. They show that the commander of the United Nations force is head in the chain of command and is answerable to the United Nations. The functions of the force as a whole are international. But its individual component forces have their own national duty and discipline and remain in their own national service. The Government of Cyprus (see letter 31 March 1964, para 36).

> "will, upon the request of the commander, assist the force in obtaining equipment, provisions, supplies and other goods and services required from local sources for its subsistence and operation ... Members of the force and United Nations officials may purchase locally goods necessary for their own consumption",

and so forth. Nowhere is there a suggestion that the United Nations are primarily liably for anything in respect of the payment or provisioning or accommodation of the forces. The financial liability of the United Nations Secretary-General is that (regulation 16):

> "Within the limits of available voluntary contributions he shall make provision for the settlement of any claims arising with respect to the force that are not settled by the governments providing contingents or the Government of Cyprus."

This is the antithesis of assuming primary financial responsibility ...'

Lord Morris of Borth-y-Gest:

'... In one of the helpful attempts to undertake the difficult task of giving a definition of an act of state (*Halsbury's Laws of England*, Vol VII para 593, p279) there are the words

> "An act of the executive as a matter of policy performed in the course of its relations with another state including its relations with the subjects of that state unless they are temporarily within the allegiance of the Crown."

For reasons which I have already indicated I do not think that such actions as securing food or shelter in peace time for troops situated abroad are to be regarded as acts of the executive performed in the course of relations with another state within the conception of the above definition ...

The remaining question raised in the preliminary issue relates to the period after 27 March 1964. British troops continued in occupation of the hotel until 5 May 1964, when they handed it over to Finnish troops. I see no reason for imposing liability after that date. The position was, however, that between 27 March 1964 and 5 May 1964, the British troops were contingents of the United Nations Force. The preliminary issue which is raised is whether on that basis and upon the facts pleaded in paragraph 5 of the defence there is a 'good defence in law' to the claims made. Paragraph 5 of the defence sets out that early in March 1964, the Security Council recommended the creation of a United Nations Peace-Keeping Force in Cyprus and that the Cyprus Government consented to this. There followed an agreement between the Secretary-General and the Government of Cyprus concerning the legal status of the United Nations Force. The terms of that agreement are contained in a letter dated 31 March 1964, from the Secretary-General to the Foreign Minister of Cyprus. It is said that the agreement became effective from 27 March, and that it was later ratified by a law passed in Cyprus. If there was at that time any liability in the appellant towards the plaintiff (which is the question to be determined in the action) I cannot see how that liability is affected by the terms of an agreement between the Secretary-General and the Cyprus Government. If, of course, some arrangement was concluded and was carried out under which liability towards Mr Nissan was assumed and was discharged then pro tanto Mr Nissan could not in a claim against the appellant assert any loss. These considerations would, I think, apply even if it were correct, as seems to be asserted, that the United Nations must be deemed to be a Sovereign state that took over from the British Government when the British troops became part of the United Nations Peace-Keeping Force. But that does not represent the true position. The United Nations is not a state or a sovereign: it is an international organisation formed (inter alia) to maintain international peace and security and to take effect collective measured for the prevention and removal of threats to peace: it is based on the principle of the sovereign equality of all its members: it does not intervene in matters which are essentially within the domestic jurisdiction of a state.

If the letter from the Secretary-General to the Cyprus Foreign Minister is being considered I do not find in its terms any provisions that would relieve the appellant from liability. Though that letter is the only document referred to in paragraph 5 of the defence (and therefore the only document that is directly relevant in this preliminary issue) attention was also given to the regulations for the United Nations Force in Cyprus issued by the Secretary-General. They were dated April 25th 1964. Reference was also made to letters passing in February 1966 between the Secretary-General and the United Kingdom Permanent Representative to the United Nations. From the various documents published in Command 3017 it appears that when the Security Council passed this resolution of March 4th 1964, they recommended that all costs pertaining to the United Nations force should be met in a manner to be agreed upon by the Governments providing contingents and by the Government of Cyprus though the Secretary-General was able to accept voluntary contributions in respect of the costs. From the documents it appears further that, though national contingents were under the authority of the United Nations and subject to the instructions of the commander, the troops as members of the force remained in their national service. The British forces continued, therefore, to be soldiers of Her Majesty. Members of the United Nations force were subject to the exclusive jurisdiction of their respective national states in respect of any criminal offences committed by them in Cyprus. The Cyprus Government agreed that upon a request from the commander of the United Nations force they (the Government) would assist the force in obtaining equipment, provisions, supplies and other goods and services required from local sources for its subsistence and operation.'

Lord Pearson:

'... As to the alleged agency, in my opinion this is not established by the assumed facts. It must have been in the interests of the United Kingdom, Greece and Turkey as well as Cyprus that the outbreak or the continuance of civil disturbance or civil war in Cyprus, which might lead to a wider conflict, should be prevented. Therefore, the truce force entered and was stationed in Cyprus in order to assist the Cyprus government in its efforts to secure the preservation of cease-fire and the restoration of peace. There is no indication that the truce force was to be subordinated in the Cyprus government and take and carry out its instructions. There would naturally be co-operation and consultation on an equal footing.

As to the alleged act of state, it is necessary to consider what is meant by the expression "act of state" even if it is not expedient to attempt a definition. It is an exercise of sovereign power. Obvious examples are making war and peace, making treaties with foreign Sovereigns, and annexations and cessions of territory. Apart from these obvious examples, an act of state must be something exceptional. Any ordinary governmental act is cognisable by an ordinary court of law (municipal not international): if a subject alleges that the governmental act was wrongful and claims damages or other relief of it, his claim will be entertained and heard and determined by the court. An act of state is something not cognisable by the court: if a claim is made in respect of it, the court will have to ascertain the facts but if it then appears that the act complained of was an act of state the court must refuse to adjudicate on the claim. In such a case the court does not come to any decisions as to the legality or illegality, or the rightness or wrongness, of the act complained of: the decision is that, because it was an act of state, the court has no jurisdiction to entertain a claim in respect of it. This is a very unusual situation and strong evidence is required to prove that it exists in a particular case.

I think that the question whether some governmental act was an act of state depends on the nature of the act and (sometimes at any rate) on the intention with which it was done, and the intention is to be inferred from words and conduct and surrounding circumstances. Some extracts from a leading judgment in this branch of the law will assist to show what is involved.

In the *Tanjore* case (*Secretary of State in Council of India* v *Kamachee Boye Sahaba*) (1) Lord Kingsdown said:

"... the main point taken, and that on which their Lordships think that the case must be decided, was this, that the East India Company, as trustees for the Crown, and under certain restrictions, are empowered to act as a Sovereign State in transactions with other Sovereign States in India; that the Rajah of Tanjore was an independent Sovereign in India; that on his death, in the year 1855, the East India Company, in the exercise of their sovereign power, thought fit, from motives of State, to seize the Raj of Tanjore and the whole of the property the subject of this suit, and did seize it accordingly; and that over an act so done, whether rightfully or wrongfully, no Municipal Court has any jurisdiction. The general principle of law was not, as indeed it could not, with any colour of reason, be disputed. The transactions of independent States between each other are governed by other laws than those which Municipal Courts administer: such Courts have neither the means of deciding what is right, nor the power of enforcing any decision which they may make."

He further said:

"The next question is, what is the real character of the act done in this case? Was it a seizure by arbitrary power on behalf of the crown of Great Britain, of the dominions and property of a neighbouring State, an act not affecting to justify itself on grounds of Municipal law? Or was it, in whole or in part, a possession taken by the Crown under colour of legal title of the property of the late Rajah of Tanjore, in trust for those who, by law, might be entitled to it on the death of the last possessor? If it were the latter, the defence set up, of course, has no foundation."

The importance of intention appears from a later passage of Lord Kingsdown's judgment where he said:

"But whatever may be the meaning of this letter, it affords no argument in favour of the judgment of the Court; but rather an argument against it. It shows that the Government intended to seize all the property which actually was seized, whether public or private, subject to an assurance that all which, upon investigation, should be found to have been improperly seized, would be restored. But, even with respect to property not belonging to the Rajah, it is difficult to suppose that the Government intended to give a legal right of redress to those who might think themselves wronged, and to submit the conduct of their officers, in the execution of a political measure, to the judgment of a legal tribunal. They intended only to declare the course which a sense of justice and humanity would induce them to adopt. With respect to the property of the Rajah, whether public or private, it is clear that the Government intended to seize the whole, for the purposes which they had in view required the application of the whole. They declared their intention to make provision for the payment of his debts, for the proper maintenance of his widows, his daughters, his relations and dependants; but they intended to do this according to their own notions of what was just and reasonable, and not according to any rules of law to be enforced against them by their own Courts."

There is also a passage in the judgment of Turner LJ in *Secretary of State in Council of India* v *Hari Bhanji* which affords some guidance as to the character of an act of state (although there is an error if and insofar as it is implied than an act of state could be committed against a subject within the realm). He said:

> "Acts done by the Government in the exercise of the sovereign powers of making peace and war and of concluding treaties obviously do not fall within the province of municipal law, and although in the administration of domestic affairs the Government ordinarily exercises powers which are regulated by that law, yet there are cases in which the supreme necessity of providing for the public safety compels the Government to acts which do not pretend to justify themselves by any canon or municipal law ... Acts thus done in the exercise of sovereign powers but which do not profess to be justified by municipal law are what we understand to be acts of state of which municipal courts are not authorised to take cognisance."

There are, of course, also more modern authorities, but I think it will be sufficient, for the sake of brevity, to cite the headnote of *Salaman* v *Secretary of State in Council of India*(2).

> "Where the East India Company, as representing the Crown, has done acts of such a nature, and under such circumstances, as to lead to the conclusion that those acts were done in the exercise of supreme power, as acts of State, and to negative any intention to give thereby legal rights, whether contractual or otherwise, to an individual or individuals as against the Company, the municipal Courts have no jurisdiction to question the validity of those acts, or to entertain any claim in respect thereof by an individual against the Secretary of State for India, as the successor of the East India Company."

In the relevant pleading (the last sentence of para 4 of the defence) and in the argument, reliance was placed on the fact that the acts complained of were done in performance of the treaty (agreement) between the Cyprus Government and the British, Greek and Turkish governments. No doubt the making of the treaty was an act of state, and the performance of it must to some extent involve acts of state. But I think the things that were done by the United Kingdom government had to some extent the character of acts of state in themselves, apart from the fact that they were done under a treaty. A British army was despatched into the territory of a independent sovereign power with orders to assist in the preservation of cease-fire and the restoration of peace. That was a military operation, involving the use of armed force, so far as might be necessary to keep the peace. It could not be justified under municipal law; it was outside the sphere of municipal law, being in the sphere of international relations.

But it does not follow that everything which the truce force, or elements of it, did in the foreign territory constituted an act of state. It is not alleged that the truce force had to engage in any fighting or that there was any urgent military necessity to occupy the hotel. The mere stationing of the truce force in the territory may have been sufficient to keep the peace. The truce force would nevertheless need supplies and accommodation. Conceivably they might have seized the supplies and accommodation in a high-handed, extra-legal manner as an act of state with the intention of denying to those affected any right of redress in any municipal court. But it is unlikely that they would so act in a friendly country, being present there with the consent and for the assistance of the government of the country. It is not reasonable to infer an intention that the occupation of the hotel should be an act of state. The probable intention was to take the hotel for the needs of the army and to leave those affected to pursue whatever legal remedies they might have. In my opinion, the assumed facts do not show that there was an act of state.

I wish to reserve the question whether an act done outside the realm could ever be an act of state in relation to a British subject. The dicta in decided cases are important, but not decisive, and there are problems involved. Should the same rule apply to acts on the high seas and to acts in independent sovereign countries? What is the position if, in a foreign country, a British army or truce force seizes in one operation a row of ten houses of which one belongs to a British subject and the other nine to foreigners? What is the position if, in a foreign country, a British army or truce force siezes a building and goods both belonging to a partnership, of which some partners are British subjects and others are foreigners? Then there is the case of the person of British nationality who has settled in a foreign country and there acquired a business and made a home for himself and his family: he belongs to the community of that country: any damage to his property there is a blow to the economy of that country and any compensation paid to him is a benefit to the economy of that country: the government of that country has an interest in his welfare: he owes local allegiance to that Government and is entitled to its protection, if the law of that country is the same as English law. How does the rule in regard to acts of state apply in his case?

Another problem is this: If the plea of act of state is not available in any circumstances against a British subject, what is the meaning of the expression "British subject" for this purpose? Does it mean only a citizen of the United Kingdom and colonies? Or does it include anyone who is a "British subject" within the wide definition in s1 of the British Nationality Act 1948? Or does it have some other meaning? ...'

Lord Reid:

'It is sometimes said, or at least suggested, that an act of the executive obtains some additional protection if it is done in execution or furtherance of some treaty. I do not see why that should be so. If the same act would be actionable if done by the executive ex proprio motu, how can it matter that the Government had agreed beforehand with some other Government that it would do that act? There is no doubt that it is within the prerogative right of the Crown to make treaties and no subject, whether within or outside the realm, can object on the ground that the making of the treaty has caused him loss. As a result of a treaty certain exports to the other country might cease because the other country would not receive them. But a British manufacturer whose former customers ceased to buy from him as a result of the making of the treaty could not complain. He could not found on the treaty as the cause of his loss. But it would be quite another matter if the Crown infringed his ordinary legal rights and founded on its obligations under a treaty as a defence. That was made clear by the decision in W*alker* v *Baird* (3). A somewhat similar point arose in *Rustomjee* v *The Queen* (4) and in *Civilian War Claimants Association Ltd* v *The King* (5). Under treaties the Crown received sums of money as compensation for damage done to British subjects, but that fact did not entitle those subjects to sue. The Crown had not made itself a trustee and the subject could not found on the treaty: there had been no infringement of any right of the claimants. And I may refer in this connection to *China Navigation Co Ltd* v *Attorney-General* (6) although no treaty was there involved. The Crown refused to afford armed protection to British subjects unless payment was made. The subject could not object because no legal right of theirs was infringed by the refusal of an armed escort.

I think that a good deal of the trouble has been caused by using the loose phrase "act of state" without making clear what it meant. Sometimes it seems to be used to denote any act of sovereign powr or of high policy or any act done in the execution of a treaty. That is a possible definition, but then it must be observed that there are many such acts which can be the subject of an action in court if they infringe the rights of British subjects. Sometimes it seems to be used to denote acts which cannot be made the subject of inquiry in a British court. But that does not tell us how to distinguish such acts: it is only a name for a class which has still to be defined. One definition which has been accepted in some quarters is that of Professor Wade, quoted in *Halsbury's Laws of England*, vol VII, para 593, p279:

"An act of the executive as a matter of policy performed in the course of its relations with another state including its relations with the subject of that state, unless they are temporarily within the allegiance of the Crown, is an act of state."

I do not think that this is entirely satisfactory. I am not sure what is meant by "as a matter of policy". One hopes that all acts of the executive are done as a matter of policy, and not on random decisions, and certainly it would not be possible for a court to enquire whether a particular act of the executive had or had not been done as a matter of policy. And what about acts subsequently ratified? When Captain Denman acted against the Spaniard (*Buron* v *Denman* (7)) it must have been his policy, for he acted without orders and, when his act was ratified, the policy may simply have been in those days to support Her Majesty's officers against foreigners. Then next "in the course of its relations with another state": I do not much like this as a description of a war of conquest. I think one would have to add "or against another state or a subject of that state". I have already said that I can find no reason why an act performed against a British subject should take on a different character and become an act of state because done by the Government in the course of or arising out of its relations with another state. And *Walker* v *Baird* (3) shows that it does not, at least when done within British dominions.

Professor Wade was, no doubt, merely attempting to make the best of a confused body of authority, and not attempting to make new law. If I attempted that I would certainly do no better. But I would suggest to your Lordships that we cannot rest content with that. I think we must say either that all acts of the executive are acts of state, or that acts of the executive should only be called acts of state in cases where the court will not enquire into them or give relief in respect of them, but should not be called acts of state when the court's jurisdiction is not ousted.

It is sometimes said that the question whether an act done on behalf of or ratified by the Crown – which here must mean the Government – is an act of state, depends on the nature or quality of the act, and that it is for the court to determine whether any act is an act of state. It is true that the court must determine, on such facts as are available, whether the act was done in purported exercise of a legal right: if it was it cannot be regarded as an act of state. But if it was not done in purported exercise of any legal right and was done by an officer of the Crown apparently in the course of his duty, then it appears to me that it must be for the Crown to say whether it claims that the act was an act of state. The act may appear to be of a routine or trivial character. But in a delicate situation there may be discussion and decision at the highest level about such acts, and the decision to do such an act may be a decision of high policy. If the Crown claims that such an act was done as an act of state I do not see what right the court can have to reject that claim: the court cannot enquire into or ask the Crown to disclose the reason why the act was done. And even if the act was done by a subordinate officer on his own responsibility, it is always open to the Crown to ratify it and thereby make it an act of state.

In the present case, the Crown claims that the taking and retention of possession of this hotel was an act of state. For all we know – and we cannot enquire – it may have been a matter of ministerial policy to take this hotel. One possibility might be that it was thought better as a matter of policy to take the property of British subjects, so as to avoid any question with the Cyprus Government, if the property of citizens of Cyprus was taken. Or the crown may simply have decided to ratify as an act of state the action of its officers in taking the hotel.

If I thought that any act done against the person or property of a British subject wherever situated could be an act of state in the sense that he was deprived of all right to an English court for redress, then I would think that the taking of this hotel was an act of state. But for the reasons which I have already given I am of opinion that a British subject – at least if he is also a citizen of the United Kingdom and Colonies – can never be deprived of his legal right to redress by any assertion by the Crown or decision of the court that the acts of which he complains were acts of state. It seems to me that no useful purpose is served by enquiring whether an act in respect of which a British subject claims legal redress is or is not an act of state, because a decision of that question can make no difference to the result ...'

(1)	(1859) 13 Moo PCC 22
(2)	[1906] 1 KB 613
(3)	Infra, this chapter
(4)	(1876) 2 QBD 69
(5)	[1932] AC 14

(6)   [1932] 2 KB 197

(7)   Supra, this chapter

R v Bottrill, ex parte Kuechenmeister [1947] KB 41 Court of Appeal (Scott, Tucker and Asquith LJJ)

Act of state: internment of enemy alien

Facts

K was a German national. He came to England in 1928 and was granted the right of permanent residence in 1931. He then married an English woman, by whom he had three children, all born in England. In May, 1939, he applied for British nationality. In 1939 he was interned. In 1946 he applied for a writ of habeas corpus. At the hearing of the application before the Divisional Court, the Attorney-General produced a certificate dated 2 April 1946 from the Secretary of State for Foreign Affairs which stated, inter alia:

> '... (3) No treaty of peace or declaration by the Allied Powers having been made terminating the state of war with Germany, His Majesty is still in a state of war with Germany, although, as provided in the declaration of surrender, all active hostilities have ceased.'

Held

The right of the Crown to intern, expel or otherwise control an enemy alien according to its discretion is part of the Royal Prerogative and, as such, the exercise of that right cannot be questioned or controlled in the courts.

Only the Crown can make peace with a state with which this country has been at war and a certificate of His Majesty's Secretary of State for Foreign Affairs to the effect that His Majesty is still at War is conclusive evidence that the state of war is not at an end, even though there may be facts, eg the unconditional surrender of the enemy state, which might be regarded in international law as putting an end to the state of war.

Walker v Baird [1892] AC 491 Judicial Committee of the Privy Council (Lords Hershell, Watson, Hobhouse, Macnaghten, Morris, Hannen, Shand and Sir Richard Crouch)

Royal prerogative: Act of State no defence against British subjects within then territories of the Crown

Facts

At a time when Newfoundland was British territory, the owners of a lobster factory there which had been seized by officers of a British warship acting on government authority, brought an action for trespass against the officers. The Crown pleaded Act of State.

Held

The defence could not be pleaded against British subjects in Crown territory.

10.3   Crown liability in contract

Attorney-General for Ceylon v Silva [1953] AC 461 Privy Council (Mr L M D de Silva, Lord Porter, Lord Tucker and Lord Asquith of Bishopstone)

The crown and agency

Facts

The Principal Collector of Customs of Ceylon obtained the permission of the Chief Secretary of Ceylon to sell certain steel plates, which were on customs premises, by auction. The Principal Collector was unaware that the plates had already been sold by the Crown some two months earlier. Permission to auction the steel plates had been granted to the Principal Collector under the provisions of the Ceylon Customs Ordinance. The plaintiff, Silva, purchased the steel plates at the auction and claimed damages when delivery was refused because of the prior sale.

Held

The Ordinance under which the goods were sold did not bind the Crown, therefore the Principal Collector had had no actual authority to sell the steel plates at the auction because they were Crown property. The argument that he had been acting within the scope of his apparent authority, and that the Crown was therefore still bound by his actions, was also rejected.

Mr L M D De Silva:

'Next comes the question whether the Principal Collector of Customs had ostensible authority, such as would bind the Crown, to enter into the contract sued on. All "ostensible" authority involves a representation by the principal as to the extent of the agent's authority.

No representation by the agent as to the extent of his authority can amount to a "holding out" by the principal. No public officer, unless he possesses some special power, can hold out on behalf of the Crown that he or some other public officer has the right to enter into a contract in respect of the property of the Crown when in fact no such right exists. Their Lordships think, therefore, that nothing done by the Principal Collector or the Chief Secretary amounted to a holding out by the Crown that the Principal Collector had the right to enter into a contract to sell the goods which are the subject-matter of this action ...

In advertising the goods for sale the Principal Collector no doubt represented to the public that the goods were saleable. But the question is whether this act of the Principal Collector can be said to be an act of the Crown. Their Lordships have considered whether by reason of the fact that the Principal Collector had been appointed to his office under the Customs Ordinance, and was the proper officer to administer it, he must be regarded as having had ostensible authority on behalf of the Crown to represent to the public that goods advertised for sale under the Customs Ordinance were in fact saleable under that Ordinance. It is argued that, if so, although the goods were in fact not saleable under the Ordinance because they were Crown property, or property to which the sections of the Ordinance authorizing sale were not applicable, or for some other reason, the contract would be binding on the Crown and the Crown would be liable in damages as it could not fulfil it.

Their Lordships think that the Principal Collector cannot be regarded as having any such authority. He had, no doubt, authority to do acts of a particular class, namely, to enter on behalf of the Crown into sales of certain goods. But that authority was limited because it arose under certain sections of the Ordinance and only when those sections were applicable.'

89 10

CONSTITUTIONAL AND ADMINISTRATIVE LAW

Churchward v R (1865) LR 1 QB 173 Queen's Bench (Cockburn CJ, Mellor, Shee and Lush JJ)

Contract conditional on payment by Parliament

Facts

In 1854 The Admiralty Commissioners had entered into a contract with Churchward for the carriage of mails between Dover and Calais and Dover and Ostend. The contract was to continue until 26 April 1870. However, the Government refused to honour the contract from 1863 onwards, the House of Commons refused to authorise any expenditure on it, and expressly provided in the appropriate Acts of 1863, '64, '65 and '66 that no part of the sum granted by Parliament to meet expenditure on the mail service was to be paid to Churchward as regards the period subsequent to 20 June 1863. The contract had included an express term that Churchward was to be paid 'out of the monies provided by Parliament'.

Churchward brought a petition of right against the Crown claiming £126,000 for breach of contract.

Held

In the agreement there was only a covenant by the Commissioners, on behalf of the Crown, that, in consideration of Churchward performing his part of the contract, by having vessels always ready for the service, the Crown would pay him if Parliament provided the funds. Since Parliament had not provided the funds, there was no breach of contract on the part of the Crown.

Cockburn CJ:

'... I am very far, indeed, from saying, if by express terms, the Lords of the Admiralty had engaged, whether parliament found the funds or not, to employ Mr Churchward to perform all these services, that then, whatever might be the inconvenience that might arise, such a contract would not have been binding; and I am very far from saying that in such a case a petition of right would not lie, where a public officer or the head of a department makes such a contract on the part of the crown, and then afterwards breaks it. We are not called upon to decide that in the present case, and I should be sorry to think that we should be driven to come to an opposite conclusion ...'

Shee J:

'... The Attorney-General pleaded thirdly. [The learned Judge read the third plea.] To this plea the suppliant has demurred, on the ground that the provision of moneys by parliament was not a condition precedent to the performance of the contract on the part of the commissioners, and therefore, that the absence of such condition cannot be set up as a justification of their breach of the contract. I am, however, of the opinion, for the reasons already given, that the covenant of the commissioners to pay to the suppliant out of the moneys to be provided by parliament, after the rate of £18,000 per annum, is the only covenant into which they have entered, and that it is a covenant to pay him that sum, if, and only if, it should be provided by parliament. As a matter of ordinary law, between subject and subject, a covenant so guarded would be held to be binding on the covenantor only in the event of his being supplied with funds from the source which the covenant had indicated. The cases cited by the Attorney-General of *Gurney* v *Rawling*, *Dawson* v *Wrench* and *Hallett* v *Dowdall*, are decisive on this point. In the case of a contract with commissioners on behalf of the crown to make large payments of money during a series of years, I should have thought that the condition which clogs this covenant, though not expressed, must, on account of the notorious inability of the crown to contract unconditionally for such money payments in consideration of such services, have been implied in favour of the crown ...'

Commissioners of Crown Lands v Page [1960] 2 QB 274 Court of Appeal (Lord Evershed MR, Ormerod and Devlin LJJ)

Crown's ability to deal with land in the national interest must be unfettered

00

Facts

Premises were leased to Page by the Crown for 25 years. Eight years later, acting under Defence Regulations, the premises were requisitioned by the Minister of Works. Page argued that the Crown was in breach of an implied covenant guaranteeing his quiet enjoyment of the premises.

Held

No covenant ensuring quiet enjoyment would be implied into the lease, as this would constitute a fetter on the freedom of the Crown to deal with the land and premises as might be necessitated by the national interest.

Devlin LJ:

'... When the Crown, or any other person, is entrusted, whether by virtue of the prerogative or by statute, with discretionary powers to be exercised for the public good, it does not, when making a private contract in general terms, undertake (and it may be that it could not even with the use of specific language validly undertake) to fetter itself in the use of those powers, and in the exercise of its discretion. This principle has been accepted in a number of authorities.'

The covenant for quiet enjoyment in the present case is implied, and it not dissimilar to the contractual provision considered in the two cases last cited, which were both concerned with the implied obligation on one party to a contract not to interfere with the performance by the other party of his obligations under it. In *Board of Trade* v *Temperley Steam Shipping Co Ltd* (1) the Board were the charterers of the defendants' ship, and it was contended that they had prevented the defendants from making their ship efficient for her service under the charterparty because one of the Board's surveyors had refused a licence to do certain repairs. In *William Cory & Sons Ltd* v *City of London Corporation* (2) the city corporation had a contract with the plaintiffs whereunder the plaintiffs undertook to remove refuse by means of lighters and barges. Some time later the city corporation passed a by-law concerning the fitment of vessels transporting refuse which it was agreed was such as to make the performance of the contract impossible. It was held by the Court of Appeal that the corporation was not in breach of the implied term.

I do not, however, rest my decision in the present case simply on the fact that the covenant for quiet enjoyment has to be implied. For reasons which I think will appear sufficiently in the next paragraph, I should reach the same conclusion if the ordinary covenant was expressed.

In some of the cases in which public authorities have been defendants, the judgments have been put on the ground that it would be ultra vires for them to bind themselves not to exercise their powers; and it has also been said that a promise to do so would be contrary to public policy. It may perhaps be difficult to apply this reasoning to the Crown, but it seems to me to be unnecessary to delve into the constitutional position. When the Crown in dealing with one of its subjects, is dealing as if it too were a private person and is granting leases or buying and selling as ordinary persons do, it is absurd to suppose that it is making any promise about the way in which it will conduct the affairs of the nation. No one can imagine, for example, that when the Crown makes a contract which could not be fulfilled in time of war, it is pledging itself not to declare war for so long as the contract lasts. Even if, therefore, there was an express covenant for quiet enjoyment, or an express promise by the Crown that it would not do any act which might hinder the other party to the contract in the performance of his obligations, the covenant or promise must by necessary implication be read to exclude those measures affecting the nation as a whole which the Crown takes for the public good.

... I need not examine the question whether, if the Crown sought to fetter its future action in express and specific terms, it could effectively do so. It is most unlikely that in a contract with the subject, it would ever make the attempt. For the purpose of this case it is unnecessary to go further than to say that in making a lease or other contract with its subjects, the Crown does not (at least in the absence of specific words) promise to refrain from exercising its general power under a statute or under the prerogative, or to exercise them in any particular way. That does not mean that the Crown

101

can escape from any contract which it finds disadvantageous by saying that it never promised to act otherwise than for the public good ... Here we are dealing with an act done for a general executive purpose, and not an act done for the purpose of achieving a particular result under the contract in question ...'

(1)   (1927) 27 L1 LR 230

(2)   [1951] 2 KB 476

Dunn v MacDonald [1897] 1 QB 555 Court of Appeal (Lord Denning MR, Widgery and Karminski LJJ)

Warrant of authority from the Crown

Facts

The facts were as in *Dunn v R* infra; having failed in a petition of right, Dunn sued the officer who had engaged him for breach of warrant of authority.

Held

No action lies against a servant of the Crown for such a breach. Dunn should in any event be deemed to know that the officer had no power in law to engage him for a fixed term.

New South Wales (State of) v Bardolph (1934) 52 CLR 455 Australian Court of Appeal (Evatt and Dixon JJ)

State liability in contract

Facts

The plaintiff owned a publication in which the regional tourist board for New South Wales (acting on the authority of the State Premier) contracted for the insertion of a series of advertisements over a two year period for a sum of £1,114. Shortly after this agreement was made, there was a change in the political control of the administration, and the Government now refused to pay for the advertisements. The plaintiff nevertheless continued to run them, and at the end of the contract period claimed the sum due.

Held

Although the contract had not been expressly authorised by the State Legislature, the relevant Appropriation Acts had made sums available for 'Government advertising', and the amount available far exceeded that now sought by the plaintiff. The plaintiff was therefore entitled to succeed in his action for damages.

The appeal by the State against this decision was dismissed.

Evatt J (at first instance):

'...The suggested defence that the contract was not authorized by the Government completely fails. It is only right to add that, although raised in the pleadings, this defence was not seriously pressed at the hearing.

The main, indeed the only real defence relied upon by the State of New South Wales, was that Parliament did not make public moneys available for the express purpose of paying the plaintiff for his advertising services. The defence is, of course, quite unmeritorious, and its success might tend to establish a dangerous precedent in the future. But it raises an interesting question of law, the examination of which shows that the repudiation of subsisting agreements by a new administration can seldom be ventured upon with success ...'

... The supply which Parliament made available during the year for Government advertising can be reckoned as amounting to eleven-twelfths of £6,600, plus one-twelfth of £9,900, that is £6,875 in all.

It appears from the statement prepared by Mr Kelly, Chief Accountant at the Treasury, that if payment had been made to the plaintiff in respect of the advertisements inserted before the end of the financial year, 30th June, 1932, but not paid for, the total expenditure for the service would only have amounted to £4,595.18s, a figure considerably lower than the assumed minimum supply voted by Parliament, that is £6,800 ...

Before referring to what took place in the financial year 1932–33, it is convenient to consider the legal position as it existed on and in respect of 30th June, 1932. It was argued for the State that it was a condition of the contracts with the plaintiff that all payments of money thereunder should be authorized by Act of Parliament, and it was said that no person can successfully sue the State of New South Wales in the absence of a precise or specific Parliamentary allocation of public moneys for the purpose of making payments under the contracts. It was further contended that, even in an Appropriation Act, the constitutional condition of such contracts is not fulfilled unless it can be shown that Parliament's intention was directed to the particular payment to the particular contractor ...

In the well-known case of *Churchward* v *The Queen* (1), Shee J, in a passage often cited, adopted the principle that in the case of a contract by a subject with the Crown, there should be implied a condition that the providing of funds by Parliament is a condition precedent to the Crown's liability to pay moneys which would otherwise be payable under the contract. In that case the actual promise was to pay a sum "out of the moneys to be provided by Parliament" so that the judgment of Shee J. went beyond the actual point necessary to determine the case. *Churchward*'s case was decided upon demurrer, the third plea alleging that "no moneys were ever provided by Parliament for the payment to the suppliant for, or out of which the suppliant could be paid for the performance of the said contract, for any part of the said period subsequent to the 20th June, 1863, or for the payment to the suppliant for, and in respect of, or out of which the suppliant could be paid or compensated for, in respect of any damages sustained by the suppliant by reason of any of the breaches of the said contract committed subsequent to the said 20th of June 1863".

Further, the Appropriation Acts referred to in that case expressly provided that Churchward's claim was to be excluded from the large sum of money (£950,000) thereby voted for the general purposes of providing and maintaining the Post Office Packet Service.

The judgment of Shee J has always been accepted as determining the general constitutional principle. But it should be added that Cockburn CJ said: (at p 201)

"I agree that, if there had been no question as to the fund being supplied by Parliament, if the condition to pay had been absolute, or if there had been a fund applicable to the purpose, and this difficulty did not stand in the petitioner's way, and he had been throughout ready and willing to perform this contract, and had been prevented and hindered from rendering these services by the default of the Lords of the Admiralty, then he would have been in a position to enforce his right to remuneration."

It appears clear that the first part of this passage has not been acted upon by the Courts in the cases subsequently determined, and that, even where the contract to pay is in terms "absolute" and the contract fails to state that the fund has to be "supplied by Parliament," the Crown is still entitled to rely upon the implied condition mentioned by Shee J.

The second part of Cockburn's CJ statement, that, if there is fund "applicable to the purpose" of meeting claims under the contract, the contractor may enforce his right to remuneration, has never, so far as I know, been questioned. Moreover, its correctness was assumed by the terms of the Crown's third plea in *Churchward*'s case which denies that moneys were ever provided by Parliament "out of which the suppliant could be paid for the performance of the said contract"...

In *Commercial Cable Co* v *Government of Newfoundland* (2) Viscount Haldane said:

> "For all grants of public money, either direct or by way of prospective remission of duties imposed by statute, must be in the discretion of the Legislature, and where the system is that of responsible government, there is no contract unless that discretion can be taken to have been exercised in some sufficient fashion."

This general principle adopts the main principle of *Churchward* v *The Queen* (1), though expressing it somewhat differently. However, the statement affords no guidance as to what will, under any particular circumstances, constitute a "sufficient" expression of the exercise of the Legislature's discretion to grant or withhold public moneys.

... It is abundantly clear, I think, that the *Auckland Harbour Board* case (3) does not justify the theory that, where there is nothing unlawful in a contract entered into by the Crown, and that contract is authorized by responsible Ministers, and made by them in the ordinary course of administering the affairs of Government, a detailed reference to the particular contract must be found in the statutory grant in order to satisfy the constitutional condition laid down in *Churchward*'s case ...

It has been the practice of the Government to enter into advertising contracts, the performance of which extends or may extend into more than one financial year, apart altogether from the innumerable contracts for single insertion advertisements in newspapers and periodicals. For instance, on 1st June, 1932, the Government entered into a contract with the proprietor of the Sydney Morning Herald, and accepted a heavy liability for advertisements covering the month of June in the financial year 1931–1932, and eleven months during the following financial year. Payments were made to the proprietor from time to time in accordance with the contract. But no reference whatever was made to this particular contract in any Act of Parliament. If the argument for the State is right, this money is recoverable back from the proprietor, although the contract has been fully performed on the part of the newspaper. Contracts of a like character were admitted in evidence in order to show the practice of the Government in relation to the Government advertising business of the State and in order to measure the precise surplus or deficiency in the Parliamentary grants for advertising. But the contracts also show that it has never been the practice for Parliament itself to consider with particularity that large number of contracts, payments under all of which are made in reliance upon the general Parliament grant for Government advertising ...

In the absence of some controlling statutory provision, contracts are enforceable against the Crown if:

a) the contract is entered into in the ordinary or necessary course of Goverment administration;

b) it is authorized by the responsible Ministers of the Crown; and

c) the payments which the contractor is seeking to recover are covered by or referable to a parliamentary grant for the class of service to which the contract relates.

In my opinion, moreover, the failure of the plaintiff to prove (c) does not affect the validity of the contract in the sense that the Crown is regarded as stripped of its authority or capacity to enter into the contract. Under a constitution like that of New South Wales where the legislative and executive authority is not limited by reference to subject matter, the general capacity of the Crown to enter into a contract should be regarded from the same point of view as the capacity of the King would be by the Courts of common law. No doubt the King had special powers, privileges, immunities and prerogatives. But he never seems to have been regarded as being less powerful to enter into contracts than one of his subjects. The enforcement of such contracts is to be distinguished from their inherent validity ...

In the present case, the position as it existed in 30th June 1932, was that:

a) the Crown had made contracts with the plaintiff; and

b) moneys had been made legally available by the Supply Acts, including that of June 1932. It is admitted that the advertising service vote, if otherwise sufficient to satisfy the rule in *Churchward*'s case, covered the service called for by the contracts with the plaintiff. On 30th June, therefore, there was (a) an existing contract, (b) a sufficient compliance with the rule in *Churchward*'s case, (c) a proved performance by the plaintiff of the contract on his part, (d) proved non-payment for this service for five weeks at £29 12s 6d per week, that is £148 2s 6d in all.

It cannot be too strongly emphasized at all points of this case that the plaintiff's contracts were not with the Ministers individually or collectively, but with the Crown ...

... The honour of the Crown demands that, subject to Parliament's having made one or more funds available, all contracts for the Crown's departments and services should be honoured. The position on 30th June 1932, having been examined, what was the position on 1st July 1932, the first day of the financial year 1932–1933? In my opinion, it was plainly this, that the plaintiff's contract with the Crown was still on foot ... The condition that payments thereunder depended upon moneys being made legally available by Parliament still subsisted, but the contract was not inchoate or suspended but existing...

The only question therefore, is whether in respect to the year 1932–1933 also the condition of *Churchward*'s case was satisfied ...

In order to secure a judgment declaring the Crown's liability, a person who has a subsisting contract with the Crown satisfies the constitutional doctrine laid down in *Churchward*'s case in respect of payments accruing during the financial year when he completes the performance of his contract if, at the time of such completion, there exists in respect of such financial year sufficient moneys in the vote for the relevant service to enable the payments in question to be lawfully made. I also think that the plaintiff is entitled to say that the constitutional doctrine was satisfied in respect of all payments falling due between 1st July 1932, and the date of his completing his contract if, at the date of the passing of the Appropriate Act (8th November 1932), enough moneys to pay him in full could have been lawfully paid or set aside to pay him from moneys then remaining from the parliamentary grant in respect of advertising. From a close consideration of the figures and evidence, I draw the inferences of fact that;

a) on 8th November 1932, sufficient moneys were available to pay him what was then owing to him in respect of services rendered in the year 1932–1933; and

b) sufficient moneys from the same grant were also available to pay him in full on 31st March, when he finally completed the performance of his contracts...

he above reasoning shows that the plaintiff is entitled to succeed in the argument based on *Churchward*'s case.'

On appeal per Dixon J:

'... It remains to deal with the contention that the contract is unenforceable because no sufficient appropriation of moneys has been made by Parliament to answer the contract. The general doctrine is that all obligations to pay money undertaken by the Crown are subject to the implied condition that the funds necessary to satisfy the obligation shall be appropriated by Parliament, *New South Wales* v *The Commonwealth (No 1)* (4).

But, in my opinion, that general doctrine does not mean that no contract exposes the Crown to a liability to suit ... unless and until an appropriation of funds to answer the contract has been made by the Parliament concerned, or unless some statutory authorization or recognition of the contract can be found.

... The principles of responsible government impose upon the administration a responsibility to Parliament, or rather to the House which deals with finance, for what the Administration has done. It is a function of the Executive, not of Parliament, to make contracts on behalf of the Crown. The Crown's advisers are answerable politically to Parliament for their acts in making contracts. Parliament is considered to retain the power of enforcing the responsibility of the Administration by means of its control over the expenditure of public moneys. But the principles of responsible government do not disable the Executive from acting without the prior approval of Parliament, nor from contracting for the expenditure of moneys conditionally upon appropriation by Parliament and doing so before funds to answer the expenditure have actually been made legally available. Some confusion has been occasioned by the terms in which the conditional nature of the contracts of the Crown from time to time has been described, terms chosen rather for the sake of emphasis than of technical accuracy. But, in my opinion, the manner in which the doctrine was enunciated by Isaacs CJ, when he last had occasion to state it, gives a correct as well as clear exposition of it. In *Australian Railways Union* v *Victorian Railways Commissioners* (5) he said:

> "It is true that every contract with any responsible government of His Majesty, whether it be one of a mercantile character or one of service, is subject to the condition that before payment is made out of the Public Consolidated Fund Parliament must appropriate the necessary sum. But subject to that condition, unless some competent statute properly construed make the appropriation a condition precedent, a contract by the Government otherwise within its authority is binding."

Notwithstanding expressions capable of a contrary interpretation which have occasionally been used, the prior provision of funds by Parliament is not a condition preliminary to the obligation of the contract. If it were so, performance on the part of the subject could not be exacted nor could it be, if he did perform, established a disputed claim to an amount of money under his contract until actual disbursement of the money in dispute was authorized by Parliament.

In my opinion, it is not an answer to a suit against a State ... upon a contract, that the moneys necessary to answer the liability have not up to the time of the suit been provided by Parliament. This does not mean that, if Parliament has by an expression of its will in a form which the Court is bound to notice, refused to provide funds for the purposes of the contract, it remains actionable... That question does not arise in the present case. Indeed a ground upon which the judgment of Evatt J is based is that moneys were provided by Parliament out of which the liability to the plaintiff might lawfully be discharged. I do not in any way disagree with this view, but, as I have formed a definite opinion that the contention of the Crown misconceives the doctrine upon which it is founded, I have thought it desirable to place my judgment upon the grounds I have given.

In my opinion the judgment of Evatt J is right and should be affirmed.'

(1)   Supra, this chapter

(2)   [1916] 2 AC 610

(3)   [1924] AC 318

(4)   (1930) 44 CLR 353

(5)   (1932) 46 CLR 176

Rederiaktiebolaget Amphitrite v R [1921] 3 KB 500 King's Bench Division (Rowlatt J)

The Crown cannot contract to fetter its future executive action

Facts

The suppliants were a Swedish shipowning company suing the Crown by petition of right for damages for breach of contract, the breach being that the ship 'Amphitrite' was refused a clearance to enable her to leave this country, when she had entered a British port under an arrangement whereby she was promised that she would be given clearance.

The suppliants had written to the British Legation at Stockholm and asked whether, in the event of the vessel being put in trade between Sweden and England the Legation would give them a guarantee that she would be allowed free passage without being detained in Great Britain. (At the time, during the First World War, because of the intensified blockage of British ports by the Germans, neutral ships were liable to be detained in British ports under an arrangement between the British and neutral Governments.) The Legation replied that they were 'instructed to say that the SS Amphitrite will earn her own release and be given a coal cargo if she proceed to the UK with a full cargo consisting of at least 60% approved goods'. That reply was given by the Legation after consulting the proper Authorities.

Held

The British Government's undertaking was not enforceable in a court of law since the Crown did not have the legal capacity to contract to fetter its future executive action in matters which concern the welfare of the state.

Rowlatt J:

'... That reply was given by the British Legation after consulting the proper authorities, and I must take it that it was given with the highest authority with which it could be given on behalf of His Majesty's Government. And the British Government thereby undertook that if the ship traded to this country she should not be subjected to the delays which were sometimes imposed. The letters in which that undertaking was contained were written with reference to an earlier voyage which was allowed to go through, the undertaking being on that occasion observed. But the undertaking was renewed with respect to the voyage in connection with which the present complaint arises by a letter from the British Legation, in which it was stated that "the SS Amphitrite will be allowed to release herself in her next voyage to the United Kingdom" – that is to say, upon the same terms as before. Now under those circumstances what I have to consider is whether there was anything of which complaint might be made outside a Court, whether that is to say what the Government did was morally wrong or arbitrary; that would be altogether outside my province. All I have got to say is whether there was an enforceable contract, and I am of opinion that there was not. No doubt the Government can bind itself through its officers by a commercial contract, and if it does so it must perform it like anybody else or pay damages for the breach. But this was not a commercial contract; it was an arrangement whereby the Government purported to give an assurance as to what its executive action would be in the future in relation to a particular ship in the event of her coming to this country with a particular kind of cargo. And that is, to my mind, not a contract for the breach of which damages can be sued for in a Court of law. It was merely an expression of intention to act in a particular way in a certain event. My main reason for so thinking is that it is not competent for the Government to fetter its future executive action, which must necessarily be determined by the needs of the community when the question arises. It cannot by contract hamper its freedom of action in matters which concern the welfare of the State. Thus in the case of the employment of public servants, which is a less strong case than the present, it has been laid down that, except under a less strong case than the present, it has been laid down that, except under an Act of Parliament, no one acting on behalf of the Crown has authority to employ any person except upon the terms that he is dismissable at the Crown's pleasure; the reason being that it is in the interests of the community that the ministers for the time being advising the Crown should be able to dispense with the services of its employees if they think it desirable. Again suppose that a man accepts an office which he is perfectly at liberty to refuse, and does so on the express terms that he is to have certain leave of absence, and that when the time arrives the leave is refused in circumstances of the greatest hardship to his family or business, as the case may be. Can it be conceived that a petition of right would lie for damages? I should think not. I am of opinion that this petition must fail and there must be judgment for the Crown.'

Commentary

See also *Commissioners of Crown Lands* v *Page* (1) in the Court of Appeal. Note Denning J's comments on the Amphitrite case in *Robertson* v *Minister of Pensions* (2) where he stated:

'... the doctrine of executive necessity, that is, the doctrine that the Crown cannot bind itself so as to fetter its future executive action. That doctrine was propounded by Rowlatt J in *Rederiaktiebolaget Amphitrite* v *The King* but it was unnecessary for the decision because the statement there was not a promise which was intended to be binding but only an expression of intention ...

In my opinion the defence of executive necessity is of limited scope. It only avails the Crown where there is an implied term to that effect or that is the true meaning of the contract.'

(1)   [1960] 2 QB 274

(2)   Infra, this chapter

Robertson v Minister of Pensions [1949] 1 KB 227 King's Bench Division (Denning J)

Power to bind the Crown by its agents

Facts

The plaintiff, when a serving officer, wrote to the War Office about a disability from which he suffered. They replied stating that it had been accepted as attributable to military service. He relied on that statement and did not get an independent medical opinion. The Ministry of Pensions, who were responsible for making a final decision, later decided that the disability was not attributable to war service.

Held

The letter from the War Office was binding on the Crown. It was intended to be binding, was intended to be acted on, and was so acted on.

10.4   Crown liability in tort

Addis v Crocker [1959] 2 All ER 773 Queens Bench (Gorman J)

Crown Proceedings Act s2(5): responsibilities of a judicial nature

Facts

An action for defamation was brought in respect of things said at a Law Society Disciplinary Committee hearing constituted under the Solicitors Act 1957.

Held

The Crown Proceedings Act which barred proceedings in tort against those exercising 'responsibilities of a judicial nature', applied here. The fact that the hearing was held in public was a major, though not essential, factor.

Home Office v Dorset Yacht Company Limited [1970] AC 1004

Facts

Several Borstal boys being detained under 'open' conditions escaped from supervision and damaged property belonging to the respondents. The relaxed conditions under which the boys had been detained were the result of a policy decision by the appellants. The respondents argued that the Borstal officers owed neighbouring property owners a duty of care to ensure that none of the detainees would escape. The existence of this duty of care was tried as a preliminary matter.

Held

(Viscount Dilhorne dissenting) A duty of care was owed by Borstal officers to neighbouring property owners to use reasonable care to prevent an escape of detainees, where there was a manifest risk of this.

Lord Diplock (after considering the authorities, his Lordship turned to deal with the policy/operational dichotomy:)

'The statute from which the right to detain is derived thus only gives the broadest indication of the purpose of the detention and confers upon the Home Secretary very wide powers to determine by subordinate legislation the way in which the powers of custody and control of Borstal trainees should be exercised by the officers of the prison service. In exercising his rule-making power, at any rate, it would be inconsistent with what are now recognised principles of English law to suggest that he owed a duty of care capable of giving rise to any liability in civil law to avoid making a rule the observance of which was likely to result in damage to a private citizen. For a careless exercise of his rule-making power he is responsible to Parliament alone. The only limitation on this power which courts of law have jurisdiction to enforce depends not on the civil law concept of negligence, but on the public law concept of ultra vires.

The statutory rules in force at the relevant time which deal with discipline and control limit themselves to laying down the general principles to be observed, viz:

"The purpose of Borstal training requires that every inmate, while conforming to the rules necessary for well-ordered community life, shall be able to develop his individuality on right lines with a proper sense of personal responsibility. Officers shall, therefore, while firmly maintaining discipline and order, seek to do so by influencing the inmates through their own example and leadership and by enlisting their willing co-operation."

If these instructions with their emphasis on co-operation rather than coercion are to be followed in a working party outside the confines of a "closed" Borstal or in an "open" Borstal they must inevitably involve some risk of an individual trainee's escaping from custody and indulging again in the same kind of criminal activities that led to his sentence of Borstal training and which are likely to cause damage to the property of another person. To adopt a method of supervision of trainees still subject to detention which affords them any opportunity of escape is, as Lord Dilhorne has pointed out, an act or omission which it can be reasonably foreseen may have as its consequence some injury to another person. But the same is true of every decision made by the Home Office, through the appropriate officers of the Borstal service, in the exercise of the statutory power to release a Borstal trainee from detention in less than two years from the time of his being sentenced or to release him temporarily on parole.

If one accepted the principle laid down in relation to private Acts of Parliament in the passages already cited by your Lordships from *Geddis v Proprietors of Bann Reservoir,* 3 App. Cas. 430 as a proposition of law of general application to modern statutes which confer upon government departments or public authorities a discretion as to the way in which a particular public purpose is to be achieved, the courts would be required, at the suit of any plaintiff who had in fact sustained damage at the hands of a Borstal trainee who had been released, to review the Home Office decision to release him and to determine whether sufficient consideration had been given to the risk of his causing damage to the plaintiff.

A private Act of Parliament in the nineteenth century, of which that under consideration in *Geddis* v *Proprietors of Bann Reservoir* was typical, conferred upon statutory undertakers power to construct and maintain works which interfered with the common law proprietary rights of other persons. The only conflict of interests to which the exercise of these powers could give rise was between the interests of the undertakers in achieving the physical result contemplated by the private bill which they had promoted and the interests of those other persons whose common law proprietary rights would be affected by the exercise of the powers. In construing a statute of this kind it can be presumed that Parliament did not intend to authorise the undertakers to exercise the powers in such a way as to cause damage to the proprietary rights of private citizens which could be avoided by reasonable care without prejudicing the achievement of the contemplated result. In the context of proprietary rights, the concept of a duty of reasonable care was one with which the courts were familiar in the nineteenth century as constituting a cause of action in "negligence". The analogy between the careless exercise of statutory powers conferred by a private Act of this kind and the careless exercise of powers existing at common law in respect of property was close and the issues involved suitable for decision by a jury, upon evidence admissible and adduced in accordance with the ordinary procedure of courts of law. There was no compelling reason to suppose that Parliament intended to deprive of any remedy at common law private citizens whose common law proprietary rights were injured by the careless, and therefore unauthorised, acts or omissions of the undertakers.

But the analogy between "negligence" at common law and the careless exercise of statutory powers breaks down where the act or omission complained of is not of a kind which would itself give rise to a cause of action at common law if it were not authorised by the statute. To relinquish intentionally or inadvertently the custody and control of a person responsible in law for his own acts is not an act or omission which, independently of any statute, would give rise to a cause of action at common law against the custodian on the part of another person who subsequently sustained tortious damage at the hands of the person released. The instant case thus lacks a relevant characteristic which was present in the series of decisions from which the principle formulated in *Geddis* v *Proprietors of Bann Reservoir* was derived. Furthermore, there is present in the instant case a characteristic which was lacking in *Geddis* v *Proprietors of Bann Reservoir*. There the only conflicting interests involved were those on the one hand of the statutory undertakers responsible for the act or omission complained of and on the other hand of the person who sustained damage as a consequence of it. In the instant case, it is the interest of the Borstal trainee himself which is most directly affected by any decision to release him and by any system of relaxed control while he is still in custody that is intended to develop his sense of personal responsibility and so afford him an opportunity to escape. Directly affected also are the interests of other members of the community of trainees subject to the common system of control, and indirectly affected by the system of control while under detention and of release under supervision is the general public interest in the reformation of young offenders and the prevention of crime.

These interests, unlike those of a person who sustains damage to his property or person by the tortious act or omission of another, do not fall within any category of property or rights recognised in English law as entitled to protection by a civil action for damages. The conflicting interests of the various categories of persons likely to be affected by an act or omission of the custodian of a Borstal trainee which has as its consequence his release or his escape are thus of different kinds for which in law there is no common basis for comparison. If the reasonable man when directing his mind to the act or omission which has this consequence ought to have in contemplation persons in all the categories directly affected and also the general public interest in the reformation of young offenders, there is no criterion by which a court can assess where the balance lies between the weight to be given to one interest and that to be given to another. The material relevant to the assessment of the reformative effect upon trainees of release under supervision or of any relaxation of control while still under detention is not of a kind which can be satisfactorily elicited by the adversary procedure and rules of evidence adopted in English courts of law or of which judges (and juries) are suited by their training and experience to assess the probative value.

It is, I apprehend, for practical reasons of this kind that over the past century the public law concept of ultra vires has replaced the civil law concept of negligence as the test of the legality, and consequently of the actionability, of acts or omissions of government departments or public authorities done in the exercise of a discretion conferred upon them by Parliament as to the means by which they are to achieve a particular public purpose. According to this concept Parliament has entrusted to the department or authority charged with the administration of the statute the exclusive right to determine the particular means within the limits laid down by the statute by which its purpose can best be fulfilled. It is not the function of the court, for which it would be ill-suited, to substitute its own view of the appropriate means for that of the department or authority by granting a remedy by way of a civil action at law to a private citizen adversely affected by the way in which the discretion has been exercised. Its function is confined in the first instance to deciding whether the act or omission complained of fell within the statutory limits imposed upon the department's or authority's discretion. Only if it did not would the court have jurisdiction to determine whether or not the act or omission, not being justified by the statute, constituted an actionable infringement of the plaintiff's rights in civil law.

These considerations lead me to the conclusion that neither the intentional release of a Borstal trainee under supervision, nor the unintended escape of a Borstal trainee still under detention which was the consequence of the application of a system of relaxed control intentionally adopted by the Home Office as conducive to the reformation of trainees, can have been intended by Parliament to give rise to any cause of action on the part of any private citizen unless the system adopted was so unrelated to any purpose of reformation that no reasonable person could have reached a bona fide conclusion that it was conducive to that purpose. Only then would the decision to adopt it be ultra vires in public law.

A parliamentary intention to leave to the discretion of the Home Office the decision as to what system of control should be adopted to prevent the escape of Borstal trainees must involve, from the very nature of the subject-matter of the decision, an intention that in the application of the system a wide discretion may be delegated by the Home Office to subordinate officers engaged in the administration of the Borstal system. But although the system of control, including the sub'delegation of discretion to subordinate officers, may itself by intra vires, an act or omission of a subordinate officer employed in the administration of the system may nevertheless be ultra vires if it falls outside the limits of the discretion delegated to him – i.e., if it is done contrary to instructions which he has received from the Home Office.

In a civil action which calls in question an act or omission of a subordinate officer of the Home Office on the ground that he has been "negligent" in his custody and control of a Borstal trainee who has caused damage to another person the initial inquiry should be whether or not the act or omission was ultra vires for one or other of these reasons. Where the act or omission is done in pursuance of the officer's instructions, the court may have to form its own view as to what is in the interests of Borstal trainees, but only to the limited extent of determining whether or not any reasonable person could bona fide come to the conclusion that the trainee causing the damage or other trainees in the same custody could be benefited in any way by the act or omission. This does not involve the court in attempting to substitute, for that of the Home Office, its own assessment of the comparative weight to be given to the benefit of the trainees and the detriment to persons likely to sustain damage. If on the other hand the officer's act or omission is done contrary to his instructions it is not protected by the public law doctrine of intra vires. Its actionability falls to be determined by the civil law principles of negligence, like the acts of the statutory undertakers in *Geddis* v *Proprietors of Bann Reservoir*, 3 App Cas 430.

This, as it seems to me, is the way in which the courts should set about the task of reconciling the public interest in maintaining the freedom of the Home Office to decide upon the system of custody and control of Borstal trainees which is most likely to conduce to their reformation and the prevention of crime and the public interest that Borstal officers should not be allowed to be completely disregardful of the interests both of the trainees in their charge and of persons likely to be injured by their carelessness without the law providing redress to those who in fact sustain injury.'

10.5   Crown employment

Dunn v R [1896] 1 QB 116 Court of Appeal (Lord Esher MR, Lord Herschell and Kay LJ)

Dismissal of crown servants

Facts

The petitioner was appointed a vice-consul in the Niger Protectorate under a contract, made with the consul-general for the protectorate, providing that the petitioner was to be engaged for three years certain. Before the three years had expired the consul-general gave the petitioner notice terminating his services.

Held

All persons employed in the public service of the Crown, whether in a military or civil capacity, hold their appointments at the pleasure of the Crown, unless there is some statutory provision to the contrary. Thus, notwithstanding the term of the contract to the contrary, the Crown was entitled to dismiss the petitioner at pleasure and thus the appointment had been properly terminated.

Kodeeswaran (Chelliah) v Attorney-General of Ceylon [1970] AC 1111 Privy Council (Lord Diplock, Lord Hodson, Viscount Dilhorne, Lord Donovan and Lord Pearson)

Rights of action by civil servants against the crown

Facts

The principal issue at stake was whether a civil servant had any right of action against the Crown in respect of salary due for services rendered.

Held

A civil servant could bring an action, under the common law of Ceylon, against the Crown to recover arrears of wages.

Lord Diplock:

His Lordship began by stressing that in this case English law was only relevant to the extent that it had been adopted as part of the common law of Ceylon. He continued:

'It is now well established in British constitutional theory, at any rate as it has developed since the eighteenth century, that any appointment as a Crown servant, however subordinate, is terminable at will unless it is expressly otherwise provided by legislation; but as pointed out by Lord Atkin in *Reilly* v *The King* (1),

"a power to determine a contract at will is not inconsistent with the existence of a contract until so determined".

In *Reilly's* case Lord Atkin, while finding it unnecessary to express a final opinion as to whether the relationship between the Crown and the holder of a public office was constituted by contract, remarked, at p 179:

"... that in some offices at least it is difficult to negative some contractual relations, whether it be as to salary or terms of employment, on the one hand, and duty to serve faithfully and with reasonable care and skill on the other."

Their Lordships thus see nothing inconsistent with British constitutional theory in the Governor of Ceylon being empowered by the Proclamation of 1799 to enter into a contract on behalf of the Crown with a person appointed to an office in the civil administration of the colony as to the salary payable to him, provided that such contract was terminable at will.'

After further considering the authorities, and in particular the effect of Roman-Dutch law on this problem, his Lordship concluded:

'A right to terminate a contract of service at will coupled with a right to enter into a fresh contract of service may in effect enable the Crown to change the terms of employment in future if the true inference to be drawn from the communication of the intended change to the servant and his continuing to serve thereafter is that his existing contract has been terminated by the Crown and a fresh contract entered into on the revised terms. But this cannot affect any right to salary already earned under the terms of his existing contract before its termination.'

(1)   [1934] AC 176

Mitchell v R [1896] 1 QB 121 Court of Appeal (Lord Esher MR, Fry and Lopes LJJ)

The Crown and contract

Facts

The suppliant had been a lieutenant-colonel in the Royal Engineers. On his retirement he brought an action in court claiming that the sum paid to him on retirement had not been correctly calculated in accordance with a Royal Warrant of 1884 the provision of which, he claimed, were terms of his contract with the Crown.

Held

No engagement made by the crown with any of its military or naval officers in respect of services can be enforced in a court of law.

Lord Esher MR:

'I agree with Matthew J that the law is as clear as it can be, and that it has been laid down over and over again as the rule on this subject that all engagements between those in the military service of the Crown and the Crown are voluntary only on the part of the Crown, and give no occasion for an action in respect of any alleged contract. It has been argued that this is not to be treated as an engagement between a person in the military service of the Crown and the Crown, but as a contract made between a civilian and the Crown. The answer to that contention seems to me to be that it is contrary to the truth. At the time when the engagement was made the suppliant may have been on half-pay, but he was getting half-pay for being in the military service, although he may not have had any active service to perform. The engagement which was made between him and the crown was made solely in consequence of his having previously been and still being at the time in the service of the Crown as a soldier. It was made with him as a soldier with reference to what the Crown would do for him upon his retirement because he had been a soldier in the service of the Crown. It is perfectly clear that such an engagement is within the rule which I have mentioned. The suppliant is not, it must be remembered; suing in respect of a matter which is provided for by an Act of Parliament, but of a matter which arises under the War Office Regulations. It is a matter which arises between him and the Crown in consequence of certain regulations which the crown has made with regard to its officers. It has been decided over and over again that, whatever means of redress an officer may have in respect of a supposed grievance, he cannot as between himself and the Crown take proceedings in the courts of law in respect of anything which has happened between him and the Crown in consequence of his being a soldier. The courts of law have nothing whatever to do with such a matter. The appeal must therefore be dismissed.'

Fry LJ:

'I am clearly of opinion that no engagement between the Crown and any of its military or naval officers in respect of services either present, past or future can be enforced in any court of law. That being so, I entirely agree with the Master of the Rolls.'

Commentary

Leaman v R [1920] 3 KB 663 established that the above rule applied to all soldiers and not just to officers.

Rodwell v Thomas [1944] 1 KB 596 King's Bench Division(Tucker J)

The crown as employer: civil servants

Facts

Rodwell claimed that he had been dismissed from the civil service by a procedure that was not in accordance with a Treasury circular that he claimed had been incorporated in his contract of employment.

Held

It had not been established that the procedural provisions laid down in the circular had become terms of the plaintiff's contract of employment, and even if they did, they would not be enforced by the Crown as they formed a clog on the power of the Crown to dismiss its servants at pleasure.

Tucker J:

'It is conceded by Mr Platts Mills (for the plaintiff) that an established civil servant can be dismissed at any time at the pleasure of the Crown and that he has no remedy for such a dismissal, whatever the grounds may be which have brought it about.

Having regard, however, to the argument addressed to me by Mr Platts Mills, I think that it is only right to consider whether the contents of the report can be considered to form part of the contract between the plaintiff and the defendants. By the word "contract", I mean a "legally binding contract" which would give the plaintiff a right of access to a court of law to enforce compliance with its provisions. I have not been shown any written contract which established the terms of the plaintiff's employment, but it is said that because members of the trade union which represents him have been parties to this report of the joint committee he has the right to come to a court of law and say: "Every one of the findings of this committee must be considered as part of the terms of my contract of employment for breach of which I am entitled to seek redress." It is well-known that it has been found convenient to settle questions relating to conditions of employment through the medium of a representative body such as the joint committee, but I am at a loss to understand how every matter which is disposed of by give and take in that way can be said to be incorporated into a civil servant's contract of employment, so that, on a deviation from any term or condition, there is a breach of contract affording him a cause of action.

There is a further difficulty in the plaintiff's way. The authorities show, not only that prima facie an established civil servant can be dismissed at pleasure, but that the court will disregard any term of his contract expressly providing for employment for a specified time or that his employment can only be terminated in specified ways. The court regards such a provision in a contract as a clog on the right of the Crown to dismiss at pleasure at any time. This action, being one which, in substance, seeks to establish that the plaintiff has been wrongly dismissed because the procedure adopted at the inquiry was wrong and, therefore, ineffective legally to terminate his employment, in my opinion, does amount to an attempt to interfere with the right of the Crown to dismiss an established civil servant at any time for any reason, stated or unstated. The letter of 22 February 1943, dismissing the plaintiff, whether or not it was founded on this preliminary inquiry, had the effect of lawfully terminating the plaintiff's employment, and to hold the contrary would be to support an interference with or a clog on the right of the Crown to dismiss at pleasure. For these reasons the action fails.'

10.6   Public interest immunity

Air Canada v Secretary of State for Trade [1983] 2 AC 394; [1983] 2 WLR 494 House of Lords (Lords Fraser, Wilberforce, Edmund-Davies, Scarman and Templeman)

Crown privilege and discovery of documents

Facts

Following financial directions from the Secretary of State, the British Airports Authority increased charges for the use of Heathrow Airport. The plaintiffs, a group of international airlines, brought an action against the Secretary of State and the BAA claiming declarations that the former had acted unlawfully in that his purpose was to reduce the public sector borrowing requirement and this was an improper purpose for exercising his power under the Airport Authorities Act 1975.

In order to investigate the Secretary of State's purpose, the plaintiffs sought discovery of documents for which the Secretary of State claimed public interest immunity. The documents in category A consisted of high level ministerial papers relating to the formulation of government policy and those in category B consisted of inter-departmental communications between senior civil servants. The judge at first instance held that the court's concern was to elicit the real truth regardless of whether it favoured one party or the other and that documents were necessary for the due administration of justice if they substantially assisted the court in determining the facts upon which the decision would depend. The judge decided to inspect category A. The Court of Appeal allowed the appeal by the Secretary of State. The plaintiffs appealed.

Held

The appeal would be dismissed. Where the Crown objected to the production of a class of documents on the grounds of public interest immunity, the judge should not inspect the documents until he was satisfied that the documents contained material which would give substantial support to the contention of the party seeking disclosure, on an issue which arose in the case or which would assist any of the parties to the proceedings, and which was necessary for 'disposing fairly of the cause or matter' within RSC Ord 24 & 13(1). Only if the judge were so satisfied, should he then examine the documents privately. Since it was improbable that the documents for which immunity was sought contained any material additional to what had already been published in a White Paper and in the House of Commons, those documents were unlikely to be of assistance, and accordingly, they should not be inspected by the court.

Lord Fraser:

'My Lords, I do not think it would be possible to state a test in a form which could be applied in all cases. Circumstances vary greatly. The weight of the public interest against disclosure will vary according to the nature of the particular documents in question; for example, it will in general be stronger where the documents are Cabinet papers than when they are at a lower level. The weight of the public interest in favour of disclosure will vary even more widely, because it depends upon the probable evidential value to the party seeking disclosure of the particular documents, in almost infinitely variable circumstances of individual cases. The most that can usefully be said is that, in order to persuade the court even to inspect documents for which public interest immunity is claimed, the party seeking disclosure ought at least to satisfy the court that the documents are very likely to contain material which would give substantial support to his contention on an issue which arises in the case, and that without them he might be "deprived of the means of ... proper presentation" of his case. It will be plain that that formulation has been mainly derived from Lord Edmund-Davies' speech in the *Burmah Oil*case (1) and from the opinion of McNeill J in *Williams* v *Home Office* (2). It assumes, of course, that the party seeking disclosure has already shown in his pleadings that he has a cause of action, and that he has some material to support it. Otherwise he would merely be "fishing".

The test is intended to be fairly strict. It ought to be so in any case where a valid claim has been made ... It should therefore, in my opinion, not be encouraged to "take a peep" just on the off chance of finding something useful. It should inspect documents only where it has definite grounds for expecting to find material of real importance to the party seeking disclosure.'

(1)   Infra, this chapter

(2)   Infra, this chapter

Alfred Crompton Amusement Machines Ltd v Customs and Excise Commissioners (No 2) [1974] AC 405 House of Lords (Lords Reid, Morris of Borth-y-Gest, Dilhorne, Cross of Chelsea and Kilbrandon)

Crown privilege and discovery of documents

Facts

By a letter dated 31 July 1967, the complainant company, which had for some years paid purchase tax on the wholesale values of machines made and sold by them on the basis of a formula negotiated with the Customs and Excise Commissioners, claimed that the assessment was too high and asked that the letter be treated as a request for arbitration under s36 of the Purchase Tax Act 1963. The commissioners thereupon began to investigate the company's books and affairs and obtained from customers and other sources information relevant not only to the ascertainment of the wholesale value but also (as the Court of Appeal found) to the possible arbitration. On 8 December 1969, they gave their formal 'opinion' under s3(1) of the Acton the way the tax should be computed. No agreement was reached and pleadings went ahead for arbitration. When the commissioners served their list of documents they claimed Crown privilege for a class of routine documents the disclosure of which the head of the department swore would be injurious to the public interest since they would reveal the commissioners' methods and contained confidential information from third parties supplied both voluntarily and pursuant to the exercise of the commissioners' powers under s24(6) of the Act.

Held

Disclosure would not be ordered. It was in the public interest that the documents should not be disclosed since if it was known that the commissioners could not keep the information given secret such information might not be forthcoming or might be distorted and this would be harmful to the efficient working of the 1963 Act.

Lord Cross of Chelsea:

'Plainly there is much to be said in favour of disclosure. The documents in question consistute an important part of the material on which the commissioners based their conclusion that the appellant sell to retailers. That is shown by the reply which the commissioners made to the request for particulars under paragraph 5(h) of the defence. Yet if the claim to privilege made by the commissioners is upheld this information will be withheld from the arbitrator. No doubt it will form part of the brief delivered to counsel for the commissioners and may help him to probe the appellants' evidence in cross-examination; but counsel will not be able to use it as evidence to controversy anything which the appellants' witnesses may say. It is said, of course, that the appellants cannot reasonably complain if the commissioners think it is right to tie their hands in this way. But if the arbitrator should decide against them the appellants may feel – however wrongly – that the arbitrator was unconsciously influenced by the fact that the commissioners stated in their pleadings that they had this further evidence in support of their view which they did not disclose and which the appellants had no opportunity to controvert. Moreover, whoever wins it is desirable that the arbitrator should have all the relevant material before him. On the other hand, there is much to be said against disclosure. The case is not, indeed, as strong as the case against disclosing the name of an informer – for the result of doing that would be that the source of information would dry up whereas here the commissioners will continue to have their powers under s24(6). Nevertheless, the case against disclosure is, to my mind, far stronger than it was in the *Norwich Pharmacal* (1) case. There it was probable that all the importers whose names were disclosed were wrongdoers and the disclosure of the names of any, if there were any, who were innocent would not be likely to do them any harm at all. Here, on the other hand, one can well see that the third parties who have supplied this information to the commissioners because of the existence of their statutory powers would very much resent its disclosure by the commissioners to the appellants and that it is not at all fanciful for Sir Louis to say that the knowledge that the commissioners cannot keep such information secret may be harmful to the efficient working of the Act. In a case where the considerations for and against disclosure appear to be fairly evenly balanced the courts should I think uphold a claim to privilege on the ground of public interest and trust to the head of the department concerned to do whatever he can to mitigate the ill-effects of non-disclosure ...'

(1)   Infra, this chapter

Burmah Oil Co Ltd v Governor and Company of the Bank of England [1980] AC 1090; CA [1979] 1 WLR 473; HL [1979] 3 WLR 722 House of Lords (Lords Edmund-Davies, Scarman, Keith, Wilberforce and Salmon)

Public interest and the discovery of documents

Facts

In January 1965, the Bank of England, acting in conjunction with the Government, made an agreement with Burmah Oil to assist them in resolving their financial difficulties. The agreement involved, inter alia, the transfer of stock to the Bank. In October 1976 Burmah Oil, the plaintiffs, claimed a declaration that the transfer of stock in 1975 was unconscionable, inequitable and unreasonable. They applied for an order for production of certain documents by the Bank. The Attorney-General intervened on behalf of the Crown, objecting to production.

The certificate signed by the Chief Secretary to the Treasury stated that the specified documents fell into three categories, that the minister had personally read all the documents, and that he considered that their production would be injurious to the public interest. Category A comprised communications between government ministers and concerned the formulation of government policy. Category B consisted of communications between senior civil servants and the Bank relating to policy matters described in Category A documents. Category C comprised memoranda of telephone conversations and meetings between senior businessmen, ministers, civil servants and the Bank, and referred to information given in confidence by businessmen. The High Court judge upheld the Crown's claim, and the plaintiffs appealed.

The Court of Appeal (Lord Denning dissenting) dismissed the appeal, holding that it would be contrary to public policy to order discovery of documents, such as those in Categories A and B, which related to the formulation of government policy, (*Conway* v *Rimmer*(1) applied). Documents in Category C should also be protected, since it is in the interests of good government that it should be able to receive confidential information on business matters, and an order for discovery of these documents might impede the giving of confidential information in future.

Burmah Oil appealed to the House of Lords but reduced their claim for discovery to ten of the documents in respect of which discovery had originally been sought. All ten documents were in Categories A and B.

Held

First (Lord Wilberforce dissenting), that the ten documents should be produced for inspection by the House, for the present case was one where without inspection of the documents it was not possible to decide whether the balance of public interest lay for or against disclosure.

The documents having been inspected, it was held per Lord Salmon and Lord Edmund-Davies, Lord Keith of Kinkel dubitante, that none of them contained matter of such evidential value as to make an order for their disclosure necessary for disposing fairly of the case or (per Lord Scarman) that the documents were relevant but their significance was not such as to override the public interest objections to their production.

Lords Keith of Kinkel and Scarman held that where the court inspects a document and orders disclosure the Crown should have a right to appeal against the order before the document is disclosed.

Lord Edmund-Davies:

'... A party to litigation who seeks, as here, to withhold from disclosure to the other party documents which, being included in their list or affidavit of documents, are ex concessis relevant to the litigation has, as this House made clear in *Conway* v *Rimmer* (1) and *R* v *Lewes Justices ex parte Secretary of State for the Home Department* (2), a heavy burden of proof. But it is not contended by the plaintiffs that the Chief Secretary has failed to establish a good prima facie case for withholding all the listed documents.

... But it was urged by the Attorney-General that, so expansive were the numerous admissions made in the Bank's defence and so liberal had the Bank been in supplying documents, that Burmah had all the material necessary for the presentation of their case. I do not think that is right. In the face of the Bank's umbrella denial of any inequality of bargaining power, the sale of BP stock at an undervalue, and all other forms of unconscionable conduct on their part, it could, as I think, prove a valuable reinforcement of Burmah's case if they could establish by means of some of the withheld documents that the bank had itself committed themselves to the view that the terms finally presented to Burmah were tainted by those unconscionable features of which Burmah complained.

What are the probabilities of such documentary support being in existence? Is it merely pure conjecture? If so, applying the plaintiffs' own test, production should be refused. But in my judgment, there is more to it than that. It is, at the very least, "on the cards" that, in the light of the bank's known support and advocacy of profit'sharing, they expressed their unequivocal dislike when the government expressed determination to impose its final terms upon Burmah. It was, I think, an over-simplification for the Attorney-General to submit that the only issue is whether the January agreement was in fact inequitable, and not whether the bank regarded it as inequitable. For if, faced by government obduracy despite its strong representations, the bank insisted upon the proposed contractual terms, an arguable foundation for the appellants' allegations of unconscionability against the bank itself could be laid. Then is all this merely "on the cards" simply a "fishing expedition"? If that is all there is to it, discovery should be refused. But, in my judgment the existence of such documentary material is likely. And that, in my judgment, is sufficient.

And so, as I see it, the position is reached that, on the one hand, the appellants seek disclosure of ten documents which may well contain material "necessary ... for disposing fairly of the cause or matter or for saving costs", while, on the other hand, the Attorney-General by his intervention asserts that the withholding of these ten documents (two in category A and eight in category B) is "necessary for the proper functioning of the public service". In these circumstances, the balancing exercise with which the courts of this country have become increasingly familiar since *Conway* v *Rimmer* (1) is called for and if the appellants are to succeed the scales must come down decisively in their favour: see *Alfred Crompton Amusement Machines Ltd* v *Customs and Excise Commissioners (No 2)*(3), per Lord Cross of Chelsea at p434F.

Despite the strong claims advanced by the Chief Secretary, none of the ten documents belong to those categories (such as Cabinet decisions and papers) hitherto largely regarded as totally immune from production. And acceptance of that claim does not necessarily preclude disclosure. For, as Lord Radcliffe said in *Glasgow Corporation* v *Central Land Board* (4):

> "The power reserved to the court is ... a power to order production even though the public interest is to some extent affected prejudicially ... The interests of government, for which the minister should speak with full authority, do not exhaust the public interest. Another aspect of that interest is seen in the need that impartial justice should be done in the courts of law, not least between citizen and Crown, and that a litigant who has a case to maintain should not be deprived of the means of its proper presentation by anything less than a weighty public reason. It does not seem to me unreasonable to expect that the court would be better qualified than the minister to measure the importance of such principles in application to the particular case that is before it."

My Lords, it follows, as I think, that the respondents were wrong in submitting that, if the appellants are to succeed in this interlocutory appeal, they must establish that the Chief Secretary's certificate is probably inaccurate. On the contrary, disclosure may well be ordered even though its accuracy is not impugned, for the minister's view is one-sided and may be correct as far as it goes but is yet not to be regarded as decisive of the matter of disclosure. For, as Lord Reid said in *Conway* v *Rimmer* (1):

> "The minister who withholds production of a 'class' document has no duty to consider the degree of public interest involved in a particular case by frustrating in that way the due administration of justice. If it is in the public interest in his view to withhold documents of that class, then it matters not whether the result of withholding a document is merely to deprive a litigant of some evidence on a mino issue in a case of little importance or, on the other hand, is to make it impossible to do justice at all in a case of the greatest importance."

...Yet when all is said and done and even accepting that the withheld documents are likely to contain material supportive of the allegation of unconscionability, this House is at present completely in the dark as to the cogency of such material. For example, does it clearly and substantially support the allegation, or only to an insignificant degree? Unless its evidentiary value is clear and cogent, the balancing exercise may well lead to the conclusion that the public interest would best be served by upholding the Chief Secretary's objection to disclosure. On the other hand, if the material provides strong and striking support of the plaintiff's claim, the court may conclude that when this is put against such prejudice to the public interest as is likely to arise were any disclosure made in late 1979 regarding even high policy commercial negotiations conducted in January 1975, the interests of justice demand that disclosure (complete or partial) should be ordered. A judge conducting the balancing exercise needs to know: see Lord Pearce in *Conway v Rimmer* (1):

> "... Whether the documents in question are of much or little weight in the litigation, whether their absence will result in a complete or partial denial of justice to one or other of the parties or perhaps to both, and what is the importance of the particular litigation to the parties and the public. All these are matters which should be considered if the court is to decide where the public interest lies."

No judge can profitably embark on such a balancing exercise without himself seeing the disputed documents. May he take a peep? In *Conway* v *Rimmer* (1), Lord Reid said at p953:

"It appears to me that, if the minister's reasons are such that a judge can properly weight them, he must, on the other hand, consider what is the probable importance in the case before him of the documents or other evidence sought to be withheld. If he decides that on balance the documents probably ought to be produced, I think that it would generally be best that he should see them before ordering production ... I can see nothing wrong in the judge seeing documents without their being shown to the parties ... If on reading the document he ... thinks that it ought to be produced he will order its production. But it is important that the minister should have a right to appeal before the document is produced."

Lord Upjohn said, at p995:

"... if privilege is claimed for a document upon the ground of 'class', the judge, if he feels any doubt about the reason for its inclusion for his private inspection, and to order its production if he thinks fit."

But it has been suggested that the position is otherwise where the "class" claim is not challenged. I see no reason why this should be so, once it is postulated that the withheld "class" documents are "likely" to contain material substantially useful to the party seeking discovery. That qualification is necessary, for what is no more than a "fishing expedition" ought not to be advanced by the judge's having a peep to see whether they contain an attractive catch. But, provided such reservation is rigidly adhered to, a judicial peep seems to be justifiable in both cases and may, indeed, prove vital in each if the judge is to be enabled to arrive at a just conclusion in the matter of discovery ...

In my judgment, such material as is presently available leads me to the conclusion that this Appellate Committee of your Lordships' House should not privately inspect the ten documents earlier referred to. What they contain remains to be seen ...

... If the conclusion is that they contain nothing of any significance, this appeal should be dismissed. But if, on the other hand, material evidence comes to light, your Lordships will be called on to adjudicate whether, in balancing the competing public interests, disclosure of any of the ten documents or any parts of them should be ordered. The final disposal of this appeal must await and will depend upon the nature of that adjudication.

My Lords, it was some days after I had completed and passed for typing the foregoing observations that I privately inspected the ten documents earlier referred to. Having done so, in my judgment disclosure of none of them can be described as "necessary either for disposing fairly of the cause or matter or for saving costs". It follows that I would uphold in its entirety the objection to production advanced by the Chief Secretary to the Treasury and dismiss this interlocutory appeal.'

(1)   Infra, this chapter

(2)   [1973] AC 388

(3)   Supra, this chapter

(4)   (1956) SC (HL) 1

Conway v Rimmer [1968] AC 910 House of Lords (Lords Reid, Morris of Borth-y-Gest, Hodson, Pearce and Upjohn)

Crown privilege and discovery of documents

Facts

The appellant was a probationer police constable who had been prosecuted for theft and acquitted. He had been charged by his superintendent who before charging him had urged him to resign. After his acquittal, he was dismissed from the force. He brought an action for malicious prosecution against his superintendent (the respondent). In the course of preliminary proceedings for discovery, the Home Secretary objected to disclosure of certain classes of documents which would include the probationary reports on the appellant and the report of the respondent to the chief constable which had led to the prosecution of the appellant. The objection was made in the proper form, particularizing the classes of document concerned (confidential reports of police officers and reports concerning investigation into crimes) and specifying that in the Home Secretary's opinion the production of documents of each class would be injurious to the public interest.

Held

Although *Duncan* v *Cammell Laird & Co Ltd* (1) was rightly decided on its own facts, the broader propositions for which that case had been regarded as an authority were wrong. Thus the court has jurisdiction to order the disclosure of documents for which crown privilege has been claimed by the head of a Government Department. In deciding whether to exercise this power, it is the right and duty of the court to hold the balance between, on the one hand, the interests of the public in ensuring the proper administration of justice and, on the other hand, the public interest in the withholding of documents whose disclosure would be contrary to the national interest. Thus a Minister's certificate is not conclusive against disclosure, particularly where the privilege is claimed for routine documents within a class of documents. In reaching a decision whether to order disclosure the court will give full weight to a Minister's view and if the considerations are of such a character as judicial experience is not competent to weight (eg protection of national security, maintenance of diplomatic relations) the Minister's view will prevail. However, where the considerations are not of that nature, the court will decide whether or not the public interest in the proper administration of justice outweighs the public interest in non-disclosure. In order to arrive at this decision, the court will generally be right to inspect the documents without their being shown to the parties before reaching its decision.

In the present case it was most improbable that harm would be done by the disclosure of the probationary reports on the appellant and it had not been suggested that disclosure of the contents of the report to the chief constable would be harmful after the appellant had been acquitted, and yet these reports might be of vital importance in the action; thus the production of the reports for the inspection of the court would be ordered and, if the court found on inspection that disclosure would not be prejudicial to the public interest, or that any such possible prejudice was outweighed by the public interest in the proper administration of justice, an order for disclosure of the reports should be made.

Lord Reid:

'... It is universally recognised that here there are two kinds of public interest which may clash. There is the public interest that harm shall not be done to the nation of the public service by disclosure of certain documents, and there is the public interest that the administration of justice shall not be frustrated by the withholding of documents which must be produced if justice is to be done. There are many cases where the nature of the injury which would or might be done to the nation or the public service is of so grave a character that no other interest, public or private, can be allowed to prevail over it. With regard to such cases it would be proper to say, as Lord Simon said is, that to order production of the document in question would put the interest of the state in jeopardy; but there are many other cases where the possible injury to the public service is much less and there one would think that it would be proper to balance the public interests involved. I do not believe that Lord Simon really meant that the smallest probability of injury to the public service must always outweigh the gravest frustration of the administration of justice ...

I cannot think that it is satisfactory that there be no means at all of weighing, in any civil case, the public interest involved in withholding the document against the public interest that it should be produced. So it appears to me that the present position is so unsatisfactory that this House must re-examine the whole question in light of the authorities.

Two questions will arise: first, whether the court is to have any right to question the finality of a Minister's certificate, and, secondly, if it has such a right, how and in what circumstances that right is to be exercised and made effective.

A Minister's certificate may be given on one or other of two grounds: either because it would be against the public interest to disclose the contents of the particular document or documents in question, or because the document belongs to a class of documents which ought to be withheld whether or not there is anything in the particular document in question disclosure of which would be against the public interest. It does not appear that any serious difficulties have arisen or are likely to arise with regard to the first class. However wide the power of the court may be held to be, cases would be very rare in which it could be proper to question the view of the responsible Minister that it would be contrary to the public interest to make public the contents of a particular document. A question might arise whether it would be possible to separate those parts of a document of which disclosure would be innocuous from those parts which ought not to be made public, but I need not pursue that question now. In the present case your lordships are directly concerned with the second class of documents.

... If the Minister, who has no duty to balance these conflicting public interests, says no more than that in his opinion the public interest requires concealment, and if that is to be accepted as conclusive in this field as well as with regard to documents in his possession, it seems to me not only that very serious injustice may be done to the parties, but also that the due administration of justice may be gravely impaired for quite inadequate reasons.

Lord Simon did not say that courts in England have no power to overrule the executive. He said in *Duncan*'s case (1):

> "The decision ruling out such documents is the decision of the judge ... It is the judge who is in control of the trial, not the executive, but the proper ruling for the judge to give is as above expressed."

ie to accept the Minister's view in every case. In my judgment, in considering what it is 'proper' for a court to do we must have regard to the need, shown by twenty five years' experience since *Duncan*'s case (1), that the courts should balance the public interest in the proper administration of justice against the public interest in withholding any evidence which a Minister considers ought to be withheld.

I would therefore propose that the House ought now to decide that courts have and are entitled to exercise a power and duty to hold a balance between the public interest, as expressed by a Minister, to withhold certain documents or other evidence, and the public interest in ensuring the proper administration of justice. That does not mean that a court would reject a Minister's view: full weight must be given to it in every case; and if the Minister's reason are of a character which judicial experience is not competent to weight then the Minister's view must prevail; but experience has shown that reasons given for withholding whole classes of documents are often not of that character. For example a court is perfectly well able to assess the likelihood that, if the writer of a certain class of document knew that there was a chance that his report might be produced in legal proceedings, he would make a less full and candid report than he would otherwise have done.

I do not doubt that there are certain classes of documents which ought not to be disclosed whatever their content may be. Virtually everyone agrees that cabinet minutes and the like ought not to be disclosed until such time as they are only of historical interest; but I do not think that many people would give as the reason that premature disclosure would prevent candour in the cabinet. To my mind the most important reason is that such disclosure would create or fan ill-informed or captious public or political criticism. The business of government is difficult enough as it is, and no government could contemplate with equanimity the inner workings of the government machine being exposed to the gaze of those ready to criticise without adequate knowledge of the background and perhaps with some axe to grind. That must in my view also apply to all documents concerned with policy making within departments including it may be minutes and the like by quite junior officials and correspondence with outside bodies. Further, it may be that deliberations about a particular case require protection as much as deliberation about policy. I do not think that it is possible to limit such documents by any definition; but there seems to me to be a wide difference between such documents and routine reports ... It appears to me that, if the Minister's reasons are such that a judge can properly weigh them, he must on the other hand consider what is the probable importance in the case before him of the documents or other evidence sought to be withheld. If he decides that on balance the documents probably ought to be produced, I think that it would generally be the best that he should see them before ordinary production and, if he thinks that the Minister's reasons are not clearly expressed, he will have to see the documents before ordering production. I can see nothing wrong in the judge seeing documents without their being shown to the parties.

... If on reading the document he still thinks that it ought to be produced, he will order its production.

It is important, however, that the Minister should have a right to appeal before the document is produced ...

It appears to me to be most probable that any harm would be done by disclosure of the probationary reports on the appellant or of the report from the Police Training Centre. With regard to the report which the respondent made to his chief constable with a view to the prosecution of the appellant there could be more doubt, although no suggestion was made in argument that disclosure of its contents would be harmful now that the appellant has been acquitted. As I have said, these documents may prove to be of vital importance in this litigation.

In my judgment, this appeal should be allowed and these documents ought now to be required to be produced for inspection. If it is then found that disclosure would not, in your lordships' view, be prejudicial to the public interest, or that any possibility of such prejudice is, in the case of each of the documents, insufficient to justify its being withheld, then disclosure should be ordered.'

Lord Morris of Borth-y-Gest:

'... It is, I think, a principle which commands general acceptance that there are circumstances in which the public interests must be dominant over the interests of a private individual. To the safety or the well-being of the community the claims of a private person may have to be subservient. This principle applies in litigation. The public interest may require that relevant documents ought not to be produced. If, for example, national security would be or might be imperilled by the production and consequent disclosure of certain documents then the interests of a litigant must give way. There are some documents which can readily be identified as containing material the secrecy of which it is vital to protect; but where disclosure is desired and is resisted there is something more than a conflict between the public interest and some private interest. There are two aspects of the public interest which pull in contrary directions. It is in the public interest that full effect should be given to the normal rights of a litigant. It is in the public interest that in the determination of disputes the courts should have all relevant material before them. It is, on the other hand, in the public interest that material should be withheld if, by its production and disclosure, the safety or the well-being of the community would be adversely affected. There will be situations in which a decision ought to be made whether the harm that may result from the production of documents will be greater than the harm that may result from their non-production. Who, then, is to hold the scales? Who is to adjudge where the greater weight lies?

We could have a system under which, if a Minister of the Crown gave a certificate that a document should not be produced, the courts would be obliged to give full effect to such certificate and, in every case and without exception, to treat it as binding, final and conclusive. Such a system (though it could be laid down by some specific statutory enactment) would, in my view, be out of harmony with the spirit which in this country has guided the ordering of our affairs and in particular the administration of justice. Whether in some cases the law has or has not veered towards adopting such a system is a matter that has involved the careful and detailed review of the authorities which was a feature of the helpful addresses of learned counsel. Though this case requires an answer to be given to the question whether in the last resort the decision rests with the courts or with a Minister, I see no reason to envisage friction or tension as between the courts and the executive. They both operate in the public interest. Some aspects of the public interest are chiefly within the knowledge of some Minister and can best be assessed by him. I see no reason to fear that the courts would not in regard to them be fully and readily receptive to all representations made in appropriate form and with reasonable sufficiency. If a responsible Minister stated that production of a document would jeopardise public safety, it is inconceivable that any court would make an order for its production. The desirability of refusing production would heavily outweigh the desirability of requiring it. Other examples will readily come to mind of claims to protection from production which would at once be fully conceded. But there will be cases where the balance of desirabilities will not be so clearly evident. Some one will then have to decide. Should it be the court or should it be the executive?

... It was conceded that objection on behalf of the Crown to production of a document on the ground of injury to the public interest which was shown (a) not to have been taken in good faith or (b) to have been actuated by some irrelevant or improper consideration or (c) to have been founded on a false factual premise, would not be final or conclusive and could be overriden by the court. If, as is thus conceded, the court possesses such wide powers or overruling an objection to production it would seem only reasonable and natural that it should also have the duty of assessing the weight of competing public interests.

I pass to consider whether there is any obstacle which prevents our arriving at a decision of this case in the direction in which, in my view, the necessities of justice point. Does the decision in *Duncan* v *Cammell Laird & Co Ltd* (1) constitute an obstacle which bars the way? ...

My Lords, it seems to me that that decision was binding on the Court of Appeal in the present case. Your lordships have, however, a freedom which was not possessed by the Court of Appeal. Though precedent is an indispensable foundation on which to decide what is the law, there may be times when a departure from precedent is in the interests of justice and the proper development of the law. I have come to the conclusion that it is now right to depart from the decision in *Duncan*'s case (1) ...

My Lords, I have embarked on a survey of the decisions prior to *Duncan*'s case (1), because I would have a measure of reluctance in disturbing a decision given in 1942, if it had been a re-statement of clear principles which for long had been widely accepted. It seems to me, however, that there was much authority which would have warranted an entirely different statement of principle in *Duncan*'s case, though doubtless in that particular case without leading to any different result. This circumstance when coupled with the fact that it is clear that the law in Scotland differs from that proclaimed in *Duncan*'s case affords ample warrant, in my view, to justify a new appraisement of the position. It can also be said that though courts have since 1942 been obliged to follow *Duncan*'s case they have often expressed disquiet in doing so. The case of *Ellis* v *Home Office* (2) may be mentioned as an example of this. Furthermore, the statements made by Viscount Kilmuir LC in 1956 and 1962 which we were invited to consider, show that the government, long aware of complaints concerning the previous practice, decided to make the modifications of it which were announced in the two statements. In my view, it should now be made clear that whenever an objection is made to the production of a relevant document it is for the court to decide whether or not to uphold the objection. The inherent power of the court must include a power to ask for a clarification or an amplification of an objection to production, though the court will be careful not to impose a requirement which could only be met by divulging the very matters to which the objection related. The power of the court must also include a power to examine documents privately, a power, I think, which in practice should be sparingly exercised, but one which could operate as a safeguard for the executive in cases where a court is inclined to make an order for production though an objection is being pressed. I see no difference in principle between the consideration of what have been called the contents cases and the class cases. The principle which the courts will follow is that relevant documents normally liable to production will be withheld, if the public interest requires that they should be withheld. In many cases it will be plain that documents are within a class of documents which by their very nature ought not to be disclosed. Indeed, in the majority of cases I apprehend that a decision as to an objection will present no difficulty. The cases of difficulty will be those in which it will appear that, if there is non-disclosure, some injustice may result and that if there is disclosure the public interest may to some extent be affected prejudicially. The courts can and will recognise that a view honestly put forward by a Minister as to the public interest will be based on special knowledge and will be put forward by one who is charged with a special responsibility. As Lord Radcliffe said in the *Glasgow Corpn* case, the courts will not seek on a matter which is within the sphere and knowledge of a Minister to displace his view by their own; but where there is more than one aspect of the public interest to be considered it seems to me that a court, in reference to litigation pending before it, will be in the best position to decide where the weight of public interest predominates. I am convinced that the courts, with the independence which is their strength, can safely be entrusted with the duty of weighing all aspects of public interests and of private interests and of giving protection where it is found to be due.

The objection to the production of the probationary reports has been explained as being put forward on the basis that those who make such reports expect them to be confidential, so that they will only be seen by police officers, and that if such reports could ever be subject to production then the future candour of future writers of such reports would be affected, and that this would be disadvantageous to, and therefore injurious to, the public interest. While accepting that the view is held that some measure of prejudice to the public interest would or might result from production, it may be that a greater measure of prejudice to the public interest would result from their non'production. As to the report of the chief constable of 13 January 1965, the matter is put on a somewhat different basis. That was a report of a police officer to his superior in relation to the alleged commission of a crime. Again, it must be accepted that the view is held that it would be injurious to the p-blic interest to order its production. The view is put forward that no documents within the class of 'reports by police officers to their superiors concerning investigations into the commission of crime' should ever be disclosed. It is submitted that, though the appellant in the present case has been acquitted of the offence with which he was charged, it would be unfortunate ever to make an exception from the practice of maintaining the secrecy of such reports. I think that any court must recognise the weight of the consideration that the police in their work of fighting crime, which is work that is so much in the public interest, must in no way be impeded or frustrated. Whether it would be or might be is a matter which it is well within the competence of a court to assess.

I have come to the conclusion that the appeal should be allowed, and that the best procedure to follow for weighing the public and private interests which are involved in this case will be to have an inspection of the five documents which are in question. It can then be decided whether there should or should not be an order for the production of some or all of the documents.'

Lord Pearce:

'... The Crown Proceedings Act, 1947, s28 made the ordinary rules of discovery apply to the Crown when it is a party, subject to any rule of law which authorises or requires the withholding of any document or the refusal to answer any question on the ground that the disclosure or the answering of the question could be injurious to the public interest. "The Crown may therefore be required to authorise the disclosure of official information which would otherwise be an offence under the Official Secrets Act, 1911" (Professor Wade *Administrative Law* (2nd ed) p283). It was argued that the exception as to any rule of law which authorises or requires the withholding of a document, was a statutory confirmation of *Duncan*'s case (1); but it does not create any particular rule of law. It merely preserves in the operation of the section whatever may from time to time be the courts' rule for the withholding of documents. It affirms nothing as to what that rule of law shall be or how it shall be operated. It is difficult to lay down with precision how far the court should accept the view of the executive on what should be privileged while retaining its inherent power to reject it; and how far it should inspect and form its own views, while giving due weight to the Minister's objection.

Certainly the rigidity of approach which crystallised in *Duncan*'s case (1) is very undesirable; and it has led to unsatisfactory results.

So far as concerns particular documents whose disclosure is said to be injurious to the public interest the problem is less acute. If the Crown on the ground of injury to the public objects to the production of the plans of a submarine, as in *Duncan*'s case (1), it is obvious that the court would accept the matter without further scrutiny. In a less obvious case the court might require more detailed elaboration by the Crown to show that what on the face of it seems harmless would in fact be harmful. This can as a rule be done without disclosing any secret. In the highest range of security there is provision in the Crown Proceedings Act, 1947_ whereby the Crown in really urgent cases of secrecy has a statutory right not to disclose the existence of a document if the disclosure of its existence would be injurious to the public interest, as, for instance, the disclosure of the mere existence of a secret treaty might be. In the lower ranges of importance the judge can, as did Scrutton J, in the *Asiatic Petroleum* case (3) satisfy himself by inspection.

It is in respect of documents for which privilege is claimed as a class that the real difficulty lies. Even since the date of *Duncan*'s case (1) there has been an enormous increase in the extent to which the executive impinges on the private lives of the citizens. New ministries have been created and the old have been enlarged. Inevitably the mass of documentation has proliferated. It now bears little relation to the "State Papers" or other documents of government to which some of the older cases refer. Yet the same privilege has been sought (and given) under the argument that the necessary candour cannot be obtained from civil servants if their documents are to be subjected to an outside chance of production in a court of law. Support for this argument is to be found in *Smith* v *East India Co* (4) and *Hennessy* v *Wright* (5).

Any department quite naturally and reasonably wishes, as any private business or any semi-State board must also wish, that its documents or correspondence should never be seen by any outside eye. If it can obtain this result by putting forward a general vague claim for protection on the ground of candour it can hardly be blamed for doing so. "It is not surprising" it has been said (Professor Wade *Administrative Law* (2nd ed) at p285) "that the Crown, having been given a blank cheque, yielded to the temptation to overdraw." Moreover the defect of such an argument is that discrimination and relaxation of the claim could not be acknowledged by the Crown lest it jeopardise the claim of the whole class of documents and of other classes of document. No weighing of the injury done to particular litigants (and thereby to the public at large) by a resulting denial of justice can be made. The ministry puts forward the rigid general claim. The court accepts it. The litigant ruefully leaves the lists, a victim of an injustice, great or small. In some cases this injustice is a necessary evil for the public good, in others it is unnecessary. Yet the court has not weighed the balance or considered whether the public interest in the well-being or routine of the ministry or the public interest in the fair administration of justice should have prevailed in that particular case.

... In the case of *Ellis v Home Office* (2), Crown privilege claimed on a "class" basis was upheld, but was with reason criticised at the trial and by the Court of Appeal.

... In my view, it is essential to leave the vague generalities of wide classes and get down to realities in weighing the respective injuries to the public of a denial of justice on the one side and, on the other, a revelation of governmental documents which were never intended to be made public and which might be inhibited by an unlikely possibility of disclosure. Obviously production would never be ordered of fairly wide classes of documents at a high level. To take an extreme case, production would never be ordered of cabinet correspondence, letters or reports on appointments to office of importance and the like; but why should the same yardstick apply to trivial documents and correspondence with or within a ministry?

It is conceded that under the existing practice there can be no weighing of injustice in particular cases against the general public disadvantage of disclosure and its effect on candour. But it is argued that a judge who is the only person who can properly weigh the former, is incapable of properly weighing the latter. I do not understand why he cannot do so, especially if the ministry gives some specific details of the type of document in question and some specific reasons why it is undesirable to allow production. It is a judge's constant task to weigh human behaviour and the points that tell for or against candour. He knows full well that in general a report will be less inhibited if it will never see the light of public scrutiny, and that in some cases and on some subjects this may be wholly desirable. He also knows that on many subjects this fact has little if any important effect. Against this he can consider whether the documents in question are of much or little weight in the litigation, whether their absence will result in a complete or partial denial of justice to one or other of the parties or perhaps to both, and what is the importance of the particular litigation to the parties and the public. All these are matters which should be considered, if the court is to decide where the public interest lies ...

In my opinion, the court should consider whether the document is relevant and important in a reasonable action, so that one may fairly say that the public interest in justice requires its disclosure. It must consider whether the disclosure will cause harm administratively, either because of the undesirability of publishing the particular contents or because of the undesirability of making public a particular class of documents (of which I have given examples above) or for any other valid reason. It must give due weight to any representations of the Minister which set out the undesirability of disclosure and explain the reasons. If these do not make the matter clear enough, the court should itself call for and inspect the documents before coming to a decision. If part of a document is innocuous but part is of such a nature that its disclosure would be undesirable, it should seal up the latter part and order discovery of the rest, provided that this will not give a distorted or misleading impression. In all these matters it must consider the public interest as a whole, giving due weight both to the administration of the executive and to the administration of justice.

In my opinion, the probation reports on the appellant should be disclosed. In practice they will have considerable influence on the result of the case, although in theory their effect might not be of importance. Both sides hope to get from them support in their respective contentions on the question of malice. However clearly the judge explains their absence, it will be hard to persuade a jury that the reports are not being suppressed for sinister reasons and to prevent its members from harbouring unfair suspicions against the respondent. Their suppression moreover, will entail a suppression of cross-examination on the point. This would be unfair to both parties. Clearly production is desirable in the interests of justice. Would their production harm the candour of such reports in general, and do a general harm disproportionate to the importance of justice in this particular case? I do not think so. The reports on a probationer are not on a sufficiently high level to do public harm by the disclosure. It is argued that in future if there is any possibility of disclosure such reports will not be written with candid criticism. It is stressed that such reports will not be written with effect on a probationer's future service in the force. No doubt the writer of such a report is aware of this, and this in itself, I think, would create a reluctance to make criticism which might be too harsh, a reluctance that would be more compelling than any outside possibility of disclosure. There are countless teachers at schools and universities, countless employers of labour, who write candid reports, unworried by the outside chance of disclosure, but deeply concerned, as no doubt the police are likewise, lest their criticism may be doing less than justice to the subject of their report. In my opinion, the balance of public good in the circumstances of this particular case tilts in favour of producing the reports, and their disclosure should therefore be ordered. The report to the chief constable is of obvious importance. It will probably make or mar the chances of one or other of the parties. If it is not produced I do not see how there can be any evidence in chief or cross-examination on a vital point in the case or how the case can be fairly tried. Nevertheless I see that there might be strong arguments against its disclosure. One cannot weigh these considerations on matters of abstract argument and theory without seeing more of the contents and form of the document. It is in just such a case as this that a court should inspect the document. Your lordships should, in my opinion, privately inspect it before coming to any conclusion ...'

(1)   Infra, this chapter

(2)   [1953] 2 QB 135

(3)   [1916] 1 KB 822

(4)   (1841) 1 Ph 50

(5)   (1888) 21 QBD 509

D v NSPCC [1978] AC 171 House of Lords (Lords Diplock, Hailsham and Simon, Killbrandon and Edmund-Davies)

Public interest and discovery of information

Facts

NSPCC is an independent body incorporated by royal charter in 1895 which received and investigates complaints from members of the public about cases of ill-treatment or neglect of children under an express pledge of confidentiality. It is authorised under s1(1) of the Children and Young Persons Act 1969 to bring care proceedings in respect of children. The Society (NSPCC) received a complaint from an informant about the treatment of a 14-month-old child and an inspector of the society called at the child's home. The complaint was unfounded. The mother subsequently brought an action against the NSPCC for damages for personal injuries alleged to have resulted from the society's negligence in failing properly to investigate the complaints and the manner and circumstances of the inspector's call which had caused her severe and continuing shock. The Society denied negligence and applied to the Master for an order that there should be no discovery or inspection ordered of any documents which revealed or might reveal the identity of the complainant, on the grounds, inter alia, that the proper performance by the Society of its duties under its charter and the 1969 Act required that the absolute confidentiality of information given in confidence should be preserved, that if disclosure were ordered in this action the society's sources of information would dry up and that that would be contrary to the public interest.

Held

By analogy with the rule relating to the immunity accorded to police informants, the public interest required that those who gave information about child abuse to the Society should be immune from disclosure of their identity in legal proceedings since, otherwise, the Society's sources of information would dry up. The public interest to be protected was the effective functioning of an organisation authorised by Act of Parliament to bring proceedings for the welfare of children. Public interest, as a ground of non-disclosure of documents and information, was not confined to the effective functioning of a department of Central Government. The Society was entitled to withhold from discovery documents disclosing the identity of its informant since the public interest in withholding disclosure outweighed the public interest that the mother should obtain the information she sought (which was admittedly relevant to the cause of action against the Society) and thereby possible legal redress.

Lord Diplock:

'... The fact that information has been communicated by one person to another in confidence, however, is not of itself a sufficient ground for protecting from disclosure in a court of law the nature of the information of the identity of the informant if either of these matters would assist the court to ascertain facts which are relevant to an issue upon which it is adjudicating: *Alfred Crompton Amusement Machines Ltd* v *Customs and Excise Commissioners (No 2)* (1). The private promise of confidentiality must yield to the general public interest that in the administration of justice truth will out, unless by reason of the character of the information or the relationship of the recipient of the information to the informant a more important public interest is served by protecting the information or the identity of the informant from disclosure in a court of law.

The public interest which the NSPCC relies upon as obliging it to withhold from the plaintiff and from the court itself material that could disclose the identity of the society's informant is analogous to the public interest that is protected by the well established rule of law that the identity of police informers may not be disclosed in a civil action, whether by the process of discovery, or by oral evidence at the trial: *Marks v Beyfus* (2).

The rationale of the rule as it applies to police informers is plain. If their identity were liable to be disclosed in a court of law, these sources of information would dry up and the police would be hindered in their duty of preventing and detecting crimes. So the public interest in preserving the anonymity of police informers had to be weighed against the public interest that information which might assist a judicial tribunal to ascertain facts relevant to an issue upon which it is required to adjudicate should be withheld from that tribunal. By the uniform practice of the judges which by the time of *Marks v Beyfus* (2) had already hardened into a rule of law, the balance has fallen upon the side of non-disclosure except where upon the trial of a defendant for a criminal offence disclosure of the identity of the informer could help to show that the defendant was innocent of the offence. In that case, and in that case only, the balance falls upon the side of disclosure.

My Lords, in *R v Lewes Justices ex parte Secretary of State for the Home Department* (3) this House did not hesitate to extend to persons from whom the Gaming Board received information for the purposes of the exercise of their statutory functions under the Gaming Act 1968 immunity from disclosure of their identity analogous to that which the law had previously accorded to police informers. Your Lordships' sense of values might well be open to reproach if this House were to treat the confidentiality of information given to those who are authorised by statute to institute proceedings for the protection of neglected or ill-treated children as entitled to less favourable treatment in a court of law than information given to the Gaming Board so that gaming may be kept clean. There are three categories of persons authorised to bring care proceedings in respect of neglected or ill-treated children: local authorities, constables and the NSPCC. The anonymity of those who tell the police of their suspicions of neglect or ill-treatment of a child would be preserved without any extension of the existing law. To draw a distinction in this respect between information given to the police and that passed on directly to a local authority or to the NSPCC would seem much too irrational a consequence to have been within the contemplation of Parliament when enacting the Children and Young Persons Act 1969. The local authority is under an express statutory duty to bring care proceedings in cases where this is necessary if neither the police nor the NSPCC have started them, while, as respects the NSPCC, the evidence shows that, presumably because it is not associated in the public mind with officialdom, the public are readier to bring information to it than to the police or the welfare services of the local authority itself.

Under the summons by the NSPCC for an order withholding discovery of documents to the extent that they were capable of revealing the identity of the society's informant, it is for the judge to weigh the competing public interests involved in disclosure and non-disclosure and to form his opinion as to the side on which the balance fell. In a careful judgement in which he reviewed the relevant authorities Croom-Johnson J ordered that disclosure should not be given. Upon an interlocutory summons relating to discovery this was a matter upon which the judge had a discretion with which an appellate court would not lightly interfere, but the reasoning by which his decision was supported is of wider application. It would also rule out any attempt to ascertain the identity of the NSPCC's informant by questions put to witnesses at the trial and would dispose of the plaintiff's claim to disclosure of the informant's identity as part, and perhaps to her the most important part, of the substantive relief she seeks. The interlocutory judgement thus raises matters of principle fit for the consideration of this House.

For my part I would uphold the decision of Croom-Johnson J and reverse that of the Court of Appeal. I would do so upon what in argument has been referred to as the "narrow" submission made on behalf of the NSPCC. I would extend to those who give information about neglect or ill-treatment of children to a local authority or the NSPCC a similar immunity from disclosure of their identity in legal proceedings to that which the law accords to police informers. The public interests served by preserving the anonymity of both classes of informants are analogous; they are of less in weight in the case of the former than in that of the latter class, and in my judgment are of greater weight than in the case of informers of the Gaming Board to whom immunity from disclosure of their identity has recently been extended by this House ...'

Lord Hailsham of St Marylebone:

'... The appellant society argued, in effect, for a general extension in range of the nature of the exceptions to the rule in favour of disclosure. This, it was suggested, could be summarised in a number of broad propositions, all in support of the view that, where an identifiable public interest in non-disclosure can be established, either there is a firm rule against disclosure (for example, legal professional privilege or state secrets) or the court has a discretion whether or not to order disclosure, and that this discretion must be exercised against disclosure in all cases where, after balancing the relevant considerations, the court decides that the public interest in non-disclosure outweighs the ordinary public interest in disclosure. The appellants contended that new cases will arise from time to time calling for a protection from disclosure in classes of case to which it was not previously extended, and that the courts had in practice shown great flexibility in adapting these principles to new situations as and when these arise. The appellants contended that some of those entitled to the benefits of protection had, and some had not, been subject to statutory or common law duties or been clothed with government authority or been answerable to Parliament or the executive. This contention was aimed at the majority judgements in the Court of Appeal which in substance disallowed the appellants' claim to immunity on the grounds that they are a private society clothed arguably with authority to fulfil a function but not a duty which they are compelled to perform, and that they are not in any sense either an organ of central government of part of the public service. The appellants noted that the dissenting judgement of Lord Denning MR, which was in their favour, largely relied on the confidentiality which the appellants had pledged to potential informants. Their own contention was that, while the mere fact that a communication was made in confidence did not of itself justify non-disclosure, the fact of confidentiality was relevant to reinforce the view that disclosure would be against the public interest. In this connection the appellants cited *Alfred Crompton Amusement Machines Ltd* v *Customs and Excise Commissioners (No 2)* (1). Lastly the appellants contended that there was no reported case in which the court, once it had identified a public interest in non-disclosure, had ever regarded itself as debarred from taking it into consideration or from weighing its importance against the damage to be apprehended from excluding relevant evidence.

These contentions have at least the merit of propounding a lucid and coherent system. Nevertheless, I am compelled to say that, in the breadth and generality with which they were put forward, I do not find them acceptable.

They seem to me to give far too little weight to the general importance of the principle that, in all cases before them, the courts should insist on parties and witnesses disclosing the truth, the whole truth, and nothing but the truth, where this would assist the decision of the matters in dispute. In the second place, I consider that the acceptance of these principles lead both to uncertainty and to inconsistency in the administration of justice. If they were to be accepted, we should remember that we should by laying down a large innovation not merely in the law of discovery but equally in the law of evidence, which has to be administered not merely in the High Court but in the Crown Courts, the county courts and the magistrates' courts throughout the land. What is the public interest to be identified? On what principles can it be defined? On what principles is the weighing-up process to proceed? To what extent, if at all, can the right to non-disclosure be waived? Can secondary or extraneous evidence of the facts not disclosed be permitted? To what extent should the Crown be notified of the fact that the issue has been raised? These questions are all manageable if the categories of privilege from disclosure and public interest are considered to be limited. Indeed, reported authority, which is voluminous, shows that largely they have been solved. But to yield to the appellants' argument on this part of the case would be to set the whole question once more at large, not merely over the admitted categories and the existing field but over a much wider, indeed over an undefined field.

Thirdly, and perhaps more important, the invitation of the appellants seems to me to run counter to the general tradition of the development of doctrine preferred by the English courts. This proceeds through evolution by extension or analogy of recognised principles and reported precedents. Bold statements of general principle based on a review of the total field are more appropriate to legislation by Parliament which has at its command techniques of inquiry, sources of information and a width of wordly-wise experience far less restricted than those available to the courts in the course of contested litigation between adversaries.

On the other hand, I find equally unattractive the more restricted and even, occasionally, pedantic view of the authorities advanced on behalf of the respondent. This was based on a rigid distinction, for some purposes valuable, between privilege and public interest, and an insistence on a narrow view of the nature of the interest of the public, reflected in the reasoning of the majority in the Court of Appeal, which would virtually have restricted the public interest cases to the narrower interests of the central organs of the state, or what might be strictly called the public service. The effect of the argument would not merely limit the ambit of possible categories of exception to the general rule. In my view, it would virtually ensure that the categories would now have to be regarded as effectively closed. In her printed case the respondent contended that:

"No party is protected from his obligation to disclose documents on the grounds of public interest unless there is some connection between the claim for protection and the functions of central government or the public service for the state: ... The expression 'Crown Privilege' has been criticised but, ... it accurately reflects the basic requirement that there must be a connection with the Crown or public service of the state."

In support of this contention the respondent referred inter alia to *Conway v Rimmer* (4), to *R v Lewes Justices ex parte Secretary of State for the Home Department* (3) and to *Alfred Crompton Amusement Machines Ltd v Customs and Excise Commissioners (No 2)* (1). There is, of course, a sense, which will become apparent as I proceed, in which the appellants' claim can be brought squarely within the respondents' principle. But the principle is itself, as I shall show, open to criticism.

In particular the argument was based on what was described as a fundamental principle that the exceptions to the general rule requiring disclosure all come within one or the other of two rigidly confined categories, one described as privilege, when secondary evidence could be given or the privilege could be waived, and the other as "public interest" where these possible escapes were excluded. But this, it was contended, was virtually restricted to the category formerly, but inaccurately, referred to as "Crown privilege".

The result of this is that I approach the problem with a caution greater than that contended for the appellants, but with a willingness to extend established principles by analogy and legitimate extrapolation more flexible than was admitted by the respondent ...

The authorities, therefore, seem to me to establish beyond doubt that the courts have developed their doctrine in this field of evidence. An example of this is seen in the privilege extended to editors of newspapers in the 19th century, before the present Ord.82 r.6 was passed, to refuse to answer interrogatories in defamation cases where the issue was malice and the plaintiff desired to discover their sources (cf *Hope v Brash* (5); *Hennessy v Wright* (6); *Plymouth Mutual Co-Operative and Industrial Society Ltd v Traders' Publishing Association Ltd* (7). This practice, robustly developed by the judges of the Queen's Bench Division (in contrast with the contemporary Chancery Division practice even after 1873) can only have been based on public policy. It has been stressed that these cases relate to discovery and not to questions to witness at the trial. This may well be so, at least at present, but certainly they illustrate the use of the court of a discretion, and its sensitiveness to public policy where discretion exists. Until the introduction of the new rules it is within my recollection that interrogatories and discovery on the lines disallowed in the newspaper cases were frequently allowed in other defamation cases where malice was in issue, although it was pointed out n argument that the newspaper principle was, at least one, applied, rather strangely, to MPs in *Adam* v *Fisher* (8).

In all this argument, however, two facts stand out unmistakably as true beyond dispute. The first is that the welfare of children, particularly of young children at risk of maltreatment by adults, has been, from the earliest days, a concern of the Crown as parens patriae, an object of legal charities and in latter years the subject of a whole series of Acts of Parliament, of which the Act of 1969 is only an example, and that not the latest. The second is that the information given by informants to the police or to the Director of Public Prosecutions, and now, since *R* v *Lewes Justices ex parte Secretary of State for the Home Department* (3) to the Gaming Board, is protected from disclosure in exactly the manner demanded by the appellants. The question, and it is I believe the only question, necessary to be decided in this appeal, is whether an extension of this established principle to information relating to possible child abuse supplied to the appellants is a legitimate extension of a known category of exception or not. For this purpose it is necessary to consider the position of the appellants in relation to the enforcement provisions of the Children and Young Persons Act 1969.

For the purposes of this inquiry the provisions of the Act can be shortly summarised. A child at risk in certain ways can be brought before a juvenile court in care proceedings. Such proceedings can only be brought by three classes of person, each of whom has a locus standi (see s1(1) of the Act). These classes of person are (i) a constable, (ii) the relevant local authority and, (iii) an authorised person, that is, a person authorised by the Secretary of State for the Home Department in this behalf. Other persons may of course bring prosecutions for breaches of the criminal law, and under s28 can bring proceedings to enable a child in imminent danger to be brought before the court, detained and taken to a place of safety.

But care proceedings can only be brought before the juvenile court by one of the three classes of person. It is common ground that the only "person" authorised by the Secretary of State within the meaning of s1 of the Actis the appellant society, a body founded in 1889 and incorporated since 1895 by royal charter. To that extent the society has been charged with the performance of a public responsibility by the Home Secretary under the direct authority of an Act of Parliament ...

Of the three classes with locus standi to initiate care proceedings, it is common ground that information given to the police is protected to the extent demanded by the society. This is clear from many cases including *Marks* v *Beyfus* (2) (which applied the principle to the Director of Public Prosecutions) and many of the recent cases in your Lordships' House. The rule relating to the immunity accorded to police informants is in truth much older, so old and so well established, in fact, that it was not and could not be challenged in the instant case before your Lordships. Once, however, it is accepted that information given to the police in the instant case would have been protected, it becomes, in my judgment, manifestly absurd that it should not be accorded equally to the same information if given by the same informant to the local authority (who would have been under a duty to act on it) or to the appellant society, to whom, according to the undisputed evidence, ordinary informants more readily resort ...'

Lord Simon of Glaisdale:

'... Nevertheless, invocation of "public policy" does impose even more than normal self-restraint on a court. Of course, every rule of law is a legal manifestation of public policy. But your Lordships are as counsel for the respondent rightly emphasises, instantly concerned with "public policy" in a narrower sense – namely, consideration of social interests beyond the purely legal which call for the modification of a normal legal rule (here the rule that all relevant evidence should be adduced to the court): cf Lord Wright in *Fender* v *St John-Mildmay* (9). In such circumstances the correct approach to the function of the courts is, in my view, expressed by Lord Thankerton in *Fender* v *St John-Mildmay*:

"Their duty is to expound, and not to expand, such policy. That does not mean that they are precluded from applying an existing principle of public policy to a new set of circumstances where such circumstances are clearly within the scope of the policy."

This suggests, in my judgment, that a narrow rather than a wide ground of decision would be desirable in the instant case, if the former is available; that your Lordships should primarily look to see whether the law has recognised an existing head of public policy which covers the case; and that, if so, your Lordships should if possible vindicate such policy by means already adapted by the law to vindicate some analogous head of public policy.

I turn, though, first to the argument that your Lordships are here concerned with what was formerly called "Crown Privilege" and that it was "Privilege" not "Crown" which was misleading, so that the public interest which may exclude relevant evidence is only that of the Crown or the public service of the state – "state" here being restricted to the organs or departments of central government. There seems to me to be a number of objections to these arguments. First, so to restrict the principle on which relevant evidence may be excluded runs counter to its rationale as I have ventured to submit it to your Lordships, according to which both "Crown" and "Privilege" must be misnomers. Secondly, "the state" cannot on any sensible political theory be restricted to the Crown and the departments of central government (which are indeed, part of the Crown in constitutional law). The state is the whole organisation of the body politic for supreme civil rule and government the whole political organisation which is the basis of civil government. As such it certainly extends to local – and, as I think, also statutory – bodies in so far as they are exercising autonomous rule. Thirdly, there is a recurrent transfer of functions between central, local and statutory authorities. For example, near the heart of the issue before your Lordships, the Crown as parens patriae had traditionally a general jurisdiction over children; a residue is now exercised in the High Court, but the bulk has been devolved by statute on local authorities. Recently, posts and telegraphs have ceased to be the concern of a department of central government responsible to Parliament and have become the function of a virtually autonomous statutory body. They have become a nationalised industry under a largely independent board – in no real political or legal sense the Crown or a department of central government. Some nationalised industries are carried on by regional boards; others have been, but no longer are. The delimitation proposed on behalf of the respondent would thus work out capriciously and mutably. Fourthly, a number of the cases are against the respondent's contentions. In *Adam* v *Fisher* (8) it was held, on a summons relating to interrogatories in a libel suit, that an MP's sources of information need not be disclosed. In *Conway* v *Rimmer* (10) the appeal concerned reports on a probationary police constable in a county constabulary. In *In Re D (Infants)* (11) the material protected from disclosure was case records compiled in pursuance of statutory regulation relating to a child boarded out with foster parents by a local authority. In *R* v *Lewes Justices, ex parte Secretary of State for the Home Department* (3) it was information supplied to the Gaming Board of Great Britain. *Adam* v *Fisher* (8) may be explained away as relating solely to discovery of documents, which still retains an element of its discretionary origin (see the explanations in *Attorney-General* v *Clough* (12) and in *Attorney-General* v *Mulholland*; *Attorney-General* v *Foster* (13), where Lord Denning MR described *Adam* v *Fisher* (8) as expressing a rule of practice, not law). But the other cases simply cannot be fitted into the respondent's attempted limitation of this category of excluded evidence ...

This brings me to the penultimate question. Is protection of their sources of information necessary for the proper performance of their functions by the appellants? As to this there is uncontradicted and entirely plausible evidence. The answer is "yes" ...

The final question, my Lords, is whether the appellants' sources of information can be withheld from forensic investigation by extending on strict analogy an established rule of law. I have already cited long-standing and approved authority to the effect that sources of police information are not subject to forensic investigation. This is because liability to general disclosure would cause those sources of information to dry up, so that police protection of the community would be impaired. Exactly the same argument applies in the instant case if for "police" you read "NSPCC" and for "community" you read "that part of the community which consists of children who may be in peril". There can be no material distinction between police and/or local authorities on the one hand and the appellants on the other as regards protection of children. It follows that, on the strictest analogical approach and as a matter of legal rule, the appellants are bound to refuse to disclose their sources of information ...'

(1)	Supra, this chapter
(2)	(1890) 25 QBD 494
(3)	[1973] AC 388
(4)	Supra, this chapter
(5)	[1897] 2 QB 188
(6)	(1888) 21 QBD 509
(7)	[1906] 1 KB 403
(8)	(1914) 30 TLR 288
(9)	[1938] AC 1
(10)	[1968] AC 910
(11)	[1970] 1 WLR 599
(12)	[1963] 1 QB 773
(13)	[1963] 2 QB 477

Duncan v Cammell Laird & Co Ltd [1942] AC 624 House of Lords (Viscount Simon, Lords Thankerton, Russell, Clauson, MacMillan, Wright and Porter)

Public interest and discovery of documents

Facts

The submarine 'Thetis' was built by the defendants under contract with the Admiralty. She sank during a trial dive in June 1939 owing to the flooding of her two foremost compartments. The present action was a test action brought by the dependants and relatives of the nine men killed against the defendants for negligence. The First Lord of the Admiralty, his attention having been drawn to the nature and content of certain documents relevant to the litigation, directed the defendants not to produce those documents or copies thereof but rather to object to production on the grounds of Crown privilege. The First Lord of the Admiralty swore an affidavit in which he stated 'All the said documents were considered by me with the assistance of my technical advisers and I formed the opinion that it would be injurious to the public interest that any of the said documents should be disclosed to any person ...'. The documents included the contract for the hull and machinery, letters written before the accident relating to the vessel's trim, reports as to the condition of the Thetis when she was raised, plans and specifications and a notebook of a foreman painter.

The judge refused to order production of the documents as did the Court of Appeal.

Held

An order for production would not be made. Documents relevant and otherwise liable to production need not be produced if the public interest required that they should be withheld. The public interest might require non-disclosure either (a) because of the contents of those particular documents or (b) because the documents belonged to a class of documents which in the public interest should not be disclosed since they contained information given in confidence which would not be forthcoming in future if it were known that disclosure in subsequent litigation was possible.

An objection to production duly taken by the head of a government department should be treated by the court as conclusive.

Viscount Simon LC:

'... It will be observed that the objection is sometimes based upon the view that the public interest requires a particular class of communications with, or within, a public department to be protected from production, on the ground that the condour and completeness of such communications might be prejudiced if they were ever liable to be disclosed in subsequent litigation, rather than upon the contents of the particular document itself. Several cases have been decided on this ground protecting from production documents in the files of the East India Company held in its public capacity as responsible for the government of India: see *Smith* v *East India Co* (1) and *Wadeer* v *East India Co* (2). In the former case Lord Lyndhurst LC said, at p55:

"Now it is quite obvious that public policy requires, and looking to the Act of Parliament it is quite clear that the legislature intended, that the most unreserved communication should take place between the East India Company and the Board of Control, that it should be subject to no restraint or limitations; but it is also quite obvious that if, at the suit of a particular individual, those communications should be subject to be produced in a court of justice, the effect of that would be to restrain the freedom of the communications, and to render them more cautious, guarded and reserved. I think, therefore, that these communications come within the class of official communications which are privileged, inasmuch as they cannot be subject to be communicated, without infringing the policy of the Act of Parliament and without injury to the public interests."

The principle to be applied in every case is that documents otherwise relevant and liable to production must not be produced if the public interest requires that they should be withheld. This test may be found to be satisfied either (a) by having regard to the contents of the particular document or (b) by the fact that the document belong to a class which, on grounds of public interest, must be classed as withheld from production.

Two further matters remain to be considered. First, what is the proper form in which objection should be taken that the production of a document would be contrary to the public interest? Secondly, when this objection is taken in proper form, should it be treated by the court as conclusive, or are there circumstances in which the judge should himself look at the documents before ruling as to their production?

On the first question, it is to be observed that the matter may arise at either of two stages in the course of a civil suit. It may arise (as in the present instance) before the trial begins, out of an application for inspection of documents referred to in the affidavit of one of the parties. It may also arise at the trial itself when a subpoena or corresponding process has been served calling for the production of the documents and there is a refusal to comply on the ground that production would be contrary to the public interest.

The essential matter is that the decision to object should be taken by the minister who is the political head of the department, and that he should have seen and considered the contents of the documents and himself have formed the view that on grounds of public interest they ought not to be produced, either because of their actual contents or because of the class of documents – eg departmental minutes – to which they belong. Instances may arise where it is not convenient or practicable for the political minister to act (eg he may be out of reach, or ill, or the department may be one where the effective head is a permanent official), and in such cases it would be reasonable for the objection to be taken, as it has often been taken in the past, by the permanent head. If the question arises before trial, the objection would ordinarily be taken by affidavit, and a good example is provided by the affidavit of the First Lord of the Admiralty in the present case. If the question arises on subpoena at the hearing, it is not uncommon in modern practice for the minister's objection to be conveyed to the court, at any rate in the first instance, by an official of the department who produced a certificate which the minister has signed, stating what is necessary. I see no harm in that procedure, provided it is understood that this is only for convenience and that, if the court is not satisfied by this method, it can request the minister's personal attendance.

The remaining question is whether, when objection has been duly taken, the judge should treat it as conclusive. There are cases in the books where the view has been expressed that the judge might properly probe the objection by himself examining the documents. For example, Field J said, in *Hennessy* v *Wright* (3) at p515:

> "... I should consider myself entitled to examine privately the documents to the production of which he (the head of the department) objected, and to endeavour by this means and that of questions addressed to him, to ascertain whether the fear of injury to the public service was his real notice in objecting."

In *Asiatic Petroleum Co Ltd* v *Anglo-Persian Oil Co Ltd* (4), Scrutton J when sitting in chambers, looked at the documents and so did MacNaghten J in *Spigelman* v *Hocken* (5). On the other hand, it has been several times laid down that the court ought to regard the objection, when validly and formally taken, as conclusive.

... Although an objection validly taken to production on the ground that this would be injurious to the public interest is conclusive, it is important to remember that the decision ruling out such documents is the decision of the judge. Thus, in the present case, the objection raised in the respondents' affidavit is properly expressed to be an objection to produce "except under the order of this honourable court". It is the judge who is in control of the trial, not the executive, but the proper ruling for the judge to give is as above expressed.

In this connection, I do not think it is out of place to indicate the sort of grounds which would not afford to the minister adequate justification for objecting to production. It is not a sufficient ground that the documents are "state documents" or "official" or are marked "confidential". It would not be a good ground that, if they were produced, the consequences might involve the department or the government in Parliamentary discussion or in public criticism, or might necessitate the attendance as witnesses or otherwise of officials who have pressing duties elsewhere. Neither would it be a good ground that production might tend to expose a want of efficiency in the administration or tend to lay the department open to claims for compensation. In a word, it is not enough that the minister or the department does not want to have the documents produced. The minister, in deciding whether it is his duty to object, should bear these considerations in mind, for he ought not to take the responsibility of withholding production except in cases where the public interest would otherwise be damnified, eg where disclosure would be injurious to national defence, or to good diplomatic relations, or where the practice of keeping a class of documents secret is necessary for the proper functioning of the public service.

When these conditions are satisfied and the minister feels it is his duty to deny access to material which would otherwise be available, there is no question but that the public interest must be preferred to any private consideration. The present opinion is concerned only with the production the exclusion of verbal evidence which, if given, would jeopardise the interests of the community. Indeed, the language of Lord Eldon, above quoted, implies this. After all, the public interest is also the interest of every subject of the realm, and while, in these exceptional cases, the private citizen may seem to be denied what is to his immediate advantage, he, like the rest of us, would suffer if the needs of protecting the interests of the country as a whole were not ranked as a prior obligation. I move that the appeal be dismissed, with costs.

My Lords, I am authorised by my noble and learned friends Lord Thankerton, Lord Russell of Killowen and Lord Clauson, who are not able to be present, to say that they concur in this opinion.'

(Lord MacMillan, Lord Wright and Lord Porter also concurred.)

(1)   (1841) 1 Ph 50

(2)   (1856) 8 De GM & G 182

(3)   (1888) 21 QBD 509

(4)   [1916] 1 KB 822

(5)   (1932) 50 TLR 87

Neilson v Laugharne [1981] 2 WLR 537 Court of Appeal (Lord Denning MR, Oliver and O'Connor LJJ)

Public interest and discovery of documents

Facts

N commenced proceedings in the county court against the police claiming damages for trespass, damage to property and belongings, false arrest, wrongful imprisonment and assault. The police had previously held an internal complaints inquiry and found no evidence of the claim. The police refused to allow discovery of statements taken at that inquiry on grounds of public interest immunity.

Held

The appeal was dismissed. Every case depended on balancing the public interest in the administration of justice, which demanded disclosure of all relevant material, with a competing public interest in withholding it, that confidentiality, the need for candour and frankness and the desirability of co-operation were all factors to be taken into account, and it was not right to allow N to see statements taken for use in an investigation of police conduct in order to help him make out a case for damages ...

Lord Denning MR:

'This modern development shows that, on a question of discovery, the court can consider the competing public interests involved. The case is decided by the court holding the balance between two sides. One of them is asserting that, in the interest of justice, the documents should be disclosed. The other is asserting that in the public interest they should not be disclosed. Confidentiality is often to be considered. So is the need for candour and frankness. So is the desirability of co-operation. Or any other factors which present themselves. On weighing them all the judge decides according to which side the balance comes down. Once it is decided that the public interest is in favour of non-disclosure, the decision is regarded as a precedent for later situations of the same kind. So the body of law is built up. As Lord Hailsham said in *D v NSPCC* (1) "The categories of public interest are not closed, and must alter from time to time whether by restriction or extension as social conditions and social legislation develop." '

(1)   Supra, this chapter

Norwich Pharmacal Co v Customs and Excise Commissioners [1974] AC 133 House of Lords (Viscount Dilhorne, Lords Reid, Cross, Morris of Borth-y-Gest and Kilbrandon)

Crown privilege and discovery of information

Facts

The appellants were the owners and licensees of a chemical compound known as furazoldine. It appeared that the patent was being infringed by importations of furazoldine manufactured abroad. In order to obtain the names and addresses of the importers the appellants brought actions against the Commissioners of Customs and Excise alleging infringement of the patent and seeking orders that the

Commissioners should (a) in the case of each consignment of furazoldine imported disclose the names and addresses of the consignors and consignees, the quantity of furazoldine therein and the date thereof; (b) give full and complete discovery of all documents which were or had been in their possession, custody or control relating to such imported consignments of furazoldine. Graham J at first instance ordered discovery of the names and addresses of the importers. On appeal, the Court of Appeal reversed the decision. The appellants appealed. At the hearing of the appeal the appellants abandoned the contention that they had a cause of action for infringement by the Commissioners themselves and the appeal proceeded on the basis that the case was and always had been an action solely for discovery.

Held

Where a person, albeit innocently and without incurring any personal liability, becomes involved in the tortious acts of others he comes under a duty to assist one injured by those tortious acts by giving him full information by way of discovery and disclosing the identity of the wrongdoers. For that purpose it is irrelevant whether the involvement is the result of voluntary action or merely the result of the execution of some duty statutory or otherwise. Thus, prima facie, the respondents were obliged to disclose the information sought.

In the circumstances there was no head of public policy which precluded the making of the order for discovery, which was ordered.

Lord Reid:

'... So discovery to find the identity of a wrongdoer is available against anyone against whom the plaintiff has a cause of action in relation to the same wrong. It is not available against a person who has no other connection with the wrong than that he was a spectator or has some document relating to it in his possession. But the respondents are in an intermediate position. Their conduct was entirely innocent: it was in execution of their statutory duty. But without certain action on their part the infringements could never have been committed. Does this involvement in the matter make a difference? ...

My noble and learned friends, Lord Cross of Chelsea and Lord Kilbrandon, have dealt with the authorities. They are not very satisfactory, not always easy to reconcile and in the end inconclusive. On the whole I think they favour the appellants, and I am particularly impressed by the views expressed by Lord Romilly MR and Lord Hatherley LC in *Upmann* v *Elkan* (1). They seem to me to point to a very reasonable principle that it through no fault of his own a person gets mixed up in the tortious acts of others so as to facilitate their wrong-doing he may incur no personal liability but he comes under a duty to assist the person who has been wronged by giving him full information and disclosing the identity of the wrongdoers. I do not think that it matters whether he became too mixed up by voluntary action on his part or because it was his duty to do what he did. It may be that if this causes him expense the person seeking the information ought to reimburse him. But justice requires that he should co-operate in righting the wrong if he unwittingly facilitated its perpetration.

I am the more inclined to reach this result because it is clear that if the person mixed up in the affair has to any extent incurred any liability to the person wronged, he must make full disclosure, even though the person wronged has no intention of proceedings against him. It would I think be quite illogical to make his obligation to disclose the identity of the real offenders depend on whether or not he has himself incurred some minor liability. I would therefore hold that the respondents must disclose the information now sought unless there is some consideration of public policy which prevents that ...

So we have to weigh the requirements of justice to the appellants against the considerations put forward by the respondents as justifying non-disclosure. They are twofold. First it is said that to make such disclosures would or might impair or hamper the efficient conduct of their important statutory duties. And secondly it is said that such disclosure would or might be prejudicial to those whose identity would be disclosed.

There is nothing secret or confidential in the information sought or in the documents which came into the hands of the respondents containing that information. Those documents are ordinary commercial documents which pass through many different hands. But it is said that those who do not wish to have their names disclosed might concoct false documents and thereby hamper the work of the Customs. That would require at least a conspiracy between the foreign consignor and the importer and it seems to me to be in the highest degree improbable. It appears that there are already arrangements in operation by the respondents restricting the disclosure of certain matters if the importers do not wish them to be disclosed. It may be that the knowledge that a court might order discovery in certain cases would cause somewhat greater use to be made of these arrangements. But it was not suggested in argument that that is a matter of any vital importance. The only other point was that such disclosure might cause resentment and impair good relations with other traders: but I find it impossible to believe that honest traders would resent failure to protect wrongdoers.

Protection of traders from having their names disclosed is a more difficult matter. If we could be sure that those whose names are sought are all tortfeasors, they do not deserve any protection. In the present case the possibility that any are not is so remote that I think it can be neglected. The only possible way in which any of these imports could be legitimate and not an infringement would seem to be that someone might have exported some furazoldine from this country and then whoever owned it abroad might have sent it back here. Then there would be no infringement. But again that seems most unlikely.

But there may be other cases where there is much more doubt. The validity of the patent may be doubtful and there could well be other doubts. If the respondents have any doubts in any future case about the propriety of making disclosures they are well entitled to require the matter to be submitted to the court at the expense of the person seeking the disclosure. The court will then only order discovery if satisfied that there is no substantial chance of injustice being done ...'

Viscount Dilhorne:

'... I must confess that I am not in the least impressed by the "candour" argument. I really cannot conceive it to be realistic to suggest that the vast majority of importers who do not infringe patents or do other wrongs, will be in the least deterred from giving proper information to Customs by the knowledge that pursuant to an order of the court the names of the wrongdoers are disclosed by Customs ...'

(1)   (1871) LR 12 Eq 140

Rogers v Home Secretary [1973] AC 388 House of Lords (Lords Reid, Morris of Borth-y-Gest, Pearson, Simon of Glaisdale and Salmon)

Crown privilege or public interest immunity?

Facts

The case concerned a claim that a letter written by an assistant Chief Constable to the Gaming Board should be produced in evidence.

Held

Production would not be ordered.

Lord Reid:

'... The ground put forward has been said to be Crown privilege. I think that that expression is wrong and may be misleading. There is no question of any privilege in the ordinary sense of the word. The real question is whether the public interest requires that the letter shall not be produced and whether that public interest is so strong as to override the ordinary right and interest of a litigant that he shall be able to lay before a court of justice all relevant evidence. A Minister of the Crown is always an appropriate and often the most appropriate person to assert this public interest, and the evidence or advice which he gives to the court is always valuable and may sometimes be indispensable. But, in my view, it must always be open to any person interested to raise the question and there may be cases where the trial judge should himself raise the question if no one else has done so. In the present case the question of public interest was raised by both the Attorney-General and the Gaming Board. In my judgment both were entitled to raise the matter. Indeed I think that in the circumstances it was the duty of the board to do as they have done ...'

Williams v Home Office [1981] 1 All ER 1151 Queen's Bench Division (McNeill J)

Public interest and the disclosure of documents

Facts

P was detained in a 'control unit' within a prison. He claimed that this was false imprisonment and sought a declaration that the setting up of the control unit system was ultra vires r43(2) of the Prison Rules 1964. The rule provided for authority for removal from association with other prisoners to be given for a period not exceeding one month, but that the authority might be renewed from month to month. The control unit scheme contemplated such removal for two periods of 90 days each with a 'reverter' provision for bad behaviour. The plaintiff claimed, inter alia, that this was a fetter on the discretion under r43(2).

The Home Secretary issued a certificate objecting to the discovery of certain documents concerning the formulation of government policy on control units, on the ground that discovery would be contrary to the public interest. The plaintiff applied for production of the documents for inspection.

Held

Candour of expression by those not expecting their words to be liable to disclosure was not a ground of immunity, at least in this case.

It was not true that all the issues in the case could be disposed of by simply looking at Statute and the prison rules to see whether or not the control unit scheme was ultra vires. Issues of professional opinion and issues of fact concerning, for instance, the manner in which the Secretary of State intended to exercise his discretion under rule 43(2) were relevant, and the documents might have a bearing on them.

This was not a case involving 'high policy' – it was concerned with the details of prison administration; in such a case the fact that it concerned the liberty of the subject weighed heavily in favour of P in balancing the interests involved.

The public interest in the administration of justice and in the protection of individual liberty outweighed the public interest in secret government in this case. Undue criticism of the government could be minimised by obscuring parts of documents, other parts of which could be ordered to be disclosed, and by means of the requirement that the documents disclosed should not be used for purposes other than the trial.

The 23 documents were ordered to be produced for inspection and parts of six of them were ordered to be discovered.

11 INTRODUCTION TO ADMINISTRATIVE LAW – LOCAL GOVERNMENT

11.1   The nature of judicial control

Associated Provincial Picture Houses Ltd v Wednesbury Corporation [1948] 1 KB 223
Court of Appeal (Lord Greene MR, Somervell LJ, and Singleton J)

Reasonableness in the exercise of a discretion

Facts

The Sunday Entertainments Act 1932 provided:

> '1(1) The authority having power, in any area to which this section extends, to grant licences under the Cinematograph Act 1909, may, notwithstanding anything in any enactment relating to Sunday observance, allow places in that area licensed under the said Act to be opened and used on Sundays for the purpose of cinematograph entertainments, subject to such conditions as the authority think fit to impose ...'

In granting a licence, the defendants imposed a condition that no children under the age of fifteen were to be admitted. The plaintiffs applied to the court for a declaration that the condition was ultra vires.

Held

The local authority's decision on the age condition was not so unreasonable that no reasonable local authority could have come to it, and it would only be in such circumstances that the court would be entitled to declare the decision ultra vires on grounds of unreasonableness.

Lord Greene MR:

> '... Mr Gallop, for the plaintiffs, argued that it was not competent for the Wednesbury Corporation to impose any such condition and he said that if they were entitled to impose a condition prohibiting the admission of children, they should at least have limited it to cases where the children were not accompanied by their parents or a guardian or some adult. His argument was that the imposition of that condition was unreasonable and that in consequence it was ultra vires the corporation. The plaintiffs' contention is based, in my opinion, on a misconception as to the effect of this act in granting this discretionary power to local authorities. The courts must always, I think, remember this: first, we are dealing with not a judicial act, but an executive act; secondly, the conditions which under the exercise of that executive act, may be imposed are in terms, so far as language goes, put within the discretion of the local authority without limitation. Thirdly, the statute provides no appeal from the decision of the local authority.
>
> What, then, is the power of the courts? They can only interfere with an act of executive authority if it be shown that the authority has contravened the law. It is for those who assert that the local

authority has contravened the law to establish that proposition. On the face of it, a condition of the kind imposed in this case is perfectly lawful. It is not to be assumed prima facie that responsible bodies like the local authority in this case will exceed their powers; but the court, whenever it is alleged that the local authority have contravened the law, must not substitute itself for that authority. It is only concerned with seeing whether or not the proposition is made good. When an executive discretion is entrusted by Parliament to a body such as the local authority in this case, what appears to be an exercise of that discretion can only be challenged in the courts in a strictly limited class of case. As I have said, it must always be remembered that the court is not a court of appeal. When discretion of this kind is granted the law recognised certain principles upon which that discretion must be exercised, but within the four corners of those principles the discretion, in my opinion, is an absolute one and cannot be questioned in any court of law. What then are those principles? They are well understood. They are principles which the court looks to in considering any question of discretion of this kind. The exercise of such a discretion must be a real exercise of the discretion. If, in the statute conferring the discretion, there are to be found expressly or by implication matters which the authority exercising the discretion ought to have regard to, then in exercising the discretion it must have regard to those matters. Conversely, if the nature of the subject-matter and the general interpretation of the Act make it clear that certain matters would not be germane to the matter in question, the authority must disregard those irrelevant collateral matters.

In the present case, it is said by Mr Gallop that the authority acted unreasonably in imposing this condition. It appears to me quite clear that the matter dealt with by this condition was a matter which a reasonable authority would be justified in considering when they were making up their minds what condition should be attached to the grant of this licence. Nobody, at this time of day, could say that the well-being and the physical and moral health of children is not a matter which a local authority, in exercising their powers, can properly have in mind when those questions are germane to what they have to consider. Here Mr Gallop did not, I think, suggest that the council were directing their mind to a purely extraneous and irrelevant matter, but he based his argument on the word "unreasonable", which he treated as an independent ground for attacking the decision of the authority ...

It is clear that the local authority are entrusted by Parliament with the decision on a matter which the knowledge and experience of that authority can best be trusted to deal with. The subject-matter with which the condition deals is one relevant for its consideration. They have considered it and come to a decision upon it. It is true to say that, if a decision on a competent matter is so unreasonable that no reasonable authority could ever have come to it, then the courts can interfere. That, I think, is quite right; but to prove a case of that kind would require something overwhelming, and, in this case, the facts do not come anywhere near anything of that kind. I think Mr Gallop in the end agreed that his opposition that the decision of the local authority can be upset if it is proved to be unreasonable, really meant that it must be proved to be unreasonable in the sense that the court considers it to be a decision that no reasonable body could have come to. It is not what the court considers unreasonable, a different thing altogether. If it is what the court considers unreasonable, the court may very well have different views to that of a local authority on matters of high public policy of this kind. Some courts might think that no children ought to be admitted on Sundays at all, some courts might think the reverse, and all over the country, I have no doubt on a thing of that sort honest and sincere people hold different views. The effect of the legislation is not to set up the court as an arbiter of the correctness of one view over another. It is the local authority that are set in that position and, provided they act, as they have acted, within the four corners of their jurisdiction, this court, in my opinion, cannot interfere ...'

Attorney-General v Fulham Corporation [1921] 1 Ch 440 Chancery Division (Sargant J)
Definition of ultra vires acts

Facts

The Metropolitan Borough of Fulham, purporting to exercise its powers under the Baths and Wash-houses Acts 1846 - 1878 to establish baths, wash-houses and open bathing places, issued a public notice inviting persons to become its customers and setting out a scheme under which a person could purchase a bag which would contain about 28lbs of clothes, bring the bag and its contents to the wash-house, and call for them when washed. Alternatively, customers could for a small additional charge have their bags collected and returned by the corporation's van. In effect, the corporation proposed to operate a laundry-service.

Held

The new scheme was not authorised by the Baths and Wash-houses Acts 1846 to 1878. A declaration would be issued that the corporation was not entitled to provide a laundry-service as distinct from facilities enabling others to come to the wash-house to wash their clothes, and an injunction would be issued restraining the corporation or its officers or servants from acting in contravention of that declaration.

Sargant J:

'... This is an action by the Attorney-General, at the relation of the ratepayers of Fulham, against the municipal borough of Fulham, to restrain it, to use a short phrase, from carrying on a laundry, or something in the nature of a laundry.

In considering what the corporation may do, and what it may not do, I have to take as my guiding authority the words of Lord Selborne LC in *Attorney-General* v *Great Eastern Railway Co* (1). He says:

"I assume that Your Lordships will not now recede from anything that was determined in *Ashbury Railway Co* v *Riche*. It appears to me to be important that the doctrine of ultra vires, as it was explained in that case, should be maintained. But I agree with James LJ that this doctrine ought to be reasonably, and not unreasonably, understood and applied, and that whatever may fairly be regarded as incidental to, or consequential upon, those things which the Legislature has authorised, ought not (unless expressly prohibited) to be held, by judicial construction, to be ultra vires."

That recognises that in every case it is for a corporation of this kind to show that it has affirmatively an authority to do particular acts; but that in applying that principle, the rule is not to be applied too narrowly, and the corporation is entitled to do not only that which is expressly authorised but that which is reasonably incidental to or consequential upon that which is in terms authorised. And it is, of course, for the defendant corporation to point out the authority under which it has acted in what it has done. (His Lordship stated the facts, as above set out, including the new laundry scheme, and continued:) Now that is the new scheme and the method of carrying it out, and the question I have to consider is this, whether that scheme is authorised by the Baths and Wash-houses Act 1846 and the Baths and Wash-houses Act 1847.

It is quite clear that the new scheme of the corporation is not directly authorised by those Acts, but I have also to see, whether, although it is not authorised in terms by the Acts, it is something which in the language I have cited, "may fairly be regarded as incidental to or consequent upon those things which the Legislature has authorised". For that purpose I have to look at the two Acts. I will not go in great length through them. My attention has been called to all the material sections by Mr Tomlin or Mr Mathew, but it is important to notice the preamble to the Act of 1846, which is as follows: "Whereas it is desirable for the health, comfort, and welfare of the inhabitants of towns and populous districts to encourage the establishment therein of public baths and wash-houses and open bathing places". So that the scheme of the Act appears to be to give washing facilities to persons who are not able to provide for themselves places where they may cleanse themselves or their clothes. Then there are a number of provisions with regard to baths, and so on, which I need not refer to, and then comes the power to establish the wash-houses. By s25 the Council may from time to time, on lands which they have provided for the purpose, make any open bathing places, "erect any building suitable for public baths and wash-houses, and as to such wash-houses either with or without open drying grounds, and make any open bathing places, and convert any buildings into public baths and wash-houses, and may from time to time alter, enlarge, repair and improve the same respectively, and fit up, furnish, and supply the same respectively with all requisite furniture, fittings and conveniences". That word "conveniences" has been much relied on by counsel for the corporation …

Then, by the Baths and Wash-houses Act 1847, after reciting that "it is expedient to afford additional facilities for the establishment of public baths and wash-houses and open bathing places", it is provided, by s5, that "the number of washing tubs and troughs for the labouring classes in any building or buildings under the management of the same Council ... shall not be less than twice the number of the washing tubs or troughs of any higher class, if but one, or of all the higher classes if more than one, in the same building or buildings". Then, in a schedule to the Act, which regulates the charges which may be made, the charges in the case of wash-houses for the labouring classes are these: "Every wash-house to be supplied with conveniences for washing and drying clothes and other articles. For the use by one person of one washing tub or trough, and of a copper or boiler (if any) or, where one of the washing tubs or troughs shall be used as a copper or boiler, for the use of one pair of washing tubs or troughs, and for the use of the convenience for drying: For one hour only in any one day, any sum not exceeding one penny. For two hours together, in any one day, any sum not exceeding threepence"; and there are certain other words which I need not refer to ...

Now what is the effect of that legislation? It appears to be quite clear that the whole scheme is to afford facilities for persons who have no such facilities themselves and cannot pay for them, so that they may, so far as the wash-houses are concerned, do their own washing. Throughout there is no sort of suggestion, as far as I can see, that anything is to be provided for those persons except facilities for their doing the work themselves. As regards the word "conveniences", in s25 of the Act of 1846, and the word "materials", is s26 of the same Act, on which great stress was laid, it seems to me that those words are merely limited to conveniences and materials for the purposes of the Act; and, the purposes of the Act being clearly, in my judgment, the provision of facilities for persons to do their own washing, the words "conveniences" and "materials" must be limited to that.

Under the new system which has been inaugurated what has been provided for the persons who became customers is, in my judgment, not facilities for doing their own washing, but the washing itself. It seems to me that, in view of the fact that the control of the articles in question is entirely parted with, that the articles are washed up to a certain point absolutely and entirely irrespective of the labours or attention or care of the customers, and that the articles when that process has been gone through are redelivered in their semi-finished state to the customers, it is impossible to say that the Council have been doing anything else except the washing of the clothes down to a certain point for the particular customers. Now is that something which may fairly be regarded as incidental to or consequential upon the provision of facilities for washing? In my judgment, it is not. It appears to me to be a completely different enterprise, namely the business of washing to a particular degree or stage ...'

(1)   (1880) 5 App Cas 473

Bromley London Borough Council v Greater London Council [1983] 1 AC 768; [1982] 2 WLR 62 House of Lords (Lords Diplock, Wilberforce, Keith of Kinkel, Scarman and Brandon of Oakbrook)

Ultra vires acts: abuse of power

Facts

On 7 May 1981 there was an election for the GLC. As a result, the Labour group won control and proceeded to implement their 'Fares Fair' scheme, as they had promised they would in their election propaganda. This involved a 25 per cent cut in London Transport fares. The ratepayers were to pay increased rates as a means of helping to finance the scheme. In order to enforce payment the GLC made a supplementary rate precept, an order directed at all 35 London boroughs. The London Borough of Bromley challenged the validity of the whole procedure, and applied to the Divisional Court for an order of certiorari to quash the supplementary precept.

By s1 of the Transport (London) Act 1969 the GLC was under a general duty to develop policies and encourage measures which promoted:

'... the provision of integrated, efficient, and economic transport facilities and services for Greater London.'

The responsibility for implementing those principles was, by s4, conferred on the London Transport Executive (LTE).

By s5(1) the LTE was under a general duty to provide public passenger transport facilities which best met the needs of Greater London, and to exercise and perform its functions in accordance with the principles laid down by the GLC and with due regard to 'efficiency, economy, and safety of operation'.

By s7(3)(b) if at the end of an accounting period there was a deficit in the LTE's revenue account, the LTE was required, as far as practicable, to make up that deficit in the next accounting period, although under s7(6) the GLC was entitled to 'take such action as was necessary and appropriate to enable the LTE to comply with its duty under s7(3)(b) to balance its accounts'. The GLC was further empowered by s3(1) to make grants to the LTE 'for any purpose'. In order to finance the 'Fares Fair' scheme, the GLC required the London boroughs to levy a rate of 6.1p in the pound. It was proposed that the GLC, acting under s7(6), mentioned above, would use this increase in income from the ratepayers to make a grant to the LTE to enable LTE to balance its accounts.

The GLC were aware that their fare reduction policy would result in the council losing a material part (some £50m) of the rate support grant that would otherwise be provided by the government.

The case was heard at first instance before Lord Justice Dunn and Mr Justice Phillips. They dismissed Bromley Council's application for certiorari. Bromley LBC appealed successfully to the Court of Appeal. The GLC now appealed to the House of Lords.

Held

In approving an arbitrary reduction in fares, the GLC had acted without due regard to ordinary business principles. The power of the GLC to make grants to London Transport had been given to deal with situations such as the making good of unavoidable losses, not for the furtherance of a social policy. The burden placed on ratepayers as a result of the GLC's decision was excessive. Insufficient regard had been paid to their interests.

Lord Diplock:

'It cannot be too emphatically stated that your Lordships in this appeal are not concerned with the wisdom or, indeed, the fairness of the GLC's decision to reduce by 25 per cent the fares charged in Greater London by the London Transport Executive (LTE) which made it necessary to issue the supplementary precept, or the greater part of it. All that your Lordships are concerned with is the legality of that decision: was it within the limited powers that Parliament has conferred by statute upon the GLC?

In the argument before this House, as in the courts below, this has been treated as involving two distinct questions. These have been referred to respectively as: the question of ultra vires, which has been treated as a pure question of construction of the Transport (London) Act 1969, and the question of discretion, viz. the exercise of a statutory discretion in a manner that was unlawful under what in administrative law has become known as the Wednesbury principle stated by Lord Green MR in *Associated Provincial Picture Houses Ltd* v *Wednesbury Corporation* (1), in terms that have been frequently cited ever since. The Wednesbury principle has in turn been subjected to sub-division in the course of the argument into decisions reached in the exercise of a statutory discretion that are unlawful because it can be shown that in reaching the decision the body exercising the discretion has acted on an erroneous view of the applicable law; and decisions that, looked at objectively, are so devoid of any plausible justification that no reasonable body of persons could have reached them.

My Lords, this treatment of the "question of ultra vires" and the "question of discretion" as falling into separate compartments and limiting consideration of the construction of the statute to the former question has in my view led counsel for the contesting parties to endeavour to support extreme, though opposite, contentions as to its meaning between which it was suggested your Lordships are compelled to choose. Bromley, on the one hand, says that the GLC must so exercise its powers under the Transport (London) Act 1969, as to require the LTE to adopt a general level and structure of fares charged to passengers that will maximise its income from this source, and that the power of the GLC to make grants towards the revenue account of the LTE is limited to making good any deficit on revenue account that arises despite the charging of fares that comply with this requirement. The GLC, on the other hand, contend that the Act confers on them an almost unlimited discretion to determine, as a matter of civic policy, in what proportions the revenue needed by the LTE in order to run its passenger transport services shall be obtained (1) from fares charged to passengers, and (2) from grants made by the GLC to the LTE at the cost of the ratepayers of Greater London respectively. The discretion as to what the proportions shall be, it is contended, is unfettered except that some part, however small, so long as it is in excess of what would fall to be ignored under the de minimis rule, is met out of fares.

It may well be that one would be left with no other option than to choose between these two extreme interpretations of the language of the Transport (London) Act 1969 if the Act is looked at in isolation without regard to the legal structure and status of the GLC as a local authority and the means that are available to it for raising the moneys necessary to enable it to perform its functions. These latter considerations, which have been treated in argument as lying within the compass of the question of discretion rather than the question of ultra vires are, in my view, highly relevant to the meaning of the Act itself on any purposive construction of it. Powers to direct or approve the general level and structure of fares to be charged by the LTE for the carriage of passengers on its transport system, although unqualified by any express words in the Act, may nonetheless be subject to implied limitations when expressed to be exercisable by a local authority such as the GLC that would not be implied if those powers were exercisable, for instance, by a minister of the Crown. For the GLC to act outwith any such limitations is ultra vires; and the question of discretion is, in my view, inseparable from the question of construction.'

... The GLC, like other local authorities, is an elected body and, like most of the larger ones, membership is divided upon party lines which reflect the social policies of the major national political parties. Broadly speaking, the electors comprise all adults resident in Greater London, of whom about 40 per cent are also ratepayers. Apart from income-earning assets, the GLC's principal sources of revenue are (1) rates for which it issues precepts to the London boroughs, who are under a statutory obligation to levy rates upon the ratepayers in the amount specified in the precept, and (2) grants from central government funds. Some 62 per cent of the total amount of the income of the GLC from rates is raised from ratepayers engaged in industry, business or commerce. They have no vote as electors. These structural characteristics of the GLC need to be borne in mind in applying, as I think one must, a purposive construction to the sometimes opaque and elliptical language adopted in the Transport (London) Act 1969. Its lack of clarity is demonstrated by the fact that although the House has reached a unanimous conclusion that, taken as a whole, the language of the Act leads ineluctably to the conclusion that Parliament cannot have intended to empower the GLC and LTE to adopt the course in relation to rates and fares that is the subject to the instant appeal, I have myself reached that conclusion notwithstanding that I would ascribe to some provisions of the Act, which are the subject to close analysis in each of your Lordships' speeches, a meaning that would give to the GLC considerably wider liberty of action in determining the general level and structure of fares that are to be charged by the LTE than would be available to the GLC under the construction of the Act which your Lordships favour.

... the mere fact that a grant on revenue account is made by the GLC to the LTE to enable it to comply with a direction to reduce fares to a level at which, in the absence of the grant, its revenue account could not be maintained in balance, is not of itself sufficient to render ultra vires either the grant or a precept issued by the GLC to raise the money for the grant from rates.

This brings me back to the crucial section of the Act, s1, to see what limitations (if any) it imposes upon the choice of policy by the GLC as to the relative proportions in which the cost of running the passenger transport undertaking of the LTE is to be met out of fares paid by passengers or out of rates paid by ratepayers. Central to this question is the legal structure of the GLC and the categories of persons to whom its duties, both generally and in particular in relation to public passenger transport, are owed.

When a statute speaks, as section 1 does, of a "duty" of a local authority composed of democratically elected members, it is speaking of the collective legal duty of all those members acting through the ordinary procedure of debate and resolution, to make choices of policy and of action that they believe to be in the best interests (weighing, where necessary, one against the other) of all those categories of persons to whom their collective duty is owed. This will involve identifying the persons to whom the particular duty is owed and in the event of a conflict of interest between one category and another deciding where the balance ought to lie. In the case of public passenger transport in Greater London those categories are: (1) potential passengers by bus and train in Greater London whether resident there or not; (2) residents in Greater London, who may be assumed to derive benefit from the general mobility of people living in or within commuting distance of Greater London resulting from the availability of a public passenger transport system, even though the particular resident may happen to make little or no use of it himself; and (3) ratepayers in Greater London, to the extent that they are required to contribute to the cost of the system. These three categories overlap but do not coincide. Most persons in category (2) will also be in category (1), and it will be convenient to refer to these as "passengers", but as mentioned earlier, there is no such coincidence between either of these two categories and category (3), the ratepayers. They constitute only 40 per cent of residents and that 40 per cent bears only 38 per cent of the total burden borne by all ratepayers. The conflict of interest lies between passengers and the ratepayers.

I have left out electors as such, as constituting a separate category. A council member once elected is not the delegate of those who voted in his favour only; he is the representative of all the electors (ie adult residents) in his ward. If he fought the election on the basis of policies for the future put forward in the election manifesto of a particular political party, he presumably himself considered that in the circumstances contemplated in the manifesto those policies were in the best interest of the electors in his ward, and, if the democratic system as at present practised in local government is to survive, the fact that he received a majority of votes of those electors who took enough interest in the future policies to be adopted by the GLC to cause them to cast their votes, is a factor to which considerable weight ought to be given by him when participating in the collective duty of the GLC to decide whether to implement those policies in the circumstances that exist at the time that the decision falls to be made. That this may properly be regarded as a weighty factor is implicit in the speeches in this House in *Secretary of State for Education and Science* v *Tameside Metropolitan Borough Council* (2); although the issues dealt with in that case were very different from those arising in the present appeals. In this respect, I see no difference between those members of the GLC who are members of what as a result of the election becomes the majority party and those who are members of a minority party. In neither case when the time comes to play their part in performing the collective duty of the GLC to make choices of policy or action on particular matters, must members treat themselves as irrevocably bound to carry out pre-announced policies contained in election manifestos even though, by that time, changes of circumstances have occurred that were unforeseen when those policies were announced and would add significantly to the disadvantages that would result from carrying them out.

My Lords, the conflicting interests which the GLC had to balance in deciding whether or not to go ahead with the 25 per cent reduction in fares, notwithstanding the loss of grant from central government funds that this would entail, were those of passengers and the ratepayers. It is well established by the authorities to which my noble and learned friend, Lord Wilberforce, has already referred, that a local authority owes a fiduciary duty to the ratepayers from whom it obtains moneys needed to carry out its statutory functions, and that this includes a duty not to expend those moneys thriftlessly but to deploy the full financial resources available to it to the best advantage; the financial resources of the GLC that are relevant to the present appeals being the rate fund obtained by issuing precepts and the grants from central government respectively. The existence of this duty throws light upon the true construction of the much-debated phrase in s1(1) "integrated, efficient and economic transport facilities and services". "Economic" in this context must I think mean in the economic interests of passengers and the ratepayers looked at together, ie keeping to a minimum the total financial burden that the persons in these two categories have to share between them for the provision by the LTE in conjunction with the railways board and the bus company of an integrated and efficient public passenger transport system for Greater London. As I have already indicated I think that the GLC had a discretion as to the proportions in which that total financial burden should be allocated between passengers and the ratepayers. What are the limits of that discretion and whether those limits would have been exceeded if the only effect of the GLC's decision to instruct the LTE to lower its fares by 25 per cent had been to transfer to the ratepayers the cost (amounting to some £69M) of the financial relief that was afforded to the passengers by the lowering of the fares is a difficult question on which the arguments for and against are by no means all one way. Fortunately I do not find it necessary to decide that question in the present appeals. It does not, in my view, arise, because the GLC's decision was not simply about allocating a total financial burden between passengers and the ratepayers, it was also a decision to increase that total burden so as nearly to double it and to place the whole of the increase on the ratepayers. For, as the GLC well knew when it took the decision to reduce the fares, it would entail a loss of rate grant from central government funds amounting to some £50 million, which would have to be made good by the ratepayers as a result of the GLC's decision. So the total financial burden to be shared by passengers and the ratepayers for the provision of an integrated and efficient public passenger transport system was to be increased by an extra £50 million as a result of the decision, without any equivalent improvement in the efficiency of the system, and the whole of the extra £50 million was to be recovered from the ratepayers. That would, in my view, clearly be a thriftless use of moneys obtained by the GLC from ratepayers and a deliberate failure to deploy to the best advantage the full financial resources available to it by avoiding any action that would involve forfeiting grants from central government funds. It was thus a breach of the fiduciary duty owed by the GLC to the ratepayers. I accordingly agree with your Lordships that the precept issued pursuant to the decision was ultra vires and therefore void.

I would also have held the decision and the precept to be void upon another ground, which I can deal with briefly because I find myself in entire agreement on this aspect of the matter with the judgment of Oliver LJ in which all the relevant facts and citations from documents may be found. This ground is that in exercising the collective discretions of the GLC under s11 to direct or approve a reduction of fares by 25 per cent. the members of the majority party by whose votes the effective resolutions were passed, acted upon an erroneous view of the applicable law, in that from first to last they regarded the GLC irrevocably committed to carry out the reduction, whatever might be the additional cost to the ratepayers, because a reduction of that amount had been pre-announced in the election manifesto issued by the political party whose candidates form a majority of the members elected. For reasons that I have previously stated at some length this is erroneous in law. For the reasons that I have stated I too would dismiss these appeals.'

(1)   Supra, this chapter   (2)   Infra, this chapter

Padfield v Minister of Agriculture, Fisheries and Food [1968] AC 977 House of Lords (Lords Reid, Pearce, Hodson, Upjohn and Lord Morris of Borth-y-Gest)

Exercise of a statutory discretion so as to defeat the general purposes of the legislation is ultra vires

Facts

A milk marketing scheme had been set up under the Agricultural Marketing Act 1958. The appellants, members of SE regional committee of the Milk Marketing Board, made a complaint to the Ministry of Agriculture, Fisheries and Food pursuant to s19(3)(b) of the Agricultural Marketing Act 1958, asking that the complaint be referred to the committee of investigation established under that enactment.

Section 19 provided:

'(3) A committee of investigation shall ...

(b) be charged with the duty if the Minister in any case so directs, of considering, and reporting to the Minister on ... any complaint made to the Minister as to the operation of any scheme ...

(6) If a committee of investigation report to the Minister that any provision of a scheme or any act or omission of a board administering a scheme is contrary to the interests of consumers of the regulated product, or is contrary to the interests of any persons affecting by the scheme and is not in the public interest, the Minister, if he thinks fit to do so after considering the report:

(a) may by order make such amendments in the scheme as he considers necessary or expedient for the purpose of rectifying the matter ...'

The complaint was that the board's terms and prices for the sale of milk to the board did not take fully into account variations between producers and the cost of bringing milk to a liquid market. In effect the complaint was that the inadequate differential worked unfairly against the producers in the popular SE region where the price of land was higher.

There had been many previous requests to the board, but these had failed to get the board, on which the SE producers were in a minority, to do anything about it.

The Minister declined to refer the matter to the committee. By letters of 1 May 1964 and 23 March 1965 he gave reasons which included that (in effect) his main duty had been to decide the suitability of the complaint for such investigation but that it was one which raised wide issues and which he did not consider suitable for such investigation as it could be settled through arrangements available to producers and the board within the milk-marketing scheme; that he had unfettered discretion and that, if the complaint were upheld by the committee, he might be expected to make a statutory order to give effect to the committee's recommendations.

Held (Lord Morris of Borth-y-Gest dissenting)

The matter would be remitted to the QBD with a direction to require the Minister to consider the appellants complaint according to law for the following reasons:

a) (per Lord Reid, and Lord Pearce) where a statute conferring a discretion on a Minister to exercise or not to exercise a power did not expressly limit or define the extent of his discretion and did not require him to give reasons for declining to exercise the power, his discretion must nevertheless be limited to the extent that it must not be so used, whether by reason of misconstruction of the statute or other reason as to frustrate the objects of the statute which conferred it.

b) (per Lord Hodson and Lord Upjohn) although the Minister had full or unfettered discretion under s19(3) of the Agricultural Marketing Act 1958 he was bound to exercise it lawfully, viz, not to misdirect himself in law, nor to take into account irrelevant matters, nor to omit relevant matters from consideration.

c) The complaint in the present case was a substantial and genuine complaint, neither frivolous, repetitive nor vexatious; the reason of the Minister for not referring the matter to the committee of investigation (viz that the complaint raised wide issues, that his discretion was unfettered so that, in effect, it was sufficient that he should bone fide have considered the matter) were not good reasons in law and indeed left out of account the merits of the complaint which was a relevant consideration and showed that he was not exercising his discretion in accordance with the intention of s19 of the Act of 1958. Thus the Minister had misdirected himself as to the true legal effect of s19 and had exercised his discretion so as to defeat the general purposes of the legislation which included the establishment of machinery for investigating and determining whether the scheme was operating contrary to the public interest and the possibility (under s19(6)) of the Minister amending or revoking such a scheme where he thought fit for the purpose of rectifying this.

Lord Reid:

'The question at issue in this appeal is the nature and extent of the Minister's duty under s19(3)(b) of the Act of 1958 in deciding whether to refer to the committee of investigation a complaint as to the operation of any scheme made by persons adversely affected by the scheme. The respondent contends that his only duty is to consider a complaint fairly and that he is given an unfettered discretion with regard to every complaint either to refer it or not to refer it to the committee as he may think fit. The appellants contend that it is his duty to refer every genuine and substantial complaint, or alternatively that his discretion is not unfettered and that in this case he failed to exercise his discretion according to law because his refusal was caused or influenced by his having misdirected himself in law or by his having taken into account extraneous or irrelevant considerations.

In my view, the appellants' first contention goes too far. There are a number of reasons which would justify the Minister in refusing to refer a complaint. For example, he might consider it more suitable for arbitration, or he might consider that in an earlier case the committee of investigation had already rejected a substantially similar complaint, or he might think the complaint to be frivolous or vexatious. So he must have at least some measure of discretion. But is it unfettered?

It is implicit in the argument for the Minister that there are only two possible interpretations of this provision - either he must refer every complaint or he has an unfettered discretion to refuse to refer in any case. I do not think that is right. Parliament must have conferred the discretion with the intention that it should be used to promote the policy and objects of the Act; the policy and objects of the Act must be determined by construing the Act as a whole and construction is always a matter of law for the court. In a matter of this kind it is not possible to draw a hard and fast line, but if the Minister, by reason of his having misconstrued the Act or for any other reason, so uses his discretion as to thwart or run counter to the policy and objects of the Act, then our law would be very defective if persons aggrieved were not entitled to the protection of the court. So it is necessary first to construe to the Act.

When these provisions were first enacted in 1931 it was unusual for Parliament to compel people to sell their commodities in a way to which they objected and it was easily foreseeable that any such scheme would cause loss to some producers. Moreover, if the operation of the scheme was put in the hands of the majority of the producers, distributors or a minority of the producers. So it is not surprising that Parliament enacted safeguards.

The approval of Parliament shows that this scheme was thought to be in the public interest, and in so far as it necessarily involved detriment to some persons, it must have been thought to be in the public interest that they should suffer it. But in sections 19 and 20 Parliament drew a line. They provide machinery for investigating and determining whether the scheme is operating or the board is acting in a manner contrary to the public interest ...

I must now examine the Minister's reasons for refusing to refer the appellants' complaint to the committee ...

The first reason which the Minister gave in his letter of 23 March 1965, was that this complaint was unsuitable for investigation because it raised wide issues. Here it appears to me that the Minister has clearly misdirected himself. Section 19(6) contemplates the raising of issues so wide that it may be necessary for the Minister to amend a scheme or even to revoke it. Narrower issues may be suitable for arbitration but section 19 affords the only method of investigating wide issues. In my view it is plainly the intention of the Act that even the widest issues should be investigated if the complaint is genuine and substantial, as this complaint certainly is ...

It was argued that the Minister is not bound to give any reasons for refusing to refer a complaint to the committee, that if he gives no reasons his decision cannot be questioned, and that it would be very unfortunate if giving reasons were to put him in a worse position. But I do not agree that a decision cannot be questioned if no reasons are given. If it is the Minister's duty not to act so as to frustrate the policy and objects of the Act, and if it were to appear from all the circumstances of the case that that has been the effect of the Minister's refusal, then it appears to me that the court must be entitled to act ...

As the Minister's discretion has never been properly exercised according to law, I would not allow this appeal. It appears to me that the case should now be remitted to the Queen's Bench Division with a direction to require the Minister to consider the complaint of the appellants according to law.'

Lord Pearce:

'It was obvious that the scheme and the Agricultural Marketing Act 1958, created a monopoly and imposed severe restrictions on individuals' liberty of action. With the aim of general betterment Parliament was interfering with the individual farmer's method of earning a livelihood and subjecting him to the mercies of the majority rule of the board; but (no doubt with these considerations in mind) Parliament deliberately imposed certain safeguards. Two independent committees must be appointed. (Section 19) ... The independent committee of investigation ... was ... a deliberate safeguard against injustices that might arise from the operation of the scheme ...

The appellants have ... no avenue for their complaint except through s19 and that section makes access to the committee of investigation dependent on a direction of the Minister to the committee of investigation. There is no provision as to what are the duties of a Minister in this respect. Has he a duty to further complaints of substance which have no other outlet? Or can he refuse them any outlet at all if he so chooses? Need he have any valid reason for doing so? Or if he refuses without any apparent justification, is he exempt from any interference by the courts provided that he either gives no reasons which are demonstrably bad or gives no reason at all? No express answer to these questions is given in the Act. The intention, therefore, must be implied from its provisions and its structure ...

It is quite clear from the Act that the Minister is intended to have some duty in the matter. It is conceded that he must properly consider the matter. He cannot throw it into the waste-paper basket unread. He cannot simply say (however honestly) "I think that in general the investigation of complaints has a disruptive effect on the scheme" ... An independent committee, set up for the purpose, should investigate grievances and ... their report should be available to Parliament.

The fact that the complaint raises wide issues and affects other regions was not a good ground for denying it an investigation by the committee. It is a matter which makes it very suitable for the committee of investigation, with its duty to report on the public interest and its capacity to hear representatives of all the regions ... A general abdication of that power and duty would not be in accord with Parliament's intention.'

Lord Upjohn:

'... My Lords, I believe that the introduction of the adjective "unfettered" and its reliance thereon as an answer to the appellants' claim is one of the fundamental matters confounding the Minister's attitude, bona fide though it be. First, the adjective nowhere appears in section 19. It is an unauthorised gloss by the Minister. Secondly, even if the section did contain that adjective, I doubt if it would make any difference in law to his powers, save to emphasise what he has already, namely that acting lawfully he has a power of decision which cannot be controlled by the courts; it is unfettered. But the use of that adjective, even in an Act of Parliament, can do nothing to unfetter the control which the judiciary have over the executive, namely that in exercising their powers the latter must act lawfully, and that is a matter to be determined by looking at the Act and its scope and object in conferring a discretion on the Minister rather than by the use of adjectives ...

Mr Kirk's letter ... contained this paragraph: "3. In considering how to exercise his discretion, the Minister would, amongst other things, address his mind to the possibility that if a complaint were so referred and the committee were to uphold it, he in turn would be expected to make a statutory order to give effect to the committee's recommendations ..." This fear of Parliamentary trouble (for in my opinion this must be the scarcely veiled meaning of this letter) if an enquiry were ordered and its possible results is alone sufficient to vitiate the Minister's decision which, as I have stated earlier, can never validly turn on purely political considerations; he must be prepared to face the music in Parliament if statute has cast on him an obligation in the proper exercise of a discretion conferred on him to order a reference to the committee of investigation.'

Pickwell v Camden London Borough Council [1983] 2 WLR 583 Queen's Bench Division (Ormrod LJ and Forbes J)

Unreasonableness and the effect of special circumstances

Facts

Manual workers employed by Camden London Borough Council ('the council') went on indefinite strike in February 1979. The council negotiated a pay deal with their employees in order to get them to return to work which was more generous than that achieved by local authority manual workers elsewhere in the country. At the next round of national pay negotiations for such workers an agreement was reached that they should have a £5 - £7 pay increase. The council agreed to pay this to its own workers even though they were already earning more than their counterparts elsewhere in the country. Mr Pickwell, the District Auditor, acting under s161(1) Local Government Act 1972, applied to the court for a declaration that this payment was contrary to law.

Held

Given the severity of the disruption caused by the strike it could not be said that the actions of the council were actions that no reasonable authority would have taken. The application was dismissed.

Ormrod LJ:

'In his affidavit Mr Pickwell relies primarily on the headnote to *Roberts* v *Hopwood* (1), which he quotes in full, and submits, in substance, that payments by Camden in excess of the national rate, as fixed either by the National Joint Council (NJC) or in the Clegg report, increased by 15 per cent to allow for local conditions, were excessive and so contrary to law. Mr Widdicombe, in argument on his behalf, relied chiefly on *Associated Provincial Picture Houses Ltd* v *Wednesbury Corporation* (2), on the basis that the respondents must have taken into account matters which they ought not to have taken into account, or must have failed to take into account matters which they ought to have taken into account, with the consequence that their decision to pay wages at the rates fixed by the resolution of 7 March 1979, was contrary to law. Alternatively, he submitted that the decision was one to which no reasonable authority could ever have come, and so was contrary to law.

Mr Henderson, for Camden, and Mr Scrivener, for the individual councillors, who are respondents to this application, while challenging the district auditor's assessment of the facts of the case, go further and submit that neither *Roberts* v *Hopwood* nor the *Wednesbury* case, when analysed, support the propositions of law on which the district auditor's case is based. They contend that a decision of a local authority can only be said to be "contrary to law," in a case of this kind, if it can be established that the local authority has in some way exceeded or abused its statutory powers, or the discretion given to it by statute; in other words, that it has acted ultra vires. They argue that excessive expenditure on a lawful object, or a failure to take relevant matters into account, or the taking into account of irrelevant matters is, in effect, evidence that the local authority has, or may have, acted ultra vires and, therefore, contrary to law, but does not amount in itself to illegality. In other words, there may be a failure to comply with Lord Greene MR's formula, or undoubtedly extravagant expenditure, without rendering the decision of the action of the local authority "contrary to law". However, some actions or decisions may be so far out of line with the "norm," or so self-evidently erroneous, that the court may be justified in drawing the inference that the local authority has purported to use the discretion given to it for one purpose, in reality to achieve an ulterior or collateral objective which is ultra vires. This argument directs attention to the quality or character of the decision itself, rather than to the methods by which it is reached.

In my judgment, this is the proper way to approach the question of whether an item of expenditure is "contrary to law". But there is a growing tendency to treat particular expressions used by judges in their judgments, taken out of context, as if they were propositions of law in themselves. This is especially true of the concluding passage in Lord Greene MR's judgment in the *Wednesbury* case (2), which is frequently cited without reference to the body of the judgment, and is coming to be regarded as a proposition of law in itself. This is a process which Frankfurter J once described in these words:

> "A phrase begins life as a literary expression; its felicity leads to its lazy repetition; and repetition soon establishes it as a legal formula, indiscriminately used to express different and sometimes contradictory ideas." (*Tiller* v *Atlantic Coast Line Railroad Co* (3))

With that warning in mind, I turn to the authorities, and in particular to *Roberts* v *Hopwood* (1).

The latest case is *Bromley London Borough Council* v *Greater London Council* (4). This again was an ultra vires case which involved difficult questions of construction of some obscurely worded statutory provisions. It turned, primarily, on statutory interpretation. The lengthy judgments are a mine of felicitous "literary expressions", but the ratio decidendi was that the statutory powers of the GLC did not extend far enough to enable them to institute, at the cost of the ratepayers, a very heavily subsidised fare structure for London Transport. In so far as the speeches in the House of Lords dealt with the question of discretion, they affirmed Jenkins LJ's opinion in *Prescott* v *Birmingham Corporation* (5), that local authorities owe a fiduciary duty to their ratepayers. As in Prescott's case, the existence of this duty was a relevant factor to be taken into account in determining the ambit of the statutory powers. However, it would not be right to regard this case as authority for the general proposition that this fiduciary duty opens up a route by which the courts can investigate and, if thought appropriate, interfere with any exercise of their discretionary powers by local authorities. This would completely undermine the principles of the *Wednesbury* case (2), and make nonsense of Diplock LJ's definition of the court's powers in *Luby* v *Newcastle-under-Lyme Corporation* (6).

In my judgment, therefore, if the district auditor is to succeed in his application for a declaration that Camden's expenditure, arising from their decision to pay their manual workers a minimum wage of £60 per week for a 35-hour week, was "contrary to law", he must establish that Camden was acting in excess of its statutory powers. There are only two ways by which this could be done in this case. The first is by showing that the decision was not, in reality, a decision made in the exercise of their statutory power to fix wage rates, but for some other extraneous, irrelevant, or collateral purpose, for example, to undermine the incomes policy, or to sabotage, for political purposes, the national negotiations which were proceeding simultaneously, or to achieve some other social or political objective. The second is by satisfying the court that no reasonable local authority would have made such a decision in the circumstances prevailing in Camden in February and March 1979.

The first of these alternatives has never been put forward by, or on behalf of, the district auditor, and it is right to say in the clearest terms that there is no evidence at all that Camden, or the respondent councillors, had any extraneous objective in mind. All the evidence shows that their sole purpose was to settle as quickly as possible a strike which was having a very serious effect on the inhabitants of the borough.

The second requires rather more consideration because the wage settlement undoubtedly involved a very large and immediate increase in the wages to be paid to the manual workers. The district auditor has expressed the opinion that the settlement was unreasonably high. His figures are challenged by Camden in various ways, but on any view, the increase was large, and from NUPE's point of view, the outcome of the strike was probably more favourable than they expected. But the question for this court is not whether Camden made a bad bargain for the ratepayers, or were precipitate in making the offer to the strikers, or could have achieved a cheaper settlement by waiting, or made a better bargain by different tactics. These are matters for the electorate at the next election. The question for the court is whether the evidence establishes that no reasonable local authority could have made a settlement on such terms. So to hold would require a detailed appraisal of the state of affairs in Camden in February and March 1979, comparisons with the experiences of other boroughs, and of prevailing wage rates in comparable jobs in other sectors, all of which would have to be related to the crisis which plainly existed, and in the midst of which the decision was made. The evidence before the court is, in my judgment, quite insufficient to permit the court to make any such finding of fact, which would require clear and compelling evidence, that is, assuming that the court could properly make such a finding on purely quantitative, as opposed to qualitative grounds. Such a conclusion, as Lord Greene MR recognised in the *Wednesbury* case (2), would have to amount almost to a finding that Camden and the councillors must have acted in bad faith.

Some reliance was also placed on the fiduciary duty owed by Camden to its ratepayers, but this line of attack must have a very limited application, if any, in a case in which the local authority had ample authority to determine wage rates, were genuinely acting on that authority, and on their appreciation of the problems and conditions with which they were confronted. The fiduciary duty, as I understand it, arises because councillors are entrusted with ratepayers' money to use it for duly, that is legally, authorised purposes and not otherwise, much as trustees hold the trust fund, to apply it for the purposes authorised by the trust instrument, or by statute, as the case may be.

My conclusion, therefore, is that these items of expenditure were not contrary to law, and it is not for this court to pass judgment on the wisdom or unwisdom of the wage settlement of March 1979. The application, therefore, fails.'

(1)   Infra, this chapter

(2)   Supra, this chapter

(3)   (1943) 318 US 54

(4)   Supra, this chapter

(5)   [1955] Ch 210

(6)   [1964] 2 QB 64

Roberts v Hopwood [1925] AC 578 House of Lords (Lords Sumner, Atkinson, Buckmaster, Wrenbury and Carson)

Failing to take into account relevant considerations/taking into account irrelevant considerations making acts ultra vires

Facts

Under s62 of the Metropolis Management Act 1855, the Poplar Borough Council was authorised to employ such servants as might be necessary and to allow them 'such ... wages as the (Council) may think fit'. In the exercise of this power the Council fixed the minimum wage for its lowest grade of employees, whether men or women, at £4 per week. This was the same rate that it had fixed for the previous year even though the cost of living had fallen from 176 per cent to 82 per cent above the pre-war level. In its view this was the minimum wage that a local authority ought, as a model employer, to pay its employees, and it had stated at the last election that this would be its policy if it were elected. The accounts of the Council were subject to audit by the District Auditor who was required by s247(7) of the Public Health Act 1875, to disallow any item contrary to law and to surcharge it on the person making or authorising the payment. He decided that the wages were so excessive as to be illegal and were not wages but gifts. Using the pre-war wages paid by the Council as a starting point he added an increase proportionate to the increase in the cost of living and a further £1 by way of margin and surcharged the excess, amounting to £5,000, on the councillors responsible.

Section 247(8) of the Public Health Act provided that councillors aggrieved by an auditor's decision could apply by way of certiorari to the Divisional Court. This they did. The Divisional Court (Lord Hewart CJ, Sankey and Salter JJ) upheld the auditor. Their decision was reversed by the Court of Appeal. (Scrutton and Atkin LJJ, Bankes LJ dissenting.)

Held

The phrase 'such ... wages as the (Council) may think fit' in the legislation did not mean that the Council could pay its employees wages of any amount it pleased. In deciding how much to pay it was not entitled to take into account the abstract social or political ideal that the dignity of adult labour requires at least a £4 a week wage regardless either of cost of living or the level of wages generally. In doing so it had taken into account an irrelevant consideration and omitted relevant considerations, i.e. ordinary economic considerations. The auditor's decision should be upheld since the excess payments were ultra vires the power of the local Council since they were based on principles that it was not open it to local council to take into account and in order to achieve objectives not permitted by the relevant legislation.

Lord Sumner:

'Much was said at the Bar about the wide discretion conferred by the Local Government Acts on local authorities. In a sense this is true, but the meaning of the term needs careful examination. What has been said in cases, which lie outside the provisions as to audit altogether, is not necessarily applicable to matters, which are concerned with the expenditure of public money. There are many matters, which the Courts are indisposed to question. Though they are the ultimate judges of what is lawful and what is unlawful to borough councils, they often accept the decisions of the local authority simply because they are themselves ill-equipped to weigh the merits of one solution of a practical question as against another. This, however, is not a recognition of the absolute character of the local authority's discretion, but of the limits within which it is practicable to question it. There is nothing about a borough council that corresponds to autonomy. It has great responsibilities, but the limits of its powers and of its independence are such as the law, mostly statutory, may have laid down, and there is no presumption against the accountability of the authority. Everything depends on the construction of the sections applicable ...

Their reason the respondents give as follows: "The Council did not and does not take the view that wages paid should be exclusively related to the cost of living. They have from time to time carefully considered the question of the wages and are of the opinion as a matter of policy that a public authority should be a model employer and that a minimum rate of £4 is the least wage which ought to be paid to an adult having regard to the efficiency of their workpeople, the duty of a public authority both to the ratepayer and to its employees, the purchasing power of the wages and other considerations which are relevant to their decision as to wages."

From this carefully considered answer I think it is plain that the respondents have deliberately decided not to be guided by ordinary economic (and economical) considerations. The first sentence above

CONSTITUTIONAL AND ADMINISTRATIVE LAW

quoted means that, when the cost of living passes £4 a week, the rate of wages paid will follow it upwards, but, however it may fall, the £4 rate will be stabilised and will stand ...

I express no opinion as to the merits of this view, that the dignity of adult labour requires at least £4 wage, nor has the honesty of those who entertain it been questioned, but I think it is plain that such a course, whether it be ideal or social or political or all three, forms no part of the conduct, as ordinarily understood, of such practical enterprises as borough councils are by statute authorised to engage in. No authority and no statutory provision was cited to your Lordships, which enables a borough council to give practical affect, at the ratepayers' expense, to such an abstract resolution, nor am I for my own part aware of any. I am, therefore, of opinion that on their own showing the respondents have exercised such discretion as the Metropolis Management act gives to the council in the matter of wages upon principles which are not open to the council, and for objects which are beyond their powers. Their exercise of those powers was examinable by the auditor, and on the above grounds the excess expenditure was liable to be disallowed by him as contrary to law ...'

Lord Atkinson:

'... in paragraph 9 of Mr Scurr's affidavit he ... said that they (i.e. the council) ... were of opinion that a public authority should be a model employer, and that a minimum rate of £4 per week (ie £208 per annum) is the least wage which ought to be paid to an adult ... This ... might possibly be admirably philanthropic if the funds of the council at the time they were thus administered belonged to the existing members of that body. These members would then be generous at their own expense ... The indulgence of philanthropic enthusiasm at the expense of persons other than the philanthropists is an entirely different thing from the indulgence of it at the expense of the philanthropists themselves ... A body charged with the administration for definite purposes of funds contributed in whole or in part by persons other than the members of that body owes, in my view, a duty to those latter persons to conduct that administration in a fairly businesslike manner with reasonable care, skill and caution, and with a due and alert regard to the interest of those contributors who are not members of the body. Towards these latter persons the body stands somewhat in the position of trustees or managers of the property of others. This duty is, I think, a legal duty as well as a moral one ...

At the meeting on 31 May 1923, at which a large number of ratepayers attended and objected to the allowance of such large sums of wages, it was apparently put forward that the council were only responsible to their constituents; that the scale of wages had been before the electors at the election in the previous November, and also at two recent bye-elections, and had been approved of by them; that the council should do their duty towards these electors, and not their duty towards the large ratepayers who lived outside the district and were not "in" (ie parties to, I presume) this matter at all. A gentleman named LW Key, one of the applicants in the present suit, appears from the auditor's affidavit to have put the council's case pithily and plainly in the following few words:

"We do not say we have no discretion but we say a mandate from the electorate was not to be despised."

I think the appeal succeeds.'

Secretary of State for Education and Science v Tameside Metropolitan Borough Council [1976] 3 WLR 641 House of Lords (Lords Wilberforce, Diplock, Salmon, Russell and Vixount Dilhorne)

Ultra vires unreasonableness and abuse of power

Facts

In November 1975 the Secretary of State for Education and Science ('the Minister') approved a scheme submitted by Tameside Metropolitan Borough Council ('the Council') for the comprehensivisation of the schools within its area. The scheme was to come into effect in September 1976. In May 1976 local elections were held in Tameside, and political control of the Council passed from the Labour party to the Conservatives. The Conservatives had campaigned on a policy of reversing the proposed change over to comprehensive. In June 1976 the Minister, acting under s68 of the Education Act 1944, which states:

'If the Secretary of State is satisfied, either on complaint by any person or otherwise, that any local education authority or the managers or governors of any county or voluntary school have acted or are proposing to act unreasonably with respect to the exercise of any power conferred or the performance of any duty imposed by or under this Act, he may, notwithstanding any enactment rendering the exercise of the power or the performance of the duty contingent upon the opinion of the authority or of the managers or governors, give such directions as to the exercise of the power or the performance of the duty as appear to him to be expedient ...'

directed the Council to give effect to the scheme approved in 1975. The Council refused to comply with this directive, and the Minister applied for an order of mandamus ordering the Council to comply. The Divisional Court felt that there was evidence before the Minister that the Council was proposing to act unreasonably and granted the order sought. This decision was reversed by the Court of Appeal who considered fresh evidence indicating that schools could be changed back to the selective system before September 1976 without too much disruption. The Minister appealed to the House of Lords.

Held

The appeal would be dismissed. There was insufficient evidence for the Minister's view that the Council was proposing to act unreasonably, in the sense that the change of educational policy at such a late stage would cause chaos and confusion. In any event, the parents must have been mindful of such possibilities when they voted for the policy of the Conservatives. Simply because the Minister disagreed with the Council's policy did not mean that it was necessarily unreasonable.

Lord Wilberforce (His Lordship considered s68 of the 1944 Act, and continued):

'Analysis of the section brings out three cardinal points.

(1) The matters with which the section is concerned are primarily matters of educational administration. The action which the Secretary of State is entitled to stop is unreasonable action with respect to the exercise of a power or the performance of a duty - the power and the duty of the authority are presupposed and cannot be interfered with. Local education authorities are entitled under the Act to have a policy, and this section does not enable the Secretary of State to require them to abandon or reverse a policy just because the Secretary of State disagrees with it. Specifically, the Secretary of State cannot use power under this section to impose a general policy of comprehensive education in their area, and if they have done so he cannot direct them to implement it. If he tries to use a direction under s68 for this purpose, his direction would be clearly invalid. A direction under s68 must be justified on the ground of unreasonable action in doing what under the Act the local authority is entitled to do, and under the Act it has a freedom of choice. I do not think that there is any controversy upon these propositions.

The critical question in this case, and it is not an easy one, is whether, on a matter which appears to be one of educational administration, namely whether the change of course proposed by the council in May 1976 would lead to educational chaos or undue disruption, the Secretary of State's judgment can be challenged.

(2) The section is framed in a "subjective" form - if the Secretary of State "is satisfied." This form of section is quite well known, and at first sight might seem to exclude judicial review. Sections in this form may, no doubt, exclude judicial review on what is or has become a matter of pure judgment. But I do not think that they go further than that. If a judgment requires, before it can be made, the existence of some facts, then, although the evaluation of

those facts is for the Secretary of State alone, the court must inquire whether those facts exist, and have been taken into account, whether the judgment has been made upon a proper self-direction as to those facts, whether the judgment has not been made upon other facts which ought not to have been taken into account. If these requirements are not met, then the exercise of judgment, however bona fide it may be, becomes capable of challenge: see S*ecretary of State for Employment* v *ASLEF (No 2)* (1), per Lord Denning MR at p 493.

(3)   The section has to be considered within the structure of the Act. In many statutes a minister or other authority is given a discretionary power and in these cases the court's power to review any exercise of the discretion, though still real, is limited. In these cases it is said that the courts cannot substitute their opinion for that of the minister: they can interfere on such grounds as that the minister has acted right outside his powers or outside the purpose of the Act, or unfairly, or upon an incorrect basis of fact.

But there is no universal rule as to the principles on which the exercise of a discretion may be reviewed: each statute or type of statute must be individually looked at. This Act, of 1944, is quite different from those which simply create a ministerial discretion. The Secretary of State, under s68, is not merely exercising a discretion: he is reviewing the action of another public body which itself has discretionary powers and duties. He, by contrast with the courts in the normal case, may substitute his opinion for that of the authority: this is what the section allows, but he must take account of what the authority, under the statute, is entitled to do. The authority - this is vital - is itself elected, and is given specific powers as to the kind of schools it wants in its area. Therefore two situations may arise. One is that there may be a difference of policy between the Secretary of State (under Parliament) and the local authority: the section gives no power to the Secretary of State to make his policy prevail. The other is that, owing to the democratic process involving periodic elections, abrupt reversals of policy may take place, particularly where there are only two parties and the winner takes all. Any reversal of policy if at all substantial must cause some administrative disruption - this was as true of the 1975 proposals as those of the respondents. So the mere possibility, or probability, of disruption cannot be a ground for issuing a direction to abandon the policy. What the Secretary of State is entitled, by a direction if necessary, to ensure is that such disruptions are not "unreasonable," ie, greater than a body, elected to carry out a new programme, with which the Secretary of State may disagree, ought to impose upon those for whom it is responsible. After all, those who voted for the new programme, involving a change of course, must also be taken to have accepted some degree of disruption in implementing it.

The ultimate question in this case, in my opinion, is whether the Secretary of State has given sufficient, or any, weight to this particular factor in the exercise of his judgment.'

After further considering evidence as to the viability of the Council's plans to revert to a selective secondary school system, his Lordship concluded:

'To rephrase the question: on 11 June 1976, (this is the date of the direction, and we are not entitled to see what happened thereafter) could it be said that the authority was acting unreasonably in proceeding with a selection procedure which was otherwise workable in face of the possibility of persistent opposition by teachers' unions and individual teachers, or would the only (not "the more") reasonable course have been for the authority to abandon its plans? This is, I think, the ultimate factual question in the case. And I think that it must be answered in the negative ie, that it could not be unreasonable, in June 1976, and assuming that the Secretary of State did not interfere, for the authority to put forward a plan to act on its approved procedure. The teachers, after all, are public servants, with responsibility for their pupils. They were under a duty to produce reports. These reports and the records in the primary schools are public property. I do not think that it could be unreasonable not ("was unreasonable") for the authority to take the view that if the Secretary of State did not intervene under his statutory powers the teachers would cooperate in working the authority's procedure - procedure which had, in similar form, been operated in part of this very area. On the whole case, I come to the conclusion that the Secretary of State, real though his difficulties were, fundamentally misconceived and misdirected himself as to the proper manner in which to regard the proposed action of the Tameside authority after the local election of May 1976: that if he had exercised his judgment on the basis of the factual situation in which this newly elected authority was placed - with a policy approved by its electorate, and massively supported by the parents - there was no ground however much he might disagree with the new policy, and regret such administrative dislocation as was brought about by the change - upon which he could find that the authority was acting or proposing to act unreasonably. In my opinion the judgments in the Court of Appeal were right and the appeal must be dismissed.'

(1)   [1972] 2 QB 455

11.2   Ensuring adherence to express statutory requirements

Coney v Choyce [1975] 1 WLR 422   Queen's Bench Division (Templeman J)

Procedural ultra vires does not apply to minor infringements

Facts

Regulation 2 of the County and Voluntary Schools (Notices) Regulations 1968, issued pursuant to s13 of the Education Act 1944, required the posting of notices in the vicinity of schools which were to be re-organised under a policy of comprehensivisation. In the case of two schools, the requisite notices had not been posted. The plaintiff claimed that the Secretary of State could not validly approve the comprehensivisation because of the failure to follow the required procedure.

Held

The procedural requirement of giving notice had been substantially complied with, and there was no evidence of anyone suffering substantial prejudice as a result, hence the Secretary of State's action was lawful.

Templeman J:

'Mr Harvey (for the defendants) does not dispute that if this had been a case where the failure to comply with the regulations had been deliberate; or if the breaches of the regulations were such that when the Secretary of State purported to approve the proposals she did not have before her the necessary information regarding the actual objections, or as to the weight of possible objections, then it would have been impossible for the Secretary of State validly to consider the proposals or validly to approve them. Her purported approval would be a nullity, vitiated by the fact that she was never in a position to do her duty - namely, to consider the proposals in the light of the objections. But that, says Mr Harvey, is not the case here; and I agree.

Now in those circumstances a suggested test, which Mr Harvey adopted and put forward, and with which, as a test, Mr Hames did not quarrel - although of course he disputed the consequence of applying the test - is to be found in de Smith, Judicial Review of Administrative Action, 3rd ed. (1973), 122. After hinting that the law might have been in a bit of a mess, he continues:

"When Parliament prescribes the manner or form in which a duty is to be performed or a power exercised, it seldom lays down what will be the legal consequences of failure to observe its prescriptions."

That describes the present case. Parliament has prescribed the manner in which the duty of giving public notices is to be performed, but it has not specified the consequences of failure. It has not said if the regulations are not carried out then the approval is invalid. It has left the result unspecified and in those circumstances I go back to de Smith; who says at p123:

> "The courts must therefore formulate their own criteria for determining whether the procedural rules are to be regarded as mandatory, in which case disobedience will render void or voidable what has been done, or as directory, in which case disobedience will be treated as an irregularity not affecting the validity of what has been done (though in some cases it has been said that there must be 'substantial compliance' with the statutory provisions if the deviation is to be excused as a mere irregularity). Judges have often stressed the impracticability of specifying exact rules for the assignment of a procedural provision to the appropriate category. The whole scope and purpose of the enactment must be considered, and one must assess 'the importance of the provision that has been disregarded, and the relation of that provision to the general object intended to be secured by the Act.' Furthermore, much may depend upon the particular circumstances of the case in hand. Although 'nullification is the natural and usual consequence of disobedience,' breach of procedural or formal rules is likely to be treated as a mere irregularity if the departure from the terms of the Act is of a trivial nature, or if no substantial prejudice has been suffered by those for whose benefit the requirements were introduced, or if serious public inconvenience would be caused by holding them to be mandatory, or if the court is for any reason disinclined to interfere with the act or decision that is impugned."

I accept that test, and applying it, here is an Act, which is concerned with the administration of education in which, as has been seen in the present case, the ramifications can be considerable as regards different areas and as regards a host of children. It would in my judgment be lamentable if the carrying out of the purposes of the Education Act 1944 (as amended) were hampered by a strict insistence on the letter of the regulations being carried out subject to the dire penalty of the whole thing being invalid. In my judgment, this is a case where the regulations must be treated as directory. Both the object and the terms of the regulations themselves seem to me to support that, and the consequences of the contrary also seem to me to require it.

I accept there must be substantial compliance with the regulations, and in my judgment there has been. Asking myself whether any substantial prejudice has been suffered by those for whose benefit the requirements were introduced, I am quite satisfied the answer is "No." The plaintiffs, having lost the battle on the merits, are now fighting a battle purely on the technicalities. I make no criticism. If the Education Act 1944 is so full of technicalities that the proposals can be tripped up, well, the plaintiffs are entitled to do just that. But in my judgment this is not an Act where Parliament intended that the technicalities should rule rather than the spirit of the law. The object of section 13 has been achieved, and in those circumstances it seems to me that it would be quite wrong to hold that the technical defects in compliance with the regulations make the Minister's approval invalid.'

Cullimore v Lyme Regis Corporation [1962] 1 QB 718 Queen's Bench Division (Edmund-Davies J)

Where the administrator fails to observe a specified procedure his acts are ultra vires

Facts

On 8 December 1952 a borough council, as coast protection authority, prepared a works scheme for carrying out coast protection work under s6 of the Coast Protection Act 1949, which was duly approved by the Minister. The scheme designated the contributory land in respect of which coast protection charges were payable pursuant to s7(1) of the Act. Section 7(4) and (5) provided as follows:

> '... (1) A works scheme which provides for the levying of coast protection charges shall either:

(a) ...

or (b) state that the authority by whom the scheme is prepared will, within such period after the completion of the work as may be specified in the scheme, determine the interests in land by references to which coast protection charges are to be levied and, in the case of each of those interests, the amount of the charge leviable in respect thereof ... (5) Where a works scheme contains such a statement as is mentioned in paragraph (b) of the last foregoing subsection, the authority may, at any time within the period specified in the scheme, determine the charges to be levied thereunder as mentioned in that paragraph and shall serve on each person upon whom a charge is leviable under the scheme a notice containing full particulars of their determination as to all the charges to be so levied.'

The scheme stated a six-month period under s7(4)(6). In fact the Council did not determine the interests and the amount of charges leviable until 23 months after completion of the work and one month later purported to serve a notice on the plaintiff under s7(5) that the charge for which he would be responsible amounted to £425. The plaintiff sought declarations that the determination as to charges was ultra vires, null, void and of no effect; that the notice served on him was invalid; and that in the circumstances no charges were leviable on, payable by, or due from him to the council.

Held

The Council in formulating the works scheme was exercising statutory powers and not merely performing statutory duties, and it was obligatory therefore for them to comply strictly with the mandatory provisions of s7(5). Thus the purported determination after 23 months was null and void, and the plaintiff was entitled to the declarations sought.

Even if the Council had not been exercising statutory powers but merely performing statutory duties so that the provisions as to the manner of their exercise were to be regarded as directory only, there had not, on the facts, been anything amounting to substantial compliance with those directions and substantial compliance as least was required even if the provisions were directory only.

Edmund-Davies J:

'... This case involves a short point which to my way of thinking presents no great difficulty. The conclusion I have quite firmly come to is that the plaintiff is entitled to each and every one of the declarations he has asked for. In coming to that conclusion, I have directed myself, as Denman J did in *Caldow* v *Pixell* that, in determining the sort of questions which are raised by these proceedings, the whole scope and object of the particular piece of legislation under consideration requires to be looked at, and I accordingly turn to consider the Act of Parliament, the Coast Protection Act 1949, with which we are here concerned, though fortunately not with every portion of that Act of Parliament ...

Other cases may provide some assistance in determining what the general principles to be applied are, and those general principles are conveniently stated in summary form in *Maxwell on Interpretation of Statutes*, 10th ed (1953) p376 et seq. I quote therefrom certain passages.

"It has been said that no rule can be laid down for determining whether the command is to be considered as a mere direction or instruction involving no invalidating consequences in its disregard or as imperative, with an implied nullification for disobedience, beyond the fundamental one that it depends on the scope and object of the enactment ... A strong line of distinction may be drawn between cases where the prescriptions of the Act affect the performance of a duty and where they relate to a privilege or power. Where powers, rights or immunities are granted with a direction that certain regulations, formalities or conditions shall be complied with, it seems neither unjust nor inconvenient to exact a rigorous observance of them as essential to the acquisition of the right or authority conferred, and it is therefore probable that such was the intention of the legislature. But when a public duty is imposed and the statute requires that it shall be performed in a certain manner, or within a certain time, or under other specified conditions, such prescriptions may well be regarded as intended to be directory only in cases when injustice or inconvenience to others who have no control over those exercising the duty would result if such requirements were essential and imperative."

and, a little later, quoting from a judgment of Sir Arthur Channell, in *Montreal Street Railway Co* v *Normandin*, Maxwell (at p381) continues:

"On the other hand, where the prescriptions of a statute relate to the performance of a public duty and where the invalidation of acts done in neglect of them would work serious general inconvenience or injustice to persons who have no control over those entrusted with the duty without promoting the essential aims of the legislature, such prescriptions seem to be generally understood as mere instructions for the guidance and government of those on whom the duty is imposed, or, in other words, as directory only."

I turn to the statute once more. It is quite clear that the worked scheme need not have provided for the payment of contributions at all. Section 7(1) has as its opening words: "A works scheme may indicate land (hereinafter referred to as 'contributory land') as land in respect of which coast protection charges are to be payable under the scheme ..." It is a matter for the coast protection authority to decide whether or not its work scheme will designate contributory land. It may not seek to recover contributions from people interested in such properties. There are provisions in later sections of the Act, particularly ss20 and 21, whereby the cost of carrying out a works scheme may be met by contributions or by Exchequer grants.

This conclusion that I have come to here is that most certainly the council in formulating this particular scheme were exercising powers conferred on them by the Act of 1943. They were, in formulating this particular works scheme in the form which it took, exercising powers conferred on them by s7 and particularly by subs(4) thereof. It was entirely open to them to designate, having decided to proceed under subparagraph (b) of s7(4), what period of time should be left to them for determining the interests in the lands after completion of the work. They it was who chose to fix a period of six months from the completion of the work, and, they being the unfettered judges in deciding that period, it is certainly not without relevance when one comes to deal with the subsidiary question as to whether or not there was substantial compliance in this case with the provisions of the Act, assuming that they were merely directory, that the period of time which elapsed between completion of the work and the determination of the interests and the costs exceeded the period of six months designated by nearly four times that period.

This case is and must be one virtually of first impression, and having come to the conclusion that the council were here exercising statutory powers it seems to me beyond dispute that it was obligatory on them to comply with the provisions of s7(5). In other words, it was essential for them, were they to act regularly and effectively, that within the period of six months specified in their scheme they determine the charges to be levied. That, it is admitted, they have not done, and I cannot accordingly regard their purported action as having any validity at all.

Let me turn to the second question. It is undisputed in law that if these be mere duties and if, accordingly, the provisions as to their exercise are to be regarded as directory only, it is sufficient if there has been substantial compliance with those directions. In *Smith* v *Jones* Littledale J said:

"But it has often been held, where an Act ordered anything to be performed by a public body and merely pointed out the specific time when it was to be done, that such an act was not imperative, but directory, and might be complied with in a reasonable time after the period prescribed."

And in *Caldow* v *Pixell* Denman J said that

"... where a public officer is directed by a statute to perform a duty within a specified time, the provisions as to time are only directory, and also that in considering whether a statute is imperative, a balance may be struck between the inconvenience of rigidly adhering to, and the inconvenience of sometimes departing from, its terms."

That some regard must be had to the six months period designated by the council in their own works scheme is conceded by Mr Squibb on their behalf. Almost his last words to this court were that admittedly serious inconvenience might have resulted if the determination had been indefinitely delayed, but he added that of course here the determination had not been indefinitely delayed and that a lapse of 23 months between completion of the works and determination was a substantial compliance with the provision in the works scheme that such period would be six months only. Every case must turn on its own facts. I simply cannot accept Mr Squibb's submission.'

Grunwick Processing Laboratories Ltd v ACAS [1978] AC 655 House of Lords (Lords Diplock, Salmon, Edmund-Davies, Fraser and Keith)

A statutory requirement to consult will almost invariably be mandatory

Facts

Workers at Grunwick sought recognition of their union by their employers; this was refused. The union then applied to ACAS under s11 of the Employment Protection Act 1975, which stated:

'(1) A recognition issue may be referred by an independent trade union to the Service by written application in such form as the Service may require.

(2) In this Act "recognition," in relation to a trade union, means the recognition of the union by an employer, or two or more associated employers, to any extent, for the purpose of collective bargaining.

(3) In this section and ss12 to 14 below, "recognition issue" means an issue arising from a request by a trade union for recognition by an employer, or two or more associated employers, including, where recognition is already accorded to some extent, a request for further recognition.'

ACAS then acted under ss12 and 14 of the 1975 Act, which stated (inter alia);

'12(1) Subject to subs(2) below, when a recognition issue is referred to the Service under s11 above the Service shall examine the issue, shall consult all parties who it considers will be affected by the outcome of the reference and shall make such inquiries as it thinks fit.'

'14(1) In the course of its inquiries into a recognition issue under ss12 or 13 above the Service shall ascertain the opinions of workers to whom the issue relates by any means it thinks fit, but if in any case it determines to take a formal ballot of those works or any description of such workers, the following provisions of this section shall apply.'

ACAS was only able to ascertain the views of a minority of the employees because the employer refused to provide their names and addresses. ACAS nevertheless proceeded to recommend recognition of the union. Grunwick claimed this action was invalid because of the failure to consult all the workers.

Held

The consultation requirement in s14 of the 1975 Act was mandatory, and could not be qualified by implying into it the phrase 'so far is reasonably practicable'.

Lord Diplock:

'First, as to the mandatory nature of the requirement upon ACAS to "ascertain the opinions of workers to whom the issue relates" - whatever precisely that requirement may involve. It is introduced by the word "shall." Prima facie this expression appearing in a statute is used as a term of art to impose a duty to do what is prescribed, not a discretion to do it or not according to whether it is reasonably practicable to do it, nor a discretion to do something like it instead. This is particularly so where, as in s14(1), the imposition of the duty upon ACAS is followed by an express grant of a discretion which does not derogate from the duty itself but is limited to determining the means by which the duty is to be carried out. This serves to point the contrast between what are matters of substance in a statute and what are matters of machinery. A court is less reluctant to treat "shall" as being directory rather than mandatory in a provision in which all that is involved is a mere matter of machinery for carrying out the undoubted purposes of the Act.

In considering whether the requirement that their opinions should be ascertained by ACAS is mandatory the Court of Appeal, in my opinion rightly, attached importance to the effect which a report by ACAS might have upon those workers to whom a recognition issue relates. A recognition issue is about a claim by a particular trade union to act on behalf of employees in collective bargaining with their employer upon a whole range of matters affecting their employment, and thus a large part of their daily lives. Granted the manifest policy of the Act to encourage the extension of collective bargaining, it is nonetheless unconvincing to suggest that it is of minor importance to workers which particular trade union is to negotiate their terms of employment for them and to decide whether any and, if so, what kind of industrial action they will be called upon to take in support of a claim of their own or in sympathy with other workers or even for political reasons only.

On behalf of ACAS it has been sought to minimise the importance which the Act attaches to the selection of a particular trade union to represent employees by pointing out that there is nothing to prevent an employer from agreeing to recognise a trade union for the purpose of collective bargaining on behalf of his employees without ascertaining or paying any heed to their wishes; and that even after a recognition issue has been referred to ACAS, s12(3) treats as the preferable outcome that it should be settled by agreement between the employer and the trade union concerned - which may take place before the opinions of any of the employees have been canvassed. But from the employer's point of view negotiations with a trade union which was without the membership or support of a substantial number of his employees would be futile unless his recognition of the union were pursuant to a recommendation for recognition made in a report by ACAS under s12(4). Where there is such a recommendation the union may demand of the employer that he shall negotiate with it and no one else as to the terms and conditions of employment of his employees and upon the employer's failure to carry on negotiations with that trade union, an application may be made under s16 to the Central Arbitration Committee to have terms and conditions of employment demanded by the trade union made part of the contract of employment of all employees in respect of whom it has been recommended for recognition; and the Central Arbitration Committee may so award. It is true that the terms and conditions of employment so awarded may be varied by agreement between an individual employee and the employer provided that the variation effects an "improvement" in the awarded terms; but apart from identifying what amounts to an improvement, individual bargaining of this kind as distinct from collective bargaining is seldom practicable for individual employees in industrial undertakings of any considerable size, and it conflicts with the expressed policy of the Act.

My Lords, I agree with the Court of Appeal that the requirement in s14(1) that ACAS "shall ascertain the opinion of workers to whom the issue relates" is mandatory, whatever the precise content of the requirement may be. Like the Court of Appeal I am unable to accept the qualification, which Lord Widgery CJ held to be implicit in the subsection, that the obligation to ascertain the opinions of workers extended only "so far as reasonably practicable" in the circumstances of the particular case. In the context of the exercise of statutory functions by a public authority the use by judges of such expressions as "reasonable" or "reasonably practicable" raises the question as to by whom the decision falls to be made as to what is or is not reasonable or reasonably practicable. Prima facie the decision, which is one of fact, is one which the public authority by whom the statutory functions are exercised would have jurisdiction to decide for itself, and a court of justice would have no jurisdiction to interfere with its decision except upon the third ground stated by Lord Greene MR in *Associated Provincial Picture Houses Ltd* v *Wednesbury Corporation* (1), the locus classicus in which he sets out the grounds upon which the court can hold to be ultra vires and void a decision of an administrative body made in purported exercise of a discretion which a statute has conferred on it;

> "... a person entrusted with a discretion must, so to speak, direct himself properly in law. He must call his own attention to the matters which he is bound to consider. He must exclude from his consideration matters which are irrelevant to what he has to consider ... Similarly, there may be something so absurd that no sensible person could ever dream that it lay within the powers of the authority" (sc. to reach the decision that it did.)

So to construe s14(1) of the Employment Protection Act 1975 as if it contained the words suggested by the Lord Chief Justice, would give to ACAS not only the wide discretion expressly conferred upon it by the subsection to decide upon the means by which the opinions of workers are to be ascertained but also a wide discretion, if faced by any difficulties, to dispense with obtaining the opinions of workers or of substantial groups of them, at all. For my part this implication would, in my view, do too great violence to the express words.'

(1)   Supra, this chapter

Howard v Boddington (1877) 2 PD 203 Probate Division (Lord Penzance)

Procedural ultra vires: mandatory and directory requirements

Facts

Section 9 of the Public Worship Act 1874 stated that a bishop who intended to act upon a complaint against an incumbent within his diocese had to give that incumbent a copy of the complaint within 21 days of receiving it. In this case, some seven weeks elapsed before this was done.

Held

The statutory time limit was mandatory, and failure to observe it was fatal to the legality of any subsequent proceedings.

Lord Penzance:

> '... It was contended that, although it is a positive provision of the Act that a copy of the representation shall be transmitted to the respondent within twenty-one days from the time the bishop received it, yet that that provision is only what has been called in the law courts "directory". Now the distinction between matters that are directory and matters that are imperative is well known to us all in the common language of the courts at Westminster. I am not sure that it is the most fortunate language that could have been adopted to express the idea that it is intended to convey; but still that is the recognised language, and I propose to adhere to it. The real question in all these cases is this: A thing has been ordered by the legislature to be done. What is the consequence if it is not done? In the case of statutes that are said to be imperative, the Courts have decided that if it is not done the whole thing fails, and the proceedings that follow upon it are all void. on the other hand, when the Courts hold a provision to be mandatory or directory, they say that, although such provision may not have been complied with, the subsequent proceedings do not fail. Still, whatever the language, the idea is a perfectly distinct one. There may be many provisions in Acts of Parliament which, although they are not strictly obeyed, yet do not appear to the Court to be of that material importance to the subject-matter to which they refer, as that the legislature could have intended that the non-observance of them should be followed by a total failure of the whole proceedings. On the other hand, there are some provisions in respect of which the Court would take an opposite view, and would feel that they

are matters which must be strictly obeyed, otherwise the whole proceedings that subsequently follow must come to an end. Now the question is, to which category does the provision in question in this case belong? ...

I believe, as far as any rule is concerned, you cannot safely go further than that in each case you must look to the subject-matter; consider the importance of the provision that has been disregarded, and the relation of that provision to the general object intended to be secured by the Act; and upon a review of the case in that aspect decide whether the matter is what is called imperative or only directory ...

Now, as I said just now, if twenty-one days is not to be adhered to, what limit is there to the time within which it would be lawful to serve this notice upon the respondent? That is a matter that has pressed more upon my mind than any other. It seems to me that there is no limit ...

On the other side, in opposition to those views, it has been argued, first of all, that no harm is done to the respondent. I think that everybody will admit that the continuation of a suit and its hanging over a man's head beyond the time that the legislature provided, is a harm, and the extent of that harm it is perhaps not so easy to measure exactly, but I think it is a harm; at any rate, in neither of the two cases to which I have called attention was there any harm done, because the notice really got to the right place, but what was done was not done in the form provided by the statute, and therefore it was held that the proceedings were void ...

Then, again it is said that this is a provision intended only for the benefit of the complainants, and it is no doubt considerably for the benefit of the complainants, because they file their representation, and of course they wish to go forward with their suit.

If the bishop holds it back, he is doing them a wrong, but I am unable to see that it is not also a provision intended for the benefit of the respondent, and I do not think the Court is at liberty to speculate too narrowly as to what the motives of the legislature were. They have chosen to provide a definite time within which the representation is to be served, and the question is whether, the matter being one of essential importance, the Court is at liberty to throw what the legislature have provided aside, upon some speculation that they intended it for the benefit of the complainants and not for the benefit of the respondent ...

Upon a review, therefore, of these matters, and after full attention to the excellent argument that I heard upon the subject, I have come to the conclusion that these proceedings cannot go forward. I think the statute has prescribed a particular form to be followed, and that the Court is not at liberty to cast the time mentioned aside, upon any speculation as to the possible reasons why that particular provision was adopted ...'

R v Swansea City Council, ex parte Quietlynn (1983) The Times 19 October Queen's Bench Division (Woolf J)

Statutory time limits are mandatory and action outside them is ultra vires

Facts

Section 2 of the Local Government (Miscellaneous Provisions) Act 1982 gave local authorities power to apply the sex establishment control provisions contained in Schedule 3 to the Act by passing a resolution and publishing notice of that resolution in two consecutive weeks in a local newspaper, the first publication being not later than 28 days before the day specified in the resolution for the coming into force of Schedule 3 in the area.

When the relevant provisions of the Act were applied to a local authority's area it became unlawful to operate a sex establishment without a licence - an offence punishable on summary conviction with a maximum fine of £1,000.

It was conceded by Swansea City Council that notice of the provisions coming into effect in their area had been given outside the time limits. Quietlynn applied for, inter alia, certiorari to quash Swansea City Council's refusal to grant a licence under the Act.

Held

Certiorari would be granted. The time limits would be regarded as mandatory. They were designed to give users of premises the opportunity of avoiding the commission of a criminal offence by applying for a licence. It was highly unsatisfactory that an application to the High Court was necessary before it could be decided whether or not a resolution was effective and whether a criminal offence was being committed. Mr. Justice Woolf concluded that non-compliance with the requirement as to publication in s2 rendered the resolution ineffective, even though no prejudice had been suffered by the applicants in the present case.

11.3   Controlling errors of fact

R v Fulham, Hammersmith and Kensington Rent Tribunal, ex parte Zerek [1951] 2 KB 1 King's Bench Division (Darlia J)

Ultra vires and jurisdictional error

Facts

A tenant referred his letting to a rent tribunal under the Landlord and Tenant (Rent Control) Act 1949 which gave rent tribunals the jurisdiction to assess rents for unfurnished lettings. The landlord claimed that the property had been let furnished, and was therefore outside the jurisdiction granted to rent tribunals by the 1949 Act. After considering the evidence, including a letter that the tenant had been pressurised into signing that declared the property to have been let furnished, the tribunal decided they had been let unfurnished and proceeded to reduce the rent payable. The landlord applied for an order of certiorari.

Held

The application would be refused.

Darlia J:

'... It is not disputed that proof of the fact that this is an unfurnished tenancy is a pre-requisite to the exercise by the tribunal of their jurisdiction under s1 to fix a reasonable rent. Likewise it is agreed that since the tribunal's jurisdiction depends upon the existence of an unfurnished tenancy, it cannot, in the pithy phrase that was used in *R v Bolton* (1), and before, give itself jurisdiction merely by its affirmation of the fact: see also per Coleridge, J in *Bunbury v Fuller* (2). This has been qualified in the terms laid down by Lord Esher MR in *R v Income Tax Special Commissioners* (3) but it is not suggested, and, indeed, the contrary has been settled by this court, that that qualification applies here.

It is therefore agreed that the finding of the tribunal that the tenancy was unfurnished cannot be conclusive. Mr Ashworth, on behalf of the tribunal, submits that it had a right, and, indeed, a duty, to make a finding about the nature of the tenancy, subject to review by this court. Mr Finer, for the applicant, agrees that in a proper case there may be such a right, but argues that it must be limited. It cannot extend to require or permit the tribunal to investigate questions for the determination of which they are by their constitution wholly unsuited, such as whether an agreement is a forgery or has been obtained by fraud or is a sham, which last is what they purported to decide in this case. I do not think that he was able to suggest any principle which would show where the line was to be drawn, except the rather vague one that there must be excluded from the investigation questions which it was inconvenient and undesirable that such a tribunal should investigate ...

In my opinion the argument on behalf of the applicant is based on a misconception of what it is that a tribunal in cases such as this is doing. When, at the inception of an inquiry by a tribunal of limited jurisdiction, a challenge is made to their jurisdiction, the tribunal have to make up their minds whether they will act or not, and for that purpose to arrive at some decision on whether they have jurisdiction or not. If their jurisdiction depends upon the existence of a state of facts, they must inform themselves about them, and if the facts are in dispute reach some conclusion on the merits of the dispute. If they reach a wrong conclusion, the rights of the parties against each other are not affected. For, if the tribunal wrongly assume jurisdiction, the party who apparently obtains an order from it in reality takes nothing. The whole proceeding is, in the phrase used in the old reports, coram non judice. If, for example, the applicant in this case wishes, he can sue for his 35s. rent. He will be met with the defence that by the order of the tribunal it has been reduced to 15s. He can reply that that order is bad for want of jurisdiction, and the defendant will have to justify the order on which he relies and so prove the facts which give the tribunal jurisdiction. This seems to me to be what is laid down by the decision in *Briscoe* v *Stephens* (4), and to be in accordance with the opinion of Willes J in *London Corporation* v *Cox* (5). In such an action, I apprehend, the findings of the tribunal would be irrelevant and inadmissible. They are findings in a preliminary inquiry whose only object is to enable the tribunal to decide for themselves how to act. They are findings, therefore, that cannot ultimately prejudice either party. In these circumstances, I am unable to see why the tribunal should, in making their preliminary inquiry, be restricted to any particular class of case, or how they can be restrained from investigating for their own purposes any point which they think it necessary to determine so that they can decide upon their course of action ...

Although tribunals may in my view and in default of any alternative have to determine for themselves in the first instance the extent of their jurisdiction, nothing that I have said means that they should take upon themselves unnecessarily the examination of questions such as those ... in cases where charges of fraud or forgery and the like are raised. Their own good sense will tell them that. While they will not allow every empty threat to their jurisdiction to deter them from their proper business of fixing reasonable rents, they will likewise appreciate that they are not by their nature equipped for the trial of matters which in the ordinary civil courts would be determined after pleading and discovery had been given and evidence on oath tested by cross-examination, and possibly, also, after trial by jury. The tribunal cannot be required to determine summarily such an issue if it involves a point of substance and if one or other of the parties is willing to have it determined in the ordinary civil courts; an adjournment can always be granted to allow that to be done. This will avoid an inconclusive inquiry by the tribunal and safeguard the tenant against the danger of being presented with an order which may afterwards turn out to be illusory. It may well be that if the tribunal itself insist, notwithstanding that there is a practicable alternative offered to them, in going into points of the sort which they purported to determine in *R* v *Hackney etc, Rent Tribunal; Ex parte Keats* (6) there is power in this court to prevent them from doing so. It is quite unnecessary that I should even consider that in relation to the present case, for this tribunal were quite willing that the validity of the alleged agreement should be determined by the ordinary courts, and I think that would be the attitude of most tribunals.

I need say little upon the facts of the present case, which have been fully dealt with by my Lords. Had there been a conflict of evidence, this court would probably not have interfered. But in fact the evidence was all one way and ample to justify the tribunal's conclusion that the document was not intended by the parties as a reduction into writing of their oral agreement, but as a bogus document which the landlord had brought into existence for his own purposes. Having regard to the receipt for the hire of the furniture, about which the landlord offered no explanation, the matter was in my view so clear as not to raise any serious issue. The tribunal's decision to assume jurisdiction cannot, therefore, be questioned in these proceedings.'

(1)   (1841) 1 QB 66

(2)   (1853) 9 Ex 111

(3)   (1888) 21 QBD 313

(4)   (1824) 2 Bing 213

(5)   (1867) LR 2 HL 239

(6)   [1951] 2 KB 1 at p15

White and Collins v Minister of Health [1939] 2 KB 838 Court of Appeal (Luxmoore and MacKinnon LJJ, Humphreys J)

Jurisdictional ultra vires

Facts

Ripon Borough Council exercised powers of compulsory purchase over land owned by the appellants. By s75 of the Housing Act 1936, these powers were not to be exercised over land forming part of any park, garden, or pleasure ground required for the amenity or convenience of any house. The appellants contended that some of the land over which the council had exercised its powers fell within the protection of s75 and thus could not be acquired in this way.

A public inquiry was held into objections to the scheme, but the Minister confirmed the compulsory purchase order. The land owners applied to the High Court to quash the Minister's confirmation, but Charles J held the question arising under s75 to be one of fact and that it was not open to the court to reconsider the decision. On appeal to the Court of Appeal.

Held

The order would be quashed.

Luxmoore LJ:

'The first and most important matter to bear in mind is that the jurisdiction to make the order is dependent on a finding of fact; for, unless the land can be held not to be part of a park or not to be required for amenity or convenience, there is no jurisdiction in the borough council to make, or in the Minister to confirm, the order. In such a case it seems almost self-evident that the Court which has to consider whether there is jurisdiction to make or confirm the order must be entitled to review the vital finding on which the existence of the jurisdiction relied upon depends. If this were not so, the right to apply to the Court would be illusory.

There is however ample authority that the Court is entitled so to act, for the point has been considered in a number of cases. It is sufficient to refer to the case of *Bunbury* v *Fuller* (1). In that case Coleridge J delivering the judgment of the Court of Exchequer Chamber said:

"It is a general rule, that no court of limited jurisdiction can give itself jurisdiction by a wrong decision on a point collateral to the merits of the case upon which the limit to its jurisdiction depends; and however its decision may be final on all particulars, making up together that subject-matter which, if true, is within its jurisdiction, and however necessary in many cases it may be for it to make a preliminary inquiry, whether some collateral matter be or be not within the limits, yet, upon this preliminary question, its decision must always be open to inquiry in the superior Court. Then to take the simplest case - suppose a Judge with jurisdiction limited to a particular hundred, and a matter is brought before him as having arisen within it, but the party charged contends that it arose in another hundred, this is clearly a collateral matter independent of the merits; on its being presented, the Judge must not immediately forbear to proceed, but must inquire into its truth or falsehood and for the time decide it, and either proceed or not with the principal subject-matter according as he finds on that point; but this decision must be open to question, and if he has improperly either forborne or proceeded on the main matter in consequence of an error, on this the Court of Queen's Bench will issue its mandamus or prohibition to correct his mistake."

As in *Bunbury* v *Fuller* and also in *R* v *Bradford* (2), so also in the present case, the decision on the question whether the particular land is part of a park or not is preliminary to the exercise of the jurisdiction to make and confirm the order conferred by the Housing Act 1936, s75, and is therefore open to review in this Court. Charles J in arriving at this decision stated that he agreed with the decision of du Parcq J in *In re Newhill Compulsory Purchase Order, 1937, Payne's Application* (3), and of Swift J in *Bowman's* case (4) in support of the view that he had no power to review the decision of the Minister of Health, because the question to be determined was one of fact.

... Reliance in this Court was placed on the statement of Swift J that an aggrieved person "is not entitled to come here and complain that the local authority have made a mistake of fact in making the order. He is not entitled to say that this house is not insanitary or unfit for human habitation and therefore the order should not have been made." If this statement was intended by the learned judge to be of universal application to all cases under s11 subs3, of the 1930 Act, and therefore also to all cases under the second clause of the Second Schedule to the 1936 Act, I should have no hesitation in saying that it went too far, for it ignores the rule laid down in *Bunbury* v *Fuller* to which reference has already been made: a decision which Swift J had no power to overrule; indeed no reference appears to have been made to it during the argument of *Bowman's* case. I think the remarks of Swift J must be read in the light of the facts of the case before him, and especially with regard to the provisions of the Act of 1930, s1, which appear in express terms to make the local authority the judge whether the houses in question are fit for habitation or not; for the material words of that section are: "Where a local authority upon consideration of an official representation or other information in their possession are satisfied" that the houses in the area are unfit, than an order may be made.

This provision differs materially from the present case; s75 of the Act of 1936 does not refer in terms of the local authority being satisfied that the land is not part of a park. The making of the order for compulsory purchase is prohibited if the land is part of a park, a matter which can only be proved or disproved by evidence ...

The true position with regard to applications under clause 2 of the Second Schedule to the 1936 Act appears to me to be that the judge to whom the application is made is bound to consider the available evidence, whether given at the local inquiry or by the affidavits in support of or in opposition to the motion, and if there is a conflict with regard to the facts raised, or if the evidence is insufficient to enable him to come to a conclusion, he is free to direct that oral evidence be given, whether by way of cross-examination or of additional evidence under the provisions of Order LVB rule 72.

In the present case, as I have already stated, I am satisfied that there was no evidence before the inspector sufficient to entitle the local authority or the Minister to come to a conclusion that the land in question was not part of the park of Highfield; I am further satisfied that on the affidavit evidence ... the only conclusion open to the Court is that the land was a part of the park of Highfield ... In my judgment the appeal must be allowed.'

(1)   (1853) 9 Ex 111

(2)   [1908] 1 KB 365

(3)   [1938] 2 All ER 163

(4)   [1932] 2 KB 621

11.4 Controlling errors of law

R v Knightsbridge Crown Court, ex parte International Sporting Club (London) Ltd
[1982] QB 304; [1981] 3 WLR 640 Court of Appeal (Griffiths LJ and May J)

Court's inherent jurisdiction to correct errors of law: what constitutes the record

Facts

The gaming licences of three London clubs were cancelled by the Gaming Board on the ground that the companies owning them were no longer fit to do so. Whilst appeals against these cancellations were pending before the Crown Court the ownership of the clubs changed completely, the new owners putting into effect significant changes to eradicate some previous malpractices. The Crown Court dismissed the appeals against cancellation on the grounds that the companies were not fit to hold licences on the basis of their past conduct.

Two companies applied for certiorari to quash the decision for error of law. The Gaming Board contended that the record consisted only of the formal order of the court, which could be reviewed but contained no error of law.

Held

The record included a wide range of documents in the case, certainly the judgment, and in this case it disclosed an error of law in that insufficient weight had been given to the fact that the ownership and management of the clubs had completely changed.

Griffiths LJ:

'In the ever increasing complexity of a modern society there has inevitably been a great increase in the number of tribunals required to regulate its affairs. Trained lawyers play their part in manning these bodies but it is neither possible because there are not enough lawyers, nor desirable because lawyers may lack the special expertise of people from other walks of life, that they should all be in the hands of the lawyers. Laymen play their part and will often outnumber and be able to outvote the lawyers among them when it comes to making a decision. The citizen affected by these decisions is entitled to expect that they will be given in accordance with the law and, if the rule of law is to mean anything, a court manned by trained lawyers is required to speak with authority to correct the decision where it appears that it is founded upon error of law. This function is now performed in may cases by the Divisional Court of the Queen's Bench Division by the use of an order of certiorari to quash an erroneous decision; in other cases Parliament may often give a right of appeal to the High Court.

But before the Divisional Court can exercise its supervisory jurisdiction it must be able to see what the error of law is said to be. The document to which anyone would naturally expect it to look must surely be that which records the reasons given by the court or tribunal for its decision - in this case the transcript of Judge Friend's judgment.

In the collective experience of the members of this court and the very experienced counsel appearing before us it has been the practice of the Divisional Court under the presidency of successive Lord Chief Justices over the last four decades to receive the reasons given by a court or tribunal for its decision and if they show error of law to allow certiorari to go to quash the decision. The court has regarded the reasons as part of the record. They are sometimes referred to as a "speaking order."

... In order to do justice the court has, in addition to regarding the reasons for a decision as part of the record, been prepared to regard other documents as part of the "record" where if read with the decision they will show that the tribunal has erred in law. In *Baldwin & Francis Ltd* v *Patents Appeal Tribunal* (1) Lord Denning held that the decision of the superintending examiner and two patent specifications formed part of the record of the proceedings before a patents appeal tribunal. In *R v Medical Appeal Tribunal, ex parte Gilmore* (2) the Court of Appeal held that the report of a medical specialist constituted part of the record. As Lord Denning MR said in *R* v *Preston Supplementary Benefits Appeal Tribunal, ex parte Moore* (3):

"The 'record' is generously interpreted so as to cover all the documents in the case."

Parliament has set its seal of approval on this practice of the court in the case of all those bodies to which the Tribunals and Inquiries Acts 1958 and 1971 apply. They are required to state their reasons and it is provided that the reasons constitute part of the record, and that certiorari will lie: see ss12 and 14 of the Act of 1971.

We can see no sensible reason why the court should adopt a different approach to a decision of an inferior court or other quasi-administrative body such as licensing justices from that which it is required to adopt in the cases to which the Act applies. If we were now to hold that the practice of the Divisional Court over the past 40 years was wrong and that the court could look only at the order dismissing the appeal, we should be putting the clock back to the days when archaic formalism too often triumphed over justice.

The argument for the Gaming Board is that it is only if the inferior court chooses to embody its reasons in its order that it becomes part of the record, for only then does it exist as a document for which the Court of Queen's Bench can call and examine. So if at the end of the judgment giving the reasons the judge or chairman adds the words "and I direct that this judgment be made part of the order," the court may look at it but not otherwise. It seems to us that it would be a scandalous state of affairs that, if having given a manifestly erroneous judgment, a judge could defeat any review by this court by the simple expedient of refusing a request to make his judgment part of the order. That would indeed be formalism triumphant.

It may be said that the same end can be achieved by the court refusing to give any reasons, as Judge Friend said he was entitled to do in this case. However, it is the function of professional judges to give reasons for their decisions and the decisions to which they are a party. This court would look askance at the refusal by a judge to give his reasons for a decision particularly if requested to do so by one of the parties. It does not fall for decision in this case, but it may well be that if such a case should arise this court would find that it had power to order the judge to give his reasons for his decision.

Although the old authorities do show a stricter approach to what constituted the "record", the modern authorities show that the judges have relaxed the strictness of that rule and taken a broader view of the "record" in order that certiorari may give relief to those against whom a decision has been given which is based upon a manifest error of law. We, therefore, hold that the reasons contained in the transcript of the oral judgment of the Crown Court constitute part of the record for the purposes of certiorari and we are entitled to look at it to see if they contain errors of law.

The statutory provisions governing applications to licensing justices for cancellation of a gaming licence and appeals from the decision of the licensing justices are contained in Schedule 2 to the Act. Paragraph 42 provides that the licensing justices may cancel the licence on any of the grounds specified in paragraphs 20 or 21. The grounds relevant to this application are those in paragraph 20(1)(b) that the applicant is not a fit and proper person to be the holder of a licence under this Act and in paragraph 21(1)(e) that, while the licence has been in force, the relevant premises have been used for an unlawful purpose or as a resort of criminals or prostitutes. In addition to cancelling the licence there is also a power to make a disqualification order prohibiting a licence being held in respect of the premises for a period not exceeding five years: see paragraph 49. Paragraphs 45 and 29 provide for an appeal to the Crown Court to be by way of a rehearing with a power to make any order that might have been made by the licensing justices, and provides that the judgment of the Crown Court shall be final. In passing we observe that the fact that the appeal is said to be final is no ground for refusing certiorari if error is found on the face of the record: see *R* v *Medical Appeal Tribunal, ex parte Gilmore* (2) and *South East Asia Fire Bricks Sdn Bhd* v *Non-Metallic Mineral Products Manufacturing Employees Union* (4).'

... On the question of whether or not the companies are fit and proper persons to hold the licence it is conceded that this question must be determined in the light of the circumstances existing at the time of the appeal. Past conduct will, of course, be relevant as we shall discuss more fully hereafter. There are, however, other considerations which should be taken into account particularly when the licence holder is a limited company; for instance, whether the shareholding or management of the company remain the same at the date of the material hearing as they were when the past misconduct occurred; the general character and reputation of the shareholders and directors of the company at the date of the hearing should be taken into account. So should any evidence that the "re-structured" licence holder has the capacity and intention to run the casino on different lines, or indeed that it may have already started to do so. It is conceded by the respondents that a failure to take these very material matters relating to the restructuring of the companies into account when considering an application to cancel a licence would amount to an error of law ...

We have no hesitation in saying that past misconduct by the licence holder will in every case be a relevant consideration to take into account when considering whether to cancel a licence. The weight to be accorded to it will vary according to the circumstances of the case. There may well be cases in which the wrong-doing of the company licence holder has been so flagrant and so well publicised that no amount of restructuring can restore confidence in it as a fit and proper person to hold a licence; it will stand condemned in the public mind as a person unfit to hold a licence and public confidence in the licensing justices would be gravely shaken by allowing it to continue to run the casino. Other less serious breaches may be capable of being cured by restructuring.'

(1)   [1959] AC 663

(2)   Infra, this chapter

(3)   [1975] 1 WLR 624

(4)   [1981] AC 363

R v Medical Appeal Tribunal, ex parte Carrarini [1966] 1 WLR 883 Queen's Bench Division (Lord Parker CJ, Sachs and Widgery JJ)

Court's inherent jurisdiction to correct errors of law including failures of natural justice

Facts

The applicant had suffered an eye injury at work, in respect of which an award had been made. Some time later he suffered a detached retina and sought to have his original award reconsidered on the ground that the original injury had led to the later one. At the tribunal hearing, expert evidence against his case was admitted in evidence, but the tribunal refused to permit the applicant an adjournment to produce expert evidence supporting his case.

Held

The tribunal had erred in law in not permitting the applicant an adjournment to provide counter-balancing evidence.

Lord Parker CJ:

'The approach, as it seems to me in this matter, is to look at the decision in the first instance of the medical appeal tribunal, and to ask oneself whether in exercising that discretion they acted judicially; that of course would embrace the question whether what they did was, as it is sometimes put, contrary to natural justice.

Mr Bridge for the Ministry has urged that if one considers the whole position here, the medical appeal tribunal were perfectly entitled, acting judicially, to refuse to adjourn for two reasons; he says in the first instance that they are an expert body, that they are entitled to use their own expertise, and that the nature of the proceedings is one of inquest rather than action. That is undoubtedly true, but Mr Bridge goes further and says, as I understand it, that there may be cases where, upon their own expertise, they can say the matter is so clear that they could indeed refuse to hear any medical evidence that was tendered.

For my part I find it very difficult to conceive of any such situation. In almost every medical question, even when primary facts are agreed, there is room for a difference of opinion, particularly on this very difficult question of causation; whether or not it can be said affirmatively that a present condition is wholly unconnected with an original accident. But, of course, the tribunal did not seek to rely entirely on their own expertise because they had before them the opinion of Mr Kent and, as it seems to me, once they got into the realm of expert opinion on one side, it would require very strong circumstances to entitle them to refuse expert evidence tendered on the other side.

Indeed, in my opinion, if Mr Murray himself had been outside the door of the room, and the applicant asked for him to be called, the tribunal would really be under a duty to allow him to be called and to hear what he said. Prima facie, then, it seems to me that when informed of Mr Murray's report and assuming, as their decision would indicate, that that report was in the applicant's favour, they should, as I have said, have adjourned to enable Mr Murray's report to be produced.

The second ground, as I understand it, that is put forward is this; whereas we know the difficulties under which the applicant suffered, in that there was, as it were, a lack of liaison between the appellant's solicitor, Barlow for the union, and the applicant himself in connection with this report of Mr Murray, the medical appeal tribunal could only act on what appeared to them, and they were never told of these particular circumstances. I understand that point very well; it is in general always for an applicant to show good reason not attributable to his fault for obtaining an adjournment. But it is to be observed in this decision, to which I return, that the medical appeal tribunal did not refuse an adjournment on that ground. If they had said: "there appeared to us to be no reason why Mr Murray's report was not available at the hearing, it must have been the fault of the applicant himself and we are not going to adjourn", that is one thing and a thing which I could understand. But what they say in their decision is nothing of the sort. They say:

> "In these circumstances no good purpose could be served by allowing an adjournment to enable Mr Murray's report to be produced."

In those circumstances it seems to me that it cannot now be said that they were entitled to refuse to adjourn because the applicant, as it were, had not proved his case for an adjournment. So much for the medical appeal tribunal.

I then come to the decision of the deputy commissioner. In my view of what I have said, it seems to me that the deputy commissioner's decision could only have been arrived at because he misdirected himself in some way as to the law or as to the facts. Put another way, once the decision of the medical appeal tribunal is analysed, and once one directs oneself properly as to the law, the only conclusion which any reasonable tribunal could come to is that the medical appeal tribunal were not acting judicially in refusing the adjournment, and accordingly that the appeal should have been allowed on the ground of that error of law.

For those reasons which I have endeavoured to state shortly, I think this is a case where on its very particular facts an order of certiorari ought to go to quash both decisions. I would like to emphasise that I am certainly not conscious of going, and certainly do not wish to go, outside the well-settled principles dealing with interference with the exercise of the discretion by a tribunal. I decide this case solely on its own particular facts.'

R v Medical Appeal Tribunal, ex parte Gilmore [1957] 1 QB 574 Court of Appeal (Denning, Romer and Parker LJJ)

Court's inherent jurisdiction to correct errors of law: the force of the record

Facts

The applicant injured his left eye at work and applied for disablement benefit under the National Insurance (Industrial Injuries) Act 1946. As a result of an earlier accident he was already injured in his left eye and almost blind in his right. The sum total of his injuries was that he was almost totally blind. Having referred to various specialist reports and statutory instruments the tribunal made an award to the applicant. He now sought to challenge this decision on the basis that there was an error of law in so far as the tribunal had not considered the injury to his right eye. The application for certiorari was refused by the Divisional Court; on appeal to the Court of Appeal

Held

The order of certiorari would be issued. The decision to award a 20 per cent aggravation of injury would not be supported by the evidence.

Denning LJ:

'... The first point is whether the error of the tribunal appears on the face of the record. It does not appear on the face of their written adjudication of 13 June 1956. There is not a word there about the right eye, or even the left eye for that matter. But the tribunal gave an extract from the specialist's report and thereby, I think, they made that report a part of the record. Just as a pleading is taken to incorporate every document referred to in it, so also does an adjudication. Once the specialist's report is read with the record, we have before us the full facts about the previous injury to the right eye and the subsequent injury to the left. These facts are sufficient to disclose the error in law: for it is then apparent that the award of 20 per cent must be wrong. No reasonable person, who had proper regard to regulation 2(5), could have come to such a conclusion. It is now settled that when a tribunal come to a conclusion which could not reasonably be entertained by them if they properly understood the relevant enactment, then they fall into error in point of law: see *Edwards (Inspector of Taxes) v Bairstow* (1).

When the primary facts appear on the record, an error of this kind is sufficiently apparent for it to be regarded as an error on the face of the record such as to warrant the intervention of this court by certiorari.

I may add that, even if we had not been able to have recourse to the specialist's report, we would have been able to get the facts by ordering the tribunal to complete the record by finding the facts, as the regulations require them to. By regulation 13 of the National Insurance (Industrial Injuries) (Determination of Claims and Questions) Regulations 1948, it is enacted that

"A tribunal shall in each case record their decision in writing ... and shall include in such record ... a statement of the reasons for their decision, including their findings on all questions of fact material to the decision."

It seems to me that the tribunal cannot, by failing to find the material facts, defeat an application for certiorari. The court has always had power to order an inferior tribunal to complete the record. Abbot CJ long ago gave very good reasons in this behalf. He said:

"If an inferior court ... send up an incomplete record, we may order them to complete it ... If we are not to order, or allow the officers of the court below to make a perfect record, which unquestionably they are at liberty to do, it will be in their power, by making an imperfect record, to defeat a writ of error whenever it shall be brought. The power of doing that lies in their hands, unless we prevent it."

Likewise a tribunal could defeat a writ of certiorari unless the courts could order them to complete or correct an imperfect record. So the courts have power to give such an order.'

(1)   [1956] AC 14

R v Minister of Housing and Local Government, ex parte Chichester Rural District Council [1960] 1 WLR 587 Queen's Bench Division (Lord Parker CJ, Gorman and Ashworth JJ)

Court's inherent jurisdiction to correct errors of law

Facts

The local authority sought an order of certiorari to quash a Minister's confirmation that certain land should be made the subject of a purchase notice within s19(1) of the Town and Country Planning Act 1947, which stated:

'Where permission to develop any land is refused, whether by the local planning authority or by the Minister, on an application in that behalf made under this Part of this Act ... then if any owner of the land claims - (a) that the land has become incapable of reasonably beneficial use in its existing state; ... he may ... serve on the council of the county borough or county district in which the land is situated a notice (hereinafter referred to as a "purchase notice") requiring that council to purchase his interest in the land in accordance with the provisions of this section. (2) Where a purchase notice is served on any council under this section, that council shall forthwith transmit a copy of the notice to the Minister, and ... the Minister shall, if he is satisfied that the conditions specified in paragraphs (a) to (c) of the foregoing subsection are fulfilled, confirm the notice ...'

Held

The minister's confirmation would be quashed as he had applied the wrong test in law.

Lord Parker CJ (his Lordship considered s19 and continued):

'The Minister's letter setting out his decisions reads: "The inspector's report stated that in view of the legal complications involved in the case, he did not consider that he was in a position to make a comprehensive recommendation. He went on, however, 'The existing use of the site is a mixture of holiday, caravan and residential use, some of which has only temporary planning permission. The planning application in respect of this site was for "redevelopment of building sites for residential purposes". Because of this my feeling is that the land in its existing state and with its existing permissions is substantially less useful to the server than it would be with permission for the permanent redevelopment for residential purposes'." Pausing there, I think it is quite clear that that of itself is not the test. I suppose that in every case where land is worth developing and permission to develop is refused, the existing use of the land will be of less beneficial use, it will be less useful to the owner, than if it were developed. The test is whether it has become incapable of reasonably beneficial use in its existing state.

It may be that the word "reasonably" invokes some comparison, but the fact that the land is less useful, to use a comprehensive term, in its present state than if developed is clearly not the test. The Minister continues: "The Minister therefore accepts his inspector's view that the land in its existing state and with the benefit of the temporary planning permissions that have been granted is of substantially less use and value to its owner than it would be if planning permission had been granted (without limitation as to time) for the rebuilding of the buildings which stood on the land on the appointed day, or which formerly stood there and have been demolished since 7 January, 1937. He is accordingly satisfied that the conditions specified in paragraphs (a) to (c) of subs(1) of s19 of the Act are fulfilled."

In my judgment that passage discloses an error of law in this speaking order. It is not, as I have said, a question of whether the land is of less use or substantially less use in its present state than if developed, and it is a non-sequitur to say that because it is of substantially less use than if developed, therefore the conditions specified in the paragraph are fulfilled. I prefer to say nothing more about the case, because it may well be that there would have been other grounds for justifying the confirmation of this purchase notice, but I am satisfied that the ground, and the only ground, stated by the Minister, is not a valid ground at all and accordingly in my judgment this decision will have to be quashed.'

R v Northumberland Compensation Appeal Tribunal, ex parte Shaw [1952] 1 KB 338
Court of Appeal (Denning, Singleton and Morris LJJ)

The courts have inherent jurisdiction to correct errors of law

Facts

By the passing of the National Health Service Act 1946, the applicant, Thomas Shaw, lost his employment as clerk to the west Northumberland Joint Hospital Board. Aggrieved by the amount of compensation awarded to him by the compensating authority, the Gosforth Urban District Council, he referred the matter to the tribunal designated by the National Health Service (Transfer of Offices and Compensation) Regulations 1948. It became the duty of the tribunal to consider the matter so referred 'in accordance with the provisions' of the regulations and 'to determine accordingly whether any and, if so, what compensation ought to be awarded to the claimant' (see regulation 12). The tribunal therefore were bound by the definition of 'service' contained in the regulations.

The order of the tribunal set out the period of the applicant's service with the hospital board as being from 7 October 1936 to 31 March 1949. It set out the contention of the compensating authority that the compensation payable should be based on that period of service with the hospital board, and the tribunal stated that they agreed that this service was the only service to be taken into account. The decision did not set out the contention of the applicant, who was clerk to the Gosforth Urban District Council, that the whole of his local government service should be taken into account. And the tribunal dismissed the appeal from the decision of the compensating authority.

Thereupon the applicant applied to the Divisional Court for an order of certiorari to remove the decision of the tribunal into the King's Bench Division that it might be quashed. Before the Divisional Court it was admitted by counsel for the tribunal that there was error on the face of the decision given by the tribunal, but he contended that certiorari would lie to such a statutory tribunal only in the case of want or excess of jurisdiction. The Divisional Court granted the order for certiorari and the tribunal appealed. The Gosforth Urban District Council did not appeal.

Held

The tribunal's decision could be reviewed and quashed by the High Court on the ground that there was an error of law on the face of the record.

Denning LJ:

'The question in this case is whether the Court of King's Bench can intervene to correct the decision of a statutory tribunal which is erroneous in point of law. No one has ever doubted that the Court of King's Bench can intervene to prevent a statutory tribunal from exceeding the jurisdiction which Parliament has conferred on it; but it is quite another thing to say that the King's Bench can intervene when a tribunal makes a mistake of law. A tribunal may often decide a point of law wrongly whilst keeping well within its jurisdiction. If it does so, can the King's Bench intervene?

There is a formidable argument against any intervention on the part of the King's Bench at all. The statutory tribunals, like this one here, are often made the judges both of fact and law, with no appeal to the High Court. If, then, the King's Bench should interfere when a tribunal makes a mistake of law, the King's Bench may well be said to be exceeding its own jurisdiction. It would be unsurping to itself an appellate jurisdiction which has not been given to it. The answer to this argument, however, is that the Court of King's Bench has an inherent jurisdiction to control all inferior tribunals, not in an appellate capacity, but in a supervisory capacity. This control extends not only to seeing that the inferior tribunals keep within their jurisdiction, but also to seeing that they observe the law. The control is exercised by means of a power to quash any determination by the tribunal which, on the face of it, offends against the law. The King's Bench does not substitute its own views for those of the tribunal, as a Court of Appeal would do. It leaves it to the tribunal to hear the case again, and in a proper case may command it to do so. When the King's Bench exercises its control over tribunals in this way, it is not unsurping a jurisdiction which does not belong to it. It is only exercising a jurisdiction which it has always had ...

Of recent years the scope of certiorari seems to have been somewhat forgotten. It has been supposed to be confined to the correction of excess of jurisdiction, and not to extend to the correction of errors of law; and several judges have said as much. But the Lord Chief Justice has, in the present case, restored certiorari to its rightful position and shown that it can be used to correct errors of law which appear on the face of the record, even though they do not go to jurisdiction. I have looked into the history of the matter, and find that the old cases fully support all that the Lord Chief Justice said. Until about 100 years ago, certiorari was regularly used to correct errors of law on the face of the record. It is only within the last century that it has fallen into disuse, and that is only because there has, until recently, been little occasion for its exercise. Now, with the advent of many new tribunals, and the plain need for supervision over them, recourse must once again be had to this well-tried means of control. I will endeavour to show how the writ of certiorari was used in former times, so that we can take advantage of the experience of the past to help us in the problems of the present.'

His Lordship then considered the authorities at some length and continued:

'It will have been seen that throughout all the cases there is one governing rule: Certiorari is only available to quash a decision for error of law if the error appears on the face of the record. What, then, is the record? It has been said to consist of all those documents which are kept by the tribunal for a permanent memorial and testimony of their proceedings: see Blackstone's Commentaries, Vol III at p24. But it must be noted that, whenever there was any question as to what should, or should not be, included in the record of any tribunal, the Court of King's Bench used to determine it.

Following these cases, I think the record must contain at least the document which initiates the proceedings; the pleadings, if any; and the adjudication; but not the evidence, nor the reasons, unless the tribunal chooses to incorporate them. If the tribunal does state its reasons, and those reasons are wrong in law, certiorari lies to quash the decision.

The next question which arises is whether affidavit evidence is admissible on an application for certiorari. When certiorari is granted on the ground of want of jurisdiction, or bias, or fraud, affidavit evidence is not only admissible, but it is, as a rule, necessary. When it is granted on the ground of error of law on the face of the record, affidavit evidence is not, as a rule, admissible, for the simple reason that the error must appear on the record itself: Affidavits were, however, always admissible to show that the record was incomplete as, for instance, that a conviction omitted the evidence of one of the witnesses or did not set out the fact that the justices had refused to hear a competent witness for the defence whereupon the court would either order the record to be completed, or it might quash the conviction at once.

Notwithstanding the strictness of the rule that the error of law must appear on the face of the record, the parties could always by agreement overcome this difficulty. If they both desired a ruling of the Court of King's Bench on a point of law which had been decided by the tribunal, but which had not been entered on the record, the parties could agree that the question should be argued and determined as if it were expressed in the order.

We have here a simple case of error of law by a tribunal, an error which they frankly acknowledge. It is an error which deprives Mr. Shaw of the compensation to which he is by law entitled. So long as the erroneous decision stands, the compensating authority dare not pay Mr. Shaw the money to which he is entitled lest the auditor should surcharge them. It would be quite intolerable if in such case there were no means of correcting the error. The authorities to which I have referred amply show that the King's Bench can correct it by certiorari. It is true that the record which has been sent up to the court does not distinctly disclose the error, but that is only because the record itself is incomplete. The tribunal has sent up its decisions, but it has not sent up the claim lodged with the compensating authority or the order made by them on it or the notice of appeal to the tribunal. Those documents would, I think, properly be part of the record. They would, I understand, have disclosed the error. If it had been necessary, the court could have ordered the record to be completed. But that is unnecessary, having regard to the fact that it was admitted in open court by all concerned that the decision was erroneous. I am clearly of opinion that an error admitted openly in the face of the court can be corrected by certiorari as well as an error that appears on the face of the record. The decision must be quashed, and the tribunal will then be able to hear the case again and give the correct decision.

In my opinion the appeal should be dismissed.'

12 THE APPLICATION FOR JUDICIAL REVIEW

An Bord Bainne Co-operative Ltd (Irish Dairy Board) v Milk Marketing Board (1984) The Times 22 May Court of Appeal (Sir John Donaldson MR, Slade and Parker LJJ)

Judicial review: Order 53 inappropriate where damages are sought on a private law right

Facts

The plaintiffs sought an injunction restraining the defendants, an English statutory corporation, from differentiating between the prices at which they sold milk destined for butter manufacture according to whether the butter was sold to an intervention agency or into the United Kingdom domestic market. They also claimed damages which in July 1983 were particularized at slightly more than £12m 'and continuing'.

In paragraphs 3 to 6 of their points of claim the plaintiffs alleged inter alia, that the defendants by selling milk at differential prices had acted contrary to their obligations under European law and the common organisation of the market in milk and milk products and in breach of Council Regulations (EEC) No 1422/78 and/or Commission Regulation (EEC) 1565/79 and/or in breach of the Milk Marketing Scheme (Amendments) Regulations (SI 1981 No 323). In paragraph 7 to 11 the plaintiffs alleged that the defendants had abused their dominant position in the English market and had distorted competition contrary to articles 86 and 92 of the Treaty of Rome. Paragraph 12 alleged that the plaintiffs had suffered damages by each of the specified 'breaches of Community law'.

The defendants had sought to strike out paragraphs 3 to 6 upon the ground that they involved 'an abuse of the process of the court'. The basis of that contention was that paragraphs 3 to 6 alleged a cause of action in, or mainly in, the field of public law or should only be pursued by the judicial review procedure provided by Order 53 of the Rules of the Supreme Court.

At first instance Mr Justice Neill had refused the application deciding that in the exercise of his discretion it would be inappropriate to strike out the paragraphs.

The defendants appealed. A prompt decision was required because the Commercial Court was very shortly to be asked to refer certain questions of law to the European Court of Justice.

Held

The procedure of judicial review under Order 53 of the Rules of the Supreme Court was wholly inappropriate where a claim for damages was based on alleged private law rights and the case could be made good on the facts and the private law, without the court having a discretion whether or not to grant relief. The prosecution of such a claim was in no way a 'misuse' of the process of the court.

The Master of the Rolls, giving the reserved reasons of the court, said that the scope of any such reference would or might be considerably affected by the fate of paragraphs 3 to 6. The court had decided unanimously that the appeal should be dismissed with costs but, since the appeal might be thought to raise issues of some general importance, had taken time to put the court's reasons into writing.

The appeal was the latest in a line of cases stemming from the decision of the House of Lords in *O'Reilly* v *Mackman* (1). In that case the plaintiff prisoners had no remedy in private law. They had, however, sufficient interest to be entitled to invoke the assistance of the court under its public or administrative supervisory jurisdiction. The sole issue was whether consideration of public policy required that a particular procedure should be invoked in asking the court for assistance. The decision had nothing to do with substantive rights. It had everything to do with how effect should be given to those rights. That was put with the utmost clarity by Lord Diplock in his speech in pp274G to 275A. It was of fundamental importance that the prisoners in *O'Reilly* v *Mackman* (1) had to ask the court to exercise its discretion if they were to be granted relief.

The procedure provided by Order 53 was geared to the grant of discretionary relief, since all the remedies available by judicial review were discretionary. Leave had to be obtained before an application for relief could be made. It was against a background of a 'blatant attempt' to seek relief by actions rather than by way of judicial review so as to avoid the protections which Order 53 provided for defendants such as the Board of Visitors of Hull Prison that Lord Diplock, with the agreement of the other members of the House, had formulated the general rule.

Lord Diplock had said (p285E) that it would 'be contrary to public policy, and as such an abuse of the process of the court, to permit a person seeking to establish that a decision of a public authority infringed rights to which he was entitled to protection under public law to proceed by way of ordinary action and by this means to evade the provisions of Order 53 for the protection of such authorities'. He had emphasised that it was a general rule, subject to exceptions to be evolved on a 'case to case' basis, and not a rule of universal application, drawing particular attention to the possibility of exceptions where all parties consented or where the invalidity of the public law decision arose as a collateral issue in a claim for infringement of a right of a plaintiff arising under private law.

O'Reilly v *Mackman* (1) was followed by *Cocks* v *Thanet District Council* (2) in which the general rule was applied. In *Davy* v *Spelthorne Borough Council* (3) a claim in negligence was allowed to proceed by action.

The court regarded the majority decision of the Court of Appeal in *Wandsworth London Borough Council* v *Winder* (4) as an illustration of the fact that the rule in *O'Reilly* v *Mackman* (1) was subject to exceptions where, although the principal issue was one of public law, private law rights were involved and it could cause the citizen injustice to be required to use the judicial review procedure.

In every case the court had to have regard to considerations of public policy in the light of the guidance given by *O'Reilly* v *Mackman* (1).

In the present case the plaintiffs' claim for damages was admittedly based on alleged private law rights whether or not it was also based on public law rights. If they could make good their case on the facts and private law, the court would have no discretion whether or not to grant relief.

The Order 53 procedure was wholly inappropriate to any non-discretionary claim and the prosecution of such a claim by the procedure of an action was in no way to abuse, or as the court preferred to style it, a "misuse" of the process of the court. It was a completely proper use of that process. The claim for an injunction did enable the court to exercise a discretion, but only as to the choice of remedy, damages or an injunction, not as to granting any remedy at all.

In the present case as it was put in argument, the public and private law issues were not even collateral one to another. They were inextricably mixed.

The court saw no ground for interfering with the judge's discretionary decision which was plainly right.

(1)   Infra, this chapter

(2)   Infra, this chapter

(3)   Infra, this chapter

(4)   Infra, this chapter

Barrs v Bethell [1981] 3 WLR 874 Queen's Bench Division (Warner J)

Declaration sought by ratepayers: proper procedure

Facts

(inter alia) The plaintiffs, all Camden London Borough ratepayers, sought declarations, by way of action, claiming that the council had adopted ruinous financial policies in its administration of services, thereby increasing the burden on ratepayers. The defendants applied to have the writ struck out as disclosing no reasonable cause of action.

Held

An individual ratepayer could only bring such an action by way of judicial review or by way of a relator action with leave of the Attorney-General.

Warner J:

'... [The] authorities, unless they are for some reason no longer good law, appear to me clearly to establish that a ratepayer, leaving aside proceedings for prohibition, certiorari or mandamus, or now for judicial review, and leaving aside the audit procedure under the Local Government Act 1972, cannot sue a local authority or its members without the consent of the Attorney-General unless he can show either an interference with some private right of his or an interference with a public right from which he has suffered damage peculiar to himself. That view was also taken, more recently, after a review of some of the English cases, in particular *Boyce* v *PaddingtonBorough Council* (1) by the Supreme Court of New Zealand in *Collins* v *Lower Hutt City Corporation* (2).'

... To my mind the crucial difference between an action of the present kind and an application for judicial review is that the former can be brought as of right whereas the latter requires the leave of the court. It appears to me, with respect, illogical to say that, because a person has a "sufficient interest" to apply for a declaration or an injunction in proceedings for judicial review, he has a sufficient right to apply for the same relief in an action brought, without leave, in his own name. Nor do I think that the substantial difference between the two kinds of proceedings can be disregarded on the ground that at the end of the day the court has a discretion as to the relief to be given. As it was put by Woolf J in *Covent Garden Community Association Ltd* v *Greater London Council* (unreported), 2nd April 1980:

> "The fact that leave is required in judicial review proceedings and was required before prerogative orders prior the new rule, is a significant factor to be taken into account in the approach to locus standi, since the requirement of leave provides a necessary filter to prevent frivolous actions by persons who have no sufficient interest in the result of the proceeding."

In *Heywood* v *Board of Visitors of Hull Prison* (3), Goulding J said:

> "Secondly, RSC, Order 53, rule 5(1) requires a would-be applicant for judicial review to obtain preliminary leave ex parte from a Divisional Court of the Queen's Bench Division or in vacation from a judge at chambers. There are very good reasons (among them an economy of public time and the avoidance of injustice to persons whom it is desired to make respondents) for that requirement of preliminary leave. If an action commenced by writ or originating summons is used instead of the machinery of RSC, Order 53, that requirement of leave is circumvented."

More recently still, in *R* v *Inland Revenue Commissioners, Ex parte National Federation of Self-Employed and Small Businesses Ltd* (4), Lord Wilberforce observed that the right for the court to refuse a person, at the threshold, leave to apply for judicial review "... is an important safeguard against the courts being flooded and public bodies harassed by irresponsible applications." The court's discretion as to the relief to be given does not afford a prospective defendant the same kind of protection. It does not protect him from the burden of being subjected to litigation or from the risk of having to bear all or part of the costs of it because the plaintiff may not be good for them and because, in any case, only party and party costs will normally be recoverable from him. There, are many sectors in which the law recognises a need for total or partial immunity from suit. Manifestly local authorities and their members are particularly vulnerable to actions by busybodies and cranks, and I do not think that the law can be criticised for providing, in their case, a filter in the form of a requirement that either the consent of the Attorney-General to a relator action or the leave of the court for an application for judicial review should be obtained.'

(1)   [1903] 1 Ch 109

(2)   [1961] NZLR 250

(3)   [1980] 1 WLR 1386

(4)   Infra, this chapter

Cocks v Thanet District Council [1983] 2 AC 286; [1982] 3 All ER 1135 House of Lords (Lord Bridge of Harwich, Lord Diplock, Lord Fraser of Tullybelton, Lord Keith of Kinkel and Lord Brightman)

Judicial review: procedure: public law rights

Facts

The plaintiff applied to the defendant council for re-housing under the Housing (Homeless Persons) Act 1977. Under the Act, the council's first duty was to enquire into the circumstances of the applicant's homelessness, and then to supply housing on the basis of that finding. The council found the applicant to be 'intentionally homeless' and thus entitled only to 'limited' accommodation rights. The plaintiff sought a remedy from the court by way of writ.

Held

He must apply for judicial review.

Lord Bridge:

'I have already indicated my agreement with the views of my noble and learned friend Lord Diplock, as expressed in *O'Reilly*'s case (1), and I gratefully adopt all his reasons for the conclusion that:

"... it would ... as a general rule be contrary to public policy, and as such an abuse of the process of the court, to permit a person seeking to establish that a decision of a public authority infringed rights to which he was entitled by protection under public law to proceed by way of an ordinary action and by this means to evade the provision of Order 53 for the protection of such authorities."

Does the same general rule apply, where the decision of the public authority which the litigant wishes to overturn is not one alleged to infringe any existing right but a decision which, being adverse to him prevents him establishing a necessary condition precedent to the statutory private law right which he seeks to enforce? Any relevant decision of a housing authority under the 1977 Act which an applicant for accommodation wants to challenge will be of that character. I have no doubt that the same general rule should apply to such a case. The safeguards built into the Order 53 procedure which protect from harassment public authorities on whom Parliament has imposed a duty to make public law decisions and the inherent advantages of that procedure over proceedings begun by writ or originating summons for the purposes of investigating whether such decisions are open to challenge are of no less importance in relation to this type of decision than to the type of decision your Lordships have just been considering in *O'Reilly*'s case. I have in mind, in particular, the need to obtain leave to apply on the basis of sworn evidence which makes frank disclosure of all relevant facts known to the applicant; the court's discretionary control of both discovery and cross-examination; the capacity of the court to act with the utmost speed when necessary; and the avoidance of the temptation for the court to substitute its own decision of fact for that of the housing authority. Undue delay in seeking a remedy on the part of an aggrieved applicant for accommodation under the 1977 Act is perhaps more often likely to present a problem, but since this appeal, unlike *O'Reilly*'s case, arises from proceedings commenced after the coming into operation of the Supreme Court Act 1981, it is an appropriate occasion to observe both that s31 of that Act removes any doubt there may have been as to the vires of the 1977 amendment of Order 53 and also that s31(6), by expressly recognising that delay in seeking the public law remedies obtainable by application for judicial review may be detrimental to good administration, lends added weight to the consideration that the court, in the control of its own process, is fully justified in confining litigants to the use of procedural machinery which affords protection against such detrimental delay.'

(1)   Infra, this chapter

Davy v Spelthorne Borough Council [1983] 3 All ER 278 House of Lords (Lords Fraser, Wilberforce, Roskill, Brightman and Brandon)

Where public law remedies excluded, private law actions may survive separately

Facts

In September 1977 the plaintiff, owner of premises used to produce concrete, applied to the council for permission to continue using his site for this purpose for another ten years. This was rejected, but as a result of further negotiations with Council officers an agreement was reached in November 1979 under which the council would issue an enforcement notice directing him to lease his user of the land, but the operation of his notice would be suspended for three years. In exchange the plaintiff promised not to exercise his statutory right of appeal against the notice, which had to be exercised within 35 days of its being issued. In October 1980 the notice was issued in accordance with the agreement.

In August 1982 the plaintiff issued a writ against the Council seeking:

a) an injunction to stop the notice taking effect;

b) damages for negligent advice;

c) the setting aside of the notice.

The plaintiff argued that the agreement was ultra vires the council and therefore void.

The Court of Appeal struck out (a) and (c) on the ground that the correct procedure for obtaining such remedies was an application for judicial review under Ord 53. The court allowed the claim for damages to survive. The council appealed.

Held

The private action for damages would survive. It was not a public law question anymore because the plaintiff was no longer contesting the validity of the enforcement notice, but the nature of the advice that led to his failing to challenge it. If the case still had a public law element it was no more than collateral to the main action and this came within the exceptions envisaged by Lord Diplock in *O'Reilly* v *Mackman* (1).

Furthermore, the court had no power to transfer the action to proceed as if it had been commenced under Ord 53, with the result that if the writ was struck out, the plaintiff would have to start afresh with an application under Ord 53. This might prejudice the plaintiff as he would be out of time; at very least such a course of action would be uncertain.

(1)   Infra, this chapter

Law v National Greyhound Racing Club Ltd [1983] 1 WLR 1302 Court of Appeal (Fox, Lawton and Slade LJJ)

Judicial review: purpose of Supreme Court Act 1981 s31 & Order 53

Facts

The defendants acted as a judicial body for the conduct and discipline of greyhound racing in Great Britain. They administered a code of rules which were enforced by stewards. All who wished to take part in greyhound racing in stadia licensed by the defendants were deemed under rule 2 of the Rules of Racing to have read the rules and to have submitted to them and to the jurisdiction of the defendants. By a disciplinary decision given by the stewards on 9 December 1982 after an inquiry which the plaintiff attended, the plaintiff's trainer's licence was suspended for six months on the ground that he had in his charge a greyhound which showed presence in its tissues of substances which would affect its performance, in breach of rule 174(a)(ii) of the Rules of Racing. By an originating summons the plaintiff sought, inter alia, a declaration that the stewards' decision was void and ultra vires in that the suspension amounted to a breach of the implied term of the agreement between him and the defendants that all actions taken by the stewards which could deprive him of his licence would be reasonable and fair and made on reasonable grounds. The defendants sought to have the proceedings struck out for want of jurisdiction, claiming that by s31(1) and (2) of the Supreme Court Act 1981 the application for the declaration should have been made by way of judicial review under RSC Ord 53, r1.

At first instance Walton J dismissed the motion. On appeal by the defendants:

Held

The appeal would be dismissed. The authority of the stewards to suspend the plaintiffs licence was derived wholly from a contract between him and the defendants. The status of the stewards was that of a domestic tribunal albeit their decisions might affect the public, so that the process of judicial review would not have been open to the plaintiff before the Supreme Court Act 1981 was passed. Section 31 of that Act did not enlarge the jurisdiction of the court to enable it to review the decisions of domestic tribunals either by way of orders of mandamus, certiorari or prohibition, or by granting a declaration or injunction by way of judicial review. The process of judicial review still applied only to public law matters and therefore, the plaintiff had properly brought an action seeking a declaration in the High Court.

Lord Justice Fox said that the authority of the stewards to suspend the licence of the plaintiff derived wholly from a contract between the plaintiff and the NGRC. He saw nothing to suggest that the NGRC had rights or duties relating to members of the public as such. What the NGRC did in relation to the control of greyhound racing might affect a section of the public but their powers in relation to the matters with which the present case was concerned were contractual.

Apart from the alteration of the Rules of the Supreme Court in 1978 and the provisions of the Supreme Court Act 1981, the prerogative orders would not lie to a tribunal set up by the NGRC because the powers of the tribunal derived from contract only.

As to the effect produced by the amendments to the Rules of Court and by the 1981 Act, it seemed to his Lordship that the power under Order 53 to grant an injunction or to make a declaration was only exercisable in cases where, before the change in the rules, the applicant could have obtained a prerogative order, and the remedy was in the realm of public law only.

His Lordship saw nothing in the Supreme Court Act 1981 which suggested any parliamentary intention to extend the scope of the prerogative orders. He agreed that the appeal should be dismissed.

O'Reilly v Mackman [1982] 3 WLR 1096 House of Lords (Lord Diplock, Lord Fraser of Tullybelton, Lord Keith of Kinkel, Lord Bridge of Harwich and Lord Brightman)

Protection of public authority from frivolous actions: Order 53

Facts

The four plaintiffs, prisoners in Hull prison, were charged with disciplinary offences before the board of visitors to the prison. In the case of each plaintiff the board held an inquiry, found the charges proved and imposed penalties (loss of remission). Three of the plaintiffs brought writ actions in the QBD against the board alleging that it had acted in breach of the Prison Rules and the rules of natural justice and claiming a declaration that the board's findings against them and the penalties awarded were void. The fourth plaintiff started proceedings by summons in the Chancery Division against the Home Office and the board of visitors alleging bias by a member of the board and claiming a declaration that the board's adjudication was void for want of natural justice. The defendants applied to strike out all four proceedings. The CA struck out the proceedings on the grounds that they were an abuse of the process of the court and their proper remedy was by way of Order 53.

Held

The appeals were dismissed. All the remedies for the infringement of rights protected by public law could be obtained on an application for judicial review under Order 53. It would be contrary to public policy and an abuse of process for a plaintiff complaining of a public authority's infringement of his public law rights to seek redress by ordinary action and that, accordingly, since in each case the only claim made by the plaintiff was for a declaration that the board of visitors' adjudication against the plaintiff was void, it would be an abuse of process to allow the actions to proceed and thereby avoid the protection afforded to statutory tribunals.

This was because the commencing of the action by writ or by summons in effect enable the plaintiff to circumvent the protections afforded by O.53 to the public authority, which were:

a) An obligation to apply for leave to make an application, and to support the application for leave by affidavits verifying the facts relied on, protected public authorities from groundless claims proceeding to trial and imposing a long period of suspense regarding the validity or otherwise of an authority's decision pending the outcome of the trial.

b) Order 53 r4 gave the court a discretion to refuse leave, or any relief sought, on the ground of unreasonable delay on the part of the applicant likely to cause eg substantial hardship to another or be detrimental to good administration. The actions and decisions of public authorities were protected from being questioned or upset at an undesirably late stage.

c) The discretionary nature of all remedies available under Order 53 allowed the court to protect the decisions of public authorities from unmeritorious attacks.

Lord Diplock:

'Order 53 does not expressly provide that procedure by application for judicial review shall be the exclusive procedure available by which the remedy of a declaration or injunction may be obtained for infringement of rights that are entitled to protection under public law; nor does s31 of the Supreme Court Act 1981. There is great variation between individual cases that fall within Order 53, and the Rules Committee and subsequently the legislature were, I think, for this reason content to rely upon the express and the inherent power of the High Court, exercised upon a case to case basis, to prevent abuse of its process whatever might be the form taken by that abuse. Accordingly, I do not think that your Lordships would be wise to use this as an occasion to lay down categories of cases in which it would necessarily always be an abuse to seek in an action begun by writ or summons a remedy against infringement or rights of the individual that are entitled to protection in public law ...

My Lords I have described this as a general rule; for though it may normally be appropriate to apply it by the summary process of striking out the action, there may be exceptions, particularly where the invalidity of the decision arises as a collateral issue in a claim for infringement of a right of the plaintiff arising under private law, or where none of the parties object to the adoption of the procedure by writ or summons. Whether there should be other exceptions should, in my view, at this stage in the development of procedural public law, be left to be decided on a case to case basis.'

R v British Broadcasting Corporation, ex parte Lavelle [1983] 1 WLR 23 Queen's Bench Division (Woolf J)

Courts have no power to review the acts of private corporations

Facts

(inter alia) Lavelle was an employee of the BBC who was dismissed by an internal disciplinary body, after a finding that she had breached her contract of employment. She now sought an order of certiorari to quash the internal appeal body's confirmation of her dismissal.

Held

(inter alia) Despite the changes introduced by the new Ord 53, and s31 of the Supreme Court Act 1981, the courts had no power to review the actions of private bodies or domestic tribunals as these were not public law matters.

Woolf J:

'The application raises a number of points which are of general importance. The points are:

1) whether judicial review is the appropriate procedure for an employee to adopt if he wishes to challenge the legality of disciplinary proceedings conducted by his employers into alleged misconduct;

2) whether the court has jurisdiction in the appropriate proceedings to grant an injunction to restrain a disciplinary tribunal set up by an employer to investigate alleged misconduct by an employee which would justify the dismissal of that employee;

3) if there is such jurisdiction, whether it should be exercised to stay the hearing before the disciplinary tribunal until after the conclusion of criminal proceedings against the employee which raised the same issues as before the disciplinary tribunal.

Rule 1 has since received statutory confirmation in almost identical terms in s31 of the Supreme Court Act 1981. There is nothing in r1 or s31 which expressly extends the circumstances in which the prerogative remedies of mandamus, prohibition or certiorari are available. Those remedies were not previously available to enforce private rights but were, what could be described as, public law remedies. They were not appropriate, and in my view remain inappropriate remedies, for enforcing performance of ordinary obligations owed by a master to his servant. An application for judicial review has not and should not be extended to a pure employment situation. Nor does it, in my view, make any difference that what is sought to be attacked is a decision of a domestic tribunal such as the series of disciplinary tribunal provided for the BBC.

Support for this approach can be found in the judgment of Denning LJ in *Lee* v *Showmen's Guild of Great Britain* (1). That was a case where an action was brought and there was no application for a prerogative writ. Therefore what Denning LJ said is, strictly speaking, obiter. However, while he made it clear that a remedy by way of declaration and injunction could be available in respect of domestic tribunals, the remedy by certiorari does not lie in domestic tribunals.

The matter was dealt with very clearly by Lord Parker CJ in *R* v *Criminal Injuries Compensation Board, Ex parte Lain* (2), a passage of his judgment:

"The position as I see it is that the exact limits of the ancient remedy by way of certiorari have never been and ought not to be specifically defined. They have varied from time to time being extended to meet changing conditions. At one time the writ only went to an inferior court. Later its ambit was extended to statutory tribunals determining a lis inter partes. Later again it extended to cases where there was no lis in the strict sense of the word but where immediate or subsequent rights of a citizen were affected. The only constant limits throughout were that it was performing a public duty. Private or domestic tribunals have always been outside the scope of certiorari since their authority is derived solely from contract, that is, from the agreement of the parties concerned. Finally, it is to be observed that the remedy has now been extended, see *R* v *Manchester Legal Aid Committee, Ex parte RA Brand & Co Ltd* (3), to cases in which the decision of an administrative officer is only arrived at after an inquiry or process of a judicial or quasi-judicial character. In such a case this court has jurisdiction to supervise that process. We have as it seems to me reached the position when the ambit of certiorari can be said to cover every case in which a body of persons of a public as opposed to a purely private or domestic character has to determine matters affecting subjects provided always that it has a duty to act judicially."

Notwithstanding the present wording of Order 53, r1 and s31 of the Act of 1981, the position remains the same and if this application had been confined to an application for an order of certiorari, in my view there would have been no jurisdiction to make the order sought. However, in seeking a stay, the applicant is seeking, in effect, an injunction. The matter was argued before me on the basis that relief by way of an injunction was being sought on the application for judicial review. Order 53, r1(2) does not strictly confine applications for judicial review to cases where an order for mandamus, prohibition or certiorari could be granted. It merely requires that the court should have regard to the nature of the matter in respect of which such relief may be granted. However, although applications for judicial review are not confined to those cases where relief could be granted by way of prerogative order, I regard the wording of Order 53, r1(2) and s30(2) of the Act of 1981 as making it clear that the application for judicial review is confined to reviewing activities of a public nature as opposed to those of a purely private or domestic character. The disciplinary appeal procedure set up by the BBC depends purely upon the contract of employment between the applicant and the BBC, and therefore it is a procedure of a purely private or domestic character.

Accordingly, it is my view that it was inappropriate to seek relief by way of judicial review in the circumstances of this case. However, when I indicated in the court of argument this could be my view, I also indicated that, if the parties were agreeable, I would be prepared to go on and consider the other issues so as to avoid the unnecessary expense and delay which would arise from the proceedings being aborted.

Power to proceed where a declaration or an injunction or damages is sought as if the action has begun by writ is provided for by Order 53, r9(5) and, accordingly, with the consent of the parties I will now consider the remaining issues on the basis that the action had been begun by writ.'

(1)   [1952] 2 QB 329

(2)   [1967] 2 QB 864

(3)   [1952] 2 QB 413

R v Dairy Product Quota Tribunal, ex parte Caswell [1990] 2 WLR 1320 House of Lords (Lord Bridge of Harwich, Lord Griffiths, Lord Ackner, Lord Goff of Chieveley and Lord Lowry)

Judicial review: delay in seeking remedies: declaratory relief

Facts

The applicant was a dairy farming partnership to whom milk quotas had been awarded on an exceptional hardship basis. A applied for judicial review and an increase in quota, which the court of first instance awarded. The tribunal appealed on the point that the partnership had delayed three years in applying and should not be awarded substantive relief as there would be a large number of similar cases, and to review all the cases would cause administrative difficulties for the tribunal since, although the available quota would be sufficient to meet this claim, it would not be sufficient to meet all of the anticipated similar claims. The Court of Appeal granted only declaratory relief: A appealed.

Held

The appeal would be dismissed.

Lord Goff of Chieveley:

'... in the present case the fact that the single judge had granted leave to the appellants to apply for judicial review despite the lapse (long before) of three months from the date when the ground for their application first arose did not preclude the court from subsequently refusing substantive relief on the ground of undue delay in the exercise of its discretion under s31(6) [of the Supreme Court Act 1981]. This was the approach adopted by both courts below, applying (as they were bound to do) the decision of the Court of Appeal in *R* v *Stratford-on-Avon DC, ex parte Jackson* [1985] 1 WLR 1319. Before your Lordships counsel for the appellants submitted that the principles stated in *Ex p Jackson* were erroneous; but ... I am unable to accept that submission.

It follows that there is no doubt that in the present case there was undue delay within s31(6). No suggestion has been made that substantial hardship or substantial prejudice were likely to be caused by the grant of the relief sought. The only questions which remained on the appeal were (1) whether the Court of Appeal should reject the judge's conclusion that the grant of such relief would be detrimental to good administration and (2) if not, whether it should interfere with the judge's exercise of his discretion to refuse such relief. The Court of Appeal decided against the appellants on both of these points.

On the question of detriment to good administration, the judge reviewed with care the evidence before him ... the judge expressed his conclusion on this point in the following passage in his judgment:

"It is obvious that if there are a number of applications the problem of reopening these claims, going back now three years, is going to be very great ... I have come to the clearest view that there will be a detriment to good administration if this application were granted."

The judge's conclusion, on the evidence before him, that there was likely to be a very real problem in relation to a number of cases was a finding of fact with which I can see no reason to interfere. Once that conclusion was reached, it seems to me inevitable that to grant the relief sought in the present case would cause detriment to good administration. As Lloyd LJ pointed out in his judgment, two things emerged from the evidence with sufficient clarity: first that, if the appellant's application for substantive relief were to be successful, there would be a significant number of further applications and second that, if a significant number of applications were granted, then all previous years back to 1984 would have to be reopened (see [1989] 1 WLR 1089 at 1099). These facts disclose, in my opinion, precisely the type of situation which Parliament was minded to exclude by the provision in s31(6) relating to detriment to good administration. Lord Diplock pointed out in *O'Reilly* v *Mackman* [1983] 2 AC 237 at 280-281:

"The public interest in good administration requires that public authorities and third parties should not be kept in suspense as to the legal validity of a decision the authority has reached in purported exercise of decision-making powers for any longer period than is absolutely necessary in fairness to the person affected by the decision."

I do not consider that it would be wise to attempt to formulate any precise definition or description of what constitutes detriment to good administration. This is because applications for judicial review may occur in many different situations, and the need for finality may be greater in one context than in another. But it is of importance to observe that s31(6) recognises that there is an interest in good administration independently of hardship, or prejudice to the rights of third parties, and that the harm suffered by the applicant by reason of the decision which has been impugned is a matter which can be taken into account by the court when deciding whether or not to exercise its discretion under s31(6) to refuse the relief sought by the applicant. In asking the question whether the grant of such relief would be detrimental to good administration the court is at that stage looking at the interest in good administration independently of matters such as these. In the present context that interest lies essentially in a regular flow of consistent decisions, made and published with reasonable dispatch; in citizens knowing where they stand, and how they can order their affairs in the light of the relevant decision. Matters of particular importance, apart from the length of time itself, will be the extent of the effect of the relevant decision, and the impact which would be felt if it were to be reopened ...

Finally, I can, like the Court of Appeal, see no basis for interfering with the judge's exercise of his discretion. The judge took into account the relevant factors, including in particular the financial hardship suffered by the appellants by reason of the erroneous approach adopted by the tribunal, and in particular the imposition on them of substantial superlevy in the years 1986-87 and 1987-88. He then balanced the various factors and, as he said, came down firmly against the view of the appellants. I can perceive no error here which would justify interference with the judge's conclusion.'

R v East Berkshire Health Authority, ex parte Walsh [1984] 3 WLR 818 Court of Appeal (Sir John Donaldson MR, May and Purchas LJJ)

Employment by a public body does not make the contract of employment a public law matter subject to judicial review

Facts

Walsh had been a senior nursing officer at Wexham Park Hospital. He was dismissed as a result of alleged misconduct, after an unsuccessful appeal against the decision of a disciplinary body established pursuant to statute. He applied for judicial review for a declaration and order of certiorari to quash the purported dismissal. The authority argued that as the relationship between the parties arose out of contract it was a private law matter and an application under Ord 53 was an abuse of the court process - Walsh should have proceeded by way of writ.

At first instance the application was allowed to proceed. The authority appealed to the Court of Appeal.

Held

The appeal would be allowed. Simply because Walsh was employed in a great public service did not make his dismissal from it a matter of public law. The only rights under consideration here arose from Walsh's contract of employment which was not a public law matter.

Sir John Donaldson MR:

'I now return to the main issue, namely whether the applicant's complaints give rise to any right to judicial review. They all relate to his employment by the health authority and the purported termination of his employment and of his contract of employment. Essentially they fall into two distinct categories. The first relates to Miss Cooper's power to act on behalf of the authority in dismissing him. The second relates to the extent to which there was any departure from the rules of natural justice in the procedures which led up to that dismissal. Both fall well within the jurisdiction of an industrial tribunal. The first goes to whether or not the applicant was dismissed at all within the meaning of s55 of the Employment Protection (Consolidation) Act 1978. The second goes to whether the dismissal, if such there was, was unfair. Furthermore, both are issues which not uncommonly arise when the employer is a company or individual, as contrasted with a statutory authority. However, this only goes to the exercise of the court's discretion, whether or not to give leave to apply for and whether or not to grant judicial review. As the authority seek to have the proceedings dismissed in limine, if they are to succeed they can only do so on the basis that, accepting all the applicant's complaints as valid, the remedy of judicial review is nevertheless wholly inappropriate and the continuance of the applicant for judicial review would involve a misuse - the term "abuse" has offensive overtones - of the procedure of the court under RSC, Order 53.

The remedy of judicial review is only available where an issue of "public law" is involved, but, as Lord Wilberforce pointed out in *Davy* v *Spelthorne Borough Council* (1), the expressions "public law" and "private law" are recent immigrants and, whilst convenient for descriptive purposes, must be used with caution, since English law traditionally fastens not so much upon principles as upon remedies. On the other hand, to concentrate on remedies would in the present context involve a degree of circularity or levitation by traction applied to shoe-strings, since the remedy of certiorari might well be available if the health authority is in breach of a "public law obligation, but would not be if it is only in breach of a "private law" obligation.

The judge referred carefully and fully to *Vine* v *National Dock Labour Board* (2); *Ridge* v *Baldwin* (3) and *Malloch* v *Aberdeen Corporation* (4). He seems to have accepted that there was no "public law" element in an "ordinary" relationship of master and servant and that accordingly in such a case judicial review would not be available. However, he held, on the basis of these three cases and, in particular, *Malloch*'s case, that the applicant's relationship was not "ordinary." He said:

"The public may have no interest in the relationship between servant and master in an 'ordinary' case, but where the servant holds office in a great public service, the public is properly concerned to see that the authority employing him acts towards him lawfully and fairly. It is not a pure question of contract. The public is concerned that the nurses who serve the public should be treated lawfully and fairly by the public authority employing them ... It follows that if in the exercise of my discretion I concluded that the remedy of certiorari is appropriate, it can properly go against the respondent authority."

The judge then said that if he was wrong in this conclusion, it would be appropriate to allow the proceedings to continue as if they had been begun by writ: see RSC, Order 53, r9(5).

None of the three decisions of the House of Lords to which I have referred was directly concerned with the scope of judicial review under RSC, Order 53. Two, *Ridge* v *Baldwin* (3) and *Malloch* v *Aberdeen Corporation* (4), were concerned with whether or not the plaintiff had a right to be heard before being dismissed and the third, *Vine* v *National Dock Labour Board* (2), with whether the body purporting to dismiss was acting ultra vires. *Vine's* case and *Ridge's* case were actions begun by writ. *Malloch's* case was a Scottish proceeding in which the remedy of "production and reduction" was claimed. This is indeed akin to certiorari, but it is available whether or not the claim involves "public" or "administrative" law. There are, however, dicta, particularly in the speech of Lord Wilberforce in *Malloch's* case, which may be thought to point the way in which we should go.

In *Ridge* v *Baldwin* (3), Lord Reid classified dismissals under three heads in terms of the right to be heard. They were: (a) dismissal by a master; (b) dismissal from an office held during pleasure; and (c) dismissal from an office where there must be something against a man to warrant his dismissal. He held that in case (b) there was no right to be heard and that in case (c) there was always a right to be heard. Dealing with master and servant cases (case (a) above) he said, at p65:

"The law regarding master and servant is not in doubt. There cannot be specific performance of a contract or service, and the master can terminate the contract with his servant at any time and for any reason or for none. But if he does so in a manner not warranted by the contract he must pay damages for breach of contract. So the question in a pure case of master and servant does not at all depend on whether the master has heard the servant in his own defence: it depends on whether the facts emerging at the trial prove breach of contract. But this kind of case can resemble dismissal from an office where the body employing the man is under some statutory or other restriction as to the kind of contract which it can make with its servants, or the grounds on which it can dismiss them."

Lord Reid was also a party to the decision in *Malloch's* case. He said:

"An elected public body is in a very different position from a private employer. Many of its servants in the lower grades are in the same position as servants of a private employer. But many in higher grades or "offices" are given special statutory status or protection. The right of a man to be heard in his own defence is the most elementary protection of all and, where a statutory form of protection would be less effective if it did not carry with it a right to be heard, I would not find it difficult to imply this right. Here it appears to me that there is a plain implication to that effect in the 1882 Act."

Lord Wilberforce said:

"One may accept that if there are relationships in which all requirements of the observance of rules of natural justice are excluded (and I do not wish to assume that this is inevitably so), these must be confined to what have been called 'pure master and servant cases,' which I take to mean cases in which there is no element of public employment or service, no support by statute, nothing in the nature of an office or a status which is capable of protection. If any of these elements exist, then, in my opinion, whatever the terminology used, and even though in some inter partes aspects the relationship may be called that of master and servant, there may be essential procedural requirements to be observed, and failure to observe them may result in a dismissal being declared to be void.

... Statutory provisions similar to those on which the employment rested would tend to show, to my mind, in England or in Scotland, that it was one of a sufficiently public character, or one partaking sufficiently of the nature of an office, to attract appropriate remedies of administrative law."

In all three cases there was a special statutory provision bearing directly upon the right of a public authority to dismiss the plaintiff. In *Vine* v *National Dock Labour Board* (2) the employment was under the statutory dock labour scheme and the issue concerned the statutory power to dismiss given by that scheme. In *Ridge* v *Baldwin* (3) the power of dismissal was conferred by statute: s191(4) of the Municipal Corporations Act 1882 (45 & 46 Vict c50). In *Malloch* v *Aberdeen Corporation* (4) again it was statutory: s3 of the Public Schools (Scotland) Teachers Act 1883 (45 & 46 Vict c18). As Lord Wilberforce said ... it is the existence of these statutory provisions which injects the element of public law necessary in this context to attract the remedies of administrative law. Employment by a public authority does not per se inject any element of public law. Nor does the fact that the employee is in a "higher grade" or is an "officer." This only makes it more likely that there will be special statutory restrictions upon dismissal or other underpinning of his employment see per Lord Reid in *Malloch* v *Aberdeen Corporation* (4). It will be this underpinning and not the seniority which injects the element of public law. Still less can I find any warrant for equating public law with the interest of the public. If the public through Parliament gives effect to that interest by means of statutory provisions, that is quite different, but the interest of the public per se is not sufficient.

I have therefore to consider whether and to what extent the applicant's complaints involve an element of public law sufficient to attract public law remedies, whether in the form of certiorari or a declaration. That he had the benefit of the general employment legislation is clear, but it was not contended that this was sufficient to attract administrative law remedies. What is relied upon are statutory restrictions upon the freedom of the authority to employ senior and other nursing officers on what terms it thought fit. This restriction is contained in the National Health Service (Remuneration and Conditions of Service) Regulations 1974 (SI 1974 No 296) which provides by regulation 3(2):

"Where conditions of service, other than conditions with respect to remuneration, of any class of officers have been the subject to negotiations by a negotiating body and have been approved by the Secretary of State after considering the result of those negotiations, the conditions of service of any officer belonging to that class shall include the conditions so approved."

The conditions of service of, inter alios, senior nursing officers were the subject of negotiations by a negotiating body, namely the Whitley Council for the Health Service (Great Britain) and the resulting agreement was approved by the Secretary of State. It follows, as I think, that if the applicant's conditions of service had differed from those approved conditions, he would have had an administrative law remedy by way of judicial review enabling him to require the authority to amend the terms of service contained in his contract of employment. But that is not the position. His notification of employment dated 12 May 1975, which is a memorandum of his contract of employment, expressly adopted the Whitley Council agreement on conditions of service.

When analysed, the applicant's complaint is different. It is that under those conditions of service Miss Cooper had no right to dismiss him and that under those conditions he was entitled to a bundle of rights which can be collectively classified as "natural justice." Thus he says, and I have to assume for present purposes that he is correct, that under section XXXIV of the Whitley Council's agreement on conditions of service, his position as a senior nursing officer is such that his employment can only be terminated by a decision of the full employing authority and that this power of dismissal cannot be delegated to any officer or committee of officers. I do not think that he relies upon any express provision of those conditions when claiming the right to natural justice, but if he has such a right, apart from the wider right not to be unfairly dismissed which includes the right to natural justice, it clearly arises out of those conditions and it implicit in them.

The ordinary employer is free to act in breach of his contracts of employment and if he does so his employee will acquire certain private law rights and remedies in damages for wrongful dismissal, compensation for unfair dismissal, an order for reinstatement or re-engagement and so on.

Parliament can underpin the position of public authority employees by directly restricting the freedom of the public authority to dismiss, thus giving the employee "public law" rights and at least making him a potential candidate for administrative law remedies. Alternatively it can require the authority to contract with its employees on specified terms with a view to the employee acquiring "private law" rights under the terms of the contract of employment. If the authority fails or refuses to thus create "private law" rights for the employee, the employee will have "public law" rights to compel compliance, the remedy being mandamus requiring the authority so to contract or a declaration that the employee has those rights. If, however,the authority gives the employee the required contractual protection, a breach of that contract is not a matter of "public law" and gives rise to no administrative law remedies.

At one stage in the argument, I did wonder whether the issuing of the "personal policy" document whereby the authority authorised district nursing officers, such as Miss Cooper, to "hire and fire" senior nursing officers, such as the applicant, could be regarded as a breach of a "public law" duty of the authority, but came to the conclusion that it could not. If the applicant is right in his claim to be dismissible only by the authority itself, the issuing of this document was an anticipatory breach of his contract of employment which became a final breach when Miss Cooper acted on it. I say this because the authority was not purporting to vary his conditions of service, but only to act consistently with them. In any event, no relief was claimed by the applicant in respect of the issuing of this policy document.

I therefore conclude that there is no "public law" element in the applicant's complaints which could give rise to any entitlement to administrative law remedies. I confess that I am not sorry to have been led to this conclusion, since a contrary conclusion would have enabled all National Health Service employees to whom the Whitley Council agreement on conditions of service applies to seek judicial review. Whilst it is true that the judge seems to have though that this right would be confined to senior employees, I see no grounds for any such restriction in principle. The most that can be said is that only senior employees could complain of having been dismissed in the exercise of delegated authority, because it is only senior employees who are protected from such dismissal. All employees would however have other rights based upon the fact that Parliament had intervened to specify and, on this view, protect those conditions of service as a matter of "public law".'

(1)   Supra, this chapter

(2)   [1957] AC 488

(3)   Infra, chapter 14

(4)   [1971] 1 WLR 1578

R v Hull Prison Board of Visitors, ex parte St Germain [1979] QB 425 Court of Appeal (Megaw, Shaw and Waller LJJ)

Availability of certiorari

Facts

Following disturbances in various prisons, the applicants were disciplined by boards of visitors, and subsequently sought certiorari on the ground that the hearings had been in breach of natural justice.

The Divisional Court refused the relief sought and the applicants appealed to the Court of Appeal.

Held

In determining cases under prison rules the boards could be acting in a judicial capacity, and hence its decisions were amenable to certiorari.

Megaw LJ (His Lordship considered the judgment of Lord Widgery CJ in the Divisional Court, and continued):

'The Lord Chief Justice, as I have said, accepted that in this context the board of visitors had a duty to act judicially. He then cited a passage from the judgment of Lord Parker CJ in *R v Criminal Injuries Compensation Board, ex parte Lain* (1). The paragraph, set out in full, is as follows:

"The position as I see it is that the exact limits of the ancient remedy by way of certiorari have never been and ought not to be specifically defined. They have varied from time to time being extended to meet changing conditions. At one time the writ only went to an inferior court. Later its ambit was extended to statutory tribunals determining a lis inter partes. Later again it extended to cases where there was no lis in the strict sense of the word but where immediate or subsequent rights of a citizen were affected. The only constant limits throughout were that it was performing a public duty. Private or domestic tribunals have always been outside the scope of certiorari since their authority is derived solely from contract, that is, from the agreement of the parties concerned."

The concluding words of that paragraph make it clear that Lord Parker CJ's exception of "private or domestic tribunals" was related to the agreement of the parties; a factor which, of course, does not apply in the present case.

Lord Widgery CJ commented, at p690, "... if one wanted encouragement to extend the scope of certiorari, one could hardly find a more powerful phrase to constitute that encouragement ...". He then went on to ask: "What is to be said on the other side?"

The answer which the board of visitors had given, and which the Lord Chief Justice and his brethren in the Divisional Court accepted, was that there was an exception to the general rule as to the scope of certiorari, which prevents it from going, even though the circumstances otherwise appear entirely suitable and appropriate for it.

"That exception," he said, at p690: "is where the order under challenge is an order made in private, disciplinary proceedings where there is some closed body, and a body which enjoys its own form of discipline and its own rules, and where there is a power to impose sanctions within the scope of those rules donated as part of the formation of the body itself. If one gets that situation, it is possible, in my judgment, on the authorities to say that certiorari will not go even though in other respects the case is suitable for it."

The principal authority which, as he himself said, moved the Lord Chief Justice was a decision of the Divisional Court, presided over by Lord Goddard CJ in *Ex parte Fry* (2). With all respect, I think that the criticism made before us of the judgment of Lord Goddard CJ in that case is well founded, at least as regards dicta therein. Though the decision in *Ex parte Fry* was upheld by this court, that approval was expressed to be on the basis of another ground given by the Divisional Court: namely, that in any event the exercise of the discretion to grant the remedy would not be appropriate on the facts of the case. It is right also to emphasise that the decision of the Divisional Court in *Ex parte Fry*, so far as it deals with the question of jurisdiction, as distinct from discretion, appears to have been, at least partly, founded on an earlier decision of that court, *R v Metropolitan Police Commissioner, ex parte Parker* (3). In my view, it would be unsafe to treat that decision as still being good law, having regard both to what was said in the speeches in *Ridge v Baldwin* (4) and the observations of Lord Denning MR in a judgment concurred in by Lord Wilberforce and Phillimore LJ in *R v Gaming Board for Great Britain, ex parte Benaim and Khaida* (5). So far as *Ex parte Fry* itself is concerned, its authority, in relation to the question of jurisdiction, is at any rate rendered doubtful by the observations of Lord Denning MR, obiter dicta, in *Buckoke v Greater London Council* (6).

Nevertheless, it is in my view open to this court, particularly in the light of the very special nature of these "private law" provisions as to offences against discipline in prisons, to consider as a matter of public policy whether or not in principle certiorari should be allowed to go in respect of awards of boards of visitors. It is for the courts, subject to overriding statutory provisions, to say where the limits lie. There is no authority binding on this court which either requires us to accept or prevents us from accepting that the present cases fall inside or outside those limited.

Lord Widgery CJ would, as I read his judgment, have held that the awards of boards of visitors may be subject to judicial review, but for his view that, if this were to be accepted as regards boards of visitors, it would have to be accepted also as regards awards by governors. If I have thought that that consequence followed, I should have agreed with the decision of the Divisional Court. But, with great respect, in my judgment that consequence does not follow.

Mr Collins and Mr Beloff both submitted, though not as their primary argument, that a valid distinction could be drawn between awards by the governor and awards by the board of visitors. I think that is right. It is at that point, and for that reason, that I would, respectfully, part company from the Divisional Court in deciding this issue of law. I would hold that judicial review of awards of boards of visitors in respect of offences against discipline is in principle available by way of certiorari.

To my mind, contrary to the submission put forward by the board of visitors in their respondents' notice, while the board of visitors have numerous other functions connected with the administration of the prison, their function in acting as a judicial tribunal in adjudicating on charges of offences against discipline, and in making awards consequent on findings of guilt, is properly regarded as a separate and independent function, different in character from their other functions. It is materially different, in my judgment, from the function of the governor in dealing with alleged offences against discipline. While the governor hears charges and makes awards, his position in so doing corresponds to that of the commanding officer in military discipline or the schoolmaster in school discipline. His powers of summary discipline are not only of a limited and summary nature but they are also intimately connected with his functions of day-to-day administration. To my mind, both good sense and the practical requirements of public policy make it undesirable that his exercise of that part of his administrative duties should be made subject to certiorari. But the same does not apply to the adjudications and awards of boards of visitors who, to quote from Mr Beloff's alternative submission on this part of the case, "are enjoined to mete out punishment only after a formalised inquiry and/or hearing." It may be difficult to define the distinction as a strict matter of logic. But I think that, as a matter of the proper practical application of the law in the general interest, not forgetting the legitimate interest of prisoners, that is where the line should be drawn, in respect of this "private law" disciplinary machinery. I think that, after giving full weight to all that has been said and done over recent years affecting the extension of the scope of the remedy of certiorari, there is nothing in existing law which requires us to decline to draw that line of distinction.'

(1)   [1967] 2 QB 864

(2)   [1954] 1 WLR 730

(3)   [1953] 1 WLR 1150

(4)   Infra, chapter 14

(5)   Infra, chapter 14

(6)   [1971] Ch 655

R v Independent Broadcasting Authority, ex parte Whitehouse (1985) The Times 4 April
Court of Appeal (Sir John Donaldson MR, Watkins LJ)

Public corporations, judicial review and locus standi

Facts

The Director General of the IBA had decided not to refer his decision to screen the film 'Scum' to other members of the IBA. After the film was broadcast, Mrs Whitehouse applied for judicial review of the Director General's decision, claiming that he had acted in breach of s4(1) of the Broadcasting Act 1981.

At first instance declarations were granted that the Director General of the IBA had committed a grave error in not consulting other members of the institutions, and that the IBA itself had failed to fully inform the Director General on the procedures relating to referral of controversial films. The IBA appealed to the Court of Appeal.

Held

The IBA had fulfilled its duties under s4 of the 1981 Act. The court would not interfere with the Director General's decision. The appeal was allowed.

Sir John Donaldson MR:

'The relevant duty of the IBA is set out in s4(1), namely, "to satisfy themselves that, so far as possible, the programmes broadcast by the Authority comply with" certain requirements. Those requirements are none of them precise. All require value judgments.

The parliamentary intention seems to have been to create a statutory body, the IBA, consisting of a number of responsible persons as members who occupy a position analogous to that of the Governors of the BBC. The role of the IBA is to control independent broadcasting and the role of the members to act as policy-makers and supervisors.

In using the phrase "it shall be the duty of the Authority to satisfy themselves" Parliament has created what might be described qualitatively as a "best endeavours" obligation and has left it to the members to adopt methods of working, or a system, which, in their opinion, is best adapted to securing the requirements set out in s4(1).

If the court is to be asked to intervene, it can only be on the basis that the IBA and its members have failed to fulfil that duty or have exceeded it and that involves satisfying the court that they have misdirected themselves as to the duty or, which amounts to the same thing, that no reasonable body of members properly directing themselves as to the duty could have devised or operated the system in fact adopted.

Mr Smyth submitted that any such view is inconsistent with the decision of the Court of Appeal in *Attorney General ex rel McWhirter* v *IBA* (1) and, in particular, the judgment of Lord Denning, Master of the Rolls, which, he submitted, requires the court to hold that the IBA and its members are in breach of their duty in failing to view a film such as Scum.

We can find nothing in that decision to contradict our view of the statutory duty of the IBA and its members. Certainly it affirmed that in some circumstances, an example of which is provided by the facts of the case, the members of the IBA would need to view a programme themselves, but that was not denied by the IBA and was inherent in the system which they had adopted.

It is always dangerous to confuse a decision on what the law is with a decision as to the application of the law to particular facts. The former, if a decision of the Court of Appeal or of the House of Lords, is binding. Unless the factual situation is wholly indistinguishable, the latter is only of persuasive authority, the degree of persuasion varying according to the extent to which the facts are distinguishable. In the instant appeal there was nothing known to the IBA or its members to put anyone sufficiently on inquiry as to the correctness of the Director General's decision to create a need for the members to be invited to view the programme or for them to take such an initiative.

However, there still remains the issue of whether the system in fact adopted by the IBA in purported fulfilment of its duty under s4(1) is one which calls for intervention by the court, either in the terms of the declaration granted by the Divisional Court or otherwise.

The way in which the system operates, and is intended to operate, is not in dispute. The sole question is thus whether no reasonable body of members of the IBA, properly directing themselves as to their duty, could have devised and operated such a system. The Divisional Court seems to have accepted that the IBA scheme would have been unimpeachable if it had provided for controversial programmes, or programmes as controversial as Scum, being referred to the members for personal decision. But what is a controversial programme or one as controversial as Scum? Lord Justice Watkins said; "It is not possible to identify exhaustively all the situations in which referral should be made."

That is precisely why the scheme left it to the Director General to decide when programmes should be referred to the members, for personal decision, subject to monitoring by the members in the light of their own home viewing, audience and newspaper reactions, programme intervention reports and discussions with the Director General and other senior officers at the IBA's monthly meetings. The IBA's duty is to devise and operate a system designed to ensure that the statutory requirements are met. The court's right and duty to interfere only arises if the system so devised is not operated or if it is such as no reasonable person could have adopted in compliance with the IBA's statutory duty. We are quite unpersuaded that the system falls into that category.

In our judgment the application for judicial review should have been dismissed. Accordingly the appeal will be allowed and the declaration by the Divisional Court set aside.'

(1)   [1973] QB 629

R v Inland Revenue Commissioners, ex parte National Federation of Self-employed and Small Businesses Ltd [1982] AC 617 House of Lords (Lords Wilberforce, Diplock, Fraser, Scarman and Roskill)

Locus standi and Order 53

Facts

About 6,000 men in Fleet Street did casual work for newspapers. Some signed their pay dockets with fictitious names (eg 'Mickey Mouse' - hence the nickname of 'The Mickey Mouse Case') to hide their true identities so that they would not be discovered by the taxman. Revenue had been defrauded of about £1m a year. The Inland Revenue gave these men an 'amnesty' for much of the past but required that in future they were to give their true names and pay their taxes. Many people, especially self-employed and small business owners, objected. Through the Federation they sought by judicial review a declaration that the IRC had acted unlawfully in granting the amnesty and an order to the IRC to compel them to collect the tax. On appeal as to whether the Federation had 'locus standi' to bring such proceedings.

Held

The appeal would be allowed.

In an application for judicial review under RSC Order 53, the locus standi issue should not be decided at the hearing of the case as a preliminary issue, but should be considered together with the merits of the application. This was so because the Order required that the plaintiff have 'sufficient interest in the matter to which the application relates' and an examination of the evidence was required to establish the nature of the 'matter'.

The appeal must be allowed since, looking at the matter as a whole, the Divisional Court ought, having regard to the matter raised, to have found that (per Wilberforce, Fraser, Roskill) the Federation merely as a body of taxpayers had shown no sufficient interest in the matter to justify its application for relief; (per Diplock) the Federation had completely failed to show any conduct of the revenue that was ultra vires or unlawful; (per Scarman) the Federation, having failed to show any grounds for believing that the revenue had failed to do its statutory duty, had not shown an interest sufficient in law to justify any further proceedings by the court on its application.

Lord Wilberforce:

'I think that it is unfortunate that this course (to take LS as a preliminary point) has been taken. There may be simple cases in which it can be seen at the earliest stage that the person applying for judicial review has no interest at all, or no sufficient interest to support the application: then it would be quite correct to refuse him leave to apply. The right to do so is an important safeguard against the courts being flooded and public bodies harassed by irresponsible applications. But in other cases this will not be so. In these it will be necessary to consider the powers or the duties in law of those against whom the relief is asked, the position of the applicant in relation to those powers or duties, and to the breach of those said to have been committed. In other words, the question of sufficient interest cannot, in such cases, be considered in the abstract, or as an isolated point: it must be taken together with the legal and factual context ... Order 53 ... requires sufficient interest in the matter to which the application relates. This, in the present case, necessarily involves the whole question of the duties of the Inland Revenue and the breaches or failure of those duties of which the respondents complain ... For all cases the test (of LS in the Order) is expressed as one of sufficient interest ... etc. As to this I would state two negative propositions. First, it does not remove the whole - and vitally important - question of LS into the realms of pure discretion. The matter is one of decision, a mixed decision of fact and law, which the court must decide on legal principles. Secondly, the fact that the same words are used to cover all the forms of remedy allowed by the rule does not mean that the test is the same in all cases. When Lord Parker CJ said that in cases of mandamus the text may well be stricter (than in certiorari) - the *Beaverbrook Newspapers* case (1) - and in *Cook*'s case (2) "on a very strict basis", he was not stating a technical rule - which can now be discarded - but a rule of common sense, reflecting the different character of the relief asked for. It would seem obvious enough that the interest of a person seeking to compel an authority to carry out a duty is different from that of a person complaining that a judicial or administrative body has, to his detriment, exceeded its powers. Whether one calls for a stricter rule than the other may be a linguistic point: they are certainly different and we should be unwise in our enthusiasm for liberation from procedural fetters to discard reasoned authorities which illustrate this ...'

Lord Diplock, allowing the appeal on the basis of no ultra vires being shown, thought Lord Wilberforce wrong on differing standards of locus standi for the various orders:

'It would be very much to be regretted if ... anything that is said by your Lordships today were to be understood as suggesting that the new Order 53 has the effect of reviving any of those technical rules of LS to obtain the various forms of prerogative writs that were applied by judges up to and during the first half of the present century, but which have been so greatly liberalised by judicial decision over the last 30 years ... Your Lordships can take judicial notice of the fact that the main purpose of the new Order 53 was to sweep away these procedural differences including, in particular, differences as to locus standi; to substitute for them a single simplified procedure for obtaining all forms of relief, and to leave to the court a wide discretion as to what interlocutory directions, including orders for discovery, were appropriate to the particular case.'

Lord Fraser agreed with Lord Wilberforce that the claim fails for want of locus standi, but said:

'The new Order 53 ... no doubt had the effect of removing technical and procedural difference between the prerogative orders, and of introducing a remedy by way of declaration and injunction in suitable cases, but I do not think it can have had the effect of throwing over all the older law and of leaving the grant of judicial review in the uncontrolled discretion of the court.'

Lord Scarman, agreeing with Lord Diplock, seems to suggest a liberal test of locus standi for all orders, and goes on to say that if ultra vires is proved by the applicant then he has locus standi, and if not, he has not. This seems to be a proverbial chicken and egg situation:

'The Federation, having failed to show any grounds for believing that the revenue has failed to do its statutory duty, have not, in my view, shown an interest sufficient in law to justify any further proceedings by the court on its application. Had they shown reasonable grounds for believing that the failure to collect tax from the Fleet Street casuals was an abuse of the revenue's managerial discretion or that there was a case to that effect which merited investigation and examination by the court, I would have agreed with the Court of Appeal that they had shown a sufficient interest ...'

Lord Roskill, believing that 'the Federation did not have sufficient interest' within the meaning of Order 53 but not agreeing with Wilberforce's differing standards, said:

'In my opinion it is now clear that the solution to the present appeal must lie in the proper application of the principles enshrined in Order 53, in the light of modern judicial policy ... to the facts of the present case without excessive regard to the fetters seemingly previously imposed by earlier decisions long before that modern policy evolved or Order 53 was enacted.'

(1)   [1969] 1 QB 342

(2)   [1970] 1 WLR 450 at 455

R v Panel on Take-overs and Mergers, ex parte Datafin plc [1987] 2 WLR 699 Court of Appeal (Sir John Donaldson MR, Lloyd and Nicholls LJJ)

Judicial review of a body not created by statute or prerogative

CONSTITUTIONAL AND ADMINISTRATIVE LAW

Facts

The Panel on Take-overs and Mergers is a self-regulating unincorporated association which supervises a code of conduct to be observed in the take-overs of listed public companies. The panel has no direct statutory, prerogative or common law powers but its powers are supported by certain statutory powers and penalties introduced after the creation of the Panel. The applicants sought leave to apply for judicial review of a decision of the Panel but leave was refused on the ground that the court had no jurisdiction to hear the application. The applicants appealed. The Panel argued, inter alia, that the supervisory jurisdiction of the court was confined to bodies whose powers derived solely from legislation or the exercise of the prerogative, and that therefore judicial review did not extend to the Panel.

Held

The Panel, despite being a self-regulating unincorporated association lacking any direct statutory, prerogative or common law powers, was a body subject to judicial review. In determining whether a body was amenable to review, and in particular the order of certiorari, regard was to be had to the functions of the body and not simply the source of its power. The Panel was amenable to certiorari because it was exercising public law functions, and in the absence of any other means of controlling the Panel, it was in the public interest for the court to extend its supervisory function.

Sir John Donaldson MR:

'The principal issue in this appeal, and the only issue which may matter in the longer term, is whether this remarkable body is above the law. Its respectability is beyond question. So is its bona fides. I do not doubt for one moment that it is intended to and does operate in the public interest and that the enormously wide discretion which it arrogates to itself is necessary if it is to function efficiently and effectively. While not wishing to become involved in the political controversy on the relative merits of self-regulation and governmental or statutory regulation, I am content to assume for the purposes of this appeal that self-regulation is preferable in the public interest. But that said, what is to happen if the panel goes off the rails? Suppose, perish the thought, that it were to use its powers in a way which was manifestly unfair. What then? Mr Alexander submits that the panel would lose the support of public opinion in the financial markets and would be unable to continue to operate. Further, or alternatively, Parliament could and would intervene. Maybe, but how long would that take and who in the meantime could or would come to the assistance of those who were being oppressed by such conduct?'

The Master of the Rolls then dealt with the question of 'reviewability' and, having explained how bodies such as the Criminal Injuries Compensation Board were brought with in the scope of judicial review, continued:

'The Criminal Injuries Compensation Board, in the form which it then took, was an administrative novelty. Accordingly it would have been impossible to find a precedent for the exercise of the supervisory jurisdiction of the court which fitted the facts. Nevertheless, the court not only asserted its jurisdiction, but further asserted that it was a jurisdiction which was adaptable thereafter. This process has since been taken further in *O'Reilly* v *Mackman* (1) by deleting any requirement that the body should have a duty to act judicially, in *Council of Civil Service Unions* v *Minister for the Civil Service* (2) by extending it to a person exercising purely prerogative power, and in *Gillick* v *West Norfolk and Wisbech Area Health Authority* (3), where Lord Fraser and Lord Scarman expressed the view obiter that judicial review would extend to guidance circulars issued by a department of state without any specific authority. In all the reports it is possible to find enumerations of factors giving rise to the jurisdiction, but it is a fatal error to regard the presence of all those factors as essential or as being exclusive of other factors. Possibly the only essential elements are what can be described as a public element, which can take many different forms, and the exclusion from the jurisdiction of bodies whose sole source of power is a consensual submission to its jurisdiction.

In fact, given its novelty, the panel fits surprisingly well into the format which this court had in mind in *R v Criminal Injuries Compensation Board* (4). It is without doubt performing a public duty and an important one. This is clear from the expressed willingness of the Secretary of State for Trade and Industry to limit legislation in the field of take-overs and mergers and to use the panel as the centrepiece of his regulation of that market. The rights of citizens are indirectly affected by its decisions, some, but by no means all of whom, may in a technical sense be said to have assented to this situation, eg the members of the Stock Exchange. At least in its determination of whether there has been a breach of the code, it has a duty to act judicially and it asserts that its raison d'etre is to do equity between one shareholder and another. Its source or power is only partly based on moral persuasion and the assent of institutions and their members, the bottom line being the statutory powers exercised by the Department of Trade and Industry and the Bank of England. In this context I should be very disappointed if the courts could not recognise the realities of executive power and allowed their vision to be clouded by the subtlety and sometimes complexity of the way in which it can be exerted.

Given that it is really unthinkable that, in the absence of legislation such as affects trade unions, the panel should go on its way concooned from the attention of the courts, in defence of the citizenry, we sought to investigate whether it could conveniently be controlled by established forms of private law, eg torts such as actionable combinations in restraint of trade, and, to this end, pressed (counsel for the applicants) to draft a writ. Suffice it to say that the result was wholly unconvincing and, not surprisingly, Mr Alexander (counsel for the panel) did not admit that it would be in the least effective.

In reaching my conclusion that the court has jurisdiction to entertain applications for the judicial review of decisions of the panel, I have said nothing about the substantial arguments put forward by (counsel for the panel) based on the practical problems which are involved. These, in my judgment, go not to the existence of the jurisdiction, but to how it should be exercised ...'

Lloyd LJ delivered a concurring judgment. It is interesting to note his observations on the 'source of power' debate:

'But suppose I am wrong; suppose that the courts are indeed confined to looking at the source of the power, as (counsel for the panel) submits. Then I would accept the submission of (counsel for the applicants) that the source of the power in the present case is indeed government, at least in part. (Counsel for the panel) argued that, so far from the source of the power being government, this a case where the government has deliberately abstained from exercising power. I do not take that view. I agree with (counsel for the applicants) when he says that there has here been an implied devolution of power. Power exercised behind the scenes is power none the less. The express powers conferred on inferior tribunals were of critical importance in the early days when the sole or main ground for intervention by the courts was that the inferior tribuanal had exceeded its powers. But those days are long since past. Having regard to the way in which the panel came to be established, the fact that the Governor of the Bank of England appoints both the chairman and the deputy chairman, and the other matters to which Sir John Donaldson MR has referred, I am persuaded that the panel was established "under authority of (the) government", to use the language of Diplock LJ in *Lain*'s case (4). If in addition to looking at the source of the power we are entitled to look at the nature of the power, as I believe we are, then the case is all the stronger.'

Nicholls LJ also delivered a concurring judgment.

(1) [1983] 2 AC 237

(2) [1985] AC 374

(3) [1986] AC 112

(4) [1967] 2 QB 864

R v Secretary of State for the Home Department, ex parte Benwell [1984] 3 WLR 843
Queen's Bench Division (Hodgson J)

Employment under a statutory provision may be subject to judicial review

Facts

The applicant sought an order of certiorari to quash the decision of the Secretary of State confirming his dismissal from the prison service on the ground that the procedure before the disciplinary bodies concerned had been in breach of natural justice.

Held

The applicant was entitled to use judicial review to challenge the decision of the Home Secretary. As a prison officer he had no contract of employment that could be enforced in civil proceedings. The Home Secretary's power to deal with the disciplinary proceedings arose under statutory provisions, and was therefore within the sphere of public law. The application was granted.

Hodgson J:

'I now come to the question whether this court can do anything to remedy this injustice. Until a few days ago I should have found the judgment of Hodgson J in *R v East Berkshire Health Authority, ex parte Walsh*, The Times, 15 November, 1983, as persuasive as Sir John Donaldson MR would have found the decision of Sir John Donaldson in *Sanders v Ernest A Neale Ltd* (1) but that assistance is no longer available to me and I must now look to the decision of the Court of Appeal in *R v East Berkshire Health Authority, ex parte Walsh* (2).

The question whether the applicant's complaints in this case give rise to any right to judicial review is as I have indicated, of great general importance. The reason is this; because of his status of constable, a prison officer cannot resort to the industrial tribunals under the Employment Protection (Consolidation) Act 1978: see *Home Office v Robinson* (3). Save to the extent that Parliament has by statute provided a Crown servant with some special entitlement, he is dismissible at pleasure and has no private law remedy. It follows that, unless a prison officer can seek leave to move for judicial review, he is without remedy if he is unlawfully dismissed (unless as Mr Lester points out in certain circumstances the officer is black or a woman). But these disadvantages go only, it seems, to the question whether this court should exercise its discretion to grant relief. They do not directly affect the jurisdiction point: see Sir John Donaldson MR in *R v East Berkshire Health Authority, ex parte Walsh* (2). So the position is that, unlike Mr Walsh (who can now start proceedings by writ with all the procedural advantages he thereby gains) the applicant, if he is turned away empty-handed from this court, has nowhere else to go in this country.

At first sight, at any rate, the position of a nurse and a prison officer have much in common. The Code of Discipline for prison officers which governs the discipline of prison officers and provides sanctions for offences against prison discipline derive their authority from the statute in much the same way as the disciplinary procedures relating to nurses. The Prison Act 1952 provides in s47(1):

"The Secretary of State may make rules for the regulation and management of prisons, remand centres, detention centres and Borstal institutions respectively, and for the classification, treatment, employment, discipline and control of persons required to be detained therein."

At first I thought that s47(2) was relevant, but it is not; it deals only with prisoners. The National Health Service Act 1977 provides by s12 and Part III of Sch 5, para 10(1):

"An authority ... may employ, on such terms as it may determine in accordance with regulations and such directions as may be given by the Secretary of State, such officers as it may so determine ..."

Under the power granted by s47(1) the Home Secretary made the Prison Rules 1964. Part II deals with officers of prisons. Rules 77 to 83 deal with matters of discipline of prison officers. Rule 84 reads:

> "The Secretary of State may approve a code of discipline to have effect in relation to officers, or such classes of officers as it may specify setting out the offences against discipline, the awards which may be made in respect of them and the procedure for dealing with charges."

The Home Secretary has approved a code of discipline: it includes offences, failure to comply with rules 77 to 83 and adds many more. The code of discipline for nurses is found in section XXXIV of the agreement of the General Council of the Whitley Council for the Health Services: these were approved by the Secretary of State under regulations made under the power granted to him by statute. I set the complete statutory process out in my judgment in *Ex parte Walsh*.

There are, however, differences between nurses and prison officers. Nurses enter into a contract of employment with health authorities whereas prison officers are appointed by the Home Secretary: s47(1) of the Prison Act 1952 and article 3(2) of Schedule 1 to the Prison Commissioners Dissolution Order 1963 (SI 1963 No 597). It seems to me that this may point the way I should go. Second, as I have said, nurses have remedies in civil law which are not available to prison officers and, although this fact only goes directly to discretion, it may be some indication that Parliament intended questions of the exercise of the Home Secretary's powers and duties under the code to be in the public sector. It was under and purportedly in compliance with that Code of Discipline that the department issued the applicant with notice of its intentions to dismiss him and the Home Secretary decided to implement that decision. The question is whether that is a sufficient statutory underpinning to inject the element of public law into this application: see Sir John Donaldson MR in *Ex parte Walsh* (2).

Mr Lester submits that a distinction between this case and *Ex parte Walsh* can be found in the fact that in *Ex parte Walsh* the conditions of employment were contractual conditions incorporated by collective bargaining and approved by a minister, whereas this case is not concerned with contractual rights but only with the public law duty of the Home Secretary to follow the Code of Discipline and apply it. Mr Brown, with an explicit lack of enthusiasm, contends the contrary. He says that there are three findings I could make. The first that what he calls the "entirety of the matter" is justiciable; the second, that the procedures are justiciable, but not the substantive decision to dismiss; the last, that neither the procedures nor the substantive decision are justiciable. With respect, I think that Mr Brown in his submissions is confusing two thins: the power of the Home Secretary to dismiss a prison officer for other than disciplinary reasons (and I have not been told what, if any, restraints are placed upon the Home Secretary in this regard); and the power of the Home Secretary to implement a disciplinary award of dismissal. That second power would be equally subject (or not subject) to review by this court if the award was one of severe reprimand or reduction in rank.

It seems to me that the reason why the Court of Appeal came to the conclusion it did in *Ex parte Walsh* was that the disciplinary procedures in section XXXIV were incorporated into the contract of service and that it was this incorporation which deprived the procedures and compliance with them of any possible public law character: see Sir John Donaldson MR at p827F-G, May LJ at p834D-G, and Purchas LJ at pp837G-H, 839H-840A, 841A-C, 843B-D. The applicant in this case was a civil servant appointed by the Home Secretary whose employment was governed by the Code of Discipline and, no doubt, by the standing orders formulated by the Prison Department of the Home Office and circular instructions amending standing orders and making provision for matters of detail: see generally Halsbury's Laws of England, 4th ed, vol 37 (1982), paras 1101 to 1121. In *Ex parte Walsh* Purchas LJ said, at p837G-H:

> "There is a danger of confusing the rights with their appropriate remedies enjoyed by an employee arising out of a private contract of employment with the performance by a public body of the duties imposed upon it as part of the statutory terms under which it exercises its powers. The former are appropriate for private remedies inter partes whether by action in the

High Court or in the appropriate statutory tribunal, whilst the latter are subject to the supervisory powers of the court under RSC, Order 53."

Clearly, the Court of Appeal in *Ex parte Walsh* did not consider the purported dismissal on disciplinary grounds of Mr. Walsh to be the performance of any duty imposed upon the authority as part of the statutory terms under which it exercised its powers.

In this case, however, it is my opinion that in making a disciplinary award of dismissal, the Home Office (to use a comprehensive term to include the department and the Secretary of State so distinguished by the respondent itself in this case) was performing the duties imposed upon it as part of the statutory terms under which it exercises its power. I conclude therefore that this court in the exercise of its supervisory jurisdiction can come to the aid of the applicant in this case and I am glad that it can. I can only hope that my gladness is longer lived than the gladness I was foolhardy enough to express in *Ex parte Walsh*.'

(1)   [1974] ICR 565

(2)   Supra, this chapter

(3)   [1982] ICR 31

Wandsworth London Borough Council v Winder [1984] 3 WLR 1254 House of Lords (Lord Fraser of Tullbelton, Lord Scarman, Lord Keith of Kinkel, Lord Roskill and Lord Brandon of Oakbrook)

Judicial review: public and private rights: procedure

Facts

The council let one of their council flats to the appellant on a weekly tenancy. In 1981, in pursuance of their statutory obligation under the Housing Act 1957, they resolved to increase the rent and served the appellant with a notice of increase. The appellant considered it excessive and continued to pay the original rent. The following year there was a further resolution by the council and a further notice of increase of rent was served on the tenant, who again refused to pay the increase. A notice seeking possession was served on him followed by a claim for possession in the county court on the ground of failure to pay rent. The defendant denied that he owed any sums to the council, contending that the council's decisions to make the increases were ultra vires and void and each of the notices was likewise ultra vires and void.

The council applied to strike out the defence and counterclaim on the ground that they were an abuse of the process of the court, relying on *O'Reilly* v *Mackman* (1). The tenant contended that that decision only dealt with the initiation of proceedings and the rule of public policy which it declared did not apply to a defendant wishing to raise a defence involving a matter of public law. The county court judge, on the council's appeal from the registrar's decision, held that there was no distinction to be drawn between the raising of an issue of public law by way of a claim or by way of defence, and allowed the appeal. The tenant appealed and the Court of Appeal allowed his appeal. The council appealed.

Held

The appeal would be dismissed.

Lord Fraser of Tullybelton:

'The respondent seeks to show in the course of his defence in these proceedings that the appellants' decisions to increase the rent were such as no reasonable man could consider justifiable. But your Lordships are not concerned in this appeal to decide whether that contention is right or wrong. The only issue at this stage is whether the respondent is entitled to put forward the contention as a defence in the present proceedings. The appellants say that he is not because the only procedure by which their decision could have been challenged was by judicial review under RSC Order 53. The respondent was refused leave to apply for judicial review out of time and (say the appellants) he has lost the opportunity to challenge the decisions. The appellants rely on the decisions of this House in *O'Reilly* v *Mackman* [1983] 2 AC 237 and *Cocks* v *Thanet DC* [1983] 2 AC 286. The respondent accepts that judicial review would have been an appropriate procedure for the purpose, but he maintains that it is not the only procedure open to him, and that he was entitled to wait until he was sued by the appellants and then to defend the proceedings, as he has done.

In order to deal with these contentions, it is necessary to consider what was decided by the House in those two cases ... There are two important differences between the facts in *O'Reilly* v *Mackman* and those in the present case. First, the plaintiffs in *O'Reilly* v *Mackman* had not suffered any infringement of their rights in private law; their complaint was that they had been ordered to forfeit part of their remission of sentence but they had no right in private law to such a remission, which was granted only as a matter of indulgence. Consequently, even if the Board of Visitors had acted contrary to the rules of natural justice when making the award, the members of the board would not have been liable in damages to the prisoners. In the present case what the respondent complains of is the infringement of a contractual right in private law. Second, in *O'Reilly* v *Mackman* the prisoners had initiated the proceedings, and Lord Diplock, throughout in his speech, treated the question only as one affecting a claim for infringing a right of the plaintiff while in the present case the respondent is the defendant. The decision on *O'Reilly* v *Mackman* is therefore not directly in point in the present case, but the appellants rely particularly on a passage in a speech of Lord Diplock [in which Lord Diplock outlined possible exceptional cases where a private law action might be permitted] ...

The question for your Lordships is whether the instant appeal is an exception to the general rule. It might be possible to treat this case as falling within one of the exceptions suggested by Lord Diplock, if the question of the invalidity of the appellants decision had arisen as a collateral issue in a claim by the respondent (as defendant) for infringement of his right arising under private law to continue to occupy the flat. But I do not consider that the question of invalidity is truly collateral to the issue between the parties. Although it is not mentioned in the appellants' statement of claim, it is the whole basis of the respondent's defence and it is the central issue which has to be decided. The case does not therefore fall within any of the exceptions specifically suggested in *O'Reilly* v *Mackman*.

Immediately after the decision in *O'Reilly* v *Mackman*, the House applied the general rule in *Cocks* v *Thanet DC*. The proceedings in *O'Reilly* v *Mackman* had begun before the Supreme Court Act 1981 (especially s31) was passed. The proceedings in *Cocks* v *Thanet DC* were begun after that Act was passed, but for the present purpose nothing turns on that distinction ... The essential difference between that case and the present is that the impugned decision of the local authority did not deprive the plaintiff of a pre-existing private law right; it prevented him from establishing a new private right law. There is also the same distinction as in *O'Reilly* v *Mackman*, namely that the party complaining of the decision was the plaintiff.

Although neither *O'Reilly* v *Mackman* nor *Cocks* v *Thanet DC* is an authority which directly applies to the facts of the instant appeal, it is said on behalf of the appellants that the principle underlying those decisions applies here, and that, if the respondent is successful, he will be evading that principle. My Lords, I cannot agree. The principle underlying those decisions, as Lord Diplock explained in *O'Reilly* v *Mackman*, is that there is a:

> "need, in the interest of good administration and of third parties who may be indirectly affected by the decision, for speedy certainty as to whether it has the effect of a decision that is valid in public law."

The main argument urged on behalf of the appellants was that this is a typical case where there is a need for speedy certainty in the public interest. I accept, of course, that the decision in this appeal will directly affect many third parties including many of the appellants' tenants, and perhaps most if not all of their ratepayers because if the appellants' impugned decisions are held to be invalid, the basis of their financial administration since 1981 will be upset. That would be highly inconvenient from the point of view of the appellants, and of their ratepayers, and it would be a great advantage to them if persons such as the respondent who seek to challenge their decision were limited to doing so by procedure under Ord 53. Such procedure is speedy and avoids prolonged uncertainty about the validity of decisions. An intending applicant for judicial review under Ord 53 has to obtain leave to apply, so that unmeritorious applications can be dismissed in limine and an application must normally be made within a limited period of three months after the decision which has impugned, unless the court allows an extension of time in any particular case. Procedure under Ord 53 also affords protection to public authorities in other ways, which are explained in *O'Reilly* v *Mackman* and which I need not elaborate here. It may well be that such protection to public authorities tends to promote good administration. But there may be other ways of obtaining speedy decisions; for example in some cases it may be possible for a public authority itself to initiate proceedings for judicial review. In any event, the arguments for protecting public authorities against unmeritorious or dilatory challenges to their decisions have to be set against the arguments for preserving the ordinary rights of private citizens to defend themselves against unfounded claims.

It would in my opinion be a very strange use of language to describe the respondent's behaviour in relation to this litigation as an abuse or misuse by him of the process of the court. He did not select the procedure to be adopted. He is merely seeking to defend proceedings brought against him by the appellants. In so doing he is seeking only to exercise the ordinary right of any individual to defend an action against him on the ground that he is not liable for the whole sum claimed by the plaintiff. Moreover, he puts forward his defence as a matter of right, whereas in an application for judicial review, success would require an exercise of the court's discretion in his favour. Apart from the provisions of Ord 53 and s31 of the Supreme Court Act 1981, he would certainly be entitled to defend that action on the ground that the plaintiff's claim arises from a resolution which (on his view) is invalid: see for example *Cannock Chase DC* v *Kelly* [1978] 1 WLR 1, which was decided in July 1977, a few months before Ord 53 came into force (as it did in December 1977). I find it impossible to accept that the right to challenge the decision of a local authority in course of defending an action for payment can have been swept away by Ord 53, which was directed to introducing a procedural reform. As Lord Scarman said in *IRC* v *National Federation of Self-Employed and Small Businesses Ltd* [1982] AC 617 at 647:

> "The new RSC Ord 53 is a procedural reform of great importance in the field of public law, but it does not, indeed cannot, either extend or diminish the substantive law. Its function is limited to ensuring 'ubi jus ibi remedium'."

Lord Wilberforce spoke to the same effect (see [1982] AC 617 at 631). Nor, in my opinion, did s31 of the Supreme Court Act 1981 which refers only to "an application" for judicial review have the effect of limiting the rights of a defendant sub silentio. I would adopt the words of Viscount Simonds in *Pyx Granite Co Ltd* v *Ministry of Housing and Local Government* [1960] AC 260 at 286 as follows:

> "It is a principle not by any means to be whittled down that the subject's recourse to Her Majesty's courts for the determination of his rights is not to be excluded except by clear words."

The argument of the appellants in the present case would be directly in conflict with that observation.

If the public interest requires that persons should not be entitled to defend actions brought against them by public authorities, where the defence rests on a challenge to a decision by the public authority, then it is for Parliament to change the law.'

13 THE ULTRA VIRES DOCTRINE – IRRATIONALITY

13.1 Irrationality – Taking into account irrelevant considerations – Failing to take into account relevant considerations – Acting on no evidence.

13.2 Using a power for an improper purpose

13.3 Failing to exercise discretion: policy and delegation

13.1 Irrationality – Taking into account irrelevant considerations – Failing to take into account relevant considerations – Acting on no evidence

Backhouse v Lambeth LBC (1972) 116 Sol Jo 802 Queen's Bench Division (Melford Stevenson J)

Ultra vires acts where no reasonable authority would so proceed: abuse of power

Facts

Under ss63 and 64 of the Housing Finance Act 1972, local authorities were required to increase council house rents. Section 63 further provided that such increases would not have to be made if the local authority made a general rent increase in the first half of 1972-3 which produced £26 or more per dwelling in 1972-73. The council hoped to avoid having to increase rents generally, by increasing the rent in respect of one house (unoccupied) from £7 per week to £18,000 per week, and thus producing the average rent increase required by s63. Backhouse, the leader of the council tenants, applied for a declaration to the effect that the increase was valid.

Held

The increase was ultra vires. It was an increase that no reasonable local authority would have sanctioned. Alternatively it was motivated by irrelevant considerations, a desire to circumvent the provisions of the Act.

Coleen Properties Ltd v Minister of Housing and Local Government [1971] 1 WLR 433 Court of Appeal (Lord Denning MR, Sachs and Buckley LJJ)

Ultra vires acts based on insufficient evidence

Facts

Coleen Properties Ltd owned Clark House which was made the subject of a clearance order by Tower Hamlets LBC on the ground that the acquisition of it was reasonably necessary for the purpose of the satisfactory development or use of the clearance area. Coleen Properties objected, and produced evidence at the subsequent local inquiry to support its case that acquisition of Clark House was unnecessary. The inquiry inspector recommended that it should not be made part of the clearance order, but the Minister rejected this contention and approved the clearance order, including Clark House. Coleen Properties applied to the High Court for the order to be quashed. Lyell J dismissed the application, and the company appealed.

Held

The appeal would be allowed and the clearance order quashed in so far as it applied to Clark House. There was no evidence to justify the Minister overruling the Inspector.

Lord Denning MR:

'In my opinion the Minister was in error in reversing the inspector's recommendation. The Minister had before him only the report of the inspector. He did not see the premises himself. To my mind there was no material on which the Minister could properly overrule the inspector's recommendation. Clark House if a first class new property. It has shops with flats over. In order to acquire it compulsorily, the local authority must show that the acquisition "is reasonably necessary for the satisfactory development or use of the cleared area." In order to show it, they ought to have produced some evidence to the inspector as to what kind of development would be a "satisfactory development" of the area. and to show how the acquisition of Clark House is "reasonably necessary." I do not say that they ought to have produced a detailed plan of the proposed development. I realise well enough that in many cases that may not be practicable. For instance, when an area is to be developed for industrial purposes, you cannot go into details until you have the business men wanting the factories. But, when an area is to be developed for residential purposes - for the council's own housing plans - it ought to be possible to give an outline plan of the proposed development. I cannot myself see that the council could get any more dwellings on to the site of Clark House than the six flats which are already there. The council may desire to make a neat and tidy development of these two streets, including Clark House, but this may well be possible whilst leaving Clark House standing. At any rate, I am quite clear that the mere ipse dixit of the local council is not sufficient. There must be some evidence to support their assertion. And here there was none.

Then there is the report of the inspector. He was clearly of opinion that the acquisition of Clark House was not reasonably necessary. I can see no possible justification for the Minister in overruling the inspector. There was no material whatever on which he could so do. I know that on matters of planning policy the Minister can overrule the inspector, and need not send it back to him, as happened in *Luke* v *Minister of Housing and Local Government* (1). But the question of what is "reasonably necessary" is not planning policy. It is an inference of fact on which the Minister should not overrule the inspector's recommendation unless there is material sufficient for the purpose. There was none here. In my judgment the Minister was wrong and this court should intervene and overrule him ...'

Sachs LJ:

'The need for evidence to be available to a Minister before he can act has been the subject of earlier decisions. The question before him was not, to my mind, one of "policy": it was in essence a question of fact that had to be established as a condition precedent to the exercise of the powers to take away the subject's property. It was no less a question of fact because it involved forming a judgment on matters on which expert opinion can and indeed ought to be given. (I rather doubt whether there is much material difference between the view I have just expressed and that of Mr Slynn who has argued that the question was simply a matter of planning judgment which had to be based on evidence.) As long ago as the *Sheffield* case (*Sheffield Burgesses* v *Minister of Health* (2) Swift J said:

"... it is for the court, if the matter is brought before it, to say whether there is any material on which the Minister could have come to the conclusion that it was reasonably necessary. If the court comes to the conclusion that there is no such material, then it will not hesitate to quash the Minister's order."

That passage coincides with those passages in the judgment of Lord Denning MR in the *Ashbridge* case (3) to which he has referred.

The Minister, therefore, cannot come to a conclusion of fact contrary to that which the inspector found in this case unless there was evidence before the latter on which he (the Minister) could form that contrary conclusion. Upon the inquiry, an inspector is, of course, entitled to use the evidence of his own eyes, evidence which he as an expert, in this case he was an architect, can accept. The Minister, on the other hand, can only look at what is on the record. He cannot, as against the subject, avail himself of other expert evidence from within the Ministry - at any rate, without informing the subject and giving him an opportunity to deal with that evidence on the lines which are set out in regard to a parallel matter in the Compulsory Purchase by Local Authorities (Inquiries Procedure) Rules 1962. Whilst the inspector, even if not an architect, may well be looked on as an expert for the purpose of forming an opinion of fact, the Minister is in a different position. It is by no means intended as a criticism to say with all respect that no Minister can personally be an expert on all matters of professional opinion with which his officers deal from day to day.'

(1)   [1968] 1 QB 172

(2)   (1935) 52 TLR 171

(3)   [1965] 1 WLR 320

13.2   Using a power for an improper purpose

Congreve v Home Office [1976] QB 629 Court of Appeal (Lord Denning MR, Roskill and Geoffrey Lane LJJ)

Exercise of a discretionary power for an improper purpose

Facts

The plaintiff was the owner of a colour television set for which he held the appropriate licence, which was due to expire on 31 March 1975.

In January 1975 it was announced that the fee for the issue of a colour television licence was to be increased from £12 to £18. On 20 February the Home Secretary made the Wireless Telegraphy (Broadcast Licence Charges and Exemption) (Amendment) Regulations which gave effect to that increase. Those regulations were expressed to come into operation on 1 April 1975.

In order to avoid payment of the increased fee, the plaintiff decided to obtain a new licence before the expiry of his existing licence. On 26 March he obtained a new licence from the Post Office and paid the prescribed fee of £12. The licence was dated 26 March and was expressed on its face to expire on 29 February 1976.

A considerable number of licence holders were taking the same course as the plaintiff and in consequence a substantial part of the anticipated revenue from the issue of licences was being lost to the Crown. Accordingly, the Licence Records Office, as agent for the Home Secretary, wrote to the plaintiff, in common with other licence holders who had taken the same action, demanding payment of an additional sum of £6 for the licence issued to him on 26 March and threatening that, if that additional sum were not paid, the Home Secretary, in the exercise of his power under s1(4) of the Wireless Telegraphy Act 1949, would revoke the plaintiff's licence.

(Section 111(4) - 'A wireless telegraphy licence may be revoked, or the terms, provisions or limitations thereof varied, by a notice in writing of the Postmaster General * served on the holder of the licence'. (*The Home Secretary had become the relevant Minister rather than the Postmaster General.))

By a subsequent letter dated 11 November, the Records Office told the plaintiff that, if he did not pay the additional £6, his licence would be allowed to run for eight months from 31 March and thereafter the licence would be revoked as from 1 December.

The plaintiff refused to pay the £6, and brought an action against the Home Office claiming a declaration that revocation of the licence would be unlawful, invalid and of no effect.

Held

The licence issued to the plaintiff on 26 March had been obtained lawfully and was a valid licence for the period expressed on its face. At the date when it was issued the Home Office had no lawful authority to require, as a condition of its issue, a sum greater than the fee that was then current, ie £12. It followed that the subsequent demand on the plaintiff for the payment of an additional sum of £6 was an unlawful demand and it would be an unlawful exercise of the Home Secretary's power of revocation to revoke, or to threaten to revoke, the licence as a means of enforcing that demand. In effect, it amounted to using the Home Secretary's power of revocation in order to levy a tax that Parliament had not given the Executive authority to levy. (*Attorney-General* v *Wilts United Dairies Ltd* [1922] (1); *Associated Provincial Picture Houses Ltd* v *Wednesbury Corporation* [1948] (2); and *Padfield* v *Minister of Agriculture, Fisheries and Food* [1968] (3) applied.)

(1)   91 LJKB 897

(2)   Supra, chapter 11

(3)   Supra, chapter 11

Sydney (Municipal Council of) v **Campbell** [1925] AC 338 Privy Council (Viscount Cave, Lord Blanesburgh, Sir Adrian Knox and Duff J)

Ultra vires acts where powers exercised for an improper purpose

Facts

Under s16 of the Sydney Corporation Amendment Act 1905 the local authority could exercise its powers of compulsory purchase to improve or remodel parts of the city. A compulsory purchase order was issued in respect of the respondent's land, although no plans for remodelling or improving the site existed. The council sought to benefit from the increase in the value of the land that would accrue once a proposed highway extension was completed.

Campbell applied for an injunction to restrain proceedings on the compulsory purchase order, and this was granted at first instance. The council now appealed to the Privy Council.

Held

The appeal would be dismissed.

Duff J:

'... Their Lordships think it not reasonably disputable that at the time of the passing of the resolution in June, the Council conceived it to be within its powers to resume lands not needed for the extension itself, but solely for the purpose of appropriating the betterments arising from the extension; and that, as Street CJE found, the Council had not at that time applied itself to the consideration of any other object in connection with the resumption of the residual lands ...

The legal principles governing the execution of such powers as that conferred by s16, in so far as presently relevant, are not at all in controversy. A body such as the Municipal Council of Sydney, authorised to take land compulsorily for specified purposes, will not be permitted to exercise its powers for different purposes, and if it attempts to do so, the Courts will interfere. As Lord Loreburn said, in *Marquess of Clanricarde* v *Congested Districts Board* (1): "Whether it does so or not is a question of fact." Where the proceedings of the Council are attacked upon this ground, the party impeaching those proceedings must, of course, prove that the Council, though professing to exercise its powers for the statutory purpose, is in fact employing them in furtherance of some ulterior object.

Their Lordships think that the conclusion of the learned Chief Judge in Equity upon this question of fact is fully sustained by the evidence.'

(1)   (1914) 79 JP 481

Westminster Corporation v London and North-Western Railway Co [1905] AC 426
House of Lords (Lord Macnaghten, Lord James, Earl of Halsbury LC and Lord Lindley)

Ultra vires acts where powers are exercised for an improper purpose

Facts

Westminster Corporation was empowered by the Public Health (London) Act 1891 to provide and maintain public conveniences. The corporation proceeded to construct public lavatories underground in the middle of Parliament Street. The lavatories were described by Lord Macnaghten in the following terms:

'The plan of the construction is this: On each side of the roadway there is an entrance, five feet nine inches wide, protected by railings and leading by a staircase of the same width to a passage or subway, ten feet wide and eight feet high, which runs the whole way across on a level with the underground conveniences. Out of this subway there are openings - two for men and one for women - into spacious chambers, were the usual accommodation (politely described as lavatories and cloak-rooms) is provided on a large and liberal scale. All the arrangements seem to have been designed and carried out with due regard to decency, and with every possible consideration for the comfort of wayfarers in need of such accommodation.'

The railway company objected to this construction on a number of grounds, but the essence of its complaint was that the corporation had used its power to construct lavatories in order to achieve its real aim, which was the construction of a subway under Parliament Street. After much involved argument at first instance and before the Court of Appeal the matter came before the House of Lords.'

Held (Lord James dissenting)

The construction of conveniences was within the scope of the statutory power. The fact that the public might use the means of access at either side of the road as a subway did not mean, in the absence of any further evidence, that the corporation had exceeded its powers.

Lord Macnaghten (on the question of whether the corporation acted in good faith, or whether it had in mind the attainment of some ultra vires goal):

'That is a very serious charge. It is not enough to shew that the corporation contemplated that the public might use the subway as a means of crossing the street. That was an obvious possibility. It cannot be otherwise if you have an entranced on each side and the communication is not interrupted by a wall or a barrier of some sort. In order to make out a case of bad faith it must be shewn that the corporation constructed this subway as a means of crossing the street under colour and pretence of providing public conveniences which were not really wanted at that particular place. That was the view of their conduct taken by the Court of Appeal. "In my judgment," says Vaughan Williams LJ, "it is not true to say that the corporation have taken this land which they have taken with the object of using it for the purposes authorised by the Legislature." "You are acting mala fide," he added, "if you are seeking to acquire and acquiring lands for a purpose not authorised by the Act of Parliament." So you are; there can be no doubt of that. The other learned Lords Justices seem to take the same view of the conduct of the corporation. Now this, as I said, is a very serious charge. A gross breach of public duty, and all for a mere fad! The learned judge who tried the case had before him the chairman of the works committee. That gentleman declared that his committee considered with very great care for a couple of years or more the question of these conveniences in Parliament Street. He asserted on oath that "the primary object of the committee was to provide these conveniences." Why is this gentleman not to be believed? The learned judge who saw and heard him believed his statement. The learned judges of the Court of Appeal have discredited his testimony, mainly, if not entirely, on the ground of two letters about which he was not asked a single question ... The letter of the surveyor was a foolish letter, which the writer seems to have thought clever. The letter of the temporary representative of the acting town clerk, if you compare the two letters, seems to have derived its inspiration from the same source. I cannot conceive why the solemn statement of the chairman of the committee should be discredited on such a ground. I do not think there is anything in the minutes tending to disprove his testimony. I entirely agree with Joyce J that the primary object of the council was the construction of the conveniences with the requisite and proper means of approach thereto and exit therefrom ...'

Lord James (dissenting):

'...[T]he question to be solved seems to be thus formulated: Was the so-called tunnel an approach to the convenience only, or was it something more? (1) Was it a subway distinct from the approach, or (2) was it a subway in combination with the approach used for two distinct purposes?

In my judgment the construction in question comes within one or other of the two latter alternatives. Possibly within the first, certainly within the second.

If this finding on the facts be correct, the works, so far as they constitute the subway, are constructed without legal authority. The Legislature has not thought it right to confer on local bodies the power to compulsorily take land or impose rates for the purpose of constructing subways. In this case some land has been taken which would not have been required if the approach had not been enlarged into a subway, and an unauthorised burden has been imposed upon the ratepayers in consequence of this enlargement.

Thus it is, in my opinion, that the appellants have acted beyond their powers and without justification.'

13.3   Failing to exercise discretion: policy and delegation

Barnard v National Dock Labour Board [1953] 2 QB 18 Court of Appeal (Denning LJ, Singleton and Romer LJJ)

Ultra vires acts: delegation of judicial functions

Facts

The National Dock Labour Board (NDLB) was created by the Dock Workers (Regulation of Employment) Order 1947 and was required to delegate to local boards (inter alia) the function of disciplining dock workers who failed to comply with the rules of the dock work scheme. The London Board passed a resolution the effect of which was to delegate this disciplinary power to Mr Hogger, the port manager. The plaintiffs had been suspended for alleged misconduct by Mr Hogger, and now sought declarations that his actions were ultra vires. They were unsuccessful at first instance and appealed to the Court of Appeal.

Held

The appeal would be allowed. The disciplinary function was judicial and could thus not be delegated by local boards to port managers. The notices of suspension received by the plaintiffs were therefore invalid.

Denning LJ:

'... It was urged on us that the local board had power to delegate their functions to the port manager on the ground that the power of suspension was an administrative and not a judicial function. It was suggested that the action of the local board in suspending a man was similar in character to the action of an employer in dismissing him. I do not accept this view. Under the provisions of the scheme, so far from the board being in the position of an employer, the board are put in a judicial position between the men and the employers; they are to receive reports from the employers and investigate them; they have to inquire whether the man has been guilty of misconduct, such as failing to comply with a lawful order, or failing to comply with the provisions of the scheme; and if they find against him they can suspend him without pay, or can even dismiss him summarily. In those circumstances they are exercising a judicial function just as much as the tribunals which were considered by this court in the corn-porters' case, *Abbot* v *Sullivan* (1) and in *Lee* v *Showmen's Guild of Great Britain* (2) the only difference being that those were domestic tribunals, and this is a statutory one. The board, by their procedure, recognise that before they suspend a man they must give him notice of the charge and an opportunity of making an explanation. That is entirely consonant with the view that they exercise a judicial function and not an administration one, and we should, I think, so hold.

While an administrative function can often be delegated, a judicial function rarely can be. No judicial tribunal can delegate its functions unless it is enabled to do so expressly or by necessary implication. In *Local Government Board* v *Arlidge* (3) the power to delegate was given by necessary implication; but there is nothing in this scheme authorising the board to delegate this functions, and it cannot be implied. It was suggested that it would be impracticable for the board to sit as a board to decide all these cases; but I see nothing impracticable at all; they have only to fix their quorum at two members ad arrange for two members, one from each side, employers and workers, to be responsible for a week at a time: probably each pair would only have to sit on one day during their week.

So far as the decision to suspend is concerned, as I see it, we are not asked to interfere with the decision of a statutory tribunal; we are asked to interfere with the position of a usurper. The port manager (if he will forgive my saying so) is a usurper, or, at any rate, is in the position of a usurper. I do not mean this unkindly, because I know that he acted in good faith on the authority of the board; nevertheless, he has assumed a mantle which was not his, but that of another. This is not a case of a tribunal which has a lawful jurisdiction and exercises it; it is a case of a man acting as a tribunal when he has no right to do so. These courts have always had jurisdiction to deal with such a case. The common law courts had a regular course of proceeding by which they commanded such a person to show by what warrant - quo warranto - he did these things. Discovery could be had against him, and if he had no valid warrant, they ousted him by judgment of ouster. In modern times proceedings by quo warranto have been abolished and replaced by declaration and injunction: see s9 of the Administration of Justice Act, 1938. Side by side with the common law jurisdiction of quo warranto the courts of equity have always had power to declare the orders of a usurper to be invalid and to set them aside. So at the present day we can do likewise. We can declare that the suspension ordered by the port manager was unlawful and void. We can declare it to be the nullity which in law it was.'

(1)   [1952] 1 KB 189

(2)   [1952] 2 QB 329

(3)   [1915] AC 120

British Oxygen Ltd v Board of Trade [1971] AC 610 House of Lords (Lords Reid, Morris of Borth-y-Gest, Viscount Dilhorne, Lords Wilberforce and Diplock)

Where an administrative power is granted the administrator may validly fetter it

Facts

The Industrial Development Act 1966 provided:

'1(1) Subject to the provisions of this section, the Board of Trade ... may make to any person carrying on a business in Great Britain a grant towards approved capital expenditure incurred by that person in providing new machinery or plant ... (a) for carrying on a qualified industrial process in the course of that business ...'

The appellants had applied for a grant and their application had been considered but rejected by the Board on the basis, inter alia, of a rule that the board had laid down itself that items costing less than £25 should not qualify.

Held

The Board had considered the appellants' application and, this being so, it was not an abuse of their power to refuse the application in accordance with the general rule or policy that items costing less than £25 should not qualify.

Lord Reid:

'... Section 1 of the Act provides that the Board of Trade "may" make grants. It was not argued that "may" in this context means "shall", and it seems to me clear that the Board were intended to have a discretion. But now were the Board intended to operate that discretion? Does the Act read as a whole indicate any policy which the Board is to follow or even give any guidance to the Board? If it does when the Board must exercise its discretion in accordance with such a policy or guidance *Padfield* v *Minister of Agriculture, Fisheries and Food* (1). One generally expects to find that Parliament has given some indication as to how public money is to be distributed. In this Act Parliament has clearly laid down the conditions for eligibility for grants and it has clearly given to the Board a discretion so that the Board is not bound to pay to every person who is eligible to receive a grant. But I can find nothing to guide the board as to the circumstances in which they should pay or the circumstances in which they should not pay grants to such persons ...

It was argued on the authority of *Rex* v *Port of London Authority, ex parte Kynoch Ltd* (2) [1919] 1 KB 176 that the Minister is not entitled to make a rule for himself as to how he will in future exercise his discretion.

Bankes LJ said, at p184:

"There are on the one hand cases where a tribunal in the honest exercise of its discretion has adopted a policy, and, without refusing to hear an applicant, intimates to him what its policy is, and that after hearing him it will in accordance with its policy decide against him, unless there is something exceptional in his case. I think counsel for the applicants would admit that, if the policy has been adopted for reasons which the tribunal may legitimately entertain, no objection could be taken to such a course. On the other hand, there are cases where a tribunal has passed a rule, or come to a determination, not to hear any application of a particular character by whomsoever made. There is a wide distinction to be drawn between these two classes."

I see nothing wrong with that. But the circumstances in which discretions are exercised vary enormously and that passage cannot be applied literally in every case. The general rule is that anyone who has to exercise a statutory discretion must not "shut his ears to an application" (to adapt from Bankes LJ on p183). I do not think there is any great difference between a policy and a rule. There may be cases where an officer or authority ought to listen to a substantial argument reasonably presented urging a change of policy. What the authority must not do is to refuse to listen at all. But a Ministry or large authority may have had to deal already with a multitude of similar applications and then they will almost certainly have evolved a policy so precise that it could well be called a rule. There can be no objection to that, provided the authority is always willing to listen to anyone with something new to say - of course I do not mean to say that there need be an oral hearing. In the present case the respondent's officers have carefully considered all that the appellants have had to say and I have no doubt that they will continue to do so ...'

Viscount Dilhorne:

'... In this case it was not challenged that it was within the power of the Board to adopt a policy not to make a grant in respect of such an item. That policy might equally well be described as a rule. It was both reasonable and right that the Board should make known to those interested the policy it was going to follow. By doing so fruitless applications involving expense and expenditure of time might be avoided. The Board says that it has not refused to consider any application. It considered the appellants'. In these circumstances it is not necessary to decide in this case whether, if it had refused to consider an application on the ground that it related to an item costing less than £25, it would have acted wrongly.

I must confess that I feel some doubt whether the words used by Bankes LJ in the passage cited above are really applicable to a case of this kind. It seems somewhat pointless and a waste of time that the Board should have to consider applications which are bound as a result of its policy decision to fail. Representations could of course be made that the policy should be changed.

I cannot see any ground on which it could be said that it was ultra vires of the Board to decide not to make grants on items costing less than £25.'

(1)   Supra, chapter 11

(2)   Infra, this chapter

Ellis v Dubowski [1921] 3 KB 621 King's Bench Division (Lawrence CJ, Avory and Sankey JJ)

Ultra vires delegation of powers to another body

Facts

Acting under the Cinematograph Act 1909, a local authority licensing committee granted a licence subject to the condition that:

'No film be shown which has not been certified for public exhibition by the British Board of Film Censors.'

The cinema owner challenged the validity of the condition.

Held

The condition was unreasonable and ultra vires; it delegated the power to decide whether a film should be shown to another body.

Lawrence CJ:

'The condition sets up an authority whose ipse dixit is to control the exhibition of films. The effect is to transfer a power which belongs to the County Council and can be delegated to committees of the Council or to district councils or to justices sitting in petty sessions alone. I think that such a condition is unreasonable, and that the committee had no power to impose it. The first five branches of this condition are quite proper; then follows the sixth, as to the film being certified by the British Board of Film Censors, which is, in my opinion, bad. I am prepared to assume that the powers of the Board are exercised wisely and discreetly. But the committee have no power to create an absolute body from which no right of appeal exists. If, as was suggested by Sankey J in the course of the argument, the condition had reserved to the committee the right to review the decisions of the Board, it would seem to be a reasonable condition. Upon that Mr Giveen's answer did not convince me; for it is reasonable that no film should be shown which has not been passed by some body. But that body should not be made the final dictator, and a condition putting the matter into the hands of a third person or body not possessed of statutory or constitutional authority is ultra vires the committee. The committee are a responsible body, as also are the justices in petty sessions, both being recognised as such by statute: the British Board of Film Censors have no such authority. For these reasons it appears to me that the condition is invalid and that the appeal must be dismissed.'

Mills v London County Council [1925] 1 KB 213 King's Bench Division (Hewart CJ, Shearman and Salter JJ)

Permissible delegation of part of powers not ultra vires

Facts

The London County Council (LCC) acting under the Cinematograph Act 1909 granted a licence to Mr Mills, a cinema owner, subject to a condition:

'That no film - other than photographs of current events - which has not been passed for universal exhibition by the British Board of Film Censors shall be exhibited in the premises without the express consent of the Council during the time that any child under or appearing to be under the age of 16 is therein: provided that this condition shall not apply in the case of any child who is accompanied by a parent or bona fide adult guardian of such child.'

Mr Mills complained that by this condition the LCC had unlawfully delegated its certifying powers.

Held

The condition was valid, as the LCC had not completely divested itself of the power to decide whether or not a particular film should be shown. Everything depended on the wording of the condition.

Lord Hewart CJ:

'In the present case the criticism which is directed against this condition by Mr Giveen with a high degree of ingenuity aims at three points. It is said, first of all, that this condition is bad, because it means that the London County Council have delegated, or transferred, to the British Board of Film Censors no small part of the duties of the London County Council under the Act, and reference is made to *Ellis* v *Dubowski* (1). In that case the condition which was attached to the licence was in these terms: "That no film be shewn ... which has not been certified for public exhibition by the British Board of Film Censors." It was held with some doubt that that condition was unreasonable and ultra vires. Avory J, for example, spoke (ibid p 626) of the considerable doubt and hesitation which he had in holding that the condition was so unreasonable as to be ultra vires the licensing authorities. But one thing was made very plain by that Court, both in the course of the argument and also in the judgment, that different considerations would have applied if the condition had been so framed as to make the certificate or the decision of the British Board of Film Censors not final, but subject to review. It was said, for example, by Lawrence CJ (as he then was) (ibid p 625): "If, as was suggested by Sankey J in the course of the argument, the condition had reserved to the Committee the right to review the decisions of the Board, it would seem to be a reasonable condition. Upon that Mr Giveen's answer did not convince me for it is reasonable that no film should be shewn which has not been passed by somebody. But that body should not be made the final dictator, and a condition putting the matter into the hands of a third person or body not possessed of statutory or constitutional authority is ultra vires the Committee." In the present case that mischief is avoided. This condition with which we are now concerned provides an exception where the express consent of the Council is given. In other words, there is an appeal in the matter from the decision of the British Board of Film Censors to the Council itself. In my opinion, therefore, the first objection fails ...'

(1)   Supra, this chapter

R v Port of London Authority, ex parte Kynoch [1919] 1 KB 176 Court of Appeal (Bankes, Warrington and Scrutton LJJ)

Proper consideration of policy before a decision is not ultra vires

Facts

Kynoch Ltd sought to challenge a decision of the Authority refusing them a licence to construct a deep water wharf on the Thames. The decision was a result of a policy adopted by the Authority of not granting licences for the type of work that it carried out itself. The Divisional Court refused Kynoch Ltd mandamus, and the company appealed to the Court of Appeal.

Held

The appeal would be dismissed. The Authority had properly considered the application before refusing it in accordance with its policy.

Banks LJ:

'The main ground was that the Port Authority had not heard and determined the application of 8 June 1917, for permission to carry out works of a very important character with a very extensive frontage to the river ...

Every case must depend on its own particular circumstances; but decided cases furnish some rules which ought to govern the Court in the exercise of its discretion to grant or refuse the prerogative writ of mandamus. There must be something in the nature of a refusal to exercise jurisdiction by the tribunal or authority to whom the writ is to be directed. A refusal may be conveyed in one of two ways: there may be an absolute refusal in terms, or there may be conduct amounting to a refusal. In the latter case it is often difficult to draw the line between those cases where the tribunal or authority has heard and determined erroneously upon grounds which it was entitled to take into consideration and those cases where it has heard and determined upon grounds outside and beyond its jurisdiction; but this conclusion may be drawn from decided cases, that there is no refusal to hear and determine unless the tribunal or authority has in substance shut its ears to the application which was made to it, and has determined upon an application which was not made to it. On this point I would refer to the words of Farwell LJ in *R v Board of Education* (1):

"If the tribunal has exercised the discretion entrusted to it bona fide, not influenced by extraneous or irrelevant considerations, and not arbitrarily or illegally, the Courts cannot interfere; they are not a Court of Appeal from the tribunal, but they have power to prevent the intentional usurpation or mistaken assumption of a jurisdiction beyond that given to the tribunal by law, and also the refusal of their true jurisdiction by the adoption of extraneous considerations in arriving at their conclusion or deciding a point other than that brought before them, in which cases the Courts have regarded them as declining jurisdiction."

Again, in *R v Bowman* (2), where licensing justices had allowed their decision to be influenced by extraneous considerations, Wills J said:

"There has been no real hearing, and the mandamus must therefore go."

Those two cases furnish a rough test for deciding when a tribunal, in considering matters outside its jurisdiction, has refused to exercise its true and proper jurisdiction.

In the present case there is another matter to be borne in mind. There are on the one hand cases where a tribunal in the honest exercise of its discretion has adopted a policy, and, without refusing to hear an applicant, intimates to him what its policy is, and that after hearing him it will in accordance with its policy decide against him, unless there is something exceptional in his case. I think counsel for the applicants would admit that, if the policy has been adopted for reasons which the tribunal may legitimately entertain, no objection could be taken to such a course. On the other hand there are cases where a tribunal has passed a rule, or come to a determination, not to hear any application of a particular character by whomsoever made. There is a wide distinction to be drawn between these two cases ... '

His Lordship referred to *R* v *Sylvester* (3), and *R* v *LCC* (4).

'Now to apply these principles to the facts of this case. There is the letter of 2nd November written on behalf of the Port Authority by their secretary, and much relied on by the prosecutors, and there is his affidavit. It negatives the suggestion that the only matter considered by the Port Authority was that specified in the letter. We must decide this case upon the affidavit. Read carefully and fairly it amounts to a statement that the Port Authority did nothing which could be properly described as a refusal to hear and determine. But I go a step further. Even assuming that the letter contains the only ground on which the application was refused, I think, considering the position of the Port Authority, that the matters involved in that decision were rightly and properly considered by them and warrant the adoption of a general policy in granting licences for works of this particular class.'

(1)   [1910] 2 KB 165

(2)   [1898] 1 QB 663

(3)   31 LJ (MC) 93

(4)   [1918] 1 KB 68

14 THE ULTRA VIRES DOCTRINE – NATURAL JUSTICE

14.1   The right to be heard

14.2   The rule against bias

14.1   The right to be heard

Andrews v Mitchell [1905] AC 78 House of Lords (Earl of Halsbury LC, Lord Davey, Lord James of Hereford and Lord Robertson)

Natural justice and the requirement of a fair hearing on the relevant matter

Facts

(inter alia) The respondent was a member of a friendly society who was in receipt of sickness benefit when he was found out of doors after 9.00 pm, contrary to the society's rules. He was summoned to a disciplinary hearing and the case against him was found proven. The society rules prescribed a fine of 2s 6d for this transgression. The hearing, having considered his case, determined to expel the respondent from the society on the basis that he had acted fraudulently and made false statements. The respondent sued the society for damages for wrongful expulsion and an injunction. The appellants sought an order of prohibition to prevent the County Court hearing the action, but this was refused at first instance and by the Court of Appeal. The society now appealed to the House of Lords.

Held

(inter alia) The decision to expel the respondent was null and void, because he had been summoned before the hearing committee to face one charge and found himself being expelled on a different matter.

Earl of Halsbury LC:

'I think it is manifest that (the society) proceeded far too hastily in this case, and, apart from imputing to them any prejudice or any desire to do wrong, I think that the mode in which the whole thing arose and was disposed of was so slipshod and irregular that it might lead to injustice. It is quite possible that if the case, instead of being disposed of in the summary way in which it was disposed of, had been considered by them somewhat more maturely and not while their minds were all inflamed against the very outrageous falsehood told by this man, they might not have taken the extreme measure they did. At all events, treating it as a matter arising in a court of law, one cannot say that this charge was a charge which was ever made against this man; it arose in the course of the investigation, and they then and there proceeded to deal with it in his absence, and to pronounce a verdict upon it, not having heard him except in the summary way alleged by themselves. He had been told to retire, and he was called in, not for the purpose of further investigation, not for the purpose of hearing what he had to say upon the matter, but simply to be told that the result of the investigation was that he was expelled. My Lords, that as a matter of substance seems to me to be a course of proceeding which it is impossible to support.

When one looks to see what the course of procedure must necessarily be in order to justify an expulsion, Mr. Lawrence points out that there is a rule which certainly does justify expulsion, but it justifies expulsion upon the express proviso that the charge has been made as provided by the rules.

In this case the charge never was made as provided by the rules; and if you have no power given under the rules to expel a member except upon a charge made and tried according to the rules, you have no power to expel in a case like this.

My Lords, it seems to me that under these circumstances it would be undesirable to go into those questions which were raised in *Palliser* v *Dale* (1), because to my mind this most important principle ought to be brought home to the minds of these courts, presided over as they are by comparatively uneducated men, that some of these forms are matters of substance, and that you must summon a man, and you must give him time to consider what he has got to do, and you must give him the charge against him in writing. Those are all matters of substance, and not mere matters of form. They are the foundation of the subsequent litigation arising between the parties, and if they were neglected in this case, it appears to me that there was no jurisdiction to entertain that charge at the time. It is a remarkable thing that the secretary, when he writes to inform the respondent of his expulsion, puts into his letter that which shews clearly enough what in his mind was necessary in order to establish the charge, because he states in plain terms that the charge was made against him by an officer by the direction of the arbitration committee, and that it was investigated and he was found guilty. I do not impute to the secretary when he wrote that any intention of writing what was false, but it was inaccurate. It shews, however, that the secretary knew what the regular course of procedure ought to have been, but it was not pursued.

My Lords, the result to my mind is that the arbitration committee had no jurisdiction to entertain this question, and under those circumstances I think the county court had jurisdiction to do what it did; and therefore this appeal must be dismissed, and I move your Lordships accordingly.'

(1)   [1897] 1 QB 257

Bushell v Secretary of State for the Environment [1981] AC 75   House of Lords (Lord Diplock, Viscount Dilhorne, Lord Edmund-Davies, Lord Fraser of Tullbelton and Lord Lane)

Nature of statutory enquiry: requirement of natural justice

Facts

Objectors into a proposed motorway attended an inquiry held under s11 of the Highways Act 1959, and sought to cross-examine the witnesses from the Department of the Environment on the need for the motorway. In particular they sought to question the validity of the Department's traffic flow predictions. The inquiry inspector refused to allow cross-examination of the Departmental witnesses on the grounds that government policy could not be questioned at the inquiry, and their cross-examination on the accuracy of the traffic flow forecasts would serve no useful purpose.

After the close of the inquiry the Department found its method of calculating traffic flow to be deficient, and consequently revised this. The new methods of prediction showed that the capacity of existing roads was far greater than had been thought. The objectors claimed that in the light of these facts the inquiry should be re-opened, but the Minister refused. The objectors then applied under para 2 of Sch 2 to the Highways Act 1959 to have the scheme for the motorway quashed.

The application was dismissed at first instance, but allowed by the Court of Appeal. The Secretary of State now appealed to the House of Lords.

Held

The appeal would be allowed. It was wrong to equate public inquiries with courts of law, in terms of the procedure that had to be followed to ensure compliance with natural justice. The refusal of cross-examination on certain points had not been unfair.

Lord Diplock:

'... The essential characteristics of a "local inquiry", an expression which when appearing in a statute has by now acquired a special meaning as a term of legal art, are that it is held in public in the locality in which the works that are the subject of the proposed scheme are situated by a person appointed by the minister upon whom the statute has conferred the power in his administrative discretion to decide whether to confirm the scheme. The subject matter of the inquiry is the objections to the proposed scheme that have been received by the minister from local authorities and from private persons in the vicinity of the proposed stretch of motorway whose interests may be adversely affected, and in consequence of which he is required by Schedule 1, para 9, to hold the inquiry. The purpose of the inquiry is to provide the minister with as much information about those objections as will ensure that in reaching his decision he will have weighed the harm to local interests and private persons who may be adversely affected by the scheme against the public benefit which the scheme is likely to achieve and will not have failed to take into consideration any matters which he ought to have taken into consideration.

Where rules regulating the procedure to be followed at a local inquiry held pursuant to a particular statutory provision have been made by the Lord Chancellor under s11 of the Tribunals and Inquiries Act 1971, the minister and the inspector appointed to hold the inquiry must observe those rules; but no such rules were applicable in the instant case - they had not yet been made. The Highways Act 1959 being itself silent as to the procedure to be followed at the inquiry, that procedure, within such limits as are necessarily imposed by its qualifying for the description "local inquiry", must necessarily be left to the discretion of the minister or the inspector appointed by him to hold the inquiry on his behalf, or partly to one and partly to the other. In exercising that discretion, as in exercising any other administrative function, they owe a constitutional duty to perform it fairly and honestly and to the best of their ability, as Lord Greene MR pointed out in his neglected but luminous analysis of the quasi-judicial and administrative functions of a minister as confirming authority of a compulsory purchase order made by a local authority, which is to be found in *B Johnson & Co (Builders) Ltd* v *Minister of Health* (1). That judgment contains a salutary warning against applying to procedures involved in the making of administrative decisions concepts that are appropriate to the conduct of ordinary civil litigation between private parties. So rather than use such phrases as "natural justice" which may suggest that the prototype is only to be found in procedures followed by English courts of law, I prefer to put it that in the absence of any rules made under the Tribunals and Inquiries Act 1971, the only requirement of the Highways Act 1959, as to the procedure to be followed at a local inquiry held pursuant to Sch 1, para 9, is that it must be fair to all those who have an interest in the decision that will follow it whether they have been represented at the inquiry or not. What is a fair procedure to be adopted at a particular inquiry will depend upon the nature of its subject matter.

What is fair procedure is to be judged not in the light of constitutional fictions as to the relationship between the minister and the other servants of the Crown to serve in the government department of which he is the head, but in the light of the practical realities as to the way in which administrative decisions involving forming judgments based on technical considerations are reached. To treat the minister in his decision-making capacity as someone separate and distinct from the department of government of which he is the political head and for whose actions he alone in constitutional theory is accountable to Parliament is to ignore not only practical realities but also Parliament's intention ... Discretion in making administrative decisions is conferred upon a minister not as an individual but as the holder of an office in which he will have available to him in arriving at his decision the collective knowledge, experience and expertise of all those who serve the Crown in the department of which, for the time being, he is the political head. The collective knowledge, technical as well as factual, of the civil servants in the department and their collective expertise is to be treated as the minister's own knowledge, his own expertise ... This is an integral part of the decision-making process itself; it is not to be equiparated with the minister receiving evidence, expert opinion or advice from sources outside the department after the local inquiry has been closed ...

In the instant case the public inquiries into the two schemes which were for two adjoining stretches of the national motorway network were held together. There were 170 objections to the schemes which had not been withdrawn when the combined inquiry began. There were about 100 different parties who took part in it and made representations to the inspector orally or in writing in objection to or in support of the schemes. Many of these called witnesses in support of their representations. The hearing of the inquiry by the inspector took 100 working days between June 1973 and January 1974. He made his report to the minister on 12 June 1975.

It is evident that an inquiry of this kind and magnitude is quite unlike any civil litigation and that the inspector conducting it must have a wide discretion as to the procedure to be followed in order to achieve its objectives. These are to enable him to ascertain the facts that are relevant to each of the objections, to understand the arguments for and against them and, if he feels qualified to do so, to weigh their respective merits, so that he may provide the minister with a fair, accurate and adequate report on these matters.

Proceedings at a local inquiry at which many parties wish to make representations without incurring the expense of legal representation and cannot attend the inquiry throughout its length ought to be as informal as is consistent with achieving those objectives. To "over-judicialise" the inquiry by insisting on observance of the procedures of a court of justice which professional lawyers alone are competent to operate effectively in the interests of their clients would not be fair. It would, in my view, be quite fallacious to suppose that at an inquiry of this kind the only fair way of ascertaining matters of fact and expert opinion is by the oral testimony of witnesses who are subjected to cross-examination on behalf of parties who disagree with what they have said. Such procedure is peculiar to litigation conducted in courts that follow the common law system of procedure; it plays no part in the procedure of courts of justice under legal systems based upon the civil law, including the majority of our fellow member states of the European Community; even in our own Admiralty Court it is not availed of for the purpose of ascertaining expert opinion on questions of navigation ... So refusal by an inspector to allow a party to cross-examine orally at a local inquiry a person who has made statements of facts or has expressed expert opinions is not unfair per se.

Whether fairness requires an inspector to permit a person ... to be cross-examined by a party to the inquiry who wishes to dispute a particular statement must depend on all the circumstances. In the instance case, the question arises in connection with expert opinion upon a technical matter. Here the relevant circumstances in considering whether fairness requires that cross-examination should be allowed include the nature of the topic upon which the opinion is expressed, the qualifications of the maker of the statement to deal with that topic, the forensic competence of the proposed cross-examiner, and, most important, the inspector's own views as to whether the likelihood that cross-examination will enable him to make a report which will be more useful to the minister in reaching his decision than it otherwise would be is sufficient to justify any expense and inconvenience to other parties to the inquiry which would be caused by any resulting prolongation of it.

The circumstances in which the question of cross-examination arose in the instant case were the following. Before the inquiry opened each objector had received a document containing a statement of the minister's reasons for proposing the draft scheme ... The second paragraph of the minister's statement of reasons said: "The government's policy to build these new motorways" (sc. for which the two schemes provided) "will not be open to debate at the forthcoming inquiries: the Secretary of State is answerable to Parliament for this policy."

"Policy" as descriptive of departmental decisions to pursue a particular course of conduct is a protean word and much confusion in the instant case has, in my view, been caused by a failure to define the sense in which it can properly be used to describe a topic which is unsuitable to be the subject of any investigation as to its merits at an inquiry at which only persons with local interests affected by the scheme are entitled to be represented. A decision to construct a nationwide network of motorways is clearly one of government policy in the widest sense of the term. Any proposal to alter it is appropriate to be the subject of debate in Parliament, not of separate investigations in each of scores of local inquiries before individual inspectors up and down the country upon whatever material happens to be presented to them at the particular inquiry over which they preside. So much the respondents readily concede.

At the other extreme the selection of the exact line to be followed through a particular locality by a motorway designed to carry traffic between the destinations that it is intended to serve would not be described as involving government policy in the ordinary sense of that term. It affects particular local interests only and normally does not affect the interests of any wider section of the public ... It is an appropriate subject for full investigation at a local inquiry and is one on which the inspector by whom the investigation is to be conducted can form a judgment on which to base a recommendation which deserves to carry weight with the minister in reaching a final decision as to the line the motorway should follow.

Between the black and white of these two extremes, however, there is what my noble and learned friend, Lord Lane, in the course of the hearing described as a "grey area". Because of the time that must elapse between the preparation of any scheme and the completion of the stretch of motorway that it authorises, the department, in deciding in what order new stretches of the national network ought to be constructed, has adopted a uniform practice throughout the country of making a major factor in its decision the likelihood that there will be a traffic need for that particular stretch of motorway in 15 years from the date when the scheme was prepared. This is known as the "design year" of the scheme. Priorities as between one stretch of motorway and another have got to be determined somehow. Semasiologists may argue whether the adoption by the department of a uniform practice for doing this is most appropriately described as government policy or as something else. But the propriety of adopting it is clearly a matter fit to be debated in a wider forum and with the assistance of a wider range of relevant material than any investigation at an individual local inquiry is likely to provides; and in that sense at least, which is the relevant sent for present purposes, its adoption forms part of government policy ...

If the analogy of a lis inter partes be a false analogy even where the scheme which is the subject of the local inquiry is not a departmental scheme but one of which a public authority other than the minister is the originator, the analogy is even farther from reflecting the essentially administrative nature of the minister's functions when, having considered in the light of the advice of his department the objections which have been the subject of a local inquiry and the report of the inspector, he makes his decision in a case where the scheme is one that has been prepared by his own department itself and which it is for him in his capacity as head of that department to decide whether it is in the general public interest that it should be made or not. Once he has reached his decision he must be prepared to disclose his reasons for it, because the Tribunals and Inquiries Act 1971 so requires; but he is, in my view, under no obligation to disclose to objectors and give them an opportunity of commenting on advice, expert or otherwise, which he receives from his department in the course of making up his mind. If he thinks that to do so will be helpful to him in reaching the right decision in the public interest he may, of course, do so; but if he does not think it will be helpful - and this is for him to decide - failure to do so cannot in my view be treated as a denial of natural justice to the objectors.

In the instant case the respondents were in fact aware of the advice the minister had received from his department upon two matters after the local inquiry had closed and before he made his decision ...

... [W]hat the respondents really wanted to do in seeking the re-opening of the local inquiry was to hold up authorisation of the constructions ... until the revised methods adopted by the department for estimating the comparative traffic needs for stretches of the national network of motorways which have not yet been constructed had been the subject of investigation at the reopened inquiry. For reasons that I have already elaborated, a local inquiry does not provide a suitable forum in which to debate what is in the relevant sense a matter of government policy. So the minister was in my view fully justified in refusing to re-open the local inquiry ... So the second ground on which the respondents claim they have suffered a denial of natural justice in my view also fails.

The schemes were, in my view, validly made by the minister ... and I would allow the appeal ...'

(1)   [1947] 2 All ER 395

Cinnamond v British Airports Authority [1980] 1 WLR 582 Court of Appeal (Lord Denning MR, Shaw and Brandon LJJ)

Natural justice does not require a hearing for every administrative decision

Facts

The Airways Authority Act 1975 provides in s2(1) that 'It shall be the duty of the Authority to provide at its aerodromes such services and facilities as are in its opinion necessary or desirable for their operation' and in s2(3) that 'The Authority shall have power to do anything which is calculated to facilitate the discharge of its duties under this Act'. Section 9(1) provides 'The Authority may ... make bye-laws for regulating the use and operation of the aerodrome, and in particular ... (3) for prohibiting or restricting access to any part of the aerodrome ...'

By bye-laws made in 1972: 'No person shall loiter, frequent or remain on the aerodrome ... without reasonable cause' (5(23)); 'No person shall, without the permission of the Authority ... offer anything for sale or hire or make any offer of services ' (5(55)); 'No person shall enter the aerodrome, except as a bona fide airline passenger, whilst having been prohibited from entering by an authorised officer of the Authority ' (5(59)).

The Airports Authority notified the plaintiffs, (six minicab drivers who had been convicted many times for loitering and touting at Heathrow Airport) that 'they were prohibited from entering the airport for any purpose other than as a bona fide airline passenger' until further notice. The plaintiffs claimed (inter alia) a declaration that the notices were invalid and of no effect.

Held

The six minicab drivers often went to Heathrow Airport sometimes to take an airline passenger to catch a flight, sometimes not. They touted for passengers without the permission of the Authority as required by bye-law 5(55). They charged a great deal more than the regular taxi fare. They had been convicted scores and scores of times under 5(55) and 5(23). They had enormous outstanding fines unpaid. What did natural justice demand in such a case? Not every administrative decision called for a hearing. If minicab drivers were of good character, coming into the airport under a licence and they were suddenly prohibited, it would only be fair that they should have a chance of putting their case. But the six men in the present case had convictions and outstanding fines. It was not a necessary preliminary that they should be given a further hearing. They could have made representations when they received the letter of 23 November. The simple duty of the Authority was to act fairly and reasonably and they had so acted.

Cooper v Wandsworth Board of Works (1863) 143 ER 414 King's Bench (Eme CJ)

No-one may be deprived of his property without being heard

Facts

Section 76 of the Metropolis Local Management Act 1855 provided:

'Before beginning to lay or dig out the foundation of any new house or building within any such parish or district (a) or to rebuild any house or building therein ... seven days' notice in writing shall be given to the vestry or board by the person intending to build or rebuild such house or building ... and every such foundation shall be laid at such level as will permit the drainage of such house or building in compliance with this act, and as the vestry or board shall order ... and, in default of such notice... it shall be lawful for the vestry or board to order such house or building to be demolished or altered ...'

The plaintiff failed to give seven days' notice of his intention before beginning to lay the foundations. The defendants demolished the building without giving the plaintiff an opportunity to be heard. The plaintiff sued the defendants for trespass.

Held

Natural justice required that the defendants should give the plaintiff an opportunity of being heard before demolishing the building. Their act of demolition in the absence of such an opportunity constituted a trespass.

Eme CJ:

'... This was an action of trespass by the plaintiff against the Wandsworth district board, for pulling down and demolishing his house, and the ground of defence that has been put forward by the defendants has been under the 76th section of the Metropolis Local Management Act 18 & 19 Vict C 120. By the part of that section which applies to this case, it enacted that, before any person shall begin to build a new house, he shall give seven days' notice to the district board of his intention to build; and it provides at the end that, in default of such notice it shall be lawful for the district board to demolish the house. The district board here say that no notice was given by the plaintiff of his intention to build the house in question, wherefore they demolished it. The contention on the part of the plaintiff has been that, although the words of the statute, taken in their literal sense, without any qualification at all, would create a justification for the act which the district board has done, the powers granted by that statute are subject to a qualification which has been repeatedly recognised, that no man is to be deprived of his property without his having a opportunity of being heard ...

I think that the power which is granted by the 76th section is subject to the qualification suggested. It is a power carrying with it enormous consequences. The house in question was built only to a certain extent. But the power claimed would apply to a complete house. It would apply to a house of any value, and completed to any extent; and it seems to me to be a power which may be exercised most perniciously, and that the limitation which we are going to put upon it is one which ought, according to the decided cases, to be put upon it, and one which is required by a due consideration for the public interest. I think the board ought to have given notice to the plaintiff, and to have allowed him to be heard. The default in sending notice to the board of the intention to build, is a default which may be explained. There may be a great many excuses for the apparent default. The party may have intended to conform to the law. He may have actually conformed to all the regulations which they would wish to impose, though by accident his notice may have miscarried; and, under those circumstances, if he explained how it stood, the proceeding to demolish, merely because they had ill-will against the party, is a power that the legislature never intended to confer. I cannot conceive any harm that could happen to the district board from hearing the party before they subjected him to a loss so serious as the demolition of his house; but I can conceive a great many advantages which might arise in the way of public order, in the way of doing substantial justice, and in the way of fulfilling the purposes of the statute, by the restriction which we put upon them, that they should hear the party before they inflict upon him such a heavy loss. I fully agree that the legislature intended to give the district board very large powers indeed: but the qualification I speak of is one which has been recognised to the full extent. It has been said that the principle that no man shall be deprived of his property without an opportunity of being heard, is limited to a judicial proceeding, and that a district board ordering a house to be pulled down cannot be said to be doing a judicial act. I do not quite agree with that; neither do I undertake to rest my judgment solely upon the ground that the district board is a court exercising judicial discretion upon the point; but the law, I think, has been applied to many exercises of power which in common understanding would not be at all more a judicial proceeding than would be the act of the district board in ordering a house to be pulled down ...'

Enderby Town Football Club Ltd v Football Association Ltd [1971] 1 Ch 591 Court of Appeal (Lord Denning MR, Fenton Atkinson and Cairns LJJ)

Natural justice, legal representation and the relations between domestic tribunals and the courts

Facts

The Football Association Ltd (the FA) controlled association football. County associations were affiliated to it. The plaintiff club were fined and censured by their county association. The club appealed to the FA and claimed the right to be represented by solicitor and counsel when the appeal was heard. The FA rejected the claim relying on their rule 38(b) which excluded legal representation save where the lawyer was chairman or secretary of the club to be represented.

The club claimed an injunction restraining the FA from hearing the appeal unless the club were permitted to be legally represented.

Held

The club were not entitled to an injunction since the Football Association were not acting contrary to natural justice in refusing to allow the club to be legally represented. Difficult points of law could be dealt with by the courts in an action by the club for a declaration.

Per Lord Denning MR and Cairns LJ. The FA Rule 40(b) purporting to prevent legal proceedings without the consent of the FA council is contrary to public policy and invalid.

QUAERE: Whether a domestic tribunal can make an absolute rule not to hear legal representatives.

Lord Denning MR:

'... Mr Sparrow's next submission was that, if the rule went so far as to exclude legal representation, it should not be applied in this particular case. The facts, he said, were undisputed. The only points at issue were points of law. There were of much complexity and difficulty. They could not be properly argued except by a lawyer. Accordingly he submitted that the club should be represented by a lawyer. In order to appreciate this argument, I will set out the principal points which Mr Sparrow desires to raise.

(1) He said that the charge against the club was not properly formulated. The first count, for instance, was 'that directors' fees were paid to Messrs H Jacques, B Jacques and K Moore' without pointing to any rule which says that directors' fees may not be paid. There is, in fact, no such rule.

(2) He said that the charge was heard by three men who had no jurisdiction to hear it. The rules of the country association gave jurisdiction to the whole council of the association. There was no power to delegate to a commission of three.

(3) Rule 45 (vi) of the FA Rules says that club companies must contain an article preventing a director from receiving remuneration. Mr Sparrow said that that rule applies only to companies hich are members of the FA. It does not apply to this club, which is not a member of the association.

I quite appreciate Mr Sparrow's submission that these are difficult points of law on which there are authorities to be cited and rules to be construed.

So much so that I do not think the FA is itself a suitable body to decide them. It would be much better, I should think, for the club to bring these points straight away before the court in an action for a declaration. That is a course which they are perfectly entitled to take at once before the appeal is heard by the FA: see *Lawlor v Union of Post Office Workers* (1); *Dickson v Pharmaceutical Society of Great Britain* (2) per Lord Upjohn. In any such action before the court the club would, of course, be entitled to be represented by counsel and solicitors. As an alternative the club could wait until after the hearing of the appeal by the FA and then bring an action for a declaration. They would not be prejudiced by so doing: see *Annamunthodo v Oilfields Workers' Trade Union* (3). But either way, the points of law would be better decided by the courts than by the FA. As Romer LJ said in *Lee* v *Showmen's Guild of Great Britain* (4):

> "The proper tribunals for the determination of legal disputes in this country are the courts, and they are the only tribunals which, by training and experience, and assisted by properly qualified advocates are fitted for the task."

Although it is open to the club to come to the court to decide the points, they have not done so. They are sticking to their appeal to the FA They ask that the points be decided by that body. They want to have counsel and solicitor to argue them before the FA. The FA decline ...

A preliminary point arises here. Has the court any power to go behind the wording of the rule and consider its validity? On this point Sir Elwyn Jones made an important concession. He agreed that if the rule was contrary to natural justice, it would be invalid. I think this concession was rightly made and I desire to emphasise it. The rules of a body like this are often said to be a contract. So they are in legal theory. But it is a fiction - a fiction created by the lawyers so as to give the courts jurisdiction. This is no new thing. There are many precedents for it from the time of John Doe onwards. Putting the fiction aside, the truth is that the rules are nothing more nor less than a legislative code - a set of regulations laid down by the governing body to be observed by all who are, or become, members of the association. Such regulations, though said to be a contract, are subject to the control of the courts. If they are in unreasonable restraint of trade, they are invalid: see *Dickson* v *Pharmaceutical Society of Great Britain* (2). If they seek to oust the jurisdiction of the court, they are invalid: see *Scott* v *Avery* (5). If they unreasonably shut out a man from his right to work, they are invalid: see *Nagle* v *Feilden* (6); *Edwards* v *Society of Graphical and Allied Traders* (7). If they lay down a procedure which is contrary to the principles of natural justice, they are invalid: see *Faramus* v *Film Artistes' Association* (8) per Lord Pearce. All these are cases where the judges have decided, avowedly or not, according to what is best for the public good. I know that over 300 years ago Hobart CJ said that "Public policy is a unruly horse". It has often been repeated since. So unruly is the horse, it is said (per Burrough J in *Richardson* v *Mellish* (9), that no judge should ever try to mount it lest it ran away with him. I disagree. With a good man in the saddle, the unruly horse can be kept in control. It can jump over obstacles. It can leap the fences put up by fictions and come down on the side of justice, as indeed was done in *Nagle* v *Feilden* (6). It can hold a rule to be invalid even though it is contained in a contract.

Take an instance from this present case. The FA have a rule 40(b) which says:

> "The rules of the association are sufficient to enable the council as the governing authority to deal with all cases of dispute, and legal proceedings shall only be taken as a last resort, and then only with the consent of the council."

If that rule were valid, it would prevent the club from bringing any action in the courts without the consent of the council. But the rule is plainly invalid. Foster J said that "it is against public policy to make provisions ousting the jurisdiction of the court". Lord Kilbrandon in Scotland said simply that it is "contrary to public policy": see *St Johnstone Football Club Ltd* v *Scottish Football Association Ltd* (10).

Seeing that the courts can inquire into the validity of the rule, I turn to the next question: Is it lawful for a body to stipulate in its rules that its domestic tribunal shall not permit legal representation? Such a stipulation is, I think, clearly valid so long as it is construed as directory and not imperative: for that leaves it open to the tribunal to permit legal representation in an exceptional case when the justice of the case so requires. But I have some doubt whether it is legitimate to make a rule which is so imperative in its terms as to exclude legal representation altogether, without giving the tribunal any discretion to admit it, even when the justice of the case requires it. Suppose a case should arise when both the parties and the tribunal felt that it was essential in the interests of justice that the parties should be legally represented, and that the tribunal should have the assistance of a lawyer. Would not the tribunal be able to allow it, or, at any rate, to allow the rule to be waived? I do not find it neccesary to express any opinion on this point. I will know how to decide when it arises. But in this case, no matter whether the rule is construed as directory or imperative, I am of opinion that the court should not insist on legal representation before the tribunal of the FA. The points which the club wishes to raise are points of law which should be decided by the courts and not by the tribunal. The club is at liberty to bring these points before the courts at once and have them decided with the aid of skilled advocates. If they choose not to bring them before the courts but prefer to put them before a lay tribunal, they must put up with the imperfections of that tribunal and must abide by their ruling that there be no legal representation. On this ground I would dismiss the appeal.'

(1)   [1965] Ch 712

(2)   [1967] Ch 708 & [1970] AC 403

(3)   [1961] AC 945

(4)   [1952] 2 QB 329

(5)   (1856) HL Cas 811

(6)   [1966] 2 QB 633

(7)   [1971] Ch 354

(8)   [1964] AC 925

(9)   (1824) 2 Bing 229

(10)   1965 SLT 171

Franklin v Minister of Town and Country Planning [1948] AC 87 House of Lords (Lords Thankerton, Porter, Uthwatt, du Parcq and Normand)

Personal bias irrelevant to Minister's duty to undertake non-judicial function

Facts

The appellants were owners and occupiers of dwelling-houses and land in Stevenage. On 3 August 1946, the respondent, as Minister of Town and Country Planning, prepared the draft Stevenage New Town (Designation) Order 1946 under para 1 of Sch 1 of the New Towns Act 1946. Thereafter, objections were received from a number of persons, including the appellants. Accordingly, the respondent instructed an inspector to hold a public local inquiry as prescribed by para 3 of Sch 1. The inspector made his report to the respondent; attached thereto was a complete transcript of the inquiry proceedings. On 11 November 1946 the respondent made the order designating Stevenage as a site for a 'new town'. The appellants applied to the High Court to have the order quashed on the ground that the order was not within the powers of the New Towns Act 1946 in that (inter alia) before considering the objections of the appellants the Minister had stated at a public meeting in Stevenage that he would make the said order using such phrases as 'The project will go forward ... While I will consult as far as possible all the local authorities, at the end, if people are fractious and unreasonable, I shall have to carry out my duty ...' and that the Minister was thereby biased in the consideration of any objections.

Available before the court was an affidavit sworn by the Minister:

'Before causing the said order to be made, I personally carefully considered all the objections made by the objectors ... together with submissions made and evidence given on their behalf as appearing in the said transcript. I also carefully considered the report of the (inspector).'

Held

In considering the report of the inspector who had held a public local inquiry under Sch 1, para 3 of the New Towns Act 1946, the duty imposed on the Minister of Town and Country Planning was not judicial or quasi-judicial, so that considerations of bias in the execution of that duty was irrelevant. His duty was only to genuinely consider the report and the objections.

Lord Thankerton:

'... In my opinion, no judicial, or quasi-judicial, duty was imposed on the respondent, and any reference to judicial duty, or bias, is irrelevant in the present case. The respondent's duties under section 1 of the Act and Schedule I thereto are, in my opinion, purely administrative, but the Act prescribes certain methods of or steps in, discharge of that duty. It is obvious that, before making the draft order, which must contain a definite proposal to designate the area concerned as the site of a new town, the respondent must have made elaborate inquiry into the matter and have consulted any local authorities who appear to him to be concerned, and obviously other departments of the Government, such as the Ministry of Health, would naturally require to be consulted. It would seem, accordingly, that the respondent was required to satisfy himself that it was a sound scheme before he took the serious step of issuing a draft order. It seems clear also, that the purpose of inviting objections, and, where they are not withdrawn, of having a public inquiry, to be held by someone other than the respondent, to whom that person reports, was for the further information of the respondent, in order to the final consideration of the soundness of the scheme of the designation; and it is important to note that the development of the site, after the order is made, is primarily the duty of the development corporation established under s2 of the Act. I am of opinion that no judicial duty is laid on the respondent in discharge of these statutory duties, and that the only question is whether he has complied with the statutory directions to appoint a person to hold the public inquiry, and to consider that person's report. On this contention of the appellants no suggestion is made that the public inquiry was not properly conducted, nor is there any criticism of the report by Mr Morris. In such a case the only ground of challenge must be either that the respondent did not in fact consider the report and the objections, of which there is here no evidence, or that his mind was so foreclosed that he gave no genuine consideration to them, which is the case made by the appellants. Although I am unable to agree exactly with the view of the respondent's duty expressed by the learned judge, or with some of the expressions used by the Court of Appeal in regard to the matter, it does appear to me that the issue was treated in both courts as being whether the respondent had genuinely considered the objections and the report, as directed by the Act.

My Lords, I could wish that the use of the word "bias" should be confined to its proper sphere. Its proper significance, in my opinion, is to denote a departure from the standard of even-handed justice which the law requires from those who occupy judicial office, or those who are commonly regarded as holding a quasi-judicial office, such as an arbitrator. The reason for this clearly is that, having to adjudicate as between two or more parties, he must come to his adjudication with an independent mind, without any inclination or bias towards one side or other in the dispute. As Lord Cranworth LC says in *Ranger* v *Great Western Ry Co*:

"A judge ought to be, and is supposed to be, indifferent between the parties. He has, or is supposed to have, no bias inducing him to lean to the one side rather than to the other. In ordinary cases it is a just ground of exception to a judge that he is not indifferent, and the fact that he is himself a party, or interested as a party, affords the strongest proof that he cannot be indifferent."

To this may be added the statement by Lord Hewart CJ in *R* v *Sussex Justices, ex parte McCarthy* (1):

"It is said, and, no doubt, truly, that when that gentleman (the deputy clerk) retired in the usual way with the justices, taking with him the notes of the evidence in case the justices might desire to consult him, the justices came to a conclusion without consulting him, and that he scrupulously abstained from referring to the case in any way. But while that is so, a long line of cases shows that it is not merely of some importance but is of fundamental importance that justice should not only be done, but should manifestly and undoubtedly be seen to be done. The question therefore is not whether in this case the deputy clerk made any observation or offered any criticism which he might not properly have made or offered; the question is whether he was so elated to the case in its civil aspect as to be unfit to act as clerk to the justices in the criminal matter. The answer to that question depends not upon what actually was done but upon what might appear to be done."

This was followed in *R* v *Essex Justices, ex parte Perkins* (2). But, in the present case, the respondent having no judicial duty, the only question is what the respondent actually did, that is, whether in fact he did genuinely consider the report and the objections.

Coming now to the inference of the learned judge from the respondent's speech in 6 May, that he had not then a mind open to conviction, the learned judge states it thus:

"If I am to judge by what he said at the public meeting which was held very shortly before the Bill, then published, became an Act of Parliament, I could have no doubt but that any issue raised by objectors was forejudged. The Minister's language leaves no doubt about that. He was not only saying there must and shall be satellite towns, but he was saying that Stevenage was to be the first of them."

It seems probable that the learned judge's mind was influences by his having already held that the respondent's function was quasi-judicial, which would raise the question of bias, but, in any view, I am clearly of opinion that nothing said by the respondent was inconsistent with the discharge of his statutory duty, when subsequently objections were lodged, and the local public inquiry took place, followed by the report of that inquiry, genuinely to consider the report and the objections. The only passages in the speech quoted in the appellants' case are contained in the third quotation I have made from the speech, and are as follows:

"I want to carry out in Stevenage a daring exercise in town planning (jeers). It is no good your jeering: it is going to be done ... After all this new town is to be built in order to provide for the happiness and welfare of some sixty thousand men, women and children ... The project will go forward, because it must go forward. It will do so more surely and more smoothly and more successfully with your help and co-operation. Stevenage will in a short time become world famous. People from all over the world will come to Stevenage to see how we here in this country are building for the new way of life."

The only two additional passages founded on by the appellants' counsel at the hearing before this House were the sentence in my first quotation, "In anticipation of the passage of the Bill - and I have no doubt that it will go through", and, in my fourth quotation, "But we have a duty to perform, and I am not going to be deterred from that duty. While I will consult as far as possible all the local authorities, at the end, if people become fractious and unreasonable, I shall have to carry out my duty - (voice: Gestapo!)." My Lords, these passages in a speech, which was of a political nature, and of the kind familiar in a speech on second reading, demonstrate (1) the speaker's view that the Bill would become law, that Stevenage was a most suitable site and should be the first scheme in the operation, and that the Stevenage project would go forward, and (2) the speaker's reaction to the hostile interruptions of a section of the audience. In my opinion, these passages are not inconsistent with an intention to carry out any statutory duty imposed on him by Parliament, although he intended to press for the enactment of the Bill, and thereafter to carry out the duties thereby involved, including the consideration of objections which were neither fractious nor unreasonable. I am, therefore of opinion that the first contention of the appellants fails, in that they have not established either that in the respondent's speech he had forejudged any genuine consideration of the objections or that he had not genuinely considered the objections at the later stage when they were submitted to him ...'

(1)   Infra, this chapter

(2)   [1927] 2 KB 475

Glynn v Keele University [1971] 1 WLR 487 Chancery Division (Pennycuick V-C)

Natural justice and the requirement of a fair hearing: quasi-judicial powers

Facts

The applicant was an undergraduate who had been found besporting himself, naked, in the university precincts. Exercising his powers under the university statutes, the vice-chancellor wrote to the applicant informing him that he had been fined £10, and excluded from residence at the university for one year. The applicant was also notified of his right of appeal. The applicant lodged his notice of appeal but did not return from his foreign holiday until after the appeal committee of the university council had considered his case and upheld the vice-chancellor's decision. On his return the student sought an injunction to restrain the university from excluding him.

Held

Whilst the vice-chancellor was acting quasi-judicially and did have to observe the rules of natural justice, the student had nevertheless failed to avail himself of the appeal procedures, and in any event had lost only the chance to enter a plea in mitigation. The penalty awarded was perfectly fair in the circumstances and the injunction would be refused.

Pennycuick V-C:

'I now come to the question which has been most debated on this motion, and which I find a very difficult one. The question is whether, when the vice-chancellor takes a decision under s6, he is acting in a quasi-judicial capacity, and if that question is answered in the affirmative, whether there has been some failure of the requirements of natural justice in the present case. The two questions as to what constitutes a quasi-judicial capacity, and the duty to comply with the requirements of natural justice, are very closely inter-related.

I was referred to *Ridge* v *Baldwin* (1), in which Lord Reid, at p63, made a lengthy and thorough survey of the principles applicable in this connection. I do not think it would be useful to quote from that case for the present purpose. I was also referred on the matter of general principles to *Durayappah* v *Fernando* (2). I will read one passage from the judgment of Lord Upjohn in that case. The passage is addressed to the principle of audi alteram partem, but it is I think applicable to the allied question whether any given body or person is acting in a quasi-judicial capacity. He said, at p349:

"Their Lordships were of course referred to the recent case of *Ridge* v *Baldwin* (1) where this principle was very closely and carefully examined. In that case no attempt was made to give an exhaustive classification of the cases where the principle audi alteram partem should be applied. In their Lordships' opinion it would be wrong to do so. Outside well-known cases such as dismissal from office, deprivation of property and expulsion from clubs, there is a vast area where the principle can only be applied upon most general considerations. For example, as Lord Reid when examining *R* v *Electricity Commissioners* (3) pointed out, Bankes LJ at p198, inferred the judicial element from the nature of the power, and Atkin LJ, at pp206-7, did the same. Pausing there, however, it should be assumed that their Lordships do not necessarily agree with Lord Reid's analysis of that case or with his criticism of *Nakkuda Ali* v *Jayaratne* (4). Outside the well-known classes of cases, no general rule can be laid down as to the application of the general principle in addition to the language of the provision. In their Lordships' opinion there are three matters which must always be borne in mind when considering whether the principle should be applied or not. These three matters are: first, what is the nature of the property, the office held, status enjoyed or services to be performed by the complainant of injustice. Secondly, in what circumstances or upon what occasions is the person claiming to be entitled to exercise the measure of control entitled to intervene. Thirdly, when a right to intervene is proved, what sanctions in fact is the latter entitled to impose upon the other. It is only upon a consideration of all these matters that the question of the application of the principle can properly be determined."

The context of educational societies involves a special factor which is not present in other contexts, namely the relation of tutor and pupil: that is to say the society is charged with the upbringing and supervision of the pupil under tuition, be the society a university or college, or a school. Where this relationship exists it is quite plain that on the one hand in certain circumstances the body or individual acting on behalf of the society must be regarded as acting in a quasi-judicial capacity - expulsion from the society is the obvious example. On the other hand, there is a wide range of circumstances in which the body or individual is concerned to impose penalties by way of domestic discipline. In these circumstances it seems to me that the body or individual is not acting in a quasi-judicial capacity at all but in a magisterial capacity, ie, in the performance of the rights and duties vested in the society as to the upbringing and supervision of the members of the society. No doubt there is a moral obligation to act fairly, but this moral obligation does not, I think, lie within the purview of the court in its control over quasi-judicial acts. Indeed, in the case of a schoolboy punishment the contrary could hardly be argued.

... The later case was concerned with an action which, although not in form expulsion, was tantamount to expulsion from the society ...

I must next decide whether in exercising his powers in the present case the vice-chancellor complied with the requirements of natural justice. I regret that I must answer that question without hesitation in the negative. It seems to me that once one accepts that the vice-chancellor was acting in a quasi-judicial capacity, he was clearly bound to give the plaintiff an opportunity of being heard before he reached his decision on the infliction of a penalty, and if so what penalty. In face he did not do so. I have already read his account of what happened. It seems to me that having by 29 and 30 June received clear and reliable evidence that the incident had indeed occurred and that the offenders included the plaintiff, he ought as a matter of natural justice to have sent for him before he left Keele, and given him an opportunity to present this own case. With all respect to the vice-chancellor I think he failed in his duty by omitting to send for the plaintiff, and instead, by writing him a letter merely announcing his decision.

The next step in the matter is the appeal to the council under section 19 of the statutes. It is unfortunate that the plaintiff failed to make the necessary arrangements to enable him to attend a meeting of the council if and when convened, but I do not think it is possible to reach the conclusion that in this respect he has been deprived of his right of appeal. He chose to go away either without leaving an address or, if he did leave an address, without coming home, and I think so far as that is concerned one must treat the decision of the council as effective. I would add that a different position might well have arisen if on his return home the plaintiff had applied for a fresh hearing before the council and his request had been refused ...

I have again after considerable hesitation, reached the conclusion that in this case I ought to exercise my discretion by not granting an injunction. I recognise that this particular discretion should be very sparingly exercised in that sense where there has been some failure in natural justice. On the other hand, it certainly should be exercised in that sense in an appropriate case, and I think this is such a case. There is no question of fact involved as I have already said. I must plainly proceed on the footing that the plaintiff was one of the individuals concerned. There is no doubt that the offence was one of a kind which merited a severe penalty according to any standard current even today. I have no doubt that the sentence of exclusion of residence in the campus was a proper penalty in respect of that offence. Nor has the plaintiff in his evidence put forward any specific justification for what he did.

So the position would have been that if the vice-chancellor had accorded him a hearing before making the decision, all that he, or anyone on his behalf, could have done would have been to put forward some plea by way of mitigation. I do not disregard the importance of such a plea in an appropriate case, but I do not think the mere fact he was deprived of throwing himself on the mercy of the vice-chancellor in that way is sufficient to justify setting aside a decision which was intrinsically a perfectly proper one.'

(1)   Infra, this chapter

(2)   [1967] 2 AC 337

(3)   [1924] 1 KB 171

(4)   Infra, this chapter

HK (An Infant), Re [1967] 2 QB 617 Queen's Bench Divisional Court (Lord Parker CJ, Salmon LJ and Blain J)

Natural justice satisfied where subject knows what information is required and has an opportunity to provide it

Facts

HK was an infant travelling on a Pakistani passport on which his date of birth was stated to be 29 February 1951, a non-existent date. On 21 November 1966 he arrived at London Airport accompanying AR. AR claimed that HK was his eldest son and under 16 years of age. If this were so then HK was entitled to enter the UK under s2(2)(b) of the Commonwealth Immigrants Act 1962. Since HK appeared to the immigration officer to be well over 15 years old, he referred the boy to the port medical officer whose opinion was that the boy was over 17 years. AR and HK were further interviewed separately by the immigration authorities, including the chief immigration officer who, his suspicion having increased during the interviews, decided to refuse HK admission into the UK. On the next day, 22 November, after learning that HK had in his possession a school-leaving certificate which also showed his date of birth to be 29 February 1951, the chief immigration officer again interviewed both AR and HK and as a result of that interview the officer, being still not satisfied that HK was under 16 years of age, directed that the boy be returned to Pakistan.

AR applied for a writ of habeas corpus to secure HK's release from the custody of the chief immigration officer and for certiorari to quash the officer's decision to refuse HK admission to the UK on the grounds that in deciding whether or not he was satisfied that the boy was under 16 years, the immigration officer was acting in a judicial or quasi-judicial capacity, and that the rules of natural justice therefore applied and required that before reaching his decision the officer should have given the boy full opportunity to remove the impression he had formed that the boy was over 16 years.

Held

Even if an immigration officer was not acting in a judicial or quasi-judicial capacity, the rules of natural justice applied to the limited extent allowed by the circumstances of any particular case and within the legislative framework under which the administrator was working. What natural justice required in the present case was that the immigration officer should act fairly and dispassionately, and give the immigrant an opportunity of satisfying him of the matters in s2(2)(b) of the 1962 Act and for that purpose to let the immigrant know what his immediate impression was, so that the immigrant might disabuse him. However, as both father and son knew the facts of which they had to satisfy the authorities and had been given ample opportunity to do so, the decision made on 21 November was arrived at validly.

McInnes v Onslow-Fane [1978] 1 WLR 1520 Chancery Division (Megarry V-C)

Where natural justice does not require a hearing but only that a decision be reached fairly

Facts

The plaintiff applied to the British Boxing Board of Control to be granted a boxers' manager's licence, asking for an oral hearing and prior information of anything that might militate against a favourable decision. The board refused his application without having given him an oral hearing or any reasons for their refusal. The plaintiff had previously held a promoter's licence, a trainer's licence and a Master of Ceremonies' licence, but in May 1973 all his licences had been withdrawn, and he had made five unsuccessful previous applications for a manager's licence. He applied to court for a declaration that in refusing this application the Board had acted unfairly and in breach of natural justice (i) in failing to inform him of the case against him so that he could answer it before the board considered in application, and (ii) in failing to grant him an oral hearing.

Held

The declaration was refused, because while there was no contract between the parties and no statute governed the case, nevertheless the board was obliged to observe the appropriate requirements of natural justice or fairness. However, since the case was not one involving forfeiture of an existing right or deprivation of an existing position nor one where the plaintiff had any legitimate expectation that his application would succeed, fairness (or natural justice) only required that the Board reached an honest conclusion without bias and not in pursuance of any capricious policy. They were under no obligation to give the plaintiff even the gist of their reasons for proposing to refuse his application and similarly were under no obligation to grant him an oral hearing; the refusal of a licence cast no slur upon his character nor did he have a statutory entitlement to a licence dependent upon the board's finding on some specific issue. The board had to decide the general issue of whether it was right to grant this licence to this applicant. The board was the best judge of the desirability of granting the licence and in the absence of any impropriety such as dishonesty, bias or caprice, the court ought not to interfere. *R v Gaming Board for GB, ex parte Benaim and Khaida* (1) and *In Re HK (An Infant)* (2) distinguished.

Megarry V-C:

'... Second, where the court is entitled to intervene, I think it must be considered what type of decision is in question. I do not suggest that there is any clear or exhaustive classification; but I think that at least three categories may be discerned. First, there are what may be called the forfeiture cases. In these, there is a decision which takes away some existing right or position, as where a member of an organisation is expelled or a licence is revoked. Second, at the other extreme there are what may be called the application cases. These are cases where the decision merely refuses to grant the applicant the right or position that he seeks, such as membership of the organisation, or a licence to do certain acts. Third, there is an intermediate category, which may be called the expectation cases, which differ from the application cases only in that the applicant has some legitimate expectation from what has already happened that his application will be granted. This head includes cases where an existing licence-holder applies for a renewal of his licence, or a person already elected or appointed to some position seeks confirmation from some confirming authority: see, for instance, *Weinberger v Inglis* (3); *Breen v Amalgamated Engineering Union* (4), and see *Schmidt v Secretary of State for Home Affairs* (5) and *R v Barnsley Metropolitan Borough Council, ex parte Hook* (6).

It seems plain that there is a substantial distinction between the forfeiture cases and the application cases. In the forfeiture cases, there is a threat to take something away for some reason: and in such cases, the right to an unbiased tribunal, the right to notice of the charges and the right to be heard in answer to the charges (which in *Ridge v Baldwin* (7), Lord Hodson said were three features of natural justice which stood out) are plainly apt. In the application cases, on the other hand, nothing is being taken away, and in all normal circumstances there are no charges, and so no requirement of an opportunity of being heard in answer to the charges. Instead, there is the far wider and less defined question of the general suitability of the applicant for membership or a licence. The distinction is well-recognised, for in general it is clear that the courts will require natural justice to be observed for expulsion from a social club, but not on an application for admission to it. The intermediate category, that of the expectation cases, may at least in some respects be regarded as being more akin to the forfeiture cases than the application cases: for although in form there is no forfeiture but merely an attempt at acquisition that fails, the legitimate expectation of a renewal of the licence or confirmation of the membership is one which raises the question of what it is that has happened to make the applicant unsuitable for the membership or licence for which he was previously thought suitable ...

... Third, there is the question of the requirements of natural justice or fairness that have to be applied in an application case such as this. What are the requirements where there are no provisions of any statute or contract either conferring a right to the licence in certain circumstances, or laying down the procedure to be observed, and the applicant is seeking from an unofficial body the grant of a type of licence that he has never held before and though hoping to obtain it, has no legitimate expectation of receiving?

I do not think that much held is to be obtained from discussing whether "natural justice" or "fairness" is the more appropriate term. If one accepts that "natural justice" is a flexible term which imposes different requirements in different cases, it is capable of applying appropriately to the whole range of situations indicated by terms such as "judicial", "quasi-judicial" and "administrative". Nevertheless, the further the situation is away from anything that resembles a judicial or quasi-judicial situation, and the further the question is removed from what may reasonably be called a justiciable question, the more appropriate it is to reject an expression which includes the word "justice" and to use instead terms such as "fairness" or "the duty to act fairly"; see *In re HK (An Infant)* (2), per Lord Parker CJ; in *Re Pergamon Press Ltd* (2), per Lord Denning MR; *Breen's* case (9), per Edmund Davies LJ ("fairly exercised"); *Pearlberg* v *Varty* (10), per Viscount Dilhorne, and ... per Lord Pearson. The suitability of the term "fairness" in such cases is increased by the curiosities of the expression "natural justice". Justice is far from being a "natural" concept. The closer one goes to a state of nature, the less justice does one find. Justice, and with it "natural justice" is in truth an elaborate and artificial product of civilisation which varies with different civilisations: see *Maclean* v *Workers' Union* (11), per Maugham J. To Black J, "natural justice" understandably meant no more than "justice" without the adjective: see *Green* v *Blake* [12]. However, be that as it may, the question before me is that of the content of "the duty to act fairly" (or of "natural justice") in this particular case. What does it entail? In particular, does it require the board to afford the plaintiff not only information of the "case against him" but also an oral hearing?

Before I turn to these heads, I should say that at the outset of his submission Mr Moses accepted, and asserted, that the board were under a duty to reach an honest conclusion, without bias, and not in pursuance of any capricious policy. To this extent the board were under a duty to act fairly. But that duty, he said, did not require the board either to inform the plaintiff of "the case against him" or to give him an oral hearing. Mr Beloff, on the other hand, contended that both of these requirements were constituent elements of "fairness" in cases of this kind. He disclaimed any submission that the board were required to give any reasons for their past rejection of applications, or that, once the decision was made, there was any obligation to give reasons in order to enable the plaintiff to apply to the courts to set it aside. He also made no positive attack on the substance of the board's decision, as distinct from the procedure adopted.

I therefore take as the fourth point the alleged obligation of the board to give the plaintiff information as to the case against him, or, as it was sometimes put during argument, information about what was troubling them. Mr Beloff accepted that there was no authority directly in point. But he contended that some authorities assisted him, and so far as authority was against him he said that it was distinguishable.

I think it is clear that there is no general obligation to give reasons for a decision. Certainly in an application case, where there are no statutory or contractual requirements but a simple discretion in the licensing body, there is no obligation on that body to give their reasons. In *Nagle* v *Feilden* (13) ... Salmon LJ made this plain: see at pp653-655. The point is also carried by *R* v *Gaming Board for Great Britain, ex parte Benaim and Khaida* (1). In the latter case, the gaming board were under a statutory obligation to have regard only to certain criteria. For this purpose the board were under a statutory obligation to take into consideration in particular "the character, reputation and financial standing" of the applicants (and of certain other persons) for what in effect was the certificate of fitness that was requisite on application for a licence. The Court of Appeal held that the board were under a duty to act fairly which required the board to give the applicants a sufficient indication of any relevant objections raised against them to enable to applicants to meet them. On the other hand, the board need not reveal the details or the sources of the information, nor when the board came to decide the application need the board give any reasons. The board had exercised their statutory power to regulate their procedure, and under the procedure that the board had adopted they gave the applicants a hearing at which the board revealed in outline what was troubling them. The applicants were then given the opportunity of making further representations in writing before the application was decided: and the Court of Appeal held that this procedure satisfied the duty of the board to act fairly which flowed from the statutory obligation of the board to "have regard only" to the specified matters: see at p430.

Mr Beloff, of course, relied on this decision. He also relied on *In re HK (An Infant)* (2). There the question was whether an immigrant was under 16 years old, and so, as the son of a Commonwealth citizen ordinarily resident in the United Kingdom, had a statutory right of entry into the United Kingdom. Lord Parker CJ held that the immigration officer was under a duty to give the immigrant an opportunity of satisfying him of the matters in the relevant subsection, and for that purpose to let him know what his immediate impression was so that the immigrant could disabuse him. On the facts, it was held that this duty has been discharged.

These cases seem to me to be very different from the case before me. In each there was a statute which conferred the power and the duty to decide upon some defined issue. Here there is no statute and no defined issue but merely a general discretion. In the *Gaming Board* case (1), the character, reputation and financial standing of the applicants were in issue, so that the refusal of the certificate of fitness would be a slur on the applicants. In *In re HK (An Infant)* (2), the question was whether or not the immigrant had a statutory right of entry. Here, there is no statutory or, indeed, any other true right; and certainly the refusal of a licence by no means necessarily puts any slur on the plaintiff's character. There are may reasons why a licence might be refused to an applicant of complete integrity, high repute and financial stability. Some may be wholly unconnected with the applicant, as where there are already too many licenses for the good of boxing under existing conditions. Others will relate to the applicant. They may be discreditable to him, as where he is dishonest or a drunkard; or they may be free from discredit, as where he suffers from physical or mental ill-health, or is too young, or too inexperienced, or too old, or simply lacks the personality or strength of character for what no doubt may be an exacting occupation. There may be no "case against him" at all, in the sense of something warranting forfeiture or expulsion; instead, there may simply be the absence of enough in favour of granting the licence. Indeed, in most cases the more demanding and responsible the occupation for which the licence is required, the greater will be the part likely to be played by considerations of moral or other blemishes. The more important these general considerations are, the less appropriate does it appear to be to require the licensing body to indicate to the applicant the nature of the "case against him". I think that this applies in the present case.

Let the distinctions between this case and the authorities that I have mentioned be accepted. There still remains the question whether in this case the board's procedure was fair ...

What, then, does the requirement to act fairly mean in this type of case?

As I have said, Mr Moses accepted that the board were under a duty to reach an honest conclusion without bias and not in pursuance of any capricious policy. That, I think, is right: and if the plaintiff showed that any of these requirements had not been complied with, I think the court would intervene. Mr Beloff accepted that the burden of proof would have been on him if any such questions had arisen. But assume a board acting honestly and without bias or caprice: why should a duty to act fairly require them to tell an applicant the gist of the reasons (which may vary from member to member) why they think he ought not to be given a licence? Is a college or university, when selecting candidates for admission or awarding scholarships, or a charity when making grants to the needy, acting "unfairly" when it gives no reason to the unsuccessful? Are editors and publishers "unfair" when they send out unreasoned rejection slips? Assume that they are under no enforceable duty to act fairly, and it may still be a matter of concern to them if they are to be told that they are acting "unfairly" in not giving the gist of their reasons to the rejected. Again, do judges act unfairly when, without any indication of their reasons, they refuse leave to appeal, or decide questions of costs?

I find some assistance in *Breen* v *Amalgamated Engineering Union* (4) on which Mr Moses strongly relied. That was a legitimate expectation type of case ...

Now of course that case is not this case. In one sense it is a fortiori the board's contentions in this case; for this, of course, is a mere application case, and not a legitimate expectation case. In *Breen*'s case (4) the plaintiff, having been elected by his fellow members, had a legitimate expectation of confirmation by the committee. If even in a legitimate expectation case there is no general right to notice of what is against the applicant, and the chance of meeting it, in a mere application case there could hardly be a greater right. On the other hand, *Breen*'s case concerned not the "right to work" but a right to hold office as a stop steward. However, the loss of such an office is no triviality in the trade union world. It is something, as Lord Denning MR said in his dissent (on which Mr Beloff relied in several respects) which "strikes deep, and not the less so because it may not strike at the pocket": p193. Furthermore, as I have indicated, I am not at all sure how far the "right to work" can be said to include the "right" to begin a new career of the worker's choice, as distinct from continuing with an existing mode of employment. On the whole, I think that *Breen*'s case provides at least a useful parallel to important factors in the case before me, and probably something more.

Looking at the case as whole, in my judgment there is no obligation on the board to give the plaintiff even the gist of the reasons why they refused his application, or proposed to do so. This is not a case in which there has been any suggestion of the board considering any alleged dishonesty or morally culpable conduct of the plaintiff. A man free from any moral blemish may nevertheless be wholly unsuitable for a particular type of work. The refusal of the plaintiff's application by no means necessarily puts any slur on his character, nor does it deprive him of any statutory right. There is no mere narrow issue as to his character, but the wide and general issue whether it is right to grant this licence to this applicant. In such circumstances, in the absence of anything to suggest that the board have been affected by dishonesty or bias or caprice, or that there is any other impropriety, I think that the board are fully entitled to give no reasons for their decision, and to decide the application without any preliminary indication to the plaintiff of those reasons. The board are the best judges of the desirability of granting the licence, and in the absence of any impropriety the court ought not to interfere.

There is a more general consideration. I think that the courts must be slow to allow any implied obligation to be fair to be used as a means of bringing before the courts for review honest decisions of bodies exercising jurisdiction over sporting and other activities which those bodies are far better fitted to judge than the courts. This is so even where those bodies are concerned with the means of livelihood of those who take part in those activities. The concepts of natural justice and the duty to be fair must not be allowed to discredit themselves by making unreasonable requirements and imposing undue burdens. Bodies such as the board which promote a public interest by seeking to maintain high standards in a field of activity which otherwise might easily become degraded and corrupt ought not to be hampered in their work without good cause. Such bodies should not be tempted or coerced into granting licences that otherwise they would refuse by reason of the courts having imposed on them a procedure for refusal which facilitates litigation against them. As Lord Denning MR said in *In re Pergamon Press Ltd* (8) "No one likes to have an action brought against him, however unfounded." The individual must indeed be protected against impropriety; but for any claim of his for anything more must be balanced against what the public interest requires.'

(1)	Infra, this chapter	(8)	[1971] Ch 388
(2)	Supra, this chapter	(9)	[1971] 2 QB 175
(3)	[1919] AC 606	(10)	[1972] 1 WLR 534
(4)	[1971] 2 QB 175	(11)	[1929] 1 Ch 602
(5)	[1969] 2 Ch 149	(12)	[1948] IR 242
(6)	Infra, this chapter	(13)	[1966] 2 QB 633
(7)	Infra, this chapter		

Maynard v Osmond [1977] QB 240 Court of Appeal (Lord Denning MR, Waller and Orr LJJ)

A fair hearing and the question of legal representation

Facts

A number of charges relating to indiscipline and the making of a false statement were laid against Maynard, a police constable. His request to be legally represented at the hearing of these charges was refused. The plaintiff constable sought, inter alia, a declaration that under the Police Discipline Regulations 1965 he was entitled to legal representation, or that the disciplinary body at least had discretion to grant him such representation.

Held

Legal representation was not available at such hearings. Where Parliament had intended that it should be available it had expressly provided for it, as in the case of disciplinary proceedings against senior officers.

Lord Denning MR:

'On principle, if a man is charged with a serious offence which may have grave consequences for him, he should be entitled to have a qualified lawyer to defend him. Such has been agreed by the government of this country when it adhered to the European Convention on Human Rights. But also, by analogy, it should be the same in most cases when he is charged with a disciplinary offence before a disciplinary tribunal, at any rate when the offence is one which may result in his dismissal from the force or other body to which he belongs; or the loss of his livelihood; or, worse still, may ruin his character for ever.

I gave the reason in *Pett* v *Greyhound Racing Association Ltd* (1):

"If justice is to be done, he ought to have the help of some one to speak for him. And who better than a lawyer who has been trained for the task?"

He should, therefore, be entitled to have a lawyer if he wants one. But, even if he should not be entitled as of right, I should have thought that as a general rule the tribunal should have a discretion in the matter. Legal representation should not be forbidden altogether. The tribunal should have a discretion to permit him to have a lawyer if they think it would assist. They are the master of their own procedure: and, unless clearly forbidden, should have a discretion to permit it. I said so in *Enderby Town Football Club Ltd* v *Football Association Ltd* (2). I recall myself an inquiry in which I had a discretion, and allowed a solicitor to speak for his client. He was able to correct a wrong impression that I had formed, and I was very glad of it. But I have to recognise that it is permissible for Parliament to decree otherwise, or for a minister to do so when making regulations, or even a domestic body itself. That is what is said in this case. It is said that in the disciplinary regulations the minister has forbidden legal representation to a policeman. He has allowed it to high-ranking officers, such as chief constables, their deputies or assistants, but not to any one of lower rank, not even to an inspector or a superintendent, let alone to a sergeant or a constable.

Apart from these points of construction, it seems to me that in these disciplinary proceedings, fairness can be obtained without legal representation. We have been given an affidavit by the deputy chief constable of Hampshire which shows that good provision is made for the defence of any officer who is accused of a disciplinary offence. The accused man will readily be assisted by the deputy chief constable and by the Police Federation to find a first-rate officer of good standing to defend him. It may be a senior officer from another police force altogether. He will regard it as his duty to defend the accused with courage and independence. He will be ready to cross-examine and criticise as well as any lawyer. He will probably do it better than a lawyer because of his knowledge of the inner workings of the police force. With such representation, the accused man can be assured of being well defended. In addition, arrangements have been made for the tribunal to be presided over by the chief constable of a force other than Hampshire. So he can be assured of a fair trial by an independent and impartial tribunal.'

Orr LJ:

'Mr Ross-Munro claimed that on the true construction of the discipline regulations (SI 1965 No 543) an accused police officer has a right of legal representation or alternatively that the chief constable has a discretion to allow him legal representation and should have exercised such discretion in the present case. I do not doubt that if such a discretion exists this would be an appropriate case in which to exercise it, but I find it impossible to construe the regulations as conferring either a right to legal representation or a discretion to permit it. Looking first at the discipline regulations themselves, regulation 8(3) provides that the case against the accused "shall be presented by a member of a police force" and regulation 8(6) provides that "The accused may conduct his defence either in person or by a member of a police force selected by himself on his behalf." Mr Ross-Munro in part of his argument relied on an alleged contrast between the word "shall" in the first of these provisions and the word "may" in the second, but in my judgment "may" is in any event appropriate in the second provision since the accused is not bound to defend the charges; and to construe regulation 8(6), by reason of the use of the word "may" and not "shall," as allowing legal representation as of right, or alternatively in the discretion of the chief constable, would in my judgment lead to an absurdity in that "shall" in regulation 8(3) would remain a barrier against legal representation, either as of right or in the exercise of a discretion, for the prosecution, and it cannot, in my judgment, have been intended that one party should be entitled to legal representation but not the other. But if any doubt remains on this matter it is, in my judgment, resolved by the provisions of the other regulations. Regulation 6(4) of the senior officers' regulations (SI 1965 No 544) provides:

"The accused may conduct his defence either in person or by counsel, a solicitor or a member of a police force selected by himself on his behalf";

and regulation 5(1) of the Police (Appeals) Rules (SI 1965 No 618) provides with respect to an inquiry ordered by the minister that: "The appellant shall have the right to appear at the inquiry in person, by a serving member of a police force or by counsel or a solicitors." Both these provisions clearly indicate, in my view, that when it is intended to allow legal representation it is specifically so provided. Further, the provisions of regulations 4(2) and 6(1) of the appeal rules indicate, in my judgment, that when it is intended to confer a discretion in derogation of accepted practice (rule 4(2)) or of a rule contained in the regulations (rule 6(1)) specific provision is so made.

For these reasons I find it impossible to construe the regulations as conferring either a right to legal representation or a discretion in the tribunal to allow it, and on the authorities I do not find it possible to hold that in failing to confer such a right or discretion the regulations are ultra vires either as failing to meet a requirement of natural justice or on any other ground. No authority cited to us lends any support to the view that the denial either of a right to legal representation or of a discretion to allow it contravenes the rules of natural justice, and while we are concerned in this case with regulations made by a minister under statutory powers and not with a domestic tribunal constituted by contract, I am inclined to agree with the view provisionally expressed by Cairns LJ in *Enderby Town Football Club Ltd* v *Football Association Ltd* (2), that: "... it is open to an organisation to make an absolute rule that a tribunal set up by it is not to hear legal representatives."

It was argued by Mr Ross-Munro that the discipline regulations and the senior officers' discipline regulations involve an unfair discrimination against junior police officers in that in disciplinary proceedings against a senior officer of the rank of assistant chief constable or above the accused is given a right to legal representation whereas on the construction which I have accepted of the discipline regulations there is, in the case of an officer below that rank, neither a right to be legally represented nor any discretion of the court to allow such representation. But this argument ignores, in my judgment, the clear fact that the right to legal representation was not granted to senior officers as a privilege of their rank but only as the necessary consequences of a decision, which I have no doubt was rightly taken, that because officers of and above the rank of assistant chief constable may be in day-to-day contact with the members of the police authority it was appropriate that the prosecution of such officers should be conducted by a lawyer, and that as a necessary consequence of that decision, embodied in regulation 6(1) of the senior officers' discipline regulations, the defendant should equally be entitled to legal representation.'

(1)   Infra, this chapter

(2)   Supra, this chapter

Maxwell v Department of Trade and Industry [1974] 1 QB 523 Court of Appeal (Lord Denning MR, Orr and Lawton LJJ)

When the courts will not grant a declaration

Facts

(inter alia) The plaintiff sought declarations that an investigation carried out by Department of Trade inspectors into companies of which he was chief executive had been unfair, in that he had not had an opportunity of refuting criticisms made of him by witnesses. He also sought an injunction to prevent any further action being taken on the inspectors' report.

Held

The investigation had been conducted fairly. Natural justice did not require the inspectors to provide the plaintiff with an opportunity to comment on their tentative conclusions.

Lord Denning MR:

'It must be remembered that the inspectors are doing a public duty in the public interest. They must do what is fair to the best of their ability. They will, of course, put to a witness the points of substance which occur to them - so as to give him the chance to explain or correct any relevant statement which is prejudicial to him. They may even recall him to do so. But they are not to be criticised because they may on occasion overlook something or other. Even the most skilled advocate, expert in cross-examination, forgets now and again to put this or that point to a witness. And we all excuse him, knowing how difficult it is to remember everything. The inspector is entitled to at least as much consideration as the advocate. To borrow from Shakespeare, he is not to have "all his faults observed, set in a notebook, learn'd, and conn'd by rote," to make a lawyer's holiday. His task is burdensome and thankless enough as it is. It would be intolerable if he were liable to be pilloried afterwards for doing it. No one of standing would ever be found to undertake it.

The public interest demands that, so long as he acts honestly and does what is fair to the best of his ability, his report is not to be impugned in the courts of law.

This disposes also of Mr Ogden's other complaint. He said that, early on in the inquiry, the inspectors gave an assurance that they would put their tentative conclusions to the witness - and nevertheless failed in the later stages to do so, without giving any warning. But Mr Le Quesne pointed out that, when the passages were read at large in their context, the inspectors gave no such assurance. In any case, any failure to do so was an oversight which did not result in any unfairness.

I would only say one word about the relief asked. Mr Ogden recognised that the court could not set aside the report, in whole or in part. It could not declare it, or any part of it, to be null and void. At most he asked for a declaration that natural justice had not been observed in the making of it. Whilst I would not restrict in any way the court's jurisdiction to grant a declaration, the case must be very rare in which it would be right to make such a bare declaration in the air. This is certainly not a case for it.

In conclusion, I would say this: I have studied all the points of detail which have been put to us. And I have read the judgment of Wien J upon them. I would like to express my appreciation of it and endorse all that he said. This is nothing more nor less than an attempt by Mr Maxwell to appeal from the findings of the inspectors to the courts. But Parliament has given no appeal. So Mr Maxwell has tried to get round it by attacking the conduct of the inspectors themselves. In this he has failed utterly. To my minds the inspectors did their work with conspicuous fairness. They investigated all the matters with the greatest care. They went meticulously into the details of these complicated transactions. They put to Mr Maxwell all the points which appeared to call for an explanation or an answer. They gave him every opportunity of dealing with them. If there were one or two points which they overlooked, these were as nothing in relation to the wide field which they covered. I regret that, having done their work so well, they should now be harassed by this attack upon them. It has never been done before in all the many inquiries under the Companies Act. And I hope it will never happen again. I would dismiss the appeal.'

Lawton LJ:

'As to what was done, once it became apparent to the inspectors that the plaintiff might be open to criticism in their report, on many occasions they put to him the substance of what other witnesses had said about him which could, if they accepted the evidence, be the basis for criticism. On a few occasions they did not, and by the standards of perfection it might have been better if they had. In putting the substance of what had been said by other witnesses the inspectors were, no doubt, trying to do what those holding inquiries have been enjoined to do by Lord Loreburn LC in *Board of Education* v *Rice* (1), namely, to give any one in the plaintiff's position a fair opportunity for correcting or contradicting any relevant statement prejudicial to his view.

What they did not do was to give the plaintiff an opportunity of correcting or contradicting the opinions which they were minded to report to the department as to what evidence they thought credible and what inferences they should draw from such evidence. The plaintiff submits they should have done so, and that their omission constituted unfairness. I do not agree. The plaintiff's submission was founded on some observations made by Sachs LJ during the hearing of what was the first of a series of proceedings which have been started by the plaintiff in respect of this inquiry: see *In re Pergamon Press Ltd* (2). Sachs LJ was there commenting on what the court, of which he was a member, had been told the inspectors had promised to do. The inspectors had said more than what had been reported and that which had not been reported altered the case. Further, endorsing with his approval what the inspectors were reported to have said was not necessary for the purpose of deciding the appeal. The researches of counsel have not produced any other case which has suggested that at the end of an inquiry those likely to be criticised in a report should be given an opportunity of refuting the tentative conclusions of whoever is making it. Those who conduct inquiries have to base their decisions, findings, conclusions or opinions (whichever is the appropriate word to describe what they have a duty to do) on the evidence. In my judgment they are no more bound to tell a witness likely to be criticised in their report what they have in mind to say about him than has a judge sitting alone who has to decide which of two conflicting witnesses is telling the truth. The judge must ensure that the witness whose credibility is suspected has a fair opportunity of correcting or contradicting the substance of what other witnesses have said or are expected to say which is in conflict with his testimony. Inspectors should do the same but I can see no reason why they should do any more.'

(1) [1911] AC 179

(2) Infra, this chapter

Nakkuda Ali v Jayaratne [1951] AC 66 Privy Council (Lord Radcliffe, Lord Porter, Lord Oaksey, Sir John Beaumont and Sir Lionel Leach)

Administrative non-judicial acts not subject to natural justice

Facts

The respondent was the Controller of Textiles in Ceylon. He had cancelled the appellant's textile licence under reg 62 of the Defence (Control of Textiles) Regulations 1945 which empowered him to do so 'where the Controller has reasonable grounds to believe that any dealer is unfit to be allowed to continue as a dealer'. The appellant applied for a writ of certiorari to quash the cancellation order.

Held

Certiorari could only be granted to quash decisions which were required to be taken following a judicial process or a process analogous to the judicial. Although the words in reg 62 'where the Controller has reasonable grounds to believe' were to be treated as imposing a condition that there must in fact exist reasonable grounds, the Controller in acting under reg 62 was not acting judicially and might arrive at his reasonable belief without a course of conduct analogous to the judicial process. Thus he might have reasonable grounds of belief without ever having notified the licence holder of the case against him or giving him an opportunity to answer that case. There was nothing in the context of conditions of the Controller's jurisdiction which suggested that he must regulate his action by analogy to judicial rules.

When he cancelled a licence the Controller was not determining a question, he was taking executive action to withdraw a privilege because he believed, and had reasonable grounds to believe, that the holder was unfit to retain it. Certiorari could not be granted.

Commentary

Compare this case with *R v Barnsley Metropolitan Borough Council, ex parte Hook* (1) where the Court of Appeal held that in revoking the stall-holder's licence the Council was under a duty to act judicially. Note also that it now seems to be accepted that it is 'not necessary to show a judicial act in order to get certiorari' (per Lord Widgery CJ in the Divisional Court in *R v Board of Visitors of Hull Prison, ex parte St Germain and Others* (2).

(1) Infra, this chapter

(2) [1978] QB 78

Ostreicher v Secretary of State for the Environment [1978] 1 WLR 810 Court of Appeal (Lord Denning MR, Shaw and Waller LJJ)

What constitutes a fair opportunity to be heard, so as to satisfy natural justice

Facts

In June 1974, a local authority made a compulsory purchase order in respect of properties owned by the applicant and her husband in a clearance area. On 2 December 1975 the applicant's surveyors lodged a written objection. The Secretary of State decided to hold a public inquiry.

By a letter of 5 February 1976 the applicant's surveyors were informed that an inquiry was to be held on 21 April 1976, over 42 days notice being given in accordance with rule 4(2) of the Compulsory Purchase by Local Authorities (Inquiries Procedure) Rules 1962. On 1 April, the applicant's surveyors wrote to the Secretary of State that due to religious reasons O was unable to attend on 21 April, briefly stated O's objections and asked for a special hearing to be arranged. On 7 April, the Secretary of State wrote that it was not possible for a special hearing to be arranged, assured the surveyors that full account would be taken of the written objection and pointed out that O could be represented at the inquiry. In fact O was prohibited by her religion from working or employing anybody to do so, but no letter was written in response to the Secretary of State's letter of 7 April.

The inquiry was held, the inspector considering the written objections of the applicant and visiting the properties. The compulsory purchase order was confirmed by the Secretary of State in accordance with the inspector's recommendations.

The applicant applied for the order to be quashed under the provisions of Schedule 4 of the Housing Act 1957 on two grounds: (1) that the inspector should not have gone ahead with the inquiry without the applicant being represented, and (2) that the inspector had made manifest errors in his conclusions.

Held

While it was a basic principle of natural justice that every party or objector should be given a fair opportunity of being heard, the applicant had been given such an opportunity. No objection was made to the date for about two months after the date was fixed and the applicant did not reply to the letter of 7 April explaining that representation would be impossible and requesting an adjournment. In the circumstances, and considering that the inspector considered the applicant's written objection, there was no failure to observe natural justice.

Since the inspector had inspected the properties and come to a conclusion that, on the evidence, was reasonable, there was no reason for quashing the compulsory purchase order on the second ground either.

Payne v Lord Harris of Greenwich [1981] 1 WLR 754 Court of Appeal (Lord Denning MR, Shaw and Brightman LJJ))

Natural justice and the requirement to give reasons for a decision

Facts

The plaintiff had been convicted of murder in 1968, but was now regarded as a 'model prisoner.' Having been refused release on licence, the plaintiff now sought from the Parole Board the reasons for the refusal so that he could better prepare his next application. The plaintiff applied for declarations that he was entitled to the information. The declarations were refused at first instance, and the plaintiff appealed.

Held

The appeal would be dismissed. There was no specific requirement upon the Board to supply the information. Natural justice did not, in this context, require the giving of reasons.

Lord Denning MR:

> 'No doubt it is the duty of all those concerned - from the member of the local review committee, to the Parole Board, to the Secretary of State - to act fairly. That is the simple precept which now governs the administrative procedure of all public bodies. But the duty to act fairly cannot be set

down in a series of set propositions. Each case depends on its own circumstances. As Sachs LJ said, in *In re Pergamon Press Ltd* (1):

> "In the application of the concept of fair play, there must be real flexibility, so that very different situations may be met without producing procedures unsuitable to the object in hand."

Sometimes fairness may require that the man be told the outline of the case against him. As in *R* v *Gaming Board for Great Britain, ex parte Benaim and Khaida* (2), I said:

> "... without disclosing every detail, I should have thought that the board ought in every case to be able to give to the applicant sufficient indication of the objections raised against him such as to enable him to answer them."

'That is what Mr Turner-Samuels urged here.

At other times it may not be necessary to have a hearing or even to tell the man the case against him, because it must be obvious to him. As, for instance, in *Cinnamond* v *British Airports Authority* (3); and *R* v *Secretary of State for the Home Department, ex parte Santillo* (4).'

There are equally strong submissions to the contrary. The first is the practical difficulty of giving the reasons of a body of five members. One or two may have a different reason from the other three or four. Some may be spoken. Other unspoken. The next is the danger that the reasons, if given, would tend to become short and stereotyped, rather than full and informative. So they would be of little avail. If they were full and informative, they would give the prisoner an opening with which he could challenge the refusal. He could lodge an application for judicial review complaining that the board took things into account which they should not have done - or that their decision was unreasonable. If he were refused judicial review, he would harbour a grievance which should become obsessive just as much as if he is refused parole without reasons being given.

Apart from these practical considerations, I would suppose that in most cases the man will know the reasons well enough himself. He will have known the gravity of his crime. He will know whether he is thought to be a danger or not. He will know whether he has behaved well in prison or not. He will be able to deal with all these points in the representation which he is allowed to make. If there should be any new factor adverse to him - of which he is unaware - the Parole Board might well arrange for one of their members to interview him so as to ascertain his reaction to it. This is contemplated by s59(4)(b) of the Act of 1967. Thus fairness will be ensured here just as we envisaged in the *Santillo* case (4).

In the end I think the problem comes down to this: what does public policy demand as best to be done? To give reasons or to withhold them? This is more a matter for the Secretary of State than for the courts. But, so far as I can judge of the matter, I should think that in the interests of the man himself - as a human being facing indefinite detention - it would be better for him to be told the reasons. But, in the interests of society at large - including the due administration of the parole system - it would be best not to give them. Except in the rare case when the board itself think it desirable, as a matter of fairness, to ask one of the members to interview him. That member may then think it appropriate to tell him.'

Brightman LJ:

'So far as natural justice is concerned, both the board and the committee accept that they are under a duty to act fairly in the exercise of their statutory functions. So the question that has to be asked is whether fairness requires that a prisoner in the situation of the plaintiff ought to be apprised of the reasons why he has not heretofore been recommended by the board for release on licence, or at least the gist of the reasons, or of matters which may tend to weigh against him.

In *Kanda* v *Government of Malaya* (5) the plaintiff, an inspector of police, had under the constitution of the Federation a right to be heard before being dismissed from the police service. The Judicial

Committee observed, at p337: "If the right to be heard is to be a real right which is worth anything, it must carry with it a right in the accused man to know the case which is made against him." That is the basis of the plaintiff's claim in this present action. In my judgment there is no close comparison between the two cases. The function of the Parole Board is to make a recommendation and of the local review committee to make a suitability report. In neither case is it to investigate charges. The board and the committee will each, no doubt, make an assessment of the prisoner's character and his likely reaction to a free environment; and also, perhaps more importantly, an assessment of the public interest. According to the undisputed evidence, the committee's suitability report, and the board's recommendation, will be based on a consideration of the prisoner's file, including all reports which have been made from time to time by prison staff and reports specially prepared for the review, and also the representations (if any) made by the prisoner. The suitability report of the local review committee and the representations of the prisoner form part of the material placed before the Parole Board to enable it to exercise an advisory function. I can see no principle of fairness which requires that the prisoner should be informed, even in outline, of the reasons which accompanied previous suitability reports of the local review committee or recommendations of the Parole Board, or of the adverse matters which may weigh against him. Indeed, the prisoner will be only too well aware of the adverse factors likely to feature in reports made about him. He will not be better able to formulate effective representations because he has been told of the character assessments and the assessments of the public interest which may also feature in the file.

The scope and extent of the principles of natural justice depend on the subject matter to which they are sought to be applied: see *R v Gaming Board for Great Britain, ex parte Benaim and Khaida* (2). They apply to the present case, as conceded, to the extent that they impose on the board and the committee, and each member of it, a duty to act fairly. That duty does not, in my judgment, require that any disclosure is made to the prisoner of adverse material which the board and the committee have in their possession to assist them in their advisory and reporting functions.

There are other problems in applying the principles of natural justice so as to produce the result which the plaintiff seeks. One problem would be to define in legally intelligible language the limits of the disclosure which must be made if the plaintiff is right. The local review committee's report will be a report on the plaintiff's suitability for release on licence. It is not claimed that he is to be given a copy of that report. Is he to be given a precis of it? If so, why not the whole report? If not a precis, how is one to define in legal language what has to be given? Much the same questions must be asked in relation to disclosure of the Parole Board's conclusions upon which its recommendation is founded.'

(1)   Infra, this chapter

(2)   Infra, this chapter

(3)   Supra, this chapter

(4)   [1981] 2 WLR 362

(5)   [1962] AC 332

Pergamon Press Ltd, Re [1971] Ch 388 Court of Appeal (Lord Denning MR, Sachs and Buckley LJJ)

Duty to act fairly in an administrative matter

Facts

(inter alia) The case concerned the conduct of inspectors carrying out an investigation of the company pursuant to s165 (b) of the Companies Act 1948.

Held

The inspectors had to act fairly, even though they were acting in an administrative capacity.

Lord Denning MR:

'... It is true, of course, that the inspectors are not a court of law. Their proceedings are not judicial proceedings: see *In re Grosvenor & West-End Railway Terminus Hotel Co Ltd* (1). They are not even quasi-judicial, for they decide nothing; they determine nothing. They only investigate and report. They sit in private and are not entitled to admit the public to their meetings: see *Hearts of Oak Assurance Co Ltd* v *Attorney-General* (2). They do not even decide whether there is a prima facie case, as was done in *Wiseman* v *Borneman* (3).

But this should not lead us to minimise the significance of their task. They have to make a report which may have wide repercussions. They may, if they think fit, make findings of fact which are very damaging to those whom they name. They may accuse some; they may condemn others; they may ruin reputations or careers. Their report may lead to judicial proceedings. It may expose persons to criminal prosecutions or to civil actions. It may bring about the winding up of the company, and be used itself as material for the winding up: see *In re SBA Properties Ltd* (4). Even before the inspectors make their report, they may inform the Board of Trade of facts which tend to show that an offence has been committed: see s41 of the (Companies) Act 1967. When they do make their report, the Board are bound to send a copy of it to the company; and the board may, in their discretion, publish it, if they think fit, to the public at large.

Seeing that their work and their report may lead to such consequences, I am clearly of the opinion that the inspectors must act fairly. This is a duty which rests on them, as on many other bodies, even though they are not judicial, or quasi-judicial, but only administrative: see *R* v *Gaming Board for Great Britain, ex parte Benaim and Khaida* (5). The inspectors can obtain information in any way they think best, but before they condemn or criticise a man, they must give him a fair opportunity for correcting or contradicting what is said against him. They need not quote chapter and verse. An outline of the charge will usually suffice.

This is what the inspectors here propose to do, but the directors of the company want more. They want to see the transcripts of the witnesses who speak adversely of them, and to see any documents which may be used against them. They, or some of them, even claim to cross-examine the witnesses.

In all this the directors go too far. This investigation is ordered in the public interest. It should not be impeded by measures of this kind. Witnesses should be encouraged to come forward and not hold back. Remember, this not being a judicial proceeding, the witnesses are not protected by an absolute privilege, but only by a qualified privilege: see *O'Connor* v *Waldron* (6). It is easy to imagine a situation in which, if the name of a witness were disclosed, he might have an action brought against him, and this might deter him from telling all he knew. No one likes to have an action brought against him, however unfounded. Every witness must, therefore, be protected. He must be encouraged to be frank. This is done by giving every witness an assurance that his evidence will be regarded as confidential and will not be used except for the purpose of the report. This assurance must be honoured. It does not mean that his name and his evidence will never be disclosed to anyone. It will often have to be used for the purpose of the report, not only in the report itself, but also by putting it in general terms to other witnesses for their comments. But it does mean that the inspectors will exercise a wide discretion in the use of it so as to safeguard the witness himself and any others affected by it. His evidence may sometimes, though rarely, be so confidential that it cannot be put to those affected by it, even in general terms. If so, it should be ignored so far as they are concerned. For I take it be axiomatic that the inspectors must not use the evidence of a witness so as to make it the basis of an adverse finding unless they give the party affected sufficient information to enable him to deal with it ...'

(1)   (1898) 76 LT 337

(2)   [1932] AC 392

(3)   [1971] AC 297

(4)   [1967] WLR 799

(5)   Infra, this chapter

(6)   [1935] AC 76

Pett v Greyhound Racing Association (No 1) [1970] 1 QB 46 Queen's Bench Division (Lyell J)

Natural justice does not require legal representation at a private hearing

Facts

The National Greyhound Racing Club issued licences to persons concerned in greyhound racing, including proprietors of racecourses and trainers of greyhounds, and a holder of their licences agreed to be bound by their rules, the Rules of Racing. The rules provided for the holding of inquiries and gave power to withdraw or suspend licences, but they did not provide for the procedure to be adopted at an inquiry or deal with the rights of their licence holders to be legally represented. The defendants owned and operated a racecourse licensed by the club and the plaintiff held a club's trainer's licence. Pursuant to rule 48 of the Rules of Racing, the defendants intended to hold an inquiry, on 19 September 1967, into the alleged drugging of a greyhound trained by the plaintiff. The plaintiff's solicitor wrote to the defendants asking for the plaintiff to be legally represented and the defendants replied agreeing to adjourn the hearing until 3 October 1967. On 3 October the plaintiff attended with his counsel and solicitor, but the defendants informed the plaintiff that they intended to hold the inquiry on 31 October, when they would not permit him to be legally represented.

The plaintiff sought, inter alia, a declaration that the defendants were acting ultra vires in refusing to allow him legal representation and an injunction restraining them from holding an inquiry unless he was allowed to be so represented.

Held

The defendants had not acted contrary to the rules of natural justice in refusing to allow the plaintiff to be legally represented at the inquiry for it was only in a society which had reached some degree of sophistication in its affairs that the right to be legally represented was an elementary feature of the fair dispensation of justice. Accordingly, since the defendants intended to hold a domestic inquiry which in all other respects was a fair one and the plaintiff had no common law right to be legally represented before such a tribunal, albeit the decision of the tribunal might affect his livelihood and reputation, the plaintiff's action failed.

R v Aston University, ex parte Roffey [1969] 2 QB 538 Queen's Bench Division (Donaldson J)

Natural justice and the court's discretion to refuse relief

Facts

The applicants were students at the university who had failed in referred examinations. Under the regulations, the examiners had a discretion to allow the students to re-sit the examinations at the end of the following academic year, or request them to withdraw from the course. In the light of their examination performance, the examiners asked the applicants to withdraw from the course, and this decision was subsequently upheld by the university senate in December 1967. In July 1968 the applicants sought orders of certiorari to quash these decisions, and mandamus to compel the university to consider their cases according to law.

Held

The university had acted in breach of natural justice in not allowing the students to give evidence on personal matters before a final decision was made, but as thestudents had delayed in applying for relief the court would exercise its discretion to refuse the orders sought.

Donaldson J:

'In Mr Forbes' submission, a student who has failed occupies a position analogous to one holding office at pleasure.

In my judgment it is not right to treat the principle of audi alteram partem as something divorced from the concept of natural justice, although it will certainly not apply in every case in which there is a right to natural justice. Where, however, it does apply, it is an integral part of natural justice and may indeed lie at its heart. Lord Upjohn delivering the report of the Judicial Committee of the Privy Council in *Durayappah* v *Fernando* (1), said that outside well known cases such as dismissal from office, deprivation of property and expulsion from clubs there existed a vast area within which the principle could only be applied upon most general considerations. In considering its applicability regard had to be had to the wording of the provisions concerned - in this case the special regulations - and to three matters, namely, first, what is the nature of the property, the office held, status enjoyed or services to be performed by the complainant; second, in what circumstances or upon what occasions is the person claiming to be entitled to exercise the measure of control entitled to intervene; thirdly, when a right to intervene is proved, what sanction in fact is the latter entitled to impose upon the other?

The first and third of these matters fall to be considered together in this case. Mr Pantridge was a student member of the university enjoying the rights and privileges of that status with the chance of achieving graduate status in due time. The sanctions which the university was entitled to impose was total deprivation of that status and of the chance of improving it thereafter. Furthermore, as Mr Pantridge found to his cost, an ex-student member of a university may well be in a more disadvantageous position that one who aspires for the first time to student status. There have been more momentous decisions than that made by the examiners in the case of Mr Pantridge, but there can be no denying its gravity from his point of view.

The second matter falls to be considered with and in the context of the special regulations governing the course. There is much force in Mr Forbes' contention that examinations are meant to be passed and that those who fail to do so at a university prima facie should expect to be sent down. I am quite prepared to accept it as a background against which the special regulations fall to be construed. They, however, provide a most elaborate code which almost effaces the background. We are concerned with the qualifying year which determines whether the student moves on to study for an honours degree, to study for a pass degree, or has to leave the university. It is only in the latter case that membership of the university a body with some of the attributes of a club - is in question. If the student passes in all major subjects at honours standard and in subsidiary subjects at pass standard, he moves on to the honours degree course automatically (regulation 4(b)). If he achieves pass standards in all subjects, he moves on to a pass degree course (regulation 4(c)). If he fails to achieve a pass standard in a major subject, he may be permitted to take a referred examination in that subject at the discretion of the examiners and, if successful, will move on to the pass course (regulation 4(d)). If he fails to achieve pass standards in either or both subsidiary subjects and, I assume although it is not so stated, achieves honours standards in the major subjects, he may on the recommendation of the examiners be permitted to take referred examinations in these subjects and, if successful, may be permitted to proceed on the honours course (regulation 4(e)). It is not stated to whom the recommendation is to be made and who decides, or why under this regulation the examiners recommend rather than exercise their own discretion. If he fails in more than one major subject (of which there are three and Mr

Pantridge was successful in them all) or fails in a referred examination (which Mr Pantridge did in the case of one subsidiary subject) he may at the sole discretion of the examiners re-sit the whole examination or may be required to withdraw from the course. In the event of his being successful in the re-sit examination he would normally proceed to the pass degree only regulation 4(f)). The regulations enjoin examiners in deciding whether to allow students to retake examinations to have regard to their performance in non-examinable subjects (regulation 4(g)) and end with an escape clause providing that students may not normally proceed to the second year of the course until they have satisfied the examiners in the examinations as a whole (regulation 4(h)). They could quite properly have provided, but did not provide, that the examiners should be under no obligation to afford the students any opportunity to make representations to them, before making a decision. Had the regulations taken this form, no problem would have arisen.

I have dealt with these regulations at length because it seems to me that they largely destroy the prima facie approach of "pass or go down." Their elaboration continues in relation to the honours course, the honours final, the pass degree course and the pass final. Of these, regulation 6.4(b) which applies to the pass degree course is important, not because it is of direct application, but because it shows a contrasting approach to that indicated by regulation 4(f) under which Mr Pantridge was sent down. That regulation provides that:

> "Any student who fails to satisfy the examiners in not more than two subjects may at the discretion of the examiners be permitted to take a referred examination in these subjects. Students failing to reach pass standard in three or more subjects, or who fail a referred examination may not normally proceed further on the course."

Here alone is the "pass or go down" approach to be seen.

Scarcely a body in the university failed to make a recommendation or a decision in the case of Mr Pantridge and his fellow students. No doubt their interventions were inspired by the most laudable of motives, although their lack of unanimity was in many ways unfortunate. The fact remains that whilst other bodies might be able to practice to temper the wind to the failed student, the only body invested by the regulations with the power and discretion to decide whether or not Mr Pantridge should be sent down was "the examiners." For my part I am inclined to think that as the regulations stand this means the full board of examiners but the decision was in fact taken by a smaller body and no objection has been taken on that account. For the purposes of this case, I shall assume that theirs was the discretion and theirs the decision.

I can understand it being argued on the regulations that regard was to be had primarily and possible exclusively to the examination results and performances in non-examinable subjects. However, the examiners themselves did not adopt this approach, as I think rightly, and they considered a wide range of extraneous factors, some of which by their very nature, for example personal and family problems, might only have been known to the students themselves. In such circumstances and with so much at stake, common fairness to the students, which is all that natural justice is, and the desire of the examiners to exercise their discretion upon the most solid basis, alike demanded that before a final decision was reached the students should be given an opportunity to be heard either orally or in writing, in person or by their representatives as might be most appropriate. It was, in my judgment, he examiners' duty and the students' right that such audience be given. It was not given and there was a breach of the rules of natural justice.

In the course of the argument it was submitted that students who had failed their examinations were in no better position than those who applied for admission as students, the latter plainly having no right to be heard, but this in my judgment overlooks the accrued status of the students as members of the university. Reference was also made to the immigrant cases such as *In re HK (An Infant)* (2), *In re Mohammed Arif (An Infant)* (3), and *Schmidt* v *Secretary of State for Home Affairs* (4), but these are not really analogous. The industry of counsel enabled us to be referred to a decision of the courts of New South Wales, *Ex parte Forster, In re Sydney University* (5), which bore a striking similarity on its facts, but there the issue was not a right of audience, but an alleged absolute right to remain a member of the university irrespective of examination results. The court denied the existence of any such right, but its existence has not been suggested in the present case.

This by no means concludes the matter in Mr Pantridge's favour, because it is not in all circumstances that a breach of the requirements of natural justice will give rise to prerogative redress. The remedies are discretionary and a very important factor is the likelihood that the ultimate decision would have been any different, if a right of audience had been extended to Mr Pantridge. It is in this context that the history of the affair after the initial decision is of relevance, but is difficult to evaluate. In the course of the argument Mr Moncaster was asked whether there was any further information which Mr Pantridge wished to place before the court, but, after taking instructions, Mr Moncaster said that there was none.

The fact remains that the examiners who reached the initial, and as I think the only directly relevant, decision were wholly unaware of the widespread allegations that the students had been misled by members of the staff as to what was at stake when they prepared, or failed to prepare, for the examinations in the subsidiary subjects and for the referred examinations in those subjects. Would the knowledge have made any difference? It may well be thought that Mr Pantridge achieved only derisory marks (17 per cent in the referred examination) but students with 22 per cent and 25 per cent were permitted to repeat the first year. When one tries to assess the probable outcome on the basis of the attitude of the full board of examiners, the board of the faculty, the academic advisory committee, the senate and the council, all of whom knew of the allegations and either had investigated them or knew the results of such investigations, the problem becomes more difficult still. None of these bodies regarded the allegations as proved, but some clearly took the view that the students honestly believed in their truth. The board of faculty, acting on the basis of the professors' interview with the students, intended to exercise the discretion which they mistakenly thought that they possessed in favour of the students. The academic advisory committee clearly thought that the principles of good administration required that both students and staff be heard by the senate.

In my judgment it is impossible to project subsequent attitudes backwards in point of time and to determine what the examiners would have done if they had heard the students' allegations, before making a decision.

In this situation I regard the time factor as decisive. The prerogative remedies are exceptional in their nature and should not be made available to those who sleep upon their rights. Mr Pantridge's complaint is that he was not allowed to re-sit the whole examination in June, 1968, and, if successful, proceed to the pass degree in the 1968-69 academic year, yet he did not even apply to move this court until July, 1968. By such inaction, in my judgment he forfeited whatever claims he might otherwise have had to the court's intervention.

I would therefore refuse the relief sought.'

(1)   [1967] 2 AC 337

(2)   Supra, this chapter

(3)   [1968] Ch 643

(4)   [1969] 2 Ch 149

(5)   (1963) SR (NSW) 723

R v Barnsley Metropolitan Borough Council, ex parte Hook [1976] 1 WLR 1052 Court of Appeal (Denning MR, Scarman LJ and Sir John Pennycuick)

Where natural justice requires that no one judge his own cause (nemo judex in causa sua)

Facts

In October 1974 the applicant, who was a stallholder in an ancient town market under an oral licence from the borough council, the owners, had his licence terminated by letter from the market manager. His appeal to two council committees was dismissed without any specific reasons being given to him. The market manager was present throughout the two appeal proceedings. The applicant applied to the Divisional Court for an order of certioari to quash the decision on the ground that there had been a denial of natural justice in that he had not been told what, if any, rule or practice of the market he was alleged to have breached; that the committee meetings had been held substantially in his absence; and that neither he nor his representative had had an opportunity to hear or question the evidence, if any, on which the market manager's decision had been confirmed.

The Divisional Court dismissed the application on the ground that the council's decision was administrative and within its powers.

On the applicant's appeal, the court received further evidence, including the Barnsley Corporation Act 1969 and byelaws made under the Act which contained no express provisions about, inter alia, the determination of revocation of the stallholder's licence or the terms on which it was held.

Held

Where the council was exercising its discretionary power under the Act of 1969 to regulate the common law public right to buy and sell in a market, it was not merely dealing with the contractual relationship but also with the common law right of a man to earn his living in the market; that in those circumstances it was under a duty to act judicially, and that the appeal hearings had been conducted in breach of the rules of justice because the market manager, who was in effect in the position of the prosecutor, was present throughout the appeal proceedings whilst the applicant was not and this offended against the principle 'nemo judex in causa sua'.

Lord Denning MR:

'... so it was quite right for the committee to hold the hearings. I will assume that Mr Hook was given sufficient notice of the charge to be able to deal with it. But, nevertheless, each of the hearings was, to my mind, vitiated by the fact that the market manager was there all the time. He was the one who gave evidence - the only one who did - and hearsay evidence, too. His evidence was given privately to the committee, not in the presence of Mr Hook or his representatives. Mr Hook was not himself in the room. His representatives were there, and they were heard. But when the committee discussed the case and came to their decision, the market manager was there all the time. His presence at all their deliberations is enough to vitiate the proceedings. It is contrary to natural justice that one who is in the position of a prosecutor should be present at the deliberations of the adjudicating committee. That is shown by *R v London County Council, ex parte Akkers Dyk, ex parte Fermenia* (1) and *Cooper v Wilson* (2).'

Scarman LJ:

'... In my judgment, the local authority was in breach of one rule of natural justice which is so old that it can be put in the Latin language: nemo debet esse judex in causa propria ...

Mr Howard relied on *R v Gaming Board for Great Britain, ex parte Benaim and Khaida* (3), to support the proposition, with which I agree, that the requirements of natural justice have to be considered always in the particular circumstances of the case. I think it is certainly possible to envisage cases in which the presence of somebody like Mr Fretwell at a hearing might not constitute a breach of natural justice. One has to see what it is that is being considered and what is the subject matter for decision.

In the present case the corporation was considering something very like dismissing a man from his office, very like depriving him of his property, and they were charging him with doing something wrong. It was the revocation of a licence because of misconduct that they had under consideration -

not merely the man's fitness or capacity for the grant of a licence. There was, therefore, a situation here in which (using the terms broadly) Mr Hook was on trial, and on trial for his livelihood. There was a complainant, the market manager. The market manager had a professional interest in the matter since he was concerned to protect his employees, or the employees for whom he was responsible, from abuse and misconduct by stallholders in the market. Mr Fretwell was a prosecutor, a complainant; Mr Hook was a man, albeit in an administrative field, who was on trial not for his life but for his livelihood.

If ever there was a case in which it was imperative that the complainant or the prosecutor should not participate in the adjudication, I should have thought it was this one ...'

(1)   [1892] 1 QB 190

(2)   [1937] 2 KB 309

(3)   Infra, this chapter

R v Gaming Board for Great Britain, ex parte Benaim and Khaida [1970] 2 QB 417 Court of Appeal (Lord Denning MR, Lord Wilberforce and Phillimore LJ)

Requirements of natural justice and disclosure of sources of information

Facts

Two French nationals who in 1967 took up residence in the UK, contracted to buy the controlling shares in Crockford's, an old-established London gaming club, and later became joint managing directors of the club. They applied to the Gaming Board for a certificate of consent to entitle them to apply for a licence for the premises as required by the Gaming Act 1968. Schedule 2 para 4 stated that in determining whether to issue a certificate of consent:

'(5) ... the Board shall have regard only to the question whether, in their opinion, the applicant is likely to be capable of, and diligent in, securing that the provisions of this Act and of any regulations made under it will be complied with, that gaming on those premises will be fairly and properly conducted, and that the premises will be conducted without disorder or disturbance.

(6) For the purposes of sub-paragraph (5) ... the Board shall in particular take into consideration the character, reputation and financial standing - (a) of the applicant, and (b) of any person (other than the applicant) by whom ... the club ... would be managed, or for whose benefit ... that club would be carried on, but may also take into consideration any other circumstances appearing to them to be relevant in determining whether the applicant is likely to be capable of, and diligent in, securing the matters mentioned in that sub-paragraph.'

On 11 December 1969, at a four hour interview with the Board, the applicants were asked and answered a wide range of questions based on information already in the board's possession. The source and detailed content of this information were not disclosed to the applicants. They were invited to supply further information in writing and did so. On 9 January 1970, the Board refused the certificate. On 13 February 1970 the applicants' solicitors wrote asking for the reasons for the Board's decision. The Board replied by letter, summarising the five matters which had been discussed at the interview on 11 December and stating that the Board had made it clear that these were the matters troubling them, that the applicants were given every opportunity to answer at length and were also invited to make further written representations. The applicants' solicitors wrote again asking the Board to indicate which of the five matters were still troubling the Board. The Board refused to do this.

The applicants moved for an order of certiorari to quash the Board's decision and of mandamus to require the Board to give them sufficient information to enable them to answer any case against them, on the ground that the board had acted unfairly and contrary to natural justice in a matter which would deprive the applicants of valuable rights of property.

Held

The requirement that the Board in determining whether to issue a certificate of consent should have regard 'only' to the matters specified in para 4(5) of sch 2 of the 1968 Act imposed on the board the duty to act fairly by giving an applicant a sufficient indication of the objections against him to answer them. The Board had done this. The Board were not obliged to disclose the sources or details of their information to an applicant who was not being required to meet charges but only to satisfy the Board as to his fitness to apply for a licence. The Board were not obliged to give their reasons for forming the opinion that a certificate should be refused to a particular applicant. Certiorari and mandamus refused.

Lord Denning MR:

'... Counsel for the applicants puts this case, I think, too high. It is an error to regard Crockford's as having any right of which they are being deprived. They have not had in the past, and they have not now, any right to play these games for chance - roulette, chemin-de-fer, baccarat and the like - for their own profit. What they are really seeking is a privilege - almost, I might say, a franchise - to carry on gaming for profit, a thing never hitherto allowed in this country. It is for them to show that they are fit to be trusted with it.

If counsel for the applicants went too far on his side, I think that counsel for the board went too far on the other. He submitted that the Board are free to grant or refuse a certificate as they please. They are not bound, he says, to obey the rules of natural justice any more than any other executive body, such as, I suppose, the Board of Trade, which grants industrial development certificates, or the Television Authority, which awards television programme contracts. I cannot accept this view. I think that the board are bound to observe the rules of natural justice. The question is: what are those rules?

It is not possible to lay down rigid rules as to when the principles of natural justice are to apply; nor as to their scope and extent. Everything depends on the subject-matter; see what Tucker LJ said in *Russell* v *Duke of Norfolk* (1) and Lord Upjohn in *Durayappah* v *Fernando* (2). At one time it was said that the principles only apply to judicial proceedings and not to administrative proceedings. That heresy was scotched in *Ridge* v *Baldwin* (3). At another time it was said that the principles do not apply to the grant or revocation of licences. That, too, is wrong. *R* v *Metropolitan Police Comr, ex parte Parker* (4) and *Nakkuda Ali* v *MF de S Jayaratne* (5) are no longer of authority for any such proposition. See what Lord Reid and Lord Hodson said about them in *Ridge* v *Baldwin* (3). So let us sheer away from these distinctions and consider the task of the board and what they should do ...

The Act provides in terms that, in determining whether to grant a certificate, the board "shall have regard only" to the matters specified. It follows, I think, that the board have a duty to act fairly. They must give the applicant an opportunity of satisfying them of the matters specified in Schedule 2, paragraph 4(5). They must let him know what their impressions are so that he can disabuse them. But I do not think that they need quote chapter and verse against him as if they were dismissing him from an office (*Ridge* v *Baldwin*) (3) or depriving him of his property, as in *Cooper* v *Wandsworth Board of Works* (6). After all, they are not charging him with doing anything wrong. They are simply enquiring as to his capability and diligence and are having regard to his character, reputation and financial standing. They are there to protect the public interest, to see that persons running the gaming clubs are fit to be trusted.

Seeing the evils that have led to this legislation, the board can, and should, investigate the credentials of those who make application to them. They can, and should, receive information from the police in this country and abroad, who know something of them. They can, and should, receive information from any other reliable source. Much of it will be confidential. But that does not mean that the applicants are not to be given a chance of answering it. They must be given the chance, subject to this qualification: I do not think that they need tell the applicants the source of their information; if that would put their informant in peril or otherwise be contrary to the public interest. Even in a criminal trial, a witness cannot be asked who is his informer. The reason was well given by Eyre CJ in *R* v *Hardy* (7):

> "... there is a rule which has universally obtained on account of its importance to the public for the detection of crimes, that those persons who are the channel by means of which that detection is made, should not be unnecessarily disclosed ..."

And Buller J added:

> "... if you call for the name of the informer in such cases, no man will make a discovery, and public justice will be defeated."

That rule was emphatically re-affirmed to *A-G* v *Briant* (8) and *Marks* v *Beyfus* (9). That reasoning applies with equal force to the enquiries made by the board. That board was set up by Parliament to cope with disreputable gaming clubs and to bring them under control. By bitter experience it was learned that these clubs had a close connection with organised crime, often violent crime, with protection rackets and with strong-arm methods. If the board were bound to disclose their sources of information no one would "tell on" those clubs, for fear of reprisals. Likewise with the details of the information. If the board were bound to disclose every detail, that might itself give the informer away and put him in peril. But, without disclosing every detail, I should have thought that the board ought in every case to be able to give to the applicant sufficient indication of the objections raised against him such as to enable him to answer them. That is only fair, and the board must at all costs be fair. If they are not, these courts will not hesitate to interfere.

Accepting that the board ought to do all this, when they come to give their decision the question arises, are they bound to give their reasons? I think not. Magistrates are not bound to give reasons for their decisions: see *R* v *Northumberland Compensation Appeal Tribunal, ex parte Shaw* (10). Nor should the board be bound. After all, the only thing that they have to give is their opinion as to the capability and diligence of the applicant. If they were asked by the applicant to give their reasons, they could answer quite sufficiently: "In our opinion, you are not likely to be capable of or diligent in the respects required of you." Their opinion would be an end of the matter.

Tested by those rules, applying them to this case, I think that the board acted with complete fairness. They put before the applicants all the information which led them to doubt their suitability. They kept their sources secret, but disclosed all the information. Sir Stanley Raymond said so in his affidavit; and it was not challenged to any effect. The board gave the applicants full opportunity to deal with the information. And they came to their decision. There was nothing whatever at fault with their decision of 9 January 1970. They did not give their reasons. But they were not bound to do so ...'

(1)	[1949] 1 All ER 109	(6)	Supra, this chapter
(2)	[1967] AC 337	(7)	(1794) 24 St Tr 199
(3)	Infra, this chapter	(8)	(1846) 15 M & W 169
(4)	[1953] 1 WLR 1150	(9)	(1890) 25 QBD 494
(5)	Supra, this chapter	(10)	[1952] 1 KB 388

R v Secretary of State for Home Affairs, ex parte Hosenball [1977] 1 WLR 766 Divisional Court; [1977] 1 WLR 776 Court of Appeal (Lord Denning MR, Lane and Cumming-Bruce LJJ)

Rules of natural justice modified in security cases where Minister's decision is sufficient

Facts

The applicant, H, a US citizen, had worked as a journalist in England for nearly three years on a paper featuring investigative journalism. In July 1976 he started work as a reporter for a London evening newspaper. By a letter of 15 November 1976 the Home Office informed him that the Secretary of State had decided in the interests of national security to make a deportation order against him under the Immigration Act 1971. The letter stated that, by virtue of s15(3) of the Act, H was not entitled to appeal against the decision to make a deportation order, but that if he wished he could make representations to an independent advisory panel. A Home Office statement accompanying the letter stated merely that the Secretary of State had considered information that H, while resident in the UK, had sought and obtained for publication information harmful to the security of the UK including information prejudicial to the safety of the servants of the Crown. On 14 December, H's solicitors requested particulars of what was alleged against him but the Secretary of State refused to add anything to the statement in the letter of 15 November. Following a hearing before an advisory panel in January at which H made representations and called witnesses, the Secretary of State made a deportation order against him on 16 February 1977.

H applied for an order of certiorari to quash the deportation order on the ground that there was a breach of natural justice in the refusal to supply him with particulars of the allegations which he had to meet. An affidavit on behalf of the Secretary of State stated that he had made the deportation order on the ground that it would be conducive to the public good after considering the advice of a panel of advisers and the representations made on H's behalf; and that the Secretary of State had personally considered H's request for further information of the allegations against him but considered that it was not in the interests of national security to add anything to the statement in the letter of 15 November 1969.

Held

Where national security was involved the ordinary principles of natural justice were modified for the protection of the realm. Public policy required the preservation of confidentiality for security information, and, since the Secretary of State, who was answerable to Parliament, had given the matter his personal consideration, the application for an order of certiorari to quash the deportation order must be dismissed.

Ridge v Baldwin [1964] AC 40 House of Lords (Lords Reid, Morris of Borth-y-Gest, Hodson, Devlin and Evershed)

Denial of natural justice by failure to provide a quasi-judical hearing

Facts

By s191 of Municipal Corporations Act 1882:

'(1) the watch committee shall from time to time appoint a sufficient number of fit men to be borough constables ... (4) The watch committee may at anytime suspend and ... dismiss any borough constable whom they think negligent in the discharge of his duty or otherwise unfit for the same.'

In 1956 the appellant was appointed chief constable of a borough police force, the appointment being subject to the Police Acts and regulations. On 25 October 1957 he was arrested and charged, together with other persons, with corruption. On 28 October, he was dismissed from duty by the borough watch committee.

On 28 February 1958 he was acquitted by jury on criminal charges against him, but Donovan J, in passing sentence on two police officers who were convicted, said that the facts admitted in the course of trial 'establish that neither of you had that professional and moral leadership which both of you should have had and were entitled to expect from the chief constable'. On 6 March on a charge alleging corruption against the appellant, on which no evidence was offered, the judge referred to the borough's police force and remarked on its need for a leader 'who will be a new influence and who will set a different example from that which was lately obtained'.

After his acquittal, the applicant applied to be reinstated, but on 7 March the watch committee at a meeting decided that he had been negligent in the discharge of his duties as chief constable, and in purported exercise of the powers conferred on them by s191(4) of the Act of 1882, dismissed him from that office.

No specific charge was formulated against him either at that meeting or at another on 18 March (when the appellant's solicitor did address the committee) but the watch committee, in arriving at their decision, considered (inter alia) his own statements in evidence and the observations made by Donovan J on 28 February and 6 March. The appellant appealed to the Home Secretary. By s2(3) of the Police Appeals Act 1927 the Home Secretary's decision was 'final and binding on the parties'. The Home Secretary's decision was 'that there was sufficient material on which the committee could properly exercise their power of dismissal under s191(4)'. The appellant then brought an action against the members of the watch committee for a declaration that his dismissal was illegal, ultra vires and void.

Held (Lord Evershed dissenting)

The decision to dismiss was null and void. Although the Home Secretary's decision was final under s2(3) of the 1927 Act, that decision could not give validity to the previous void decision. The decision of the respondents was a nullity since (per Lords Reid, Morris and Hodson) the appellant was not the servant of the respondents, so they could only dismiss him under their statutory powers. As they dismissed him on the ground of neglect of duty, they were bound to observe the principles of natural justice by informing the appellant of the charges against him and giving him an opportunity of being heard, and that they had not done.

Lord Hodson:

'My Lords, I have reached the conclusion, apart from the application of the Police Act of 1919 and the regulations which followed, that this appeal should succeed upon the ground that the appellant was entitled to and did not receive natural justice at the hands of the watch committee of Brighton when he was dismissed on 7 March 1958 ...

The Court of Appeal took a different view and held that the watch committee were not bound in taking the executive action of dismissing their chief constable to hold an inquiry of a judicial or quasi-judicial nature (per Lord Pearce LJ) Harman LJ was of opinion that the watch committee were acting in exercise of their administrative functions just as they were when they made the appointment under section 191(1) of the Act, and that the principles of natural justice did not come into the case ...

The topic is, however, not as simple as would seem. A large number of authorities were cited to your Lordships beginning with *Bagg*'s case and extending to the present day. I will not travel over the field of the authorities, which I am bound to say are not easy to reconcile with one another, for if I did, I should surely omit some which might be thought to be of equal or greater importance than those I mentioned, but certain matters seem to me clearly to emerge. One is that the absence of a lis or dispute between opposing parties is not a decisive feature although, no doubt, the presence of a lis would involve the necessity for the applications of the principles of natural justice. Secondly, the answer in a given case is not provided by the statement that the giver of the decision is acting in an executive or administrative capacity as if that was the antithesis of a judicial capacity. The cases seem to me to show that persons acting in a capacity which is not on the face of it judicial but rather executive or administrative have been held by the courts to be subject to the principles of natural justice. Perhaps the most striking example is to be found in the old case of *Capel* v *Child* which is referred to at length by North J in *Fisher* v *Jackson* ...

The matter which, to my mind, is relevant in this case is that where the power to be exercised involves a charge made against the person who is dismissed, by that I mean a charge of misconduct, the principles of natural justice have to be observed before the power is exercised ...'

Lord Evershed (dissenting):

'It has been said many times that the exact requirements in any case of the so-called principles of natural justice cannot be precisely defined: that they depend in each case upon the circumstances of that case. According to Sir Frederick Pollock, the meaning of the phrase "natural justice" is "the ultimate principle of fitness with regards to the nature of man as a rational and social being", and he went on to point out that the origin of the principles could be traced to Aristotle and the Roman jurists. (*Jurisprudence and Legal Essays* (1961) p124). Your Lordships were, therefore, not unnaturally referred to a great many cases, but, as I believe that your Lordships agree, it is by no means easy to treat these decisions as entirely uniform and still less easy to be able to extract from them the means of propounding a precise statement of the circumstances or of the cases in which the princples can be invoked before the courts. I am, however, content to assume that the invocation should not be limited to cases where the body concerned, whether a domestic committee or some body established by a statute, is one which is exercising judicial or quasi-judicial functions strictly so-called; but that such invocation may also be had in cases where the body concerned can properly be described as administrative - so long as it can be said, in Sir Frederick Pollock's language, that the invocation is required in order to conform to the ultimate principle of fitness with regard to the nature of man as a rational and social being ... '

Willis v Childe (1851) 13 Beav 117 Chancery (Lord Langdale MR)

Natural justice and the requirement of a hearing

Facts

The trustees of a school delegated to a committee the task of investigating a complaint against a master without giving any notice of this decision. The committee reported against him. The trustees resolved to implement the report and dismiss the master without giving him an opportunity to present his case. A second meeting of the trustees was convened to confirm the dismissal at which the master was present and allowed a hearing, but the dismissal was still upheld. The master applied for an injunction to restrain the dismissal on the ground that he had not had a fair hearing.

Held

The injunction would be granted as the master had not been allowed any proper opportunity to represent himself.

Lord Langdale MR:

'Upon the merits, I find it very difficult to form any conclusive opinion, upon the truth or falsehood of many of the allegations which are stated; but after reading the affidavits, I observe that some difference having arisen between the master and the usher, the trustees, not troubling themselves to promote any means of conciliation or adjustment, seem to have been disposed to impute the principal fault to the plaintiff; and, instead of instituting an inquiry in his presence, which might have afforded him the means of explanation and defence, they, without his knowledge, commenced proceedings against him by referring the matter to the school committee to consider the case. The committee proceeded to investigate the case in his absence and without his knowledge, and reported against him. The report was not communicated to him; but the trustees met, and, as they say, considered the report; and, in his absence and without hearing him, they confirmed the report, and resolved to remove him, and stated the grounds and reasons for his removal.

The trustees having thus committed themselves, having thus condemned the Plaintiff unheard, ordered another meeting to be summoned for Wednesday the 20th day of February then next, for the purpose of submitting the foregoing resolution for confirmation. The trustees did not even then think it necessary to communicate their proceedings to the plaintiff: but the plaintiff having, by some means, become acquainted with the proceedings, he, on the 18th February, two days before the meeting appointed for the 20th, wrote to the trustees a letter, which ought to have induced them to pause and to consider whether they were proceeding with due caution and justly. The only effect which it seems to have had was, to induce them, at twelve o'clock on the day of the meeting, to inform him that they had received his letter, and were ready to hear what he had to say on the subject of it. He did accordingly attend, and said what he could or thought of under such circumstances; and after so hearing him, and without any other hearing or enquiry in his presence, they confirmed the former resolution to remove him, and this confirmation was signed by the same fourteen trustees who had signed the resolutions of January.

Care was taken to observe the mere form required by the fourteenth regulation; but I own that it appears to me perfectly clear that Mr Willis had not proper opportunity afforded him of defending himself; no sufficient means of explanation; no means of proving his defence, if he had any. The evidence which is before me does not enable me to determine whether Mr. Willis had a good defence or not; and it is a most serious misfortune to the welfare of this school, that a matter of such importance should remain in suspense: but I think, that upon their own shewing, the trustees have taken upon themselves to remove Mr Willis without giving him a proper hearing; and the facts which are disclosed in the affidavits though not such as to enable me to come to a satisfactory conclusion, are at least such, as to make it not improbable, that Mr. Willis may be able to shew that he ought not to have been removed.

I therefore grant the injunction to restrain the defendants from enforcing the resolution of the 16th January, confirmed on the 20th February.'

14.2   The rule against bias

Dimes v Grand Junction Canal Proprietors (1852) 3 HL Cas 759 House of Lords (Lord Cottenham LC, Lord Campbell and Lord Brougham)

Natural justice and possible bias

Facts

During the years 1838-50 the Lord Chancellor, Lord Cottenham, confirmed various decrees prohibiting Aimes from obstructing the company's land. In 1849 Aimes discovered that the Lord Chancellor held shares worth several thousands of pounds in the canal company. Aimes challenged all the decrees on the ground of interest.

Held

(inter alia) The Lord Chancellor's decrees could not stand.

Lord Campbell:

'... No one can suppose that Lord Cottenham could be, in the remotest degree, influenced by the interest that he had in this concern; but, my Lords, it is of the last importance that the maxim that no man is to be a judge in his own cause should be held sacred. And that is not to be confined to a cause in which he is a party, but applies to a cause in which he has an interest. Since I have had the honour to be Chief Justice of the Court of Queen's Bench, we have again and again set aside proceedings in inferior tribunals because an individual, who had an interest in a cause, took a part in the decision. And it will have a most salutary influence on these tribunals when it is known that this high Court of last resort, in a case in which the Lord Chancellor of England had an interest, considered that his decree was on that account a decree not according to law, and was set aside. This will be a lesson to all inferior tribunals to take care not only that in their decrees they are not influenced by their personal interest, but to avoid the appearance of labouring under such an influence.'

Hannam v Bradford Corporation [1970] 1 WLR 937 Court of Appeal (Cross, Sachs and Widgery LJJ)

Natural justice and possible bias from dual functions

Facts

Hannam was dismissed from his post as a teacher by the school governors. The local education authority had the power to prevent the dismissal taking effect, and instructed an education sub-committee to consider the matter. The sub-committee, which required three members in order to be quorate, consisted of ten persons, three of whom were also school governors at the school at which Hannam had taught. The sub-committee resolved not to interfere with the decision of the school governors, and this was ratified by the full council. Hannam brought an action for breach of contract, claiming (inter alia) that the decision of the sub-committee was vitiated by bias. At first instance this contention (at least in part) succeeded. The corporation appealed.

Held

The appeal would be allowed.

Sachs LJ:

'The county court judge applied the test as to whether "a reasonable man would say that a real danger of bias existed." Mr Duncan asserted that that test was erroneous and that, anyway, no real danger existed. This court was referred to the well-known series of authorities, not all of which had been cited to the county court judge, ranging from *R v Rand* (1) through the case of *R v Camborne Justices, ex parte Pearce* (2) to *Metropolitan Properties Co (FGC) Ltd v Lannon* (3), a recent decision of this court ...'

... Those judgments involve, in effect, somewhat of a swing back towards the principle enunciated in the *Sussex Justices'* case (4), which had to some account been discounted in some previous decisions. For my part, I doubt whether in practice materially different results are produced by the "real likelihood of bias" test urged by Mr Duncan or that adopted by the county court judge. If there is such a difference, I uphold the latter and respectfully adhere to the school of thought adopted in *Lannon's* case (3), for the reasons there given by Lord Denning MR I agree, too, that the county court judge applied the test correctly to the facts.

I would, however, add that there is a slightly different ground on which it was abundantly clear that the staff subcommittee decision could not stand. No man can be a judge of his own cause. The governors did not, upon donning their subcommittee hats, cease to be an integral part of the body whose action was being impugned, and it made no difference that they did not personally attend the governors' meeting of 19 December. The fallacy of any contrary view is exemplified by considering what the position would be if there had been a quorum meeting of three members of the subcommittee, all of whom had been governors. To say that a decision of such a trio could stand would be to produce an absurdity. There thus fails the argument that was put in the forefront of his case by Mr Duncan in his attack on the decision on liability made at first instance by the county court judge ...'

Widgery LJ:

'So far as bias is concerned, I, like my Lord (Sachs LJ), am satisfied that there was a real likelihood of bias in this case. I do not wish to add to the somewhat confusing welter of authority on what is meant by "bias" in this connection by attempting any further definition myself, because I think that whichever of the tests adumbrated in *Metropolitan Properties Co (FGC) Ltd* v *Lannon* (3) is properly to be applied in this case, the plaintiff had made out his allegation. I am much impressed by the fact that when the subcommittee sat down to consider what the plaintiff could regard as an appeal, the chairman was a member of the governors against whose decision this so-called appeal was being brought. I think that if it had been disclosed at the outset that no less a person than the chairman of the subcommittee was a member of the governors in question, the immediate reaction of everyone would have been that some real likelihood of bias existed. I say that with every respect to the distinguished gentleman who chaired the subcommittee on this occasion; but when one is used to working with other people in a group or on a committee, there must be a built-in tendency to support the decision of that committee, even though one tries to fight it, and this is so even though the chairman was not sitting on the occasion when the decision complained about was reached.'

(1)   Infra, this chapter

(2)   [1954] 1 QB 41

(3)   Infra, this chapter

(4)   Infra, this chapter

Metropolitan Properties Ltd v Lannon [1969] 1 QB 577 Court of Appeal (Lord Denning MR, Danckwerts and Edmund-Davies LJJ)

Natural justice and bias: family interest

Facts

Mr Lannon, a solicitor, lived in a block of flats known as Regency Lodge which was owned by a company belonging to the 'Freshwater Group.' His son John Lannon sat as chairman of a rent assessment committee, determining a dispute between tenants of Oakwood Court and their landlords, a company that was also a member of the 'Freshwater Group.' When the committee determined a rent for Oakwood Court below that contended for by the landlords, they applied for an order of certiorari to have the decision quashed for bias.

Held

The decision of the committee would have to be quashed. The appearance of bias was fatal to its proceedings.

Lord Denning MR:

'... A man may be disqualified from sitting in a judicial capacity on one of two grounds. First, a "direct pecuniary interest" in the subject-matter. Second, "bias" in favour of one side or against the other.

So far as "pecuniary interest" is concerned, I agree with the Divisional Court that there is no evidence that Mr John Lannon had any direct pecuniary interest in the suit. He had no interest in any of the flats in Oakwood Court. The only possible interest was his father's interest in having the rent of 55 Regency Lodge reduced. It was put in this way: if the committee reduced the rents of Oakwood Court, those rents would be used as "comparable" for Regency Lodge, and might influence their being put lower than they otherwise would be. Even if we identify the son's interest with the father's, I think this is too remote. It is neither direct nor certain. It is indirect and uncertain.

So far as bias is concerned, it was acknowledged that there was no actual bias on the part of Mr Lannon, and no want of good faith. But it was said that there was, albeit unconscious, a real likelihood of bias. This is a matter on which the law is not altogether clear: but I start with the oft-repeated saying of Lord Hewart CJ in *R* v *Sussex Justices, ex parte McCarthy* (1):

> "It is not merely of some importance, but is of fundamental importance that justice should not only be done, but should manifestly and undoubtedly be seen to be done."

In *R* v *Barnsley Licensing Justices, ex parte Barnsley and District Licensed Victuallers' Association* (2) Devlin J appears to have limited that principle considerably, but I would stand by it. It brings home this point: in considering whether there was a real likelihood of bias, the court does not look at the mind of the justice himself or at the mind of the chairman of the tribunal, or whoever it may be, who sits in a judicial capacity. It does not look to see if there was a real likelihood that he would, or did, in fact favour one side at the expense of the other. The court looks at the impression which would be given to other people. Even if he was as impartial as could be, nevertheless if right-minded persons would think that, in the circumstances, there was a real likelihood of bias on his part, then he should not sit. And if he does sit, his decision cannot stand: see *R* v *Huggins* (3); and *R* v *Sunderland Justices* (4) per Vaughan Williams LJ. Nevertheless there must appear to be a real likelihood of bias. Surmise or conjecture is not enough: see *R* v *Camborne Justices, ex parte Pearce* (5) and *R* v *Nailsworth Licensing Justices, ex parte Bird* (6). There must be circumstances from which a reasonable man would think it likely or probable that the justice, or chairman, as the case may be, would, or did, favour one side unfairly at the expense of the other. The court will not inquire whether he did, in fact, favour one side unfairly. Suffice it that reasonable people might think he did. The reason is plain enough. Justice must be rooted in confidence: and confidence is destroyed when right-minded people go away thinking: "The judge was biased."

Applying these principles, I ask myself: Ought Mr. John Lannon to have sat? I think not. If he was himself a tenant in difference with his landlord about the rent of his flat, he clearly ought not to sit on a case against the selfsame landlord, also about the rent of a flat, albeit another flat. In this case he was not a tenant, but the son of a tenant. But that makes no difference. No reasonable man would draw any distinction between him and his father, seeing he was living with him and assisting him with his case.

Test it quite simply: if Mr. John Lannon were to have asked any of his friends: "I have been asked to preside in a case about the rents charged by the Freshwater Group of Companies at Oakwood Court. But I am already assisting my father in his case against them, about the rent of his flat in Regency Lodge, where I am living with him. Do you think I can properly sit?" The answer of any of his good friends would surely have been: "No, you should not sit. You are already acting, or as good as acting, against them. You should not, at the same time, sit in judgment on them."

No man can be an advocate for or against a party in one proceeding, and at the same time sit as a judge of that party in another proceeding. Everyone would agree that a judge, or a barrister or solicitor (when he sits ad hoc as a member of a tribunal) should not sit on a case to which a near relative or a close friend is a party. So also a barrister or solicitor should not sit on a case to which one of his clients is a party. Nor on a case where he is already acting against one of the parties. Inevitably people would think he would be biased.

I hold, therefore, that Mr John Lannon ought not to have sat on this rent assessment committee. The decision is voidable on that account and should be avoided ...'

Edmund-Davies LJ:

'... The appellants submit that the Divisional Court "misdirected itself in holding that on the facts proved or admitted there were no sufficient grounds for the appellant applicants to believe that the said John Lannon" - that is, the chairman of the committee - "could not give them an unbiased hearing." Not until a late stage in the hearing of this appeal was that matter touched upon. What had chiefly been contested was whether such complaint (be it well founded or not) poses the correct question in law. Mr Slynn submits that it does not. Resting himself upon such decisions as *R* v *Camborne Justices (5)* and *R* v *Barnsley Licensing Justices (2)* he propounds the correct test as being: Was there a real likelihood that the chairman was biased in his participation in the committee's decision? He submits that the possibility of bias is insufficient, and so is the suspicion thereof, even though reasonably held by right-thinking people.

It cannot be made too clear that the appellants expressly disclaim actual bias in the chairman. But if Mr Slynn be right, what becomes of the principle which remains transcended despite its enshrinement in the excessively quoted words of Lord Hewart in *R* v *Sussex Justices* (1) that

"justice should not only be done, but should manifestly and undoubtedly be seen to be done"?

As Professor de Smith has written ("Judicial Review of Administrative Action" (1959), p150):

"The courts have often quashed decisions on the strength of the reasonable suspicions of the party aggrieved, without having made any finding that a real likelihood of bias in fact existed."

But, after referring to *R* v *Camborne Justices* (5), the writer continues:

"In so far as the 'real likelihood' and 'reasonable suspicion' tests are inconsistent with each other, it is submitted that the former is to be preferred; the reviewing court should make an objective decision, on the basis of the whole evidence before it, whether there was a real likelihood that the inferior tribunal would be biased. That members of an independent tribunal are likely to have been biased is a serious allegation. The public interest will not be served by relaxing the conditions under which it may be successfully made."

Nor in my judgment will the public interest be served if, in the light of all the circumstances as they finally emerge, it appears to right-thinking people that there are solid grounds for suspecting that a member of the tribunal responsible for the decision may (however unconsciously) have been biased.

But it must be conceded that the tide of judicial opinion is to some extent in favour of the professor. Thus, in *Healey* v *Rauhina* (7) Hutchinson J, after reviewing the cases, said :

"... the weight of authority now is that the test to be applied is that of real likelihood of bias, and that reasonable suspicion of bias is insufficient."

And in *R* v *Barnsley Licensing Justices* (2) referring to the dissenting judgment of Salmon J in the Divisional Court, Devlin LJ said:

"I am not quite sure what test Salmon J applied. If he applied the test based on the principle that justice must not only be done but manifestly be seen to be done, I think he came to the right conclusion on that test ... But ... it is not the test. We have not to enquire what impression might be left on the minds of the present applicants or on the minds of the public generally. We have to satisfy ourselves that there was a real likelihood of bias - not merely satisfy ourselves that that was the sort of impression that might reasonably get abroad. The term 'real likelihood of bias' is not used, in my opinion, to import the principle in *R* v *Sussex Justices* (1) to which Salmon J referred. It is used to show that it is not necessary that actual bias should be proved. It is unnecessary ... to investigate the state of mind of each individual justice. 'Real likelihood' depends on the impression which the court gets from the circumstances in which the justices were sitting. Do they give rise to a real likelihood that the justices might be biased? The court might come to the conclusion that there was such a likelihood, without impugning the affidavit of a justice that he was not in fact biased. Bias is or may be an unconscious thing ... The matter must be determined upon the probabilities to be inferred from the circumstances in which the justices sat."

With profound respect to those who have propounded the "real likelihood" test, I take the view that the requirement that justice must manifestly be done operates with undiminished force in cases where bias is alleged and that any development of the law which appears to emasculate that requirement should be strongly resisted. That the different tests, even when applied to the same facts, may lead to different results is illustrated by *R v Barnsley Licensing Justices* (2) itself, as Devlin LJ made clear in the passage I have quoted. But I cannot bring myself to hold that a decision may properly be allowed to stand even although there is reasonable suspicion of bias on the part of one or more members of the adjudicating body.

Adopting that approach in relation to the facts of the present case, the circumstances already adverted to by my Lords are such that I regard it as most unfortunate that this particular chairman sat to try these appeals. The reality of the situation emerges clearly from the record of the committee itself, for when it sat on 19 January 1967, its clerk began his notes of the hearing by transcribing as the landlords of the Oakwood Court flats not "Metropolitan Properties Co (FGC) Ltd" but "The Freshwater Group of Companies." To that same group belonged the Swiss Cottage flat tenanted by Mr Lannon senior, on whose behalf his son had written to the rent officer only six days before the hearing in terms critical of the landlords. It is indeed difficult to see how the chairman could have failed to be aware of the ambiguous position in which he was placing himself by so soon thereafter proceeding to adjudicate on the Oakwood Court applications. Be that as it may, the result of his having sat is highly unfortunate. It is conceivable that, although "startling," the decisions of the committee were nevertheless correct - that remains to be seen. But it is not manifest that they were just, and they therefore ought not to be allowed to stand. I concur with my Lords in holding that they should be quashed.'

(1)   Infra, this chapter

(2)   [1960] 2 QB 167

(3)   [1895] 1 QB 563

(4)   [1901] 2 KB 357

(5)   [1955] 1 QB 41

(6)   [1953] 1 WLR 1046

(7)   [1958] NZLR 945

R v Liverpool City Justices, ex parte Topping [1983] 1 WLR 119 Queen's Bench Division (Ackner LJ and Webster J)

Natural justice and tests for bias: reasonable suspicion

Facts

Topping was convicted of criminal damage by magistrates who had read, from court register forms printed out by computer, that there were, at the time of the trial, seven other charges pending against the defendant. The defendant applied for review of the conviction on the ground that the justices would have been prejudiced against him as a result of reading of the other charges.

Held

The application would be granted. The justices should have asked themselves whether a fair-minded person, with knowledge of the circumstances would have a reasonable suspicion that the proceedings were biased, this they had failed to do.

Ackner LJ:

'As regards the appropriate test, as far back as *Allinson* v *General Council of Medical Education and Registration* (1), there was authority that the test of actual bias, as distinct from the appearance of bias, is inappropriate:

"The question is not, whether in fact he was or was not biased. The court cannot inquire into that ... In the administration of justice, whether by a recognised legal court or by persons who, although not a legal public court, are acting in a similar capacity, public policy requires that, in order that there should be no doubt about the purity of the administration, any person who is to take part in it should not be in such a position that he might be suspected of being biased" (per Lord Esher MR).

More recently Lord Denning MR has preferred the test of the appearance of bias to that of actual bias. In *Metropolitan Properties Co (FGC) Ltd* v *Lannon* (2) he said:

"In considering whether there was a real likelihood of bias, the court does not look at the mind of the justice himself or at the mind of the chairman of the tribunal, or whoever it may be, who sits in a judicial capacity. It does not look to see if there was a real likelihood that he would, or did, in fact favour one side at the expense of the other. The court looks at the impression which would be given to other people. Even if he was as impartial as could be, nevertheless if right-minded persons would think that, in the circumstances, there was a real likelihood of bias on his part, then he should not sit ... There must be circumstances from which a reasonable man would think it likely or probable that the justice, or chairman, as the case may be would, or did, favour one side unfairly at the expense of the other. The court will not inquire whether he did, in fact, favour one side unfairly. Suffice it that reasonable people might think he did. The reason is plain enough. Justice must be rooted in confidence: and confidence is destroyed when right-minded people go away thinking: 'The judge was biased'."

In our view, therefore, the correct test to apply is whether there is the appearance of bias, rather than whether there is actual bias.

In the past there has also been a conflict of view as to the way in which that test should be applied. Must there appear to be a real likelihood of bias? Or is it enough if there appears to be a reasonable suspicion of bias? (For a discussion on the cases see de Smith's Judicial Review of Administrative Action, 4th ed (1980), pp262-264 and Wade, Administrative Law, 5th ed, (1982), pp430-432.) We accept the view of Cross LJ expressed in *Hannam* v *Bradford Corporation* (3) that there is really little, if any, difference between the two tests:

"If a reasonable person, who had no knowledge of the matter beyond knowledge of the relationship which subsists between some members of the tribunal and one of the parties, would think that there might well be bias, then there is in his opinion a real likelihood of bias. Of course, someone else with inside knowledge of the characters of the members in question might say: 'Although things don't look very well, in fact there is no real likelihood of bias.' That, however, would be beside the point, because the question is not whether the tribunal will in fact be biased, but whether a reasonable man with no inside knowledge might well think that it might be biased."

'We conclude that the test to be applied can conveniently be expressed by slightly adapting the words of Lord Widgery CJ in a test which he laid down in *R* v *Uxbridge Justices, ex parte Burbridge*, apparently only reported in The Times, 20 June 1972, but referred to by him in *R* v *McLean, Ex parte Aikens* (4): Would "a reasonable and fair-minded person sitting in court and" knowing all the relevant facts have a "reasonable suspicion that a fair trial for" the application "was not possible"?

Assuming, therefore, that the justices had applied the test advised by Mr. Pearson - do I fell prejudiced? - then they would have applied the wrong test, exercised their discretion on the wrong principle and the same result, namely, the quashing of the conviction, would follow.'

(1)   [1984] 1 QB 750

(2)   Supra, this chapter

(3)   Supra, this chapter

(4)   (1974) 139 JP 261

R v Nailsworth Licensing Justices ex parte Bird [1953] 1 WLR 1047 Queen's Bench Divisional Court (Lord Goddard CJ, Parker and Donovan JJ)

Natural justice and possible bias

Facts

One of a number of licensing justices who granted a liquor licence was discovered, by a party opposed to the grant of the licence, to have signed a petition in favour of the licence being granted. Certiorari was now sought to quash the grant of the licence on grounds of bias.

Held

Certiorari would not be granted. It had not been established that there was any such degree of bias on the part of the justice who had signed the petition such as would make her unfit to sit.

Lord Goddard CJ:

'It is undesirable that a justice of the peace should sign a petition in favour of something which may come before the court, and then sit and adjudicate on that matter. No one suggests here that Mrs Waine knew about this matter when she came to the court, and I do not attach any blame to her. She was brought in in an emergency to sit as a justice. But it is said that justice was not seen to be done because the parties discovered while the justices were out of court that Mrs Waine had signed the petition. It is obvious from the affidavit of the clerk to the justices that while the justices had retired, one of the licensed victuallers who was instructing the solicitors to oppose the application for the licence called the solicitor's attention to the fact that the name of Mrs Waine appeared on the petition. The solicitor did not take his objection then and it seems clear that he decided to let the matter go on, taking the view that this was a heaven sent opportunity of getting the order quashed if the committee found in favour of the application. That would be sufficient ground for refusing this application because certiorari is a discretionary remedy even where there is jurisdiction.

The more important point is whether or not the court is bound to quash this order on the ground of bias simply because one of the justices had signed the petition. I do not in the least wish to depart from what my predecessors have said about the necessity of justice being seen to be done because it is most important that it should be seen to be done, but it is not everything which may raise suspicion in somebody's mind that is enough to set aside a decision of justices. I need not put it as it was put by Day J in *R v Taylor, ex parte Vogwill* (1) where he said: "Anything at any time which could make fools suspect." It is not anything that raises doubt in somebody's mind that is enough to set aside an order or a judgment of justices; there must be something in the nature of real bias. If a person has a proprietary or a pecuniary interest in the subject-matter that is before the court and that person does not disclose it, that has always been held to be enough to upset the decision, but the mere fact that a justice may be thought to have formed some opinion beforehand is not, in my opinion, enough to upset the decision. As I pointed out in the course of the argument, licensing matters are left by Parliament to local justices for the very best of reasons, that is to say, because justices have local knowledge, and it is impossible to suppose that any justice coming on to the bench at a licensing meeting when he knows that there is an application for a licence or that there is opposition to the renewal of a licence, has not formed his own private views as to whether the licence ought to be granted or refused as the case may be. The anomaly has often been pointed out that whereas no person interested in a brewery may sit as a licensing justice, a person who is a very active teetotaller may sit as a justice; but it cannot be said that because an application is refused the justice necessarily acted improperly because he happens to be a total abstainer. In all these cases it must be a question of degree.

The attention of the court has been drawn to *R v Caernarvon Licensing Justices* (2) in which the court, consisting of myself, Hilbery and Birkett JJ, granted an order of certiorari to set aside a decision of justices refusing a licence. In that case, one of the justices was a deacon of a chapel, which had called a meeting for the express purpose of considering whether the grant of the licence should be opposed, and although the justice did not actually vote at the meeting, he took part in it. The court took the view that in those circumstances, where a man was practically making himself a party to the body which intended to oppose the licence, it was not right that he should sit on the bench. In the present case, all that happened was that Mrs Waine at some time - it is not clear when - went into a grocer's shop and signed a petition which indicated that she thought that an off-licence would be justified. We do not think, in those circumstances, that we ought to say that she was so biased that she was unfit to sit on the bench. The application is refused, therefore, on two ground, first, because it was not established that there was any real bias on the part of Mrs Waine, or that anything was done which would make it appear improper for her to sit, although it was undesirable that she should do so - there is no reason to suppose that she would have signed this petition had she known that she was going to sit; secondly, because there was ample opportunity for objection to have been taken before the decision was given, and no objection was taken.'

(1)   (1898) 14 TLR 185

(2)   (1948) 113 JP 23

R v Rand (1866) LR 1 QB 230 Queen's Bench Divisional Court (Cockburn CJ, Blackburn and Shee JJ)

Natural justice and bias: remoteness of interest

Facts

Two justices who granted a certificate enabling Bradford Corporation to draw water from a certain source were also trustees of institutions which held Bradford Corporation bonds.

Held

The justices were not prevented from acting by virtue of any pecuniary interest, as this was too remote. The court also held that there was no real likelihood of bias.

R v Sussex Justices, ex parte McCarthy [1924] 1 KB 256 King's Bench Divisional Court (Lord Hewart CJ, Lush and Sankey JJ)

Justice must not only be done, but be seen to be done

Facts

A collision occurred between a motor-vehicle belonging to the applicant and one belonging to W. A summons was taken out by the police against the applicant for having driven his motor vehicle in a manner dangerous to the public. At the trial before the magistrates, the acting clerk to the justices was a member of the firm of solicitors who were acting for W in a claim for damages against the applicant for injuries received in the collision. At the conclusion of the evidence the magistrates retired to consider their decision, the acting clerk retiring with them in case they should desire to be advised on any point of law. The magistrates convicted the applicant, but stated on affidavit that they came to their conclusion without consulting the clerk. The applicant applied for certiorari to quash the conviction on the basis that it was improper for the acting clerk, having regard to his firm's relation to the case, to be present with the justices when they were considering their decision.

Held

The conviction must be quashed on the basis that justice should not only be done, but should manifestly and undoubtedly be seen to be done.

Lord Hewart CJ:

'... It is said, and, no doubt, truly, that when that gentleman retired in the usual way with the justices, taking with him the notes of the evidence in case the justices might desire to consult him, the justices came to a conclusion without consulting him and that he scrupulously abstained from referring to the case in any way. But while that is so, a long line of cases shows that it is not merely of some importance but is of fundamental importance that justice should not only be done, but should manifestly and undoubtedly be seen to be done. The question therefore is not whether in this case the deputy clerk made any observation or offered any criticism which he might not properly have made or offered; the question is whether he was so related to the case in its civil aspect as to be unfit to act as clerk to the justices in the criminal matter. The answer to that question depends not upon what actually was done but upon what might appear to be done. Nothing is to be done which creates even a suspicion that there has been an improper interference with the course of justice ...'

Steeples v Derbyshire County Council [1985] 1 WLR 256 Queen's Bench Division (Webster J)

Natural justice and tests for bias

Facts

(inter alia) An agreement was entered into by the Council and KLF Ltd under which the company would develop a leisure complex on land owned by the council, provided planning permission could be obtained. Under the terms of the agreement, the council were to pay the company £116,000 in compensation should planning permission not be obtained. The planning committee granted the application, although at the time of its decision it had not been informed of the terms of the agreement. The plaintiff claimed, inter alia, that the planning committee's decision was vitiated by the appearance of bias.

Held

(inter alia) The decision of the planning committee was vitiated by there being a real likelihood of its having been influenced by the terms of the agreement.

Webster J:

'The plaintiff contends that the decision of 10 December 1979, failed to comply with the requirements of natural justice in one respect only; namely that, primarily because of the terms of the contract made with KLF, it was not seen to have been fairly made, in that - and here I am both summarising and amplifying his contentions - the public had reason to suspect that the decision was a mere formality, to suspect that its outcome had been prejudged or predetermined, to suspect at the very least that when the decision was made there was a strong bias in favour of the decision which was in fact made, and to suspect accordingly that it was not a proper decision at all.

The plaintiff does not contend that the decision was in fact not fairly made. He did not seriously challenge the evidence of Mr Crowther, the chairman of the planning committee, which was to the effect that the meeting at which the decision was made was open to the public and that about fifty members of the public attended it, that his committee had considered the objections received, that in the morning before debating the matter they visited the site and spoke to people there, that he, Mr Crowther, thought that the contract with KLF was subject to the obtaining of planning permission, that the committee looked at the matter only from the planning point of view and that the committee could have turned down the county council's application. I accept the evidence of Mr Crowther and I am satisfied that the decision was in fact fairly and properly made.

But to satisfy the requirements of natural justice it must not only have been properly made, it must also be seen to have been fairly made. The plaintiff says that it was not seen to have been fairly made, but that, on the contrary, it was seen or was seen by the public at large to have been pre-judged, because having agreed with KLF to use their best endeavours to obtain the permission or permissions in question, and by having undertaken a liability in damages if they failed to use those best endeavours, and generally by reason of the terms of the contract which I have recited, they had given the appearance of having imposed upon themselves and upon the planning committee a fetter or restraint on their freedom to discharge that duty in the way prescribed by the Regulations and the Act of 1971.

This appearance was underlined, says the plaintiff, by the desire exhibited by the officers of the county council in the correspondence, to some of which I have referred, to expedite the decision and in their perseverance in pursuing the procedures leading up to the decision, despite being cautioned by the Friends of Shipley Park that they were not complying properly with those processes; and he says that the appearance that the matter had been pre-judged looked all the more unfair in circumstances in which, operating the procedures under regulations 4 and 5, they were in effect judges in their own cause - circumstances in which, says the plaintiff, they should have been particularly scrupulous to avoid any appearance of unfairness.

In support of his contentions he relied upon the persuasive authority of *Lower Hutt City Council* v *Bank* (1), a decision of the Court of Appeal of New Zealand in which, in circumstances very similar though not identical to the facts of this case, that court upheld the decision of Wild CJ that by entering into a contract with the third party by which they agreed, inter alia, to take all steps necessary to stop certain streets the city council had so situated themselves that it appeared there was a real likelihood that they would feel constrained to disallow objections made under the relevant legislation to stopping those streets, and that accordingly a writ of prohibition should be granted restraining the council from proceeding to inquire into and dispose of those objections.

Mr Mann, on behalf of the county council, resisted the plaintiff's contentions on a number of grounds. The requirements of fairness, he says, are to be seen in the context of the specific express statutory obligations of the county council which, he says, extend only to the advertising, and to the giving of notice of their intention to seek permission and to consulting with the district council about it. He particularly draws attention to the fact that there is no equivalent, under regulation 4 or 5, to the requirements of section 29(2) and (3) of the Act of 1971 that the county council should take into account representations relating to the application, although he concedes, as he must, that in the light of the express obligations to advertise and give notice of the application there must be an implied obligation to consider any representations made in response.

He contends that in deciding this issue I should take account of the fact that there is no evidence - and there is none - that any member of the public knew until discovery in this action of the terms or effect of the clause of the contract which exposed the county council to liability for liquidated damages if they failed to use their best endeavours to obtain the necessary planning permission. He contends that the public must be taken to have known of the separation of powers within the county council and in particular that the planning committee were statutorily required to consider the matter from a planning points of view.

Finally he submits that the relevant test was whether the county council had done anything which could cause a reasonable member of the public to believe that the authority had precluded its relevant decision making organ, that is, the planning committee, from considering whether there was anything in the representations received which could deter it from following the council's chosen course.

Before choosing between these rival contentions, I have to decide on the appropriate tests to apply and to look for the authority to guide my choice.

First, in deciding whether the decision is to be seen to be fair, through whose eyes do I look? It seems that I should look through the eyes of a reasonable person hearing of the relevant matters: see *Metropolitan Properties Co (FGC) Ltd* v *Lannon* (2), per Lord Denning MR, and per Danckwerts LJ.

Secondly, what knowledge should I impute to the reasonable person? There are alternatives. The first is that he is to be taken to know only of matters known to the public to have occurred before the decision (perhaps including matters known to the public before the issue of proceedings). The second alternative is that he is to be taken to know of matters, whether in fact known or available to members of the public or not, which are in evidence at the trial. In my view the second alternative is the lower one. That is to say in my view, and subject to my answer to the sixth question I ask below, he is to be taken to know of all matters, whether in fact known or available to the public or not, which are in evidence at the trial. I rely for that conclusion on the dictum of Danckwerts LJ to which I have just referred, in which he said, "a person subsequently" - subsequently to the making of the decision in question - "hearing of these matters which might reasonably feel doubts," but I also rely on the principle and common sense of the matter which is: that the body in question, before it makes its decision, must ensure that after it has made that decision it will be seen to the public at large, in the person of a hypothetical reasonable member of the public, to have acted fairly; that for that purpose it must be taken to assume that all facts, whether confidential or not, are or will become available to the public, if only to members or employees of the authority in question in their capacity as members of the public; and that it would be impossible to cast upon the court the burden of deciding which of the actual facts are and which are not to be deemed to be known to the public or to its hypothetical reasonable member.

Thirdly, is a decision unfair only if it is actually seen to be unfair? Or is it unfair if there is a real likelihood that it would be seen to be unfair? Or is it enough in order to show that it is unfair, that there is a reasonable suspicion that it will be seen to be unfair? Which of these tests is to be applied may depend, in my view, on the nature of the decision-making body in question. Where the body is a judicial tribunal it may be that any doubt that justice is seen to be done is enough: see the dictum of Lord Hewart CJ in *R* v *Sussex Justices, ex parte McCarthy* (3):

> "it is not merely of some importance but is of fundamental importance that justice should not only be done, but should manifestly and undoubtedly be seen to be done."

At the other end of the scale, where the body in question is primarily administrative, it may be that its decisions are invalid (when they are in fact fair) only when they actually appear to be unfair. In *Lannon's* case (2), where the body in question was a rent assessment committee, Lord Denning MR appears to have applied the test of real likelihood and Edmund Davies LJ, that of reasonable suspicion: see p606D. For the purposes of the present case, where, as it seems to me, the body has more of an administrative function and less of an adjudicative one than has a rent assessment committee, I shall apply the test of likelihood.

Fourthly, what amounts to a fetter upon the discretion in question? In the absence of direct authority on this question it seems to me that anything constitutes a fetter for this purpose at the very least if a reasonable man would regard it as being likely to have a material and significant effect one way or another on the outcome of the decision in question; and it may very well be that something appearing to have less of an effect than that might constitute a fetter.

Fifthly, what knowledge is to be imputed to a hypothetical reasonable man about the workings of the county council and their committees? The answer to this question is, in view of the conclusion which I am about to reach, not determinant of my final conclusion on the issue of natural justice (which would be the same whichever way I answered this question), but I am inclined to the view that if, as I have decided, that hypothetical reasonable man is to be taken to know all the relevant facts, then there is no good reason why those facts should exclude the fact that the county council have delegated their planning powers to, inter alia, the planning committee in question.

Sixthly and finally, is the hypothetical reasonable man to be taken to have attended the meeting or to know of my conclusion that the decision was in fact fairly made? In my view, for the same sort of reasons which I have given for my answers to the second of these six questions, although this question is apparently inconsistent with my answer to that question, he is not to be taken to have attended the meeting or to know that in fact the decision was fairly made.

Moreover, if, without taking into account the circumstances of the meeting at which the decision was made, that decision on all the evidence is not to be regarded as having been seen to be unfair by the public at large, it would be illogical and wrong to avoid that conclusion simply because a minute proportion of that public actually attended the meeting, and because that minute proportion would have seen that the decision was in fact fair.

In conclusion, therefore, and applying the tests to which I have just referred, in my judgment it is probable that a reasonable man, not having been present at the meeting when the decision was made, and not knowing of my conclusion as to the actual fairness of it, knowing of the existence and of all the terms of the contract (but without regard to the question whether they would in law have been enforceable), would think that there was a real likelihood that those provisions in the contract which require the county council, and for that matter the joint venture committee, to use their best endeavours to obtain planning permission, and the contract as a whole in the light of its provisions to which I have referred, had had a material and significant effect on the planning committee's decision to grant the permission; and accordingly, on that ground, I hold that that decision was either voidable or void.

I would like to add one or two footnotes under the heading of natural justice. First, as I have said, it was the plaintiff's submission that because of the procedure under regulations 4 and 5 the county council were permitted to grant themselves planning permission and therefore, in a sense, to be judges in their own cause, and that because of this it was necessary for them to be more scrupulous than might otherwise have been necessary to be seen to be fair. Mr Mann puts precisely the opposite contention. The effect of those regulations, he says, is that inevitably the planning committee will approach its decision with a predisposition to make it and it is allowed to do so. I reject that argument. When the county council decide to seek planning permission they can do so without regard to any statutory obligations under the Town and Country Planning Acts; but when they come to grant it, by their planning committee, they must have regard to the considerations and provisions of s29(1) of the Act of 1971. The fact that the county council have already decided to seek permission is not, in my view, "any other material consideration" within the meaning of that expression in s29(1). I reject, therefore, Mr Mann's test, to which I have already referred, and particularly the words in that test which I emphasised, and I agree with Mr McLaren that in operating the procedures under regulations 4 and 5 the planning authority must be particularly scrupulous to ensure that their decision is seen to be fair, particularly when it is at all controversial.

Secondly, both parties relied upon the preceding history which I set out at some length at the beginning of this judgment. The plaintiff said that the applications made in 1979 were materially different from the proposals current in the middle 1970s, and that, therefore, the decision of 10th December 1979 was a significant one. The county council say that the decision differed little in principle from the planning permission they granted themselves in 1973. In my view the plaintiff is right. If the decision of December 1979 had been made at the end of 1973, its significance, and therefore the need to have ensured that the considerations involved were being objectively and fairly considered, would have been much less; but by 1979, after the publications of the pamphlets in the middle 1970s, I am satisfied that it constituted in the eyes of many members of the public a significantly new proposal. In my view the significance of the decision in question is a matter which affects, in each particular case, the question whether the decision is to be seen to have been properly considered and therefore to have been fair. That is why I dwelt on the preceding history at some length.

Thirdly, the county council ask what else they could have done. One answer comes to mind immediately. They could have avoided committing themselves to KLF in any way until after the planning decision had been properly made or, if they were to make a contract with them, they could have ensured that the contract was subject to planning permission, that they had no obligation of any sort in connection with the obtaining of planning permission, and that they would be under no liability of any sort should planning permission not be obtained.

Against the background of a contract already made, however, at least two further alternative courses come to mind as being far from inappropriate. They could have let KLF make the application, possibly - I am not sure because the matter has not been canvassed - to the Amber Valley District Council, or they could have decided to hold a public meeting at which they, with members of the planning committee present, explained their proposals and the reasons for them and at which objectors were given an opportunity to air their views.

Finally, in concluding, as I do, that the requirements of natural justice were not fulfilled, I have not relied upon the evidence of any witness in this case. I have done so relying on inferences to be drawn from the facts to which I have referred; but I regard Mr. Steeples, the plaintiff, as a witness of the utmost reliability and good sense, and his evidence that he thought that it had all been cut and dried before the formal decision was made, or words to that effect, fortifies me in my conclusion.'

(1)   (1974) 1 NZLR 545

(2)   Supra, this chapter

(3)   Supra, this chapter

15 REMEDIES – EXCLUSION OF JUDICIAL REVIEW – ESTOPPEL

15.1   Remedies

15.2   Exclusion of judicial review

15.3   Estoppel in public law

15.1   Remedies

Dunlop v Woollahra Municipal Council [1982] AC 158   Privy Council (Lords Diplock, Simon, Edmund-Davies, Scarman and Bridge)

Local authorities: liability in damages for ultra vires acts

Facts

(as related by Lord Diplock)

'The action in which this appeal to Her Majesty in Council is brought by the unsuccessful plaintiff, Dr Dunlop, is the sequel to the previous action between the self-same parties tried before Wootten J in which the plaintiff was successful: *Dunlop* v *Woollahra Municipal Council* (1). From that judgment the defendant, the council, did not appeal. Both that action and the present action arose out of two resolutions which the council passed on 10 June 1974, in purported exercise of their powers under ss308 and 309 respectively in Part XI of the Local Government Act 1919, to fix a building line for the plaintiff's property at No 8 Wentworth Street, Point Piper, and to regulate the number of storeys which might be contained in any residential flat building erected on that property.

In the first action the plaintiff sought and obtained from Wootten J on 26 September 1975, declarations that each of the resolutions was invalid and void: the resolution fixing a building line because a procedural requirement as to giving notice to the plaintiff had not been satisfied, the resolution regulating the number of storeys because it was ultra vires. The judge expressly rejected the plaintiff's allegation that in passing the resolutions the council were not acting bona fide. In the instant case, which was tried by Yeldham J, the plaintiff claimed to recover from the council damages which he alleged he had sustained as a result of the invalid resolutions during the period from the passing of the resolutions on 10 June 1974, to 25 October 1975, this being the last day on which the council might have appealed against the judgment of Wootten J ...'

Held

Lord Diplock:

'The basis of the plaintiff's allegation of negligence by the council in passing the resolution regulating the number of storeys that might be contained in any flat building on (No 8) Wentworth Street at not more than three, was that they owed him a duty to take reasonable care to ascertain whether such a resolution was within their statutory powers. The breach of this duty of are that was alleged was the council's failure to seek proper detailed legal advice.

After discussing a number of Australian, English and Canadian cases Yeldham J felt considerable doubt, which their Lordships share, as to the existence of any such duty of care owed to the plaintiff, but he found it unnecessary to go into this interesting jurisprudential problem since he was clear that even assuming the existence of such a duty no breach of it had been proved. The council's resolution of 10 June 1974, limiting the number of storeys was passed on the initiative and advice of their solicitors, as a lawful means of preventing the erection of residential flat buildings of more than three storeys on the properties in question if they were satisfied that this was desirable on planning grounds. What more could the council be reasonably expected to do than to obtain the advice of qualified solicitors whose competence they had no reason to doubt? It is true that Wootten J held the legal advice which the council had received from their solicitors had been wrong but it is only fair to the reputation of the solicitors, who gave it, to add that until that judgment made the matter res judicata between the parties, the question of law, which turned on the construction to be placed on two clauses in the planning scheme and in particular on whether or not a restriction upon the maximum number of storeys in residential flat buildings was inconsistent with a restriction upon the maximum height above sea level of all building was an evenly balanced one and, in their Lordships' view, to answer it either way at any time before that judgment, could not have amounted to negligence on the part of a solicitor whose advice was sought upon the matter.

As respects the resolution which purported to fix the building lines the only ground on which Wootten J held this to be void was because the council had failed to give the plaintiff the kind of hearing to which he was entitled before they passed it, and, in particular, because he should have been specifically informed, but was not, that the council were contemplating exercising their powers under s308 to fix building lines. This question too was not an easy one, as is shown by the fact that it took Wootten J 20 closely reasoned pages of his judgment and the citation of some two score of authorities to reach the conclusion that he did. Yeldham J held that failure by a public authority to give a person an adequate hearing before deciding to exercise a statutory power in a manner which will affect him or his property, cannot by itself amount to a breach of a duty of care sounding in damages. Their Lordships agree. The effect of the failure is to render the exercise of the power void and the person complaining of the failure is in as good a position as the public authority to know that that is so. He can ignore the purported exercise of the power. It is incapable of affecting his legal rights. In agreement with Yeldham J their Lordships are of opinion that the claim in negligence fails ...'

(1)   (1975) 2 NSWLR 446

Healey v Minister of Health [1955] 1 QB 221 Court of Appeal (Denning, Morris and Parker LJJ)

Limitations on the jurisdiction to grant a declaration

Facts

The Minister had determined, under regulation of the NHS (Superannuation) Regulations 1960, that Healy was not a mental health officer within the meaning of the legislation, and was thus not entitled to more favourable terms of superannuation. Healy thereupon sought a declaration that he was a mental health officer.

Held

The Court had no jurisdiction to grant the remedy sought, as Healey was not alleging any illegality on the part of the Minister; to grant a declaration would be tantamount to allowing an appeal from the Minister's decision, for which Parliament had not provided. A declaration even if granted in favour of Healy would simply result in two conflicting decisions, causing confusion.

Denning LJ:

'The relief which is sought does not include a declaration that the Minister's determination was invalid. It seeks only a declaration that the plaintiff is and was a mental health officer. It is obvious that if the court were to consider granting this declaration it would have to hear the case afresh. Mr

Healey would have to give evidence showing how he spent his time, and the Minister would have to be allowed to give evidence in answer to it. In short, the court would have to rehear the very matter which the Minister has decided. If the court were to embark on a rehearing of this sort there is no telling where it would stop. Every person who was disappointed with a Minister's decision could bring an action for a rehearing. That would be going much too far. And suppose that the court did rehear the matter and decide in Mr Healey's favour, and grant the declaration for which he asks, what would happen to the Minister's decision? So far as I can see, it would still stand unless the Minister chose of his own free will to revoke it. There would then be two inconsistent findings, one by the Minister and the other by the court. That would be a most undesirable state of affairs. In my opinion, if the court were to entertain this declaration, it would be going outside its province altogether. It would be exercising a jurisdiction to "hear and determine" which does not belong to it but to the Minister.'

Merricks v Heathcote-Amory and the Minister of Agriculture [1955] 1 Ch 567 Chancery Division (Upjohn J)

Court's ability to interfere with a Minister of the Crown

Facts

The plaintiff moved for an injunction against the Minister to restrain a draft scheme for the marketing of potatoes being laid before the Houses of Parliament. It was argued inter alia that the court was being asked to proceed against a Minister of the Crown, contrary to the Crown Proceedings Act, and against a Member of Parliament with respect to proceedings of Parliament, contrary to the privileges of Parliament.

Held

The court could not interfere.

Upjohn J:

'I have heard full argument ... and I think in those circumstances I can express my own views as to the capacity in which the Minister acts in carrying out or proposing to carry out the relevant functions ... It seems to me clear that ... he is acting as a representative or as an officer of the Crown.

... It was his duty in his capacity as Minister of Agriculture and not merely as a delegated person ... to lay a draft scheme before the Houses of Parliament ... That being so, it is conceded that no injunction can be obtained against him, and therefore the motion fails in limine.

A number of points of great interest have been argued. Among them was the question whether the court had any jurisdiction, and if so, whether it would be proper in any event to interfere with the proceedings now in Parliament by making an order on the Minister to withdraw the draft scheme ... I say no more than this, I see great force in the arguments put forward by the Attorney-General; but in this delicate and difficult branch of the law it is much better not to express an opinion on any matter which does not arise directly for decision. As I have come to the clear conclusion that the Minister throughout is acting as a Minister of the Crown, when it is conceded that no injunction can be granted, it is much better that I should say no more.'

See now *Factortame Ltd v Secretary of State for Transport,* extracted in Chapter 5.

R v Electricity Commissioners, ex parte London Electricity Joint Committee Co (1920) Ltd [1924] 1 KB 171 Court of Appeal (Bankes, Younger and Atkin LJJ)

Scope and availability of prohibition and certiorari

Facts

(inter alia) A number of electricity companies sought orders of prohibition and certiorari in respect of a scheme for the supply of electricity contained in a draft order made by the Electricity Commissioners.

Held

The scheme was ultra vires. (The real significance of this decision, as indicated in the extracts below, is the discussion of the scope and availability of remedies.)

Bankes LJ:

'... the Court will issue the writ to a body exercising judicial functions, though that body cannot be described as being in any ordinary sense a Court. There are, I think, three dicta of learned judges which may usefully be borne in mind in approaching an examination of the decisions which bear most closely upon the present case. There is the dictum of Brett LJ, as he then was in *R v Local Government Board* (1) where he says:

"My view of the power of prohibition at the present day is that the Court should be chary of exercising it, and that wherever the Legislature entrusts to any body of persons other than to the superior Courts the power of imposing an obligation upon individuals, the Courts ought to exercise as widely as they can the power of controlling those bodies of persons if those persons admittedly attempt to exercise powers beyond the powers given to them by Act of Parliament."

There is the dictum of Lord Sumner in *In re Clifford and O'Sullivan* (2), where he says:

"It is agreed also that, old as the procedure by writ of prohibition is, and few are older, there is not to be found in the very numerous instances of the exercise of this jurisdiction any case in which prohibition has gone to a body which possessed no legal jurisdiction at all."

Lastly there is the dictum of Fletcher Moulton LJ in *R v Woodhouse* (3) where he is discussing what, in his opinion, constitutes a judicial act. He there says:

"Other instances could be given, but these suffice to show that the procedure of certiorari applies in many cases in which the body whose acts are criticizes would not ordinarily be called a Court, nor would its acts be ordinarily termed 'judicial acts.' The true view of the limitation would seem to be that the term 'judicial act' is used in contracts with purely ministerial acts. To these latter the process of certiorari does not apply, as for instance to the issue of a warrant to enforce a rate, even though the rate is one which could itself be questioned by certiorari. In short, there must be the exercise of some right or duty to decide in order to provide scope for a writ of certiorari at common law."

In that case the Lord Justice was dealing with an application for a writ of certiorari, but his observations here quoted apply in my opinion equally to prohibition ...'

Atkin LJ:

'The question now arises whether the persons interested are entitled to the remedy which they now claim in order to put a stop to the unauthorised proceedings of the Commissioners. The matter comes before us upon rules for writs of prohibition and certiorari which have been discharged by the Divisional Court. Both writs are of great antiquity, forming part of the process by which the King's Courts restrained courts of inferior jurisdiction from exceeding their powers. Prohibition restrains the tribunal from proceeding further in excess of jurisdiction; certiorari requires the record or the order of the court to be sent up to the King's Bench Division, to have its legality inquired into, and, if necessary, to have the order quashed. It is to be noted that both writs deal with questions of excessive jurisdiction, and doubtless in their origin dealt almost exclusively with the jurisdiction of what is described in ordinary parlance as a Court of Justice. But the operation of the writs has extended to control the proceedings of bodies which do not claim to be, and would not recognised as, courts of Justice. Wherever any body of persons having legal authority to determine questions affecting the rights of subjects, and having the duty to act judicially, act in excess of their legal authority they are subject to the controlling jurisdiction of the King's Bench Division exercised in these writs ... I can see no difference in principle between certiorari and prohibition, except that the latter may be invoked at an earlier stage. If the proceedings establish that the body complained of its exceeding its jurisdiction by entertaining matters which would result in its final decision being subject to being brought up and quashed in certiorari, I think that prohibition will lie to restrain it from so exceeding its jurisdiction ...

In the present case the Electricity Commissioners have to decide whether they will constitute a joint authority in a district in accordance with law, and with what powers they will invest that body. The question necessarily involves the withdrawal from existing bodies of undertakers of some of their existing rights, and imposing upon them of new duties, including their subjection to the control of the new body, and new financial obligations. It also provides in the new body a person to whom may be transferred rights of purchase which at present are vested in another authority. The Commissioners are proposing to create such a new body in violation of the Act of Parliament, and are proposing to hold a possibly long and expensive inquiry into the expediency of such a scheme, in respect of which they have the power to compel representatives of the prosecutors to attend and produce papers. I think that in deciding upon the scheme, and in holding the inquiry, they are acting judicially in the sense of the authorities I have cited, and that as they are proposing to act in excess of their jurisdiction they are liable to have the writ of prohibition issued against them.

It is necessary, however, to deal with what I think was the main objection of the Attorney-General. In this case he said the Commissioners come to no decision at all. They act merely as advisers. They recommend an order embodying a scheme to the Minister of Transport, who may confirm it with or without modifications. Similarly the Minister of Transport comes to no decision. He submits the order to the Houses of Parliament, who may approve it with or without modifications. The Houses of Parliament may put anything into the order they please, whether consistent with the Act of 1919, or not. Until they have approved, nothing is decided, and in truth the whole procedure, draft scheme, inquiry, order, confirmation, approval, is only part of a process by which Parliament is expressing its will, and at no stage is subject to any control by the Courts ... In the provision that the final decision of the Commissioners is not to be operative until it has been approved by the two Houses of Parliament I find nothing inconsistent with the view that in arriving at that decision the Commissioners themselves are to act judicially and within the limits prescribed by Act of Parliament, and that the Courts have power to keep them within those limits. It is to be noted that it is the order of the Commissioners that eventually takes effect; neither the Minister of Transport who confirms, nor the Houses of Parliament who approve, can under the statute make an order which in respect of the matters in question has any operation. I know of no authority which compels me to hold that a proceeding cannot be a judicial proceeding subject to prohibition or certiorari because it is subject to confirmation or approval, even where the approval has to be that of the Houses of Parliament.'

(1)   (1882) 10 QBD 309

(2)   [1921] 2 AC 570

(3)   [1906] 2 KB 501

Williams v Home Office (No 2) [1981] 1 All ER 1211 Queen's Bench Division (Tudor Evans J)

Declaration: no practical use

Facts

The plaintiff sought, inter alia, a declaration that the Home Office had acted ultra vires and unlawfully in setting up and operating the control unit: see *Williams* v *Home Office* chapter 13, supra.

Held

His claim could not succeed.

Tudor Evans J:

'With respect to declaratory relief, I have a discretion whether to make an order. In this case, in the exercise of my discretion, I do not consider that I should make a declaration for these reasons: first, I have held that the Secretary of State had power to act under r43; second, the action of false imprisonment has failed and any breach of the rules did not go to the validity of the plaintiff's detention. The highest point of the plaintiff's case could, in my judgment, have been that there was a breach of the Prison Rules which are regulatory and not mandatory. Third, and most important, it is well established that it is inappropriate to grant declarations which are academic and of no practical value. In *Merricks* v *Nott-Bower* [1965] 1 QB 57 at 67 Lord Denning MR stated the approach which should be adopted to the granting of declarations. He said: "If a real question is involved, which is not merely theoretical, and on which the court's decision gives practical guidance, then the court in its discretion can grant a declaration."

The control unit at Wakefield was closed in October 1975 and the plaintiff left it in February of that year. The chances of its return seem to me on the evidence to be very remote. It is true that at the very end of his cross-examination Mr Emes said that in 1975 the Secretary of State had retained the option to reopen the unit. This was made in answer to a Parliamentary question. Mr Emes said that he had no knowledge of any intention to reopen the control units. No one can, of course, say what a Secretary of State may decide to do at some future time, but on all the present information I think that a declaration would be of no practical use.

For the reasons I have given, the claims for ... a declaration must fail.'

15.2   Exclusion of judicial review

Anisminic v Foreign Compensation Commission [1969] AC 147 House of Lords (Lords Reid, Morris of Borth-y-Gest, Pearce, Wilberforce and Pearson)

Ouster of the courts from administrative cases not applicable where the administrator acts ultra vires and his act is void

Facts

The appellants owned a mining property in Egypt. On 1 November 1956 property in Egypt belonging to British subjects was sequestrated by the Egyptian Government. On 29 April 1956, the Egyptian Government authorised a sale of the appellants' property and it was sold to an Egyptian organisation, TEDO. A treaty was made, on 28 February 1959, between the UK and the United Arab Republic whereby the latter paid to the British Government £27,500,000 out of which the British Government was to compensate British subjects whose property had been sequestrated and sold by the Egyptian authorities. The Foreign Compensation Commission had been set up by the Foreign Compensation Act 1950 to determine claims when compensation agreements of this type were made. An Order in Council, the Foreign Compensation (Egypt) (Determination and Registration of Claims) Order, was made by the UK Government in 1962. Article 4(1) provided that the applicant must satisfy the Commission that (inter alia) he was the person referred to in Annex E as the owner of the property sold or was the successor in title of such person; and that the original owner and any successor in title were British nationals. The Commission construed this latter provision as requiring them to enquire, even when the applicant was the original owner, whether the applicant had any successor in title and to refuse the applicant's claim if he had a successor in title who was not a British national. The appellants made an application for compensation. The Commission held that their successor in title was TEDO and since TEDO was not a British national, that the appellants' claim should be rejected. The appellants applied to the court for declarations that the determination of the Commission was a nullity and that they were entitled to participate in the compensation fund, their contention being that the Commission had misconstrued the Order in finding that TEDO was their successor in title. The Commission contended that, under s4(4) of the Foreign Compensation Act 1950, the court had no jurisdiction to entertain the proceedings. Section 4(4) read:

'The determination by the commission of any application made to them under this Act shall not be called in question in any court of law.'

Held

1) (Lord Morris of Borth-y-Gest dissenting): The word 'determination' in s4(4) was not to be construed as including everything which purported to be a determination but was not in fact a determination but rather a nullity due to the Commission having stepped outside its jurisdiction by basing its decision on some matter that it was not entitled by the Order in Council to take into account. Thus, the court was not precluded by s4(4) from inquiring whether a decision of the Commission was a nullity due to the Commission having stepped outside the limits of its jurisdiction as defined by the Order in Council and could declare such a decision to be a nullity.

2) (Lord Pearson dissenting): The expression 'successor in title' could not refer to any person whilst the original owner was still in existence and thus, since the appellants came within Annex E as the original owners of the property, the commission stepped outside its jurisdiction in even considering whether the appellants had a successor in title and in basing their decision on this matter.

3) The appellants were entitled to the declarations sought.

Lord Reid:

'... It is a well established principle that a provision ousting the ordinary jurisdiction of the court must be construed strictly - meaning, I think, that, if such a provision is reasonably capable of having two meanings, that meaning shall be taken which preserves the ordinary jurisdiction of the court.

Statutory provisions which seek to limit the ordinary jurisdiction of the court have a long history. No case has been cited in which any other form of words limiting the jurisdiction of the court has been held to protect a nullity ...

Undoubtedly such a provision protects every determination which is not a nullity. But I do not think that it is necessary or even reasonable to construe the word "determination" as including everything which purports to be a determination but which is in fact no determination at all ...

The case which gives the most difficulty is *Smith* v *East Elloe Rural District Council* (1) where the form of ouster clause was similar to that in the present case. But I cannot regard it as a very satisfactory case. The plaintiff was aggrieved by a compulsory purchase order. After two unsuccessful actions she tried again after six years. As this case never reached the stage of a statement of claim we do not know whether her case was that the clerk of the council had fraudulently misled the council and the Ministry, or whether it was that the council and the Ministry were parties to the fraud. The result would be quite different, in my view, for it is only if the authority which made the order had itself acted in mala fide that the order would be a nullity. I think that the case which it was intended to present must have been that the fraud was only the fraud of the clerk because almost the whole of the argument was on the question whether a time limit in the Act applied where fraud was alleged; there was no citation of the authorities on the question whether a clause ousting the jurisdiction of the court applied when nullity was in question, and there was little about this matter in the speeches. I do not therefore regard this case as a binding authority on this question. The other authorities are dealt with in the speeches of my noble and learned friends, and it is unnecessary for me to deal with them in detail. I have come without hesitation to the conclusion that in this case we are not prevented from inquiring the order of the commission was a nullity.

It has sometimes been said that it is only where a tribunal acts without jurisdiction that its decision is a nullity. But in such cases the word "jurisdiction" has been used in a very wide sense, and I have come to the conclusion that it is better not to use the term except in the narrow and original sense of the tribunal being entitled to enter on the inquiry in question. But there are many cases where, although the tribunal had jurisdiction to enter on the inquiry, it has done or failed to do something in the course of the inquiry which is of such a nature that its decision is a nullity. It may have given its decision in bad faith. It may have made a decision which it had no power to make. It may have failed in the course of inquiry to comply with the requirements of natural justice. It may in perfect good faith misconstrued the provisions giving it power to act so that it failed to deal with the question remitted to it and decided some question which was not remitted to it. It may have refused to take into account something which it was required to take into account. Or it may have based its decision on some matter which, under the provisions setting it up, it had to right to take into account. I do not intend this list to be exhaustive.

... If, on a true construction of the Order, a claimant who is an original owner does not have to prove anything about successors in title, then the commission made an enquiry which the Order did not empower them to make, and they based their decision on a matter which they had no right to take into account. If one uses the word "jurisdiction" in its wider sense, they went beyond their jurisdiction in considering this matter. It was argued that the whole matter of construing the Order was something remitted to the commission for their decision. I cannot accept that argument. I find nothing in the Order to support it. The Order requires the commission to consider whether they are satisfied with regard to the prescribed matters. That is all they have to do. It cannot be for the commission to determine the limits of its powers. Of course if one party submits to a tribunal that its powers are wider than in fact they are, then the tribunal must deal with that submission. But if they reach a wrong conclusion as to the width of their powers, the court must be able to correct that - not because the tribunal has made an error of law, but because as a result of making an error of law they have dealt with and based their decision on a matter with which, on a true construction of their powers, they had no right to deal. If they base their decision on some matter which is not prescribed for their adjudication, they are doing something which they have no right to do and if the view which I expressed earlier is right, their decision is a nullity. So the question is whether on a true construction of the Order the applicants did or did not have to prove anything with regard to successors in title. If the commission were entitled to enter on the enquiry whether the applicants had a successor in title, then their decision as to whether TEDO was their successor in title would, I think, be unassailable whether it was right or wrong: it would be a decision of a matter remitted to them for their decision. The question I have to consider is not whether they made a wrong decision but whether they enquired into and decided a matter which they had no right to consider.

I have great difficulty in seeing how in the circumstances there could be a successor in title of a person who is still in existence ...'

Lord Morris of Borth-y-Gest (dissenting):

'There is no question here of a sham or spurious or merely purported determination. Why, then, is it said to be null and void? The answer given is that it contains errors in law which have caused the commission to exceed their jurisdiction. When analysed this really means that it is contended that when the commission considered the meaning of certain words in article 4 of the Order in Council they gave them a wrong construction with the consequence that they had no jurisdiction to disallow the claim of the applicants.

It is not suggested that the commission were not acting within their jurisdiction when they entertained the application of the appellants and gave it their consideration nor when they heard argument and submissions for four days in regard to it. The moment when it is said that they strayed outside their allotted jurisdiction must, therefore, have been at the moment when they gave their "determination".

The control which is exercised by the High Court over inferior tribunals (a categorising but not a derogatory description) is of a supervisory but not of an appellate nature. It enables the High Court to correct errors of law if they are revealed on the face of the record. The control cannot, however, be exercised if there is some provision (such as a "no certiorari" clause) which prohibits removal to the High Court. But it is well settled that even such a clause is of no avail if the inferior tribunal acts without jurisdiction or exceeds the limit of its jurisdiction.

In all cases similar to the present one it becomes necessary, therefore, to ascertain what was the question submitted for the determination of a tribunal. What were its terms of reference? What was its remit? What were the questions left to it or sent to it for its decision? What were the limits of its duties and powers? Were there any conditions precedent which had to be satisfied before its functions began? If there were, was it or was it not left to the tribunal itself to decide whether or not the conditions precedent were satisfied? If Parliament has enacted that provided a certain situation exists then a tribunal may have certain powers, it is clear that the tribunal will not have those powers unless the situation exists. The decided cases illustrate the infinite variety of the situations which may exist and the variations of statutory wording which have called for consideration. Most of the cases depend, therefore, upon an examination of their own particular facts and of particular sets of words. It is, however, abundantly clear that questions of law as well as of fact can be remitted for the determination of a tribunal.

If a tribunal while acting within its jurisdiction makes an error of law which it reveals on the face of its recorded determination, then the court, in the exercise of its supervisory function, may correct the error unless there is some provision preventing a review by a court of law. If a particular issue is left to a tribunal to decide, then even there it is shown (in cases where it is possible to show) that in deciding the issue left to it the tribunal has come to a wrong conclusion, that does not involve that the tribunal has gone outside its jurisdiction. It follows that if any errors of law are made in deciding matters which are left to a tribunal for its decision such errors will be errors within jurisdiction. If issues of law as well as of fact are referred to a tribunal for its determination, then its determination cannot be asserted to be wrong if Parliament has enacted that the determination is not to be called in question in any court of law ...

If, therefore, a tribunal while within the area of its jurisdiction committed some error of law and if such error was made apparent in the determination itself (or, as it is often expressed, on the face of the record) then the superior court could correct that error unless it was forbidden to do so. It would be so forbidden if the determination was "not to be called in question in any court of law". If so forbidden it could not then even hear argument which suggested that error of law had been made. It could, however, still consider whether the determination was within "the area of the inferior jurisdiction".

So the question is raised whether in the present case the commission went out of bounds. Did it wander outside its designated area? Did it outstep the confines of the territory of its inquiry? Did it digress away from its allotted task? Was there some preliminary inquiry upon the correct determination of which its later jurisdiction was dependent?

For the reasons which I will endeavour to explain it seems to me that at no time did the commission stray from the direct path which it was required to tread. Under article 4 of the Order in Council the commission was under a positive duty to treat a claim under Part III as established if the applicant satisfied them of certain matters ...

They could not come to a conclusion as to whether they were satisfied as to the specified matters unless and until they gave meaning to the words which they had to follow. Unless such a phrase as "successor in title" was defined in the Order - and it was not - it was an inescapable duty of the commission to consider and to decide what the phrase signified. Doubtless they heard ample argument before forming a view. The same applies in regard to many other words and sequences of words in article 4. But the forming of views as to these matters lay in the direct path of the commission's duties. They were duties that could not be shirked. They were central to the exercise of their jurisdiction. When their fully reasoned statement of their conclusions (which in this case can be regarded as a part of their "determination") is studied it becomes possible for someone to contend that an alternative construction of article 4 should be preferred to that which was thought correct by the commission. But this calling in question cannot, in my view, take place in any court of law. Parliament has forbidden it ...

In the present case the commission could be controlled if being "satisfied" of the matters referred to "them" they failed to obey the mandatory direction of the Order in Council. But in deciding whether or not they were satisfied of the matters they were working within the confines of their denoted delegated and remitted jurisdiction. In the exercise of it very many questions of construction were inevitably bound to arise. At no time was the commission more centrally within their jurisdiction than when they were grappling with those problems. If anyone could assert that in reaching honest conclusions in regard to the questions of construction they made any error, such error would, in my view, be an error while acting within their jurisdiction and while acting in the discharge of their function within it.'

(1)   Infra, this chapter

Minister of Health v R (on the prosecution of Yaffe) [1931] AC 494 House of Lords (Viscount Dunedin, Lords Warrington of Clyffe, Tomlin, Thankerton and Lord Russell of Killowen)

Powers of the court to intervene in administrative matters

Facts

The Corporation of Liverpool submitted to the Minister of Health for confirmation a document purporting to be an improvement scheme under s35 of the Housing Act 1925, in respect of an unhealthy area within the city. The first part of this document, after defining the area proposed to be dealt with, empowered the Corporation, in clause 5, to make and widen and stop up or deviate any street in the area, directed them to appropriate other parts of the land to the erection of dwellinghouses for the working classes, and provided that any lands not required for these purposes might be disposed of as the Corporation might think fit. The second part contained estimates of the cost of acquiring the land and of the lay-out, and stated that there were no surplus lands. No lay-out plan was sent to the Minister when he was asked to confirm the scheme. The Minister, after holding a public enquiry, made an order modifying the scheme by providing (inter alia), in lieu of clause 5, that the whole of the lands in the area should, subject to the provision of any necessary streets and approaches, be used for the purposes of rehousing, and confirming the scheme as so modified.

Section 40(5) of the Housing Act 1925 provided 'The Order of the Minister when made shall have effect as if enacted in this Act.'

The owner of two houses which it was proposed to acquire compulsorily under the scheme on account of their sanitary condition applied for a writ of certiorari to quash the order of the Minister as being made without jurisdiction since the scheme which the order purported to confirm was not an improvement scheme within the meaning of the Act because (i) it was not accompanied by a lay-out plan and (ii) it provided that land within the area might be disposed of as the Corporation might think fit.

Held (Lord Russell of Killowen dissenting)

i) Section 40(5) did not preclude the Court from calling in question the order of the Minister where the scheme presented to him for confirmation is inconsistent with the provisions of the Act.

ii) The Act did not require a lay-out plan to be submitted to the Minister when his confirmation of the scheme was requested.

iii) The scheme, as presented to the Minister, even if it had defects, eg the provision in clause 5 that any lands not required for the specified purposes might be disposed of as the Corporation might think fit, was an improvement scheme within the meaning of the Act. *R* v *Minister of Health, ex p Davis* (1) distinguished. The Minister, according to the Act, could confirm the scheme 'with or without ... conditions or modifications' and this included alteration of any provision which, if left untouched, would not be in conformity with the Act. Any defects in the scheme has been cured by the order of the Minister.

Viscount Dunedin:

'... Now before the Divisional Court it was held by a majority that the first argument was good. The order was protected as having the authority of an Act of Parliament. Swift J dissented. He did not need to go into the second point, because at that time the Attorney-General admitted that the scheme, as presented, was bad. When the case came before the Court of Appeal the Attorney-General withdrew that admission, but of course still maintained his first point. On the first point the Court of Appeal reversed the judgement of the Divisional Court, and on the second point they held that the case was practically ruled by the case of *The King* v *Minister of Health ex parte Davis* (1) and held the scheme bad.

The first question, and it is a very important and far-reaching one, is, therefore, as to the effect of s40, subs5. Has it the effect of preventing any enquiry by way of certiorari proceeding of a scheme confirmed by the Minister? It is evident that it is inconceivable that the protection should extend without limit. If the Minister went out of this province altogether, if, for example, he proposed to confirm a scheme which said that all the proprietors in a scheduled area should make a per capita contribution of £5 to the municipal authority to be applied by them for the building of a hall, it is repugnant to common sense that the order would be protected, although if there were an Act of Parliament to that effect, it could not be touched. Now, the high water mark of inviolability of a confirmed order is to be found in a case in this House which necessarily binds your Lordships. It is the case of the *Institute of Patent Agents* v *Lockwood* (2). That case arose under the Patents, Designs and Trade Marks Act. By that Act the Board of Trade was empowered to pass such general rules as they thought expedient for the purposes of the Act. Such rules were, "subject as hereinafter prescribed", to be of the same effect as if they were contained in the Act, and were to be judicially noticed. The "as hereinafter prescribed", was that the rules were to be laid before Parliament for forty days, and if, within forty days, either House disapproved of any rule, it was to be of no effect. The Board of Trade made rules as to the register of patent agents, which were laid before Parliament for forty days and were not objected to. The rules provided that an annual subscription should be paid by all registered patent agents, and prescribed a penalty for any one calling himself a patent agent who was not on the register.

The respondent in the case, who was duly registered, refused to pay the subscription and was put off the register. He continued to practise and call himself a patent agent. The Institute of Patent Agents raised an action for a declaration and an injunction. In defence, the respondent pleaded that the rule was ultra vires of the Board of Trade. The House of Lords held that the provision as to the rules being of like effect as if they had been enacted in the Act, precluded enquiry as to whether the rules were ultra vires or not.

Now, there is an obvious distinction between that case and this, because there Parliament itself was in control of the rules for forty days after they were passed, and could have annulled them if motion were made to that effect, whereas here there is no Parliamentary manner of dealing with the confirmation of the scheme by the Minister of Health. Yet, I do not think that that distinction, obvious as it is, would avail to prevent the sanction given being an untouchable sanction. I think the real clue to the solution of the problem is to be found in the opinion of Herschell LC who says this: "No doubt there might be some conflict between a rule and a provision of the Act. Well, there is a conflict sometimes between two sections to be found in the same Act. You have to try and reconcile them as best you may. If you cannot, you have to determine which is the leading provision and which the subordinate provision, and which must give way to the other. That would be so with regard to the enactment, and with regard to rules which are to be treated as if within the enactment. In that case, probably the enactment itself would be treated as the governing consideration and the rule as subordinate to it.'

What that comes to is this: The confirmation makes the scheme speak as if it was contained in an Act of Parliament, but the act of Parliament in which it is contained is the Act which provides for the framing of the scheme, not a subsequent Act. If therefore the scheme, as made, conflicts with the Act, it will have to give way to the Act. The mere confirmation will not save it. It would be otherwise if the scheme had been, per se, embodied in a subsequent Act, for then the maxim to be applied would have been "Posteriora derogant prioribus". But as it is, if one can find that the scheme is inconsistent with the provisions of the Act which authorises the scheme, the scheme will be bad, and that only can be gone into by way of proceedings in certiorari ...

To turn now to the objections urged. They are really two in number. The first is that the scheme, as submitted to the Minister, did not contain a lay-out plan, and the second is that in clause 5 of the scheme, as originally presented, the Council was given untrammelled powers, a defect which the Minister had no right to cure ...

The real objection which is urged is that it is a fatal defect in the scheme that it did not, as submitted to the Minister, include the lay-out plan. The expression "a lay-out plan" is nowhere to be found in the statute ...

My view of the matter is that there is no cut and dried form in which a scheme must be propounded. The essentials are that it should clearly show the area which, in its present condition, is treated as the unhealthy area, and that, further, it should show that the municipality have bona fide proposals in sight, but that all particulars, and the precise form that reconstruction may take, are left over for the decision of the Minister, who can impose such conditions as he desires.

Now, when I apply this view to the facts in the present case, so far from finding something which resembles *Davis*'s case (1), I find a very definite proposal. The scheme, as sent to the Minister, not only clearly showed that the cost of reconstruction had been minutely gone into, by the mention of the figure 261,5001, but also that the whole area was going to be used for reconstruction by the fact that "no surplus land" was expressed, and it was accompanied, when sent, with all the reports, including the report of the housing director, which really gave every detail ...

So far, I have dealt with what may be styled the suggested sin of omission in the scheme. I now deal with what I may call a sin of commission, which forms the ground of the second objection urged. As proffered to the Minister, the scheme contained this clause: "After obtaining possession of the land authorised to be taken by this scheme the Corporation may remove the whole of the buildings standing thereon, and may make and widen streets and approaches in such lines and situations as the Corporation may prescribe, and may stop up or deviate any street or streets included in any of the areas, and the Corporation shall appropriate other parts of the said land to the erection of dwellinghouses for the accommodation of such number of persons of the working class, as, in the opinion of the Corporation, may require such accommodation, and any lands not required for the purposes aforesaid may be appropriated to such public purposes as the Corporation may direct, or be sold, leased, or otherwise disposed of, as the Corporation may think fit."

It was this clause that made several of the judges in the Court below say that they thought the case was ruled by *ex parte Davis* (1). I have already dealt with the clause in *Davis*'s case, and it is impossible, in my opinion, to say that this is the same. In *Davis*'s case, the municipality need never have used the area for reconstruction at all. Here, under the clause, they must, and it is only the ground possibly not wanted for reconstruction which is left to their free will. But I will assume that this clause gives a wider freedom to the municipality than they ought to have. That wider freedom disappears in the scheme as confirmed. The whole area is accounted for in reconstruction, and it is clearly my opinion that, if the Minister finds a good scheme, but disfigures by a blot upon it which would make it possible to call the legality of the scheme in question, he is absolutely entitled to remove that blot. That, upon the supposition that this clause was a blot, he has done.'

(1)   [1929] 1 KB 619

(2)   [1894] AC 347

Pearlman v Keepers and Governors of Harrow School [1978] 3 WLR 736 Court of Appeal (Lord Denning MR, Geoffrey Lane and Eveleigh LJJ)

Jurisdictional error: when the courts may intervene

Facts

Mr Pearlman was the tenant of a house held on a long lease from the respondents. He installed central heating in the house, and applied under the Housing Act 1974 Schedule 8 to have the rateable value reduced on the ground that he had carried out structural alterations. The County Court judge, differing from a previous County Court ruling, held that the work had not constituted a 'structural alteration' and refused to make any declaration concerning a reduction in the rateable value of the property. Under paragraph 2(2) of Schedule 8 to the 1974 Act:

'Where ... any of the following matters has not been agreed in writing between the landlord and the tenant, that is to say - (a) whether the improvement specified in the notice is an improvement to which this Schedule applies: ... the county court may on the application of the tenant determine that matter, and any such determination shall be final and conclusive.'

The Divisional Court refused Mr Pearlman's application for an order of certiorari to quash the judge's determination. On appeal to the Court of Appeal:

Held

The installation of central heating was a structural alteration. Further (Geoffrey Lane LJ dissenting) the judge had made an error of law upon which his jurisdiction depended, hence his decision was ultra vires and not protected by paragraph 2(2).

Lord Denning MR:

In addition to paragraph 2(2) of the 1974 Act, his Lordship considered s107 of the County Courts Act 1959 which stated:

'Subject to the provisions of any other Act relating to county courts, no judgment or order of any judge of county courts, nor any proceedings brought before him or pending in his court, shall be removed by appeal, motion, certiorari or otherwise into any other court whatever, except in the manner and according to the provisions in this Act mentioned.'

He then turned to consider the question of jurisdictional error.

'But even if s107 does apply to this case, it only excludes certiorari for error of law on the face of the record. It does not exclude the power of the High Court to issue certiorari for absence of jurisdiction. It has been held that certiorari will issue to a county court judge if he acts without jurisdiction in the matter: see *R v Hurst, ex parte Smith* (1). If he makes a wrong finding on a matter on which his jurisdiction depends, he makes a jurisdictional error; and certiorari will lie to quash his decision: see *Anisminic Ltd v Foreign Compensation Commission* (2), per Lord Wilberforce. But the distinction between an error which entails absence of jurisdiction - and an error made within the jurisdiction - is very fine. So fine indeed that it is rapidly being eroded. Take this very case. When the judge held that the installation of a full central heating system was not a "structural alteration ... or addition" we all think - all three of us - that he went wrong in point of law. He misconstrued those words. That error can be described on the one hand as an error which went to his jurisdiction. In this way: if he had held that it was a "structural alteration ... or addition" he would have had jurisdiction to go on and determine the various matters set out in paragraph 2(2)(b)(c) and (d) of Schedule 8. By holding that it was not a "structural alteration ... or addition" he deprived himself of jurisdiction to determine those matters. On the other hand, his error can equally well be described as an error made by him within his jurisdiction. It can plausibly be said that he had jurisdiction to inquire into the meaning of the words "structural alteration ... or addition"; and that his wrong interpretation of them was only an error within his jurisdiction, and not an error taking him outside it.

That illustration could be repeated in nearly all these cases. So fine is the distinction that in truth the High Court has a choice before it whether to interfere with an inferior court on a point of law. If it chooses to interfere, it can formulate its decision in the words: "The court below had no jurisdiction to decide this point wrongly as it did." If it does not choose to interfere, it can say: "The court had jurisdiction to decide it wrongly, and did so." Softly be it stated, but that is the reason for the difference between the decision of the Court of Appeal in *Anisminic Ltd v Foreign Compensation Commission* (2) and the House of Lords.

I would suggest that this distinction should now be discarded. The High Court has, and should have, jurisdiction to control the proceedings of inferior courts and tribunals by way of judicial review. When they go wrong in law, the High Court should have power to put them right. Not only in the instant case to do justice to the complainant, but also so as to secure that all courts and tribunals, when faced with the same point of law, should decide it in the same way. It is intolerable that a citizen's rights in point of law should depend on which judge tries his case, or in which court it is heard. The way to get things right is to hold thus: no court or tribunal has any jurisdiction to make an error of law on which the decision of the case depends. If it makes such an error, it goes outside its jurisdiction and certiorari will lie to correct it. In this case the finding - that the installation of a central heating system was not a "structural alteration" - was an error on which the jurisdiction of the county court depended: and, because of that error, the judge was quite wrong to dismiss the application outright. He ought to have found that the installation was an "improvement" within Schedule 8, paragraph 2(2)(a), and gone on to determine the other matters referred to in Schedule 8, paragraph 2(2)(b)(c) and (d).

On these grounds I am of opinion that certiorari lies to quash the determination of the judge, even though it was made by statute "final and conclusive".'

Geoffrey Lane LJ (dissenting):

'What then is the effect of the words of Schedule 8, paragraph 2(2), of the Housing Act - "such determination shall be final and conclusive"? Since there is in any event no appeal on fact, the words of the Schedule can only apply to questions of law and one must therefore conclude that they are effective to bar an appeal on a point of law. There is nothing else to which they can apply.

It follows from that reasoning that the only circumstances in which this court can correct what is to my mind the error of the judge is if he was acting in excess of his jurisdiction (as opposed to merely making an error of law in his judgment) by misinterpreting the meaning of "structural alteration ... or addition".

In order to determine the ambit of the words "excess of jurisdiction" one must turn to the decision of the House of Lords in *Anisminic Ltd v Foreign Compensation Commission* (2). The effect of the majority speeches in that case may perhaps be expressed as follows: where words in a statute purport to oust the jurisdiction of the High Court to review the decision of an inferior tribunal they must be construed strictly. That is to say, if there is more than one way in which they can reasonably be construed, the construction which impairs the power of the High Court the least should be selected. A provision to the effect that the determination of a tribunal "shall not be called in question in any court of law" does not exclude the power of the High Court to quash a decision which has been reached by the tribunal acting in excess of its jurisdiction. Jurisdiction in this sense has a wide meaning. It includes any case where the apparent determination of the tribunal turns out on examination to be a nullity, because it cannot properly be called a determination at all ...

In that case the Foreign Compensation Commission in adjudicating upon the appellants' claim to compensation considered that they were bound by the relevant order to determine whether the appellants had a "successor in title" and if so whether that successor was a British national. Having decided that there was such a successor and that he was not a British national they considered themselves obliged to reject the claim. In fact the order did not require them to make any determination at all about "successors in title" or their nationality and the commission was basing its decision "on some matter which, under the provisions setting it up, it had no right to take into account". Therefore the apparent or purported determination was a nullity and no determination at all and was not protected by the words of ouster.'

... For my part I am unable to see what the judge did which went outside the proper area of his inquiry. He seems to have taken the view that the word "structural" qualifies the following words, "alteration, extension or addition" and does not qualify the part of the house to which the alterations etc, are made. That is to say the words do not mean "non-structural alterations" or "additions to a structure". Assuming he was wrong in that method of interpreting the words of the Schedule, it does not seem to me to be going outside his terms of reference in any way at all, nor does it contravene any of the precepts suggested by Lord Reid and Lord Wilberforce which I have already cited. The question is not whether he made a wrong decision, but whether he inquired into and decided a matter which he had no right to consider: see Lord Reid at p174E.

The judge summarised matters in the final passage of his judgment as follows:

> "I think in the final analysis it is a matter of first impression tested by argument, analogy and illustration and finally it is a question of fact. There can be little doubt. I do not intend to give any definition at all."

In short what he is saying is that in his view the works executed by Mr Pearlman did not amount to structural alteration or addition, within the ordinary meaning of those words. I am, I fear, unable to see how that determination, assuming it to be an erroneous determination, can properly be said to be a determination which he was not entitled to make. The judge is considering the words in the Schedule which he ought to consider. He is not embarking on some unauthorised or extraneous or irrelevant exercise. All he has done is to come to what appears to this court to be a wrong conclusion upon a difficult question. It seems to me that, if this judge is acting outside his jurisdiction, so then is every judge who comes to a wrong decision on a point of law. Accordingly, I take the view that no form of certiorari is available to the tenant. I am fortified in this view of the matter by the fact that Mr Read on behalf of the tenant accepted that the judge was acting within his jurisdiction, and added that "the nature of the judge's error was within his jurisdiction and was in relation to his interpretation and construction of the Schedule." Consequently Mr Dawson did not feel himself obliged to address us on the *Anisminic* (2) line of argument. Indeed for that reason alone I would have been reluctant to allow the appeal.'

(1)   [1960] 2 QB 133

(2)   Supra, this chapter

R v Secretary of State for the Environment, ex parte Ostler [1977] 1 QB 122 Court of Appeal (Lord Denning MR, Goff and Shaw LJJ)

Statutory regulation of judicial intervention in administration

Facts

The applicant had business premises in a certain old town. He applied for leave to move for an order of certiorari to quash a road scheme order made under the Highways Act 1959 and a compulsory purchase order made under the Acquisition of Land (Authorisation Procedure) Act 1946. Both orders had already been confirmed by the Secretary of State for the Environment. The applicant claimed that he had not objected these original proposals because they did not appear to affect his property and therefore he had not attended the public inquiry in respect of them. However, after these orders had been confirmed a proposed supplementary order had been published which would, if carried out, affect his premises. He had therefore objected at the public inquiry held in respect of this supplementary order but the supplementary order had been confirmed. He further alleged that, after the confirmation of the supplementary order, it had come to his knowledge that before the earlier enquiry there had been a secret agreement between an Officer of the department for the Environment and the local wine merchants (who were intending to object to the original proposals) guaranteeing that if the original orders were confirmed, the supplementary proposal would be made. The applicant contended that if he had known of the secret agreement he would have objected to the original orders and that, since he had been deprived of the opportunity to object, the original orders as confirmed were invalidated by lack of natural justice and bad faith verging on fraud.

A preliminary objection was taken on behalf of the Secretary of State that whatever the facts, any attack on the validity of the original orders as confirmed was barred in any legal proceedings whatever because the prescribed six-week period under para 2 of Sch 2 to the Act of 1959 and under para 15 of Sch 1 to the Act of 1946 for questioning the orders had expired.

Held

Parliament had by the relevant provisions of Sch 2 to the Act of 1959 and Sch 1 to the Act of 1946 given a person aggrieved by a confirmed scheme or order six weeks in which to question its validity in the High Court, but that after that period had expired the court could not entertain any proceedings to question its validity on any ground whatsoever. Provisions of that type were appropriate in relation to orders involving administrative decisions where the public interest required that they should be acted on promptly. The two orders were made within the jurisdiction of the relevant administrative bodies and thus were not void. They were voidable if challenged successfully within the time limit allowed but, thereafter, were immune from any challenge to their validity. The application for certiorari, therefore, could not proceed. *Smith v East Elloe RDC* (1) applied; *Anisminic Ltd v Foreign Compensation Commission* (2) distinguished.

Lord Denning MR:

'We are here presented with a nice question. Is Smith v East Elloe Rural District Council (1) a good authority or has it been overruled by Anisminic v Foreign Compensation Commission (2)?

... The Foreign Compensation Act 1950 s4(4) said:

"The determination by the commission of any application made to them under this Act shall not be called in question in any court of law."

The House held that that clause only applied to a real determination. It did not apply to a purported determination. They held that there had been no determination, properly so called, by the commission. So their decision could be called in question.

Some of their Lordships seem to have thrown doubt on *Smith v East Elloe Rural District Council* (1): see what Lord Reid said. But others thought it could be explained on the ground on which Browne J explained it. Lord Pearce said, at p201: "I agree with Browne J that it is not a compelling authority in the present case", and Lord Wilberforce said: "After the admirable analysis of the authorities made by Browne J ... no elaborate discussion of authority is needed."

I turn therefore to the judgment of Browne J. His judgment is appended as a note to the case at p223 et seq. He put *Smith* v *East Elloe Rural District Council* (1), as one of the "cases in which the inferior tribunal has been guilty of bias, or has acted in bad faith, or has disregarded the principles of natural justice". He said of those cases:

> "It is not necessary to decide it for the purposes of this case, but I am inclined to think that such decisions are not nullities but are good until quashed (cf the decision of the majority of the House of Lords in *Smith* v *East Elloe Rural District Council* (1), that a decision made in bad faith cannot be challenged on the ground that it was made beyond powers and Lord Radcliffe's dissenting speech,"

In these circumstances, I think that *Smith* v *East Elloe Rural District Council* (1) must still be regarded as good and binding on this court. It is readily to be distinguished from the *Anisminic* case (2). The points of difference are these:

First, in the *Anisminic* case (2) the Act ousted the jurisdiction of the court altogether. It precluded the court from entertaining any complaint at any time about the determination. Whereas in the *East Elloe* case (1) the statutory provision has given the court jurisdiction to inquire into complaints so long as the applicant comes within six weeks. The provision is more in the nature of a limitation period than of a complete ouster. That distinction is drawn by Professor Wade, *Administrative Law* 3rd ed 1971 pp152-153, and by the late Professor SA de Smith in the latest edition of *Halsbury's Laws of England*, 4th ed col 1 (1973) para 22, note 14.

Second, in the *Anisminic* case (2) the House was considering a determination by a truly judicial body, the Foreign Compensation Tribunal, whereas in the *East Elloe* case (1) the House was considering an order which was very much in the nature of an administrative decision. That is a distinction which Lord Reid himself drew in *Ridge* v *Baldwin* (3). There is a great difference between the two.. In making a judicial decision, the tribunal considers the rights of the parties without regard to the public interest. But in an administrative decision (such as a compulsory purchase order) the public interest plays an important part. The question is, to what extent are private interests to be subordinated to the public interest.

Third, in the *Anisminic* case (2) the House had to consider the actual determination of the tribunal, whereas in the *Smith* v *East Elloe* (1) case the House had to consider the validity of the process by which the decision was reached.

So, *Smith* v *East Elloe Rural District Council* (1) must still be regarded as the law in regard to this provision we have to consider here. I would add this: if this order were to be upset for want of good faith or for lack of natural justice, it would not to my mind be a nullity or void from the beginning. It would only be voidable. And as such, if it should be challenged promptly before much has been done under it, as Lord Radcliffe put it forcibly in *Smith* v *East Elloe Rural District Council* (1):

> "But this argument is in reality a play on the meaning of the word nullity. An order," - and he is speaking of an order such as we have got here - "even if not made in good faith, is still an act capable of legal consequences. It bears no brand of invalidity upon its forehead. Unless the necessary proceedings are taken at law to establish the cause of invalidity and to get it quashed or otherwise upset, it will remain as effective for its ostensible purpose as the most impeccable of orders. And that brings us back to the question that determines this case: Has Parliament allowed the necessary proceedings to be taken?"

The answer which he gave was "No". That answer binds us in this court today ...'

Goff LJ:

'... for the purposes of the present interlocutory application, we have to assume that a case of fraud or mala fides could be established. The question then arises whether the statutory provisions to which Lord Denning avoid MR has referred bar any such case ...

In my judgment, in *Smith* v *East Elloe Rural District Council* (1) the majority did definitely decide that those statutory provisions preclude the order from being challenged after the statutory period allowed, then by para15, and now by para2, and we are bound by that unless *Anisminic Ltd* v *Foreign Compensation Commission* (2) has so cut across it that we are relieved from the duty of following *Smith* v *East Elloe Rural District Council* (1) and indeed, bound not to follow it.

That raises a number of problems. With all respect to Lord Denning MR and Professor Wade, I do myself find difficulty in distinguishing *Anisminic* (2) on the ground that in that case there was an absolute prohibition against recourse to the court, whereas in the present case there is a qualified power for a limited period, because the majority in the *Smith* case (1) said either that fraud did not come within para15, so that, in effect, it was an absolute ouster, or that it made no difference to the construction if it did.

Nevertheless, it seems to me that the *Anisminic* case (2) is distinguishable on two grounds. First, the suggestion made by Lord Pearce, that *Anisminic* dealt with a judicial decision, and an administrative or executive decision might be different. I think it is. It is true that the Minister has been said to be acting in a quasi judicial capacity, but he is nevertheless conducting an administrative or executive matter, where questions of policy enter into and must influence his decision.

I would refer in support of that to a passage from the speech of Lord Reid in the well-known case of *Ridge* v *Baldwin* (3). I need not read it. It sets out what I have been saying.

Where one is dealing with a matter of that character and where, as Lord Denning MR has pointed out, the order is one which must be acted upon promptly, it is, I think, easier for the courts to construe Parliament as meaning exactly what it said - that the matter cannot questioned in any court, subject to the right given by para2, where applicable, and where application is made in due time - than where, as in *Anisminic* (2), one is dealing with a statute setting up a judicial tribunal and defining its powers and the question is whether it has acted within them ...

The second ground of distinction is that the ratio in the *Anisminic* case (2) was that the House was dealing simply with a question of jurisdiction and not a case where the order is made within jurisdiction, but it is attacked on the ground of fraud or mala fides. There are, I am fully conscious, difficulties in the way of that distinction, because Lord Somervell of Harrow in *Smith* v *East Elloe Rural District Council* (1), in his dissenting speech, said that fraud does not make the order voidable but a nullity. Lord Reid said the same in the *Anisminic* case (2); and Lord Pearce equated want of natural justice with lack of jurisdiction.

Nevertheless, despite those difficulties, I think there is a real distinction between the case with which the House was dealing in *Anisminic* (2) and the case of *Smith* v *East Elloe Rural District Council* (1) on that ground, that in the one case the determination was a purported determination only, because the tribunal, however eminent, having misconceived the effect of the statute, acted outside its jurisdiction, and indeed without any jurisdiction at all, whereas here one is dealing with an actual decision made within jurisdiction though sought to be challenged.

It cannot be gainsaid that some of the speeches in *Anisminic* (2) do appear to cast doubts upon the correctness of the decision in *Smith* v *East Elloe Rural District Council* (1) but it certainly was not expressly overruled, nor did any of their Lordships, as I see it, say that it was wrong. There are substantial differences, such as Lord Denning MR and I have indicated, between the two cases, and it seems to me that *Smith* v *East Elloe Rural District Council* (1) stands, is binding on this court, and is a decision directly in point ...'

(1)   Infra, this chapter

(2)   Supra, this chapter

(3)   Supra, chapter 14

Smith v East Elloe RDC [1956] AC 736 House of Lords (Viscount Simonds, Lords Morton of Henryton, Reid, Radcliffe and Somervell of Harrow)

Where the jurisdiction of the courts may be ousted in administrative matters

Facts

By para 15(1) of Part IV of Sch I to the Acquisition of Land (Authorisation Procedure) Act 1946: 'If any person aggrieved by a compulsory purchase order desired to question the validity thereof ... on the ground that the authorisation thereby granted is not empowered to be granted under this Act ... he may, within six weeks from the date on which notice of confirmation or making of the order ... is first published ... make an application to the High Court ...' By para 16: 'Subject to the provisions of the last foregoing paragraph, a compulsory purchase order ... shall not ... be questioned in any legal proceedings whatsoever ...' Land belonging to the appellant was made the subject of a compulsory purchase order. She brought an action more than six weeks after notice of its confirmation had been published, against the local authority which had obtained it, the clerk to the local authority and the Government Department which had confirmed it, claiming damages, an injunction against further trespass on the land, a declaration that the order was made and confirmed wrongfully and in bad faith and that the clerk acted wrongfully and in bad faith in procuring the order and its confirmation.

Held

1) (Per Viscount Simonds, Lord Morton of Henryton and Lord Radcliffe; Lord Reid and Lord Somervell of Harrow dissenting) the action against the council and the Government Department could not proceed because of the clear prohibition in para16 against questioning the validity of the order which operated to oust the jurisdiction of the court.

2) (unanimously) the action might proceed against the clerk to the council for damages.

Viscount Simonds:

'... In this House a more serious argument was developed. It was that, as the compulsory purchase order was challenged on the ground that it had been made and confirmed "wrongfully" and "in bad faith" para16 had no application. It was said that the paragraph, however general its language, must be construed so as not to oust the jurisdiction of the court where the good faith of the local authority or the Ministry was impugned and put in issue. Counsel for the appellant made his submission very clear. It was that where the words "compulsory purchase order" occur in these paragraphs they are to be read as if the words "made in good faith" were added to them.

My Lords, I think that anyone bred in the tradition of the law is likely to regard with little sympathy legislative provisions for ousting the jurisdiction of the court, whether in order that the subject may be deprived altogether of remedy or in order that his grievance may be remitted to some other tribunal. But it is our plain duty to give the words of an Act their proper meaning and, for my part, I find it quite impossible to qualify the words of the paragraph in the manner suggested. It may be that the legislature had not in mind the possibility of an order being made by a local authority in bad faith or even the possibility of an order made in good faith being mistakenly, capriciously or wantonly challenged. This is a matter of speculation. What is abundantly clear is that words are used which are wide enough to cover any kind of challenge which an aggrieved person may think fit to make. I cannot think of any wider words. Any addition would be mere tautology. But, it is said, let those general words be given their full scope and effect, yet they are not applicable to an order made in bad faith. But, my Lords, no one can suppose that an order bears upon its face the evidence of bad faith.

It cannot be predicated of any order that it has been made in bad faith until it has been tested in legal proceedings, and it is just that test which para16 bars. How, then, can it be said that any qualification can be introduced to limit the meaning of the words? What else can "compulsory purchase order" mean but an act apparently valid in the law, formally authorised, made, and confirmed?

It was urged by counsel for the appellant that there is a deep-rooted principle that the legislature cannot be assumed to oust the jurisdiction of the court, particularly where fraud is alleged, except by clear words, and a number of cases were cited in which the court has asserted its jurisdiction to examine into an alleged abuse of statutory power and, if necessary, correct it. Reference was made, too, to Maxwell on the Interpretation of Statutes to support the view, broadly stated, that a statute is, if possible, so to be construed as to avoid injustice. My Lords, I do not refer in detail to these authorities only because it appears to me that they do not override the first of all principles of construction, that plain words must be given their plain meaning. There is nothing ambiguous about paragraph 16; there is no alternative construction that can be given to it; there is in fact no justification for the introduction of limiting words such as "if made in good faith" and there is the less reason for doing so when those words would have the effect of depriving the express words "in any legal proceedings whatsoever" of their full meaning and content ...

I come, then, to the conclusion that the court cannot entertain this action so far as it impugns the validity of the compulsory purchase order, and it is no part of my present duty to attack or defend such a provision of an Act of Parliament. But two things may, I think, fairly be said. First, if the validity of such an order is open to challenge at any time within the period allowed by the ordinary Statute of Limitations with the consequence that it and all that has been done under it over a period of many years may be set aside, it is not perhaps unreasonable that Parliament should have thought fit to impose an absolute bar to proceedings even at the risk of some injustice to individuals. Secondly, the injustice may not be so great as might appear. For the bad faith or fraud upon which an aggrieved person relies is that of individuals, and this very case shows that, even if the validity of the order cannot be questioned and he cannot recover the land that has been taken from him, yet he may have a remedy in damages against those individuals. Here the appellant by her writ claims against the personal defendant a declaration that he knowingly acted wrongfully and in bad faith in procuring the order and its confirmation, and damages, and that is a claim which the court clearly has jurisdiction to entertain ...'

Lord Reid (dissenting):

'... In my judgment, para16 is clearly intended to exclude, and does exclude entirely, all cases of misuse of power in bona fide. But does it also exclude the small minority of cases were deliberate dishonesty, corruption or malice is involved? In every class of case that I can think of the courts have always held that general words are not to be read as enabling a deliberate wrongdoer to take advantage of his own dishonesty. Are the principles of statutory construction so rigid that these general words must be so read here? Of course, if there were any other indications in the statute of such an intention beyond the mere generality of the words that would be conclusive: but I can find none.

There are many cases where general words in a statute are given a limited meaning. That is done, not only when there is something in the statute itself which requires it, but also where to give general words their apparent meaning would lead to conflict with some fundamental principle. Where there is ample scope for the words to operate without any such conflict it may very well be that the draftsman did not have in mind and Parliament did not realise that the words were so wide that in some few cases they could operate to subvert a fundamental principle. In general, of course, the intention of Parliament can only be inferred from the words of the statute, but it appears to me to be well established in certain cases that, without some specific indication of an intention to do so, the mere generality of words used will not be regarded as sufficient to show an intention to depart from fundamental principles. So, general words by themselves do not bind the Crown, they are limited so as not to conflict with international law, they are commonly read so as to avoid retrospective infringement of rights, and it appears to me that they can equally well be read so as not to deprive the court of jurisdiction where bad faith is involved ...

I think that there is still room for reason to point out that the general words in this case must be limited so as to accord with the principle, of which Parliament cannot have been ignorant, that a wrongdoer cannot rely on general words to avoid the consequences of his own dishonesty...'

15.3   Estoppel in public law

Lever (Finance) Ltd v Westminster City London Borough Council [1971] 1 QB 222
Court of Appeal (Lord Denning MR, Sachs and Megaw LJJ)
Local authority estopped from exercising powers by the action of its officer

Facts

Lever Finance Ltd ('the company') applied for planning permission for the building of fourteen houses. Permission was duly granted, and at a later date the architect acting for the company approached the planning authority's planning officer with variations to the original approved plans, showing a number of modifications, including the siting of a house seventeen feet nearer to existing dwellings than the original plans envisaged. The planning officer, who had lost the relevant file, telephoned the company's architect confirming that the alterations were merely incidental and within the scope of the original planning permission. As building of the houses proceeded, residents objected to the modifications and the company, supported by the planning officer applied for new planning permission. The application was refused by the planning authority and an enforcement notice issued. The company sought a declaration that it had planning permission for the development and an injunction to prevent execution of the enforcement notices. This relief was granted by Bridge J at first instance, and the authority appealed to the Court of Appeal.

Held

The appeal would be dismissed. There was a previous history here of minor modifications to developments being agreed to informally by planning officers, without new applications having to be made. The consent given by the planning officer was within the scope of his ostensible authority.

Lord Denning MR:

'Mr Chavasse for the city council accepted – as he must accept – that is the practice. But he says it is not binding on the planning committee. He says that Parliament has entrusted these important planning decisions to the planning authority and not to the planning officer of the council; and, no matter that the planning officers tell a developer that a variation is not material, it is not binding on the planning authority. They can go back on it. Mr Chavasse says that it is for the developer's architect to shoulder the responsibility. He must make up his own mind whether it is material. He can take the opinion of the planning officer, but it is eventually the architect's own responsibility. If the variation should turn out to be a material variation, and he has not got permission for it from the planning committee, then so much the worse for him. He ought not to have relied on the planning officer's opinion. The planning authority, he said, are quite entitled to throw over the opinion of their planning officer.

I can see the force of Mr Chavasse's argument, but I do not think it should prevail. In my opinion a planning permission covers work which is specified in the detailed plans and any immaterial variation therein. I do not use the words "de minimis" because that would be misleading. It is obvious that, as the developer proceeds with the work, there will necessarily be variations from time to time. Things may arise which were not foreseen. It should not be necessary for the developers to go back to the planning committee for every immaterial variation. The permission covers any variation which it not material. But then the question arises: Who is to decide whether a variation is material or not? In practice it has been the planning officer. This is a sensible practice and I think we should affirm it. If the planning officer tells the developer that a proposed variation is not material, and the developer acts on it, then the planning authority cannot go back on it. I know that there are authorities which say that a public authority cannot be estopped by any representations made by its officers. It cannot be estopped from doing its public duty: see, for instance, the recent decision of the Divisional Court in *Southend-on-Sea Corporation* v *Hodgson (Wickford) Ltd* (1). But those statements must now be taken with considerable reserve. There are many matters which public authorities can now delegate to their officers. If an officer, acting within the scope of his ostensible authority, makes a representation on which another acts, then a public authority may be bound by it, just as much as a private person would be. A good instance is the recent decision of this court in *Wells* v *Minister of Housing and Local Government* (2).

So here it has been the practice of the local authority, and of many others, to allow their planning officers to tell applicants where a variation is material or not. Are they now to be allowed to say that that practice was all wrong? I do not think so. It was a matter within the ostensible authority of the planning officer; and, being acted on, it is binding on the council.

I would only add this: the conversation with Mr Carpenter took place early in May 1969. At that date there had been in force for one month at least, since 1 April 1969, the provisions of the Town and Country Planning Act 1968. Section 64 enables a local authority as from 1 April 1969, to delegate to their officers many of their functions under the Planning Acts. An applicant cannot himself know, of course, whether such a delegation has taken place. That is a matter for the "indoor management" of the planning authority. It depends on the internal resolutions which they have made. Any person dealing with them is entitled to assume that all necessary resolutions have been passed. Just as he can in the case of a company: see *Royal British Bank* v *Turquand* (3). It is true that s64(5) speaks of a notice in writing. But this does not alter the fact that much authority can now be delegated to planning officers.

I do not think this case can or should be decided on the new Act: for there was no notice in writing here. I think it should be decided on the practice proved in evidence. It was within the ostensible authority of Mr Carpenter to tell Mr Rottenberg that the variation was not material. Seeing that the developers acted on it by building the house, I do not think the council can throw over what has been done by their officer, Mr Carpenter.

I can see how the trouble has arisen. Mr Carpenter had lost the file. He made a mistake. He told Mr Rottenberg that a variation was not material, when he ought to have told him that it was material and required planning permission. He made a mistake. That is unfortunate for the neighbours. They may feel justly aggrieved. But it is not a mistake for which the developers should suffer. The developers put up this house on the faith of this representation made to them. I do not think an enforcement notice should be launched against them. I think the judge was right and I would dismiss the appeal.'

Sachs LJ:

'... On matters such as those raised in this appeal the court must, of course, hold a careful balance between two po___ ___lly conflicting principles.

Both of ___ ___ are ___ ___trated in the judgments delivered in *Wells* v *Minister of Housing and Local Go___ment* ___ ___ ___ ___he one hand, the court must be careful to remember "The local planning ___ ___ ___ ___ ___t to waive statutory requirements in favour of (so to speak) an adversary: it ___ ___ing system." (See the dissenting judgment of Russell LJ at p1015.) The ___ ___ the public interest must not be impaired. Hence the attitude of the courts on the matter of estoppel. On the other hand, the courts must likewise take care that those who deal reasonably with the council's officers cannot afterwards be trapped by the council saying:

"You ought to have completed a series of procedural technicalities, and, although we by our officers normally do not insist on them, we can always turn round and say that what has happened as between us and yourselves is of no effect."

That is the basis upon which Lord Denning MR said in the *Wells* case (2):

"I take the law to be that a defect in procedure can be cured, and an irregularity can be waived, even by a public authority, so as to render valid that which would otherwise be invalid."

The general position on the exercise in planning matters of powers by the officers of the corporation has, of course, been affected by s64 of the Act of 1968. That section gives power to delegate to officers of a corporation where delegation was not previously possible. For my part, I do not wish to generalise as to when an officer can be deemed to have authority for the actions which he takes in the course of exercising what would appear to persons dealing with him to be a natural authority. In the present case one can look at the combined effect of past practice and the powers of delegation which have now been provided and see how the matter works in this particular instance, for we are now dealing with a conversation that took place just after s64 came into operation.'

[His Lordship referred to the practice that prevailed before s64 came into effect, as described by Bridge J at first instance.]

No change in that procedure was made when s64 came into force. Whatever may have been the position before that date, the unimpeded continuance of a practice that had previously existed resulted after that date in an implied delegation no less than if there had been an express delegation.

In those circumstances in essence what technically happened was that there was a delegation of power to deal with an application under s43 of the Act of 1962 as to whether any further planning permission was required. For such an application it would be otiose to send in forms such as had previously been filled in, probably in triplicate, which were already available on the files of the corporation and which would show all the material necessary for dealing with the case except the modification of the original plan, which was set out in the amended plan - here plan No 2. In those circumstances it would be appalling if every time there was such an application it was necessary to clutter the files of architect and authority alike with a mass of additional paper. Given good faith on the part of those concerned - and there is not the slightest suggestion that this is a case which was other than one of good faith - it is enough that the decision be recorded by the respective parties. I would however say for future reference that it would have been much better if there had been an xchange of short notes on the subject. But in practice the conversation of early May 1969, operated in the same way as if all s43 formalities had been observed.

On those grounds accordingly I too would dismiss this appeal. I thus do not feel it necessary nor indeed do I feel qualified without further consideration to go into the other interesting points which have been raised by Mr Chavasse.'

(1)   Infra, this chapter

(2)   [1967] 1 WLR 1000

(3)   (1856) 6 E & B 327

Southend-on-Sea Corporation v Hodgson (Wickford) Ltd [1962] 1 QB 416 Queen's Bench Divisional Court (Parker CJ, Winn and Widgery JJ)

Estoppel should not prevent the exercise of a statutory power for the public benefit

Facts

The owner of a building company wrote to the borough engineer of the local authority concerning the use of a piece of land as a builder's yard. He received a reply to the effect that permission for such use had already been granted, and on the strength of this the builder purchased the land and used it as a builder's yard. Shortly afterwards the authority served an enforcement notice on the builder to stop use of the land as a builder's yard, on the ground that no valid planning permission had been granted for such a use. The builder contended that the authority was estopped from denying the existence of permission on the basis of the borough engineer's letter. At first instance the court upheld the estoppel argument. The authority appealed to the Divisional Court.

Held

The appeal would be allowed. Estoppel could not be raised to prevent a public body such as a local authority from exercising its powers for the public benefit.

Lord Parker CJ:

'... The broad submission made by Mr Bridge on behalf of the appellants is that estoppel cannot operate to prevent or hinder the performance of a statutory duty or the exercise of a statutory discretion which is intended to be performed or exercised for the benefit of the public or a section of the public. It is further said that the discretion of a local planning authority to serve an enforcement notice under s23 in respect of development in fact carried out without permission is a statutory discretion of a public character. It is perfectly clear that the proposition is sound, at any rate to this extent, that estoppel cannot operate to prevent or hinder the performance of a positive statutory duty. That, indeed, is admitted by Mr Forbes on behalf of the respondents, but he maintains that it is limited to that and that it does not extend to an estoppel which might prevent or hinder the exercise of a statutory discretion ...

... I can see no logical distinction between a case such as that of an estoppel being sought to be raised to prevent the performance of a statutory duty and one where it is sought to be raised to hinder the exercise of a statutory discretion. After all, in a case of discretion there is a duty under the statute to exercise a free and unhindered discretion. There is a long line of cases to which we have not been specifically referred which lay down that a public authority cannot by contract fetter the exercise of its discretion. Similarly, as it seems to me, an estoppel cannot be raised to prevent or hinder the exercise of the discretion ...

There are many matters which public authorities can now delegate to their officers. If an officer, acting within the scope of his ostensible authority, makes a representation on which another acts, then a public authority may be bound by it, just as much as a private concern would be. A good instance is the recent decision of this court in *Wells* v *Minister of Housing and Local Government* (1). It was proved in that case that it was the practice of planning authorities, acting through their officers, to tell applicants whether or not planning permission was necessary. A letter was written by the council engineer telling the applicants that no permission was necessary. The applicants acted on it. It was held that the planning authority could not go back on it. I would like to quote what I then said, at p1007:

"It has been their practice to tell applicants that no planning permission is necessary. Are they now to be allowed to say that this practice was all wrong and their letters were of no effect? I do not think so. I take the law to be that a defect in procedure can be cured, and an irregularity can be waived, even by a public authority so as to render valid that which would otherwise be invalid."

So here it has been the practice of the local authority, and of many others to allow their planning officers to tell applicants whether a variation is material or not. Are they now to be allowed to say that that practice was all wrong? I do not think so. It was a matter within the ostensible authority of the planning officer; and, being acted on, it is binding on the council.'

(1)   [1967] 1 WLR 1000

Western Fish Products v Penwith District Council [1981] 2 All ER 204 Court of Appeal (Megaw, Lawton and Browne LJJ)

Limitations on estoppel of local authority exercise of powers

Facts

The plaintiff purchased a factory for processing fish products and inquired of the local planning authority whether or not existing use rights were in force in respect of such activities. The planning officer, Mr Giddens, replied by letter that the proposed use of the factory was within existing use rights, and in reliance on this the plaintiff company commenced use of the factory.

At a later date the planning authority wrote to the plaintiffs requesting them to apply for planning permission for their use of the factory. The subsequent application was refused and an enforcement notice issued. The plaintiff sought a declaration claiming, inter alia, that the planning authority was estopped from denying the existing user rights by Mr Giddens' letter. The application was unsuccessful at first instance, and the plaintiffs appealed to the Court of Appeal.

Held

The appeal would be dismissed. The planning officer could not make a decision that had been entrusted by Parliament to the planning authority. The situation might be different had the power to grant planning permission been delegated to the officer under s101(1) of the Local Government Act 1972.

An estoppel might arise where an officer acted within the scope of his ostensible authority and there is evidence over and above his mere holding of an office to justify the person dealing with him in believing that the officer had the power to make the decision in question. Further, estoppel might be allowed where all that was involved was the waiving of a mere technicality. The extension of estoppel beyond these two exceptions could not be justified.

16 THE PARLIAMENTARY COMMISSIONER FOR ADMINISTRATION

R v Local Commissioner for Administration for the North and East Area of England, ex parte Bradford Metropolitan City Council [1979] QB 287 Court of Appeal (Lord Denning MR, Eveleigh LJ and Sir David Cairns)

The nature of maladministration; discretion

Facts

The Local Commissioner investigated complaints against the local authority that had been made by the mother of two children, the children having been taken into care by the authority. Despite the complaints being brought after the twelve months limitation period, the Lord Commissioner exercised his discretion to consider the complaints. The authority applied for an order of prohibition to prevent the local Commissioner's investigation.

Held

The order of prohibition should not be made. The Local Commissioner had exercised his discretion to investigate properly. The complainant had no alternative legal remedy, and her personal problems did constitute special circumstances.

Lord Denning MR:

'... This brings me to the substantial point in this case. Has there been a sufficient claim of maladministration such as to justify investigation by the commissioner? The governing words of each statute are the same. There must be a written complaint made by or on behalf of a member of the public "who claims to have suffered injustice in consequence of maladministration."

But Parliament did not define "maladministration." It deliberately left it to the ombudsman himself to interpret the word as best he could: and to do it by building up a body of case law on the subject. Now the Parliamentary ombudsman, Sir Edmund Compton, has acknowledged openly that he himself gained assistance by looking at the debates in Parliament on the subject. He looked at Hansard and, in particular, at a list of instances of maladministration given by Mr. Crossman, the Lord President of the Council. It is called the "Crossman Catalogue": and is used by the ombudsman and his advisers as a guide to the interpretation of the word. Now the question at once arises: Are we the judges to look at Hansard when we have the self-same task? When we have ourselves to interpret the word "mal-administration". The construction of that word is beyond doubt a question of law. According to the recent pronouncement of the House of Lords in *Davis* v *Johnson* (1), we ought to regard Hansard as a closed book to which we as judges must not refer at all, not even as an aid to the construction of statutes.

By good fortune, however, we have been given a way of overcoming that obstacle. For the ombudsman himself in a public address to the Society of Public Teachers of Law quoted the relevant passages of Hansard (734 HC Deb, col 51 (18 October 1966)) as part of his address: and Professor Wade has quoted the very words in his latest book on Administrative Law, 4th ed (1977), p82. And we have not yet been told that we may not look at the writings of the teachers of law. Lord Simonds was as strict upon these matters as any judge ever has been but he confessed his indebtedness to their writings, even very recent ones: see *Jacobs* v *London County Council* (2). So have other great judges. I hope therefore that our teachers will go on quoting Hansard so that a judge may in this way have the same help as others have in interpreting a statute.

So this is the guide suggested to the meaning of the word "maladministration". It will cover "bias, neglect, inattention, delay, incompetence, ineptitude, perversity, turpitude, arbitrariness and so on." It "would be a long and interesting list," clearly open-ended, covering the manner in which a decision is reached or discretion is exercised; but excluding the merits of the decision itself or of the discretion itself. It follows that "discretionary decision, properly exercised, which the complainant dislikes but cannot fault the manner in which it was taken, is excluded": see Hansard, 734 HC Deb, col 51.

In other words, if there is no maladministration, the ombudsman may not question any decision taken by the authorities. He must not go into the merits of it or intimate any view as to whether it was right or wrong. This is explicitly declared in s34(3) of the Act of 1974. He can inquire whether there was maladministration or not. If he finds none, he must go no further. If he finds it, he can go on and inquire whether any person has suffered injustice thereby ...'

Eveleigh LJ:

'... Maladministration according to the Shorter Oxford English Dictionary means "faulty administration" or 'inefficient or improper management of affairs, esp public affairs" ...

Section 34 (3) of the Act reads:

"It is hereby declared that nothing in this part of this Act authorises or requires the Local Commissioner to question the merits of a decision taken without maladministration by an authority in the exercise of a discretion vested in that authority."

[Counsel for the Council] says that the matters complained of were the result of decisions arrived at with authority and that the complaint in effect seeks to question the merits of the decision or decisions ...

Action that is taken may or may not be the result of a particular administrative decision. If it is an act that is complained of I do not think that the commissioner can be denied the right to investigate merely by contending that the act is the result of a decision. When the party alleges injustice as a result of administrative action which the party claims is faulty the commissioner may investigate. In the course of that investigation he may come across a number of decisions that have been taken. Section 34 does not say that he may not investigate those decisions. It says that he may not question the merits of a decision taken without maladministration. It will often not be possible to say if a decision was taken with or without maladministration until it has been investigated. That is the whole purpose of the role of a commissioner. It is to investigate what has gone on in administrative quarters so that members of the public can be satisfied that public affairs are properly conducted. I therefore do not think that s34 provides any obstacle. If the commissioner carries out his investigation and in the course of it comes personally to the conclusion that a decision was wrongly taken, but is unable to point to any maladministration other than the decision itself, he is prevented by s34(3) from questioning the decision. Consequently his investigations into the complaint in whatever direction his inquiries might lead will have to be conducted upon the basis that the decision in question was validly taken. Administrative action therefore which is based upon or dictated by that decision will not amount to maladministration simply because someone in the exercise of his discretion has come to a wrong decision. If the decision itself is affected by maladministration, different consequences will follow.'

(1)   [1978] 2 WLR 553

(2)   [1950] AC 361

17 ORGANISATION AND ACCOUNTABILITY OF THE POLICE

R v Chief Constable of Devon and Cornwall, ex parte Central Electricity Generating Board [1981] 3 WLR 967 Court of Appeal (Lord Denning MR, Lawton and Templeman LJJ)

Mandamus will not lie on a policy decision

Facts

The Electricity Board were unable to carry out a survey of farm land as a possible site for a nuclear power station, due to the continuing activities of objectors. In a written reply to complaints from the Board, the Chief Constable stated that he was unwilling to act against the objectors in the absence of stronger evidence of illegal action on their part.

The Board applied for an order of mandamus to compel the Chief Constable to act, but this was refused. The Board appealed to the Court of Appeal.

Held

The appeal would be dismissed. The Court should not intervene to usurp the decision making function of the Chief Constable.

Lord Denning MR:

'Notwithstanding all that I have said, I would not give any orders to the chief constable or his men. It is of the first importance that the police should decide on their own responsibility what action should be taken in any particular situation. As I said in *R v Commissioner of Police of the Metropolis, ex parte Blackburn* (1):

"... it is for the Commissioner of Police of the Metropolis, or the chief constable, as the case may be, to decide in any particular case whether inquiries should be pursued, or whether an arrest should be made, or a prosecution brought. It must be for him to decide on the disposition of his force and the concentration of his resources on any particular crime or area. No court can or should give him direction on such a matter. He can also make policy decisions and give effect to them, as, for instance, was often done when prosecutions were not brought for attempted suicide. But there are some policy decisions with which, I think, the courts in a case can, if necessary, interfere."

The decision of the chief constable not to intervene in this case was a policy decision with which I think the courts should not interfere. All that I have done in this judgment is to give the "definitive legal mandate" which he sought. It should enable him to reconsider their position. I hope he will decide to use his men to clear the obstructors off the site or at any rate help the board to do so.'

(1)   Infra, this chapter

R v Commissioner of Police of the Metropolis, ex parte Blackburn [1968] 2 QB 118 Court of Appeal (Lord Denning MR, Salmon and Edmund Davies LJJ)

Enforcement of law

Facts

Raymond Blackburn sought an order of mandamus (inter alia) compelling the Commissioner to enforce the law against illegal gambling.

Held

Whilst there might be extreme cases where the courts would issue orders of mandamus directed at the Commissioner, as a general rule day to day policing policies were a matter for the police alone. In any event by the time this matter reached the Court of Appeal the policy of the Metropolitan Police had been altered.

Lord Denning MR:

'... A question may be raised as to the machinery by which he could be compelled to do his duty. On principle, it seems to me that once a duty exists, there should be a means of enforcing it. This duty can be enforced, I think, either by action at the suit of the Attorney-General or by the prerogative writ of mandamus. I am mindful of the cases cited by Mr Worsley which he said limited the scope of mandamus. But I would reply that mandamus is a very wide remedy which has always been available against public officers to see that they do their public duty. It went in the old days against justices of the peace both in their judicial and in their administrative functions. The legal status of the Commissioner of Police of the Metropolis is still that he is a justice of the peace, as well as a constable. No doubt the party who applies for mandamus must show that he has sufficient interest to be protected and that there is no other equally convenient remedy. But once this is shown, the remedy of mandamus is available, in case of need, even against the Commissioner of Police of the Metropolis.

Can Mr Blackburn invoke the remedy of mandamus here? It is I think an open question whether Mr. Blackburn has sufficient interest to be protected. No doubt any person who was adversely affected by the action of the commissioner in making a mistaken policy decision would have such an interest. The difficulty is to see how Mr. Blackburn himself has been affected. But without deciding that question, I turn to see whether it is shown that the Commissioner of Police of the Metropolis has failed in his duty ...'

Salmon LJ:

'... I am not impressed by the argument that Mr. Blackburn has an equally effective and equally convenient remedy open to him and that, therefore the order of mandamus should in any event be refused in the court's discretion. It seems to me fantastically unrealistic for the police to suggest, as they have done, that their policy decision was unimportant because Mr. Blackburn was free to start private prosecutions of his own and fight the gambling empires, possibly up to the House of Lords, single-handed ... The only doubt I should have had would have been as to whether Mr. Blackburn had a sufficient personal interest in order to obtain an order of mandamus. As it is, no order is necessary ...'

See *Ridge* v *Baldwin*, chapter 14.

R v Secretary of State for the Home Department, ex parte Northumbria Police [1988] 1 WLR 356

Facts

The Home Secretary issued a circular to all chief constables informing them that the Home Office maintained a central store of riot equipment, such as CS gas. It went on to state that if chief constables experienced difficulties in persuading their respective police authorities to sanction the supply of such equipment, it would be made directly available on request to the Home Office. The Home Secretary claimed that the power to supply such equipment was provided either by s41 of the Police Act 1964, or that he was exercising his prerogative power to maintain law and order. The police authority maintained that it alone was responsible for sanctioning the provision of such equipment to a chief constable, and that the exercise of any prerogative power by the Home Secretary was inconsistent with its own power under s4(4) of the 1964 Act. At first instance the Divisional Court held that although the Home Secretary did not have the power to supply such equipment under s41 of the Act, he could do so in the exercise of his prerogative power to maintain law and order. This had not been replaced by s4(4) of the Act. The police authority now appealed to the Court of Appeal.

Held

The Home Secretary was empowered to supply such equipment by s41 of the 1964 Act. Further, even if he was not, he could still do so in the exercise of his prerogative power to maintain law and order. This power had not been replaced by statute, because s4(4) did not provide the police authority with monopoly control over the supply of equipment.

Extracts from the judgments:

Croom-Johnson LJ (having determined that the Home Secretary could have acted within s41):

'The second question is, on the assumption that s41 gives no statutory power to the Home Secretary to supply this equipment to chief constables, then does the royal prerogative supply it?

Although there has always been what is called the war prerogative, which is the Crown's right to make war and peace, (counsel) for the police authority has submitted that there is no corresponding prerogative to enforce the keeping of what is popularly called the Queen's peace within the realm. He based his submission by reference to Chitty *A treatise on the Law of the Prerogatives of the Crown* (1820) and pointed out that there is no power referred to in it for keeping the peace. It does, however, contain an extensive section on "the King as the Fountain of Justice" and courts and gaols (see ch 7, p75 ff). The argument is that if there was no prerogative power to keep the peace in 1820, at which date no organised police force existed, then all police forces exist and are controlled only by the later statutes by which they were created, and there is no residual prerogative power to draw on in cases of necessity.

In contrast to this submission, Professor O Hood Phillips in *Constitutional and Administrative Law* (6th edn, 1978), ch 21, p399 states unequivocally:

"Although the preservation of the peace, which is a royal prerogative, is one of the primary functions of any state, the administration of the police has always been on a local basis in this country."

It may be that the King's power to establish courts and gaols and to administer justice was no more than the larger power to see that the peace was kept. There were constables long before the establishment of Peel's metropolitan police in 1829.

At all events, the assumption was early made that keeping the peace was part of the prerogative. The position of the Home Secretary is that he is one of a number of Secretaries of State through whom the prerogative power is exercised. In *Harrison* v *Bush* (1855) 5 E & B 344 at 353, 119 ER 509 at 513 Lord Campbell CJ stated:

"In practice, to the Secretary of State for the Home Department ... belongs peculiarly the maintenance of the peace within the Kingdom, with the superintendence of the administration of justice as far as the Royal prerogative is involved in it."

That case does not establish the existence of the power with regard to the police, but only the status of the Home Secretary.'

[His Lordship considered *Coomber (Surveyor of Taxes)* v *Berks JJs* (1883) 9 App Cas 61, and continued]:

'A recent instance of the exercise of the royal prerogative in the context of preserving law and order was the creation of the Criminal Injuries Compensation Board in 1964 (see *R* v *Criminal Injuries Compensation Board, ex p Lain* [1967] 2 All ER 770 at 777, 780-781, 783-784, [1967] 2 QB 864 at 881, 886, 891 per Lord Parker CJ, Diplock LJ and Ashworth J). By its very nature, the subject of maintaining the Queen's peace and keeping law and order has over the years inevitably been dealt with by statute much more than the war prerogative has been. Instances of the way in which such a prerogative may be used are more readily provided by example than by being placed in categories, but I have no doubt that the Crown does have a prerogative power to keep the peace, which is bound up with its undoubted right to see that crime is prevented and justice administered. This is subject to the next submission of (counsel) for the police authority, which was that any prerogative power may be lost by being overtaken by statute law.

(Counsel) for the police authority adopted the dictum of Dicey in *Introduction to the Study of the Law of the Constitution* (10th edn, 1959) p 424 that the prerogative is "the residue of discretionary or arbitrary authority, which at any given time is legally left in the hands of the Crown". *A-G* v *De Keyser's Royal Hotel Ltd* [1920] AC 508, [1920] All ER Rep 80 was the decision which establishes that in the exercise of the war prerogative the Crown's power to requisition property had been limited by Defence Act 1842 so as to require compensation to be paid to the subject. Lord Dunedin said ([1920] AC 508 at 526, [1920] All ER Rep 80 at 86):

"Inasmuch as the Crown is a party to every Act of Parliament it is logical enough to consider that when the Act deals with something which before the Act could be effected by the prerogative, and specially empowers the Crown to do the same thing, but subject to conditions, the Crown assents to that, and by the Act, to the prerogative being curtailed".

Lord Parmoor stated ([1920] AC 508 at 575, [1920] All ER Rep 80 at 109):

"The constitutional principle is that when the power of the Executive to interfere with the property or liberty of subjects has been place under Parliamentary control, and directly regulated by statute, the Executive no longer derives its authority from the Royal Prerogative of the Crown but from Parliament, and that in exercising such authority the Executive is bound to observe the restrictions which Parliament has imposed in favour of the subject."

(Counsel) for the police authority also placed reliance on the speech of Lord Atkinson (see [1920] AC 508 at 539, [1920] All ER Rep 80 at 92).

It is clear that the Crown cannot act under the prerogative if to do so would be incompatible with statute. What is said here is that the Home Secretary's proposal under the circular would be inconsistent with the powers expressly or impliedly conferred on the police authority by s4 of the 1964 Act. The Divisional Court rejected that submission for reasons with which I wholly agree, namely that s4 does not expressly grant a monopoly, and that granted the possibility of an authority which declines to provide equipment required by the chief constable there is every reason not to imply a parliamentary intent to create one.

The last submission of (counsel) for the police authority was that if there is a prerogative power it can only be used in emergency and that this does not allow its use beforehand in circumstances of peace and quiet.

One need only quote, and adapt, two passages from the speeches in *Burmah Oil Co (Burma Trading) Ltd* v *Lord Advocate* [1964] 2 All ER 348 at 353, 382, [1965] AC 75 at 100, 144. That was a case concerning the war prerogative, but the same point was taken. Lord Reid said: "... it would be very strange if the law prevented or discouraged necessary preparations until a time when it would probably be too late for them to be effective." Lord Pearce said:

"The prerogative power in the emergency of war must be one power, whether the peril is merely threatening or has reached the ultimate stage of crisis. Bulwarks are as necessary for the public safety when they are constructed in good time against a foreseen invasion as when they are hastily improvised after the enemy has landed. The Crown must have power to act before the ultimate crisis arises ..."

The same reasoning must apply to the provision of equipment to the police, and to their being trained in its use, in times when there is reason to apprehend outbreaks of riot and serious civil disturbance. The steps contemplated by the circular are within prerogative powers, and in my view the declaration now asked for should not be granted. I would dismiss this appeal and allow the appeal on the Home Secretary's cross-notice.'

Purchas LJ (on the nature of the prerogative power):

'The respect in which the authority asserts that the Secretary of State has exceeded his powers is that his offer is extended directly to chief officers of police forces in cases where they expect their police authority would be unwilling to make this equipment available themselves. The Secretary of State's powers in this regard must either be based on statute or be derived from the royal prerogative and exercised by the Secretary of State as a Secretary of State acting on behalf of the Crown: see the quotation already given in the judgment of Croom-Johnson LJ from Lord Campbell CJ in *Harrison* v *Bush* (1855) 5 E & B 344 at 353, 119 ER 509 at 513.

I shall return to consider the question of the exercise of prerogative powers in a little more detail later in this judgment. At this stage before considering the position under the Police Act 1964 it is convenient to notice the distinction between the underlying prerogative power which indisputably resides in the Crown to "protect the realm", "keep the Queen's peace", "make treaties" etc and the various ways in which that power is exercised and has been exercised over many centuries.

Whether the prerogative powers variously described are merely different aspects of the same fundamental power to protect the realm or are separate individual prerogative powers may be more important academically than in the resolution of the issues raised in this appeal. The exercise of the prerogative of keeping the peace and the enforcement of law and order was effected by proclamation and statute from earliest times (see the Proclamation of Humbert Walter the Justiciar in 1195 and the Statute of Winchester (13 Edw 1 (1285)). The constable's powers and duties have been described in the judgment of McCardie J in *Fisher* v *Oldham Corp* [1930] 2 KB 364, [1930] All ER Rep 96, already cited by Croom-Johnson LJ and by Lord Denning MR in *R* v *Metropolitan Police Comr, ex partie Blackburn* [1968] 1 All ER 763 at 769, [1968] 2 QB 118 at 135:

"The office of Commissioner of Police within the metropolis dates back to 1829 when Sir Robert Peel introduced his disciplined Force. The commissioner was a justice of the peace specially appointed to administer the police force in the metropolis. His constitutional status has never been defined either by statute or by the courts. It was considered by the Royal Commission on the Police in their report in 1962 (Cmnd 1728). I have no hesitation, however, in holding that like every constable in the land, he should be, and is, independent of the executive. He is not subject to the orders of the Secretary of State, save that under the Police Act 1964 the Secretary of State can call on him to give a report, or to retire in the interests of efficiency. I hold it to be the duty of the Commissioner of Police, as it is of every chief constable, to enforce the law of the land. He must take steps so to post his men that crimes may be detected: and that honest citizens may go about their affairs in peace. He must decide whether or no suspected persons are to be prosecuted; and, if need be, bring the prosecution or see that it is brought; but in all these things he is not the servant of anyone, save of the law itself. No Minister of the Crown can tell him that he must, or must not, keep observation on this place or that; or that he must, or must not, prosecute this man or that one. Nor can any police authority tell him so. The responsibility for law enforcement lies on him. He is answerable to the law and to the law alone. That appears sufficiently from *Fisher* v *Oldham Corpn* ([1930] 2 KB 364, [1930] All ER Rep 96), the Privy Council case of *A-G for New South Wales* v *Perpetual Trustee Co (Ltd)* ([1955] 1 All ER 846, [1955] AC 457)."

In carrying out these duties, the powers of the chief constables must stem from delegated power to exercise the prerogative power to keep the peace. The duty to do this is confirmed in s5(1) of the 1964 Act. How he disposes of the personnel available to him or what use he may make of any particular equipment in any given set of circumstances has not been altered by the Act. Section 48 provides that the chief constable shall in certain circumstances be vicariously liable for the acts of constables under his direction and control.'

[Having agreed with Purchas LJ that s41 empowered the Secretary of State to act as he had, his Lordship returned to consider the scope of prerogative power in this matter]:

'I will, however, add some words of my own on the issue relating to royal prerogative, on which the Divisional Court found in favour of the Secretary of State. I find this a more difficult topic. As I have already said when I touched on it at the beginning of this judgment, the 1964 Act is mainly a consolidating Act and does not, in my judgment, affect any prerogative power otherwise enjoyed by the Crown any more than any of the enactments in whose place it now stands from the Statute of Winchester (13 Edw 1 (1285)) onwards. The continued existence of prerogative has never been questioned. Indeed, the police authority has conceded that it still exists in the case of national emergency, although as a concept this was difficult to define behind the obvious extremes of war or threat of war (civil or otherwise). So far as I know, it has never been suggested that in assenting to any of the enactments referred to in this judgment the monarch has in any way derogated from the royal prerogative to maintain the peace of the realm.

As I ventured to comment at the outset in considering the powers of ministers exercising as a Secretary of State the royal prerogative, one must distinguish between the existence of the prerogative and the machinery set up to enable the expeditious and efficient use of that prerogative. Thus it was seen in *R v Pinney* (1832) 3 B & Ad 947, (1824-34) All ER Rep 125 that the magistrate was called on to act in accordance with his duties to preserve the peace. It was held that he sufficiently discharged this duty by calling on the armed forces and constables and by appointing special constables. Having done this, the manner in which those whom he marshalled discharged their respective duties was no concern of the magistrates, but at no point was the existence of the prerogative of keeping the King's peace as the origin of the resulting duties and powers put in question.

The part of the speech of Lord Blackburn in *Coomber (Surveyor of Taxes) v Berks Justices* (1883) 9 App Cas 61 at 67, already cited by Croom-Johnson LJ, clearly sets out the prerogative powers stemming from the Crown which form the basis of the jurisdiction. By the time Lord Blackburn delivered his speech the Statute of Winchester had been in existence for nearly 600 years. I am unaware that the statutory provisions for organising the police or their predecessors, the constables or custodians of the law, or for appointing commissions for the appointment of justices in the Statute of Winchester or the many subsequent Acts of Parliament have in any way eroded or derogated from the prerogative in the Crown to protect the peace of the realm.

The submissions of (counsel) for the police authority based on *A-G v De Keyser's Royal Hotel Ltd* [1920] AC 508, (1920) All ER Rep 80 deserve careful analysis.'

[Having considered this authority at length, his Lordship continued]:

'When considering *Crown of Leon (owners) v Admiralty Comrs* [1921] 1 KB 595, *A-G v De Keyser's Royal Hotel Ltd* and *Burmah Oil Co (Burma Trading) Ltd v Lord Advocate* [1964] 2 All ER 348, [1965] AC 75 the courts were dealing with the purported exercise of the war or defence prerogative to avoid a liability to compensate the subject. As Lord Reid pointed out in the *Burmah Oil* case [1964] 2 All ER 348 at 354, (1965) AC 75 at 101, the exercise of the prerogative in the the circumstances must be rare because, in recent times, powers to requisition were available under the emergency legislation. It is well established that the courts will intervene to prevent executive action under the prerogative powers in violation of property or other rights of the individual where this is inconsistent with statutory provisions providing for the same executive action. Where the executive action is directed towards the benefit or protection of the individual it is unlikely that its use will attract the intervention of the courts. In my judgment, before the courts will hold that such executive action is contrary to legislation, express and unequivocal terms must be found in the statue which deprive the individual from receiving the benefit or protection intended by the exercise of prerogative power.

In the present case the Secretary of State contends that, if he does not have the power to make equipment available to police forces under the 1964 Act, he must have this power under the royal prerogative for the purpose of promoting the efficiency of the police. In order to dispute this the police authority must contend that the combined effect of ss4(1) and (4) and 41 is to prevent the Secretary of State from supplying equipment unless it is requested by the authority. These sections have already been considered in this judgment. Even if I am not justified in holding that these sections afford positive statutory authority for the supply of equipment, they must fall short of an express and unequivocal inhibition sufficient to abridge the prerogative powers, otherwise available to the Secretary of State, to do all that is reasonably necessary to preserve the peace of the realm.

(Counsel) for the police authority referred us to Chitty *A treatise on the law of the Prerogatives of the Crown* (1820) for the purposes of demonstrating that there was then no recognisable "prerogative to provide or equip a police force". With respect to counsel for the police authority, in my judgment this argument begs the question. One is not seeking a prerogative right to do this. The prerogative power is to do all that is reasonably necessary to keep the Queen's peace. This involves the commissioning of justices of the peace, constables and the like. The author clearly identifies the prerogative powers inherent in the Crown in relation to the duty placed on the sovereign to protect his dominions and subjects. The author (at p 4) adopts the definition of prerogative by Sir William Blackstone (1 Bl Com 239):

> "By the word 'prerogative' we usually understand' observes Sir William Blackstone, 'that special pre-eminence which the King hath over and above all other persons, and out of the ordinary course of the common law, in right of his royal dignity. It signifies, in its etymology, (from prae and rogo) something that is required or demanded before, or in preference to, all others. And hence it follows, that it must be in its nature singular and eccentrical: that it can only be applied to those rights and capacities which the king enjoys alone, in contradistinction to others; and not to those which he enjoys in common with any of his subjects: for if once any one prerogative of the Crown could be held in common with the subject, it would cease to be prerogative any longer. And therefore *Finch* lays it down as a maxim, that the prerogative is that law in case of the King, which is law in no case of the subject.' The splendour, rights, and powers of the Crown were attached to it for the benefit of the people, and not for the private gratification of the sovereign: they form part of, and are, generally speaking, as antient as the law itself, and the statute 17 Ed 2 St 1 de prerogativa regis is merely declaratory of the common law."

After considering the principal and transcendent prerogatives with respect to foreign states and affairs, as supreme head of the church and as the fountain of justice the author turns to the question of the protection of the realm in these terms (Chitty p7):

> "The *duties* arising from the relation of sovereign and subject are reciprocal. Protection, that is, the security and governance of his dominions according to law, is the duty of the sovereign; and allegiance and subjection, with reference to the same criterion, the constitution and laws of the country, form, in return, the duty of the governed, as will be more fully noticed hereafter. We have already partially mentioned this duty of the sovereign and have observed that the prerogatives are vested in him for the benefit of his subjects, and that his Majesty is under, and not above, the laws."

The up to date position is summarised in 36 Halsbury's Laws (4th edn) para 320:

> "*General functions of constables.* The primary function of the constable remains, as in the seventeenth century, the preservation of the Queen's peace. From this general function stems

a number of particular duties additional to those conferred by statute and including those mentioned hereafter. The first duty of a constable is always to prevent the commission of a crime. If a constable reasonably apprehends that the action of any person may result in a breach of the peace it is his duty to prevent that action. It is his general duty to protect life and property. The general function of controlling traffic on the roads is derived from this duty ..."

The passing of the 1964 Act did nothing to affect the duties and powers of police constables, including chief officers of police forces. In my judgment, the prerogative power to take all reasonable steps to preserve the Queen's peace remains unaffected by the Act and these include the supply of equipment to police forces which is reasonably required for the more efficient discharge of their duties.

In *Burmah Oil Co (Burma Trading) Ltd* v *Lord Advocate* [1964] 2 All ER 348 at 363, [1965] AC 75 at 114-115 a passage from the speech of Viscount Radcliffe, who at the outset was careful to state that he was dealing with the war prerogative, is also relevant to the exercise of the prerogative in general:

"What, then, do we mean by the prerogative in this connexion? I say 'this connexion' because in our history the prerogatives of the Crown have been many and various, and it would not be possible to embrace them under a single description. Some of them were or came to be beneficial or sources of profit to the Crown - these, I suppose, had their origin in the military tenures and the status of the feudal superior and examples of them would be wardship and purveyance and the right to the royal minerals. Others were as much duties as rights and were vested in the Sovereign as the leader of the people and the chief executive instrument for protecting the public safety. No one seems to doubt that a prerogative of this latter kind was exercisable by the Crown in circumstances of sudden and extreme emergency which put that safety in peril. There is no need to say that the imminence or outbreak of war was the only circumstance in which that prerogative could be invoked. Riot, pestilence and conflagration might well be other circumstances; but without much recorded history of unchallenged exercises of such a prerogative I do not think that for present purposes we need say more than that the outbreak or imminence of war, provided that it carried with it the threat of imminent invasion or attack, did arm the Crown with what may be called the war prerogative."

(Counsel) for the police authority conceded that there is a residual prerogative to act in relation to the maintenance of the peace in what he describes as an emergency, in respect of which he found it difficult, understandably, to give a useful definition. As Croom-Johnson LJ has already commented, and I agree with respect, it would be idle for the Crown to have retained a prerogative right if this cannot be used except in the immediate presence of an emergency.

For these reasons I have come to the conclusion that nothing in the 1964 Act or the preceding legislation has eroded the fundamental prerogative to keep the peace, In the exercise of this power, it is, in my judgment, open to the Secretary of State to supply equipment reasonably required by police forces to discharge their functions. I would, therefore, dismiss the appeal of the police authority.'

Nourse LJ agreed.

18 FREEDOM OF ASSEMBLY –
EMERGENCY POWERS

Arrowsmith v Jenkins [1963] 2 QB 561 Queen's Bench Division (Lord Parker CJ, Ashworth and Winn JJ)

Intention in obstruction of the highway

Facts

A public meeting was held on a highway that linked two main roads and where meetings were held from time to time. The defendant was the main speaker and she addressed the crowd from about 12.35 pm until about 12.55 pm. The road and pavements were completely blocked from about 12.35 pm to 12.40 pm, when a passageway for vehicles was cleared by the police with the help of the defendant using a loudspeaker. From 12.40 pm until after 12.55 pm when the defendant concluded her address, the road remained partially obstructed. The defendant was charged with wilfully obstructing the free passage along the highway contrary to s121(1) of the Highways Act 1959. She complained that meetings had been held there before and that the police had sometimes attended to keep a free passage but that no-one had been prosecuted before. In her defence it was argued that in order to establish that she was guilty of 'wilfully' obstructing the highway, the prosecution had to establish a knowingly wrongful act on her part and that since, because of previous meetings held there without prosecution, she had believed herself to be acting in the exercise of a legal right to address a public meeting on that highway, no knowingly wrongful act had been committed by her.

Held

On the true construction of s121(1) of the Act of 1959, a person who, without lawful authority or excuse, intentionally by the exercise of his free will (as opposed to accidentally) did or omitted to do an act which caused an obstruction or the continuance of an obstruction, was guilty of the offence. A requirement of mens rea in the sense that a person would only be guilty if he knowingly did a wrongful act could not be inferred from the words 'wilfully obstructs'. The defendant had done an act which caused an obstruction since it was found as a fact that the crowd would not have remained if she had not been addressing them. She was, therefore, guilty of the offence.

Lord Parker CJ:

'... I think that the defendant feels that she is under a grievance because - and one may put it this way - she says: "Why pick on me? There have been many meetings held in this street from time to time. The police, as on this occasion, have attended those meetings and assisted to make a free passage, and there is no evidence that anybody else had ever been prosecuted. Why pick on me?" That, of course, has nothing to do with this court. The sole question here is whether the defendant has contravened s121(1) of the Highways Act 1959. That section provides:

"If a person, without lawful authority or excuse, in any way wilfully obstructs the free passage along a highway he shall be guilty of an offence and shall be liable in respect thereof to a fine not exceeding forty shillings."

I am quite satisfied that s121(1) of the Act of 1959, on its true construction, is providing that if a person, without lawful authority or excuse, intentionally as opposed to accidentally, that is, by an exercise of his or her free will, does something or omits to do something which will cause an obstruction or the continuance of an obstruction, he or she is guilty of an offence. Mr Wigoder, for the defendant, has sought to argue that if a person - and I think that this is how he puts it - acts in the genuine belief that he or she has lawful authority to do what he or she is doing then, if an obstruction results, he or she cannot be said to have wilfully obstructed the free passage along a highway.

Quite frankly, I do not fully understand that submission. It is difficult, certainly, to apply in the present case. I imagine that it can be put in this way: that there must be some mens rea in the sense that a person will only be guilty if he knowingly does a wrongful act. I am quite satisfied that that consideration cannot possibly be imported into the words "wilfully obstructs" in s121(1) of the Act of 1959. If anybody, by an exercise of free will, does something that causes an obstruction, then an office is committed. There is no doubt that the defendant did that in the present case ...'

Beatty v Gillbanks (1862) 9 QBD 308 Queen's Bench Division (Field and Cave JJ)

What constitutes unlawful assembly

Facts

It was the practice of the Salvation Army to march through Weston-super-Mare. It was also the practice for the Salvation Army to be attacked in the course of their parades by the Skeleton Army. After a particularly bad incident on 23 March 1882 the local magistrates purported to ban further parades and when the Salvation Army assembled on 26 March their procession was stopped by the police since disturbances were caused by the Skeleton Army and Beatty was told that he would be arrested if he refused to disperse the group. Beatty refused and was arrested but told the others to go on. They too were arrested. All submitted quietly to their arrests. None of them committed any act of violence. They were charged with and convicted by the magistrates of unlawful assembly and were bound over to keep the peace, but appealed.

Held

The appeal would be allowed. The Salvationists had not caused any breach of the peace. No breach of the peace would have occurred but for the unlawful and unjustifiable interference of the Skeleton Army which could not be said to be a natural and necessary consequence of the acts of the Salvationists.

Field J:

'... There is no doubt that the appellants did assemble together with other persons in great numbers ... But there was nothing so far as the appellants were concerned to show that their conduct was in the least degree "tumultuous" or "against the peace"... And it is submitted by the learned counsel for the respondent, that as regards the appellants themselves, there was no disturbance of the peace, and that their conduct was quiet and peaceable. But then it is argued that, as in fact their line of conduct was the same as had on previous similar occasions led to tumultuous and riotous proceedings with stone-throwing and fighting, causing a disturbance of the public peace and terror to the inhabitants of the town, and as on the present occasion like results would in all probability be produced, therefore the appellants, being well aware of the likelihood of such results again occurring, were guilty of the offence charged against them. Now, without doubt, as a general rule it must be taken that every person intends what are the natural and necessary consequences of his own acts, and if in the present case it had been their intention, or if it had been the natural and necessary consequence of their acts, to produce the disturbance of the peace which occurred, then the appellants would have been responsible for it, and the magistrates would have been right in binding them over to keep the peace. But the evidence as set forth in the case shows that, so far from that being the case, the acts and conduct of the appellants caused nothing of the kind, but, on the contrary, that the disturbance that did take place was caused entirely by the unlawful and unjustifiable interference of the Skeleton Army ... and that but for the opposition and molestation offered to the Salvationists by these other persons, no disturbance of any kind would have taken place. The appellants were guilty of no offence in their passing through the streets, and why should other persons interfere with or molest them? What right had they to do so? If they were doing anything unlawful it was for the magistrates and police, the appointed guardians of law and order, to interpose. The law relating to unlawful assemblies, as laid down in the books and the cases, affords no support to the view ... that persons acting lawfully are to be held responsible and punished merely because other persons are thereby induced to act unlawfully and created a disturbance ... Many examples of what are unlawful assemblies are given in Hawkins' *Pleas of the Crown*, book 1, cap 28, ss9 and 10, in all of which the necessary circumstances of terror are present in the assembly itself, either as regards the object for which it is gathered together, or in the manner of its assembling and proceeding to carry out that object. The present case, however, differs from the cases there stated; for here the only terror that existed was caused by the unlawful resistance wilfully and designedly offered to the proceedings of the Salvation Army by an unlawful organisation outside and distinct from them, called the Skeleton Army. It was suggested by the respondent's counsel that, if these Salvation processions were allowed, similar opposition would be offered to them in future, and that similar disturbances would ensue. But I cannot believe that that will be so. I hope, and I cannot but think, that when the Skeleton Army, and all other persons who are opposed to the proceedings of the Salvation Army, come to learn, as they surely will learn, that they have no possible right to interfere with or in any way to obstruct the Salvation Army in their lawful and peaceable processions, they will abstain from opposing or disturbing them. It is usual happily in this country for people to respect and obey the law when once declared and understood, and I hope and have no doubt that it will be so in the present case. But, if it should not be so, there is no doubt that the magistrates and police, both at Weston-super-Mare, and everywhere else, will understand their duty and not fail to do it efficiently, or hesitate, should the necessity arise, to deal with the Skeleton Army and other disturbers of the public peace as they did in the present instance with the appellants, for no one can doubt that the authorities are only anxious to do their duty and to prevent a disturbance of the public peace. The present decision of the justices, however, amounts to this, that a man may be punished for acting lawfully if he knows that his so doing may induce another man to act unlawfully - a proposition without any authority whatever to support it. Under these circumstances, the questions put to us by the justices must be negatively answered, and the order appealed against be discharged.'

Commentary

See, however, *Duncan* v *Jones*, infra.

Duncan v Jones [1936] 1 KB 218 Queen's Bench Division (Lord Hewart CJ, Singleton and Humphreys JJ)

Facts

At about 1 pm on 30 July 1934 about thirty people, including the appellant, collected in the road near the entrance to a training centre for the unemployed. A notice across the entrance to the street stated, inter alia, that one of the speakers was from the National Unemployed Workers' Movement. A box was placed in the road by the entrance to the training centre. Mrs Duncan, who had been an unsuccessful Communist candidate at the General Election, was about to get up on it when the local chief constable told her that the meeting could not be held there. Mrs Duncan replied that she was going to hold the meeting, stepped on to the box and started to speak. Inspector Jones took her into custody without any resistance on her part. She was later charged with wilfully obstructing the inspector in the execution of his duty. The issue for decision was whether the inspector (the respondent) was acting in the execution of his duty when he told her that she could not hold the meeting. It was admitted that on 25 May 1933 after Mrs Duncan had addressed a meeting in the same place, there had been a disturbance in the training centre. The superintendent of the centre had attributed the disturbance to the meeting.

The magistrate found Mrs Duncan guilty. Quarter Sessions dismissed her appeal. The deputy-chairman at Quarter Sessions stated: (i) that as a matter of fact (if it was material) the appellant must have known of the probable consequence of her holding a meeting - namely a disturbance and possibly a breach of the peace - and was 'not unwilling' that such consequences should ensue; (ii) that in fact the respondent reasonably apprehended a breach of the peace; (iii) that in law it thereupon became his duty to prevent the holding of the meeting; (iv) that, in fact, by attempting to hold the meeting, the appellant obstructed the respondent in the execution of his duty. Mrs Duncan appealed to the Divisional Court.

Held

The appeal would be dismissed. The deputy-chairman of Quarter Sessions was entitled to come to the conclusion he did on the facts as he found them.

Lord Hewart CJ:

'... There have been moments during the argument in this case when it appeared to be suggested that the court had to do with a grave case involving what is called the right of public meeting. I say "called" because English law does not recognise any special right of public meeting for political or other purposes. The right of assembly, as Professor Dicey put it, is nothing more than a view taken by the Court of the individual liberty of the subject. If I thought that the present case raised a question which has been held in suspense by more than one writer on constitutional law - namely, whether an assembly can properly be held to be unlawful merely because the holding of it is expected to give rise to a breach of the peace on the part of persons opposed to those who are holding the meeting - I should wish to hear much more argument before I expressed an opinion. This case, however, does not even touch that important question.

Our attention has been directed to the somewhat unsatisfactory case of *Beatty* v *Gillbanks* (1). The circumstances of that case and the charge must be remembered, as also must the important passage in the judgement of Field J, in which Cave J concurred. Field J said:

"I entirely concede that every one must be taken to intend the natural consequences of his own acts, and it is clear to me that if this disturbance of the peace was the natural consequence of acts of the appellants they would be liable, and the justices would have been right in binding them over. But the evidence set forth in the case does not support this contention ..."

"Our attention has also been directed to other authorities where the judgements in *Beatty* v *Gillbanks* have been referred to, but they do not carry the matter any further, although they more than once express a doubt about the exact meaning of the decision. In my view, *Beatty* v *Gillbanks* is apart from the present case. No such question as that which arose there is even mooted here.

The present case reminds one rather of the observations of Bramwell B in *R* v *Prebble*, where, in holding that a constable, in clearing certain licensed premises of the persons thereon, was not acting in the execution of his duty, he said:

"It would have been otherwise had there been a nuisance of disturbance of the public peace, or any danger of a breach of the peace."

The case stated which we have before us indicates clearly a casual connection between the meeting of May 1933, and the disturbance which occurred after it - that the disturbance was not only post the meeting but was also propter the meeting. In my view, the deputy-chairman was entitled to come to the conclusion to which he came on the facts which he found and to hold that the conviction of the appellant for wilfully obstructing the respondent when in the execution of his duty was right. This appeal should, therefore be dismissed.'

Humphreys J:

'I agree. I regard this as a plain case. It has nothing to do with the law of unlawful assembly. No charge of that sort was even suggested against the appellant. The sole question raised by the case is whether the respondent, who was admittedly obstructed, was so obstructed when in the execution of his duty.

It does not require authority to emphasise the statement that it is the duty of a police officer to prevent apprehended breaches of the peace. Here it is found that the respondent reasonably apprehended a breach of the peace. It then ... became his duty to prevent anything which in his view would cause that breach of the peace. While he was taking steps so to do he was wilfully obstructed by the appellant. I can conceive no clearer case ...'

Harrison v Duke of Rutland [1893] 1 QB 142 Queen's Bench Division (Lord Esher MR, Kay and Lopes LJJ)

Unreasonable use of the highway: civil trespass

Facts

The plaintiff objected to the Duke, the defendant, shooting grouse on his land, and walked up and down the highway across the grouse moor, opening and shutting his umbrella so as to frighten the birds. He was ejected by the Duke's gamekeeper on the Duke's orders, and brought an action for assault.

Held (Lord Esher MR dissenting)

He was an unreasonable user of the highway and therefore a trespasser, and the Duke was entitled to use reasonable force to eject him.

Homer v Cadman (1886) 16 Cox 51 Queen's Bench Division (Mathew and Smith JJ)

Definition of obstruction of the highway

Facts

The respondent stood on a chair in the highway and addressed a large crowd of persons who had collected round him. There was space for vehicles and foot-passengers to pass to and from outside the crowd, but to have attempted to walk or drive across that part where the appellant and the crowd stood would have been inconvenient and dangerous. The respondent was charged under s72 of the Highway Act 1835 with 'wilfully obstructing the free passage' of a highway.

Held

Although there was room to pass to and from outside the crowd, the appellant was guilty of wilful obstruction of the free passage of the highway.

Smith J:

'... The question for us to decide is, whether or not there was evidence before the justice that the appellant had wilfully obstructed the free passage of the highway. The appellant was only entitled to use the highway in an authorised manner, that is, to pass over it to and fro. He certainly had used it in an unauthorised manner, and the magistrate has found that, as no person could have gone across that part of the highway where the appellant and his band were without considerable inconvenience and danger, there was an obstruction to the highway. The fact that only a part of the highway was so obstructed seems to me to make no difference. That the whole highway was not obstructed does not make what the appellant did any the less an obstruction within the meaning of the section. The appeal must fail.'

Moss v McLachlan [1985] IRLR 77 Queen's Bench Divisional Court (Skinner and Otton JJ)

Obstruction of the police likely to cause a breach of the peace: pickets

Facts

During the miners' strike of 1984-5, the appellants were would-be pickets who ignored police requests to turn back from proposed picket sites, and attempted to force their way through a police cordon between one and a half and four miles from the picket sites.

Held

They were rightly convicted of obstructing the police, since there was ample evidence to support the police view that a breach of the peace was likely if pickets were allowed through to the picket site. The police, in deciding whether there was a reasonable apprehension of a breach of the peace, were allowed to take into account their knowledge of the course of the dispute.

O'Kelly v Harvey (1883) 15 Cox 435 Court of Appeal in Ireland (Law LC)

Actions to prevent a breach of the peace

Facts

Placards were put up announcing a meeting of the Land League (Catholic) in Ireland with Parnell as speaker. Soon afterwards other placards appeared calling upon Orangemen (Protestant) to gather together to give Parnell 'a warm reception'. When the Land League met, a local justice of the peace called upon them to disperse and when they refused put his hand on the plaintiff in an attempt to disperse the meeting. The plaintiff brought an action against the JP for assault.

Held

The duty of a justice of the peace is to preserve the peace and he is therefore bound to intervene the moment he has reasonable apprehensions of a breach of the peace being imminent. He was, therefore, entitled to disperse the meeting of the Land League - even if the threat of breach of the peace came from an opposing group who were likely to attack them if this was the only way of preserving the peace.

Law LC (delivering the judgement of the court):

'... The duty of a justice of the peace being to preserve the peace unbroken, he is, of course, entitled, and in fact bound to intervene the moment he has reasonable apprehensions of a breach of the peace being imminent ... Accordingly, in the present case, even assuming that the danger to the public peace arose altogether from the threatened attack of another body on the plaintiff and his friends, still, if the defendant believed and had just grounds for believing that the peace could only be preserved by withdrawing the plaintiff and his friends from the attack with which they were threatened, it was I think the duty of the defendant to take that course. This indeed was, as it appears to me, substantially decided here some years ago by the Court of Queen's Bench in the case of *Humphries* v *Connor* (1) ... During the argument the recent case of *Beatty* v *Gillbanks* (2) was much relied on by the plaintiff's counsel. I frankly own that I cannot understand that decision, having regard to the facts stated in the special case there submitted to the court, and which appear to me to have presented all the elements necessary to constitute the offence known as "unlawful assembly". Field J quotes a passage from Sergeant Hawkins to the effect that any meeting of great numbers of people with such circumstances of terror as cannot but endanger the public peace and raise fears and jealousies among the King's subjects, is an unlawful assembly, and suggests that, for this purpose, the "circumstances of terror" must exist in the assembly itself. Well, even supposing this to be so, what is to be said as to the paragraph of the case which stated that the particular assemblage in question was a terror to the peaceable inhabitants of the town, and especially to those then going to their respective places of worship, and was calculated to endanger, and did endanger, the public peace. I should have thought that as assemblage of that character had in itself sufficient "circumstances of terror" to make it unlawful. But, again, we find it stated that Beatty and his friends constituting this Salvation Army procession knew they were likely to be attacked on this occasion, as before, by the body which had been organised in antagonism to them, and that there would be fighting, stone-throwing and disturbance as there had been on previous occasions; and further, that they intended, on meeting such opposition, to fight and force their way through the streets and public places as they had done before. I confess I should have thought that this, too, was no bad description of an unlawful assembly. Indeed, I have always understood the law to be that any needless assemblage of persons in such numbers and manner and under such circumstances as are likely to provoke a breach of the peace, was itself unlawful: and this, I may add, appears to be the view taken by the very learned persons who revised the Criminal Code Bill in 1878. But, after all, that decision of Field and Dave JJ is no authority against the view I take of the case now before us. I assume here that the plaintiff's meeting was not unlawful. But the question still remains, was not the defendant justified in separating and dispersing it if he had reasonable ground for his belief that by no other possible means could he perform his duty of preserving the peace? For the reasons already given I think he was so justified and therefore that the defence in question is good ...'

(1)   (1864) 17 Ir CLR 1

(2)   Supra, this chapter

R v Clarke (No 2) [1964] 2 QB 315 Court of Criminal Appeal (Lord Parker CJ, Winn and Fenton Atkinson JJ)

Incitement to commit a public nuisance by obstructing the highway

Facts

The accused was charged after the police alleged that, during a demonstration against a visit by the King and Queen of Greece, he directed the movements of a crowd of about 2,000 in attempting to evade police cordons. He appealed on the grounds that the Deputy-Chairman of Quarter Sessions had asked the jury only whether there had been an obstruction of the highway, but not whether there had in the circumstances been a reasonable use of it.

Held

The appeal would be allowed and the conviction quashed.

Lord Parker CJ:

'... [Counsel] for the defendant ... refers to the Irish case of *Lowndes* v *Keaveney* (1). It is convenient to refer to that case because all the relevant earlier decisions are there mentioned and in some cases summarised. In that case the defendant was a member of a band playing tunes in the streets of Belfast who went down a street followed by a large crowd. A constable cautioned the band but they went on, persisted in playing, and the crowd followed, with the result that the free passage of foot passengers and vehicles was temporarily interrupted. It was held that the conviction must be quashed, the justices having overlooked or omitted to decide the question which was whether the user of the street was, under the circumstances, unreasonable.

Lord O'Brien CJ ... pointed out that many processions are perfectly lawful, and that no public nuisance is created by obstruction thereby unless the user of the highway in all the circumstances is unreasonable. He pointed out that there may be considerable, even complete obstruction and yet the use of the street may be quite reasonable ...

Lowndes v *Keaveney* is valuable as setting out the true position, as this court understands it, after reviewing the previous cases. Unfortunately, in the present case, as I have already said, there was no direction to the jury as to the question of reasonableness or unreasonableness. It may well be that on a proper direction this defendant would, all the same, have been convicted, but the question was really withdrawn from the jury since they were told that, if in fact there was a physical obstruction, that constituted nuisance, and that the defendant, if he incited it, was guilty.

The court feels that this is a case in which they are unable to apply the proviso to s4(1) of the Criminal Appeal Act 1907. It follows that, since there was a material misdirection as to the law, this appeal must be allowed and the conviction quashed.'

(1)   [1903] 2 IR 82

Wise v Dunning [1902] 1 KB 167 King's Bench Division (Lord Alverstone CJ, Darling and Channell JJ)

Causing a breach of the peace

Facts

The appellant called himself a Protestant 'crusader'. He went about carrying a crucifix and, of his own admission, made use of expressions very insulting to the faith of the Roman Catholic population, amongst whom he went. Riots and disturbances had resulted from his conduct previously and, on the occasion in question, the magistrate found that the language of the appellant was provocative so that disturbances were likely to occur again. Large crowds had assembled in the streets, and a serious riot was only prevented by the interference of the police. The appellant was taken before the magistrate and bound over to keep the peace and be of good behaviour for twelve months (recognisance in the sum of £100 with 2 sureties of £50 each). He appealed against this order.

Held

The appeal was dismissed. The magistrate was entitled to bind the appellant over to be of good behaviour since he had previously used language and conduct the natural consequence of which was that breaches of the peace occurred and intended to do the same again in the future.

Lord Alverstone CJ:

'... It is not necessary to go at great length into the various authorities which were cited to us; I am not able to find in those authorities any statement of a rule of law which is to be applied in all such cases as this ... For instance, our attention was called to the opinion of a very learned lawyer and writer, Mr Dicey, with respect to *Beatty* v *Gillbanks* (1), and his opinion, as I understood the passage when read, was that the view taken by the Irish courts is in conflict with that taken by Field J and Cave J in that case. But I think that, when *Beatty* v *Gillbanks* is closely examined, it lays down no law inconsistent with anything stated by the judges in the Irish cases. For this purpose it is sufficient to cite the following passage. In *Beatty* v *Gillbanks* Field J said, stating, I think, the law with absolute accuracy:

"Now I entirely concede that every one must be taken to intend the natural consequences of his own acts, and it is clear to me that if this disturbance of the peace was the natural consequence of acts of the appellants they would be liable, and the justices would have been right in binding them over. But the evidence set forth in the case does not support this contention."

O'Brien CJ in *R* v *Justices of Londonderry* said:

'No act on the part of any person was proved to shew that it was reasonably probable that the conduct of the defendants would, on the day in question, have provoked a breach of the peace."

It is, in my opinion, important to emphasise that enunciation of the necessary test, because it has been pressed upon us by the appellant's counsel that if the appellant did not intend to act unlawfully himself, or to induce other persons to act unlawfully, the fact that his words might have led other people so to act would not be sufficient ...

... Here we have distinct findings of facts that the appellant held a number of meetings in the public streets; that the highways were blocked by crowds numbering thousands of persons; that very serious contests and breaches of the peace had arisen, and that the appellant himself used, with respect to a large body of persons of a different religion, language which the magistrate has found to be of a most insulting character, and that the appellant challenged any one of them to get up and deny his statements ... In considering the natural consequences of a man's acts who has used insulting language in the public streets towards persons of a particular religion, the magistrates are bound to take into consideration the fact that there is a large body of those persons in the town. The appellant also was proved to have stated, with respect to a meeting he intended to hold, that he had received a letter informing him that the Catholics were going to bring sticks, and he told his supporters that the police had refused to give him protection, and he said that he looked to them for protection. On these facts I think no one could reasonably doubt that the police and the magistrates were right in thinking that his language and conduct went very far indeed towards inciting people to commit, or was, at any rate, language and behaviour likely to occasion, a breach of the peace. It may be true that, if this case were to be considered with reference only to any particular one of the threats or illegalities which it is suggested the appellant has committed, further evidence would have been necessary; but, in my opinion, there was abundant evidence to shew that in the public streets he had used language which had caused an obstruction, which was abusive, which did intend to bring about a breach of the peace, and that he threatened and intended to do similar acts in another place. The fact that he had promised not to hold a meeting at one place, but held it within a quarter of a mile of that place on the same day, shews, at any rate, that the magistrate was justified in taking precautions to prevent a repetition of his previous conduct ...'

Darling J:

'... Now, what was the natural consequence of the appellant's acts? It was what has happened over and over again, what has given rise to all the cases which were cited to us, and what must be the inevitable consequence if persons, whether Protestants or Catholics, are to be allowed to outrage one another's religion as the appellant outraged the religion of the Roman Catholics of Liverpool ... In my view, the natural consequence of those people's conduct has been to create the disturbances and riots which have so often given rise to this sort of case. Counsel for the appellant contended that the natural consequence must be taken to be the legal acts which are a consequence. I do not think so. The natural consequence of this "crusader's" eloquence has been to produce illegal acts, and that from his acts and conduct circumstances have arisen which justified the magistrate in binding him over to keep the peace and be of good behaviour. In the judgment of O'Brien CJ in *R* v *Justices of Londonderry* there is this passage:

> "Now I wish to make the ground of my judgment clear, and carefully to guard against being misunderstood ... The defendants were bound over in respect of an apprehended breach of the peace; and, in my opinion, there was no evidence to warrant that apprehension."

It is clear that, if there had been evidence to warrant that apprehension, the Chief Justice would have held the magistrates' decision in that case to be right. It is said that *Beatty* v *Gillbanks* (1) is in conflict with that decision. I am not sure that it is. I am inclined to think that the whole question is one of fact and evidence. But I do not hesitate to say that, if there be a conflict between these two cases, I prefer the law as it is laid down in *R* v *Justices of Londonderry*. If that be a right statement of the law, as I think it is, the magistrate was perfectly justified in coming to the conclusion he did come to in this case, even without taking into consideration the question of the local Act of Parliament to which we were referred ...'

Channell J:

'... I agree ... that the law does not as a rule regard an illegal act as being the natural consequence of a temptation which may be held out to commit it. For instance, a person who exposes his goods outside his shop is often said to tempt people to steal them, but it cannot be said that this is the natural consequence of what he does ... But I think the cases with respect to apprehended breaches of the peace shew that the law does regard the infirmity of human temper to the extent of considering that a breach of the peace, although an illegal act, may be the natural consequence of insulting or abusive language or conduct.'

(1)   Supra, this chapter

19 FREEDOM OF EXPRESSION

19.1   Contempt of court

19.2   Blasphemy

19.3   Defamation

19.1   Contempt of court

Attorney-General v British Broadcasting Corporation [1981] AC 303 House of Lords (Viscount Dilhorne, Lords Fraser, Scarman, Edmund-Davies and Salmon)

Rules of contempt and tribunal proceedings

Facts

The single issue arising here was whether the rules of the High Court dealing with contempt applied to the proceedings of a local valuation court.

Held

Viscount Dilhorne, Lord Fraser and Lord Scarman held that a valuation court discharged administrative functions and as such was not protected by the rules of contempt. The Rules of the Supreme Court that referred to 'inferior courts' included courts of law, not inferior bodies such as valuation courts.

Lord Salmon held that it was against the public interest for the rules of contempt to apply to the proceedings of modern tribunals.

Lord Scarman:

'The second question may now be re-phrased. Does a body established for an administrative purpose but required to act judicially in the achievement of that purpose attract to itself the protection of the doctrine of contempt of court?

The High Court has power to punish summarily, ie without trial by jury upon indictment, for contempt of its own proceedings. The Court of King's Bench, now a constituent part of the High Court of Justice, has power to punish summarily for contempt of inferior courts; *R* v *Parke* (1) and *R* v *Davies* (2). This jurisdiction is today regulated by RSC, Order 52, rule 1. The question for your Lordships is whether this power, which admittedly extends to inferior courts which are part of the judicial system of the Kingdom, extends to administrative courts, or to bodies not so described but required in pursuit of their administrative purpose to act judicially.

Historically, there is no reason why it should be so extended. Summary punishment by attachment for contempt of court owes its origin to the fact that the offence was that of interfering with the King's justice administered in his "aula," ie courtyard, or "curia," ie council: see Holdsworth, A History of English Law, vol III, 3rd ed, (1923) pp391-393 and Oswald's Contempt of Court, 3rd ed (1910), p13. It was an offence against the judicial power of the sovereign. In the 19th century the judicial system was developed so as to include courts established not under the royal prerogative of justice but by statute - notably, the county court and the courts of summary jurisdiction. The question arose at the beginning of the 20th century whether the High Court, which clearly could punish for contempt of its own proceedings, could also punish for contempt of inferior courts. In 1906, *R* v *Davies* (2) the King's Bench Divisional Court (Lord Alverstone CJ Wills and Darling JJ) decided that it could. The Judgment of the court was delivered by Wills J. He reviewed the law. He cited with approval a dictum of Bowen LJ in *Helmore* v *Smith* (3): contempt of court "is not to vindicate the dignity of the court ... but to prevent undue interference with the administration of justice." He concluded that the state of the authorities was such as to leave the question entirely open for the court's decision (p40). He held that the mischief to be stopped in the case of inferior courts was identical with that in superior courts. The inferior court in the case was quarter sessions: and there could be no doubt that quarter sessions (and, indeed, petty sessions) were part of the judicial system of the Kingdom. The case did not decide, nor did it give, any indication as to the true answer to the question raised by this appeal.

It is plain that in the present case the Court of Appeal, especially Lord Denning MR, though he dissented on a specific point, gave great weight to the policy considerations which impressed themselves upon the mind of Wills J in the *Davies* case (2). Inferior courts have no power to protect themselves: some of them have a very extended and important jurisdiction: "The danger is perhaps greater to them than it is to the superior courts of having their efficiency impaired by publications ..." relating to pending proceedings: see *R* v *Davies* at p48. But there are weighty considerations to be put into the balance on the other side. First, there is freedom of speech, ie, the right to express opinions and impart information with the complementary right of the public to hear opinions and receive information. Secondly, there is the danger recognised by Fry LJ in the *Royal Aquarium* case (4) of the great number of tribunals and other bodies exercising judicial functions to which the doctrine of contempt of court could be applied, if extended beyond courts in law. Appendix C of the Annual Report of the Council on Tribunals for 1978/79 reveals the very large number and variety of such tribunals. How can a newspaper or broadcasting authority ever be sure that it is not expressing an opinion or making a report upon some matter which is under considering by some tribunal or another? And it matters not that the newspaper may have a defence of innocent publication. For we are considering a policy of law designed to prevent such publications. The plethora of tribunals results in an absurdity: either the policy is a nonsense because it can seldom be enforced or it takes effect, in which event freedom of speech may be widely restricted and injustice done.

Neither the meagre authorities available in the books nor the historical origins of contempt of court require the House to extend the doctrine to administrative courts and tribunals. Legal policy in today's world would be better served, in my judgment, if we refused so to extend it. If Parliament wishes to extend the doctrine to a specific institution which it establishes, it must say so explicitly in its enactment; as it has done on occasion, eg, Tribunals of Inquiry (Evidence) Act 1921. I would not think it desirable to extend the doctrine, which is unknown, and not apparently needed, in most civilised legal systems, beyond its historical scope, namely the proceedings of courts of judicature. If we are to make the extension, we have to ask ourselves, if the United Kingdom is to comply with its international obligations, whether the extension is necessary in our democratic society. Is there "a pressing social need" for the extension? For that, according to the European Court of Human Rights, 2 EHRR 245, 275, is what the phrase means. It has not been demonstrated to me that there is.

For these reasons I would allow the appeal.

I would add a few general comments not necessary for the decision in this case but relevant to the reform of the law. The allegation of contempt with which this case is concerned is publication of matter alleged to be prejudicial to the fair trial of pending proceedings. The Attorney-General must have thought it in the public interest to secure the suppression of the broadcast - an issue on which it is not possible to express an opinion since we have not seen it. But the prior restraint of publication, though occasionally necessary in serious cases, is a drastic interference with freedom of speech and should only be ordered where there is a substantial risk of grave injustice. I understand the test of "pressing social need" as being exactly that.

Contempt "in the face of the court," ie physical interruption or a scandalising of the court, should ordinarily be the subject of criminal proceedings after the event: and the criminal law, if it does not do so already, should cover, in one way or another, the offence of obstructing or interfering with the course of proceedings in administrative courts and tribunals as well as in courts of judicature.

It is high time, I would think, that we re-arranged our law so that the ancient but misleading term "contempt of court" disappeared from the law's vocabulary.'

(1)   [1903] 2 KB 432   (3)   (1886) 35 Ch D 449

(2)   [1906] 1 KB 32   (4)   [1892] 1 QB 431

Attorney-General v English [1983] 1 AC 116 House of Lords (Lords Diplock, Elwyn-Jones, Keith of the Kinkel, Scarman and Brandon)

Contempt of Court Act: scope of strict liability (s2(2)) and discussion in good faith (s5).

Facts

The defendant editor of the Daily Mail had published an article in support of a candidate in a Parliamentary by-election. The candidate was severely handicapped and was running as a Pro-Life candidate, alleging that a practice had developed in some hospitals of killing newborn handicapped babies. The article contained a number of highly emotional phrases and accusations, and one paragraph read:

'Today the chances of such a baby surviving would be very small indeed. Someone would surely recommend letting it die of starvation or otherwise disposing of it'.

Two days before the publication of this article, the trial had opened of Dr Arthur, a consultant paediatrician, on a charge of murdering a three-day-old mongoloid child by giving instructions that a drug should be administered which caused the baby to die of starvation.

The issues were whether the article, which was clearly a publication within s2(1) of the Contempt of Court Act, but against which a deliberate intention to prejudice the trial was not alleged, was subject to strict liability because of the nature and circumstances of publication, and if so, whether the publication nevertheless escaped strict liability under s5, which protects a 'discussion in good faith of public affairs'.

The Divisional Court held that the article created a substantial risk of seriously impeding Dr Arthur's trial, as required under s2(2), and therefore strict liability applied. The onus of proving s5 applied rested on the defence, and they had not discharged it since the article contained accusations which were not necessary to a 'discussion' within the section. The defendants appealed.

Held

The nature and circumstances of the publication satisfied s2(2), since the appearance of the article on the third day of Dr Arthur's trial involved a more than remote risk (which was all that the word substantially meant to exclude) that the jury might be affected.

However, the onus of proving that s5 was satisfied did not necessarily fall on the defendants, and in the present case the section did in fact apply. The newspaper had a duty to inform electors and discuss the programme of any candidate; to hold otherwise would prevent the discussion of mercy killings anywhere in the media during the progress of the trial, and seriously prejudice the candidate's ability to present her case to the electorate.

Attorney-General v Times Newspapers Ltd [1974] AC 273 House of Lords (Lords Reid, Diplock, Cross of Chelsea, Morris of Borth-y-Gest and Simon of Glaisdale)

Contempt of court and newspaper publication

Facts

Distillers Ltd were the subject of nearly 400 claims before the courts over the use of the drug thalidomide. The Sunday Times published an article urging the company to make a general settlement of claims, and later proposed to publish an examination of the actions of the company before the drug was put on general sale. At the request of the Attorney-General, the Divisional Court granted an injunction to restrain publication, as it would create a serious interference with the company's freedom of action in the litigation. The Court of Appeal discharged the injunction, holding that the article was comment in good faith on a matter of outstanding public importance, and did not prejudice pending litigation, since the actions had been dormant for some years during negotiations. The Attorney-General appealed to the House of Lords.

Held

The injunction was restored. It was a contempt to publish an article prejudging the merits of an issue before the court where this created a real risk that a fair trial would be prejudiced. The actions were not dormant, since active negotiations were continuing. It was contempt to use improper pressure to induce a litigant to settle out of court on terms to which he did not wish to agree, or to hold a litigant up to public scorn for exercising his rights in the courts.

Commentary

The Sunday Times went to the European Court of Human Rights, claiming that the decision infringed the freedom of expression protected by Article 10 of the European Convention on Human Rights. The main discussion before the court turned on whether the ban on publication was 'necessary in a democratic society ... for maintaining the authority and impartiality of the judiciary'.

The court voted that it was not necessary, by 11 votes to nine. This led to the passing of the Contempt of Court Act 1981, to amend the English law in line with the convention.

Home Office v Harman [1983] AC 280 House of Lords (Lords Diplock, Keith of Kinkel, Roskill, Scarman and Simon of Glaisdale)

Contempt and publication of confidential material used in open court

Facts

A prisoner challenged the legality of a Home Office decision, and an order for discovery was made against the Home Office for the production of a large number of documents to the prisoner's solicitor, the defendant in this case. She undertook that the documents would only be used for the purposes of the case, but later, after some had been read out in open court, she allowed a journalist to see those which had been so used. The journalist published an article based on the documents and she was fined for contempt. She appealed to the House of Lords.

Held (Lords Simon and Scarman dissenting)

Although the documents were read in court and could have been reported by journalists who were present, the solicitor was guilty of contempt since she had used the documents for a purpose which was not necessary for the conduct of her client's case, and had broken her implied undertaking to the court that had ordered their discovery.

Secretary of State for Defence v Guardian Newspapers Ltd [1985] AC 339 House of Lords
(Lord Diplock, Lord Fraser of Tullybelton, Lord Scarman, Lord Roskill and Lord Bridge of Harwich)

Contempt of Court Act 1981: s10 protection of journalistic sources

Facts

A document entitled Deliveries of Cruise Missiles to RAF Greenham Common - Parliamentary and Public Statements was prepared in the Ministry of Defence on or about 20 October 1983. It was classified 'secret'. Only seven copies left the Ministry.

The next day a photocopy of one of the copies arrived at the news-desk of The Guardian. No one on the staff knew whence it came or who delivered it. The editor, after inquiries, decided that it was authentic. He also concluded that the national interest would not be damaged by its publication. On 31 October, he published it.

On 11 November, the Treasury Solicitor wrote to the editor asking him to deliver up the document. On 17 November The Guardian's solicitors replied saying that certain markings on the document might disclose, or assist in the identification of, the source of the information in The Guardian, although the editor did not know the source and that in accordance with the well-established convention of journalism which had statutory force by s10 of the Contempt of Court Act 1981 he was not prepared to take any steps which might lead to the disclosure. The reply stated that the editor was only concerned to protect his sources and was prepared to hand over the document with the markings excised. That was unacceptable and proceedings were begun on 22 November. Two issues arose for decision, ie, the proper construction, in general terms, of s10 of the 1980 Act and the application of that section to this particular case.

Held

Unanimously, that s10 should be given a wide interpretation so that a publisher is always safe from having to disclose his sources unless it is proved that one of the four grounds requiring disclosure applies. As to this particular case, the newspaper had to deliver up the document intact (Lord Fraser and Lord Scarman dissented on this point, but the Court of Appeal's decision ([1984] Ch 156) was upheld).

Lord Diplock:

'Section 10 thus recognises the existence of a prima facie right of ordinary members of the public to be informed of any matter that anyone thinks it appropriate to communicate to them as such, though this does not extend to that information's source. The right so recognised is, so far as members of the public are directly concerned, of imperfect obligation. It encourages purveyors of information to the public, but a member of the public as such has no right conferred on him by this section to compel purveyance to him of any information. The choice of what information shall be communicated to members of the public lies with the publisher alone. It is not confined to what, in an action for defamation would be regarded as matters of public interest, or even, going down the scale, information published in order to pander to idle curiosity and thus promote sales of the publication; nor is the section confined to publications by "the media" although no doubt the media will in practice be the chief beneficiaries of it. Provided that it is addressed to the public at large or to any section of it every publication of information falls within the section and is entitled to the protection granted by it unless the publication falls within one of the express exceptions introduced by the word "unless".

The nature of the protection is the removal of compulsion to disclose in judicial proceedings the identity or nature of the source of any information contained in the publication, even though the disclosure would be relevant to the determination by the court of an issue in those particular proceedings, and the only reasonable inference is that the purpose of the protection is the same as that which underlay the discretion vested in the judge at common law to refuse to compel disclosure of sources of information - videlicet - unless informers could be confident that their identity would not be revealed, sources of information would dry up.

The words with which the section starts, before it comes to specifying any exceptions, impose a prohibition on the court itself that is perfectly general in its terms: "No court may require a person to disclose ... the source of information contained in a publication for which he is responsible ..." This prohibition is in no way qualified by the nature of the judicial proceedings or of the claim or cause of action in respect of which such judicial proceedings, if they are civil, are brought ...

Again, what the court is prohibited from requiring is not described by reference to the form the requirement takes, but by reference to its consequences, viz disclosure of the source of information. If compliance with the requirement, whatever form it takes, will, or is sought in order to enable, another party to the proceedings to identify the source by adding to the pieces already in possession of that party to the last piece to a jigsaw puzzle in which the identity of the source of information would remain concealed unless that last piece became available to put into position. The requirement will fall foul of the ban imposed by the general words with which the section starts ...

I find myself in full agreement with the judgment of Griffiths LJ, where he says that he sees no harm in giving a wide construction to the opening words because in the latter part of the section the court is given ample powers to order the source to be revealed where in the circumstances of a particular case the wider public interest makes it necessary to do so.

So I turn next to the exceptions that the latter part of s10 provides to the general ban upon the court requiring disclosure of sources of information that is imposed by the opening words. There are only four interests, and each of these is specific, that are singled out for protection, viz: (a) justice, (b) national security (c) the prevention of disorder, and (d) the prevention of crime.

The exceptions include no reference to "the public interest" generally and I would add that in my view the expression "justice", the interests of which are entitled to protection, is not used in a general sense as the antonym of "injustice" but in the technical sense of the administration of justice in the course of legal proceedings in a court of law, or, by reason of the extended definition of "court" in s19 of the Act of 1981 before a tribunal or body exercising the judicial power of the State.

The onus of proving that an order of the court has or may have the consequence of disclosing the source of information, falls within any of the exceptions lies upon the party by whom the order is sought. The words 'unless it be established to the satisfaction of the court' make it explicit and so serve to emphasise what otherwise might have been left to be inferred from the application of the general rule of statutory construction: The onus of establishing that he falls within an exception lies upon the party who is seeking to rely upon it. Again, the section uses the word "necessary" by itself, instead of using the common statutory phrase "necessary or expedient" to describe what must be established to the satisfaction of the court - which latter phrase gives to the judge a margin of discretion; expediency, however great, is not enough; s10 requires actual necessity to be established. And whether it has or not is a question of fact that the judge has to find in favour of necessity as a condition precedent to his having any jurisdiction to order disclosure of sources of information. I find it difficult to envisage a civil action in which s10 of the Concept of Court Act 1981 would be relevant other than one for defamation or for detention of goods where the goods, as in the instant case and in *British Steel Corporation* v *Granada Television Ltd* [1981] AC 1096, consist of or include documents that have been supplied to the media in breach of confidence. The instant case does not provide a convenient occasion for saying anything about the effect of s10 on actions for defamation. As respects actions for the detention of documents s10 does not destroy the cause of action or affect its nature. What it does is to affect what interlocutory orders may be made by the court in the action, what questions witnesses may be compelled to answer and what documents (or other things) they may be required to produce at the actual trial, and what relief under the Torts (Interference with Goods) Act 1977 may be granted by the judgment given in it.'

19.2   Blasphemy

Bowman v Secular Society Ltd [1917] AC 406 House of Lords (Lord Finlay LC, Lords Dunedin, Buckmaster, Parker and Sumner)

Religion and freedom of expression

Facts

The Secular Society Ltd was registered as a company limited by guarantee, the main object, as stated in its memorandum of association, being: 'To promote ... the principle that human conduct should be based on natural knowledge, and not upon supernatural belief, and that human welfare in this world is the proper end of all thought and action.'

On the issue of whether this was blasphemous.

Held

The propagation of anti-Christian doctrines, apart from scurrility or profanity, did not constitute blasphemy.

Lord Finlay LC:

'... It may be that there has been a considerable change of public opinion with regard to the discussion of religion, but the question is whether anything has taken place to justify any Court in holding that the principle of law on this matter may be treated as obsolete. From time to time the standard as to what is decent discussion of religious subjects may vary, and in one age a jury would find that a particular publication was blasphemous in the strict sense of the term which would not be so considered in another. With regard to questions of public policy, such as those arising in connection with restraint of trade, circumstances with regard to facility of communication and of travel may so alter that the principle invalidating such contracts would apply to a particular state of circumstances in one age but not in another. But it is difficult to see how change in the spirit of the time could justify a change in a principle of law by judicial decision. Such changes in public opinion may lead to legislative interference and substantive alteration of the law, but cannot justify a departure by any Court from legal principle, however they may affect its application in particular cases.

The decisions in *Briggs* v *Harley* (1) and *Cowan* v *Milbourne* (2) are in conformity with a considerable body of authority on this subject.

It has been repeatedly laid down by the Courts that Christianity is part of the law of the land, and it is the fact that our civil policy is to a large extent based upon the Christian religion. This is notably so with regard to the law of marriage and the law affecting the family. The statement that Christianity is part of the law of the land has been often given as a reason for punishing criminally contumelious attacks upon Christianity. It is true that expressions have in some cases been used which would seem to imply that any attack upon Christianity, however decently conducted, would be criminal. For the reasons I have already given I do not think that this view can be accepted as having represented the common law of England at any time. But the fact that Christianity is recognised by the law as the basis to a great extent of our civil policy is quite sufficient reason for holding that the law will not help endeavours to undermine it ...'

(1)   (1850) 19 LJ (Ch) 416   (2)   (1867) LR 2 Ex 230

R v Lemon, R v Gay News Ltd [1979] 1 All ER 898 House of Lords (Lord Scarman, Viscount Dilhorne, Lord Edmund-Davies, Lord Diplock and Lord Russell of Killowen)

Religion and freedom of expression

Facts

The appellants, who were editor and publishers of a newspaper for homosexuals published a poem purporting to describe acts of sodomy and fellatio with the body of Christ immediately after His death and to ascribe homosexual activities during His lifetime. They were charged with blasphemous libel.

The issue was whether it was sufficient for the prosecution in order to secure a conviction of the appellants to show an intention to publish material which was in fact blasphemous, or whether it was necessary to show that the appellants intended to blaspheme.

Held (Lords Diplock and Edmund-Davies dissenting)

The offence of blasphemous libel only requires the prosecution to prove the intention to publish material which was in fact blasphemous.

Lord Scarman:

'... My Lords, I do not subscribe to the view that the common law offence of blasphemous libel serves no useful purpose in the modern law. On the contrary, I think there is a case for legislation extending it to protect the religious beliefs and feelings on non-Christians. The offence belongs to a group of criminal offences designed to safeguard the internal tranquillity of the kingdom. In an increasingly plural society such as that of modern Britain it is necessary not only to respect the differing religious beliefs, feelings and practices of all but also to protect them from scurrility, vilification, ridicule and contempt. Professor Kenny, in his brilliant article on "The Evolution of the Law of Blasphemy", gives two quotations which are very relevant to British Society today. When the Home Secretary was pressed to remit the sentence on Gott after the dismissal of his appeal, he wrote:

"The common law does not interfere with the free expression of bona fide opinion. But it prohibits, and renders punishable as a misdemeanour, the use of coarse and scurrilous ridicule on subjects which are sacred to most people in this country. Mr Shortt could not support any proposal for an alteration of the common law which would permit such outrages on the feelings of others as those of which Gott was found to be guilty."

When nearly a century earlier Lord Macaulay protested in Parliament against the way the blasphemy laws were then administered, he added: "If I were a judge in India, I should have no scruple about punishing a Christian who should pollute a mosque."

When Macaulay became a legislator in India, he saw to it that the law protected the religious feelings of all. In those days India was a plural society; today the United Kingdom is also.

I have permitted myself these general observations at the outset of my opinion because, my Lords, they determine my approach to this appeal. I will not lend my voice to a view of the law relating to blasphemous libel which would render it a dead letter, or diminish its efficacy to protect religious feelings from outrage and insult. My criticism of the common law offence of blasphemy is not that it exists but that it is not sufficiently comprehensive. It is shackled by the chains of history.

While in my judgment it is not open to your Lordships' House, even under the Lord Chancellor's policy announcement of 26 July 1966 to extend the law beyond the limits recognised by the House in *Bowman* v *Secular Society Ltd* (1) or to make by judicial decision the comprehensive reform of the law which I believe to be beneficial, this appeal does offer your Lordships the opportunity of stating the existing law in a form conducive to the social conditions of the late twentieth century rather than to those of the seventeenth, eighteenth or even the nineteenth century. This is, my Lords, no mere opportunity: it is a duty. As Lord Sumner said in his historic speech in *Bowman* v *Secular Society Ltd*:

"The words, as well as the acts, which tend to endanger society differ from time to time in proportion as society is stable or insecure in fact, or is believed by its reasonable members to be open to assault. In the present day meetings or processions are held lawful which a hundred and fifty years ago would have been deemed seditious, and this is not because the law is weaker or has changed, but because, the times having changed, society is stronger than before. In the present day reasonable men do not apprehend the dissolution or the downfall of society because religion is publicly assailed by methods not scandalous. Whether it is possible that in the future irreligious attacks, designed to undermine fundamental institutions of our society, may come to be criminal in themselves, as constituting a public danger, is a matter that does not arise. The fact that opinion grounded on experience has moved one way does not in law preclude the possibility of its moving on fresh experience in the other; nor does it bind succeeding generations, when conditions have again changed. After all, the question whether a given opinion is a danger to society is a question of the times and is a question of fact. I desire to say nothing that would limit the right of society to protect itself by process of law from the dangers of the moment, whatever that right may be, but only to say that, experience having proved dangers once thought real to be now negligible, and dangers once very possibly imminent to have now passed away, there is nothing in the general rules as to blasphemy and irreligion, as known to the law, which prevents us from varying their application to the particular circumstances of our time in accordance with that experience." '

(1)   Supra, this chapter

19.3   Defamation

Alexander v North Eastern Railway (1865) 6 B & S 340 Court of Queen's Bench (Cockburn CJ, Blackburn, Mellor and Shea JJ)

Libel: justification

Facts

The railway published a notice saying that Alexander had been convicted of riding on a train without a ticket and given the alternative of a fine or three weeks in prison. Alexander sued for libel, claiming that the notice was not justified as he had been offered the choice of a fine or two weeks in prison.

Held

The notice was in fact justified; the rest of the statement was true and the error did not make the statement libellous.

Ambard v Attorney-General for Trinidad and Tobago [1936] AC 322 Privy Council (Lord Atkin, Lord Maugham and Sir Sidney Rowlatt)

Contempt of court and discussion of judicial sentencing

Facts

The newspaper discussed the variation in sentence in two cases with very similar facts, suggesting that the reason was the personal attitudes of one of the judges. The paper was convicted of contempt, but appealed.

Held

The case did not amount to contempt.

Lord Atkin:

> 'But whether the authority and position of an individual judge, or the due administration of justice, is concerned, no wrong is committed by any member of the public who exercises the ordinary right of criticising, in good faith, in public or in private, the public act done in the seat of justice. The path of criticism is a public way: the wrong-headed are permitted to err therein: provided that members of the public abstain from imputing improper motives to those taking part in the administration of justice, and are genuinely exercising a right of criticism and not acting in malice or attempting to impair the administration of justice, they are immune. Justice is not a cloistered virtue; she must be allowed to suffer the scrutiny and respectful, even though outspoken, comments of ordinary men.'

Goldsmith v Pressdram Ltd [1977] 2 All ER 557 Queen's Bench Division (Wien J)

Limits of the law of criminal libel

Facts

The defendants were publishers of 'Private Eye' and the plaintiff sought to bring an action for criminal libel over repeated references to him. By s8 of the Law of Libel Amendment Act 1888 it is necessary to obtain leave from a judge in chambers. The respondents claimed that (a) there was no evidence that the applicants' claim could not be fully satisfied in damages; and (b) a criminal remedy would not protect the public interest; and (c) the publication was not calculated to incite a breach of the peace.

Held

The court would grant leave under s8 only where there was a clear prima facie case, and where the libel was so serious, and the public interest required, that criminal proceedings be instituted. In this case there was a serious libel of a public figure whose integrity and financial dealings had been impugned by the publication, and it had been alleged that he had committed a criminal offence which allegation had not been withdrawn.

Per curiam

In determining whether the criminal law should be invoked it is relevant, although not conclusive, to consider whether the libel is likely to cause a breach of the peace. If the criminal law should be invoked it is irrelevant whether damages might afford an adequate remedy in a civil action. Nor is it a consideration in favour of the respondent that certain defences will not be available to them in a criminal action, although it may be a consideration in favour of the applicant.

London Artists v Littler [1969] 2 QB 375 Court of Appeal (Denning MR, Edmund Davies and Widgery LJJ)

Defence of fair comment: when available

Facts

Four actors, all represented by the same agent, simultaneously gave notice to leave a West End production during its run. The production had been subject to disagreements with the impresario. He wrote to their agent alleging a conspiracy to force a closure of the play. The artists sued for defamation and the producer claimed fair comment on a matter of public interest.

Held

Although the fate of the play was a matter of public interest, the claim of conspiracy was an allegation of fact not comment, and the defence did not apply.

Youssoupoff v Metro-Goldwyn-Mayer Pictures Ltd (1934) 50 TLR 581 Court of Appeal (Slessor, Scrutton and Greer LJJ)

The scope of libel

Facts

The plaintiff alleged that a libel was contained in the sound film 'Rasputin the Mad Monk'. The issue was whether information conveyed on a film constituted libel or slander.

Held

It was a libel. Slessor LJ described the position thus:

'In my view, this action, as I have said, was properly framed in libel. There can be no doubt that, so far as the photographic part of the exhibition is concerned, that is a permanent matter to be seen by the eye and is a proper subject of an action for libel, if defamatory. I regard the speech which is synchronized with the photographic reproduction and forms part of one complex, common exhibition as an ancillary circumstance, part of the surroundings explaining that which is to be seen ...'

20 EUROPEAN CONVENTION ON HUMAN RIGHTS

Malone v Metropolitan Police Commissioner [1979] Ch 344 Chancery Division (Megarry VC)

Article 8, European Convention on Human Rights: right to privacy

Facts

Malone a London antique dealer, who had been accused of handling stolen goods, sued the police for a declaration that the police had acted unlawfully in tapping his telephone on the authority of a warrant from the Home Secretary. Malone claimed that the tapping had infringed his rights of property, privacy, and confidentiality, and also the right to respect 'for his private and family life, his home and correspondence' under the Convention, Article 8.

Held

The action would be dismissed on the ground that the right to privacy was not known to English law. The Convention had not been given domestic effect by legislation, and was therefore not justiciable in the English courts.

Uppal v Home Office (1978) The Times 21 October Chancery Division (Megarry VC)

Article 8, European Convention on Human Rights: right to family life; right of petition

Facts

The applicants were illegal immigrants about to be deported. They applied for declarations that the deportation should not be carried out until the European Commission had determined whether Article 8's right to family life would be violated thereby. They also argued that the deportation would effectively deprive them of their right to petition the Commission.

Held

The declaration would be refused.

Megarry VC:

> 'Obligations in international law which are not enforceable as part of English law cannot ... be the subject of declaratory judgments or orders.'

21 POLICE POWERS – ARREST, DETENTION, AND QUESTIONING

Kuruma, Son of Kaniu v R [1955] AC 197; [1955] 2 WLR 223 Privy Council (Lord Goddard CJ, Lord Oaksey and Mr L M D de Silva)

Evidence - method of obtaining

Facts

The appellant had been convicted of being in unlawful possession of two rounds of ammunition: he maintained that the evidence had been illegally obtained and should not have been admitted. The law provided that police officers of or above the rank of assistant inspector could stop and search; those who had stopped and searched the appellant had been below this rank.

Held

The appeal would be dismissed as the evidence had been properly admitted.

Lord Goddard CJ:

'In their Lordships' opinion, the test to be applied in considering whether evidence is admissible is whether it is relevant to the matters in issue. If it is, it is admissible and the court is not concerned with how the evidence was obtained. While this proposition may not have been stated in so many words in any English case, there are decisions which support it and, in their Lordships' opinion, it is plainly right in principle. In R v *Leatham*, an information for penalties under the Corrupt Practices Prevention Act 1854, objection was taken to the production of a letter written by the defendant because its existence only became known by answers he had given to the commissioners who held the inquiry under the Act, which provided that answers before that tribunal should not be admissible in evidence against him. The Court of Queen's Bench held that, though the defendant's answers could not be used against him, yet if a clue was thereby given to other evidence, in that case the letter, which would prove the case, it was admissible. Crompton J, said (8 Cox CC at p501):

"It matters not how you get it; did you steal it even, it would be admissible."

In their Lordships' opinion, when it is a question of the admission of evidence strictly it is not whether the method by which it was obtained is tortious but excusable, but whether what has been obtained is relevant to the issue being tried. Their Lordships are not now concerned with whether an action for assault would lie against the police officers and express no opinion on that point.'

R v Alladice (1988) NLJ 20 May Court of Appeal (Lord Lane CJ, Rose and Hazan JJ)

Criminal evidence - admissions

Facts

The appellant was convicted of robbery at a Birmingham post office and sentenced to eight years' youth custody. The foundation of the prosecution case was alleged admissions, and the appellant now contended that the judge had been wrong to admit them because he had been denied access to a solicitor, which he had requested. The denial of access had been wrongful, he maintained, because: (a) the officer who had authorised the decision was merely an acting chief superintendent; and (b) on a true construction of the Police and Criminal Evidence Act 1984 and the Code of Practice, there was no proper basis for the decision.

Held

The appeal would be dismissed. As to (a), the holder of an acting rank, at least so far as authority and powers were concerned, was to be treated as if he were the holder of the substantive rank, unless his appointment to the acting rank was a colourable pretence, which was not suggested in the present case. As to (b), there had been a breach of s58 of the 1984 Act; if the officer concerned had believed that access to a solicitor would have had any of the unwelcome results set out in s58(8)(a)-(c), there had been no reasonable grounds for that belief. However, it did not follow that the evidence would necessarily have to be excluded under ss76 or 78 of the 1984 Act.

Lord Lane CJ:

'There remained the question under s76(2)(b) whether the confession might have been obtained in consequence of the breach of s58 and, if so, whether that was likely in all the circumstances to render the confession unreliable.

Their Lordships very much doubted whether it could be said that the confession might have been obtained as a result of the refusal of access to a solicitor. Even assuming that that might have been the case, there was no reason to believe that that fact was likely in all the circumstances to render a confession unreliable.

The judge was not obliged to rule the evidence inadmissible under s76.

That left s78, under which the court could refuse to allow evidence on which the prosecution proposed to rely to be given if it appeared to the court that, having regard to all the circumstances, including the circumstances in which the evidence was obtained, the admission of the evidence would have such an adverse effect on the fairness of the proceedings that the court ought not to admit it.

If the police had acted in bad faith, the court would have little difficulty in ruling any confession inadmissible under s78, if not under s76.

If the police, albeit in good faith, had nevertheless fallen foul of s58, it was still necessary for the court to decide whether to admit the evidence would adversely affect the fairness of the proceedings and would do so to such an extent that the confession ought to be excluded. No doubt in many cases it would.

It behoved the police to use their powers of delaying access to a solicitor with great circumspection.

It was impossible to say in advance what would or would not be fair.

The judge in the instant case decided that the authorisation of delay was properly given and consequently he did not have to consider the question whether s78 was applicable in the light of a breach of s58.

The appellant said in evidence that he was well able to cope with the interviews, that he had been given the appropriate caution before each of them, that he had understood the caution and was aware of his rights. His reason for wanting a solicitor was to have some sort of check on the conduct of the police during the interview.

The judge concluded that the only difference the presence of a solicitor would have made would have been to provide additional advice as to the appellant's right to say nothing - a right which he knew and understood and indeed at times during the interview exercised.

The appellant's candour about his attitude towards the legal adviser's presence simplified the task of deciding whether the admission of the evidence "would have such an adverse effect on the fairness of the proceedings" that it should not have been admitted.

Had the solicitor been present, his advice would have added nothing to the knowledge of his rights which the appellant already had. The police, as the judge found, had acted with propriety at the interviews and, therefore, the solicitor's presence would not have improved the appellant's case in that respect.

The present case was, therefore, a case where a clear breach of s58 nevertheless did not require the court to rule inadmissible subsequent statements made by the appellants.'

Commentary

Applied: *R* v *Samuel* [1988] 2 WLR 920.

R v Fulling [1987] 2 WLR 923 Court of Appeal (Lord Lane CJ, Taylor and Henry JJ)

Criminal evidence - oppression

Facts

A woman was arrested for allegedly obtaining property by deception. While in police custody, for two days she exercised her right to say nothing in response to persistent questioning. An officer then told her that her lover had been having an affair with another woman for the last three years and, on hearing this, the accused confessed to the charge. At her trial, she contended that the confession was inadmissible under s76(2)(a) of the Police and Criminal Evidence Act 1984 because it had been obtained by oppression.

Held

This was not the case, even if her account of the alleged disclosure by the police officer was correct.

Lord Lane CJ:

'... "oppression" in s76(2)(a) should be given its ordinary dictionary meaning. The Oxford English Dictionary as its third definition of the word runs as follows: "Exercise of authority or power in a burdensome, harsh, or wrongful manner; unjust or cruel treatment of subjects, inferiors, etc; the imposition of unreasonable or unjust burdens." One of the quotations given under that paragraph runs as follows: "There is not a word in our language which expresses more detestable wickedness than oppression."

We find it hard to envisage any circumstances in which such oppression would not entail some impropriety on the part of the interrogator.'

R v Mason [1988] 1 WLR 139 Court of Appeal (Watkins LJ, Mars-Jones and Henry JJ)

Criminal evidence - confession

Facts

The appellant was arrested and questioned regarding an offence of arson - setting fire to a car. At the time of the arrest, the police had no evidence to associate the appellant with the incident, but they told him and his solicitor that his fingerprints had been found on the bottle used to perpetrate the offence. This was a deliberate falsehood, but it was sufficient to cause the appellant to confess that he had been involved. At the trial, he maintained that the confession was inadmissible, but the judge allowed the evidence to be adduced.

Held

The appeal would be allowed.

Watkins LJ:

' ... regardless of whether the admissibility of a confession falls to be considered under s76(2) [of the Police and Criminal Evidence Act 1984], a trial judge has a discretion to deal with the admissibility of a confession under s78 which, in our opinion, does no more than to restate the power which judges had at common law before the 1984 Act was passed. The power gave a trial judge a discretion whether solely in the interests of the fairness of a trial he would permit the prosecution to introduce admissible evidence sought to be relied on, especially that of a confession or an admission. That being so, we now return to the circumstances of the present case.

It is obvious from the undisputed evidence that the police practised a deceit not only on the appellant, which is bad enough, but also on the solicitor whose duty it was to advise him. In effect, they hoodwinked both solicitor and client. That was a most reprehensible thing to do. It is not however because we regard as misbehaviour of a serious kind conduct of that nature that we have come to the decision soon to be made plain. This is not the place to discipline the police. That has been made clear here on a number of previous occasions. We are concerned with the application of the proper law. The law is, as I have already said, that a trial judge has a discretion to be exercised, of course on right principles, to reject admissible evidence in the interests of a defendant having a fair trial. The judge in the present case appreciated that, as the quotation from his ruling shows. So the only question to be answered by this court is whether, having regard to the way the police behaved, the judge exercised that discretion correctly. In our judgment he did not. He omitted a vital factor from his consideration, namely the deceit practised on the appellant's solicitor. If he had included that in his consideration of the matter we have not the slightest doubt that he would have been driven to an opposite conclusion, namely that the confession be ruled out and the jury not permitted therefore to hear of it. If that had been done, an acquittal would have followed for there was no other evidence in the possession of the prosecution ...

Before parting with this case, despite what I have said about the role of the court in relation to disciplining the police, we think we ought to say that we hope never again to hear of deceit such as this being practised on an accused person, and more particularly possibly on a solicitor whose duty it is to advise him, unfettered by false information from the police.'

R v Samuel [1988] 2 WLR 920 Court of Appeal (Glidewell LJ, Hodgson and Rougier JJ)

Criminal evidence - access to a solicitor

Facts

Arrested on suspicion of robbery, that day and the next the appellant was interviewed by the police on four occasions about the robbery and two burglaries, in all of which the appellant denied any involvement. During the second interview he asked for access to a solicitor, but his request was refused on the ground of likelihood of other suspects involved in the robbery being inadvertently warned. At the fourth interview the appellant confessed to the two burglaries and he was charged with those offences at 4.30 pm. At 4.45 pm a solicitor was informed of the charges, but denied access. Shortly afterwards the appellant confessed to the robbery and the solicitor was allowed to see him one hour later. At the trial, the appellant contended that evidence of the latter confession should be excluded, but it was admitted and he was convicted of robbery.

Held

The conviction would be quashed as, in the circumstances, the refusal of access to a solicitor had been unjustified and the interview in question should not have taken place. Under the Code of Practice for Detention issued under s66 of the Police and Criminal Evidence Act 1984, access could not be denied after a person had been charged with 'a serious arrestable offence' - and one of the burglaries was such an offence.

Hodgson J:

'... a court which has to decide whether denial of access to a solicitor was lawful has to ask itself two questions: "Did the officer believe?", a subjective test; and "Were there reasonable grounds for that belief?", an objective test.

What it is the officer must satisfy the court that he believed is this: that (1) allowing consultation with a solicitor (2) will (3) lead to or hinder one or more of the things set out in paras (a) to (c) of s58(8) [of the 1984 Act]. The use of the word "will" is clearly of great importance. There were available to the draftsman many words or phrases by which he could have described differing nuances as to the officer's state of mind, for example "might", "could", "there was a risk", "there was a substantial risk" etc. The choice of "will" must have been deliberately restrictive.

Of course, anyone who says that he believes that something will happen, unless he is speaking of one of the immutable laws of nature, accepts the possibility that it will not happen, but the use of the word "will" in conjunction with belief implies in the believer a belief that it will very probably happen.

What is it that the officer has to satisfy the court he believed? The right denied is a right "to consult a solicitor privately". The person denied that right is in police detention. In practice, the only way that the person can make any of the matters set out in paras (a) to (c) happen is by some communication from him to the solicitor. For the matters set out in paras (a) to (c) to be made to happen the solicitor must do something. If he does something knowing that it will result in anything in paras (a) to (c) happening he will, almost inevitably, commit a serious criminal offence. Therefore, inadvertent or unwitting conduct apart, the officer must believe that a solicitor will, if allowed to consult with a detained person, thereafter commit a criminal offence. Solicitors are officers of the court. We think that the number of times that a police officer could genuinely be in that state of belief will be rare. Moreover it is our view that, to sustain such a basis for refusal, the grounds put forward would have to have reference to a specific solicitor. We do not think they could ever be successfully advanced in relation to solicitors generally ... We do not know who make the decision at 4.45 pm but we find it impossible to believe that whoever did had reasonable grounds for the belief required by s58(8).'

Commentary

Applied in *R* v *Alladice* (1988) NLJ 20 May.

R v Sang [1980] AC 402; [1979] 3 WLR 263 House of Lords (Lord Diplock, Viscount Dilhorne, Lord Salmon, Lord Fraser of Tullybelton and Lord Scarman)

Discretion to refuse evidence - agents provocateurs

Facts

The appellant pleaded not guilty to a charge that he conspired with others to utter forged United States banknotes. Requesting a trial within a trial, his counsel said that he hoped to establish that the appellant had been induced to commit the offence by an informer acting on the instructions of the police and that but for such persuasion the appellant would not have committed the offence. Counsel then hoped that the judge would rule, in the exercise of his discretion, that no evidence of the offence so incited should be admitted and that he would direct the entry of a not guilty verdict. The judge ruled that he had no discretion to exclude the evidence.

Held

Although a judge always had a discretion to refuse to admit evidence if he thought its prejudicial effect outweighed its probative value, here the evidence should not have been excluded, whether or not it had been obtained as a result of the activities of an agent provocateur.

Lord Diplock:

'The decisions in *R* v *McEvilly, R* v *Lee* and *R* v *Mealey, R* v *Sheridan* that there is no defence of "entrapment" known to English law are clearly right. Many crimes are committed by one person at the instigation of others. From earliest times at common law those who counsel and procure the commission of the offence by the person by whom the actus reus itself is done have been guilty themselves of an offence, and since the abolition by the Criminal Law Act 1967 of the distinction between felonies and misdemeanours can be tried, indicted and punished as principal offenders. The fact that the counsellor and procurer is a policeman or a police informer, although it may be of relevance in mitigation of penalty for the offence, cannot affect the guilt of the principal offender; both the physical element (actus reus) and the mental element (mens rea) of the offence with which he is charged are present in his case.

My Lords, this being the substantive law on the matter, the suggestion that it can be evaded by the procedural device of preventing the prosecution from adducing evidence of the commission of the offence, does not bear examination. Let me take first the summary offence prosecuted before magistrates where there is no practical distinction between a trial and a trial within a trial. There are three examples of these in the books, *Brannan* v *Peek; Browning* v *J W H Watson (Rochester) Ltd; Sneddon* v *Stevenson*. Here the magistrates in order to decide whether the crime had in fact been instigated by an agent provocateur acting on police instructions would first have to hear evidence which ex hypothesi would involve proving that the crime had been committed by the accused. If they decided that it had been so instigated, then, despite the fact that they had already heard evidence which satisfied them that it had been committed, they would have a discretion to prevent the prosecution from relying on the evidence as proof of its commission. How does this differ from recognising entrapment as a defence, but a defence available only at the discretion of the magistrates?

Where the accused is charged on indictment and there is a practical distinction between the trial and a trial within a trial, the position, as it seems to me, would be even more anomalous if the judge were to have a discretion to prevent the prosecution from adducing evidence before the jury to prove the commission of the offence by the accused. If he exercised the discretion in favour of the accused he would then have to direct the jury to acquit. How does this differ from recognising entrapment as a defence, but a defence for which the necessary factual foundation is to be found not by the jury but by the judge and even where the factual foundation is so found the defence is available only at the judge's discretion.

My Lords, this submission goes far beyond a claim to a judicial discretion to exclude evidence that has been obtained unfairly or by trickery; nor in any of the English cases on agents provocateurs that have come before appellate courts has it been suggested that it exists. What it really involves is a claim to a judicial discretion to acquit an accused of any offences in connection with which the conduct of the police incurs the disapproval of the judge. The conduct of the police where it has involved the use of an agent provocateur may well be a matter to be taken into consideration in mitigation of sentence; but under the English system of criminal justice it does not give rise to any discretion on the part of the judge himself to acquit the accused or to direct the jury to do so, notwithstanding that he is guilty of the offence. Nevertheless the existence of such a discretion to exclude the evidence of an agent provocateur does appear to have been acknowledged by the Courts-Martial Appeal Court of Northern Ireland in *R* v *Murphy*. That was before the rejection of "entrapment" as a defence by the Court of Appeal in England; and Lord McDermott CJ in delivering the judgment of the court relied on the dicta as to the existence of a wide discretion which appeared in cases that did not involve an agent provocateur. In the result he held that the court-martial had been right in exercising its discretion in such a way as to admit the evidence.

I understand your Lordships to be agreed that whatever be the ambit of the judicial discretion to exclude admissible evidence it does not extend to excluding evidence of a crime because the crime was instigated by an agent provocateur. In so far as *R* v *Murphy* suggests the contrary it should no longer be regarded as good law.

I turn now to the wider question that has been certified. It does not purport to be concerned with self-incriminatory admissions made by the accused himself after commission of the crime, though in dealing with the question I will find it necessary to say something about these. What the question is concerned with is the discretion of the trial judge to exclude all other kinds of evidence that are of more than minimal probative value ... I would hold that there has now developed a general rule of practice whereby in a trial by jury the judge has a discretion to exclude evidence which, though technically admissible, would probably have a prejudicial influence on the minds of the jury, which would be out of proportion to its true evidential value.'

Commentary

Applied: *R* v *McEvilly*, *R* v *Lee* (1973) 60 Cr App R 150 and *R* v *Mealey*, *R* v *Sheridan* (1974) 60 Cr App R 59.

Overruled: *R* v *Faulder, Foulkes and Johns* [1973] Crim LR 45, *R* v *Burnett and Lee* [1973] Crim LR 748 and *R* v *Ameer*, *R* v *Lucas* [1977] Crim LR 104.

Walters v W H Smith & Son Ltd [1914] 1 KB 595 King's Bench Division (Sir Rufus Isaacs CJ)

Arrestable offences

Facts

The plaintiff was employed by the defendants at a bookstall in King's Cross Station; he also owned a newsagent's shop (which was a breach of his contract of employment). Over a period of several months the bookstall suffered a series of thefts of money and books and, consequently, the defendants set a trap for the thief by secretly marking some of the stock, including a book entitled *Traffic*.

When they later sent an agent round to the newsagent's shop to buy a copy of the book it was found to bear the secret mark. On being interviewed by the defendants the plaintiff admitted taking the book but said that he had intended to pay for it. The defendant was arrested and he was subsequently prosecuted for theft. On being found not guilty the plaintiff sued the defendants for false imprisonment.

Held

He had been falsely imprisoned since the plaintiffs were wrong in believing that he had committed a crime.

Isaacs CJ:

'When a person, instead of having recourse to legal proceedings by applying for a judicial warrant for arrest or laying an information or issuing other process well known to the law, gives another into custody, he takes a risk upon himself by which he must abide, and if in the result it turns out that the person arrested was innocent, and that therefore the arrest was wrongful, he cannot plead any lawful excuse unless he can bring himself within the proposition of law which I have enunciated in this judgment.

In this case, although the defendants thought, and indeed it appeared that they were justified in thinking, that the plaintiff was the person who had committed the theft, it turned out in fact that they were wrong. The felony for which they had the plaintiff into custody had not in fact been committed, and, therefore, the very basis upon which they must rest any defence of lawful excuse for the wrongful arrest of another fails them in this case. Although I am quite satisfied not only that they acted with perfect bona fides in the matter but were genuinely convinced after reasonable inquiry that they had in fact discovered the perpetrator of the crime, it now turns out that they were mistaken, and it cannot be established that the crime had been committed for which they gave the plaintiff into custody; they have failed to justify in law the arrest, and there must, therefore, be judgment for the plaintiff.'

HLT PUBLICATIONS

All HLT Publications have two important qualities. First, they are written by specialists, all of whom have direct practical experience of teaching the syllabus. Second, all Textbooks are reviewed and updated each year to reflect new developments and changing trends. They are used widely by students at polytechnics and colleges throughout the United Kingdom and overseas.

A comprehensive range of titles is covered by the following classifications.

- **TEXTBOOKS**
- **CASEBOOKS**
- **SUGGESTED SOLUTIONS**
- **REVISION WORKBOOKS**

The books listed overleaf should be available from your local bookshop. In case of difficulty, however, they can be obtained direct from the publisher using this order form. Telephone, Fax or Telex orders will also be accepted. Quote your Access, Visa or American Express card numbers for priority orders. To order direct from publisher please enter cost of titles you require, fill in despatch details and send it with your remittance to The HLT Group Ltd. **Please complete the order form overleaf.**

DETAILS FOR DESPATCH OF PUBLICATIONS
Please insert your full name below

Please insert below the style in which you would like the correspondence from the Publisher addressed to you
TITLE Mr, Miss etc.   INITIALS   SURNAME/FAMILY NAME

Address to which study material is to be sent (please ensure someone will be present to accept delivery of your Publications).

POSTAGE & PACKING
You are welcome to purchase study material from the Publisher at 200 Greyhound Road, London W14 9RY, during normal working hours.

If you wish to order by post this may be done direct from the Publisher. Postal charges are as follows:

UK   - Orders over £30: no charge. Orders below £30: £2.50. Single paper (last exam only): 50p
OVERSEAS   - See table below

The Publisher cannot accept responsibility in respect of postal delays or losses in the postal systems.
DESPATCH All cheques must be cleared before material is despatched.

SUMMARY OF ORDER

Date of order:

Add postage and packing:

Cost of publications ordered:
UNITED KINGDOM:

OVERSEAS:	TEXTS		Suggested Solutions (Last exam only)	
	One	Each Extra		
Eire	£4.00	£0.60	£1.00	
European Community	£9.00	£1.00	£1.00	
East Europe & North America	£10.50	£1.00	£1.00	
South East Asia	£12.00	£2.00	£1.50	
Australia/New Zealand	£13.50	£4.00	£1.50	
Other Countries (Africa, India etc)	£13.00	£3.00	£1.50	

Total cost of order: £

Please ensure that you enclose a cheque or draft payable to
THE HLT GROUP LTD for the above amount, or charge to ❏ Access ❏ Visa ❏ American Express

Card Number

Expiry Date .... Signature ....

ORDER FORM

LLB PUBLICATIONS	TEXTBOOKS Cost £	£	CASEBOOKS Cost £	£	REVISION WORKBOOKS Cost £	£	SUG. SOL. 1985/90 Cost £	£	SUG. SOL. 1991 Cost £	£
Administrative Law	17.95		18.95				9.95		3.00	
Commercial Law Vol I	18.95		18.95		9.95		9.95		3.00	
Commercial Law Vol II	17.95		18.95							
Company Law	18.95		18.95		9.95		9.95		3.00	
Conflict of Laws	16.95		17.95							
Constitutional Law	14.95		16.95		9.95		9.95		3.00	
Contract Law	14.95		16.95		9.95		9.95		3.00	
Conveyancing	17.95		16.95							
Criminal Law	14.95		17.95		9.95		9.95		3.00	
Criminology	16.95						+3.00		3.00	
English Legal System	14.95		12.95				*7.95		3.00	
Equity and Trusts	14.95		16.95		9.95		9.95		3.00	
European Community Law	17.95		18.95		9.95		+3.00		3.00	
Evidence	17.95		17.95		9.95		9.95		3.00	
Family Law	17.95		18.95		9.95		9.95		3.00	
Jurisprudence	14.95				9.95		9.95		3.00	
Labour Law	15.95									
Land Law	14.95		16.95		9.95		9.95		3.00	
Public International Law	18.95		17.95		9.95		9.95		3.00	
Revenue Law	17.95		18.95		9.95		9.95		3.00	
Roman Law	14.95									
Succession	17.95		17.95		9.95		9.95		3.00	
Tort	14.95		16.95		9.95		9.95		3.00	

BAR PUBLICATIONS

BAR PUBLICATIONS	TEXTBOOKS Cost £	£	CASEBOOKS Cost £	£	REVISION WORKBOOKS Cost £	£	SUG. SOL. 1985/90 Cost £	£	SUG. SOL. 1991 Cost £	£
Conflict of Laws	16.95		17.95				†7.95		3.95	
European Community Law & Human Rights	17.95		18.95				†7.95		3.95	
Evidence	17.95		17.95				14.95		3.95	
Family Law	17.95		18.95				14.95		3.95	
General Paper I	19.95		16.95				14.95		3.95	
General Paper II	19.95		16.95				14.95		3.95	
Law of International Trade	17.95		16.95				14.95		3.95	
Practical Conveyancing	17.95		16.95				14.95		3.95	
Procedure	19.95		16.95				14.95		3.95	
Revenue Law	17.95		18.95				14.95		3.95	
Sale of Goods and Credit	17.95		17.95				14.95		3.95	

LAW SOCIETY FINALS

LAW SOCIETY FINALS	TEXTBOOKS	REVISION WORKBOOKS	SUGGESTED SOLUTIONS PACKS (4-5 years of papers)		ALL PAPERS PACKS
Accounts	14.95	9.95	14.95		
Business Organisations & Insolvency	14.95		14.95		
Consumer Protection & Employment Law	14.95		14.95		
Conveyancing I & II	14.95		14.95		
Family Law	14.95		14.95		
Litigation	14.95		14.95		
Wills, Probate & Administration	14.95	9.95	14.95		
Final Exam Papers (Set) (All Papers) Summer 1989					9.95
Final Exam Papers (Set) (All Papers) Winter 1990					9.95
Final Exam Papers (Set) (All Papers) Summer 1990					9.95
Final Exam Papers (Set) (All Papers) Winter 1991					9.95

CPE PUBLICATIONS

CPE PUBLICATIONS	TEXTBOOKS	
Criminal Law	14.95	
Constitutional & Administrative Law	14.95	
Contract Law	14.95	
Equity and Trusts	14.95	
Land Law	14.95	
Tort	14.95	

INSTITUTE OF LEGAL EXECUTIVES

INSTITUTE OF LEGAL EXECUTIVES	TEXTBOOKS	
Company & Partnership Law	18.95	
Constitutional Law	14.95	
Contract Law	14.95	
Criminal Law	14.95	
Equity and Trusts	14.95	
European Law & Practice	17.95	
Evidence	17.95	
Land Law	14.95	
Revenue Law	17.95	
Tort	14.95	

* 1987–1990 papers only
† 1988–1990 papers only
+ 1990 paper only